Oracle Applications DBA

Covers 11i and R12

Oracle Applications DBA

Covers 11i and R12

Joyjeet Banerjee

Principal Consultant
Oracle Consulting
California, USA

Tata McGraw-Hill Publishing Company Limited
NEW DELHI

McGraw-Hill Offices

New Delhi New York St Louis San Francisco Auckland Bogotá
Caracas Kuala Lumpur Lisbon London Madrid Mexico City
Milan Montreal San Juan Santiago Singapore Sydney Tokyo Toronto

Published by the Tata McGraw-Hill Publishing Company Limited,
7 West Patel Nagar, New Delhi 110 008.

ISBN (13): 978-0-07-007729-4
ISBN (10): 0-07-007729-0

Managing Director: *Ajay Shukla*
Head—Professional and Healthcare: *Roystan La'Porte*
Publishing Manager: *R Chandra Sekhar*
Manager—Sales and Marketing: *S Girish*
Product Manager—Trade Computing: *Rekha Dhyani*
Jr Sponsoring Editor: *Ritesh Ranjan*
Copy Editor: *Deepti Ahuja Balani*
Controller—Production: *Rajender P Ghansela*
Assistant General Manager—Production: *B L Dogra*

Typeset at Le Studio Graphique, Guru Shivir, 12, Sector 14, Gurgaon 122 001, and printed at
Pashupati Printers Pvt. Ltd., 1/429/16, Friends Colony, Shahdra, Delhi 110 095

Cover Design: Kapil Gupta, Delhi
Cover Printer: Rashtriya Printers

RAZCRDDYRBXBY

The McGraw·Hill Companies

To

the loving memory of my father
who left for the heavenly abode when the book was in progress;

my mother, my sisters Joyeeta and Tia,
my brother-in-law Sagar
and to my two months old niece Saanjh

PREFACE

With the acquisition of PeopleSoft, Siebel and JD Edwards, Oracle has emerged as one of the leaders in the ERP software market. With the exponential growth of ERP software, the demand for Oracle Apps DBAs has increased manifold. Surprisingly, though there are numerous books on Oracle Database, there are only a few on Oracle Applications.

This was the reason that motivated me to jot down my experience and learning into a book that can be used by Apps DBAs as well as people aspiring to work in this domain. This book is written in a simple language and requires no prior knowledge of Oracle Applications. It covers each and every aspect of administrating Oracle Applications starting from installation to its day-to-day maintenance. For the ease of the readers, screenshots on installation, upgradation and managing Oracle Applications have been provided. The Unix sessions for all the maintenance activities have been included to help readers understand how to manage Oracle Applications without any issues.

The most frequently asked questions are 'what is an Apps DBA' and 'how is an Apps DBA different from a regular DBA'. An Apps DBA is the person who apart from doing all the regular DBA jobs also manages the entire Oracle Application. Apps DBA is responsible for the management of Oracle Applications, both at the database level as well as the middle-tier components, keeping the business of multimillion dollar companies up and running. So an Apps DBA's job is challenging as it includes all responsibilities of Oracle DBA along with upgrading, cloning, patching, maintenance and troubleshooting of the application system. So the scope of an Apps DBA's profile is much broader. To address this, the book has tried to cover every aspect of Oracle Applications.

Initially, this book was planned for release 11*i* only, but recently Oracle announced the release of latest version of E-Business Suite R12, which introduced major changes in the technology stack and the application file system. So the next question was whether to release the book for R12 or 11*i*. While I was in the process of taking a decision, Oracle announced the launch of Apps Unlimited and providing lifetime support for the existing application systems. That meant if a customer is on 11*i* she can remain on 11*i* for lifelong and she will be given lifelong support and won't be forced to upgrade to a higher version. It also meant that 11*i* would be relevant to the market and this made it easier for me to arrive at the decision. So, I decided to cover both 11*i* as well as R12 in this book making it as comprehensive as possible by ensuring coverage of every aspect of 11*i* and R12.

The book is divided into 14 chapters and here is a summary of all the chapters:

Chapter 1 provides an overview of Oracle E-Business Suite. It explains an ERP system, advantages of an ERP system, and Oracle Applications as an ERP system.

Chapter 2 covers Oracle Applications' architecture. It explains in detail the three-tier architecture, the components of the database tier, the application tier and the desktop tier, how these servers work and how these tiers interact with each other. The chapter begins with the architecture of 11*i* Application system and then goes into the architecture of R12 and the changes made in R12.

Chapter 3 discusses the file system of Oracle Applications. It talks about the file system in the database tier as well as in the application tier and discusses about the important files that are used in Oracle Applications. It covers both the 11*i* file system and R12 file system.

Chapter 4 is about installing Oracle Applications. It discusses how to install Oracle Application in case of single node instance and multi-node instance. This chapter includes examples of an actual installation for both single node and multi-node, along with the screenshots of the installation. It is divided into two sessions—installing 11.5.10 and installing R12 file system. For both 11*i* and R12, the complete installation is shown for easier comprehension.

Chapter 5 talks about configuring Oracle Applications. It talks about how to configure the various services once the installation is completed, and how to check the various application services after the installation.

Chapter 6 talks about managing the entire instance. It talks about managing the database as well as the application services. It also mentions the various services in 11*i* and R12 Application systems and how to start/stop various services and the location of all the scripts.

Chapter 7 talks about Concurrent Manager. It discusses the various types of Concurrent Managers and their role. It explains how to define concurrent program, schedule request, start/stop Concurrent Manager, troubleshoot the Concurrent Manager. It also discusses parallel concurrent processing and generic service management.

Chapter 8 is on patching. It explains in detail the different types of patches and the different types of drivers that are available in the patch, how to apply a patch in an interactive and non-interactive mode, the options available for applying a patch, and what to do if a patch fails. The Unix session of applying a patch has been explained and all the different modes of patching have been shown with examples.

Chapter 9 talks about all the AD utilities. A detailed discussion on `adadmin`, `adctrl`, `adsplice`, `adrelink` and all the available AD utilities is included. The Unix session of all the important AD utilities has been illustrated.

Chapter 10 is on cloning. It explains in detail the various cloning methodologies, `adclone` and `rapidclone`. It also covers `autoconfig` in detail.

Chapter 11 covers Oracle Applications Manager. Using screenshots, it explains all the features of the OAM.

Chapter 12 is on upgrading Oracle Applications. This chapter is divided into two sessions. The first section discusses about upgrading to 11.5.10 for 11*i* as well as non-11*i* application system and the second section talks about upgrading to R12 for all the application systems. For the benefit of the readers all the screenshots of the upgrade process are included. The techstack upgrade has also been included in the chapter.

Chapter 13 talks about printer setup. It explains in detail about the SRW drivers and the Pasta printer utility. All the screenshots for the printer setup have been included.

Chapter 14 talks about managing applications' security. It talks about creating a user and assigning responsibilities to the user. The entire flow has been explained with screenshots.

This book is targeted at core DBAs as well as Apps DBAs. For core DBAs who don't have any knowledge about Oracle Applications, this book serves as a starting point for becoming an Apps DBA. Whatever an Apps DBA does has been covered in the book. This book will help core DBAs to keep themselves upgraded with the new technology and to enhance their knowledge. And for the Apps DBAs, this book covers everything that is there in Release 12, released a few months back.

Comments, suggestions and feedback are most welcome and would be definitely acknowledged. You can mail me all your comments and suggestions at *joyjeet.books@gmail.com*. I will make all efforts to include your feedback in the next edition.

JOYJEET BANERJEE

Acknowledgements

I am really thankful to all my friends who motivated me, as it would have been impossible to complete the book without their efforts. I would like to thank all my friends and colleagues especially Jaikant, Ravi, Hemant, Rajesh, Raja, Rajrupa, Subhodeep, Kumkum, Nirmalya, Saugata, Tanmoy, Sreelatha, Jyoti, Sugeeti, Sushma, Surbhi, Neha, Manjusha, Aparajita, Sharath, Aditya, Saurabh, Sunil, Sahil, Jyoti, Nagarjuna, Abhijat, Syed, Sanjeev, Nurul, Abhilash, Brajesh, Abhishek, Vikram, Divya, Vineet Bhatia, Vineet Fernandes, Nikhil, Kapil, Anuj, Neeraj, Vinay, Sudhanshu, Suresh, Thiagu, Channesh, Santhosh, Jayaraman, Murali, and Sandeep for extending their help every time to make this book a reality.

I would also like to thank my manager Sanjay Bheemasena Rao and Kevin Dahms for reviewing the book and helping me in getting all the approvals. I would also like to thank Sreeni Hosamane and Shanna Gazley for helping me in getting all the approvals from Oracle legal department. I would also like to thank Rick Jewell for approving the book, and would like to thank Todd Alder for giving all the relevant approvals from the legal department.

This book would not have been possible without the help of the editorial and production team at McGraw-Hill Education, India.

Joyjeet Banerjee

Contents

1

ORACLE E-BUSINESS SUITE: AN OVERVIEW

WHAT IS ERP

Enterprise Resource Planning is a management system that integrates all the different aspects of business, viz. marketing, sales, finances, accounting, manufacturing, procurement, and Human Resource. ERP is the term used to describe the integrated software that caters to the needs of an organization as a whole. It is designed to support multiple business functions such that any organization can implement and customize it to their business needs. The best part of ERP is that it fits in any type of organization, whether small scale or large scale.

The term ERP has been derived from manufacturing resource planning. There, the key area of focus was on inventory control of manufacturing systems. In the 1960s most softwares were designed to handle inventory-based traditional systems. The focus then shifted to Material Requirement Planning (MRP) in the year 1970. In 1980, the concept of MRP-II (Manufacturing Resources Planning) evolved, which was an extension of MRP to shop floor and distribution management activities. In the early 1990s, MRP-II was further extended to cover areas like finance, engineering, projects management, and HR. After this came the concept of ERP.

In non-ERP systems, each department uses a different application system and there is no integration between them. The software each department uses is unique and caters to the requirements of that particular department only. For example, the financial department uses some accounting software which can't be used by the sales department. The HR department uses another software, which can't be used by the financial department. If higher management needs some reports from the accounting and HR departments, then he has to coordinate with the respective departments. In this kind of a system, the movement of the information is not at lightning speed and it's difficult to coordinate. Even intra-department communication takes a lot of time.

In contrast, the Oracle ERP software uses a single database, which helps the various departments to share information easily and effectively. Using the ERP software, the companies can enact best practices and standardize business processes more easily. It also allows companies to understand their business better, concentrate on serving their customers and maximize their profits.

REASONS FOR MOVING TO ERP

The reasons why a company moves to an ERP based system are discussed here.

- *The manufacturing perspective*

ERP system can take care of the day to day requirements of the manufacturing process. It helps in production planning, takes care of the materials needed, and maintains the inventory. It keeps track of the customers' orders. It maintains a record of the goods in the warehouse and also tracks the movement of the goods. It also ensures tracking of the suppliers and details of the raw material. From the customer's perspective, it arranges and tracks the delivery of the finished goods to customers and keeps track of each point of the product movement. It also updates the database, so that the customer can know the status at any particular time.

- *The financial perspective*

ERP keeps the accounting information updated at all times. It keeps track of the payments due from the customers as well as the scheduled date of payment to suppliers. At any point, it can make the balance sheet of the company. The details of profits, taxes and revenues can be retrieved from the system. It keeps track of cash flows and fund flows and monitors and analyzes cash holdings, financial deals and investment risks. It also takes care of the company's assets and liabilities and helps in making the budget for any financial year. It can also aid in making a consolidated balance sheet for holdings and subsidiary companies.

- *The human resource perspective*

It helps in keeping track of each and every employee. It works on a Self-service model, wherein an employee can update all personal information and apply for leave without paperwork or having to communicate with the HR department. Thanks to this, personnel management is automated (including recruitments, headcount open etc). The salary information is also automated, and as a result there is no delay in salary payment.

- *The top management perspective*

It helps the top management in better decision making. It can get reports of various departments within a fraction of a second. The MIS reports of the ERP help in budgeting, setting and achieving the targets. ERP software systems are designed to support the resource planning section of strategic planning.

Advantages of ERP

Implementation of ERP has the following advantages.

- *Faster accessibility of data*—This allows the top management to retrieve information about any department at the click of a mouse.
- *No more redundancy of data*—ERP system enters all company data into one centralized system. For example, the employee details are shared between the HR and finance departments.
- *Faster tracking*—It allows tracking of all the information among departments, viz. production, sales, etc which helps in identifying bottlenecks.

- *Low system maintenance cost*—The implementation of ERP is expensive, but once implemented, the cost of maintenance is very less as compared to its benefits.
- *Integration of processes*—It provides an integration of the supply chain, production and administrative processes.
- *Zero downtime*—ERP systems run 24X7, so it's available all the time. It also supports customers with worldwide operations.
- *Internet enabled*—The software is internet enabled, so one need not be in the office or connected to the office network.
- *Better coordination among different departments*—With the implementation of ERP there is better coordination among departments as the transfer of information is very quick and easy.

ORACLE E-BUSINESS SUITE AS AN ERP SOLUTION

Oracle E-Business Suite is a complete, integrated set of enterprise applications. It streamlines each area of an organization—from sales and marketing to supply chain and manufacturing. Oracle E-Business Suite is one of the fastest paths to high quality enterprise intelligence. It gives the company a 360-degree view of finances, customers and supply chains and automates all its work aspects.

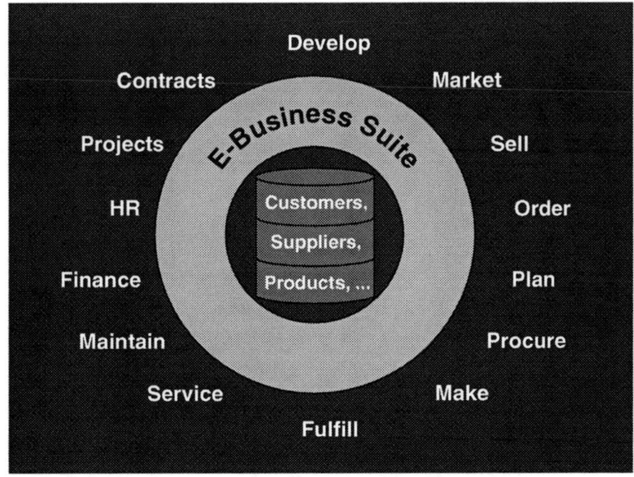

Fig. 1.1 Oracle E-Business Suite

Over thousands of new features have been added in the release version R12 in order to make it as comprehensive as possible. The Oracle ERP suite is supported by 30 languages and in 100 countries. Oracle has around 13500 customers on Oracle Applications.

Oracle Applications UI comes in two flavors—the Oracle Forms and the Oracle Self Service Application (HTML). The former provides incredibly quick learning curves for people from finance and other domains, who are used to Fox pro and dBase. The Oracle Self Service Application is an HTML based solution and specifically caters to the global organization, where Internet plays a major role.

2

ORACLE APPLICATION ARCHITECTURE

Oracle Applications have a three-tier architecture. They are comprised of a *Database Tier* which manages the Oracle database and stores all data; an *Application Tier* which hosts various servers, manages communication between the desktop and database tier and contains the application file system; and a *Client Desktop* through which users access Oracle Applications.

This architecture is shown in Figure 2.1.

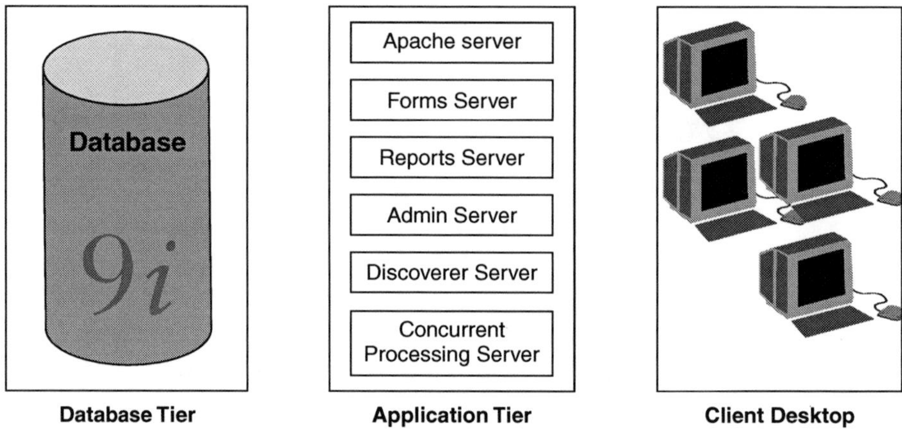

Fig. 2.1 Three-tier Architecture of Oracle Applications

A tier does not mean a physical machine. It's a logical grouping of services normally spread across more than one machine. A server is a process that runs on a single machine and provides a particular functionality. In Oracle Applications, one can install the database and the application tier on a single machine and can start all servers from that machine. Although many physical machines may be used in a configuration, scalability is derived from processing capabilities on three separate levels, namely: the desktop client tier, the application tier, and the database tier.

DATABASE TIER

The database tier contains the Oracle server. Oracle 10g database is shipped with R12 and 9*i* database is shipped with Oracle Application 11.5.10. The database tier stores all the data maintained by the Oracle Applications and runs the Oracle instance. It never interacts with the clients' desktop directly but with the various servers on the application tier.

For high availability environments, real application clusters can also be configured with Oracle Applications. In this case, more than one instance of Oracle is run. The data files are stored at a central location accessible from all of the instances.

APPLICATION TIER

The application tier is where the application software resides. It contains the servers that provide the business logic and code processing, as well as servers that interact with the database and client desktop The application tier architecture shifts software administration from the desktop to the middle tier, thus removing the burden of installing the application software for every client. It also supports load balancing between multiple Forms server and Concurrent processing server to provide optimum scalability and performance.

Six servers constitute the application tier.

- Oracle HTTP server (Apache)
- Forms server
- Reports server (Applicable only for 11*i* based systems)
- Admin server
- Concurrent processing server
- Discoverer server

Oracle HTTP Server (Apache)

The Oracle HTTP server processes all requests received from clients. The web server has some additional components, viz.—web listener, Jserv (Java servlet engine) and Java Server Pages. The web listener component accepts incoming HTTP requests from client browsers.

- The browser contacts the web listener with the URL. If possible, the HTTP listener itself services the request by returning a simple HTML page.
- If the page referenced by the URL needs advanced processing, the listener passes the request on to the servlet engine, which contacts the database server as necessary.

HTML-based Applications and the Oracle Applications Framework

Oracle HTML-based Applications are those designed in pure HTML and JavaScript. They dynamically generate HTML pages by executing Java code. They use a metadata dictionary for a flexible layout and operate by direct connection to the web server.

The Oracle Applications Framework consists of a Java-based application tier framework and associated services, designed to facilitate the rapid deployment of HTML-based applications. It includes the following components.

- Business Components for Java (BC4J) is included in Oracle Jdeveloper. It is used to create Java components that represent business logic. It allows the separation of application business logic from the user interface. It also provides a mechanism for mapping relational tables to Java objects.
- AOL/J supplies the Oracle Applications Framework with underlying security. It gives OAF its database connection and application-specific functionality.

The Framework-based applications logic is controlled by procedures executed through the Java servlet engine. The Apache JServ module provides this. The servlet engine uses the metadata dictionary in constructing the Framework UI.

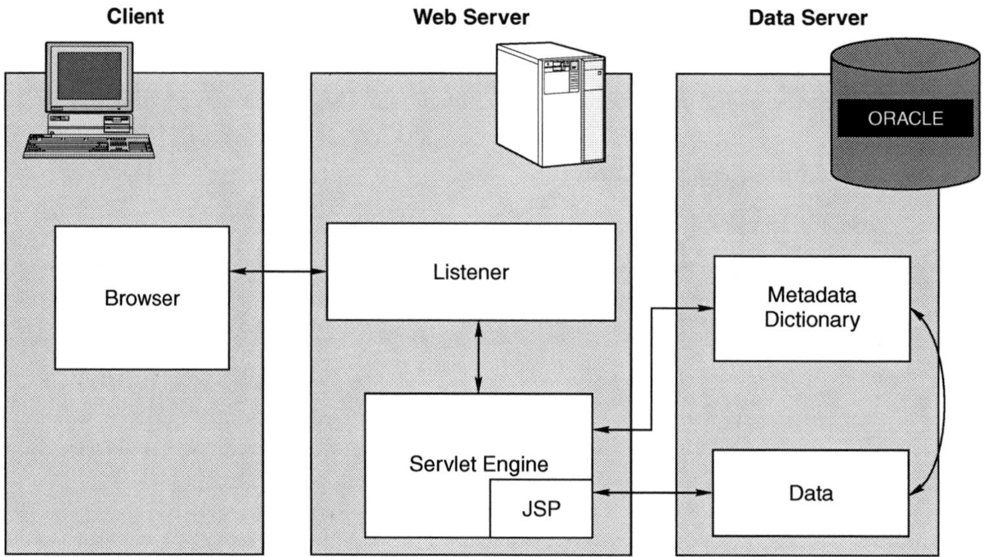

Fig. 2.2 HTML-based Application Architecture

How the Java servlet works with HTML-based Applications

- The user clicks a hyperlink in his browser from the client desktop.
- The browser connects the web listener with the URL.
- The web listener contacts the servlet engine (Jserv) and it runs a Java Server Page (JSP).
- The JSP in turn connects the Oracle database, gets information from the metadata dictionary and the content from the Application tables in order to construct the HTML page.
- The web server passes the resulting HTML page back to the browser.

In 11*i* the Java Servlet Engine is known as Jserv whereas in Release 12 it is replaced by OC4J (Oracle Container for Java).

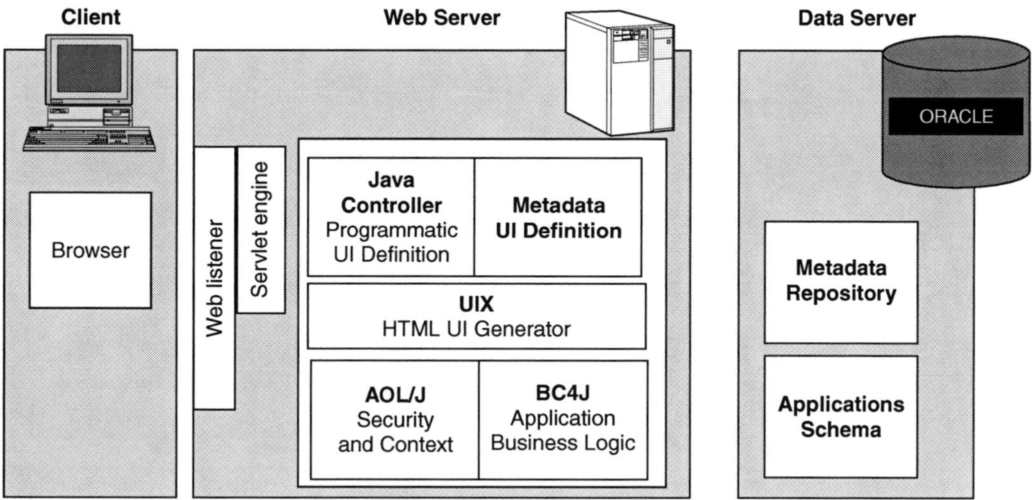

Fig. 2.3 Processing of Oracle Applications Framework

How processing of Oracle Applications Framework takes place

- The user access to the page is validated by AOL/J.
- The page definition is loaded on the application tier from the application tables in the metadata repository of the database tier.
- The BC4J objects that contain the application logic and access the database are instantiated.
- The Java Controller dynamically alters the page definition as required according to the dynamic UI rules.
- UIX (HTML UI Generator) interprets the page definition, creates the corresponding HTML in accordance with UI standards, and sends the page to the browser.

Forms Server

The Forms server also has a three-tier architecture. The client browser connects the Forms server through the Forms client Applet running on the local desktop. The Forms client Applet is a collection of Java Archive (JAR) files. When a user runs a Forms session, a thin (100% pure Java Applet) client downloads from the Forms server. The thin client handles the interface to the middle tier and the basic tasks of the user interface. The Forms server runs the server runtime engine, which passes all user interfaces to the thin client. It also maintains a database connection for the thin client.

The database tier stores all the data accessed by the Forms server for the thin client.

The Forms server also caches data and provides it to the client when needed. The Forms server communicates with the client using three protocols.

- Standard HTTP network
- Secure HTTPS network connection
- TCP/IP connection

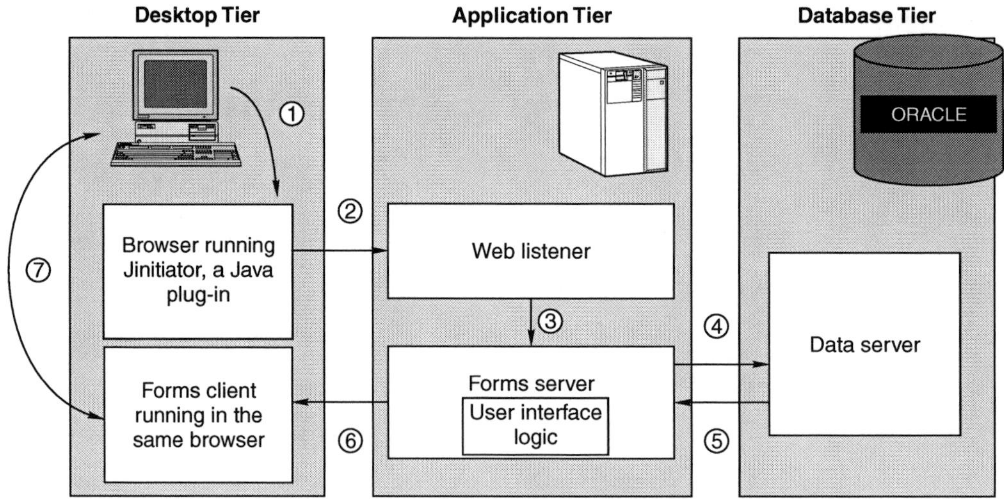

Fig. 2.4 Working of Forms Server

How the Forms server works

- Browser sends request (URL) to HTTP Listener (Apache)
- HTML page is retrieved (static) or generated (dynamic)

The web server receives and interprets the URL. If the URL points to a static file, the file will be retrieved from storage. If it points to a CGI script, the file will essentially be the same as the static version, but the CGI script will dynamically generate some pieces. If dynamic, CGI script asks Load Balancing Server for the least loaded server. The answer is used in the generation of the HTML file returned to the browser.

The Load Balancing Server is a process that monitors loading on all of the Forms servers. Each Forms server runs a Load Balancing Client which keeps the Load Balancing Server apprised of its load.

- HTTP Listener sends HTML page back to browser

Browser decodes HTML page, and detects the <APPLET> tag (indicating a Java Applet). Specifically, this is the thin client that will connect to the Forms server.

The <APPLET> tag contains the name Applet, along with numerous parameters like:

(a) The name of the form to run
(b) The name of the Forms server to use
(c) Log in information
(d) Any other parameters needed to pass to the Forms session

- Browser sends request (URL) to HTTP Listener for Java Applet

The browser asks the web server to send it the Java Applet. Java Applets are stored in class or Java Archive (JAR) files. JAR files are compressed archives that contain multiple class files. Oracle Applications use JAR files because they speed up the downloading of the Java Applet, and there are many JAR files that they must download.

- HTTP Listener returns Applet (JAR files) to browser

Browser receives Java Applet (JAR files), and begins to run them in its JVM (JInitiator). The JVM/JInitiator checks the version of the files being sent. If it is newer than the version cached on the client, JInitiator will continue the download. If the version is the same or older, JInitiator will begin to run the cached Java files. Java Applet is now running in the JVM and the browser is no longer part of the equation. The Java thin client connects to the Forms Listener via a TCP/IP socket or an HTTP port. The Forms Listener is already started, and listens for these requests.

- Forms Listener allocates a Forms Runtime Engine

When the Forms Listener gets a request, it starts a new Forms Runtime Engine for the thin client. The Forms Runtime Engine begun can either be a new process, or it can be an allocation of a running process. In the latter case, the process is greatly speeded up.

- Java Applet connection is passed from Forms Listener to Forms Runtime Engine

The Forms Listener hands-off the connection to the thin client, and has no further role in the process. Forms Runtime Engine loads the module(s) needed to run the requested form. When the thin client is connected, it passes a parameter entry, serverArgs. In that parameter entry, there is the name of the form to be run. At this point the Forms Runtime Engine loads the form and any libraries and/or menus required by that form.

- Forms Runtime Engine opens a connection to the database

The details of this connection depend on whether the Forms Runtime Engine is a newly spawned process or if it was allocated from a pool of running processes.

Reports Server (R12 does not have reports server)

The reports server is installed in the same node as the concurrent processing server. The reports server is used to produce business intelligence reports. These are present in the same directory as the regular concurrent processing reports. However, reports generated by the reports server are administered and monitored separately.

The steps involved in this process are as follows:

- The user clicks a link in the browser
- The browser contacts the web listener with the request
- The web listener contacts the reports server through the Web CGI
- The reports server starts reports runtime engine
- The reports runtime engine connects the database to query the requested information and generates the necessary reports
- The reports are shown to the user in an HTML page in the client desktop

The Reports server is obsolete in Release 12. All reports in R12 now run through the Concurrent Processing server manager via the rwrun executable, which spawns an in-process server.

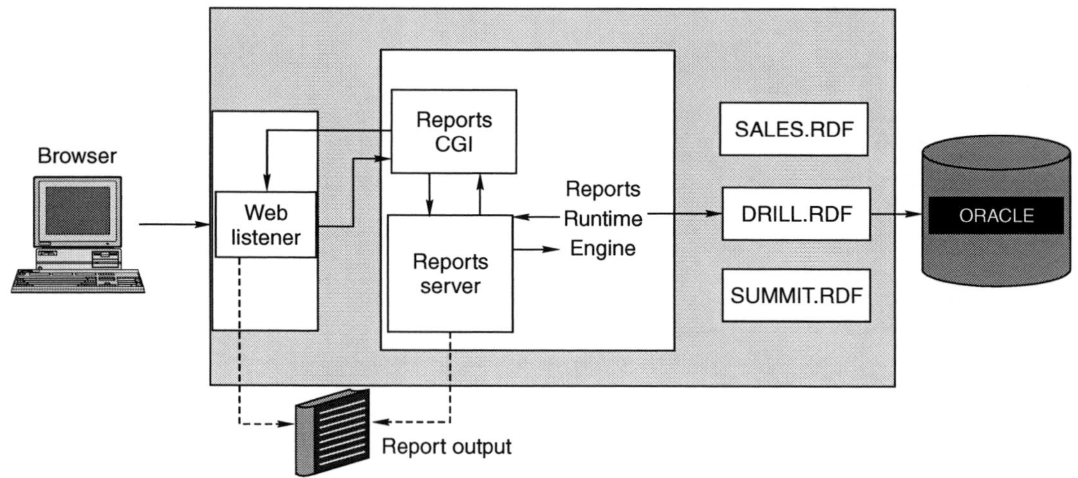

Fig. 2.5 How the Reports Server Works

Admin Server

The admin server is that node of the APPL_TOP from which all the maintenance activities for Oracle Applications are done. These are the activities done by the admin server.

- Upgrading Oracle Applications

If you are upgrading from one release to another, then you run the AutoUpgrade (adaimgr) utility from the administration server.

- Applying patches to the application system

Patches are applied using the AutoPatch (adpatch) utility. You can use adpatch for applying any type of patches, such as family packs, mini packs and maintenance packs.

- Maintaining Oracle Applications

Some features such as multi-lingual support and Multiple Reporting Currencies require regular maintenance to ensure updates are propagated to the additional schemas used by these features. All the maintenance activities of the Oracle Application are also done from the admin server using the adadmin utility.

Concurrent Processing Server

When an Oracle Application user submits a request to run a program, it is called a concurrent request. The set of programs responsible for running the concurrent requests is known as Concurrent Manager. It runs in the background and takes care of initiating and completing concurrent requests. Concurrent

Managers act as job processing administrators in Oracle Applications and employ workers in the operating system to process the application requested by the user. A manager can run any program or can be specialized to run only certain programs. We will discuss more about concurrent processing and the Concurrent Manager in Chapter 7.

Discoverer Server

Discoverer is an intuitive ad hoc query as well as a reporting, analysis, and Web-publishing tool. It empowers business users at all organizational levels to gain immediate access to information from data marts, data warehouses, online transaction processing systems and Oracle E-Business Suite. The Discoverer server is comprised of Oracle Discoverer 4i, a key component of the Oracle9*i* Application Server (9*i*AS). Discoverer 4i is well integrated with Oracle Applications. This allows users to employ Discoverer to analyze data from selected business areas in Human Resources, purchasing, etc. The Discoverer server complements the Reports server through its queries and analysis of the resulting output. It also allows users to use projections based on possible changes to the environment or other strategic factors.

Till this point the architecture is common for 11*i* and R12 based application systems. R12 introduces some changes in the architecture which are discussed below.

New Changes in R12

Release 12 techstack in the application tier has two new Oracle Homes .The web Oracle Home is now Application Server (AS) 10.1.3 which was earlier known as the `iAS_ORACLE_HOME` (8.1.7), and the `ORACLE HOME` used for Forms & Reports is AS 10.1.2 (`8.0.6 ORACLE_HOME` in previous release). These significant technology changes bring different file systems, new behaviors, and new configurations.

The following are the component of the Application Server 10.1.3

- Oracle Containers for Java (OC4J)
- Oracle Process Manager and Notification Server (OPMN)
- Oracle HTTP Server (OHS) 10.1.3.0.0 (Apache 1.3.34)

The Jserv is replaced by Oracle Containers for Java (OC4J). This is included in the 10.1.3 `ORACLE_HOME`.OC4J runs on the Java virtual machine and is based on Java 2 Enterprise Edition (J2EE) standards. You can have multiple OC4J process running each of which is referred to as a OC4J instance. The OC4J configuration is controlled via XML configuration files and OC4J properties file. An OC4J instance is referred to as a container as it provides a web container to support services like Java Server Pages (JSP), Servlets, Enterprise Java Beans (EJB) and Web Services.

The R12 creates 3 OC4J instances:

- Oacore (runs OA Framework-based applications),
- Forms (runs Forms-base applications),
- OAFM (runs the web services , mapviewer, Application server control)

Oracle Process Manager is the centralized process management mechanism in Oracle Application Server and is used to manage Oracle Application Server processes. The Process Manager is responsible for starting, restarting, stopping, and monitoring every process it manages. The Process Manager handles all requests sent to OPMN associated with controlling a process or obtaining status about a process. The Process manager is also responsible for performing death-detection and automatic restart of the processes it manages.(OPMN) manages AS components and consists of:

- Oracle Notification Server (ONS). It is the transport mechanism for failure, recovery, startup, and other related notifications between components in Oracle Application Server. It operates according to a publish-subscribe model: an Oracle Application Server component receives a notification of a certain type for each subscription to ONS. When such a notification is published, ONS sends it to the appropriate subscribers.
- Delivers notifications between components `OHS<->OPMN<->OC4J`

The following are the component of the Application Server 10.1.2

- Forms 10
- Reports 10

By default Forms Services is configured for OC4J by deploying it as a J2EE compliant application packaged in an EAR (Enterprise Archive) file called formsapp.ear. This is located in the 10.1.2 Oracle Home. The Forms and Reports are also delivered through the 10.1.2 Oracle Home but the AS 10.1.3 http server and OC4J container are used to run the Forms servlet, although the Forms runtime process (`$ORACLE_HOME_1012/bin/frmweb`, in 11*i* the forms runtime process was f60webmx) is forked into an AS 10.1.2 environment .This avoids having to run both 10.1.2 and 10.1.3 instances of the http server. The figure below shows the relationship between the two Application Server `ORACLE_HOMEs`

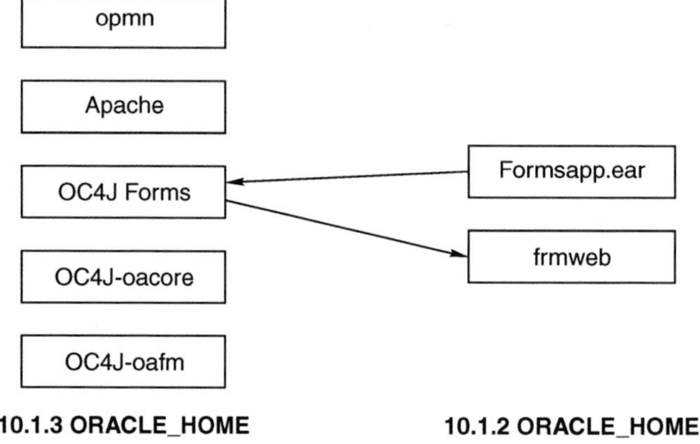

Fig. 2.6 The Two New `ORACLE_HOME` in R12

In Release 12 the following forms executables are renamed as follows.

Table 2.1 New Executables of R12

R12	11*i*
Frmweb	f60webmx
Frmcmp	f60genm
frmcmp_batch	f60gen
Frmbld.sh	f60desm

In Release 12 by default the forms service are provided by forms servlet mode. The forms servlet mode provides the following advantages.

- The dropped network connection can be re-established
- Firewall/proxy server is easy to configure
- Only a few machines and ports needs to be exposed at firewall
- Its very secured protocol in over the internet

CLIENT DESKTOP

The client interface is provided through a Java Applet using a Java enabled web browser. The client can download the Applet on demand and it is then kept in the desktop cache for future use. Users log in to the Oracle Application using the client browser. Once logged in to the E-Business suite home page, the user need not sign in again to access another part of the system.

Forms Client Applet

For running the Forms from the client PC, the Forms client Applet must run on the client desktop. The Forms client Applet supports all Oracle Application forms including the custom forms. It is a collection of JAR (Java Archive) files. All the commonly used JAR files are downloaded from the web server once in the client's first session. Thereafter it stays in the browser's local disk cache, ready for all future sessions till the Oracle Applications is upgraded to a higher release. All updates are installed on the application tier and downloaded to the client automatically through the JInitiator. Less commonly used JAR files are downloaded as and when needed.

Oracle JInitiator

Oracle JInitiator enables end users to run Oracle Forms Services Applications directly within Netscape Navigator or Internet Explorer on Windows 2000, Windows NT4.0 and Windows XP platforms._It is implemented as a plug-in (Netscape Navigator) or ActiveX Object (Microsoft Internet Explorer). Oracle JInitiator allows you to specify the use of the Oracle certified Java Virtual Machine (JVM) on web clients, instead of relying on the default JVM provided by the browser.

It is automatically downloaded in a user's machine the first time that the client web browser encounters an HTML file that specifies the use of Oracle JInitiator. The installation and updating is done using the standard plug-in mechanism provided by the browser.

Changes in the Desktop Tier in Release 12

In the desktop tier the new Sun J2SE plugin replaces the traditional Oracle Jinitiatior which was used till the 11*i* release. The J2SE plugin is automatically downloaded and installed when the forms based application are called. For example if you select the System Administrator responsibility and click the responsibility Security > User > Define then you will get a message like this for the installation of the J2SE.

```
In order to access this application, you must install the J2SE Plug-in version 1.5.0_07. To install this plug-in, click here to download the oaj2se.exe executable. Once the download is complete, double-click the oaj2se.exe file to install the plug-in. You will be prompted to restart your browser when the installation is complete.
```

Once you download and install the plug-in, you will be able to run Forms-based Applications.

The Forms client applet and commonly used JAR files are downloaded from the Web server at the beginning of the client's first session. Less commonly used JAR files are downloaded as needed. All downloaded JAR files are cached locally on the client, ready for future sessions.

In Release 12, the cache directory path is of the form:

```
<HOMEDRIVE>\Documents and Settings\<Windows User Name>\Application Data\Sun\Java\Deployment\cache
```

For example:

```
C:\Documents and Settings\jobanerj\Application Data\Sun\Java\Deployment\cache
```

ORACLE APPLICATION TECHNOLOGY LAYER

The Oracle Application technology layer provides a common basic functionality across all Oracle Application product families. The following products comprise the Oracle Application technology layer.

- Oracle Application DBA (AD)
- Oracle Application Object Library (FND)
- Oracle Common Modules (AK)
- Oracle Application Utilities (AU)
- Oracle Alert (ALR)
- Oracle Workflow (WF)
- Oracle Applications Framework (FWK)
- Oracle XML Publisher (XML)

Oracle Applications DBA (AD)

The Application DBA provides a number of tools for the maintenance of the application system. These are also known as Adutilities. They are used for installing, upgrading, patching and maintaining the Oracle Application. The main Adutilities are:

- `Adpatch`—This is used to apply patches in the Oracle application system
- `Adadmin`—This is used for maintaining Oracle applications
- `Adctrl`—It is used for controlling workers while applying patches and during adadmin
- `Auto upgrade`—This utility is used to upgrade Oracle Applications

We will discuss further about these utilities in Chapter 9.

Oracle Application Object Library (FND)

The Application object library is one of the major components of the application technology layer. It is also called the foundation (FND) of Oracle Application. It consists of various programs, database tables and reusable codes that provide common functionality across the different modules of Oracle Application.

Oracle Common Modules (AK)

The Oracle Common Modules are a data dictionary. It helps to define application components for the web and to generate many of the applications' characteristics at runtime. It can be used to develop an enquiry application for the HTML-based application, without any programming.

Oracle Application Utilities (AU)

The Oracle Application utilities are used for maintenance of the Application. The AU top also hosts a collection of files copied from other products. The installation process copies PL/SQL code from each application's PL/SQL directory into this common area. Other Oracle products use the code in these directories instead of in each product's PL/SQL subdirectory. The applications Java files are stored in this common area as well.

Oracle Alert (ALR)

Oracle alert sends alerts in the form of emails in case some error or exception or event occurs. The alerts can be customized according to the requirement of the administrator and users. In other words, Oracle Alert is a flexible, automated exception management and reporting tool that keeps you aware of critical activity in your database, helps you automate workflows and make better, quicker business decisions. Oracle Applications also come with pre-defined alerts.

Oracle Workflow (WF)

Oracle Workflow is a complete business process management solution embedded in the Oracle database. It delivers a complete workflow management system that supports business process-based integration. Its technology enables modeling, automation, and continuous improvement of business processes, since it can route information of any type according to user-defined business rules. Oracle Workflow provides customers with a scalable production workflow system tuned for the high volumes associated with enterprise applications.

The quick changes necessitated by e-business place special demands on enterprise systems. They have to manage a business process that spans trading partners, respond quickly to market innovations, support personalized business rules, streamline and automate transaction flows, and manage exceptions instead of transactions. Oracle Workflow gives the requisite capabilities through an extensible process-driven architecture. It automatically processes and routes information of any type to any person or system anywhere, whether inside or outside your enterprise. This is done according to business rules that can be changed to suit the user.

Oracle Workflow provides all parties in a business process with all the information needed to make the right decision. It can give summary and detailed information to each decision-maker in your workflow process, whether that process is a self-service transaction, a standard business document approval, or an XML document.

Oracle Workflow lets you model and maintain your business processes using a graphic workflow builder, unlike other workflow systems that simply route documents from one user to another with some approval steps. With it, one can define processes that loop, branch into parallel flows and rendezvous, decompose into sub-flows, and branch out on task results, time out, and more. Acting as a system integration hub, it can apply the business rules to control and route objects between applications and systems with minimal intrusion into those applications and systems.

Oracle Application Framework (OAF)

The Oracle Applications Framework (OA Framework) is the Oracle Applications development and deployment platform for HTML-based business applications. The OA Framework is composed of a set of middle-tier runtime services as well as a design-time extension to Oracle JDeveloper called the OA Extension.

The OA Framework provides customers with an easy-to-use personalized user interface that is accessible from all pages. The Oracle JDeveloper OA Extension wizards accomplish business logic extensions with little coding. Overall, the OA Framework personalization and extensibility features offer huge flexibility and cost savings to customers.

Oracle XML Publisher (XML)

Oracle XML Publisher is a new java-based product available with the E-Business suite. It is based on standard, well-known technologies and tools and provides end users with a template-based, easy-to-use publishing solution.

The technology is based on the W3C XSL-FO standard to transform XML data into an FO object; this contains both data and formatting information that can then be transformed into an output format like PDF.

Utilizing a set of familiar desktop tools such as Adobe Acrobat and Microsoft Word, users can create and maintain their own report formats based on development delivered XML data extracts. XML Publisher will then convert these documents to the XSL-FO format.

Users can also obtain PDF forms from third parties, e g government tax forms and merge XML data from development teams to fill the forms with the required data prior to printing.

3

ORACLE APPLICATION FILE SYSTEM

The Oracle Application files are stored on the application server, which is known as APPL_TOP. The database files are stored on the database server. Depending on the type of installation, all files can be on a single server (if it is a single node installation) and on multiple servers (if it's a multi-node installation).The client tier, viz. the desktop doesn't have any application files installed.

In this chapter, we will discuss the file system of Oracle Applications. First we will discuss 11*i* file system and then we will discuss R12 file system. Figure 3.1 shows the high level directory structure of a typical single node installation of a 11*i* installation.

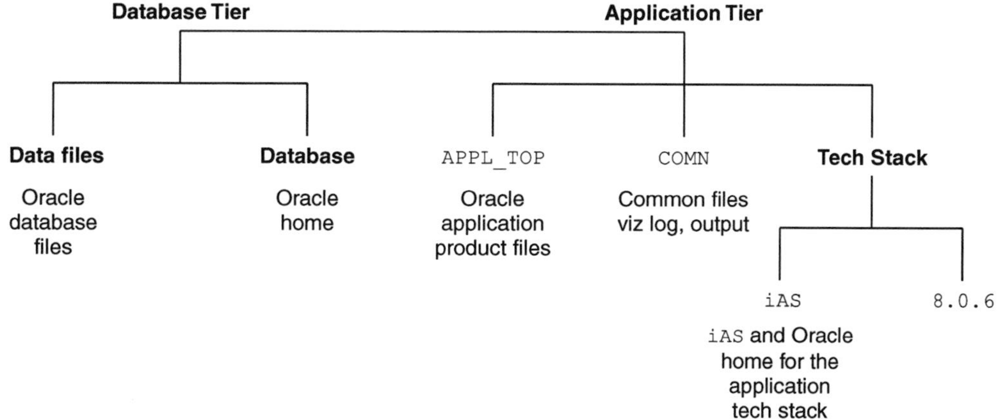

Fig. 3.1 Directory Structure of a Single Node Installation

As seen in the figure, there are five major top-level directories.

- DATA_TOP is the directory where all the datafiles are stored. The naming convention for this directory is <dbname>DATA.
- ORACLE_HOME is the directory where the ORACLE_HOME is located. It is named as <dbname>DB.
- APPL_TOP is the directory in which all application and product files are stored. This directory is named <dbname>APPL.

- COMN_TOP is the directory where the common files used across products are stored. The naming convention used here is <dbname>COMN.
- TECH_STACK contains the ORACLE_HOME for the Oracle Application Technology Stack and is named <dbname>ORA.

11*i* APPLICATION TIER FILE SYSTEM

The Application tier consists of the APPL_TOP, COMN_TOP and the Technology Stack ORACLE_HOME. We will discuss their file systems one by one.

APPL_TOP

APPL_TOP is the heart of Oracle Application. It is where all application and product files reside. It also contains some important configuration files required for the proper functioning of Oracle Applications. Figure 3.2 shows the directory structure of APPL_TOP.

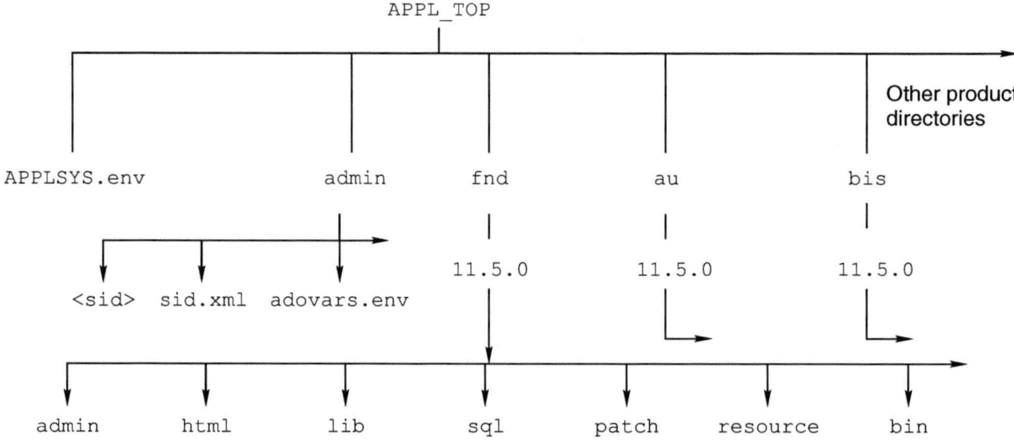

Fig. 3.2 Directory Structure of APPL_TOP

To summarize, it contains the following:

- Product files and directories
- Configuration files
- Core technology file and directories
- Language files and directory

Product directories

For each product (in the 11.5.10 release alone, there are more than 200 products), there is a separate directory in the APPL_TOP. The product files are stored in these directories. The product directories are named with the product's standard abbreviation, like 'bis' for Business Intelligence System and 'e c' for e-commerce. As seen in Figure 3.2, within each product directory there is a sub-directory, which is named using the base Oracle Application release number (viz. 11.5.0).

`<Prod_Top>` refers to the `<APPL_TOP>/<prod>/Version`, for example, `$FND_TOP=$APPL_TOP/fnd/11.5.0`.

Under each product top, there are a large number of directories. If we go to the `FND_TOP` directory, we will see the directories as shown in Figure 3.3.

```
(appmgr01) emstestappl - bash $ cd $FND_TOP

(appmgr01) 11.5.0 - bash $ pwd
/slot01/appmgr/emstestappl/fnd/11.5.0

(appmgr01) 11.5.0 - bash $ ls
3rdparty  fndenv.env  html     lib  media  patch     secure  xml
admin     forms       include  log  mesg   reports   sql     driver
bin       help        java     mds  out    resource  usrxit

(appmgr01) 11.5.0 - bash $
```

Fig. 3.3 Unix Session 3.1

Now we shall discuss the details of all the important directories in the product top and their significance.

Admin directory

This directory contains the product specific files used during the upgradation process. The admin sub-directory also has several sub-directories. The important sub directories in admin are:

- `Driver`: This folder contains the upgrade driver files (`.drv`). The upgrade process is divided into several phases. Phase driver files specify processing by phase. For example, the file `glseq.drv` creates sequences for the General Ledger (GL) product during the sequence phase; `glfile.drv` lists the GL files needed to run the application; and `gldep.drv` specifies dependencies between GL and other products so that upgrade jobs between products are processed in the correct order.
- `Import` Contains the import files which are used to upgrade seed data.
- `Odf` Contains object description files (`odf`) are used to create tables and other database objects.
- `SQL` Contains SQL scripts and PL/SQL scripts are used to upgrade data.
- Template contains the templates of all configuration files.

Bin directory

This directory contains C language programs, concurrent programs and shell scripts of each product. The most important bin directories are those of `$AD_TOP/bin` and `$FND_TOP/bin`. Some of the important files stored in the bin directories, are:

- `Adpatch` is the utility to patch the Oracle Applications is stored in `$AD_TOP/bin`
- `Adadmin` is the ad administration utility, stored in `$AD_TOP/bin`

- `FNDLIBR` is the executable Concurrent Manager and is stored in `$FND_TOP/bin`
- `Startmgr` is the shell script to start the Concurrent Manager and is found in `$FND_TOP/bin`
- `f60webmx` is the Applications form processor, stored in `$FND_TOP/bin`

Forms directory

This directory contains the Oracle Forms files. These files could be portable source files (`.fmb`) or generated runtime files (`.fmx`). The form files are generated by converting the `.fmb` source files to `.fmx` runtime files. This is taken care of by the installation utility. The source form files are stored in `$AU_TOP/` forms, so that the generation of the runtime files is convenient.

If more than one language is installed, then there is a sub-directory for each additional language. The sub-directory is named according to the language, e.g. US for American English forms, KO for Korean forms, AR for Arabic forms.

Help directory

This directory contains all the online help files. These files are imported into the database during an install or upgrade to optimize the performance of online help. Under the help directory, there is also a language directory, which stores the help file for each language installed.

HTML directory

The HTML directory contains all the HTML, Java Server Pages files (JSP), and Javascripts. These files are mainly used by products that have a Self Service Interface. The Javascripts (`.js`) and Java Server Page (`.jsp`) files are kept in the main directory. HTML files are kept in sub-directories by language.

Include directory

This directory contains the C header files (`.h` files). The files contained in the `lib` directory for relinking process often require these files. All products may not have an include directory.

Java directory

The Java directory contains all the Java and Java-dependent files. During an installation or upgrade process, all Java files are copied in the `$JAVA_TOP` in order to optimize the performance of the upgrade process.

All products that use Java contain a `JAR` sub-directory, which in turn contains all the Java Archive (`JAR`) files.

Lib directory

This directory contains all library files used during the process of re-linking. The library contains three types of files.

- Object files have an extension of '`.o`'. There is one object file per C program that has to be re-linked.
- A library file with an extension of '`.a`' is the compiled C code common to that product's programs.
- A Makefile has an extension of '`.mk`'. Makefiles specify how to relink the `.o` and the `.a` file.

Media directory

This directory contains the `.gif` files used for to display graphics.

Mesg directory

Oracle Application displays messages at the bottom of screen in the form of pop-ups. These are stored message files in form of `.msb` files. Each product's `Mesg` directory contains one or more files for the language-specific messages that the product uses, in addition to the following files:

- `.msb` files contain the binary messages used at runtime
- `<Language>.msg` files, one for each language installed (e.g. an Arabic installation will have an `AR.msg` file, while a Korean installation will have `KO.msg` file)

Patch directory

The `patch` directory is used to store the `patch` files used during updates to Oracle Applications data or data model. It contains the following sub-directories.

- `Driver`: This directory contains all the driver files used during patching and maintenance activities of Oracle Applications
- `SQL`: This directory contains SQL (`.sql`) and PL/SQL(`.pls`) scripts used to update the database
- `ODF`: This directory contains the object description files (`.odf`) used to update the data model
- `Import`: It contains the `.lct` and the `.slt` files which are used to update the seed data

PL/SQL and resource directories

These directories are used for unloading the PL/SQL libraries.

- The files in the PL/SQL sub-directory (`.pll` files) are used by Oracle Reports.
- The files in the resource sub-directory (`.pll` and `.plx` files) are used by Oracle Forms.
- After these files are unloaded, they are moved to equivalent sub-directories under the `$AU_TOP` directory.

Reports directory

This directory contains the report files for products. They are stored as portable binary `.rdf` files. For every additional language installed, there is a language-specific directory under the reports directory.

SQL directory

Oracle Application uses many SQL scripts for concurrent processing and produce reports. The scripts are stored as `.sql` files in this directory.

Log and out directories

When Concurrent Managers run Oracle Applications reports or data update programs, they write output, diagnostic log files and temporary files to directories that are defined during installation. There are two methods for storing log and output files:

- In each product's log and output directories (this is the default) or
- A common log and output sub-directory

The `log` directory holds concurrent log files from each concurrent request as well as the CM log files, while the out directory holds the concurrent report output files. The default locations for these two files are `<PROD>_TOP/log` and `<PROD>_TOP/out`. However, changing the `APPLLOG` and `APPLOUT` environment variables in the `<db name>` .env file can change the default directory and the default file names.

All product `log` and `out` files can be consolidated into one directory by defining the `APPLCSF` environment variable in the `<db name>.env`. This parameter identifies a directory to hold all log and output files.

Configuration files

Configuration files contain all information about the Oracle Application. The details of the important configuration files which are there in `$APPL_TOP` are as follows.

APPLSYS.env/<SID>.env

The name of a file varies, depending on the version of Oracle Application. In some versions, it is `APPLSYS.env`, whereas in others it is `SID.env`. These files source the `APPL_TOP`, all the product tops (product top is the top level directory for each product) and the technology stack environments. This is the most important file for the proper functioning of the Application, so we will discuss all entries of this file individually. Figure 3.4 shows a sample of the entries in this file.

```
#!/bin/sh
#
# $Header: APPLSYS_ux.env 115.66 2004/10/13 06:04:13 isikdar ship $
#
# ###############################################################
#
# This file is automatically generated by AutoConfig. It will be read and
# overwritten. If you were instructed to edit this file, or if you are not
# able to use the settings created by AutoConfig, refer to Metalink
# document 165195.1 for assistance.
#
# ###############################################################
#

#
# The APPLFENV variable is the filename of this file.
```

Contd

Fig. 3.4 Contd

```
# If you rename this file, you should change this value.
#
APPLFENV="emstest.env"
export APPLFENV
#
# The CONTEXT_FILE variable stores the location of the context file.
#
CONTEXT_FILE="/SLOTS/slot01/appmgr/emstestappl/admin/emstest.xml"
export CONTEXT_FILE
#
# The CONTEXT_NAME variable stores the value for the current context
#
CONTEXT_NAME="emstest"
export CONTEXT_NAME
#
# The PLATFORM variable is the Oracle name for this platform.
# The value below should match the value in adpltfrm.txt.
#
PLATFORM="LINUX"
export PLATFORM
# APPL_TOP is the top-level directory for Oracle Applications.
#
APPL_TOP="/slot01/appmgr/emstestappl"
export APPL_TOP
#
# FNDNAM is the name of your AOL schema.
#
FNDNAM="apps"
export FNDNAM
#
# GWYUID is the schema name and password for your public schema.
#
```

Contd

Fig. 3.4 Contd

```
GWYUID="APPLSYSPUB/PUB"
export GWYUID
# RHEL Patch
LD_ASSUME_KERNEL="2.4.19"

#
# The APPCPNAM determines how files are named by cm
# Possible values are USER and REQID.
#
APPCPNAM="REQID"
export APPCPNAM

#
# The APPLMAIL variable is needed for relinking.
# You may edit its definition, but do not remove it.
# APPLMAIL={NONE | ORACLE_INTEROFFICE}
#

APPLMAIL="NONE"
export APPLMAIL

# This is for the corner case where somebody removed the
# context file and needs to rebuild the context file.

#
# Top-level directories for all products
#

  AD_TOP="/slot01/appmgr/emstestappl/ad/11.5.0"
  export AD_TOP

  FND_TOP="/slot01/appmgr/emstestappl/fnd/11.5.0"
  export FND_TOP

#
# APPLCSF is the top-level directory in which the Concurrent Manager
# puts log and output files.
#
APPLCSF="/slot01/appmgr/emstestcomn/admin"
export APPLCSF
```

Contd

Fig. 3.4 Contd

```
#
# AFSYSCSI is the CSI number
#
AFSYSCSI="N/A"

#
# APPLLOG and APPLOUT are the subdirectories in which
# the Concurrent Manager puts log and output files.
#

APPLLOG="log/emstest"
export APPLLOG

APPLOUT="out/emstest"

APPLRGF="/slot01/appmgr/emstestcomn/rgf/emstest"
export APPLRGF

#
# APPLTMP is the directory in which Oracle Applications
# temporary files are created.
#

APPLTMP="/slot01/appmgr/emstestcomn/temp"
export APPLTMP

#
# APPLPTMP is the directory in which PL/SQL output files are created.
#

APPLPTMP="/slot01/oracle/emstestdb/9.2.0/temp"
export APPLPTMP

#
# Env variable that will be to set the LD_LIBRARY_PATH for Java
concurrent
# programs
# Env variable that will be to set the LD_LIBRARY_PATH for Java
concurrent
# programs
#
```

Contd

Fig. 3.4 Contd

```
AF_LD_LIBRARY_PATH=/slot01/appmgr/emstestora/iAS/lib:/slot01/appmgr/
emstestora/8.0.6/network/jre11/lib/i686/native_threads:/slot01/appmgr/
emstestora/8.0.6/network/jre11/lib/linux/native_threads:/slot01/appmgr/
emstestappl/cz/11.5.0/bin:${LD_LIBRARY_PATH:=}
export AF_LD_LIBRARY_PATH

#
# National Language Support environment variables
#

NLS_LANG="American_America.UTF8"
export NLS_LANG

NLS_DATE_FORMAT="DD-MON-RR"
export NLS_DATE_FORMAT

NLS_NUMERIC_CHARACTERS=".,"
export NLS_NUMERIC_CHARACTERS

NLS_SORT="BINARY"
export NLS_SORT

#
# Oracle Reports 6.0 environment variables
#

REPORTS60_TMP="/slot01/appmgr/emstestcomn/temp"
export REPORTS60_TMP
```

Fig. 3.4 Entries in APPLSYS.env

Table 3.1 Details of Environment Settings

Parameter	Details
APPLFENV	The name of the environment files viz. <sid.env>, for example emstest.env.
CONTEXT_FILE	The location of the context file, which is normally $APPL_TOP/admin/<sid>.xml.
CONTEXT_NAME	Name of the environment.
TWO_TASK	Name of the environment.
PLATFORM	The platform of the Operating System.

Contd

Table 3.1 Contd

Parameter	Details
APPL_TOP	Full pathname of the APPL_TOP.
FNDNAM	The Oracle schema to which the system responsibility connects. This is APPS by default.
GWYUID	The Oracle user ID/password used for the authentication at the first sign in of Forms. The default is APPLSYSPUB/PUB.
PROD_TOP	Full pathname of the product top directories
PATH	The path of the product directories.
APPLDCP	It tells whether the Distributed Concurrent Processing feature is used. The value of this is either yes or no.
APPLCSF	This is the top-level directory in which the CM puts the log and output files.
APPLLOG	This is the sub-directory for the CM log files. The default is log.
APPLOUT	This is the sub-directory for the CM output files. The default is out.
APPLTMP	This is the directory in which Oracle Application temporary files are created.
APPLPTMP	This is the directory for the temporary PL/SQL output files.

adovars.env

This file is located in $APPL_TOP admin directory. It contains information about JAVA_TOP, JRE files, and HTML files, as well as a few environment parameters.

Table 3.2 Details of Environment Parameters in adovars.env

Parameter	Details
JAVA_TOP	The JAVA_TOP variable indicates the top-level directory where all Java class files are copied.
OA_JRE_TOP	This variable indicates the location where the Java Runtime Environment (JRE) is installed on the machine.
AF_JRE_TOP	This variable indicates the location of a transition JVM installation on the machine.
CLASSPATH	Java requires CLASSPATH to be defined on most platforms. This is because it lists the directories and zip files to be scanned for Java class files needed at runtime.

Contd

Table 3.2 Contd

Parameter	Details
`LD_LIBRARY_PATH`	This is used on some platforms to list the directories to be scanned for dynamic library files needed at runtime.
`OAH_TOP`	The `OAH_TOP` variables define the locations for copying HTML files by Oracle Applications.
`OAD_TOP`	The `OAD_TOP` variables define the locations where Oracle Applications copies context-sensitive documentation files.

APPSORA.env/APPS<SID>.env

This file contains the entries for two files—one is `APPLSYS.env`, and the other sets the technology stack `8.0.6 ORACLE_HOME`.

SID.xml

This is the context file used by Oracle Applications and contains the following details about the `APPL_TOP`:

- The name of the application system
- The information about the various servers
- The technology stack version
- The guest user name password
- The DB host and port details
- The port number of all the components of the middle tiers
- The product top directories of all the installed products

adconfig.txt

This file is also located at the `$APPL_TOP/admin` directory. It contains the information about the configuration of tiers on the particular nodes of the `APPL_TOP` as well as details of the server and the `APPL_TOP` path. Therefore, it should not be altered manually.

adjareas.txt

This file lists the Java code libraries (areas) listed in the -areas argument passed to `adjmx`. In the C code, we only call `adjmx` with the -areas argument when generating JAR files.

The Java code libraries listed in this file are evaluated and added to the -areas argument in the exact order that they occur. This file is located in `APPL_TOP/admin` directory.

topfile.txt

This file has the information about the number of products installed and lists the product top of each. It is located in `APPL_TOP/admin` directory.

appsweb.cfg

This is the main configuration file used by the Forms, and defines the parameter values used. It is located at `$OA_HTML/bin` and contains the following details:

- Forms server name, server port, domain name
- Database connection parameters
- JInitiator version

Hostname_SID.dbc

DBC stands for database connection. This file is responsible for establishing a successful connection between the database and the `APPL_TOP`. The location of this file is `$FND_TOP`/secure.

The DBC file contains the values of `GWYUID`, `FNDNAM`, and `TWO_TASK` and `GUEST_USER_PWD`. `GWYUID` should have `APPLSYSPUB/PUB` as user ID/password. The default user ID/password for Oracle Applications is guest/guest, guest/oracle, oracle/guest. It should match the record available in the `fnd_profile_options` table.

adpltfrm.txt

This file contains name of the platform and is located in `$APPL_TOP/admin`.

Core directories

The `APPL_TOP` contains four code directories that are used for the proper functioning, maintenance and up gradation of the `APPL_TOP`. The directories are `ad`, `admin`, `au` and `fnd`.

AD directory

AD refers to Application DBA. This is a set of tools for installing, upgrading, and administering the Oracle Applications environment. This directory contains all the Adutilities such as AutoUpgrade, Auto Patch (`adpatch`) and the AD Administration (`adadmin`). All these utilities are stored in the `$AD_TOP/bin` directory. Figure 3.5 shows the content of the `$AD_TOP/bin` directory.

```
(appmgr01) bin - bash $ ls
adadmin            adcvm.cmd         admrgpch          adshell.sh
adadminnew         adcvm.sh          adncnv            adsplice
adadmin_wrapper    addefgen          adodfcmp          adsplicenew
adaimgr            addlnctl.pl       adogdgen.sh       adsplice_wrapper
adbldxml.cmd       addmimp           adownmt.sh        adsstart
adbldxml.sh        adenvch.sh        adpatch           adtmplreport.cmd
adcfginfo.cmd      adgenhfver.pl     adpatch.bak       adtmplreport.sh
adcfginfo.sh       adgenhnm          adpatchnew        adtopgen.sh
adchgatname.pl     adgennls.pl       adpatchnew.bak    aducsifm.pm
```

Contd

Fig. 3.5 Contd

```
adchgjreopt.pl      adgenpsf.pl       adpatch_wrapper    aducsifm.sh
adchkcfg.cmd        adgentns.pl       adphmigr.pl        aducssp.pl
adchkcfg.sh         adgetnode.cmd     adposclo.pm        aducssp.sh
adchkutl.sh         adgetreg          adpreclo.pm        adulong
adclonectx.pl       adident           adprmkey           adunload.sh
adclone.pl          adjava            adprocfg.pm        adupdts.cmd
adclone.sh          adjavamig.pl      adproc.sh          adupdts.sh
adconfig.cmd        adjbuild.sh       adpwhide.cmd       adurs
adconfig.pl         adjkey            adpwmask           adutils.pl
adconfig.sh         adlibin.sh        adrebase           adutils.sh
adctrl              adlibout.sh       adregenv           advldmerge.pl
adctrlnew           adlicmgr.cmd      adrelinknew.sh     adwait
adctrl_wrapper      adlicmgr.sh       adrelink.sh        adworker
adcustomizer.cmd    adlicmgr.sh.bak   adsctest.sh        adworker.bak
adcustomizer.sh     admkappsutil.pl   adshell.pl         adxerr.pl
```

Fig. 3.5 Unix Session 3.2

Admin directory

The `$APPL_TOP/admin` directory contains the scripts and files used by the Adutilities. This directory also contains the log and output files created during patching. The important files in the `$APPL_TOP/admin` directory are:

- `<sid>.xml`, a context file used by the Oracle Applications
- `adovars.env`, an important configuration file that has been discussed earlier
- `<sid>/log` contains all the log files generated during patching or running of Adutilities
- `<sid>/out` contains all the output files
- Text files pertain to the application system, which are referred to during Auto Patch

AU (applications utility) directory

This directory contains all the application utility files. The `AU_TOP` directory contains product files consolidated in a single location for optimal processing, such as:

- PL/SQL libraries used by the Oracle Forms (`$AU_TOP/resource`)
- PL/SQL libraries used by the Oracle Reports (`$AU_TOP/plsql`)
- All Oracle forms source files (`$AU_TOP/forms`)
- Reports files required by discoverer (`$AU_TOP/reports`)
- A copy of all Java files used by JInitiator when regenerating the desktop client JAR files (The public copies of all Java files are stored in `JAVA_TOP`)

FND (foundation) directory

FND is the foundation of the Application Object Library. It contains the script and programs that are used to build the data dictionary and forms of all application programs.

Language files and directory

Whenever Oracle Application is installed in a language other than English, language-specific files and directories are also created in the APPL_TOP. Each product tree contains an additional directory with the code of this language, which has the language-specific files. For example, if the additional language Arabic is installed, then in each product directory there will be a directory AR for the Arabic related files.

COMMON_TOP

The COMMON_TOP (<sid>comn) directory contains the common files used by the Oracle Applications.

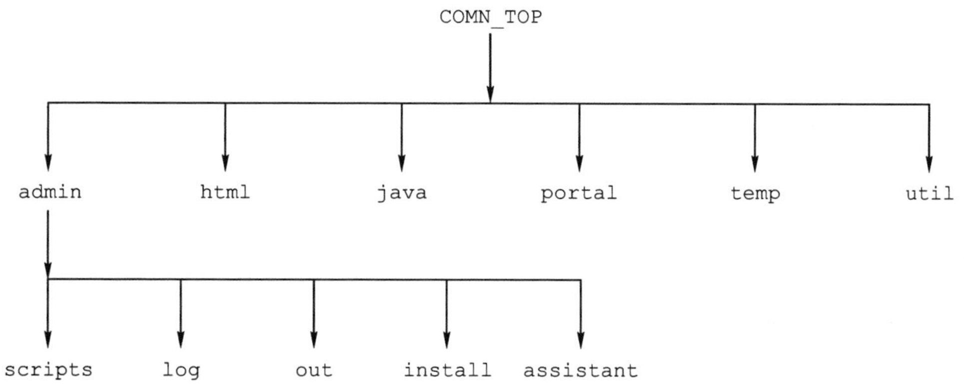

Fig. 3.6 Directory Structure of COMN_TOP

The common top contains six directories.

- Admin—This directory is the default location for the Concurrent Manager log and output files. It also contains a directory (called scripts), which contains all the scripts for managing all components of the middle tiers. The install directory under the admin directory contains the script and the log files used by the Rapid Install.
- HTML—This directory points to the environment variable $OA_HTML. The HTML-based screens and sign-on pages are stored in this directory as well as JSP files, Java Scripts and XML files.
- JAVA—This directory points to the environment variable $JAVA_TOP. All the Oracle Application JAR files are placed here by Rapid Install. It also contains some third party Java and zip files.
- Portal—This directory contains the portal files of the Rapid Install. This is the web page containing the server administration scripts, installation documents and online help page. This page comes by default by parsing the following URL at the browser—http://hostname.domain:port

- `Temp`—The temp directory contains temporary files and is also used for caching by products like Oracle reports.
- `Util`—This directory contains third party utilities like JRE, JDK and zip.

Oracle Application Technology Stack

The Oracle Application technology stack consists of two components—`8.0.6 Oracle_Home` and `iAS ORACLE_HOME`.

- `8.0.6 Oracle_Home` contains the `ORACLE_HOME` for the Developer6i products, viz. Forms, reports and graphics.
- `iAS` contains the `ORACLE_HOME` for the Oracle 9*i* Application Server and it hosts a number of middle tier components, viz. the `Apache` and `Jserv`.

R12 FILE SYSTEM

There has been a lots of changes in the file system in the new Release12. The new structure splits the Oracle Application files in three parts.

- Data
- Code
- Config

Separating these three will help in easy maintenance as configuration file changes more frequently that the code and the data. Lets start with the top level directory structure of the file system and then we will discuss the changes one by one.

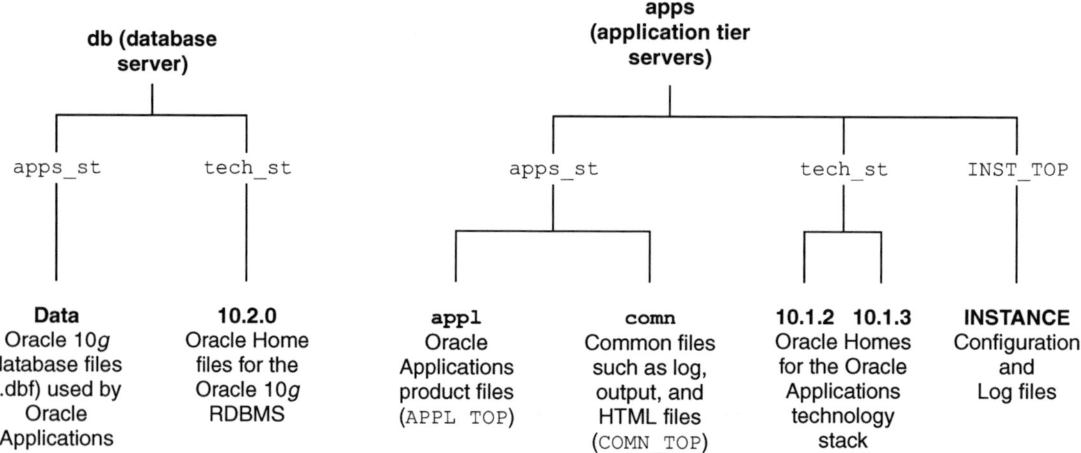

Fig. 3.7 R12 File System

- The db/apps_st/data (DATA_TOP) directory contains all the datafiles , redo log file and is located on the database node
- The db/tech_st/10.2.0 contains the ORACLE_HOME for the Oracle10g database and is located in the database node
- The apps/apps_st/appl (APPL_TOP) directory contains the product directories and files for Oracle Applications
- The apps/apps_st/comn or (COMMON_TOP or COMN_TOP) directory contains the common directories and files used across products
- The apps/tech_st/10.1.2 directory contains the ORACLE_HOME used for the Applications technology stack tools components
- The apps/tech_st/10.1.3 directory contains the ORACLE_HOME used for the Applications technology stack Java components
- The INST_TOP contains all the configuration files and all the log files. We will discuss in more details about this in the next section.

The following table shows the overview of the changes in the filesystem between 11*i* and R12

Table 3.3 11*i* and R12 Mount Points Comparison

For Applmgr User		
Mount Point	**Old**	**New**
APPL_TOP	<APPS_BASE>/<SID>appl	<APPS_BASE>/apps/apps_st/appl
COMMON_TOP	<APPS_BASE>/<SID>comn	<APPS_BASE>/apps/apps_st/comn
ORACLE_HOME	<APPS_BASE>/<SID>ora/8.0.6	<APPS_BASE>/apps/tech_st/10.1.2
IAS_ORACLE_HOME	<APPS_BASE>/<SID>ora/iAS	<APPS_BASE>/apps/tech_st/10.1.3
For Oracle User		
Mount Point	**Old**	**New**
ORACLE_HOME	<ORACLE_BASE>/<SID>db/10.2.0	<ORACLE_BASE>/db/tech_st/10.2.0
ORADATA	<ORACLE_BASE>/<SID>data	<ORACLE_BASE>/db/apps_st/data
INSTANCE_HOME		
Mount Point	**Old**	**New**
INST_TOP	NA	<APPS_BASE>/inst/apps/<context_name>

The important change that has been done in the Release 12 is the directory structures don't contain the $TWO_TASK.

Instance Home Overview

Release 12 introduces a new concept of a top-level directory for an Applications Instance which is known as Instance Home and is denoted the environment variable $INST_TOP. Instance Home contains all the config files, log files, SSL certificates etc. The addition Instance Home makes the middle tier more easy to manage and organised since the data is kept separate from the config files. The Instance Home also has the ability to share the Applications and Technology stack code across multiple instances. To create a new instance that shares an existing middle-tier, just create a new instance_top with proper config files and nfs mount the middle tier in the server.

Another advantage of the Instance Home is that the Autoconfig no longer writes anything to the APPL_TOP and ORACLE_HOME directories everything is now written in the INST_TOP as a result APPL_TOP and ORACLE_HOME can also be made read only file system if required . Earlier say the adpatch used to write the log file in APPL_TOP/admin directory but with the new model the APPL_CONFIG_HOME/admin is used.

The basic structure of the Instance Home is:

<APPS_BASE>/inst/apps/<context>/<INST_TOP>, where APPS_BASE (which does not have or need a corresponding environment variable) is the top level of the Applications installation, and <context> is the highest level at which the Applications context exists.

Instance Home Directory Structure

$INST_TOP

/admin	
/scripts	ADMIN_SCRIPTS_HOME: Find all AD scripts here
/appl	APPL_CONFIG_HOME. For standalone envs, this is set to $APPL_TOP
/fnd/12.0.0/secure	FND_SECURE: dbc files here
/admin	All Env Config files here
/certs	SSL Certificates go here
/logs	LOG_HOME: Central log file location. All log files are placed here (except adconfig)
/ora	ORA_CONFIG_HOME
/10.1.2	'C' Oracle home config, Contains tnsnames and forms listener servlet config files
/10.1.3	Apache & OC4J config home, Apache, OC4J and opmn. This is the 'Java' oracle home configuration for OPMN, Apache and OC4J
/pids	Apache/Forms server PID files here
/portal	Apache's DocumentRoot folder

Changes in COMMON_TOP Directory Structure

There has been some changes in the COMMON_TOP file system in the Release 12 . These changes are mainly related to the location of the various java files . The below illustration shows the difference between a 11*i* and R12

11*i*:

- $JAVA_TOP = $COMMON_TOP/java
    - Class
    - Archives

R12:

- $JAVA_TOP = $COMMON_TOP/java/classes
    - Classes
- $AF_JLIB = $COMMON_TOP/java/lib
    - Archives

Rapid Install installs all Oracle Applications class files in the COMMON_TOP/classes directory known as $JAVA_TOP. Release 12 introduces a new environment variable $AF_JLIB which points to $COMMON_TOP/lib where all the zip and jar files are installed .The top-level Java directory, $COMMON_TOP/java, is pointed to by the $JAVA_BASE environment variable.

The OA_HTML environment setting points to the html directory in the COMMON_TOP. The new path for the same is <diskresource>/appmgr/apps/apps_st/comn/webapps/oacore/html. Two new subdirectories META-INF and WEB-INF is introduced under the HTML directory to meet J2EE specifications.

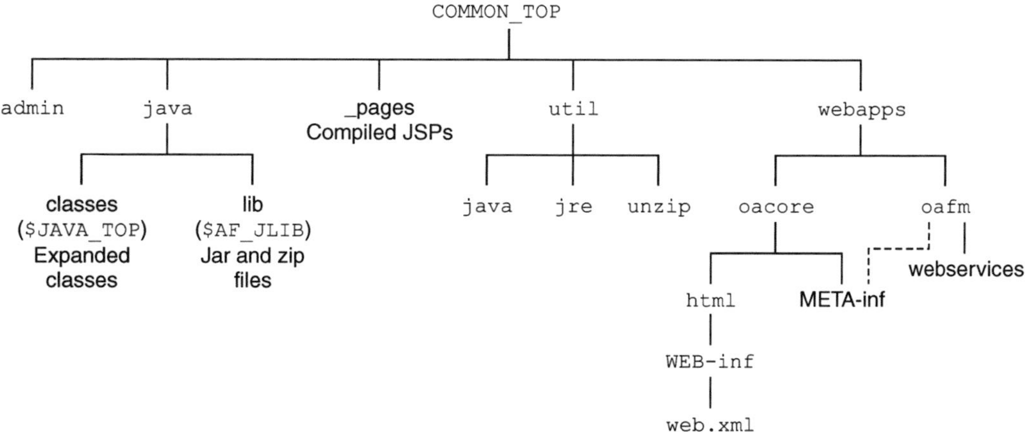

Fig. 3.8 R12 COMMON_TOP File System

Table 3.4 11*i* and R12 Environment Files/Variable Changes Comparison

ENVIRONMENT FILE/VARIABLE CHANGES		
	OLD	NEW
Env Source File	APPSORA.env	APPS<SID>.env This file executes the following env files $ORA_CONFIG_HOME/10.1.2/$TWO_TASK.env $APPL_CONFIG_HOME/$TWO_TASK.env
Context File (MT)	$APPL_TOP/admin/$TWO_TASK.xml	$APPL_CONFIG_HOME/admin/$TWO_TASK.xml
OA_HTML	$COMMON_TOP/html	$COMMON_TOP/webapps/oacore/html
JAVA_TOP, OA_JAVA	$COMMON_TOP/java	$COMMON_TOP/java/classes
AF_JLIB	N/A	$COMMON_TOP/java/lib
JAVA_BASE	N/A	$COMMON_TOP/java/
FND_SECURE	$FND_TOP/secure/<SID>/	$INST_TOP/apps/fnd/12.0.0/secure/
ADMIN_SCRIPTS_HOME	$COMMON_TOP/admin/scripts/<SID>/	$INST_TOP/admin/scripts/
LOG_HOME	$APPL_TOP/admin/<SID>/logs/	$INST_TOP/logs
FORMS_WEB_CONFIG_FILE	N/A	$INST_TOP/ora/10.1.2/forms/server/appsweb.cfg

Changes in Environment Files and Variables

The following are the changes in the env file naming convention and environment variables.

Configuration Files

For standalone instances, `$APPL_CONFIG_HOME` is set to `$APPL_TOP`. So the `config` files will be in the usual location (`$APPL_TOP/admin`). A small set of files created by `autoconfig`, that are used by `adpatch`, are still required to be in `APPL_TOP` (Context variable `s_appl_config_home`).

Hence in a multinode environment, `$APPL_CONFIG_HOME` should be set to `$APPL_TOP` in the node where `adpatch` will be run. Since the technology stack with R12 uses is AS10g so it uses a couple of XML configuration files also.

Important Configuration files are

Location: `$APPL_CONFIG_HOME/admin`

- `Topfile.txt` — `product top info`
- `adjareas.txt` — `adjareas.txt`
- `adjborg.txt` — `adjborg.txt`
- `adjborg2.txt` — `adjborg2.txt`
- `adovars.env` — `adovars.env`
- `adconfig.txt` — AD tools related parameters
- `context file` — Context file `<SID>.xml`

The XML Configuration files are

- `opmn.xml`
- `server.xml`
- `orion-application.xml`
- `orion-web.xml`

OPMN.XML

This is located at `$ORA_CONFIG_HOME/10.1.3/opmn/conf/`

- Used by Oracle Process Manager and Notification Server (OPMN)
- Contains details of all the OC4J instances deployed on the server·
- Various ports used by OPMN

SERVER.XML

This is located at `$ORA_CONFIG_HOME/10.1.3/j2ee/oacore/config/`

- Used by OC4J
- Contains details of all the Applications deployed under that OC4J instance

- Details like name of the application, where it is deployed, shared libraries if any....
- Path for the j2ee-logging configuration file, RMI configuration file, JMS configuration file....

ORION-APPLICATION.XML

This is located at `$ORA_CONFIG_HOME/10.1.3/j2ee/oacore/applications-deployment/oacore`

- Used by application instance
- Contains details of all the web-modules deployed under that Application
- Also includes library path where it should look for the java code

ORION-WEB.XML

This is located at `$ORA_CONFIG_HOME/10.1.3/j2ee/oacore/applications-deployment/oacore/html/`

- Used by web module
- Contains details of all servlet aliases and the mapping to servlet classes

APACHE CONFIGURATION FILES

Location: `$ORA_CONFIG_HOME/10.1.3/Apache/Apache/conf/`

- `httpd.conf` — This is a server configuration file which typically contains directives that affect how the server runs, such as user and group IDs it should use, and location of other files.
- `apps.conf` — Contains alias to html,media,temp etc (E-biz settings)
- `dms.conf` — Oracle iAS DMS configuration file. This config file enables you to monitor performance of site components with Oracle's Dynamic Monitoring Service (DMS).
- `mod_oc4j.conf` — OC4J Apache module config file.
- `oracle_apache.conf` — Oracle Specific HTTP server configuration file. Used for including other `config` files
- `security.conf` — Used for loading security modules

Location: `$ORA_CONFIG_HOME/10.1.3/config/`

- `ias.properties` iAS related properties in this file, like Apache home location, version, server etc.

Location: `$ORA_CONFIG_HOME/10.1.3/javacache/admin/`

- `javacache.xml config` files for `oacore apps`

Location: `$ORA_CONFIG_HOME/10.1.3/j2ee/forms/config/`

- `j2ee-logging.xml`: Logging configuration file for OC4J
- `jms.xml`: JMS Configuration file for forms application
- `oc4j-connectors.xml`: Connector Configuration file for forms application
- `oc4j.properties`: OC4J properties file for Various parameters like log filenames etc are specified here.
- `rmi.xml`: RMI Configuration file for forms application. RMI stands for Remote Method Invocation. (The Java RMI system allows an object running in one Java Virtual Machine to invoke methods on an object running in another VM)
- `server.xml`: Various directory locations are specified in this file
- `system-application.xml`: This is the global application config file that is the parent for all other applications on the server. This file imports and loads various web modules

Location: `$ORA_CONFIG_HOME/10.1.3/j2ee/oacore/application-deployments/oacore/oa_servlets/` and `$ORA_CONFIG_HOME/10.1.3/j2ee/oacore/application-deployments/oacore/html/`

- `orion-web.xml` Replacement for zone.properties. The same file is located in both the above `oa_servlets` and HTML directories

Location: `$ORA_CONFIG_HOME/10.1.3/j2ee/oacore/application-deployments/oacore/`

- `orion-application.xml` Used for applications level configuration. Used for specifying `applications.log` file location, OC4J connector context file etc.

Location: `$ORA_CONFIG_HOME/10.1.3/network/$TWO_TASK`

- `tnsnames.ora` Apache's `tnsnames.ora` file.

FORM SERVER CONFIG FILES

Location: `$ORA_CONFIG_HOME/10.1.2/forms/server`

- `appsweb.cfg` (`$FORMS_WEB_CONFIG_FILE`). This file has moved to this location. Contains info on serverName, serverPort etc.
- `default.env` Contains most of the env variables (classpath, product tops, oracle home etc)

MIDDLE TIER ORACLE HOME CONFIG FILES

Location: `$ORA_CONFIG_HOME/10.1.2/network/admin`

- `tnsnames.ora` Contains `tns` entries for `fndsm`, `db` etc
- `listener.ora` Middle-tier Oracle home `listener.ora` file

Log Files

The log file locations have also changed in the R12 . All the log files are now located in the Instance Top.

- AD Script log files `$INST_TOP/logs/appl/admin/log`
- CM Log Files `$INST_TOP/logs/appl/conc/log`
- AD tools log files `$APPL_CONFIG_HOME/admin/$TWO_TASK/log`
- OPMN Log Files `$INST_TOP/logs/10.1.3/opmn`
- Apache Log Files `$INST_TOP/logs/10.1.3/Apache/`
- OC4J Log Files (Text) `$INST_TOP/logs/10.1.3/j2ee/oacore/`
- OC4J Log Files ODL `$INST_TOP/logs/10.1.3/j2ee/oacore/log/oacore_default_group_1/oc4j`

4

INSTALLING ORACLE APPLICATIONS

INSTALLING ORACLE APPLICATIONS 11.5.10 CU2

PLANNING THE INSTALLATION

The first and foremost step for a successful installation is proper planning—a considerable amount of time should be spent in planning the business needs, the long-term growth of business, the number of concurrent users, the size of the database and the hardware and software requirements. It is important to ensure that the required hardware, software, documentation, correct operating system patches and of course the skills are available to complete the installation.

System Requirement

CPU and memory requirements

The CPU requirements for installing Oracle Applications are not fixed. They depend on a number of factors, viz. the number of parallel users, the size and the expansion required in the database, the jobs running in the background and the desired response time. Since Oracle Applications can be used for any type of business (whether large or small scale), benchmarking these is not feasible. The best way is to refer to the Oracle Consulting Service and the hardware vendor to get a proper analysis of your CPU requirements.

Disk requirement

As per Oracle Documentation, the disk space requirements for a fresh Rapid Install are as given here.

Install configures the file system and database files for all products regardless of their licensed status. The approximate file sizes in a single-node installation are:

- Application tier file system—26 GB (includes `iAS/8.0.6 ORACLE_HOME`, `COMMON_TOP` and `APPL_TOP`)
- Database tier file system (fresh install with a production database)—31 GB
- Database tier file system (fresh install with a Vision Demo database)—65 GB

- Total space for a single node system, not including stage area, is 57 GB (for a fresh install with a production database) and 91 GB (for a fresh install with a Vision Demo database)

The database tier disk space requirements for both the production database and the Vision database include database files (`.dbf`) and the database `ORACLE_HOME`.

Stage area

To run Rapid Install from a stage area, you need at least 24 GB for the files.

Language installation

Apart from what has already been mentioned, if additional languages are being installed (other than American English), you need additional space for each language. Typically, each additional language takes around 10 GB in the application file system and 800 MB in the database.

Pre-Installation Tasks

Operating system patches

One needs to check Oracle Documentation to find out which OS patches are required for the requisite platforms, and then check whether one has the right ones for an Oracle Application installation.

Creating Unix Accounts

For installing Oracle Application, two Unix accounts need to be created—one for the database (called the `Oracle` user) and the other for the Application file system (called the `applmgr` user). Both the accounts need to be created before starting the installation. In a single node installation, one needs to log in as `Oracle` user for starting the Rapid Install, while for a multi-node installation, one logs in as `root`.

Installing Java development kit

Before the Oracle Application, the relevant version of JDK needs to be installed. The latest 11.5.10 release of Oracle Application needs JDK1.4.2.

Creating the stage area

The 11.5.10 software comes in a DVD format. The individual disks included in the Release-11*i* software bundle are labeled as follows:

- Start Here—Disk 1
- `APPL_TOP`—Disk *n*
- `RDBMS`—Disk *n*
- Tools—Disk *n*
- Databases—Disk *n*

If you are an NLS customer, you should also have the NLS supplement—Disk *n* software for each additional language that you plan to install before beginning the installation. Rapid Install requires this language-specific software for completion.

For creating the stage area, insert the Start Here DVD in the DVD-ROM drive and mount the same. Run the `adautostg.pl` script as follows:

```
$ cd/mnt/cdrom/Disk1/rapidwiz
$ perl adautostg.pl
```

You *must* have perl 5.0053 installed and it should be there in your PATH. If you don't have perl installed, you can download it from www.perl.com.

At the prompt for stage directory, enter the name of the system top-level directory. The Rapid Install Stage11*i* will be created in this path. For example, if you enter `/d1` as top-level directory, the stage will be created in `/d1/stage11i`. The components that are to be staged need to be indicated next, viz. `Apps`, `DB`, `AppsDB`, `iAS`, `NLS`. If you type '`All`' at the prompt, then all components will be staged. However, this does not create the stage for the `NLS` component, which comes in a separate DVD pack. So at this point, it will ask whether or not to stage the `NLS` software component. If your response is '`yes`', then you will be prompted for the language short name (like `AR` for Arabic `KO` for Korean) and later on the script prompts you to insert the `NLS` DVD.

Stage area directory structure

The stage area created by `adautostg.pl` looks like this: a top-level directory `<Stage11i>`, with sub-directories `startCD`, `oraApps`, `oraDB`, `oraiAS`, `oraAppDB`, and `oraNLS/<LANG>` (if required).

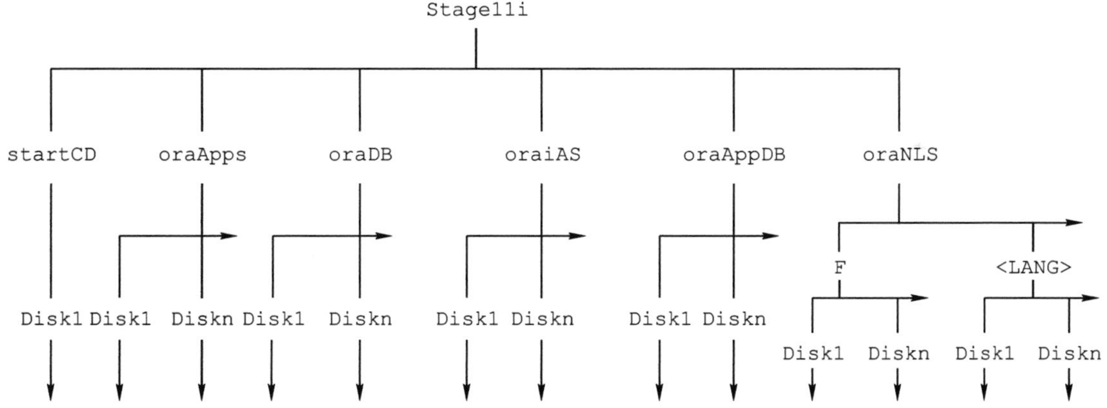

Fig. 4.1 Stage Area Directory Structure

THE INSTALLATION PROCESS

Starting the Rapid Install

Once the stage is created, we can start the Rapid Install as follows:

```
$ cd/<path of stage>/startCD/Disk1/rapidwiz
$ ./rapidwiz
```

We will examine the Rapid Install separately for single and multi-nodal installations.

Single Node Installation

Overview of single node installation

In such installations, all servers (concurrent processing, Forms, web and reports), the database and all product directories are installed on a single node. In other words, the entire Oracle Application is installed in a single server. It is generally used for smaller installations and for demonstrations.

Invoking the Rapid Install wizard starts the single node installation.

```
./rapidwiz
```

The welcome screen

The welcome screen lists the components included in the release of Oracle Application. The 11.5.10 CU2 Rapid Install comes with a 9.2.0.6 database. It can also be used to upgrade or migrate an existing database to 9.2.0.6. This is an informative screen only, so no action is required. Click 'Next' to continue.

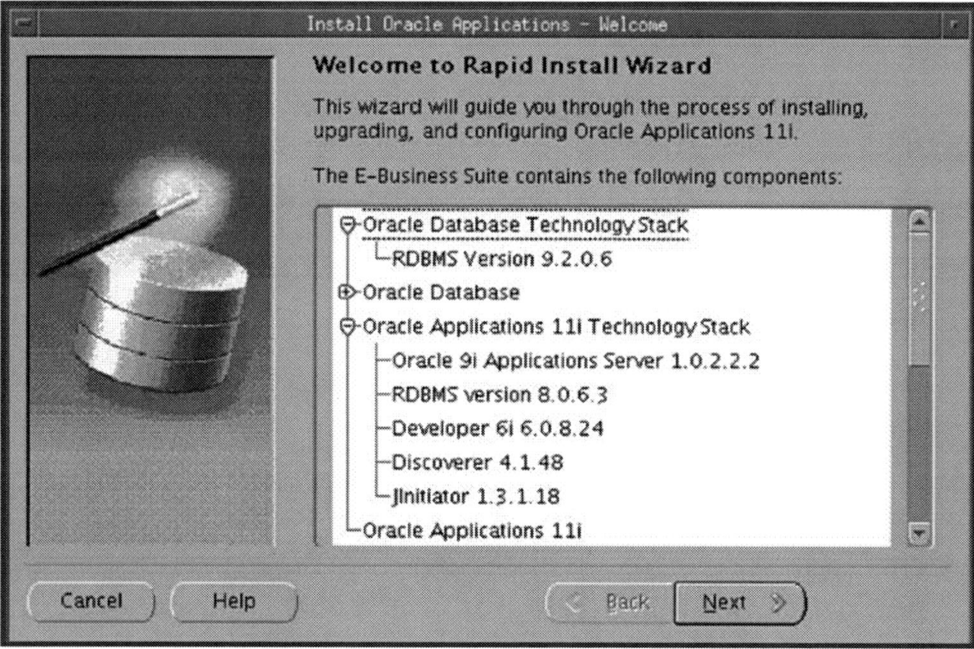

Fig. 4.2 Illustration of Welcome Screen

Selecting a wizard operation

This screen asks for the action to be performed by Rapid Install. You can choose between a fresh installation and an upgrade. Based on the response, Rapid Install performs the appropriate action and screen flow.

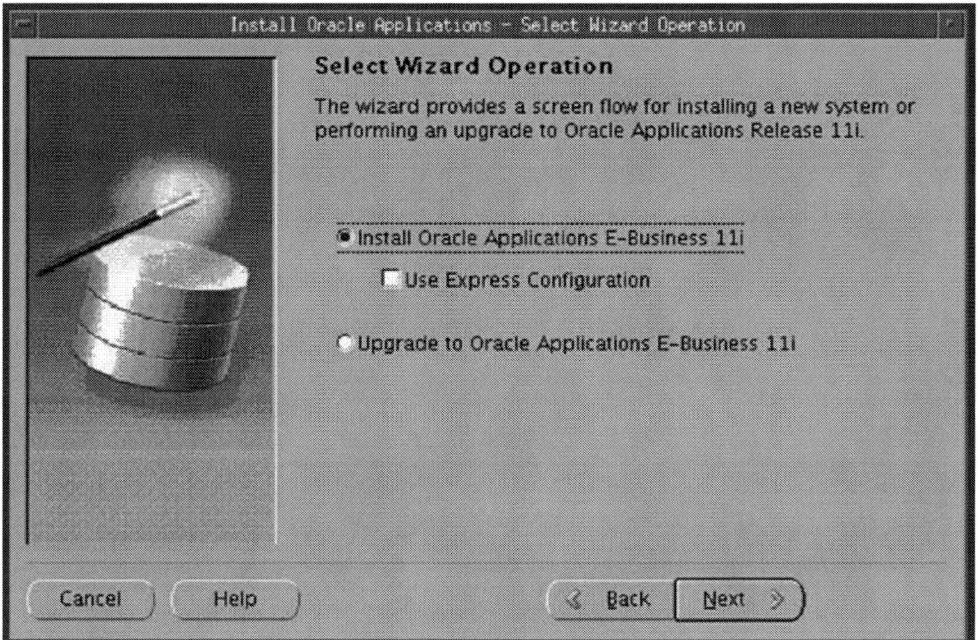

Fig. 4.3 Illustration of Selecting a Wizard Operation: Installation or Upgrade

The following are the available actions:

- Installing Fresh Oracle Applications: This action installs a fully configured system with either a fresh database or Vision Demo Database (Optional).
- Express Configuration: This action also installs a fully configured single node system with either a fresh database or Vision Demo. The only difference is that here you supply a few basic parameters such as database name, top-level install directories and port settings. The remaining directories and other settings are taken by Rapid Install using default values.
- Upgrade to Oracle Applications E-Business `11i`: Choose this option if you are upgrading your existing application system to the current version of Oracle Application.

This chapter mainly deals with fresh installations, so the last option is not recommended here. Click 'Install Oracle Application E-Business 11*i*' and press 'Next'.

Load configuration file

In this screen, you indicate whether you will be using an existing configuration file for the installation or not.

While running Rapid Install for the first time, it asks many questions from the users. It saves all the configuration parameters you enter in a new configuration file (`config.txt`). Then, it uses this to configure your system for the new installation.

If you select 'no', then Rapid Install creates a new configuration file and saves all the information in that. In case you choose 'yes', then it asks for the full path name of the configuration file. This option is chosen generally for multi-nodal installation or for restarting the Rapid Install after an interruption.

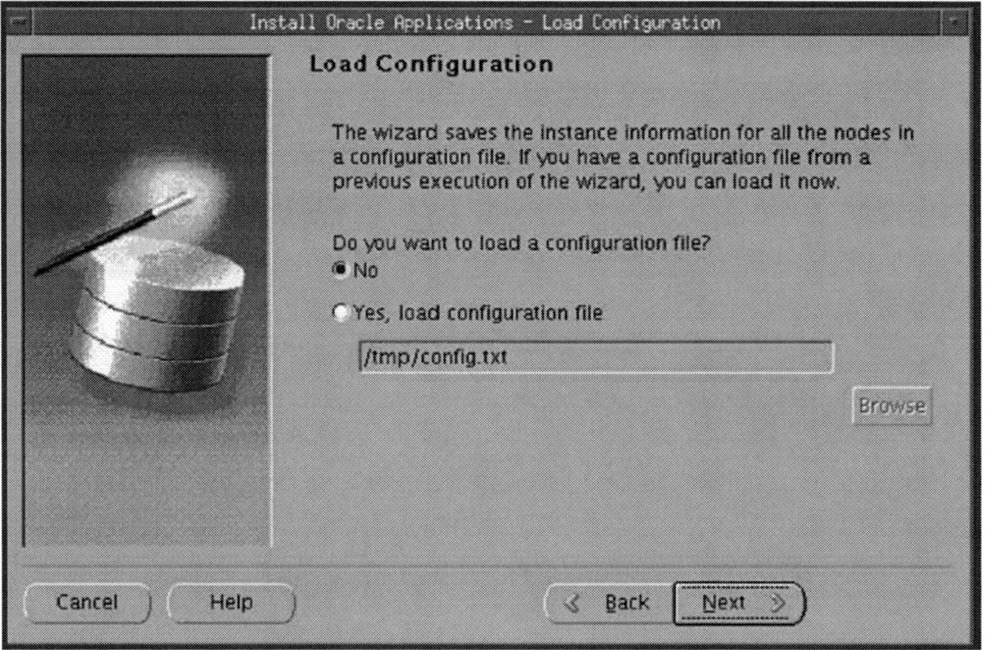

Fig. 4.4 Illustration of Load Configuration

Choosing installation type

In this screen, you indicate whether to install Oracle Application on a single node or across multiple nodes.

Since this section is about single node installation, click on 'Single node' and press 'Next'.

Database type

In this screen you indicate the database type that you want installed along with Oracle Applications. You can choose either a fresh database or a Vision Demo database.

A fresh database is a fully configurable database used for a new implementation, whereas Vision Demo database is a demonstration database having data for fictious company called Vision Enterprises. This is normally used for training or demonstration. The default name of the fresh database is `PROD`. The Vision Demo database comes with a fully configured Oracle Application System, which has already been implemented and populated with fictitious seed data.

At this stage, the user should choose 'Fresh Database', name it as `APPSTEST` and click 'Next'.

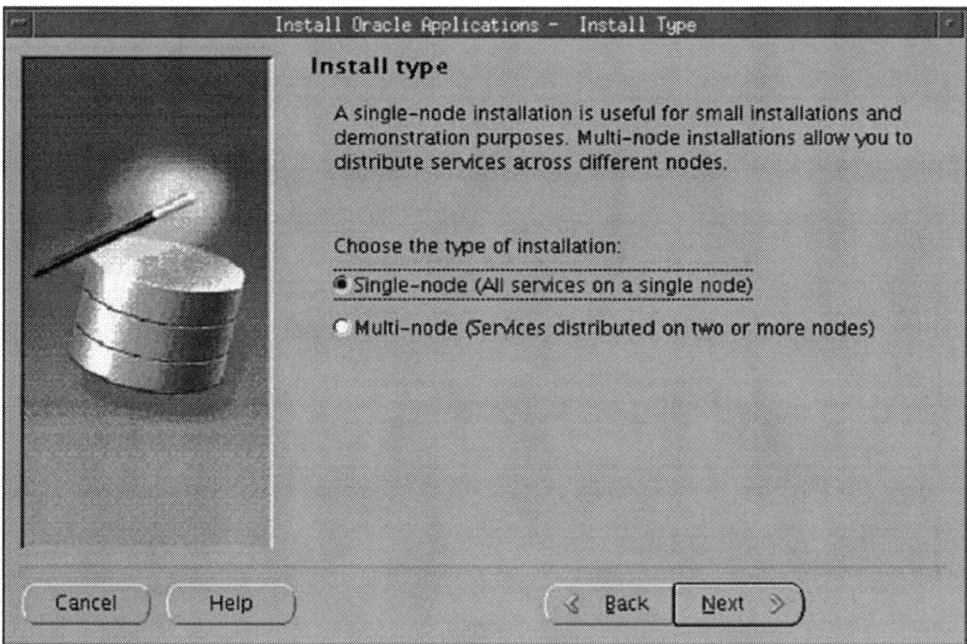

Fig. 4.5 Type of Installation

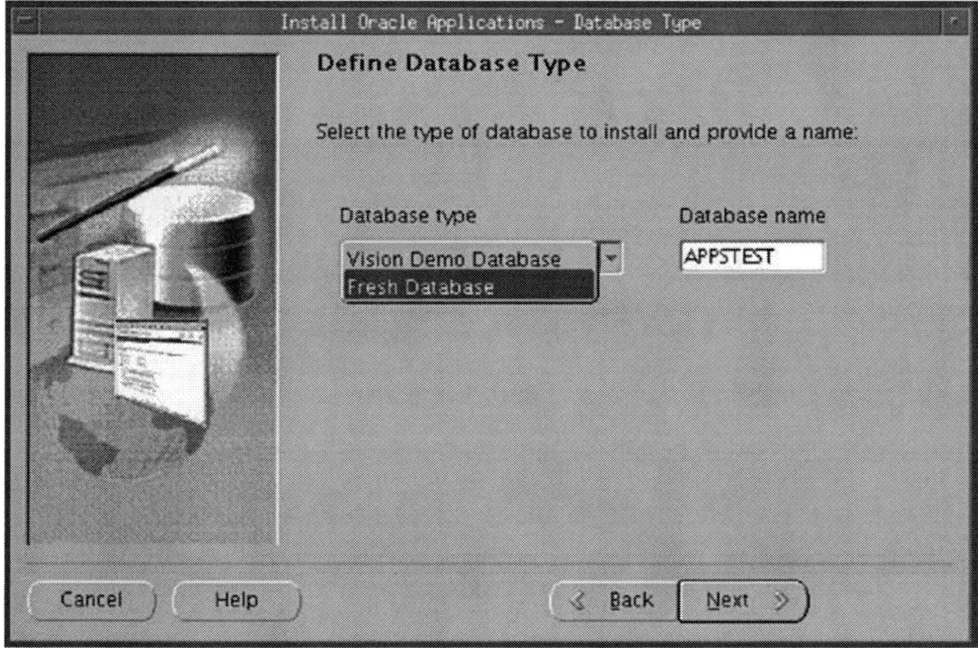

Fig. 4.6 Indicating Database Type

Database installation details

In this step, we give the database details, the storage mount points, the operating system user who will own the Oracle file system, the operating system group of the Oracle user and the Base Install directory

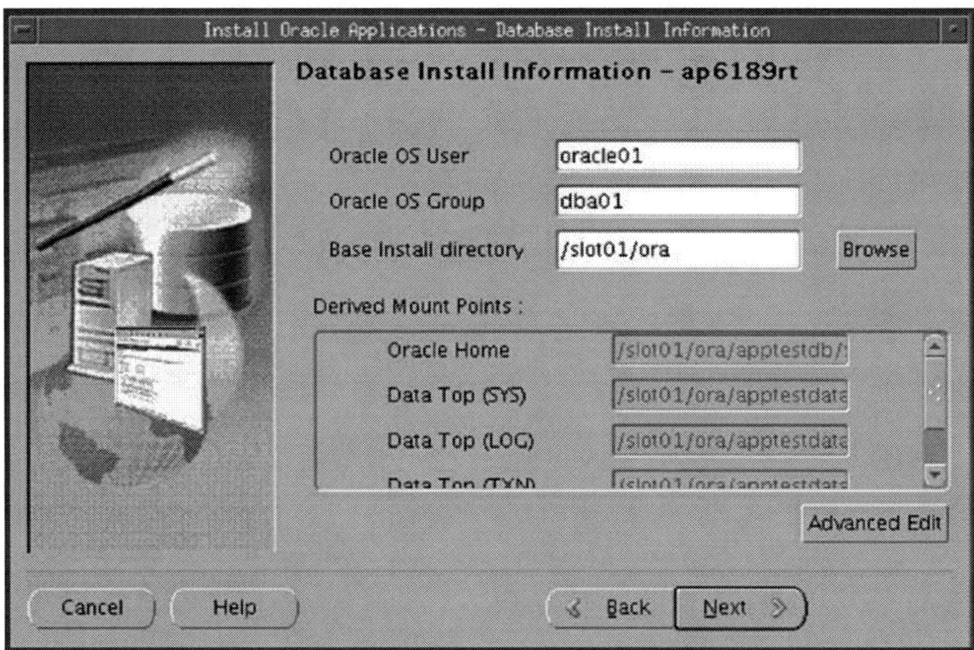

Fig. 4.7 Illustration of Database Installation

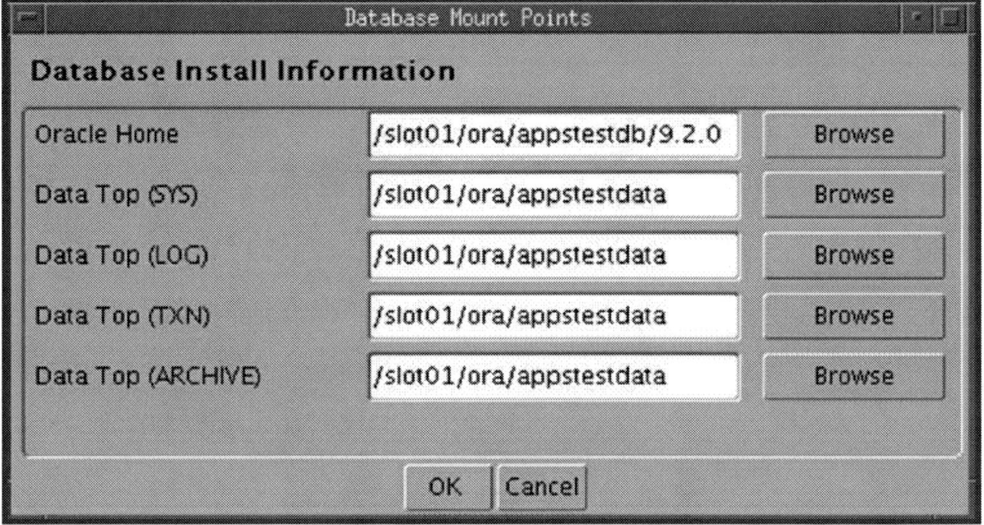

Fig. 4.8 Database Mount Points

of the Oracle. The base install directory is not the Oracle Home, it is a top-level directory which contains all the Oracle softwares.

Once the base install directory is given, Rapid Install automatically takes the default values for the Oracle Home and Data Top directories. If you want to change these values individually, it can be done using the 'Advanced Edit' button. When this button is pressed, a screen pops out where you can change the values. After making the desired changes, press the 'OK' button to return to the previous screen. Click 'Next' to continue.

Select licensing type

In this wizard, you indicate the type of licensing agreement purchased from the Oracle Corporation. Completing a licensing screen *does not* constitute a license agreement. It simply registers your products as active. You should have complete information about your product license before you complete the licensing screens.

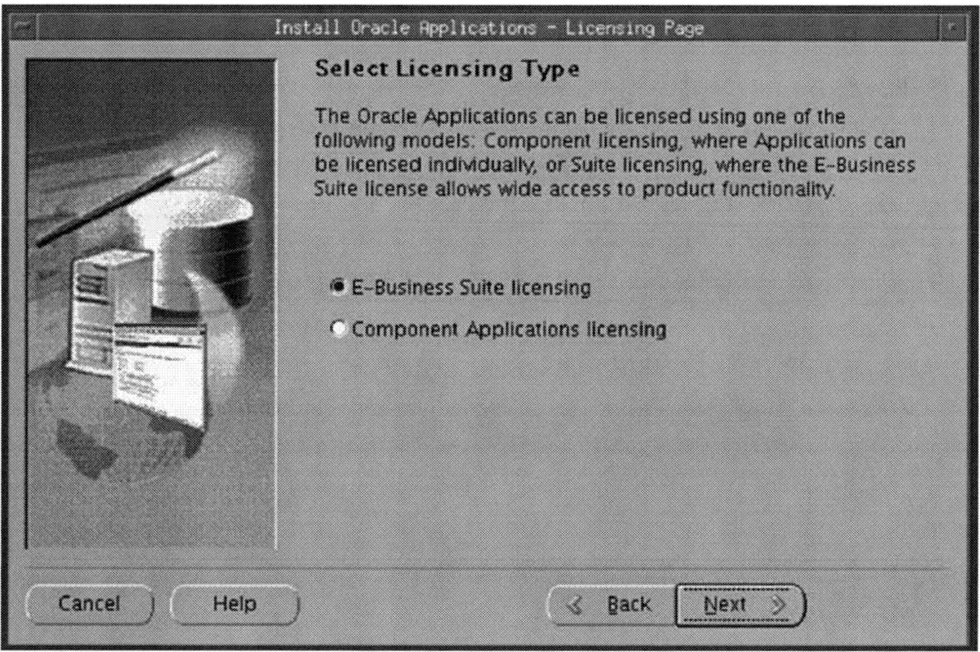

Fig. 4.9 Illustration of Licensing Page

Rapid Install installs all products automatically, regardless of their license status. However, you must register the products that you have licensed so that they are flagged in the system as active. An active flag marks products for use and inclusion in patching and other tasks to update and maintain your system after initial installation.

You can either register through E-Business Suite or Component Application Licensing in order to license your product.

If you click the E-Business Suite licensing option, the following licensing page appears.

Fig. 4.10 E-Business Suite Licensing Page

This licensing model allows wide access to Applications functionality. In effect, your choice instructs Rapid Install to automatically register all products included in the E-Business Suite price bundle. The products that are checked and grayed are licensed automatically as a part of the suite. The ones that are not must be registered separately as add-on products. Tick any add-on products that you have licensed and want to register.

You can also choose the Component Applications licensing option on the Suite Selection Screen as shown in Fig. 4.11.

Then the screen appears as shown in Fig. 4.12.

You should choose this option if the licensing agreement is for Component products of individual Applications. These products are licensed based on the number of authorized users or on the number of business transactions processed.

On this licensing page, all individual products are listed. Products that are grayed out cannot be selected unless the parent component is selected.

You can also license additional products after installation from the Oracle Application Manager by going to OAM > License Manager > License additional products.

Selecting country-specific functionality

Many application systems need country-specific or local functionality. In order to select this, choose the country from the list which is shown in the left side of the screen by using the '>' button (Fig. 4.13). Country-specific functionality can also be added at a later stage using Oracle Application Manager License Manager. In case you don't want this, just ignore this screen.

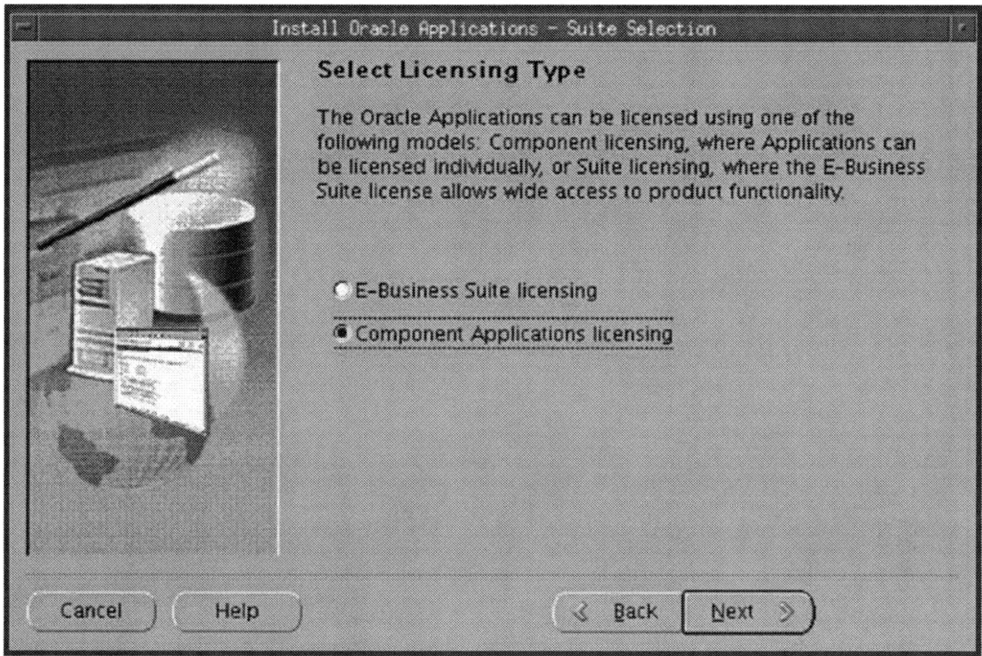

Fig. 4.11 Illustration of Choosing Component Applications Licensing Option

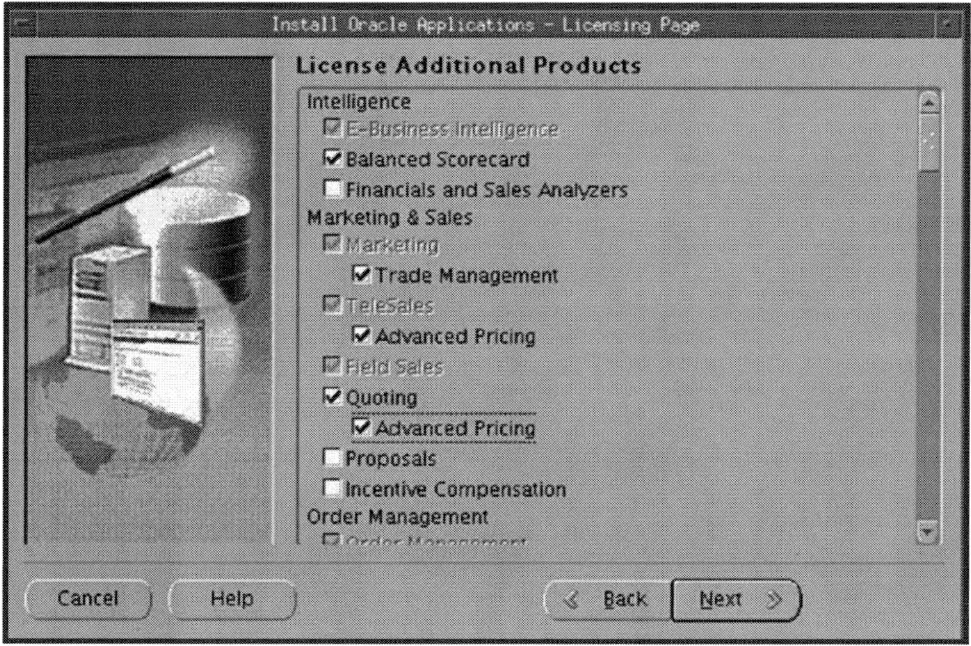

Fig. 4.12 Component Applications Licensing Page

Fig. 4.13 Selection of Country-specific Functionalities

Selecting additional languages

Using the next screen, you can install languages other than American English. As mentioned earlier, you should have the software for all the additional languages you want installed. You can also install an additional language at a later stage by making it active using Oracle Application Manager and then installing the software for it. In Fig. 4.14, it can be seen that American English is there in the first place, as it is automatically selected. Select any additional language using the '>' button. If you don't want to install an additional language, simply press 'Next'. In the illustration, we have selected two additional languages, viz. Arabic and German.

NLS settings

The next screen deals with the character set of additional languages chosen. As mentioned earlier, the base language is American English. If you select an additional language, it comes in the dropdown list in the character set column (Fig. 4.15). The character set automatically changes and includes only those compatible with the additional languages chosen.

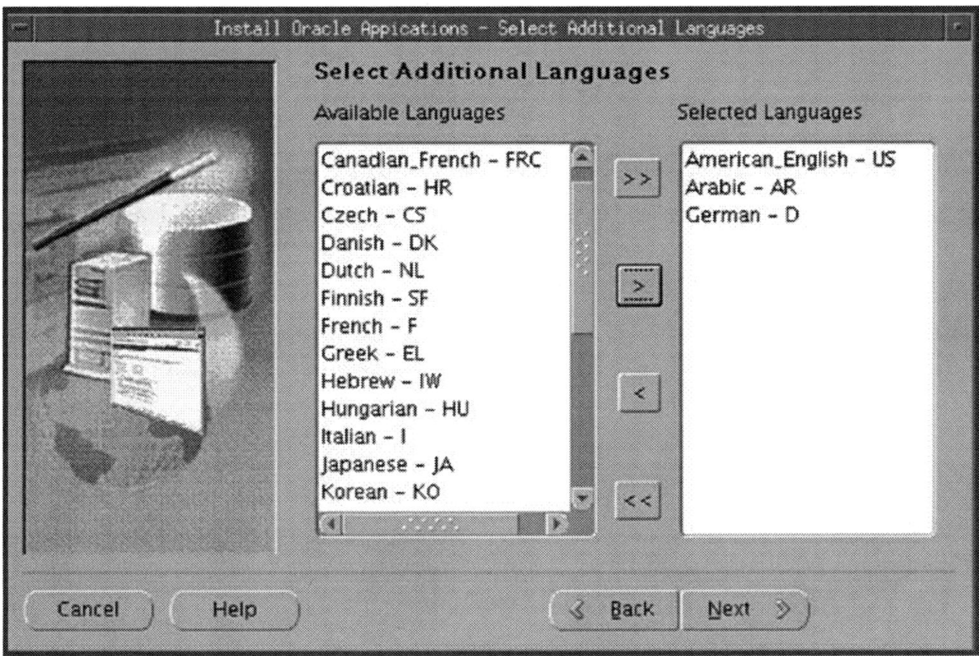

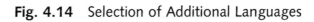

Fig. 4.14 Selection of Additional Languages

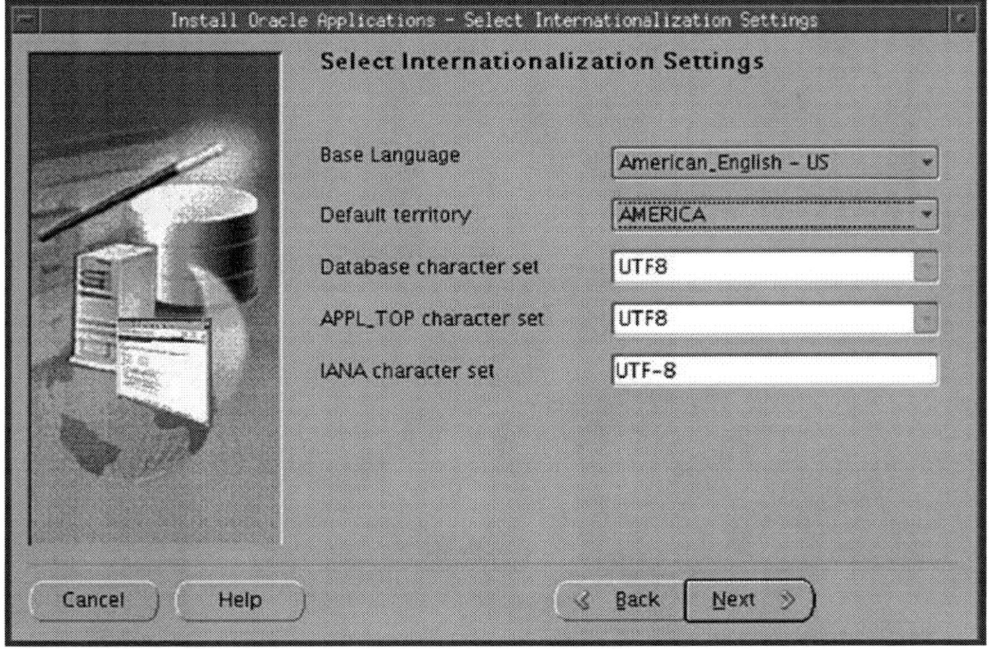

Fig. 4.15 Selection of Internationalization Settings

Box 4.1

Explanation of terms in Fig. 4.15

Base Language	The base language is the default language of the application system. If you have more than one language, then the base language field is not grayed out and you can always change it. If you have only American English as the active language then this field cannot be changed.
Default Territory	This is set to AMERICA by default and should remain so during the upgrade.
Database Character	This refers to the common character set of the database, which is compatible with all the additional languages installed.
APPL_TOP Character	This refers to the common character set of the APPL_TOP, which is compatible with all languages installed in your application system.
IANA Character	This refers to the Internet Assigned Number Authority character set. For more information about this, visit http://www.iana.org/assignments/character-sets.

Configuration information for nodes

Here you specify the top-level directory and the mount points for the APPL_TOP. Since we are doing a single node installation, all the servers are on the same node. The terms in the page are explained as follows:

- The OS user name is the operating system user who will own the Oracle Application file system

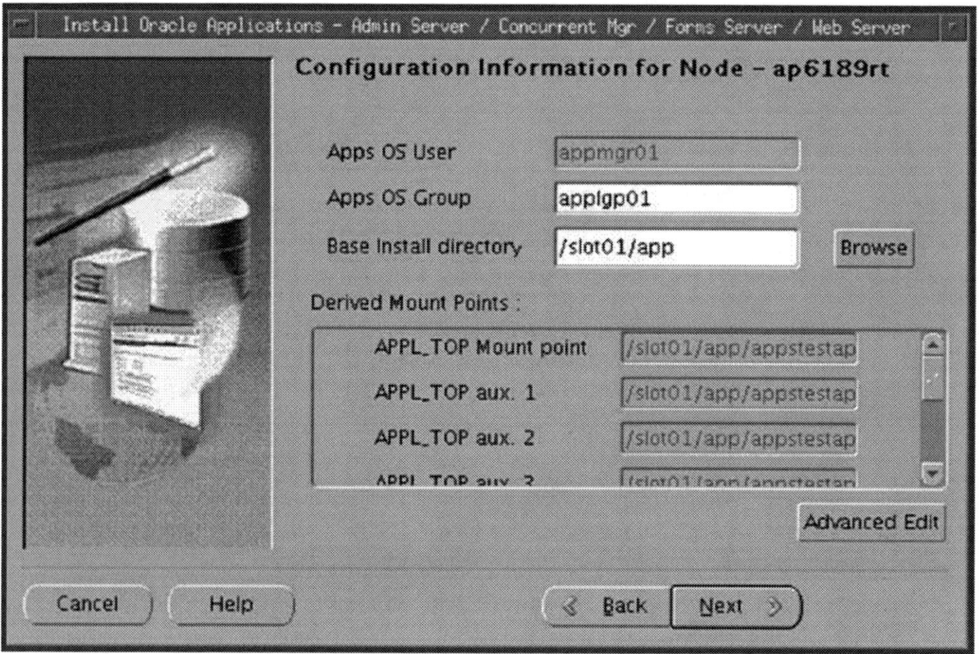

Fig. 4.16 Illustration of Configuration Information for Nodes

- The OS group is the Unix group name of the operating system user
- The Base Install directory is the top-level directory that the Rapid Install will use to derive the mount point for the `APPL_TOP`.

If you want to change any of these from the default values, then click 'Advanced Edit'. Once this button is pressed, the following screen appears.

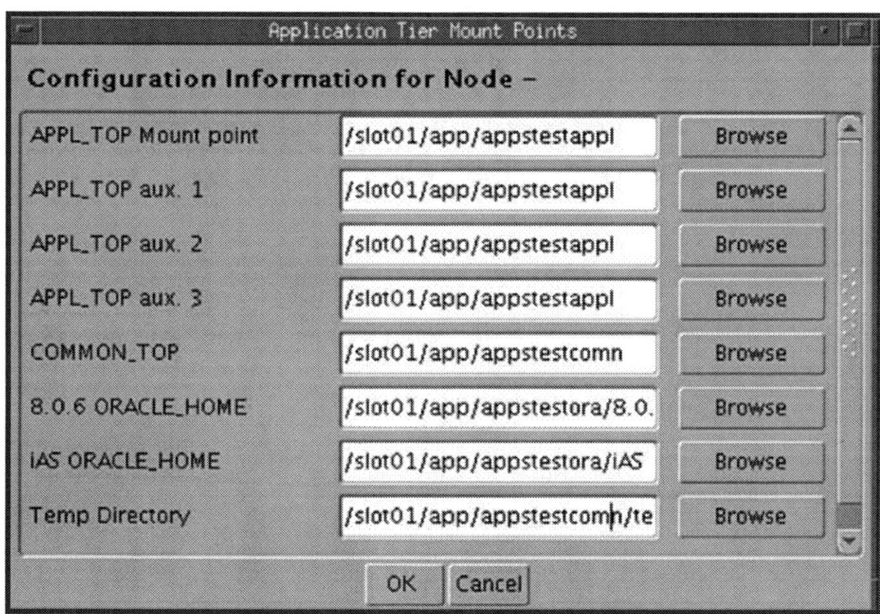

Fig. 4.17 Application Tier Mount Points

In case if you want to make separate mount points than the default one's then you can do the same by clicking the browse button and going to the exact location where you want the mount point to be, Press OK to make the changes.

Global system settings

The next screen prompts for the global domain name that will be used to connect the services and listeners.

The domain name should be such that it produces a fully qualified domain name when combined with the host name. For example, for the host `ap6189rt`, the domain name is `us.oracle.com` when combined it makes `ap6189r.us.oracle.com` (Fig. 4.18).

X Display is the default for the operating system. It should be Host name: 0,0.

This screen also shows the port number that Rapid Install will assign to various components. 'Port pool' increases the default values by adding a counter to the default port. If you assign a port pool of value five, Rapid Install will add five for all the default values of the port (Fig. 4.19). Rapidinstalls by default assigns its own port for all the services running. For example for apache it will assign a port number of 8000 for Jserv it will assing a default of 8050 and say for forms it will assign a default port of 8100. Port pool is the value by which you can increase the values of all the default ports at one go. Say we choose a port pool of 10 then the new port of apache becomes 8000 + 10 = 8010, the new value for

Jserv becomes 8050 + 10 = 8060 and similarly the values for the forms becomes 8100 + 10 = 8110. For example, for the database, if the default value is 1521 it will change to 1526.

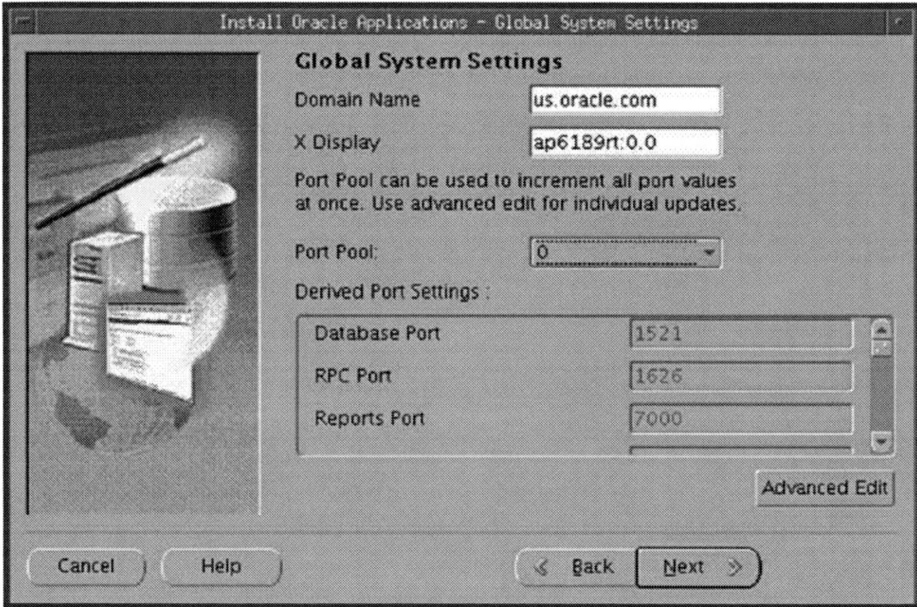

Fig. 4.18 Global System Settings

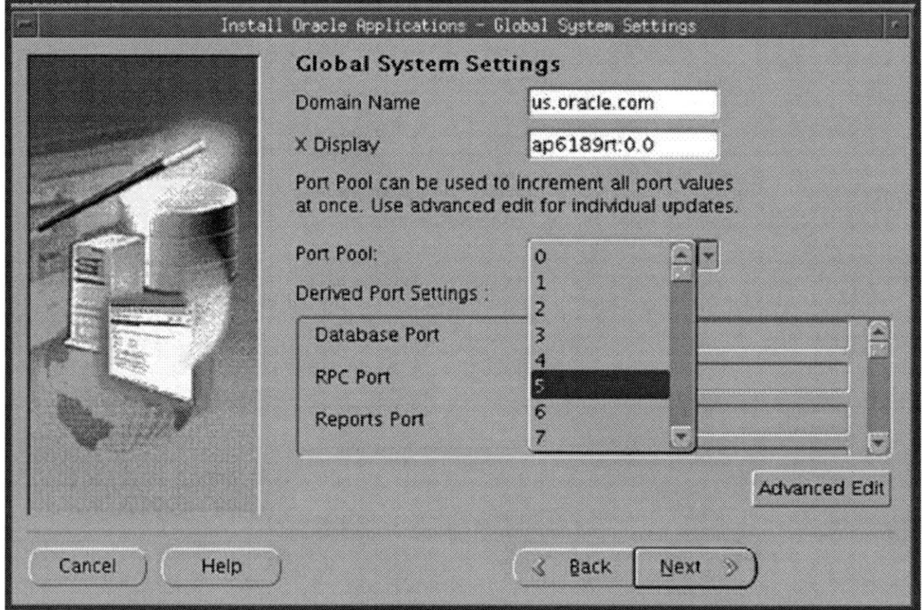

Fig. 4.19 Illustration of Global System Settings

If you want to assign different values, then click on the 'Advanced Edit' button. This shows all ports assigned by Rapid Install (Fig. 4.20).

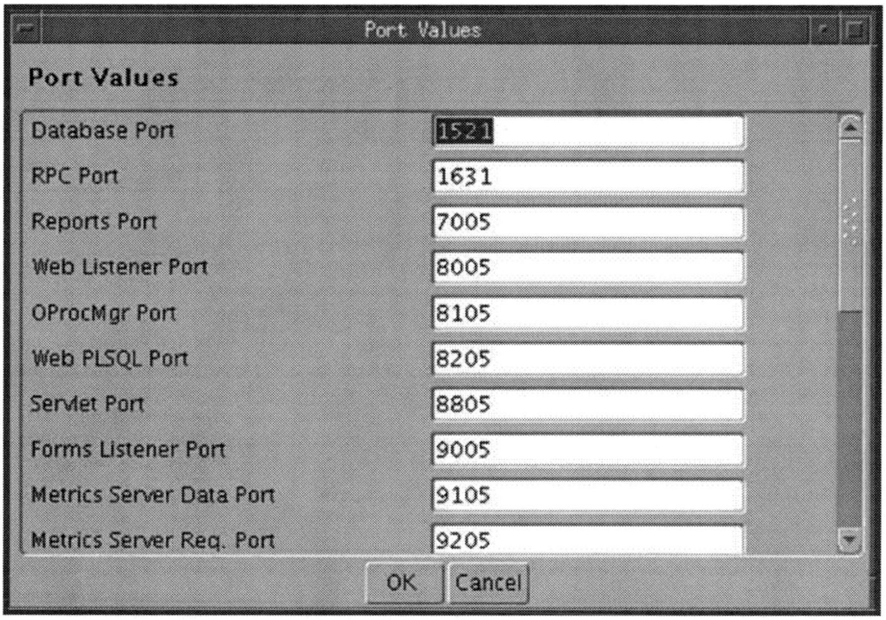

Port Values

Port Values

Database Port	1521
RPC Port	1631
Reports Port	7005
Web Listener Port	8005
OProcMgr Port	8105
Web PLSQL Port	8205
Servlet Port	8805
Forms Listener Port	9005
Metrics Server Data Port	9105
Metrics Server Req. Port	9205

OK Cancel

Fig. 4.20 Port Values

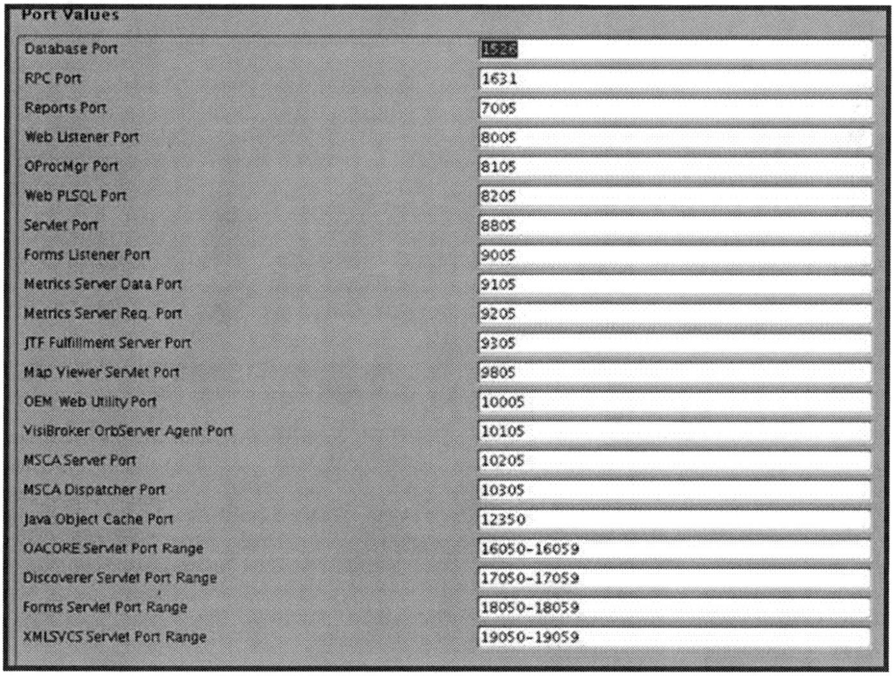

Port Values

Database Port	1526
RPC Port	1631
Reports Port	7005
Web Listener Port	8005
OProcMgr Port	8105
Web PLSQL Port	8205
Servlet Port	8805
Forms Listener Port	9005
Metrics Server Data Port	9105
Metrics Server Req. Port	9205
JTF Fulfillment Server Port	9305
Map Viewer Servlet Port	9805
OEM Web Utility Port	10005
VisiBroker OrbServer Agent Port	10105
MSCA Server Port	10205
MSCA Dispatcher Port	10305
Java Object Cache Port	12350
OACORE Servlet Port Range	16050-16059
Discoverer Servlet Port Range	17050-17059
Forms Servlet Port Range	18050-18059
XMLSVCS Servlet Port Range	19050-19059

Fig. 4.21 Port Values Assigned to Various Components

Saving the configuration file

At this point, you have given all the information required to run the Rapid Install. This is stored in a configuration file 'config.txt', which is used by Rapid Install to configure a specific Oracle Application instance. The default location of the file is in the 'tmp' directory. It is always advisable to save this file to another location, as the same file can be used in case the installation has to be repeated for any reason.

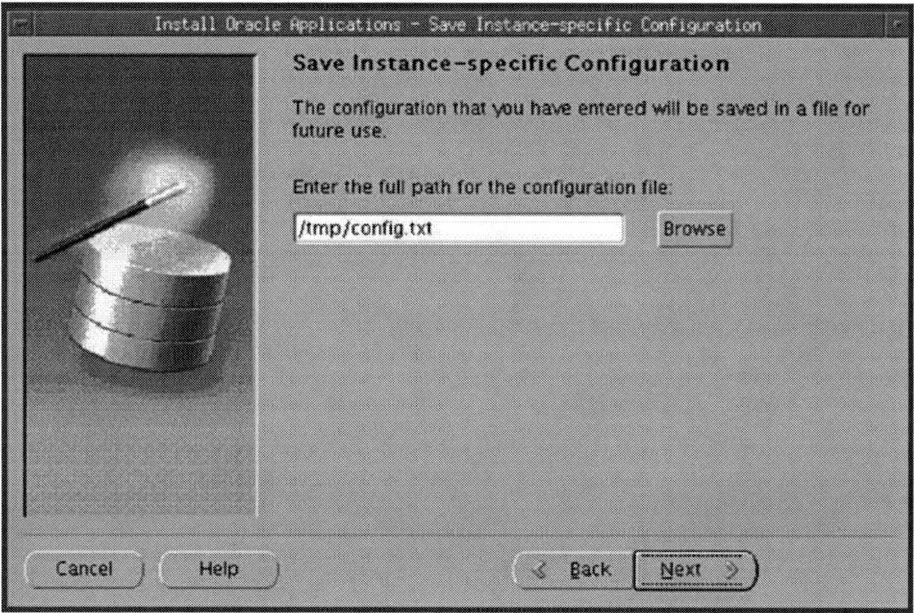

Fig. 4.22 Save Instance-specific Configuration

Pre-install checking

Before starting the installation, Rapid Install performs a number of checks in order to ensure a smooth installation process (Fig. 4.23).

It checks the system on the following parameters.

- Port availability: whether the port you have selected is available or clashing with an existing port
- Port uniqueness: that there is no duplicate defined port for the processes
- File space check: ensures that the file system has sufficient space for the installation
- OS patch check: ensures that the right Operating System patches are there
- Operating System check: checks the Operating System weather the version Oracle Applications Software chosen is compatible with the operating system or not
- File system check: checks whether the files are mounted properly and have correct permission
- Host/Domain check: verifies the host name and the domain name
- System utilities check: checks whether the linking utilities viz. make, ld and cc are available or not
- OS user and group check: checks that the OS user exists and is part of the correct group

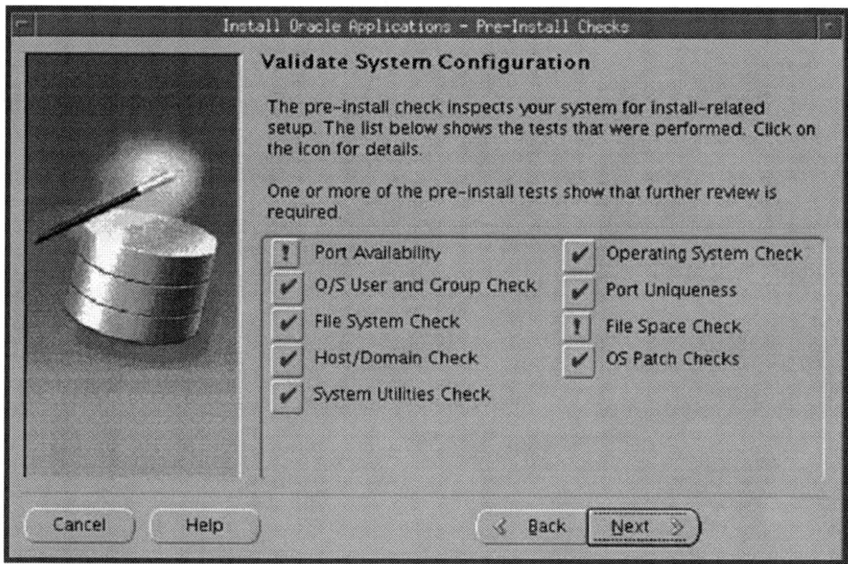

Fig. 4.23 Pre-install Checks

The results of test are labeled with check marks (✓), exclamation marks (!) or a cross (X) mark. The check mark means the system has passed the test, while the exclamation mark means the system should be checked. Points marked with a cross signify that the issues should be resolved before continuing with the installation. Here, you can click 'Yes' to continue or 'No' to review the issues.

Installation process

Rapid Install now lists all the components that it will install, based on the parameters entered earlier.

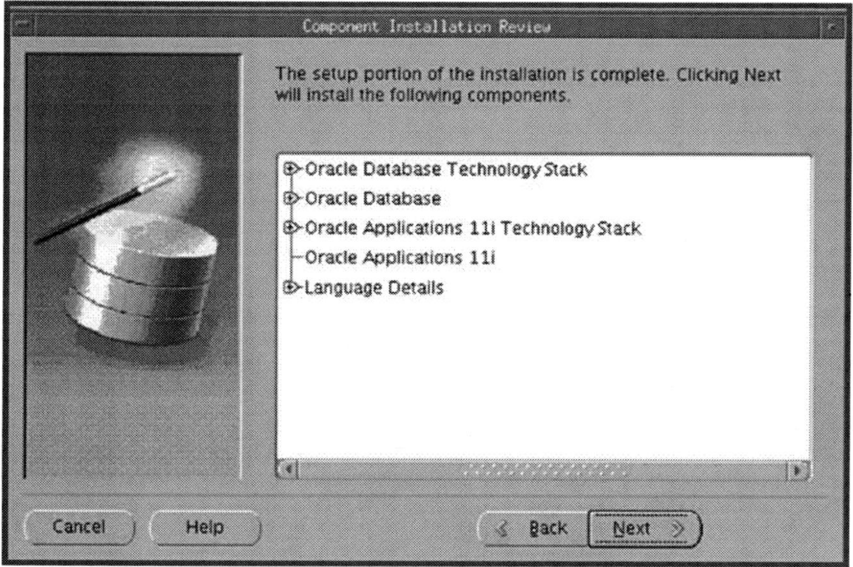

Fig. 4.24 Component Installation Review

On clicking 'Next', it displays an alert asking if you want to start the installation immediately.

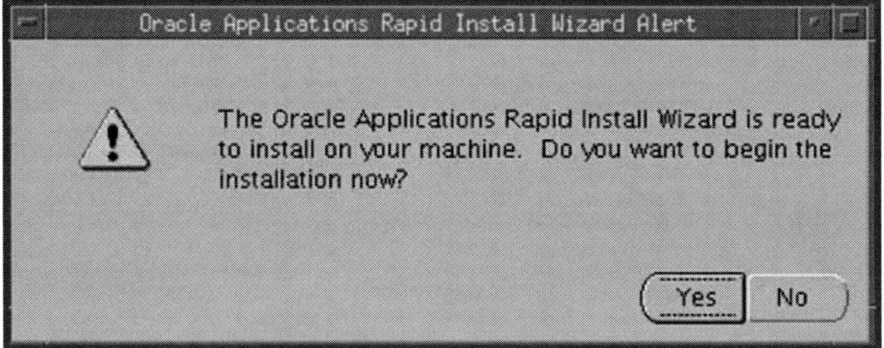

Fig. 4.25 Installation Alert

You should click 'Yes' to start the installation. Then, the status bar displays the status of the installation.

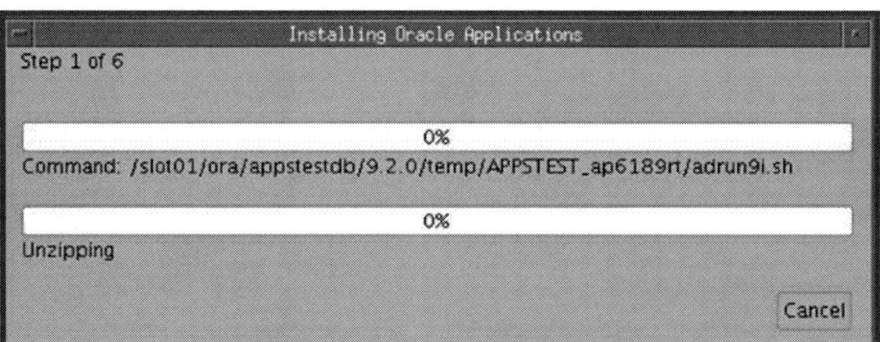

Fig. 4.26 Status of Installation

Now there is a prompt for the path name of the stage. Once this is given, Rapid Install completes the installation.

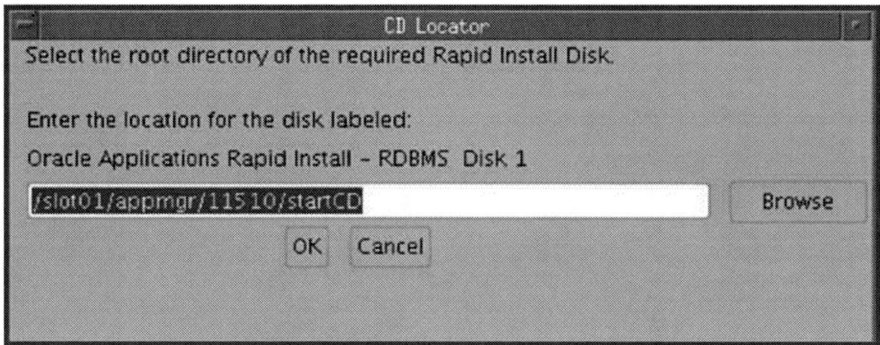

Fig. 4.27 Path Name of the Stage

Validate system configuration

Rapid Install automatically completes the installation without much user intervention. Once the installation is finished, it will validate the installed components to ensure that they have been installed properly. Once this is done, the output is shown in the Post-install check screen.

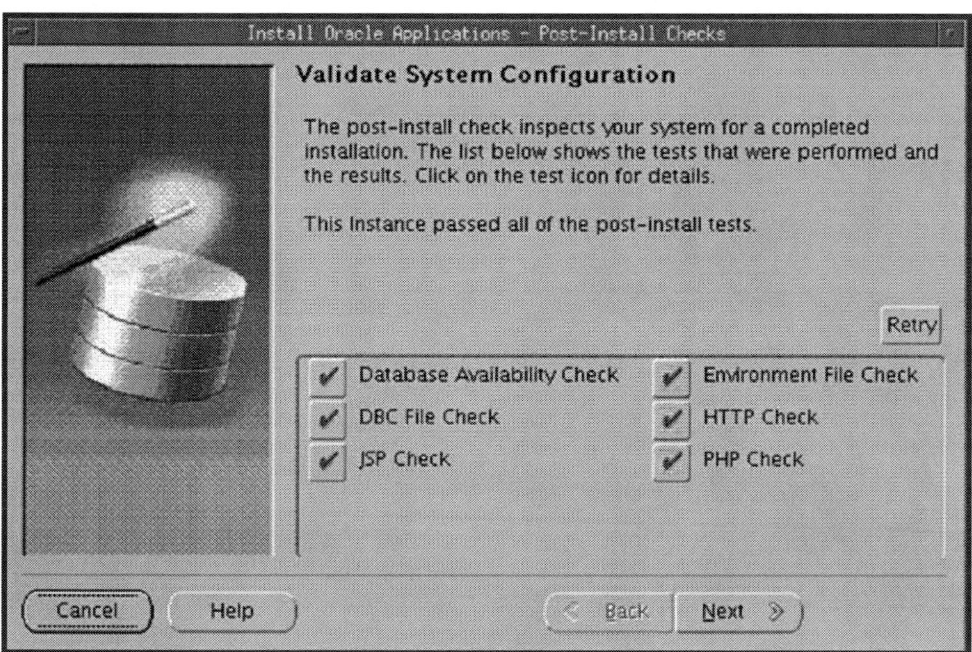

Fig. 4.28 Post-install Checks

The following components are checked at this stage.

- Database availability check to see that the database is up and running
- Environment file check whether the env file has been created properly
- DBC file check that the DBC file has been created (Location `$FND_TOP/secure`)
- HTTP check that the Apache is up and running
- JSP check to see if they are working fine
- PHP check to ensure the PHP is working fine

When you click 'Next', the finish screen comes. It lists all the components loaded by Rapid Install. Press 'Finish' to complete the installation.

The finish screen

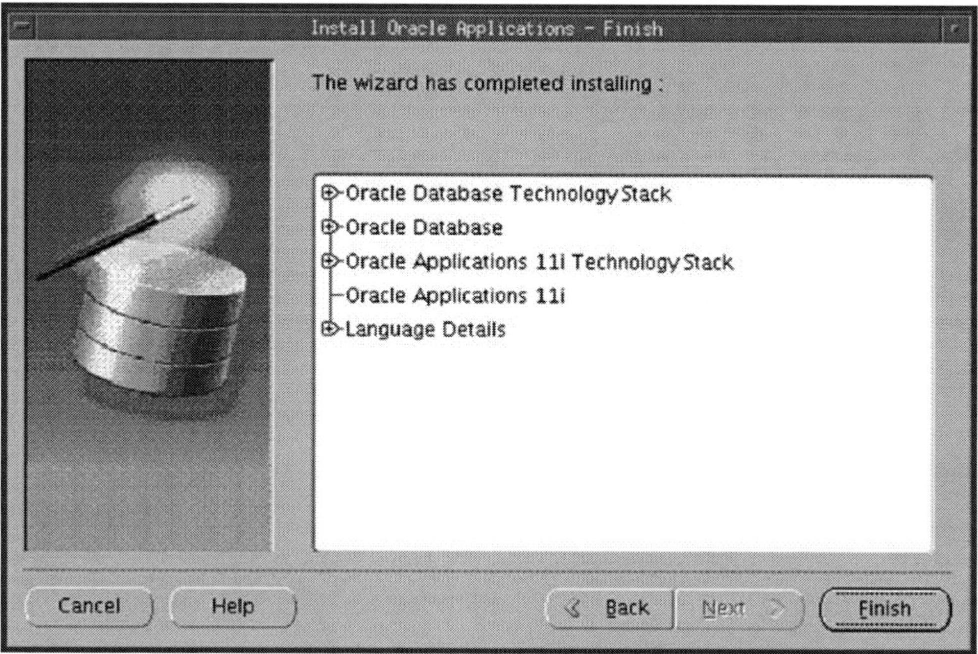

Fig. 4.29 Finish Screen

Multi-node Installation

Multi-node installation is one where the database and application tiers are installed across two or more nodes. In such an installation, the database needs to be set up first, i.e. Rapid Install needs to be run from the database server first. With the 11.5.10 release, Rapid Install creates a shared `APPL_TOP` by default for multi-node installations.

Rapid Install must be run from the database node first in case of multi node installation. In order to run Rapid Install from the database server first, '`rapidwiz`' is typed at the prompt. As discussed earlier, for this process, one should be logged on as the owner of Oracle.

Once '`rapidwiz`' is typed, the welcome screen comes as shown in Fig. 4.30.

Welcome screen

The welcome screen lists the components included in that release of Oracle Application. The 11.5.10 Rapid Install comes with a 9.2.0.6 database, which can also be used to upgrade or migrate an existing database to 9.2.0.6. This is just an informative screen. Click 'Next' to continue.

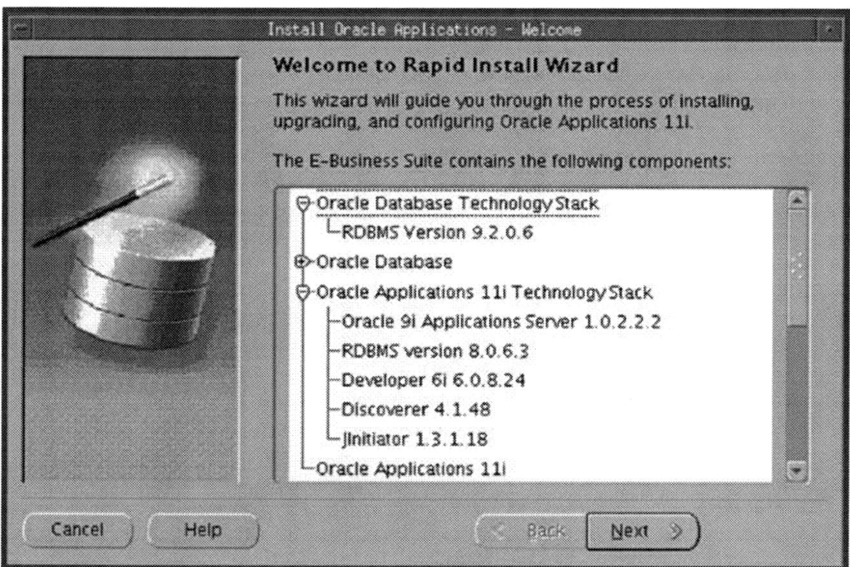

Fig. 4.30 Welcome Screen

Selecting a wizard operation

This screen asks for the action to be performed by Rapid Install. You can choose either a fresh installation or an upgrade. Based on the user's response, Rapid Install performs the appropriate action.

Since this chapter is devoted to a fresh installation, click 'Install Oracle Application E-Business `11i`' and press 'Next'.

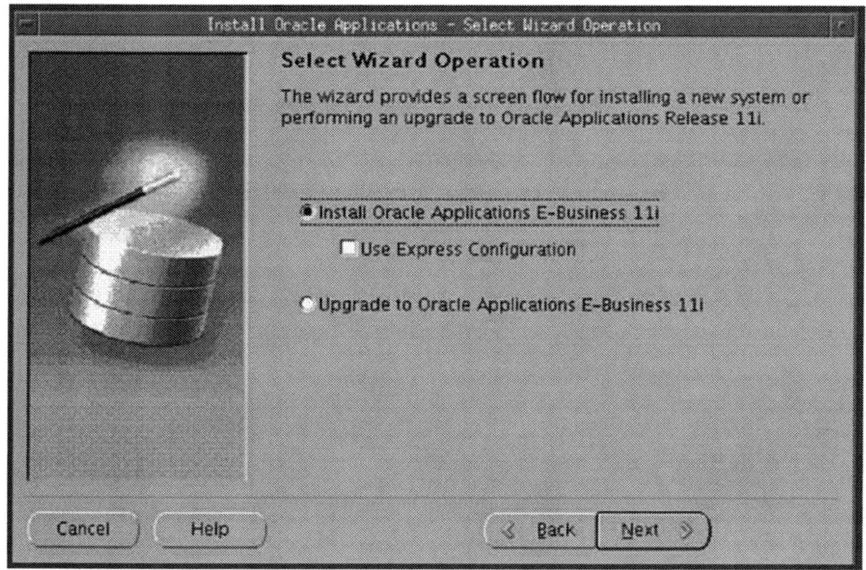

Fig. 4.31 Selecting a Wizard Operation

Load configuration file

In this screen, you indicate whether or not you will use an existing configuration file for the installation.

As shown in Fig. 4.32, if you select 'No', then Rapid Install creates a new configuration file and saves all the information in it. This can be used in the next installation.

If you choose 'Yes', it asks for the full path name of the configuration file. This option is chosen for starting the installation from the other nodes. Since we are assuming this to be a new installation, click 'No' and then 'Next'.

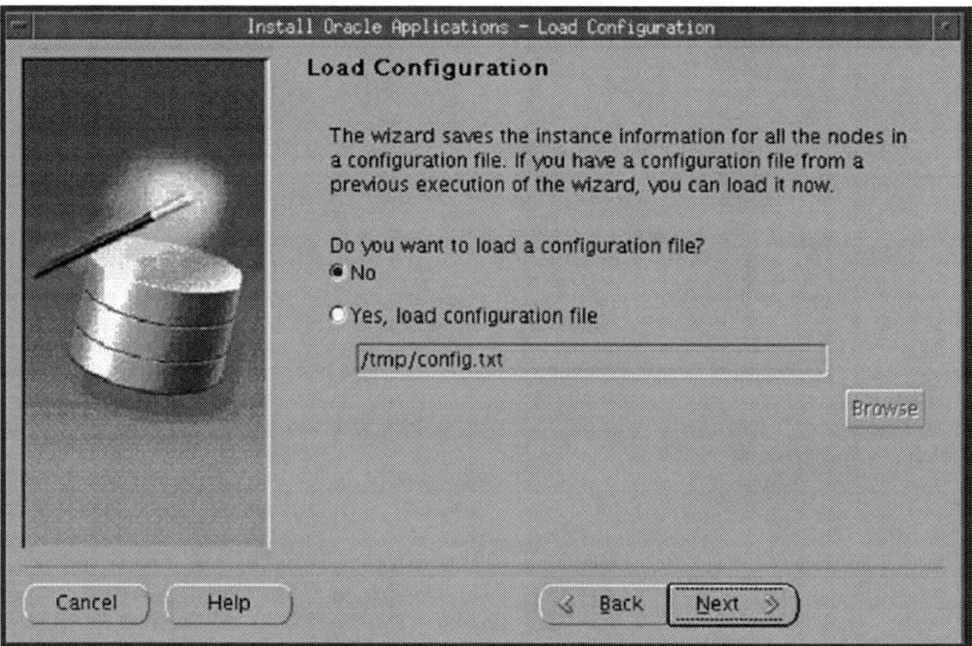

Fig. 4.32 Load Configuration

Choosing installation type

In this screen, you indicate whether to install Oracle Application on a single node or distribute the tiers across multiple nodes (Fig. 4.33).

Since we are doing a multi-node installation, we will assume this option is selected. As mentioned earlier, in a multi-node installation we can distribute the database, Forms, concurrent processing server and Apache across multiple nodes.

Load balancing

Load balancing is the feature for distribution of the load of forms and concurrent processing in multiple nodes. If this feature is implemented, then the requests are automatically directed to the server with the least load. Figure 4.34 shows the load balancing screen.

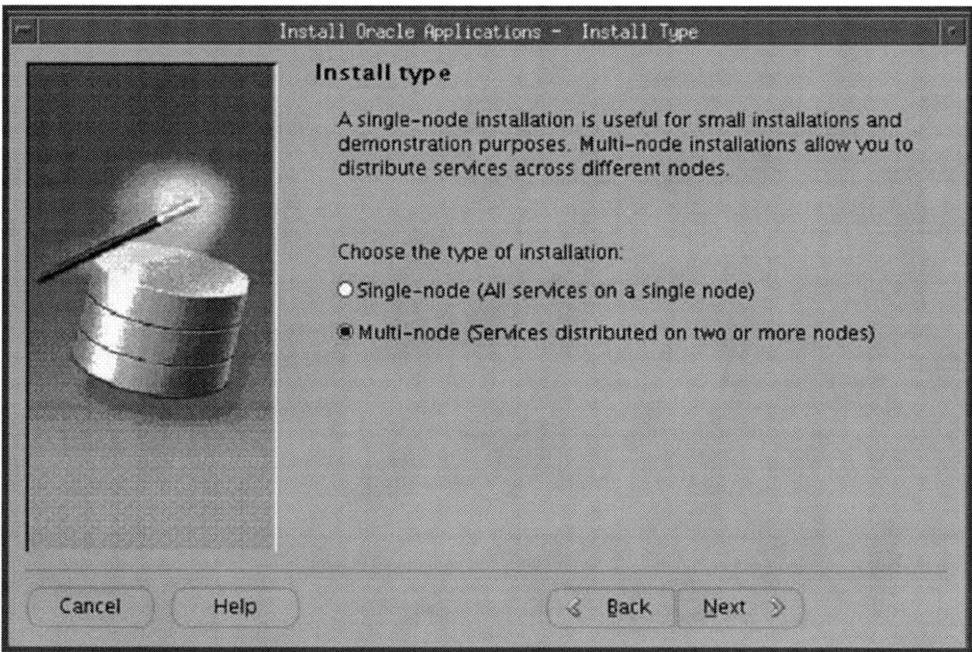

Fig. 4.33 Installation Type

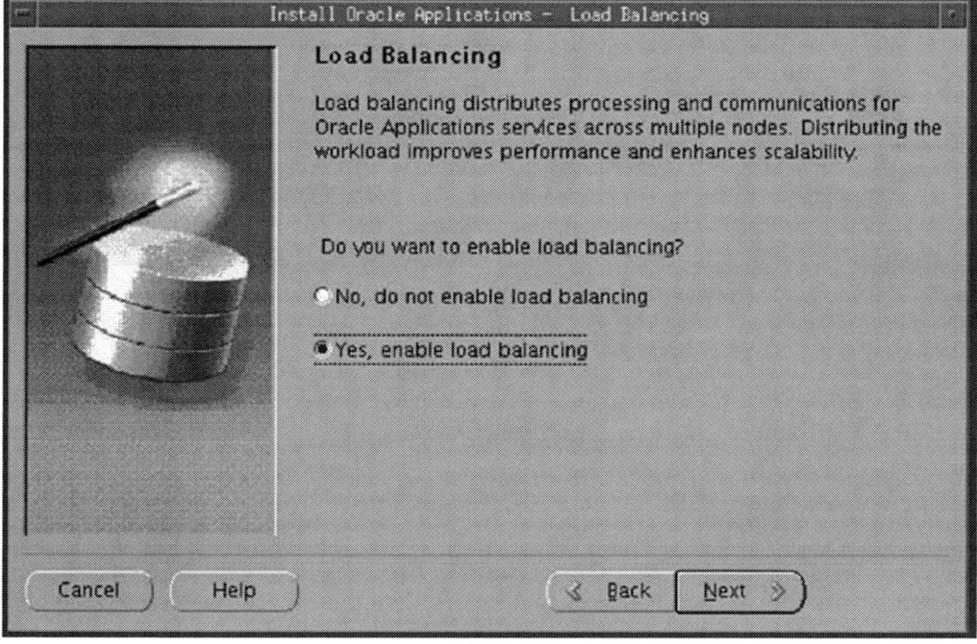

Fig. 4.34 Load Balancing Screen

Let us discuss both options, viz. enabling and not enabling load balancing.

Case 1—load balancing is enabled

In this case, Rapid Install will ask you how many nodes to assign for Forms and concurrent processing server. To ensure that the load is balanced, choose more than one node for each service type.

Node specification

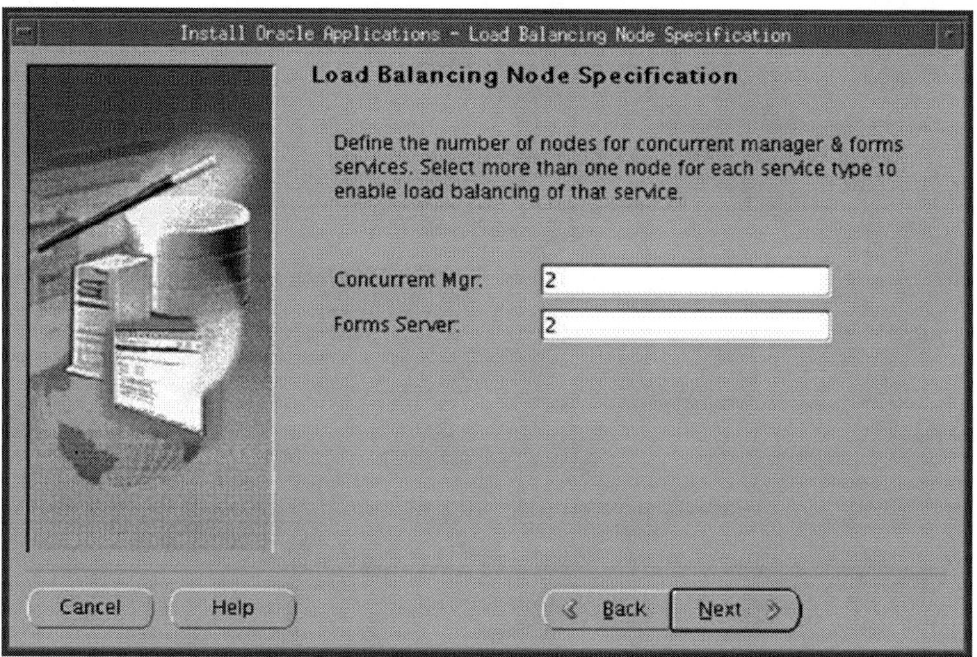

Fig. 4.35 Load Balancing Node Specification

Once the number of nodes for the Forms and Concurrent Manager are defined, Rapid Install will prompt for server details in the next screen as shown in Fig. 4.36.

Case 2—load balancing is not enabled

If you choose not to enable load balancing, Rapid Install straightaway goes to the various server information screens without checking the details of primary and secondary servers, as they are not applicable here.

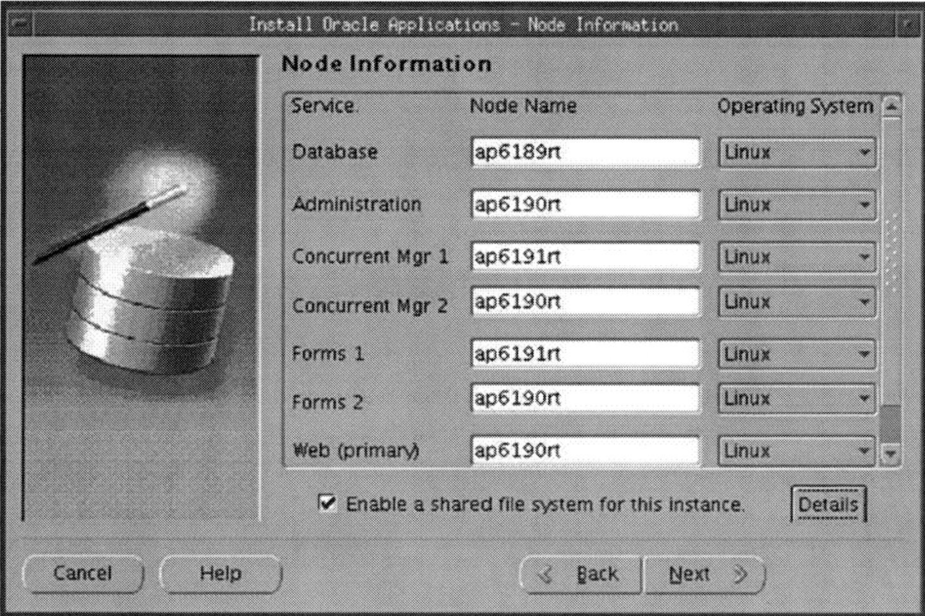

Fig. 4.36 Node Information

Load balancing

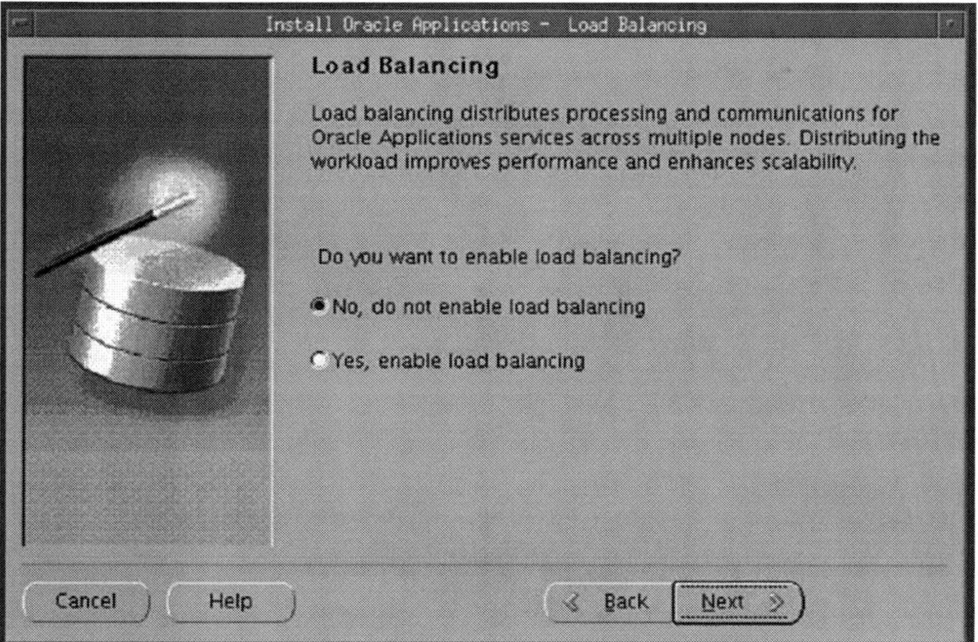

Fig. 4.37 Load Balancing is Not Enabled

Node information

In this screen, you assign the servers to individual nodes using the 'Node Name' field. As can be seen in Fig. 4.38, we have selected 'ap6189rt' as our database server. The next is the admin tier of the APPL_TOP from where we maintain the APPL_TOP file system. In this example, we have chosen 'ap6190rt' as our admin node. Then for Concurrent Manager, we have chosen 'ap6191rt'and for Forms, we have chosen 'ap6191rt'. For web, the Apache will be hosted from 'ap6190rt' server. Therefore, this is a three-node installation with DB on one server, Forms-CM on one and Admin-Web on one.

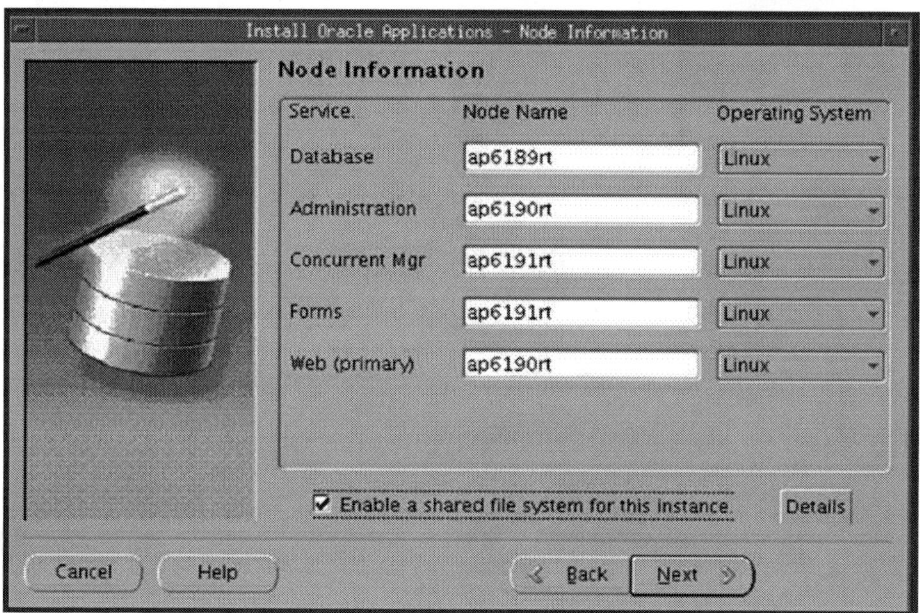

Fig. 4.38 Node Information

There is also a check box in the screen, 'Enable a shared APPL_TOP for this instance'. This means the APPL_TOP will be installed only in one node (which is also called the admin tier), but will be accessible to all nodes. This is helpful as it considerably reduces the time needed for maintenance tasks. With the 11.5.10 release, the APPL_TOP is shared by default. Of course, shared APPL_TOP is possible only if all the nodes have the same operating system. If one node has Unix and the other has Windows, then sharing of the APPL_TOP is not possible.

There is also a 'Details' button on the screen in Fig. 4.38. On clicking this, there is a screen from where you can define the node in which you want to install the APPL_TOP and the nodes where you will share it.

In Fig. 4.39, there are three options—'Node Name', 'File System Actions' and 'OS'. Node name is the physical server from which the Forms, Apache, and CM are hosted. 'File System Actions' gives two choices, 'Install' and 'Share Existing'. The former installs the APPL_TOP on that particular node and makes it available for sharing with other nodes. The node will thus serve as the admin tier. 'Share Existing' means that it won't have its own APPL_TOP, but will be using the one shared by the node marked 'Install'.

Define File System Actions

Define File System Actions

Select "Install" to create a new file system, or select "Share existing" to use another node's shared file system.

Node Name	File System Actions	OS
ap6190rt	Install	Linux
ap6191rt	Share Existing	Linux

OK Cancel

Fig. 4.39 Define File System Actions

In this example, we have chosen to install the APPL_TOP in the node 'ap6190rt'. The server 'ap6191rt' will be sharing its APPL_TOP.

Database type

Here, you indicate the type of database to be installed along with Oracle Applications. You can choose between a fresh database and a Vision Demo database.

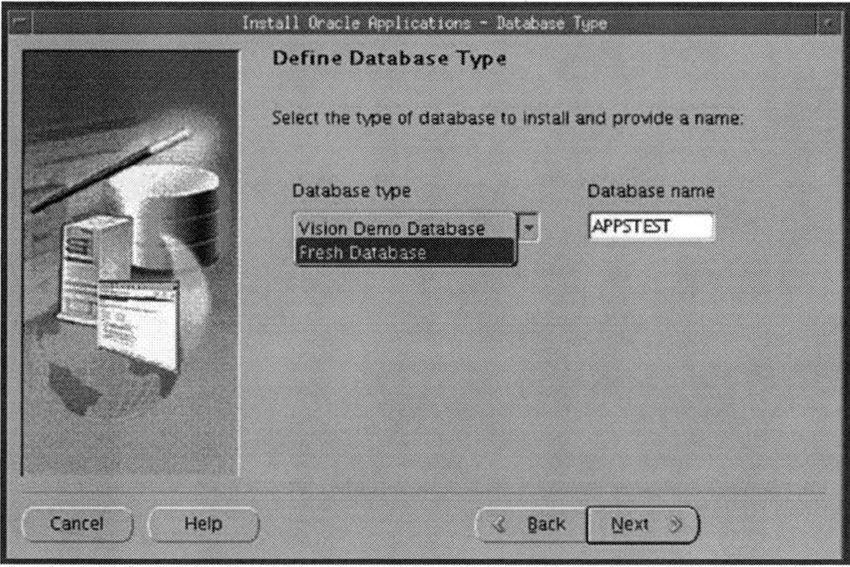

Fig. 4.40 Database Type Selection

Choose the 'Fresh Database' option, name it as 'APPSTEST' and click 'Next'.

Database installation details

Install Oracle Applications - Database Install Information
Database Install Information - ap6189rt
Oracle OS User
oracle01
Oracle OS Group
dba01
Base Install directory
/slot01/ora
Browse
Derived Mount Points :
Oracle Home
Data Top (SYS)
Data Top (LOG)
Advanced Edit
Cancel
Help
Back
Next

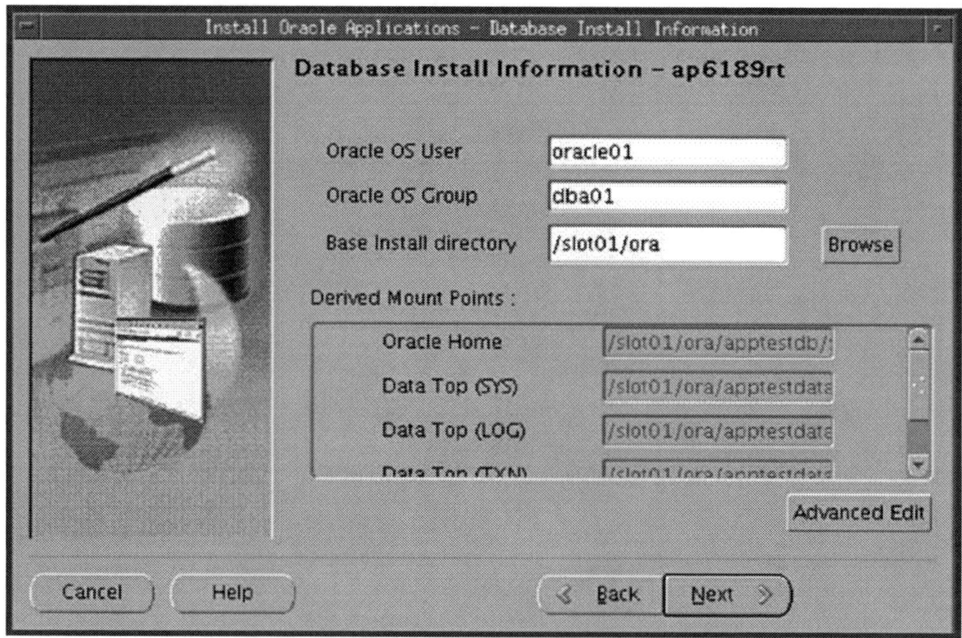

Fig. 4.41 Database Install Information

Click 'Next' to continue.

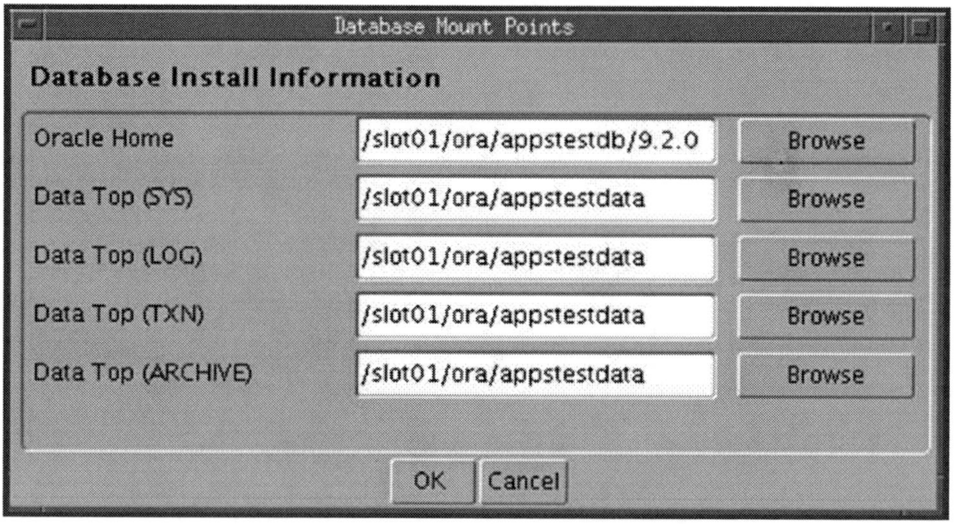

Database Mount Points
Database Install Information
Oracle Home
/slot01/ora/appstestdb/9.2.0
Browse
Data Top (SYS)
/slot01/ora/appstestdata
Browse
Data Top (LOG)
/slot01/ora/appstestdata
Browse
Data Top (TXN)
/slot01/ora/appstestdata
Browse
Data Top (ARCHIVE)
/slot01/ora/appstestdata
Browse
OK
Cancel

Fig. 4.42 Database Mount Points

Select licensing type

In this wizard, you indicate the type of licensing agreement that you have purchased from the Oracle Corporation. Completing a licensing screen does not constitute a license agreement. It simply registers your products as active. You should have complete information about your product license before you complete the licensing screens.

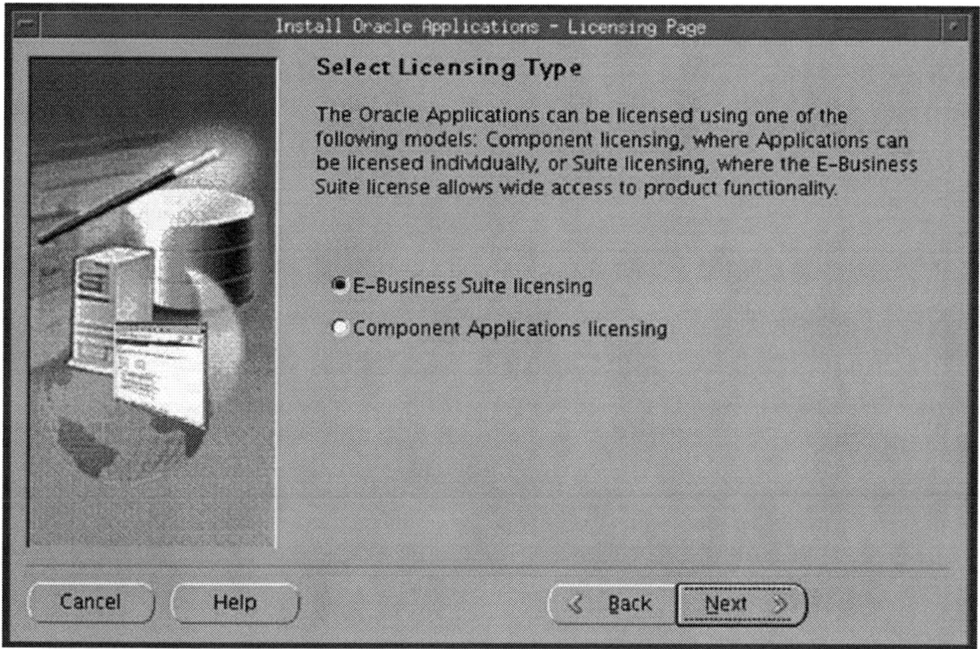

Fig. 4.43 Selection of Licensing Type

Rapid Install sets up all products automatically, regardless of their license status. However, you must register the products you have licensed so that they are flagged in the system as active. An active flag marks products for inclusion in patching and other tasks for maintenance and updating of your system.

You can either register through E-Business Suite licensing or Component Application Licensing.

If you click the E-Business Suite licensing option, the following page appears as shown in Fig. 4.44.

This licensing model allows wide access to Applications functionality. By choosing it, you tell Rapid Install to automatically register all products included in the E-Business Suite price bundle. The products that are checked and grayed are licensed automatically as a part of the suite. The ones that are not must be registered separately as add-on products. Place a check mark next to any add-on products that you have licensed and want to register.

You can also click the Component Applications licensing option on the Suite Selection Screen as shown in Fig. 4.45.

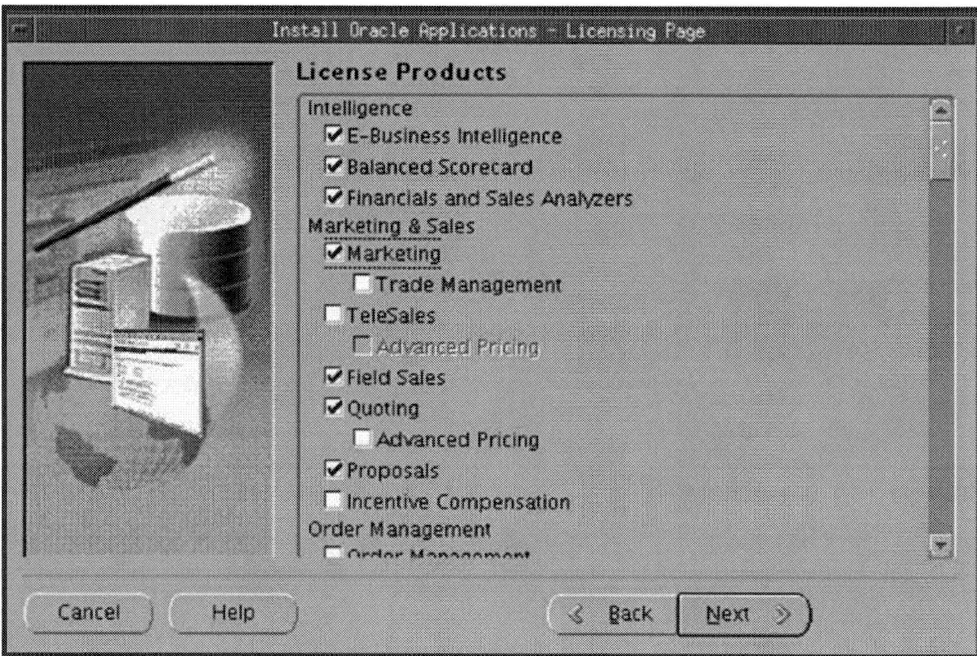

Fig. 4.44 E-Business Suite Licensing Page

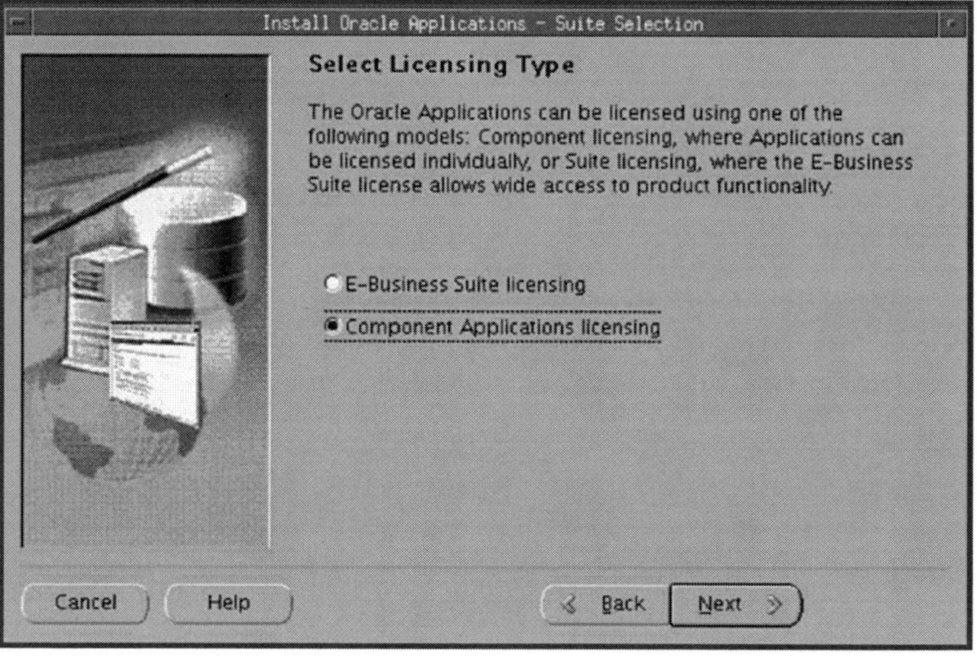

Fig. 4.45 Selection of Licensing Type

Then the following screen comes for licensing.

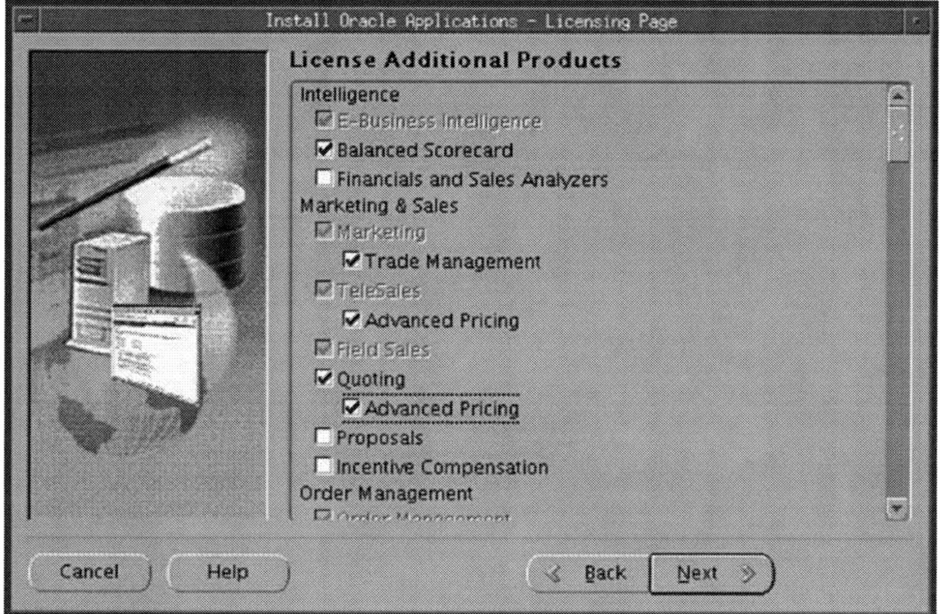

Fig. 4.46 Component Applications Licensing Page

Choose this option if your licensing agreement is for component products of individual Applications. These products are licensed based on the number of authorized users or on the number of business transactions processed. All the products are listed on this screen. Products that are grayed out cannot be selected unless the parent component is selected.

You can always license additional products after installation from the Oracle Application Manager by going to OAM > License Manager > License additional products.

Selecting country-specific functionality

Many application systems need country-specific functionality. For this, you have to select the country from the list by using the '>' button (Fig. 4.47). It can also be added at a later stage using Oracle Application Manager's License Manager. If you don't want a country-specific functionality, then simply ignore this screen.

Selecting additional languages

Using the next screen, you can install languages other than American English. You can select any number of additional languages, provided you have the software for them at the time of installation. You can also install an additional language at a later stage by making that language active using Oracle Application Manager and then installing the necessary software. In Fig. 4.48, it can be seen that American English is automatically selected first. Select any additional language using the '>' button. If you don't want to install any additional language, just click 'Next'. Here, we have selected two additional languages, viz. Arabic and German.

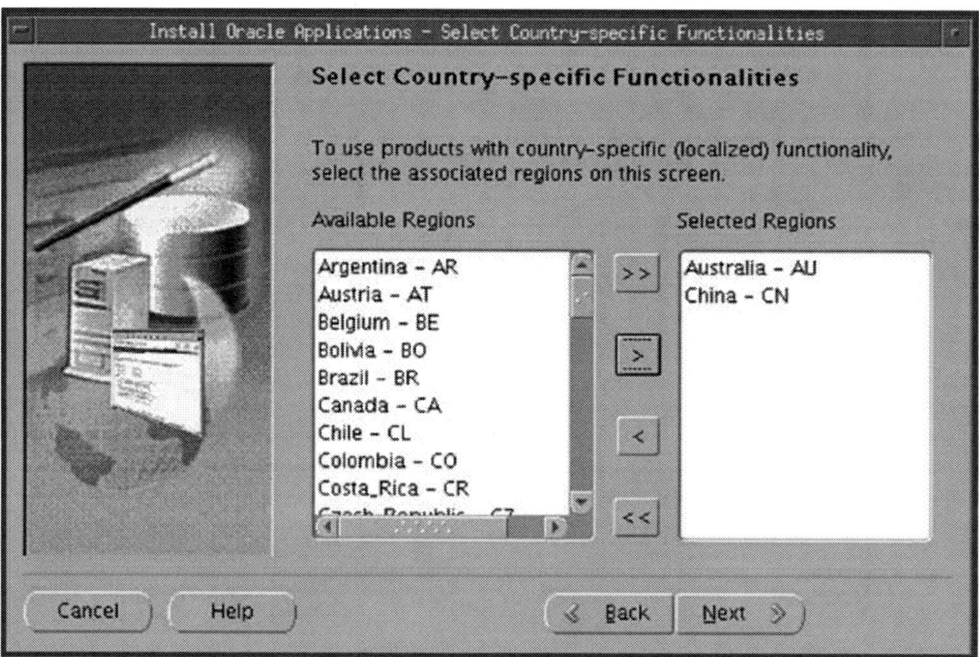

Fig. 4.47 Selection of Country-specific Functionalities

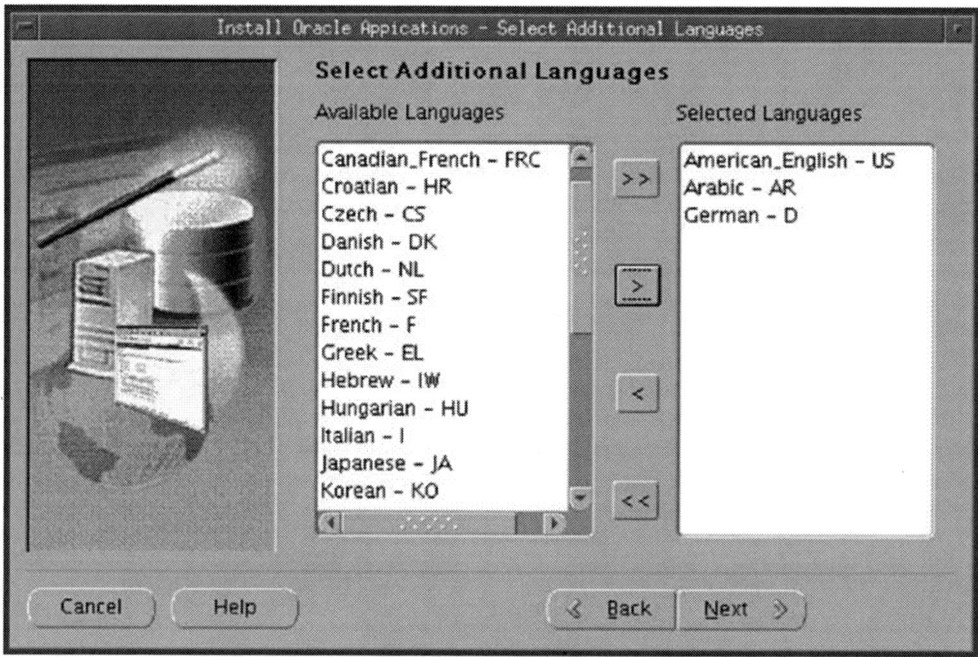

Fig. 4.48 Selection of Additional Languages

NLS settings

The next screen deals with the character set of the additional languages chosen. If you select an additional language, it comes in the drop-down list in the character set column. The character set automatically changes and includes those compatible with the additional languages which have been chosen.

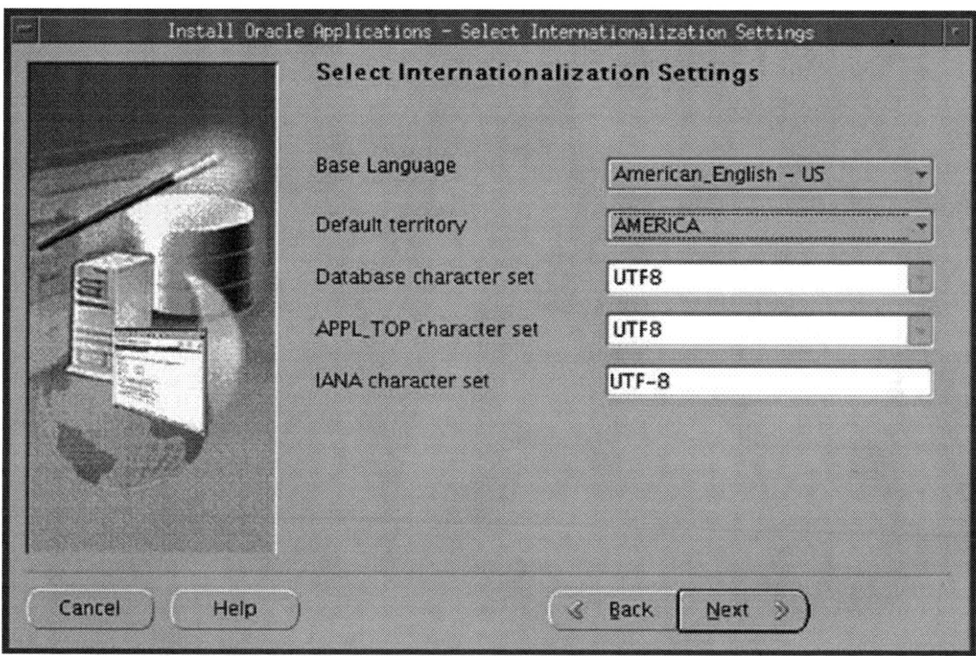

Fig. 4.49 Select Internationalization Settings

Box 4.2

Explanation of terms in Fig. 4.49

Base Language	The base language is the default language of the application system. If you have more than one language, then the base language field is not grayed out and you can always change it. If you have only American English as the active language then this field cannot be changed.
Default Territory	This is set to AMERICA by default and should remain so during the upgrade.
Database Character	This refers to the common character set of the database, which is compatible with all the additional languages installed.
APPL_TOP Character	This refers to the common character set of the APPL_TOP, which is compatible with all languages installed in your application system.
IANA Character	This refers to the Internet Assigned Number Authority character set. For more information about this, visit http://www.iana.org/assignments/character-sets.

Admin server/web server details

Since we have a two node APPL_TOP, we need to give the details of each node. Rapid Install first prompts for the information of the node where the APPL_TOP file system will be installed. In this case, it is the Admin-Web server node, i.e. 'ap6190rt' server.

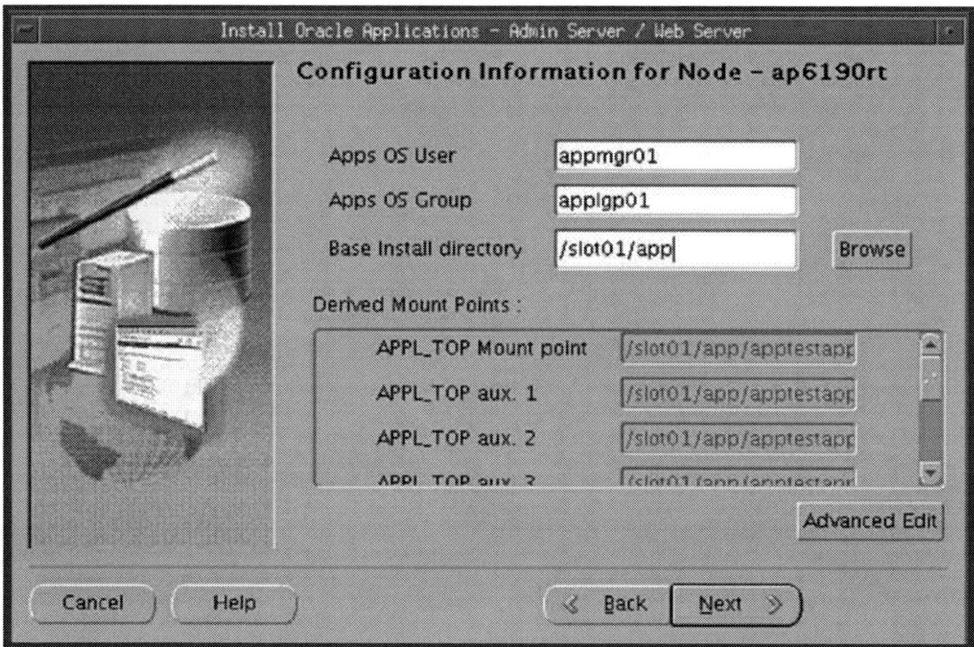

Fig. 4.50 Configuration Information for Admin Server/Web Server

Here you specify the top-level directory and the mount points for the APPL_TOP. The OS user name is the operating system user who will own the Oracle Application file system. The OS group is the Unix group name of the operating system user. The base install directory is the top-level directory that Rapid Install will use to derive the mount points for the APPL_TOP (Fig. 4.51). If you want to change the default values, click the button 'Advanced Edit'. Since you would be installing the APPL_TOP from this node so you can change the mount points of the various components if you want them to have a different path from the default value.

Concurrent Manager/Forms server

The second node of the APPL_TOP is the one that hosts the Forms and the concurrent processing servers. This node will not have APPL_TOP installed but will share it from the Web/Admin server. We have chosen the 'ap6191rt' server for the same.

From Fig. 4.52, it can be seen that it first displays the server with which it will share the file system. It is also obvious in this figure that the path locations of all the mount points are grayed out, i.e. you can't manually change them. This is because we are not installing any APPL_TOP here, but sharing the existing one.

Application Tier Mount Points

Configuration Information for Node –

APPL_TOP Mount point	/slot01/app/appstestappl	Browse
APPL_TOP aux. 1	/slot01/app/appstestappl	Browse
APPL_TOP aux. 2	/slot01/app/appstestappl	Browse
APPL_TOP aux. 3	/slot01/app/appstestappl	Browse
COMMON_TOP	/slot01/app/appstestcomn	Browse
8.0.6 ORACLE_HOME	/slot01/app/appstestora/8.0.	Browse
iAS ORACLE_HOME	/slot01/app/appstestora/iAS	Browse
Temp Directory	/slot01/app/appstestcomn/te	Browse

OK Cancel

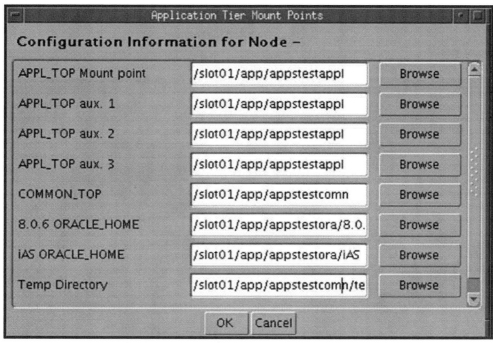

Fig. 4.51 Application Tier Mount Points

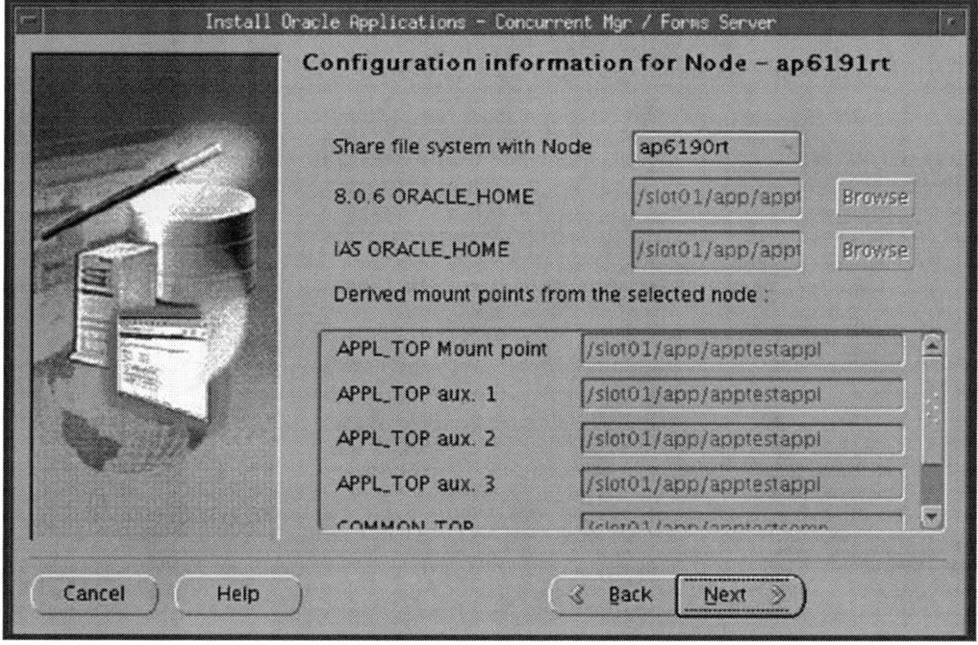

Fig. 4.52 Concurrent Manager/Forms Server

Global system settings

The next screen prompts for the global domain name that your system will use to connect the services and listeners.

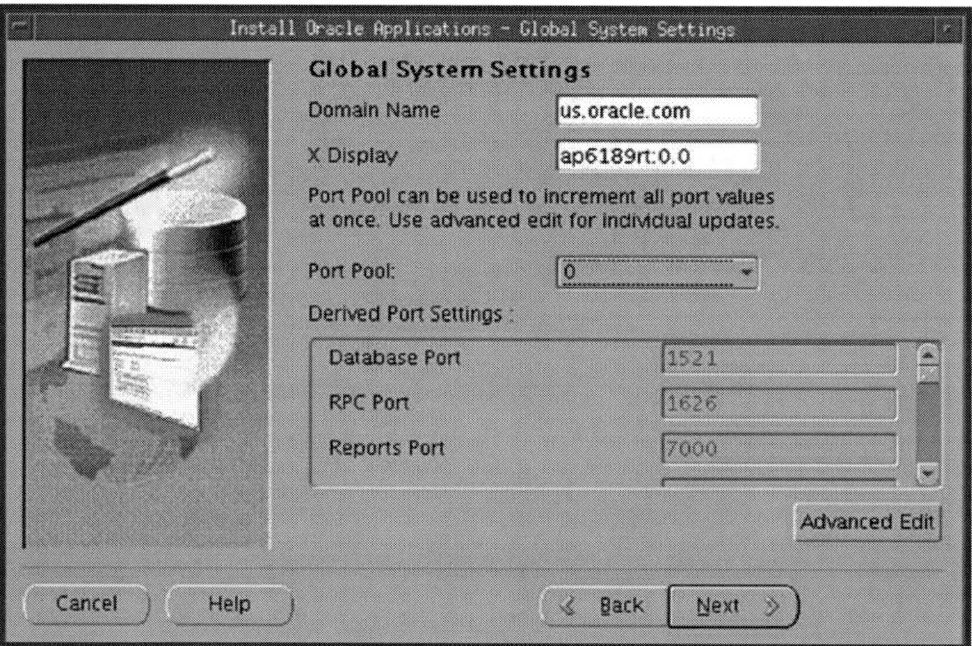

Fig. 4.53 Global System Settings

The domain name should be such that when combined with the host name, it produces a fully qualified domain name (viz. in `ap6189rt.us.oracle.com`, the domain name is `us.oracle.com`).

X Display is the default of the operating system which should be Hostname:0,0.

This screen also shows the port number that Rapid Install will be assigning for various components. Port pool option changes the default values to higher values by adding a counter to default port. If you assign a port pool of value five, Rapid Install will increase by this number all the default values of the port. For example, for the database if the default value is 1521, it will be changed to 1526. If you want to assign totally different values then click on the 'Advanced Edit' button. This shows all the ports that Rapid Install assigns (Fig. 4.54).

Saving the configuration file

At this point, you have given all the information required to run Rapid Install. All the information is stored in a configuration file '`config.txt`'. Rapid Install uses these values during the installation to create the file system, install the database, and configure and start the server processes. The default location of the file is in the temp directory. It is always advisable to save this `config.txt` file to another location, as the same file can be used for re-installation at any point (Fig. 4.55).

Port Values

Database Port	1526
RPC Port	1631
Reports Port	7005
Web Listener Port	8005
OProcMgr Port	8105
Web PLSQL Port	8205
Servlet Port	8805
Forms Listener Port	9005
Metrics Server Data Port	9105
Metrics Server Req. Port	9205
JTF Fulfillment Server Port	9305
Map Viewer Servlet Port	9805
OEM Web Utility Port	10005
VisiBroker OrbServer Agent Port	10105
MSCA Server Port	10205
MSCA Dispatcher Port	10305
Java Object Cache Port	12350
OACORE Servlet Port Range	16050-16059
Discoverer Servlet Port Range	17050-17059
Forms Servlet Port Range	18050-18059
XMLSVCS Servlet Port Range	19050-19059

Fig. 4.54 Port Values Assigned to Various Components by Rapid Install

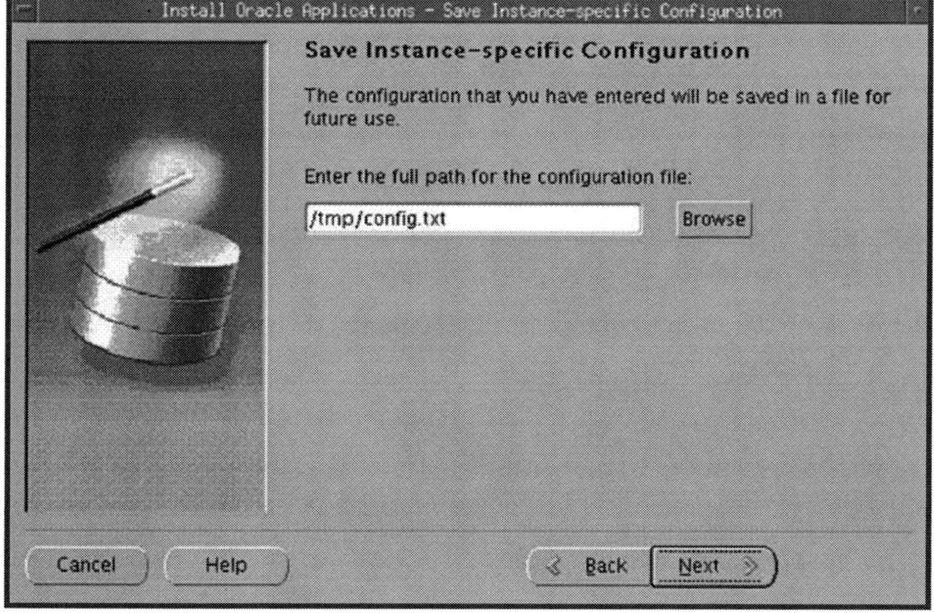

Fig. 4.55 Save Instance-specific Configuration

Pre-install checking

Before starting the installation, Rapid Install performs a number of checks in order to ensure the process is smooth.

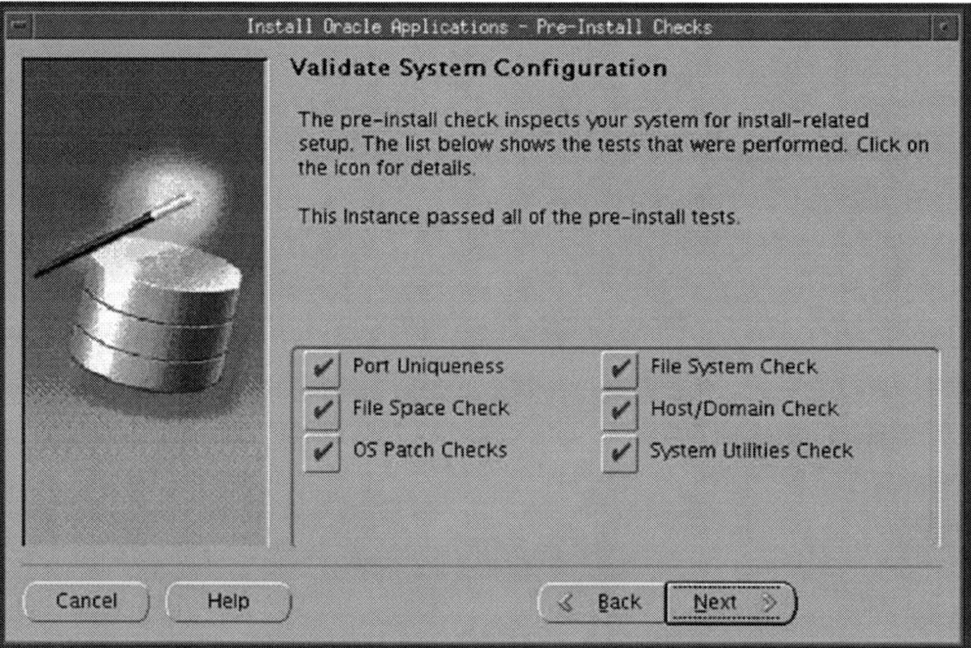

Fig. 4.56 Pre-install Checks

It checks the system on the following parameters.

- Port uniqueness: There should be no duplicate defined port for the processes.
- File space check: It ensures that the file system has sufficient space for a smooth installation.
- OS patch check: It ensures that the right Operating System patches are there.
- File system check: It checks whether the files are mounted properly and have correct permission.
- Host/domain check: It verifies the host name and the domain name.
- System utilities check: It checks whether the linking utilities, viz. make, ld and cc, are available or not.

The results of the tests are labeled with check marks (✓), exclamation marks (!), or cross marks (✕). A check mark means the system has passed the test, while the exclamation means the system should be checked at those points. Points marked with a cross mean that the issues need to be resolved before continuing with the installation. Click 'Yes' to continue and 'No' to review the issues.

Installation process

Rapid Install now lists all the components that it will install based on the parameters entered earlier (Fig. 4.57).

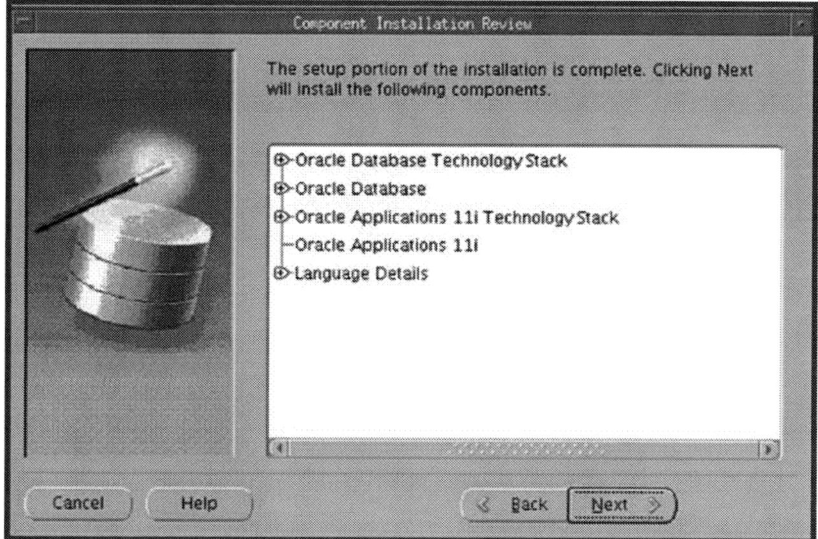

Fig. 4.57 Component Installation Review

On clicking 'Next', it displays an alert asking if you want to start the installation at this point.

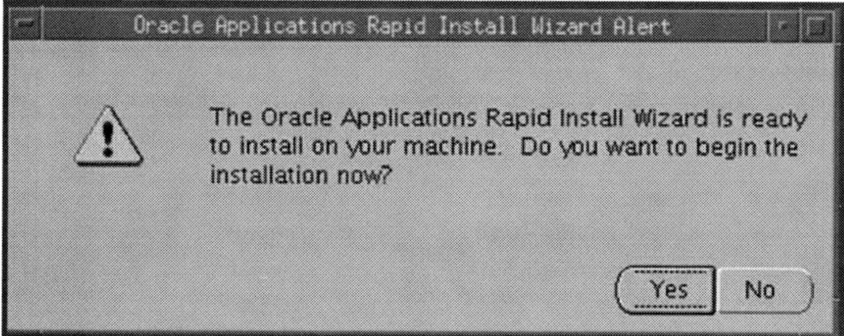

Fig. 4.58 Rapid Install Wizard Alert

Click 'Yes' to start the installation.

Once the installation has begun, a status bar is displayed.

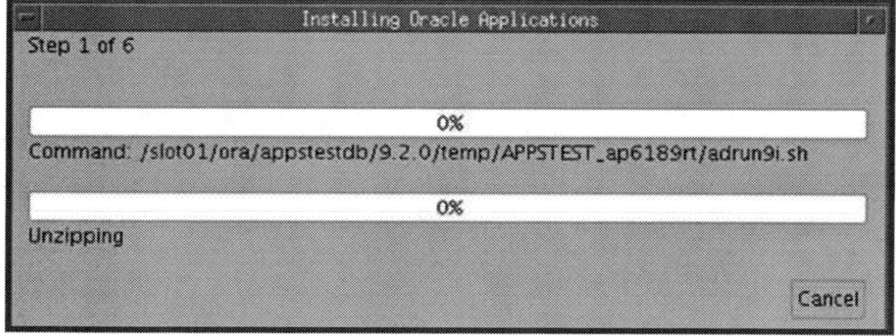

Fig. 4.59 Status Bar of Rapid Install

It prompts for the path name of the stage location. Once this is given, it completes the installation.

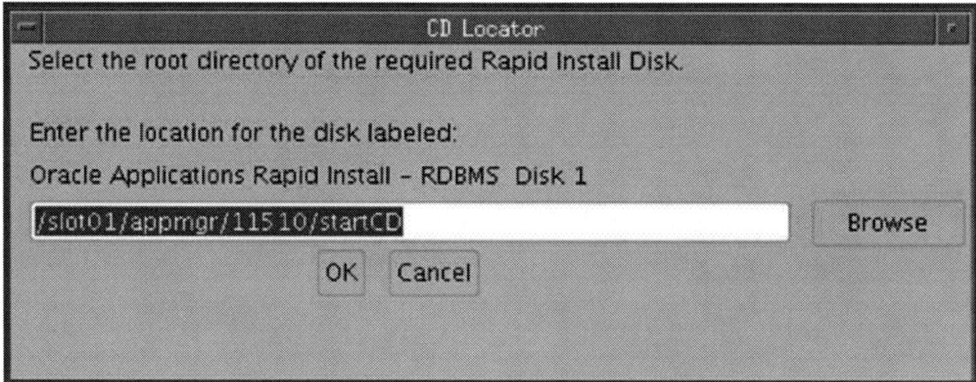

Fig. 4.60 Path Name of Stage Location

Rapid Install will automatically complete the installation without much user intervention. Once the installation is complete, it will validate the components to ensure that they have been installed properly. Once this is done, it displays the post-install check screen.

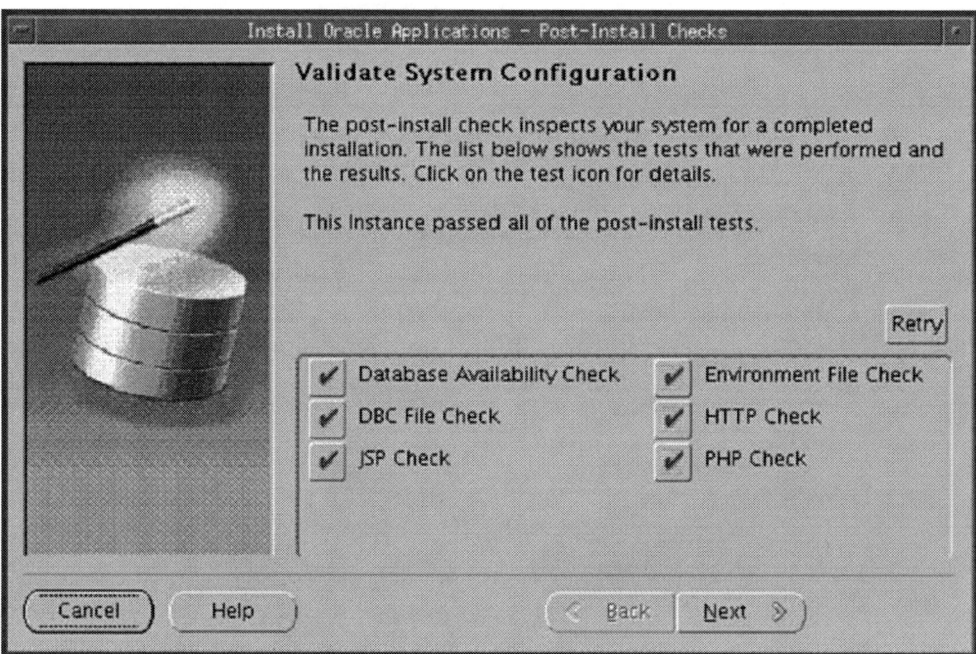

Fig. 4.61 Post-install Checks

The following components are checked in the post-install check.

- Database availability check to see that the database is up and running.
- Environment file check to ensure the env file is created properly.
- DBC file check to see whether the DBC file has been created (Location `$FND_TOP/secure`).
- HTTP check for the running status of the apache.
- JSP check to see that they are working fine.
- PHP check to ensure they are working.

Click 'Next' and the 'Finish screen' appears. It lists all the components installed. Press 'Finish' to complete the installation.

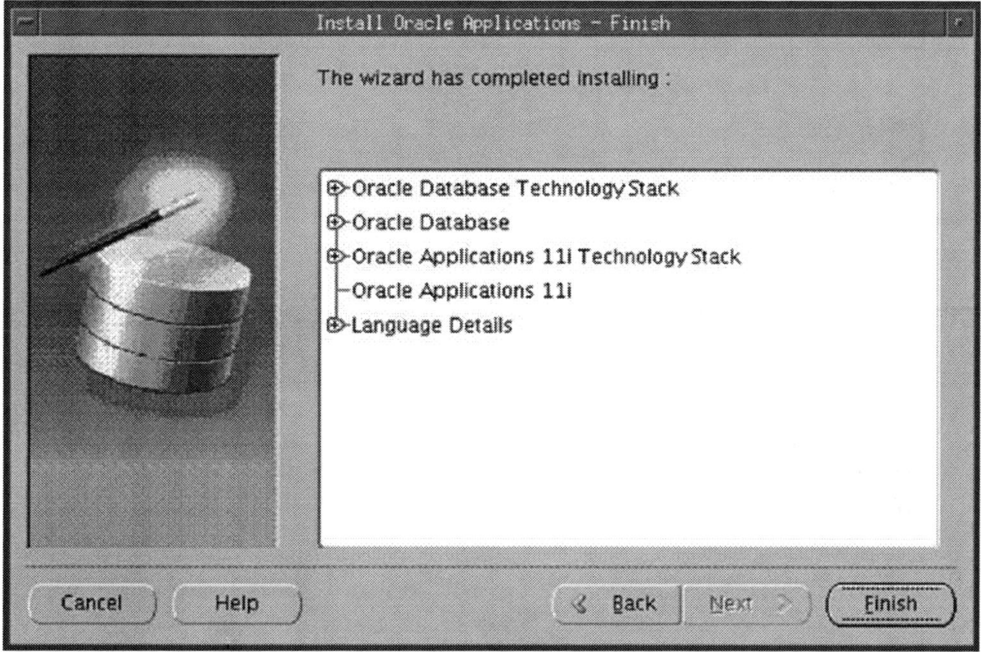

Fig. 4.62 Finish Screen

Running Rapid Install from the Second Node

In a multi-node installation, Rapid Install needs to be run from the database server first and then from each of the nodes where Oracle Application has to be installed. It is run in the same way as from the first node, with the difference that you have to use the config file that was created while running Rapid Install from the first node. Also, you need not answer all the prompts of the Rapid Install.

Here is the flow of the Rapid Install while running it from the second or third node (Fig. 4.63).

```
./rapidwiz
```

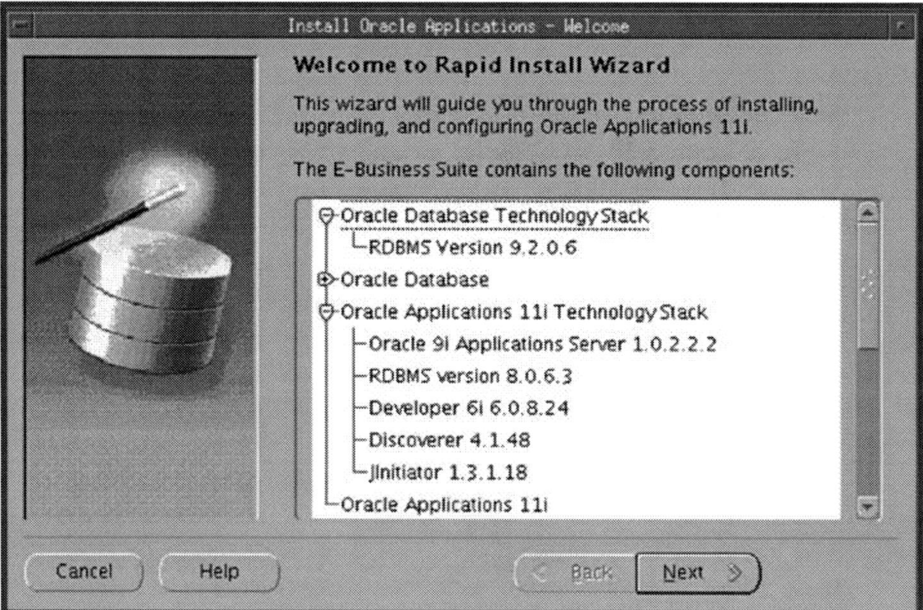

Fig. 4.63 Welcome Screen

The welcome screen is displayed first. On clicking 'Next', it prompts whether you want to do an installation or up gradation.

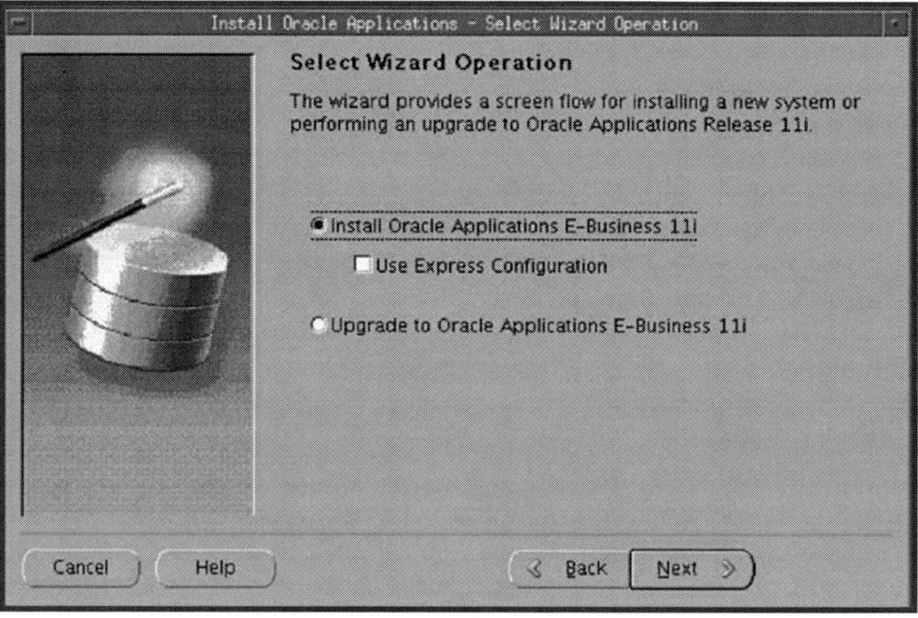

Fig. 4.64 Select Wizard Operation

Since we are installing the Oracle Application on the other node, select 'Install Oracle Applications' and press 'Next'. Choose the configuration file name that was created while running Rapid Install from the first node. As mentioned earlier, you should keep this file in a secure location.

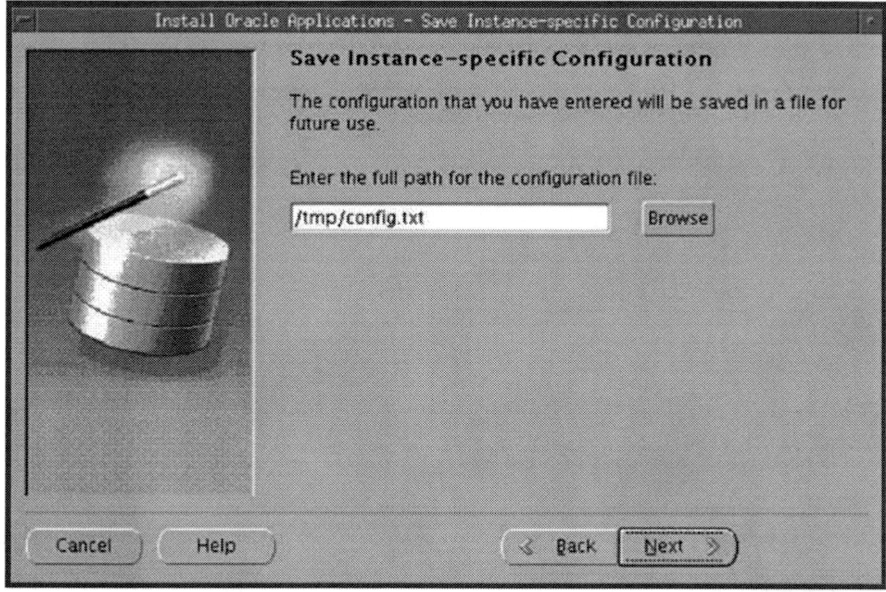

Fig. 4.65 Save Instance-specific Configuration

Once the path name of the configuration file is given, Rapid Install will start various checks and will show the results of these.

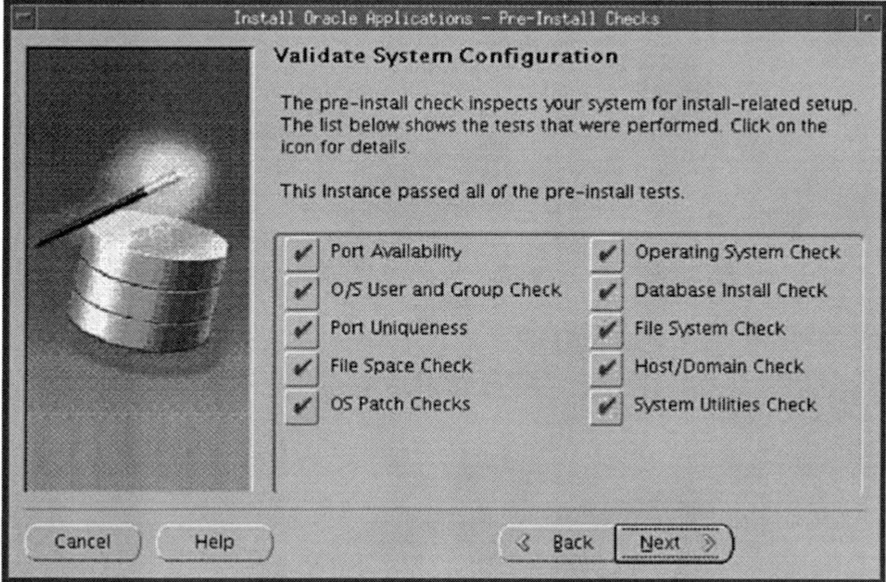

Fig. 4.66 Pre-install Checks

USING EXPRESS CONFIGURATION

Express Configuration is the fastest way to create an Application system. It can configure a single node/ single user system with either a fresh database or a Vision Demo database. It prompts for very few parameters (such as database type and name, top-level installation directory, and port increments) and takes the rest of the parameters on its own to start the installation.

The first step is to select the option 'Use Express Configuration' as shown in Fig. 4.67.

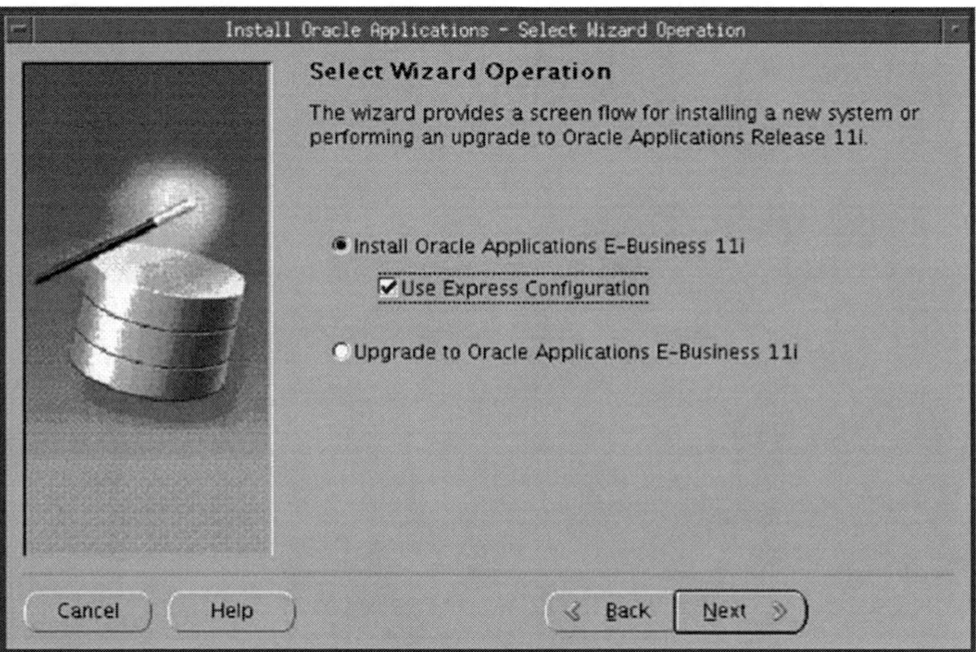

Fig. 4.67 Select Wizard Operation

In the next screen, it will prompt for the database type, database SID, the domain name, the base directory (which will be the top-level directory of Oracle Applications) and the Port Pool.

Install Oracle Applications - Express Configuration Information

Express Configuration Information

Database Type: Fresh Database

Database SID: APPTEST

Domain: us.oracle.com

Base directory: /slot01/oracle Browse

Port Pool can be used to increment the default port values select by the wizard.

Port Pool: 0

Cancel Help Back Next

Fig. 4.68 Express Configuration Information

Type the SID and Domain for your environment and the base directory where you want the Oracle Application to be installed. If you want the default ports to be assigned for your environment then choose the port pool as zero.

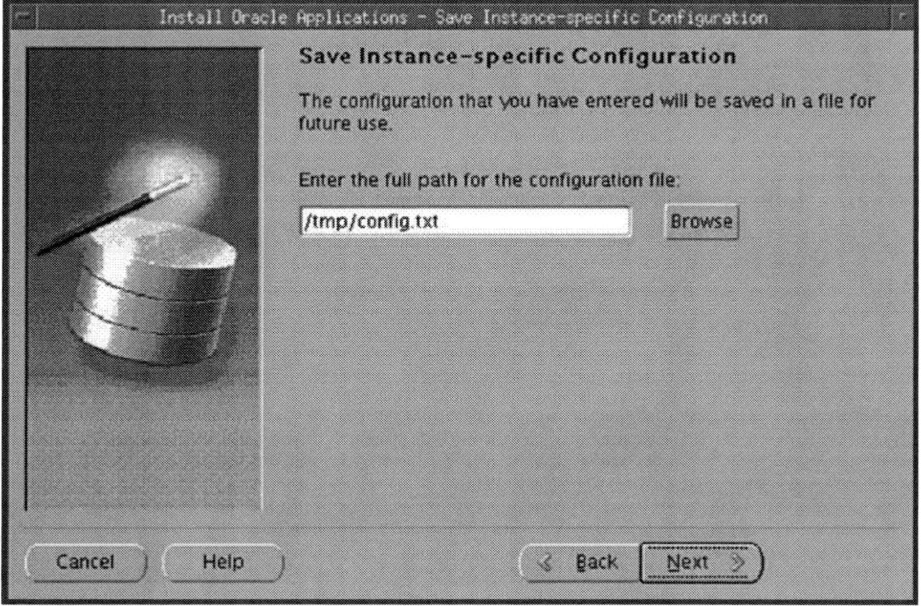

Fig. 4.69 Save Instance-specific Configuration

The configuration details are saved in a file called `config.txt`. Rapid Install prompts for the path name of the file. Enter the full path where you want this file to be created and press the button 'Next'. This file is required for restarting the installation if it fails due to any reason.

Pre-install checking

Before starting the installation, Rapid Install performs a number of checks in order to ensure a smooth install.

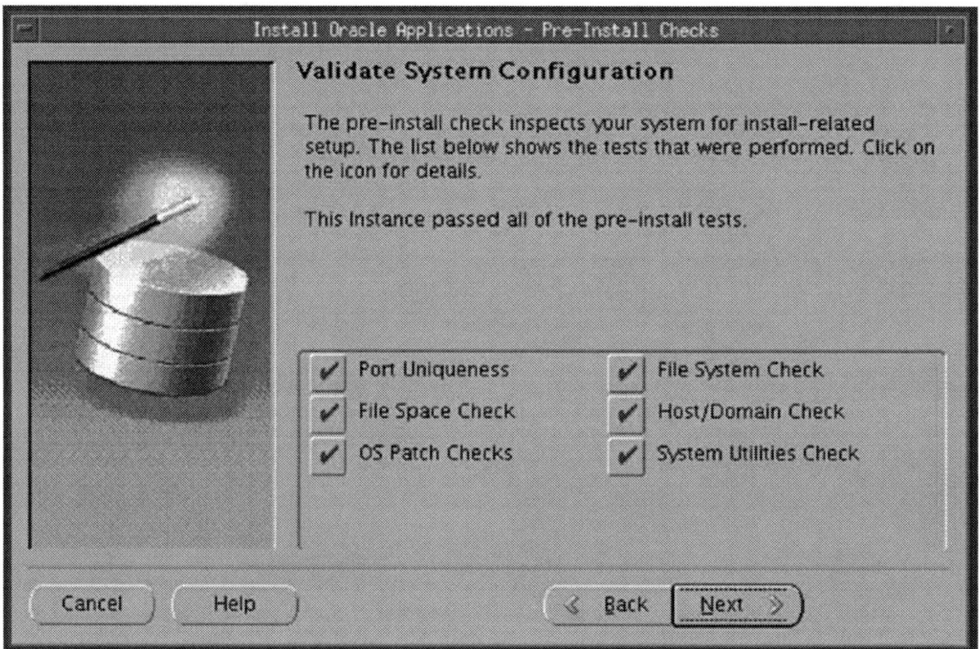

Fig. 4.70 Pre-install Checks

The system checks are the same as discussed in the earlier sections. Once the checks are completed, Rapid Install informs you about the results.

Installation process

Rapid Install now lists all the components to be installed, based on the parameters entered earlier (Fig. 4.71).

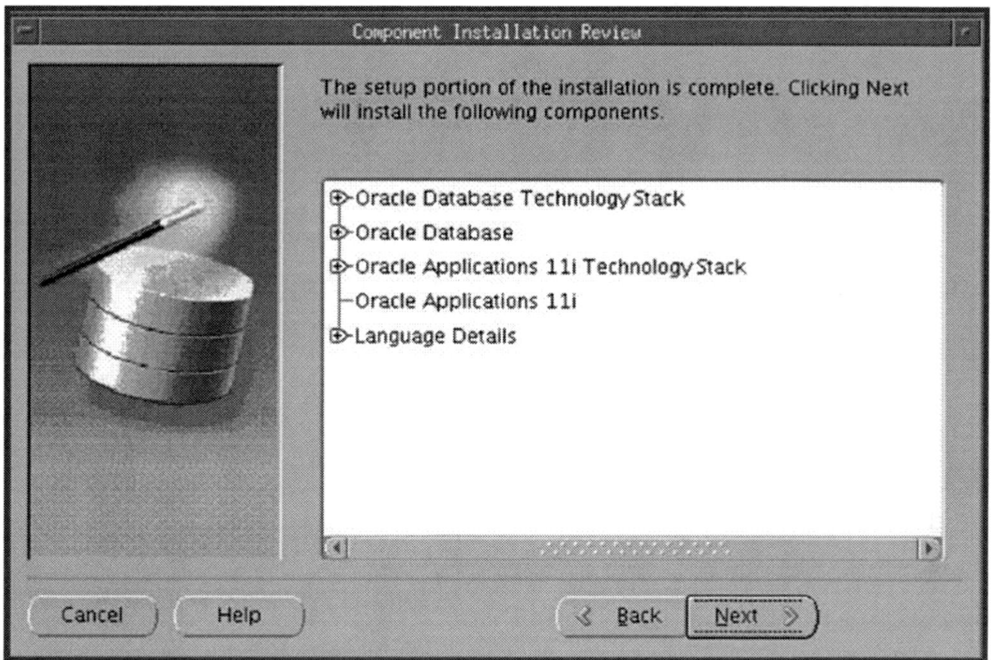

Fig. 4.71 Component Installation Review

On clicking 'Next', it displays an alert.

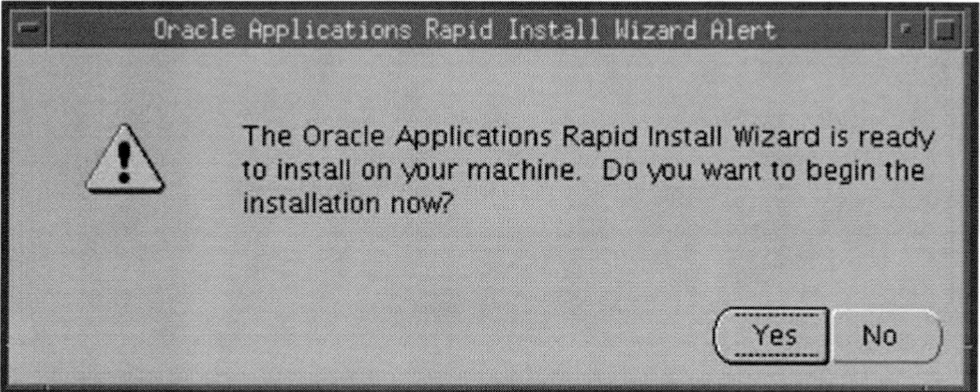

Fig. 4.72 Rapid Install Wizard Alert

Click 'Yes' to start the installation.

Once the installation is started, a status bar is displayed.

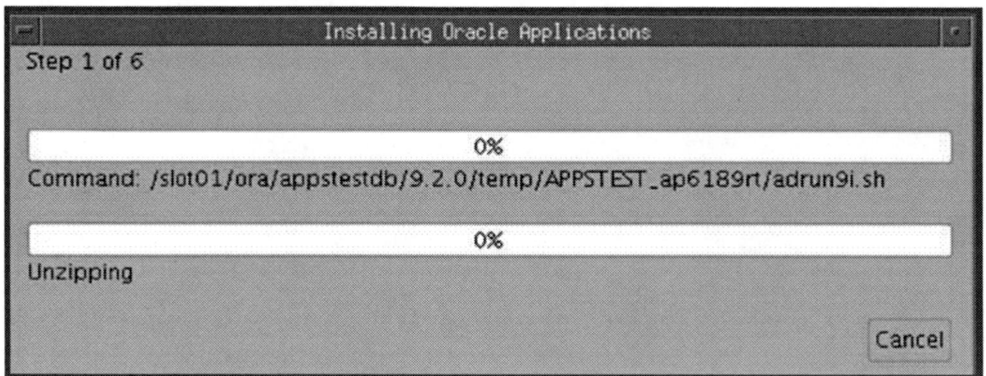

Fig. 4.73 Status Bar

It prompts for the path name of the location of the stage. Once this is given, it completes the installation.

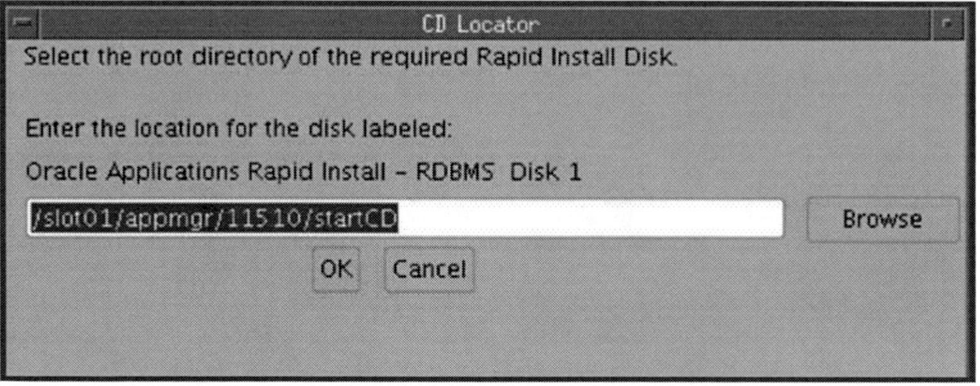

Fig. 4.74 Path Name of Location of the Stage

As discussed earlier, Rapid Install will now complete the installation on its own. After the installation is complete, it will check that they have been installed properly and display the results of these checks on the post-install check screen (Fig. 4.75).

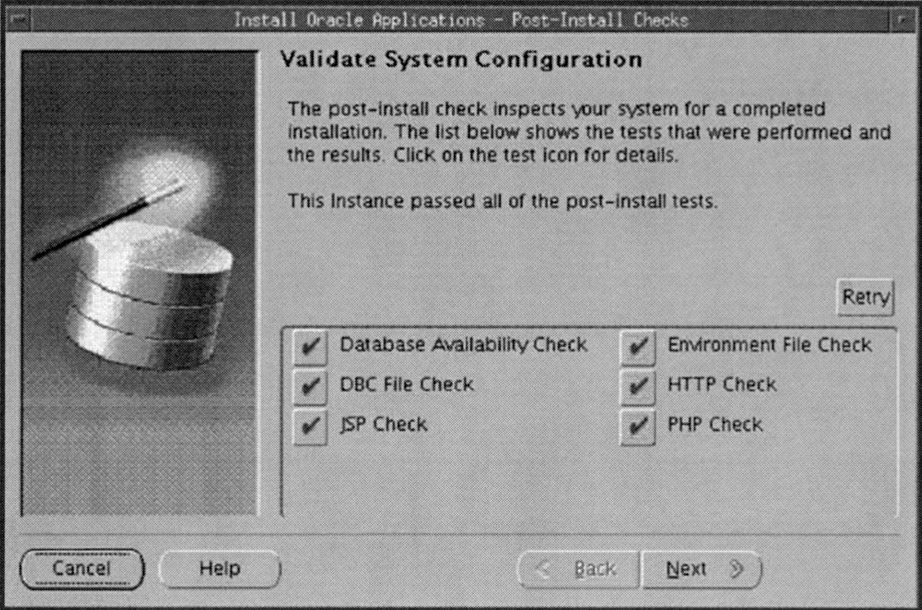

Fig. 4.75 Post-install Checks

The post-install checks are the same as covered in earlier sections. Once the checks are completed, the Finish screen appears, listing all the components installed. Press 'Finish' to complete the installation.

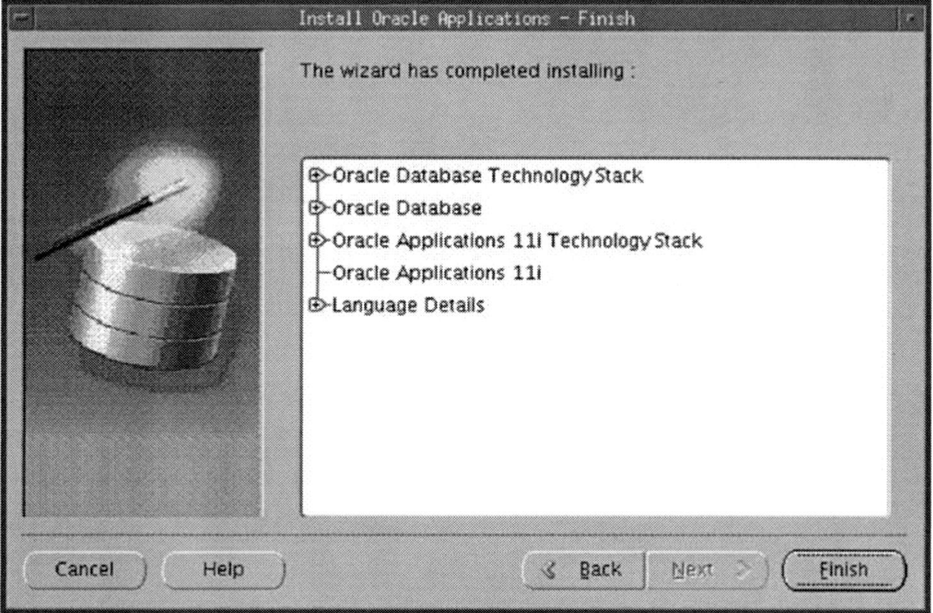

Fig. 4.76 Finish Screen

INSTALLING ORACLE APPLICATIONS RELEASE 12

PLANNING THE INSTALLATION

The first and foremost step for a successful installation is proper planning—a considerable amount of time should be spent in planning the business needs, the long-term growth of business, the number of concurrent users, the size of the database and the hardware and software requirements. It is important to ensure that the required hardware, software, documentation, correct operating system patches and of course the skills are available to complete the installation.

System Requirement

System Software requirements

The following software/maintenance tools must be installed in all the machines, and these should be available in the PATH of the user which runs the Rapid Install.

Table 4.1

Operating System	Required Maintenace Tools
Solaris (SPARC)	`ar, ld, make, X Display Server`
Linux	`ar, gcc, g++, ld, ksh, make, X Display Server`
Windows	`Microsoft C++, MKS Toolkit *, GNU make`
HP-UX	`ar, cc, aCC, make, X Display Server`
HP-UX (Itanium)	`ar, cc, aCC, make, X Display Server`
IBM AIX	`ar, cc, ld, linkxlc, make, X Display Server`

CPU requirements

The CPU requirements for installing Oracle Applications are not fixed. They depend on a number of factors, viz. the number of parallel users, the size and the expansion required in the database, the jobs running in the background and the desired response time. Since Oracle Applications can be used for any type of business (whether large or small scale), benchmarking these is not feasible. The best way is to refer to the Oracle Consulting Service and the hardware vendor to get a proper analysis of your CPU requirements.

To summarize, the following factors should be kept in mind while analyzing the CPU requirements:

- The size of the database
- The number of the concurrent users
- The average growth of the database
- The response time desired

- The type of the concurrent processing jobs that needs to be run
- What other services the server will host apart from Oracle applications
- How many nodes are planned for the architecture

Memory requirements

Apart from the CPU the memory also plays a vital role for the proper functioning of the Oracle applications. The memory requirements should be analyzed properly else it will result to slow functioning of the system or may even lead to crash of the database. The memory requirements should be calculated on the basis of the number of concurrent users as more the number of the users, more memory is required. Apart from this, the size of the database needs to be taken into consideration for calculating the memory requirement as the size of the database affects the size of SGA and the SGA directly depends on the physical RAM. Apart from that, you need to take into consideration the number of the instances that will be running, whether it will be a single instance or multiple RAC nodes. The memory requirement also depends on the number of sessions connecting the database and the amount of data processing you are planning to do on the database. It also depends on the other software you need to run on the servers apart from Oracle.

Thus to summarize, the memory requirement depends on the following factors:

- The size of the database as it affects the size of SGA
- The number of concurrent users and the number of sessions connecting to the database
- The amount of data processing you are planning to do
- Whether it will be a single instance or multi node RAC database
- Any other software you are planning to install in the server

Disk requirement

As per Oracle documentation, the disk space requirements for a fresh Rapid Install Release 12 are as given below:

Rapid Install installs the file system and database files for all products, regardless of their licensed status. The approximate file system requirements in a standard installation are:

Node	**Space Required**
Applications node file system (includes `AS 10.1.2 ORACLE_HOME, AS 10.1.3 ORACLE_HOME, COMMON_TOP, APPL_TOP, and INST_TOP`)	28GB
Database node file system (fresh install)	45 GB
Database node file system (Vision Demo database)	133 GB

The total space required for a standard system, not including the stage area, is 73 GB for a fresh install with a production database, and 161 GB for a fresh install with a Vision Demo database.

The database tier disk space requirements for both the production database and the Vision database include database files (`.dbf`) and the 10gR2 database `ORACLE_HOME`.

Stage area

To run Rapid Install from a stage area, you need at least 33 GB for the files.

Apart from this, a lot of other factors also need to be taken into consideration for calculating the disk requirement.

- Project growth: You need to anticipate the growth of the database and should plan for the disk requirement accordingly.
- Log and Output files: Oracle Applications create log files for many activities like patching, running AD utilities, starting/stopping middle tiers, running concurrent requests etc. Many of these activities create output files also, like concurrent requests. The disk space for the log and the output files depends totally on how extensively you are using the application, which creates log/output files. The files are not deleted or purged by default and you need to make a strategy for deleting the old log and output files.
- Temporary directory: Oracle Applications need temporary disk space for keeping the buffer data, which it processes. Oracle forms, reports and concurrent processing make extensive use of the temporary directory for doing all the processing during the runtime. This temporary directory is also not purged automatically and you need to make a strategy for deleting these files.
- Patches and Software: You need disk space to keep a stage where you would like to download all the patches that need to be run in the application system. Also you need space to keep the operating system software if any. You can always delete the patches and software after the application.
- Custom Application: Oracle Applications are customized by many users as per their requirement. To customize Oracle Applications you need additional space for keeping the custom files which are normally stored in the `CUSTOM_TOP`.
- Backups: You also need to take into consideration the backup size and the backup retention policy for calculating the disk requirement.
- Additional Software size: To install any other software or to integrate any third party software along with Oracle Applications the space required by the additional software also needs to be taken into account while calculating the disk requirement.
- Language Installation: If additional languages are being installed (other than American English), you need additional space for each language. Typically, each additional language takes around 10 GB in the application file system and 800 MB in the database.

Pre-Installation Tasks

Operating system patches

One needs to check Oracle documentation to find out which OS patches are required for the requisite platforms, and then check whether one has the right OS patches for an Oracle Application installation.

Creating Unix accounts

For installing Oracle Applications, two Unix accounts need to be created—one for the database (called the *Oracle* user) and the other for the Application file system (called the `applmgr` user). Both the accounts need to be created before starting the installation. In a single node installation, one needs to log in as Oracle user for starting the Rapid Install, while for a multi-node installation, one logs in as root.

Note: In Release 12, Java Development Kit (JDK) 5.0 is automatically installed by Rapid Install. You need not install the JDK separately, as was the case in Oracle11.5.10.

Creating the stage area

The Release 12 software comes in a DVD format. The individual disks included in the Release 12 software bundle are labeled as follows:

- Start Here—Disk 1
- `APPL_TOP`—Disk *n*
- RDBMS—Disk *n*
- Tools—Disk *n*
- Databases—Disk *n*

For creating the stage area, insert the Start Here DVD in the DVD-ROM drive and mount the same. Run the adautostg.pl script as follows:

```
$ cd /mnt/cdrom/Disk1/rapidwiz
$ perl adautostg.pl
```

You must have perl 5.0053 installed and it should be there in your PATH. If you don't have perl installed, you can download it from www.perl.com.

At the prompt for stage directory, enter the name of the system top-level directory. The Rapid Install Stage12 will be created in this path. For example, if you enter /d1 as top-level directory, the stage will be created in /d1/stage12. The components that are to be staged need to be indicated next, viz. `Apps`, `DB`, `AppsDB`, `iAS`. If you type 'All' at the prompt, then all the components will be staged.

Stage area directory structure

The stage area created by `adautostg.pl` looks as in Fig. 4.77. It consists of a top-level directory `<Stage12>`, with sub-directories startCD, `oraApps`, `oraDB`, `oraiAS`, `oraAppDB`, and `oraNLS/<LANG>` (if required).

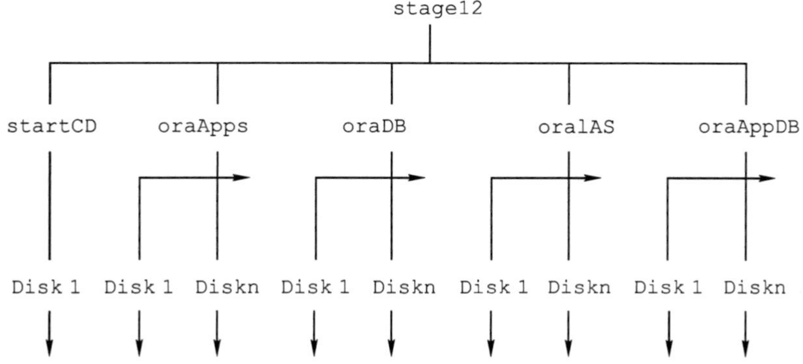

Fig. 4.77 Stage Area Directory Structure

THE INSTALLATION PROCESS

Starting the Rapid Install

Once the stage is created, we can start the Rapid Install as follows:

```
$ cd /<path of stage>/startCD/Disk1/rapidwiz
$ ./rapidwiz
./rapidwiz
```

The welcome screen

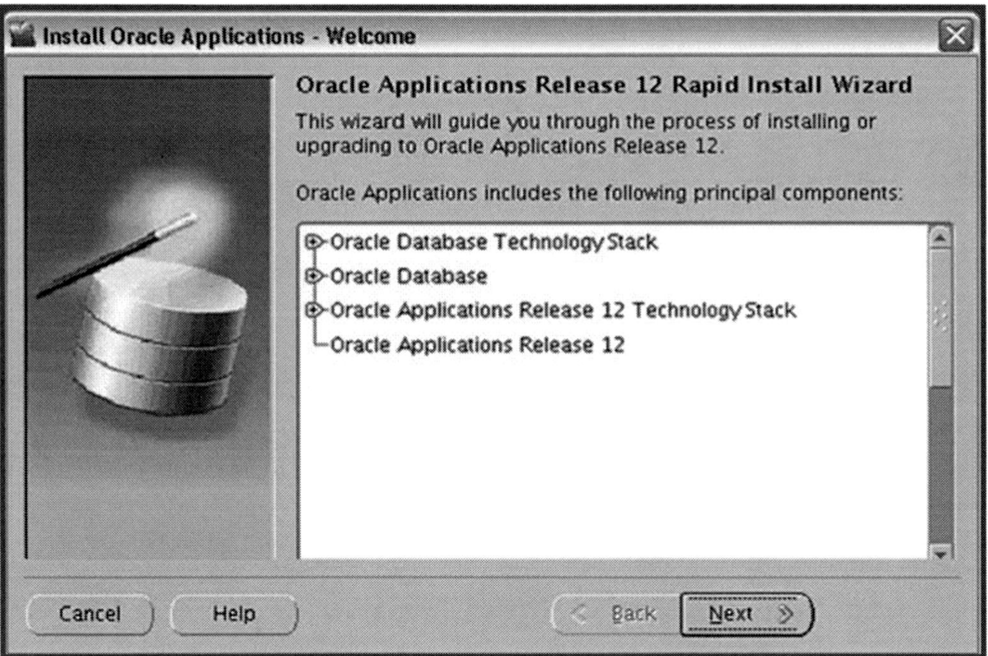

Fig. 4.78 Illustration of Welcome Screen

The welcome screen lists the components included in the release of Oracle Application. Release12 Rapid Install comes with 10gR2 database. It can also be used to upgrade or migrate an existing database to 10gR2. This is an informative screen only, so no action is required. Click 'Next' to continue.

Selecting a wizard operation

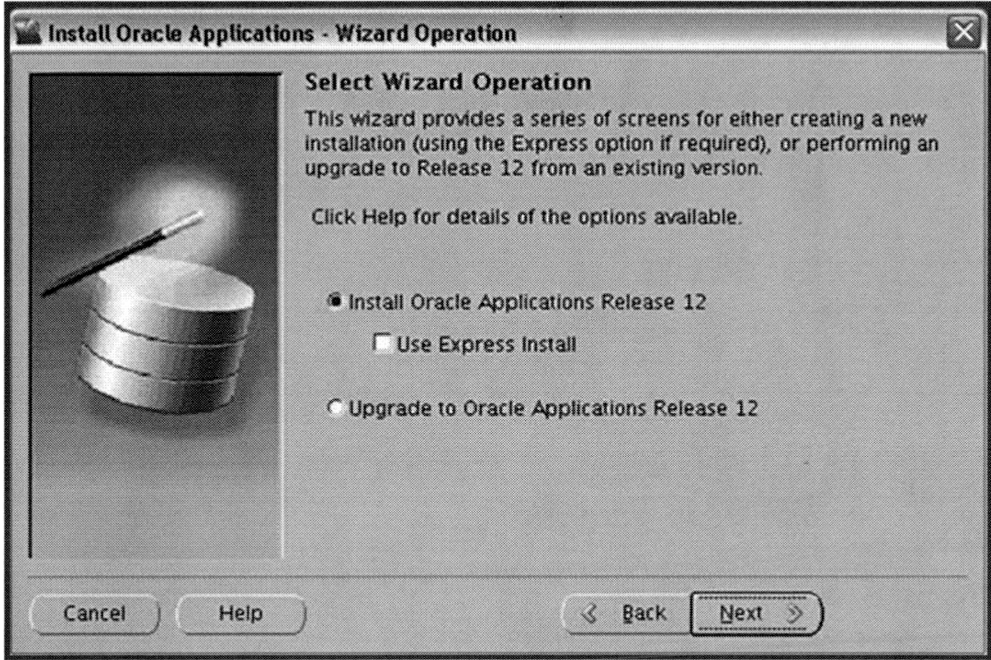

Fig. 4.79 Illustration of Selecting a Wizard Operation: Installation or Upgrade

This screen asks for the action to be performed by Rapid Install. You can choose between a fresh installation and an upgrade. Based on the response, Rapid Install performs the appropriate action and screen flows.

The following are the available actions:

- Installing Fresh Oracle Applications: This action installs a fully configured system with either a fresh database or Vision Demo Database.
- Express Configuration: This action also installs a fully configured single node system with either a fresh database or Vision Demo Database. The only difference is that here you supply a few basic parameters such as database name, top-level install directories and port settings. The remaining directories and other settings are taken by Rapid Install using default values.
- Upgrade to Oracle Applications E-Business Release12: Choose this option if you are upgrading your existing application system to the current version of Oracle Application.

This chapter mainly deals with fresh installations, so the last option is not recommended here. Click 'Install Oracle Application Release12' and press 'Next'.

Oracle Configuration Manager

Oracle Configuration Manager (OCM) is a new component that is included in the R12 Rapid Install which is designed to facilitate support for the Oracle products. It provides continuous tracking of key

Oracle and system statistics of the machine it is running on. Data collected by the Configuration Manager is sent via secured HTTPS back to Oracle Support, who can thereby maintain an updated view of your Oracle instance. OCM also automatically discovers the installed components and their configuration information.

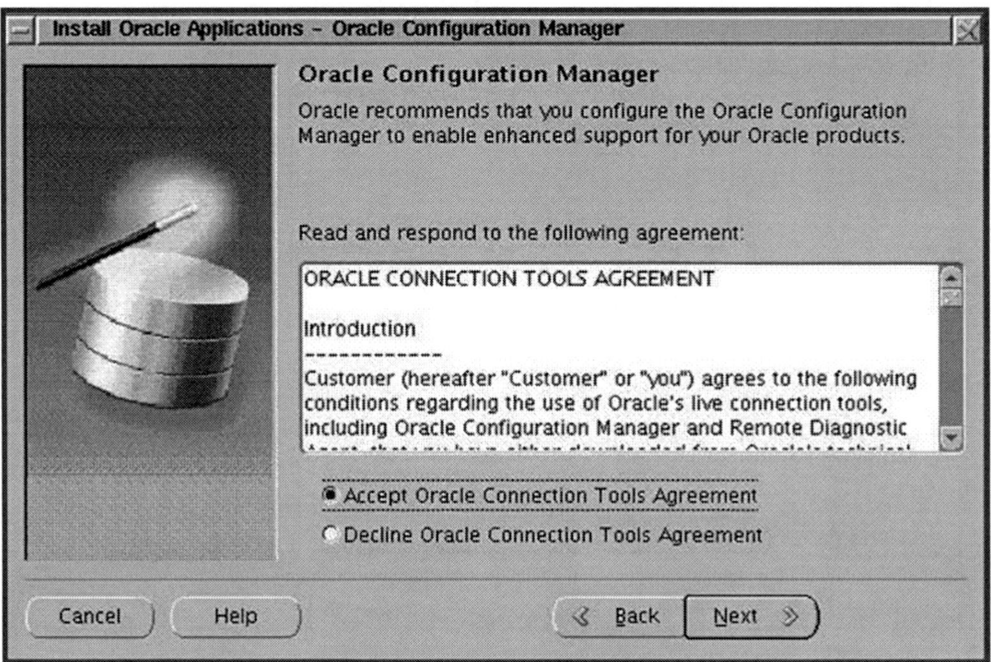

Fig. 4.80 The Oracle Configuration Manager Screen

Though Oracle recommends to deploy the OCM but this is an optional component, so you can either accept of decline to proceed or not to proceed with the OCM.

If you choose Accept, you are presented with another OCM screen.

Oracle Configuration Manager Details

The following details need to be given on the Oracle Configuration Manager Details Screen:

- Support Identifier (CSI Number): It is the unique Customer Support Identifier number provided from Oracle.
- Metalink Account: It is the email address by which your company is registered to metalink.
- Country: Select the country from the drop down list.

If you intend to use proxy server for OCM then you need to check the check box saying Configure proxy server for Oracle Configuration Manager and need to give the proxy server name and the port number.

Install Oracle Applications - Oracle Configuration Manager Details

Oracle Configuration Manager Details

Enter the setup values for Oracle Configuration Manager.

Support Identifier (CSI) 9445562122

Metalink Account jobanerj_us@oracle.com

Country United States

Configure proxy server for Oracle Configuration Manager

Proxy Server Name

Proxy Server Port

Cancel Help Back Next

Fig. 4.81 The Oracle Configuration Manager Details Screen

Load Configuration File

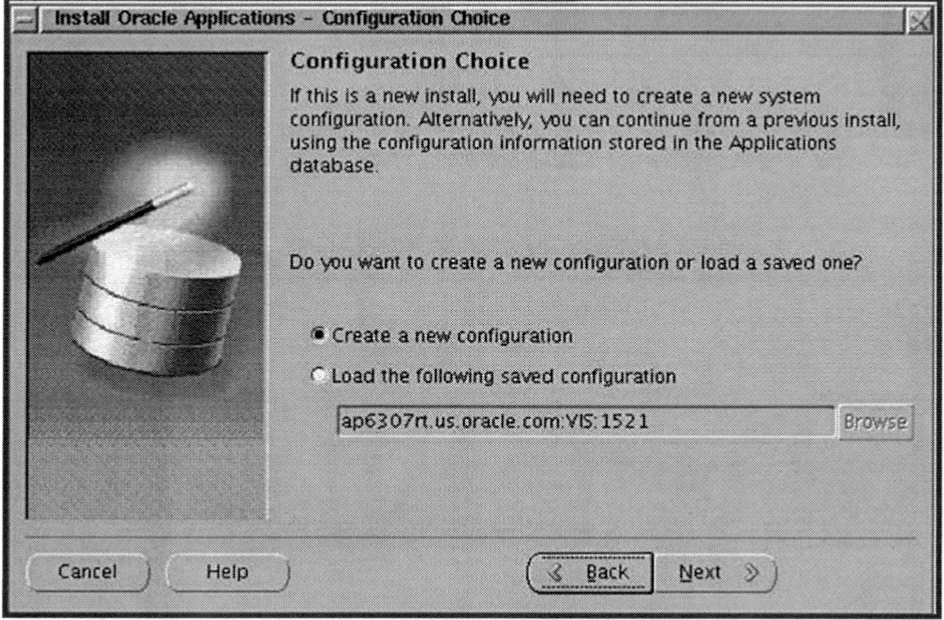

Fig. 4.82 Load Configuration Screen

In this screen the Rapid Install prompts if you would like to create a new configuration file or load an existing file. If you choose to create a new configuration then Rapid Install saves the parameter that you enter in the wizard screen in the applications database and in the configuration file (`conf_SID.txt`) which is stored in a temporary directory. The new thing in R12 is that it stores the configuration information in application database also, which was not the case in Oracle 11.5.10

If you choose to load the saved configuration, it automatically loads the configuration stored in the database by giving the database connect string. As seen in Fig. 4.82, for loading the configuration from the database you need to supply `<hostname.domain>:<SID>:<database port>` for example ap6307rt.us.oracle.com:VIS:1521. Typically, this option is chosen while performing a multi-node install, or while restarting Rapid Install after an interruption to the installation process. You can also browse and point the text configuration file in case if you don't want the configuration to be read from the database.

In Release 12 the name of this configuration file has changed, and it now includes the database `SID`, to give a file name of `conf_<SID>.txt` (for example, `conf_PROD.txt`). This file stores the information collected by Rapid Install for all database and Applications' nodes. Rapid Install stores the same `conf_<SID>.txt` file in three separate locations:

1. Database `10g R2 <ORACLE_HOME>/appsutil`: This copy is used on database nodes, on Application nodes in multi-node installs, and in upgrades. It is permanently stored and not deleted.
2. `$INST_TOP`: This copy is used on Application nodes in multi-node installs, and in upgrades. It is permanently stored and not deleted.
3. `/tmp/<time stamp>`: This copy is used by Rapid Install during the installation run. It is deleted when the installation is completed.

Global System Settings

There has been some minor changes in the Global System Settings screen. Unlike Oracle 11.5.10 this screen does not prompt for the hostname and the domain information anymore. Like11.5.10 installation, on this screen you assign the port pool for the various components.

Database Node Configuration

The Database Node Configuration details screen prompts for the following:

Database type: Fresh or Vison Demo database

Database SID

The Hostname of the database server

The Domain name

The Operating System

The Database OS User who will the own the Oracle file system

The Database OS group

The Base directory of the Oracle.

Unlike 11.5.10 this screen prompts for the Operating System, Hostname and the Domain Name information.

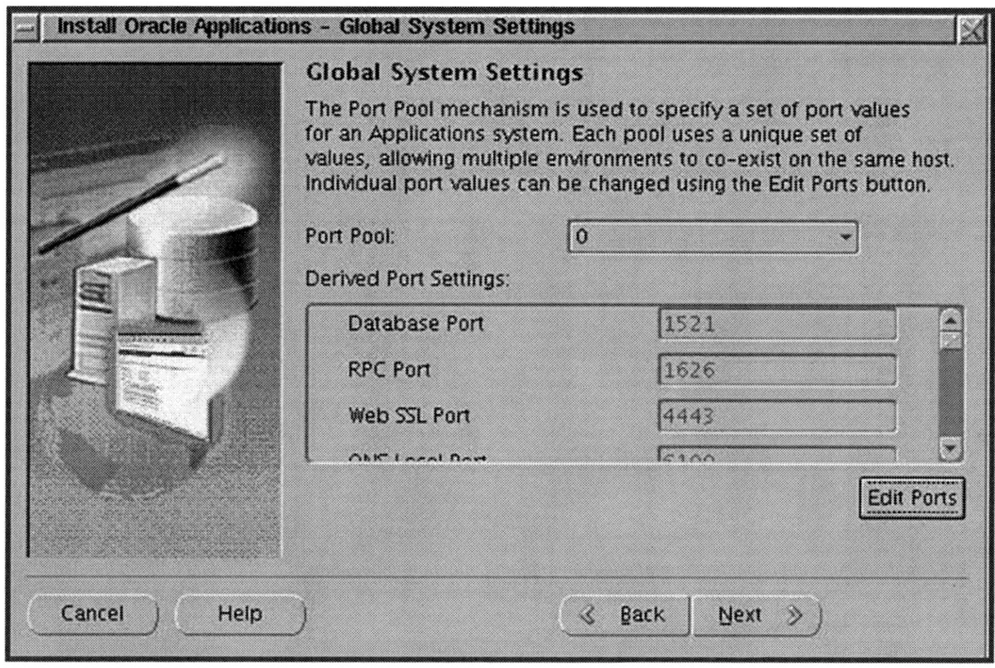

Fig. 4.83 Global System Settings

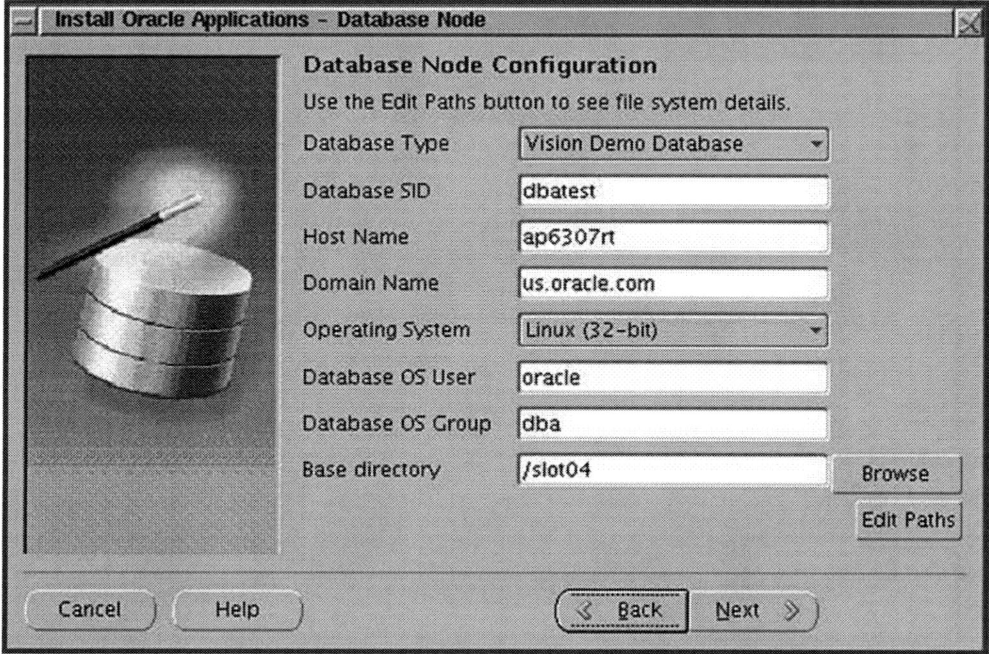

Fig. 4.84 Database Node Configuration

Select licensing type

In this wizard, you indicate the type of licensing agreement purchased from the Oracle Corporation. Completing a licensing screen *does not* constitute a license agreement. It simply registers your products as active. You should have complete information about your product license before you complete the licensing screens.

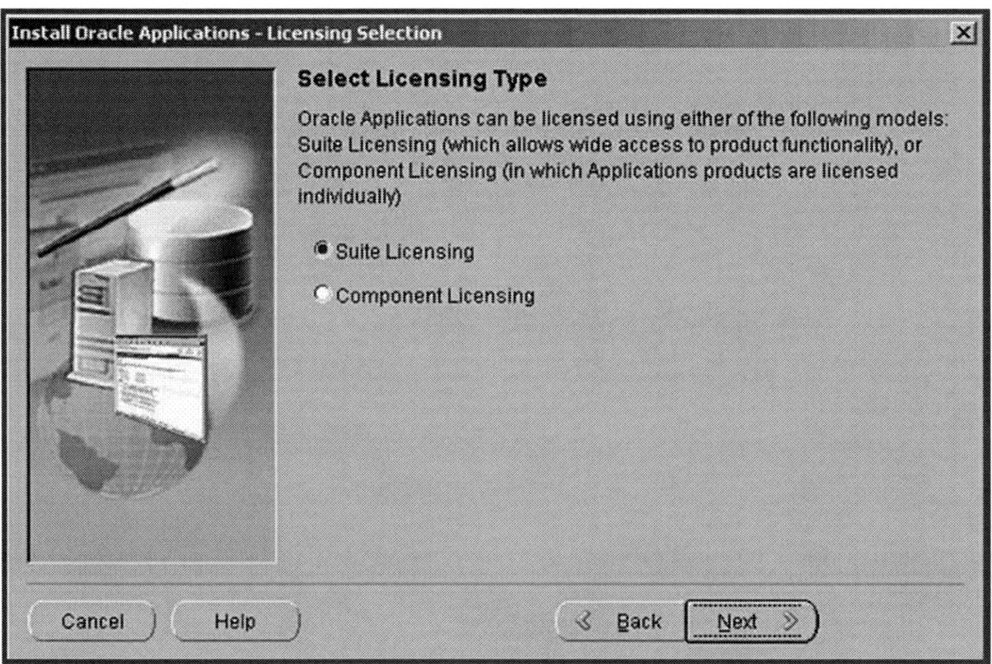

Fig. 4.85 Illustration of Licensing Page

Rapid Install installs all products automatically, regardless of their license status. However, you must register the products that you have licensed so that they are flagged in the system as active. An active flag marks the products for use and inclusion in patching and other tasks to update and maintains your system after initial installation.

You can either register through Suite or Component Application Licensing in order to license your product.

If you click the Suite licensing option, the licensing page appears as shown in Fig 4.86

This licensing model allows wide access to Applications functionality. In effect, your choice instructs Rapid Install to automatically register all products included in the E-Business Suite price bundle. The products that are checked and grayed are licensed automatically as a part of the suite. The ones that are not must be registered separately as add-on products. Tick any add-on products that you have licensed and want to register.

You can also choose the Component Applications licensing option on the Suite Selection Screen as shown. If you select the Component Applications licensing then the screen appears as shown in Fig. 4.87.

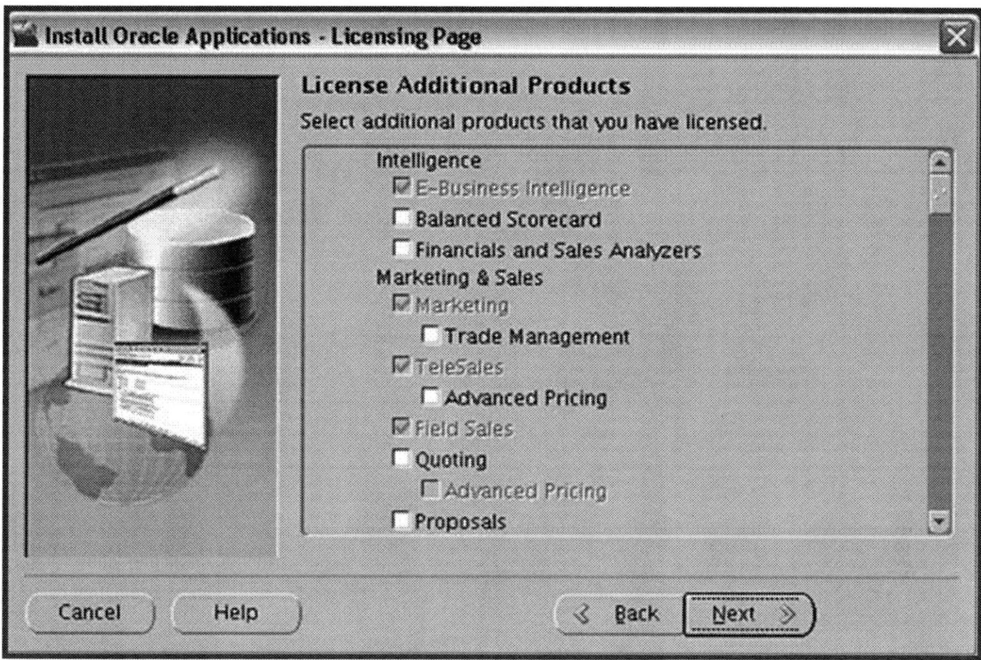

Fig. 4.86 Suite Licensing Page

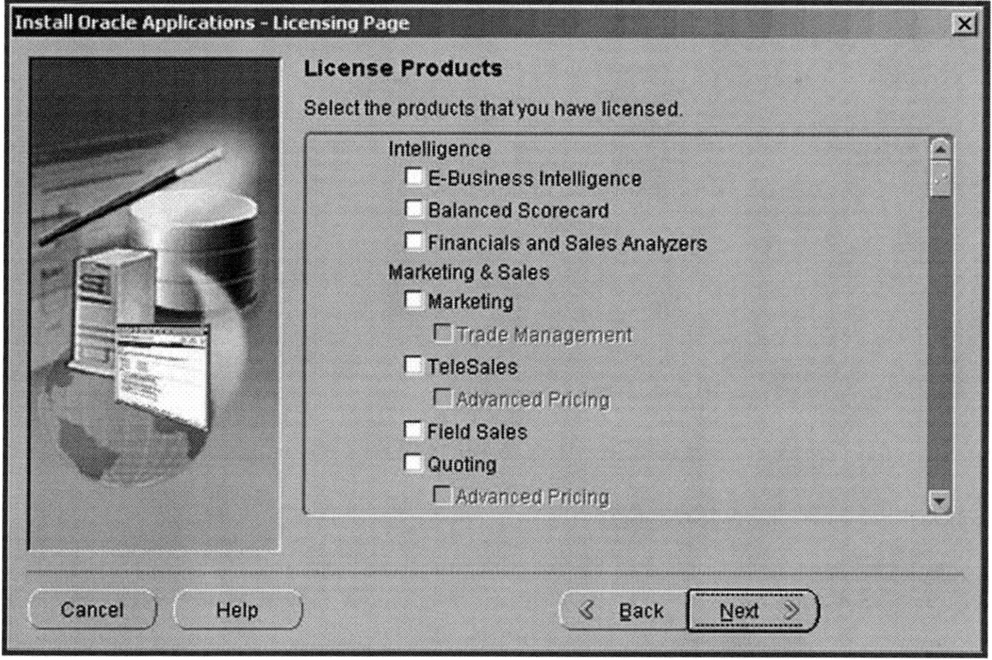

Fig. 4.87 Component Applications Licensing Page

You should choose this option if the licensing agreement is for component products of individual Applications. These products are licensed based on the number of authorized users or on the number of business transactions processed.

On this licensing page, all individual products are listed. Products that are grayed out cannot be selected unless the parent component is selected.

You can also license additional products after installation from the Oracle Application Manager by going to OAM > License Manager > License additional products.

Selecting country-specific functionality

Many application systems need country-specific or local functionality. In order to select this, choose the country from the list which is shown on the left side of the screen by using the '>' button. Country-specific functionality can also be added at a later stage using Oracle Application Manager License Manager. In case you don't want this, just ignore this screen.

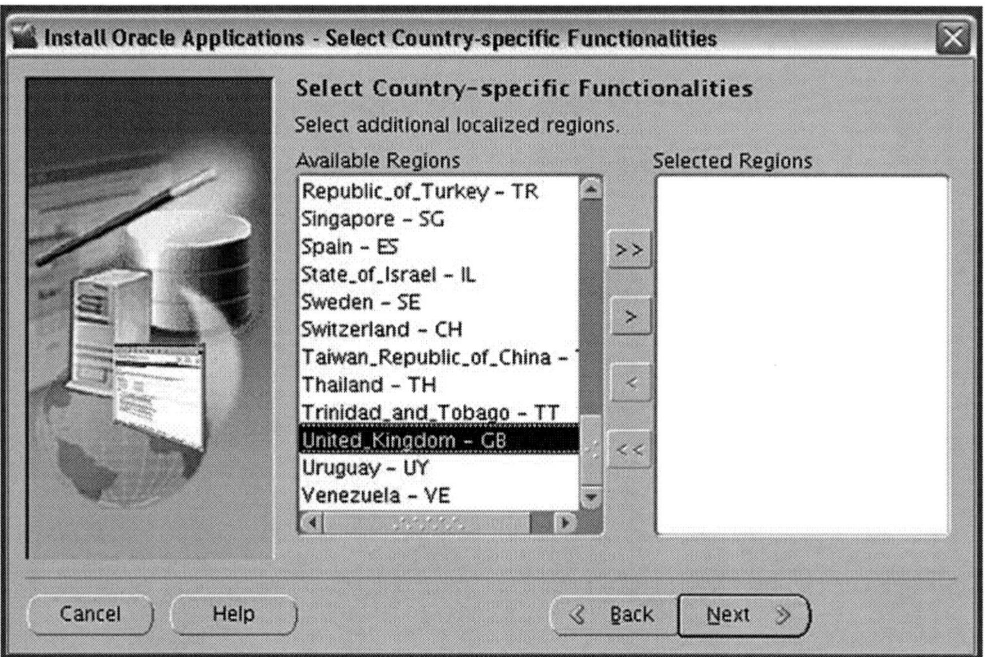

Fig. 4.88 Selection of Country-specific Functionalities

Select Internationalization Settings

Using the next screen, you can select languages other than American English. Select any additional language using the '>' button. If you don't want an additional language, press 'Next'. The languages you select determine help to the available options for the other NLS-related configuration parameters (such as territory and character set) that your system requires and can support.

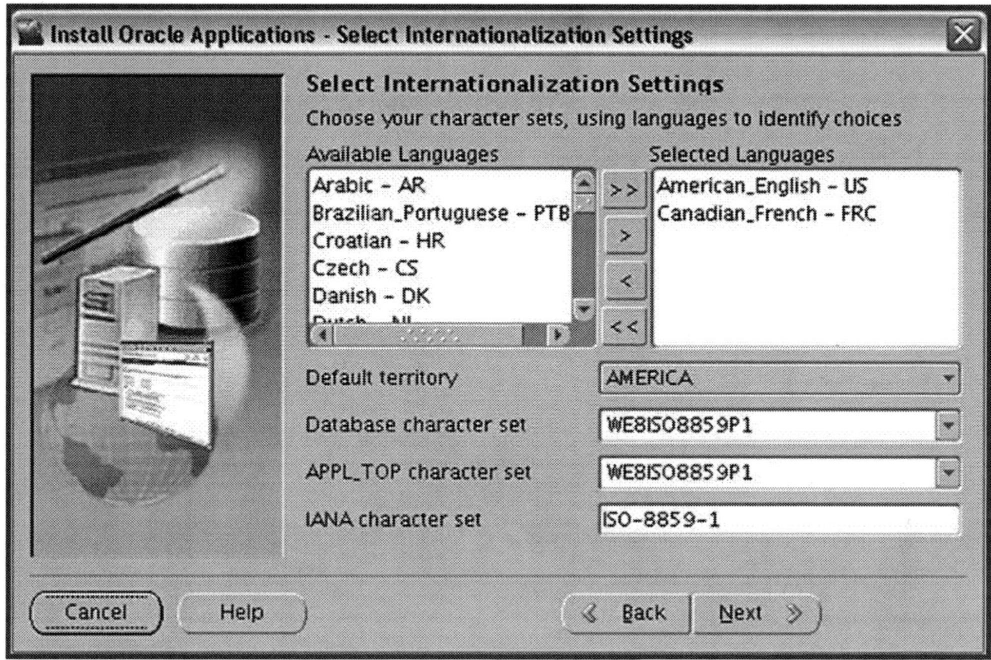

Fig. 4.89 Selection of Additional Languages

Note: Languages are no longer licensed using Rapid Install; instead, use License Manager which is available in Oracle Application Manager to license languages.

The NLS language and territory settings are stored as profile options in the database. They are configured at the site level when you run Rapid Install. The base language is used for the default language setting and the default territory is used for the territory profile option. Users inherit these values the first time they log on to Oracle Applications.

In this illustration we have chosen Canadian French as an additional language so the character set choices have changed and now include only those that are compatible with both American English and Canadian French. If you plan to install any other language after Rapid Install then you have to make sure that it should be compatible with the character set of your Applications system.

Primary Applications Node Configuration

The major change in this screen is that it has a new entry for the Instance Directory. This is the place where you give the location of the `INST_TOP`. It can be seen from Fig 4.90 that there are two buttons Edit Services and Edit Paths. By clicking the Edit Paths button you can change the mount points of the `APPL_TOP`, `COMMON_TOP`, `ORACLE_HOME` etc which we have already discussed. Edit Services is something new to the Release 12. If we click the Edit Services button we will see the services which are enabled in this node. The categories are: Root Service Group, Web Entry Point Services, Web Application Services, Batch Processing Services, and Other Service Group.

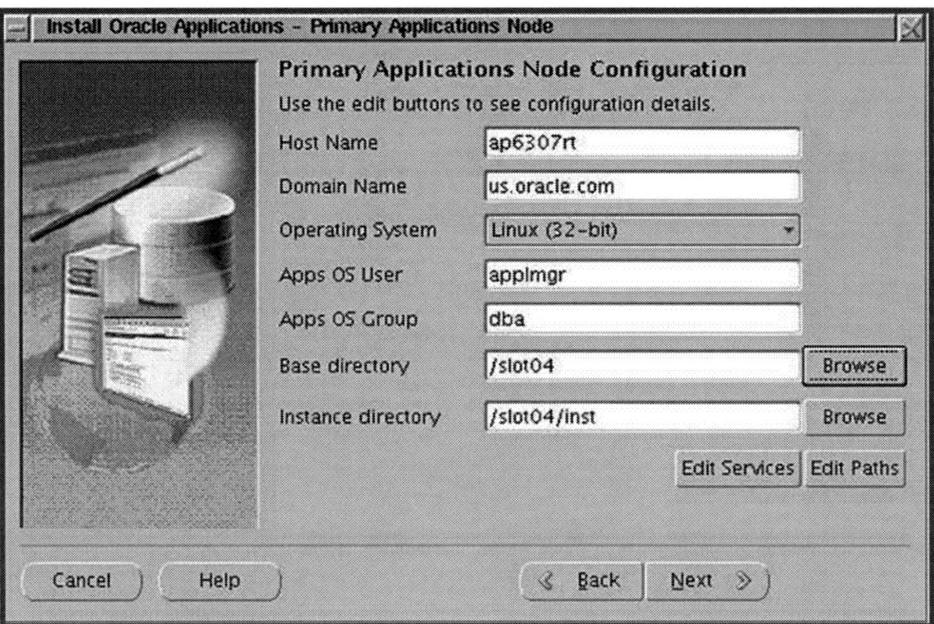

Fig. 4.90 Primary Applications Node Configuration Screen

The Edit Service screen looks like as shown in Fig. 4.91.

Application Services

Primary Applications Node Configuration

Root Service Group	enabled
Web Entry Point Services	enabled
Web Application Services	enabled
Batch Processing Services	enabled
Other Service Group	enabled

OK Cancel

Fig. 4.91 The Services Configuration Screen

The services provide the following functionality, which differs significantly from Release 11*i* and also uses new terminology:

Service Group:	**Supports:**
Root Service Group	• Oracle Process Manager (OPMN)
Web Entry Point Services	• HTTP Server
Web Application Services	• OACORE OC4J • Forms OC4J • OAFM OC4J
Batch Processing Services	• Applications TNS Listener • Concurrent Managers • Fulfillment Server
Other Service Group	• Oracle Forms Services • Oracle MWA Service

Applications nodes should have services enabled as follows:

- **Web node**: Root Service Group, Web Entry Point Services, Web Application Services
- **Forms node**: Root Service Group, Web Application Services, Other Service Group
- **Concurrent Processing node**: Root Service Group, Batch Processing Services

Let us take an example to understand it in a better way. If you want to do a two node installation in two Linux boxes, say LinuxServer1 and LinuxServer2 and want to install the database and the concurrent processing in LinuxServer1 and the Web and Forms Services in the LinuxServer2 then

- On LinuxServer1, select Root Service Group and Batch Processing Services.
- On LinuxServer2, select Root Service Group, Web Entry Point Services, Web Application Services, and Other Service Group.

In terms of `ORACLE_HOME` creation, the result will be that:

- LinuxServer1 will have an `ORACLE_HOME` for the 10g R2 Applications database, plus an `ORACLE_HOME` for Application Server 10.1.2, and an `ORACLE_HOME` for Application Server 10.1.3.
- LinuxServer2 will have an `ORACLE_HOME` for Application Server 10.1.2, and an `ORACLE_HOME` for Application Server 10.1.3.

Node Information

This screen shows the detailed information of all the nodes. From this screen you can add any number of nodes, which you want to add in your application system.

If you want to add more nodes click the button Add Server. The Add Server screen looks like as shown in Fig 4.93

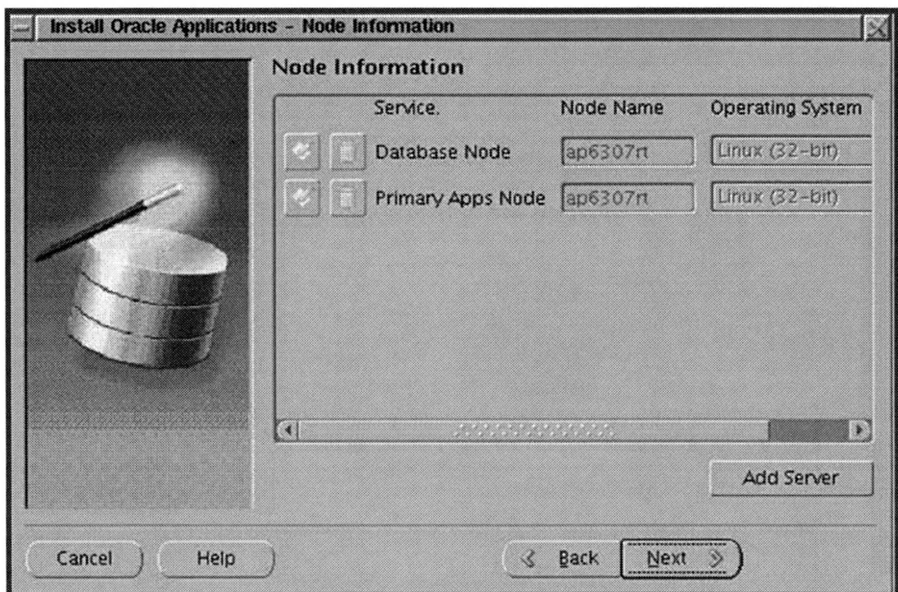

Fig. 4.92 Node Information

Additional Applications Node Configuration

Host Name ap6307rt

Domain Name us.oracle.com

Operating System Linux (32-bit)

Apps OS User applmgr

Apps OS Group dba

Base directory /slot04 Browse

Instance directory /slot04/inst

Shared File System: Not Shared

Edit Paths Edit Services

OK Cancel

Fig. 4.93 The Add Server Screen

Here, you specify details of the first additional Applications node. You can either accept the default and the suggested values, or edit them as needed.

If you want to add a few more servers then click on the Add Server button and fill in the details for the application system. With the Edit Services button you can choose which services should be enabled for the nodes you are adding.

An important feature on this screen is the Shared File System checkbox and associated drop-down list. By checking the box and selecting a node from the existing Applications nodes that appear on the drop-down list, you enable the node being added on this screen to share the Applications tier file system with the node selected from the drop-down list.

Validate System Configuration

On Clicking Next, Rapid Install starts doing all the checks and validates the system.

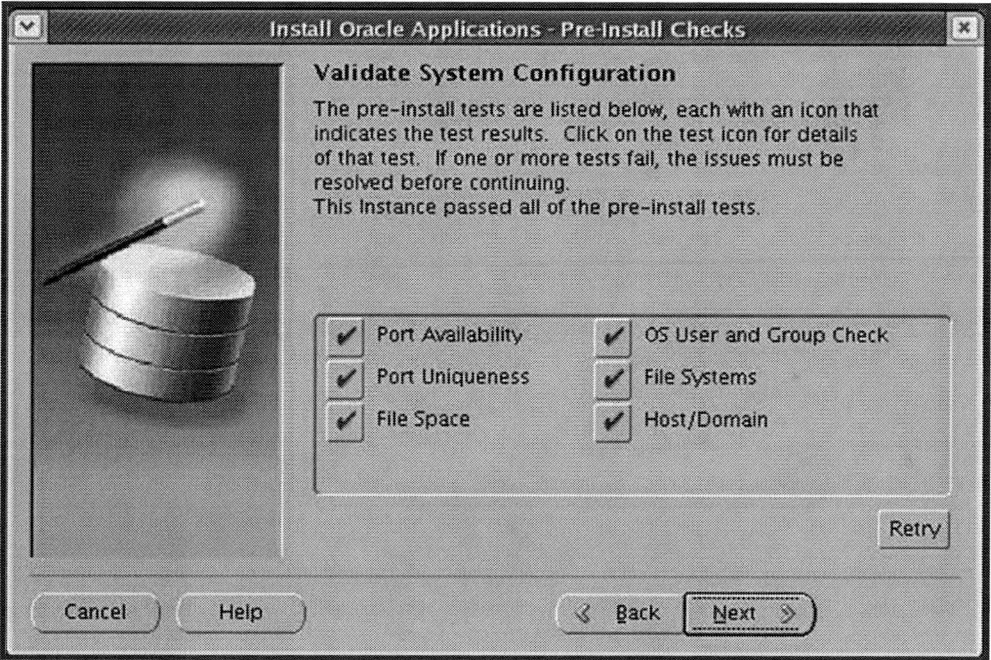

Fig. 4.94 Validate System Configuration

It checks the system on the following parameters:

- Port Availability: it checks whether the port you have selected is available or clashing with an existing port
- Port Uniqueness: it checks that there is no duplicate defined port for the processes
- File Space Check: it ensures that the file system has sufficient space for the installation
- OS User and Group Check: it checks that the OS user exists and is a part of the correct group

- File Systems Check: it checks whether the files are mounted properly and have correct permission
- Host/Domain Check: it verifies the host name and the domain name are valid.

The results of test are labeled with check marks (✓) exclamation marks (!) or a cross (×) mark. The check mark means the system has passed the test, while the exclamation mark means the system should be checked. Points marked with a cross signify that the issues should be resolved before continuing with the installation. Here, you can click 'Yes' to continue or 'No' to review the issues.

Begin the Installation

On the Component Installation Review screen, Rapid Install lists the components it will install, based on the system parameters you entered in the wizard.

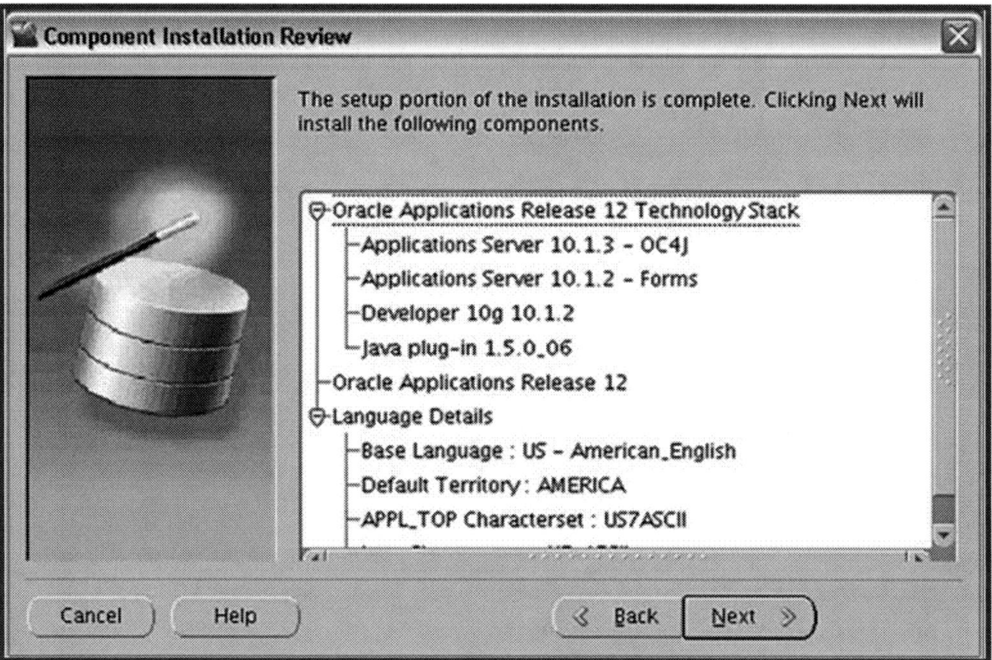

Fig. 4.95 Component Installation Review Screen

On clicking Next, Rapid Install displays another alert asking you to verify whether you are ready to begin the installation.

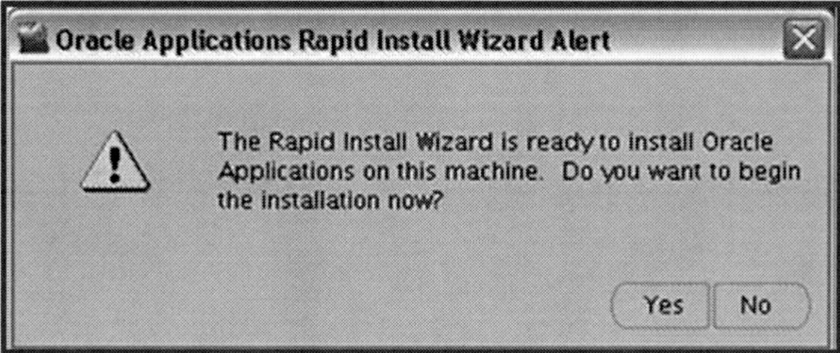

Fig. 4.96 Confirming to Start Installation

On clicking Yes, it starts the actual installation and displays the progress. Once the installation is over, it does a couple of post install checks and displays the results of the tests that were performed as a part of post install checks.

Post-Install Checks

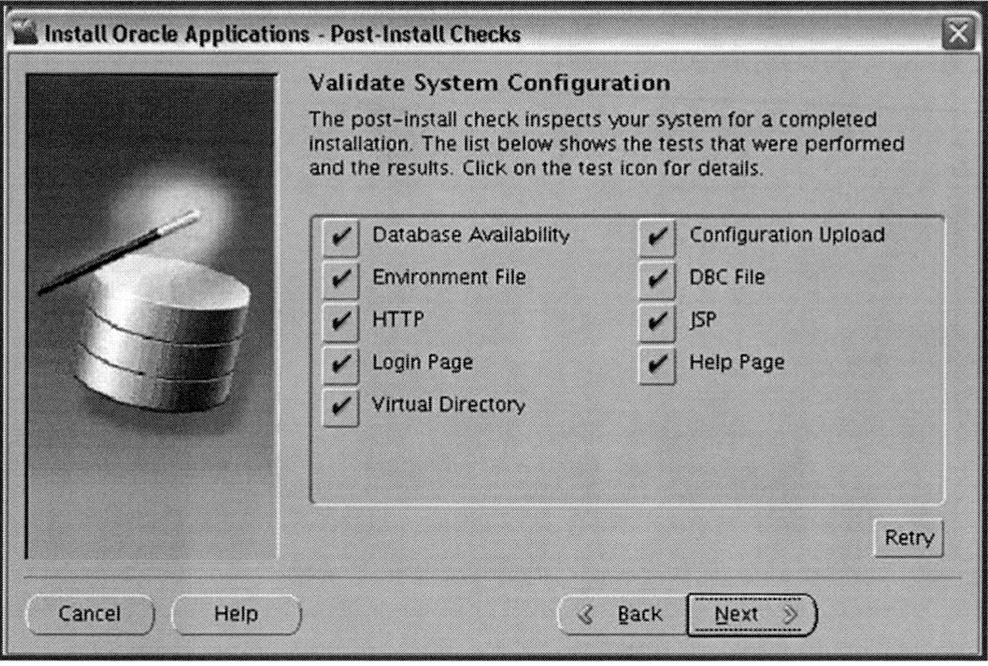

Fig. 4.97 Post-Install Checks

Rapid Install conducts the following post install checks:

Name of test	Checks
Database Availability	Database is running and allows users to log on
Environment File	Environment file has been delivered
HTTP	HTTP listener is working
Login Page	Login Page is working
DBC File	DBC file has been created
JSP	Java Server pages are working

The Finish Screen

Once the installation is complete the finish screen comes as shown in Fig 4.98

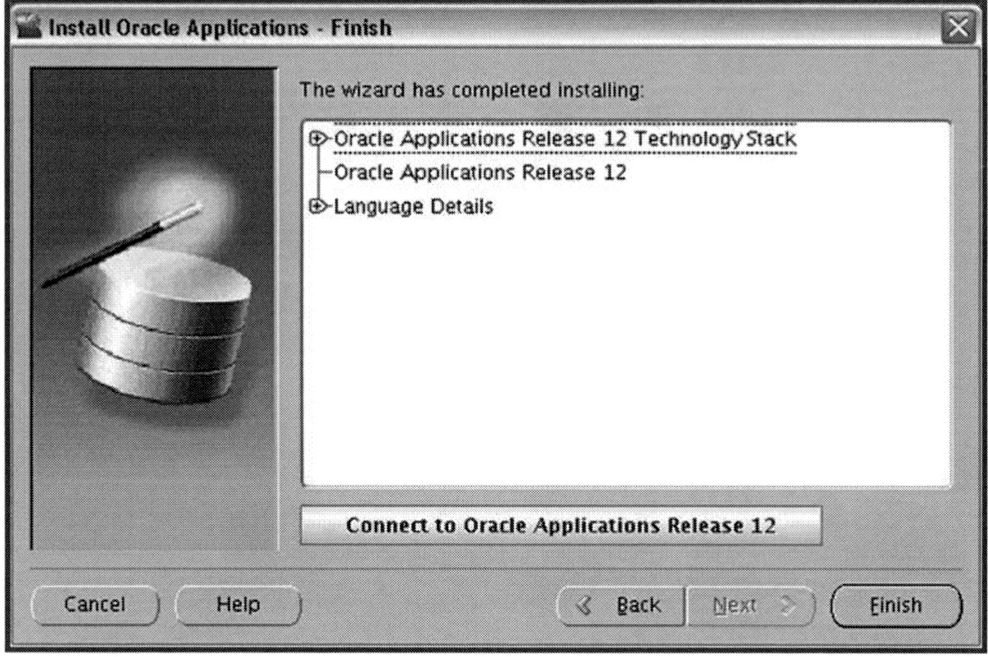

Fig. 4.98 The Finish Screen

USING EXPRESS CONFIGURATION IN R12

Express Configuration is the fastest way to create an Application system. It can configure a single node/ single user system with either a fresh database or a Vision Demo database. It prompts for very few parameters (such as database type and name, top-level installation directory, and port increments) and takes the rest of the parameters on its own to start the installation.

The Express Configuration in R12 works exactly in the same way as 11.5.10 so we won't be discussing the same again in details. The order of the R12 express configuration screens are also the same as that of 11.5.10.

Let us summarize the screens that comes while doing a R12 express configuration installation:

- Select Wizard Operation: Here you choose express configuration
- Choose Oracle Configuration Manager options
- Oracle Configuration Manager details
- Express Configuration Information: Here you give the input for Database type, Database SID, Domain, Base directory, Instance directory and port pool
- Validate System Configuration
- Alert Confirming Installation
- Post Install Checks
- Finish Screen

5

Checking and Configuring Oracle Applications

As discussed in the previous chapter, Rapid Install sets up the Oracle Application and conducts some checks at the end to ensure that the installation was successful. But it's always advisable to crosscheck if all components are running well or not before moving on to production.

In this chapter, we will manually go through all the checks to ensure that installation has occurred properly. We will also configure Oracle Applications once the manual check is finished. We will do the checks in the following order.

- Database check and database listener check
- Environment file check
- DBC file check
- HTTP check
- JSP check
- Checking Forms server

DATABASE AND LISTENER CHECK

Log in to the database server and check whether the database is up and running. This can be done by logging in to the SQL plus and issuing the following command.

```
(oracle01) oracle - -bash $ sqlplus ' / as sysdba '

SQL*Plus: Release 9.2.0.5.0 - Production on Tue Oct 11 20:56:23 2005

Copyright (c) 1982, 2002, Oracle Corporation. All rights reserved.

Connected to:
Oracle9i Enterprise Edition Release 9.2.0.5.0 - Production
```

Contd

Fig. 5.1 Contd

```
With the Partitioning, OLAP and Oracle Data Mining options
JServer Release 9.2.0.5.0 - Production

SQL> select open_mode from v$database ;

OPEN_MODE
------

READ WRITE

SQL> select name from v$database ;

NAME
------

EMSTEST
```

Fig. 5.1 Unix Session 5.1

Make sure that the database is in read-write mode and answers correctly when queried for the database name.

The next step is to check the functioning of the database listener. This is done using the listener status <env_name> command at the command prompt.

```
(oracle01) oracle - -bash $ lsnrctl status emstest

LSNRCTL for Linux: Version 9.2.0.5.0 - Production on 11-OCT-2005 21:01:28

Copyright (c) 1991, 2002, Oracle Corporation. All rights reserved.

Connecting to (ADDRESS=(PROTOCOL=IPC)(KEY=EXTPROCemstest))
STATUS of the LISTENER
--------------

Alias                  emstest
Version                TNSLSNR for Linux: Version 9.2.0.5.0 -
Production
Start Date             16-SEP-2005 22:48:47
Uptime                 24 days 22 hr. 12 min. 40 sec
Trace Level            off
Security               OFF
SNMP                   OFF
Listener Parameter File
/slot01/oracle/emstestdb/9.2.0/network/admin/emstest/listener.ora
```

Contd

Fig. 5.2 Contd

```
Listener Log File
/slot01/oracle/emstestdb/9.2.0/network/admin/emstest.log
Listening Endpoints Summary...
  (DESCRIPTION=(ADDRESS=(PROTOCOL=ipc)(KEY=EXTPROCemstest)))
(DESCRIPTION=(ADDRESS=(PROTOCOL=tcp)(HOST=ap6189rt.us.oracle.com)(PORT=1521)))
Services Summary...
Service "emstest" has 2 instance(s).
  Instance "emstest", status UNKNOWN, has 1 handler(s) for this
service...
  Instance "emstest", status READY, has 1 handler(s) for this service...
```

Fig. 5.2 Unix Session 5.2

Once the database listener has also been checked, the final step is connecting the database from a remote location. You can check for this by logging in to the APPL_TOP and then trying to connect to the database. If you are able to connect, then your database check is done and you are ready to move on to the next check. You can also do a tnsping from the APPL_TOP to check if it is pointing to the correct database.

```
(appmgr01) emstestappl - -bash $ tnsping emstest

TNS Ping Utility for Linux: Version 8.0.6.3.0 - Production on 11-OCT-2005
21:31:50

(c) Copyright 1997 Oracle Corporation. All rights reserved.

Attempting to contact
(ADDRESS=(PROTOCOL=tcp)(HOST=AP6189RT.us.oracle.com)(PORT=1521))
OK (0 msec)
(appmgr01) emstestappl - -bash $
```

Fig. 5.3 Unix Session 5.3

ENVIRONMENT FILE CHECK

The next test is to check the environment file. Log in to the APPL_TOP as the owner of the application file system and source the environment file.

Once the environment is sourced, check for the APPL_TOP, FND_TOP, AD_TOP, OA_HTML and OA_MEDIA, whether it is pointing to the correct location or not. Try connecting to the database after sourcing the APPL_TOP to check that the environment file is configured correctly.

```
(appmgr01) appmgr - -bash $ cd $APPL_TOP
(appmgr01) emstestappl - -bash $ . APPSORA.env
(appmgr01) emstestappl - -bash $
```

Fig. 5.4 Unix Session 5.4

```
(appmgr01) emstestappl - -bash $ echo $APPL_TOP
/slot01/appmgr/emstestappl
(appmgr01) emstestappl - -bash $ echo $FND_TOP
/slot01/appmgr/emstestappl/fnd/11.5.0
 (appmgr01) emstestappl - -bash $ echo $AD_TOP
/slot01/appmgr/emstestappl/ad/11.5.0
(appmgr01) appmgr - -bash $ echo $OA_HTML
/slot01/appmgr/emstestcomn/html
(appmgr01) emstest - -bash $ echo $OA_MEDIA
/slot01/appmgr/emstestcomn/java/oracle/apps/media
(appmgr01) appmgr - -bash $ sqlplus apps/apps
SQL*Plus: Release 8.0.6.0.0 - Production on Tue Oct 11 21:37:09 2005
(c) Copyright 1999 Oracle Corporation. All rights reserved.

Connected to:
Oracle9i Enterprise Edition Release 9.2.0.5.0 - Production
With the Partitioning, OLAP and Oracle Data Mining options
JServer Release 9.2.0.5.0 - Production
SQL>
```

Fig. 5.5 Unix Session 5.5

HTTP AND WEB LISTENER CHECK

Rapid Install sets up as well as configures the HTTP server of its own. You can manually crosscheck the Rapid Install configuration by logging in to the server with the iAS installation as the owner of the application file system.

Go to the `iAS` top directory, which is normally in the `<env_name>ora` directory. There will be an `xml` file, '`envname.env`; source it and echo for `ORACLE_HOME`. It should return the path of `iAS_TOP`.

```
cd /slot01/appmgr/emstestora/iAS
(appmgr01) iAS - -bash $ . emstest.env
(appmgr01) iAS - -bash $ echo $ORACLE_HOME
/slot01/appmgr/emstestora/iAS
(appmgr01) iAS - -bash $
```

Fig. 5.6 Unix Session 5.6

Testing the Virtual Directories of the Web Listener

Rapid Install creates a number of directories used by the web listener. These directories are listed in the file 'apps.conf', which is located in iAS_TOP/Apache/Apache/conf in 11*i* and $ORA_CONFIG_HOME/10.1.3/Apache/Apache/conf/ for R12. All the Apache configuration files are located in the same directory.

The locations of the following directories need to be checked in the apps.conf file.

Table 5.1 Directories in apps.conf File

Virtual Directories	Location
OA_HTML	$COMMON_TOP/html
OA_JAVA	$COMMON_TOP/java
OA_MEDIA	$COMMON_TOP/ java/oracle/apps/media
OA_TEMP	Temp Location
OA_CGI	$COMMON_TOP/ java/oracle/apps/media/bin
OA_SECURE	$COMMON_TOP/secure
Images	$iAS_TOP/portal30/images

If we open the existing apps.conf file in the current installation, we will find all the directories mentioned in Table 5.1 present there.

There are two ways of checking these virtual directories—either you open the apps.conf file with an editor, or you use your web browser to verify that the directories have been configured properly.

```
#
# $Header: apps_ux.conf 115.41 2004/09/02 10:58:16 kroychow ship $
#
# ################################################################
#
# This file is automatically generated by AutoConfig. It will be read #
and overwritten. If you were instructed to edit this file,  or if # you
are not able to use the settings created by AutoConfig, refer to #
Metalink document 165195.1 for assistance.
#
# ################################################################
#Alias /instlogs/ "/slot01/appmgr/emstestcomn/admin/install/emstest/"
#<Location /instlogs/>
#  Order allow,deny
#  Allow from all
#</Location>
Alias   /OA_JAVA/       "/slot01/appmgr/emstestcomn/java/"
<Location /OA_JAVA/>
  Order allow,deny
  Allow from all
</Location>
Alias   /OA_HTML/       "/slot01/appmgr/emstestcomn/html/"
<Location /OA_HTML/>
  Order allow,deny
  Allow from all
</Location>
Alias   /OA_SECURE/     "/slot01/appmgr/emstestcomn/secure/"
<Location /OA_SECURE/>
  Order allow,deny
  Allow from all
</Location>
Alias /media/       "/slot01/appmgr/emstestcomn/java/oracle/apps/media/"
<Location /media/>
  ExpiresActive on
  ExpiresDefault "now plus 1 day"
```

Contd

Fig. 5.7 Contd

```
  Order allow,deny
  Allow from all
</Location>

Alias /html/            "/slot01/appmgr/emstestcomn/html/"
<Location /html/>
  Order allow,deny
  Allow from all
</Location>

Alias  /OA_MEDIA/    "/slot01/appmgr/emstestcomn/java/oracle/apps/media/"
<Location /OA_MEDIA/>
  ExpiresActive on
  ExpiresDefault "now plus 1 day"
  Order allow,deny
  Allow from all
</Location>

Alias   /OA_TEMP/    "/slot01/appmgr/emstestcomn/temp/"
```

Fig. 5.7 Unix Session 5.7

Using web browser to check the virtual directories

To check the virtual directory 'OA_HTML', put this in your browser.

http://<hostname.domain>:<port>/OA_HTML/jtflogin.jsp

This will open the jtf log in screen of Oracle Applications. If the log in page appears, it means that this directory has been configured properly.

As can be seen in this screen, the address bar of the internet explorer clearly shows that it is pointing to the virtual directory OA_HTML.

For the directory 'OA_MEDIA', put the following in your browser.

http://<hostname.domain>:<port>/OA_MEDIA/FNDLOGOL.gif

This will return the Oracle Applications logo as seen in Fig. 5.9.

In order to check OA_CGI, you can type the following.

http://<hostname>.<domain>:<port no>/OA_CGI/FNDWRR.exe

This will result in the following response from the web browser.

```
Query String Parse Error.
```

To check the virtual directory 'OA_JAVA', put the following in your browser.

```
http://<hostname>.<domain>:<port>/OA_JAVA/oracle/forms/registry/Registry.dat
```

This will return a text file with Forms registry settings.

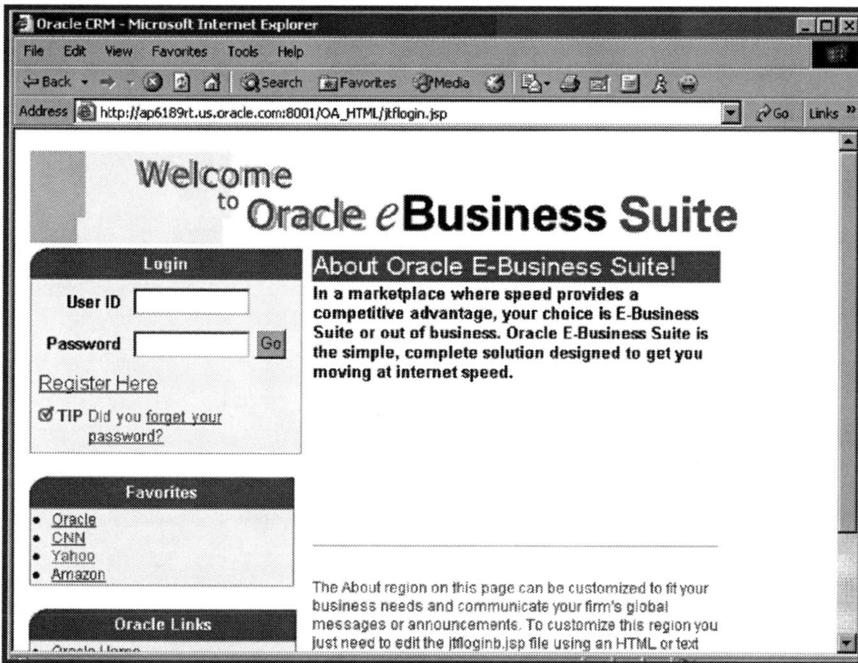

Fig. 5.8 Checking `OA_HTML` Directory

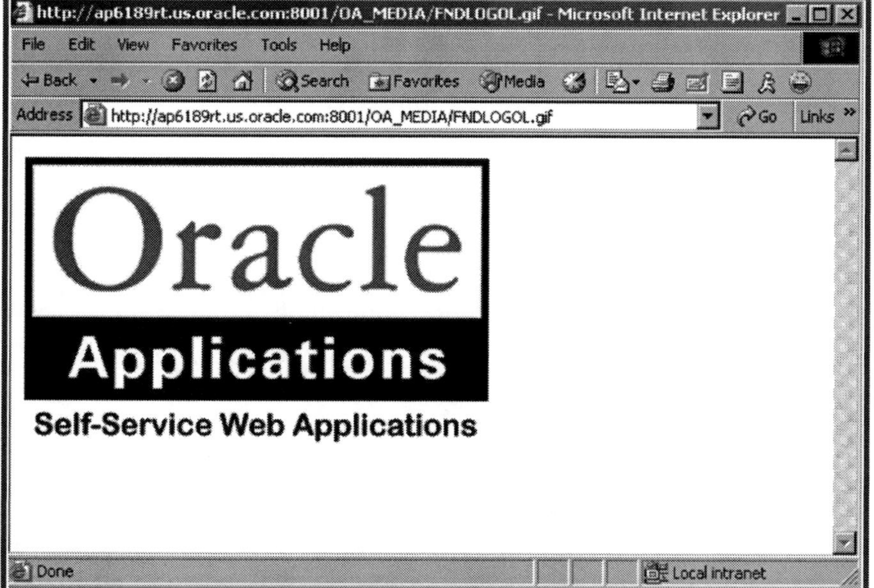

Fig. 5.9 Checking `OA_MEDIA` Directory

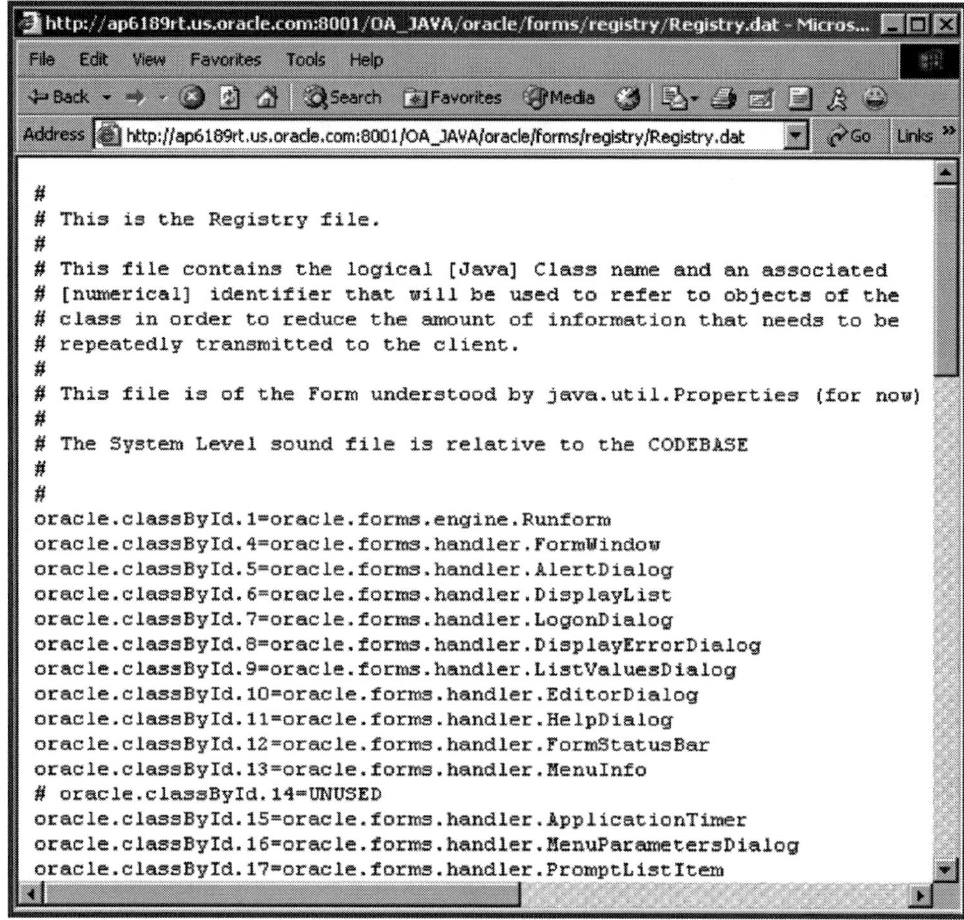

```
#
# This is the Registry file.
#
# This file contains the logical [Java] Class name and an associated
# [numerical] identifier that will be used to refer to objects of the
# class in order to reduce the amount of information that needs to be
# repeatedly transmitted to the client.
#
# This file is of the Form understood by java.util.Properties (for now)
#
# The System Level sound file is relative to the CODEBASE
#
#
oracle.classById.1=oracle.forms.engine.Runform
oracle.classById.4=oracle.forms.handler.FormWindow
oracle.classById.5=oracle.forms.handler.AlertDialog
oracle.classById.6=oracle.forms.handler.DisplayList
oracle.classById.7=oracle.forms.handler.LogonDialog
oracle.classById.8=oracle.forms.handler.DisplayErrorDialog
oracle.classById.9=oracle.forms.handler.ListValuesDialog
oracle.classById.10=oracle.forms.handler.EditorDialog
oracle.classById.11=oracle.forms.handler.HelpDialog
oracle.classById.12=oracle.forms.handler.FormStatusBar
oracle.classById.13=oracle.forms.handler.MenuInfo
# oracle.classById.14=UNUSED
oracle.classById.15=oracle.forms.handler.ApplicationTimer
oracle.classById.16=oracle.forms.handler.MenuParametersDialog
oracle.classById.17=oracle.forms.handler.PromptListItem
```

Fig. 5.10 Checking OA_JAVA Directory

DBC FILE CHECK

The DBC file is located in the `$FND_TOP/secure` area and is used to connect the application system with the database. The format of the DBC file name is `<hostname>_<twotask>.dbc`. The DBC file is automatically created by Rapid Install. In multi-node installations it is there in all nodes of the `APPL_TOP`.

The DBC file contains the following details.

- The database host name
- The database port name
- The Guest user ID and password: The Guest Applications User is a public Applications user with no responsibilities. If no such user exists, create one in the 'Define User' form. Do not have a user with active responsibilities. An important thing to note here is that this parameter is for an Applications user, NOT an Oracle user. The Guest user is seeded with `11i`.
- The `TWO_TASK`

- The APPL_SERVER_ID: This should match with the SERVER_ID column of the FND_NODES table in the database.
- FNDNAM: The Oracle User for Oracle Applications connection, viz. the apps user ID.
- The GWYUID: The public account Oracle User/Password to be used for the initial Oracle Applications connection. The GWYUID Oracle User must have an Oracle Applications privilege level of 'Public'. Its value is applsyspub/pub.

Testing DBC File

The following things need to be checked.

1. The DBC file should exist in the FND_TOP secure for 11*i* and $INST_TOP/appl/fnd/12.0.0/secure for R12.
2. The CLASSPATH should contain:

- $JAVA_TOP (Oracle Applications java code)
- $ORACLE_HOME/jdbc/lib/classes111.zip (jdbc drivers for Unix) or %JAVA_TOP%\jdbc111.zip (jdbc drivers for Windows)

The DBC file can be checked using the following command:

```
jre oracle.apps.fnd.security.AdminAppServer STATUS
DBC=<full_path_of_dbc_file>
```

This will return the value of the APPL_SERVER_ID and the status information. If this does not occur, it means that a new DBC file has to created, which can be done by issuing the following command.

```
jre oracle.apps.fnd.security.AdminAppServer ADD \
SECURE_PATH=<$FND_TOP/secure> \
GWYUID=<gateway_schema_name>/<gateway_schema_pwd> \
FNDNAM=<apps_schema_name> \
APPS_JDBC_DRIVER_TYPE=THIN \
GUEST_USER_PWD=<guest_user>/<guest_pwd> \
DB_HOST=<database_hostname> \
DB_PORT=<database_port> \
DB_NAME=<database_sid> \
[SERVER_ADDRESS=<tcp.ip address>] \
[SERVER_DESCRIPTION="Public web access server"] \
[env_name=env_value]
```

For example,

```
java oracle.apps.fnd.security.AdminAppServer apps/apps@emstest ADD FNDNAM=apps
GWYUID=applsyspub/pub TWO_TASK=emstest SECURE_PATH=$FND_TOP/secure
GUEST_USER_PWD=guest/guest APPS_JDBC_DRIVER_TYPE=THIN DB_HOST=ap6189rt
DB_PORT=1521
```

The command for Windows is as follows:

```
jre -classpath %CLASSPATH% \
oracle.apps.fnd.security.AdminAppServer \
<APPS username/password> ADD \
SECURE_PATH=<$FND_TOP/secure> \
GWYUID=<gateway_schema_name>/<gateway_schema_pwd> \
FNDNAM=<apps_schema_name> \
APPS_JDBC_DRIVER_TYPE=THIN \
GUEST_USER_PWD=<guest_user>/<guest_pwd> \
DB_HOST=<database_hostname> \
DB_PORT=<database_port> \
DB_NAME=<database_sid> \
[SERVER_ADDRESS=<tcp.ip address>] \
[SERVER_DESCRIPTION="Public web access server"] \
[env_name=env_value]
```

It can be seen from the command explained here that the AdminAppServer utility is used to create a DBC file. The same utility can be used for adding, updating, deleting and checking the status of the DBC file. It can also be used for toggling the authentication mode of the application system (we will discuss this in detail at later stage).

As seen earlier, the `$JAVA_TOP` and JDBC Classes must be there in the `CLASSPATH` to run the `AdminAppServer` utility command.

The script is run as

```
java oracle.apps.fnd.security.AdminAppServer [parameters]
```

The first parameter must be the connection string followed by the command string, for example:

```
apps/apps@dbname ADD
```

The following commands are supported by the `AdminAppServer` utility

- `ADD`—to create a new `.dbc` file
- `UPDATE`—to update an existing `.dbc` file
- `DELETE`—to delete an existing `.dbc` file
- `STATUS`—to check the server ID as well as to see if the DBC file is correct or not
- `AUTHENTICATION`—toggle authentication mode

  Apart from these there are a couple of additional parameters which are given here.
- DBC—the name of the DBC file to be modified.
- `SECURE_PATH`—this is used with the `ADD` option. This parameter specifies the directory where the DBC file will be created, and defaults to the current directory from where the command is run if not provided. This should always point to `$FND_TOP/secure` location.
- `DB_HOST`—the host machine of database.

- `DB_PORT`—the port number of database.
- `DB_NAME`—For thin drivers. The database SID.
- `APPS_JDBC_DRIVER_TYPE - THICK` or `THIN`—this parameter must be set to `THIN` in Release `11i`.
- `GUEST_USER_PWD`—any valid Applications user. This parameter defaults to the value of `GUEST_USER_PWD` profile if not provided. If passed with no arguments to an `UPDATE` call, it will refresh with the value from database.
- `GWYUID`—for thick drivers.
- `FNDNAM`—for thick drivers.
- `TWO_TASK`—for thick drivers. Name of database.
- `WALLET_PWD`—used with the TCF Socket Server in SSL mode.
- `SERVER_ADDRESS`—used with authentication.
- `SERVER_DESCRIPTION`—used with authentication.
- `FND_MAX_JDBC_CONNECTIONS`—the maximum number of open connections in the JDBC connection cache. This depends on the amount of memory available, processes parameter in the init.ora file of the database and the per-processor file descriptor limit.
- `FND_IN_USE_CONNECTION_TIMEOUT`—the maximum number of seconds a connection can be in use. If this parameter is not specified, connections in use will not be cleaned up. This should be generally set to a number larger than the time taken to complete the largest transaction.
- `FND_UNUSED_CONNECTION_TIMEOUT`—the maximum number of seconds an unused connection can remain in the cache. The connection cache will close and remove any connection that has been idle for longer than the specified limit.

The Oracle JDBC Thin driver is a 100% pure Java driver that can be used in applications and applets. Because it is written entirely in Java, this driver is platform-independent. It does not require any additional Oracle software on the client side. The Thin driver communicates with the server using TTC, a protocol developed by Oracle to access the Oracle Relational Database Management System (RDBMS).

On the other hand the thick driver is used for client-server Java applications. This driver requires an Oracle client installation, and therefore is Oracle platform-specific.

TESTING JSP

Rapid Install automatically configures Apache to run Java servlets and Java Server Pages. Once the Apache is started, it takes care of the servlet engine, without any manual intervention.

The JSP can be checking by launching the following URL:

```
http://<hosntname>.<domain>:<port_no>/OA_HTML/jsp/fnd/fndping.jsp
```

Alternatively, you can also log in to Oracle Application Manager and then check the status of the JSP agent on the overview page. The log in URL is given in the next section about configuring Oracle Applications.

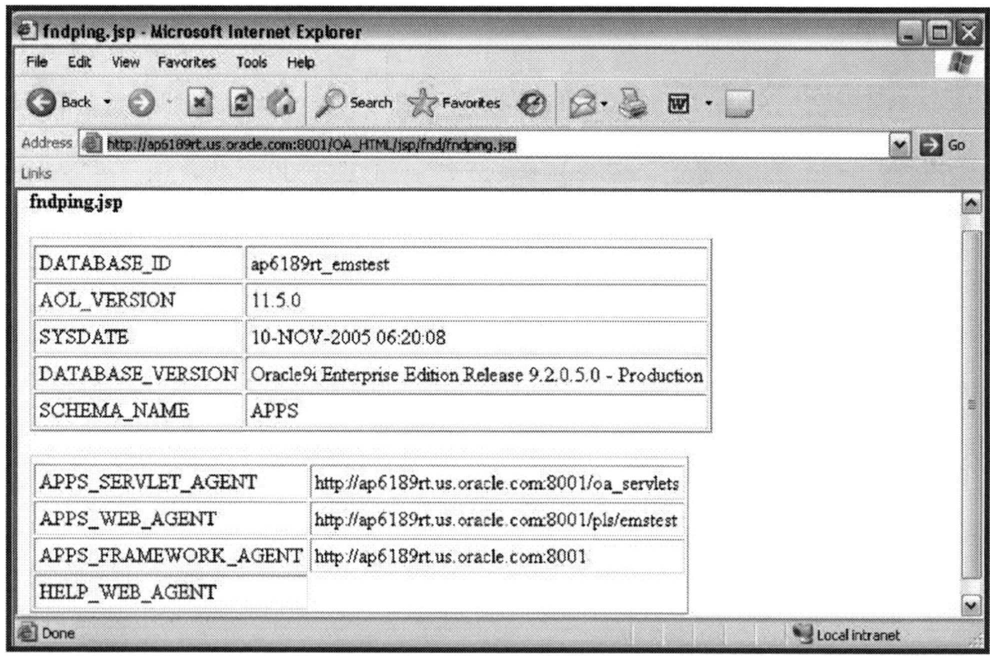

Fig. 5.11 JSP Checking

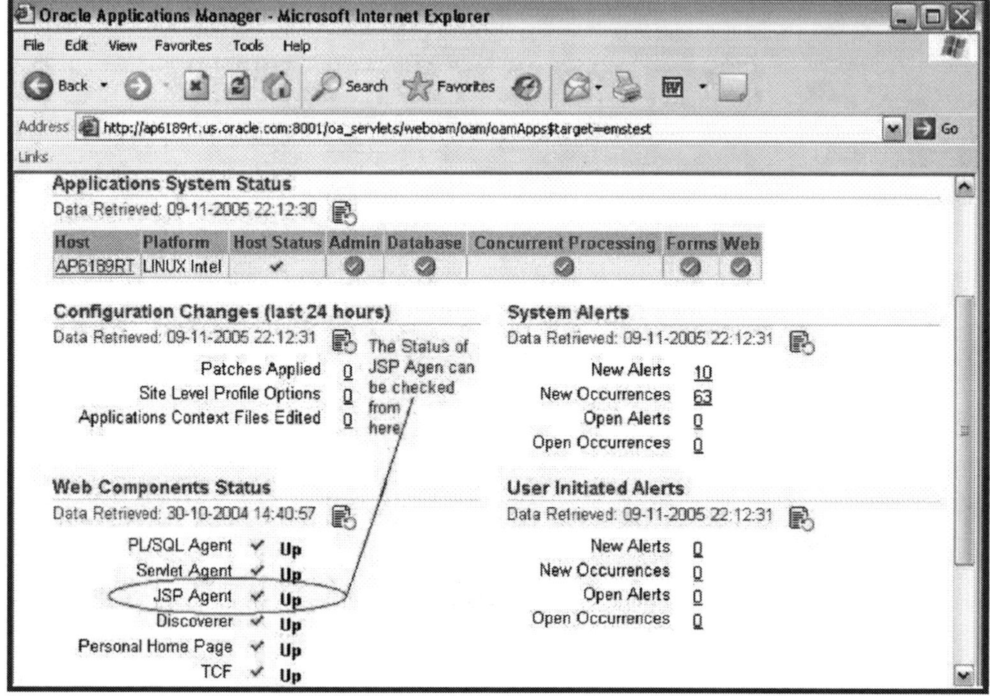

Fig. 5.12 Checking JSP from Oracle Applications Manager

CHECKING FORMS SERVER

The Forms server can be checked either by launching the direct Forms URL or by logging in to Oracle Applications and then selecting a responsibility that will launch the Forms. If the Forms are launched without any problems, it means that the Forms server is working. When the Forms are launched for the first time, the system will automatically download and install JInitiator, which we have discussed in Chapter 2. With release 11.5.10, the access of direct Forms is not allowed by default. If you want to launch the Forms directly, then you need to set the authentication off. This we will discuss in the following section.

CONFIGURING ORACLE APPLICATIONS

Configuring Client Desktops

The client desktop must be configured to run the Forms. The connection between the client desktop and the Forms is done through an applet in the browser. This applet is a collection of JAR files (Java Archive). The Forms client runs within a Java Virtual Machine on the client desktop. Thus, the executable JInitiator needs to be installed for this.

For installing JInitiator log in to Oracle Applications, select a responsibility and then select a Forms-based application. (How to log in to Oracle Applications is discussed in the next section.) Once this is done, it prompts for the download of Oracle JInitiator (orajinit.exe). You can choose to save the file in your PC and then run the setup or run the setup directly from the prompt. Once the Orajinit.exe (JInitiator) is installed, the client desktop is ready to launch the Forms-based application.

Logging in to Oracle Applications

The Applications log in can be accessed through the following URL:

```
http://<hostname>.<domain>:port>/oa_servlets/AppsLogin
```

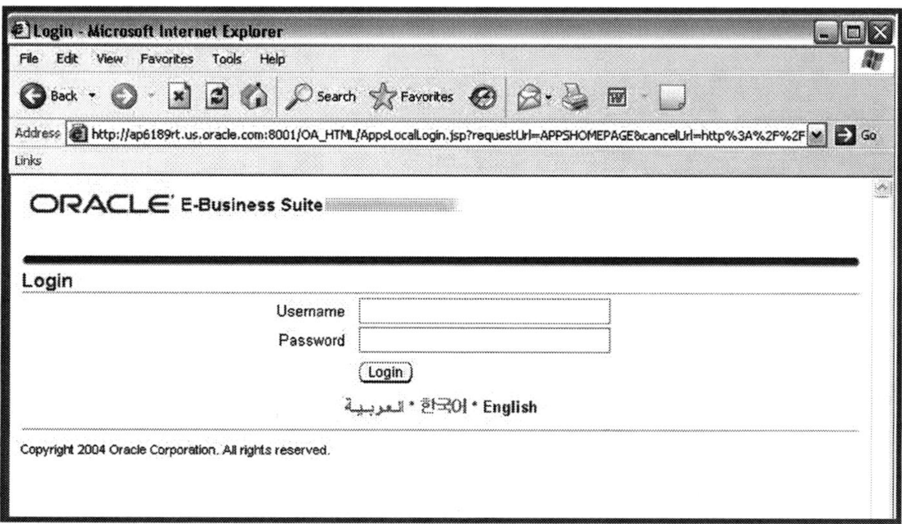

Fig. 5.13 Oracle Applications Log in Screen

The `Apps Log in` is a single point access for all HTML- and Forms-based applications. Since the access of direct Forms is not encouraged from 11.5.10 release onwards, users should access the Forms-based applications also from this URL.

The log in screen prompts for the user name and password. As seen in Fig. 5.13, it also displays languages other than English. Thus if you have installed any additional languages then this will be reflected here. You can select a language and use Oracle Applications in that language.

Once the log in button is pressed, it takes you to the responsibilities pages. These show the responsibilities available to that user. The responsibility page is shown in Fig. 5.14.

Setting Preferences

After logging in to the `Apps log in`, you can set your preferences and customize your Oracle Application. These preferences are saved and displayed each time you log in.

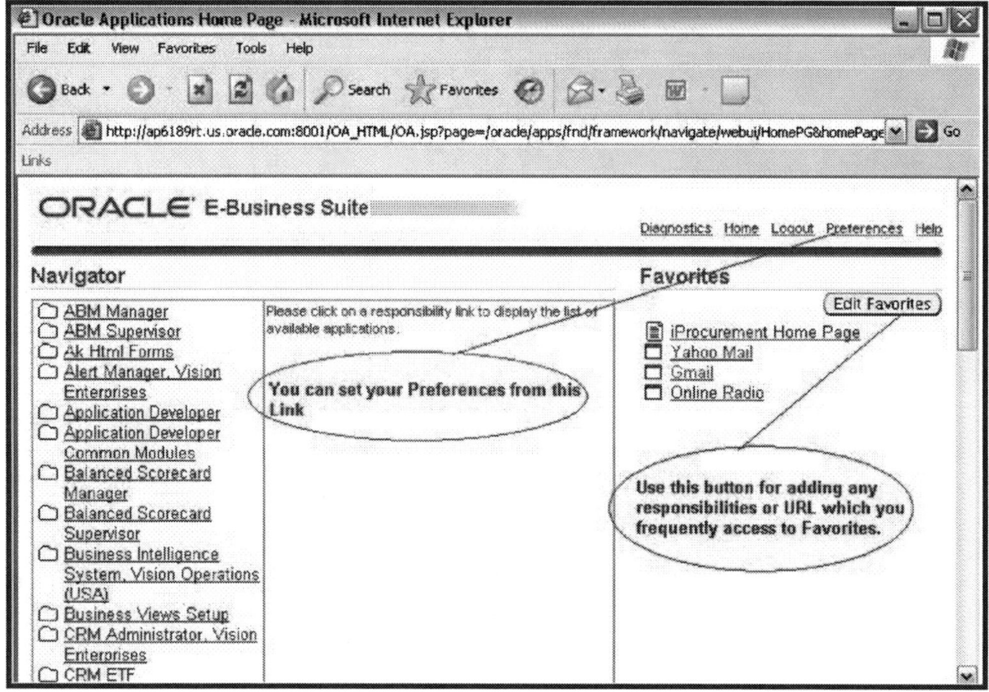

Fig. 5.14 The Responsibility Screen

Once logged in the Oracle Applications, there is a button 'Preferences' at the top right hand side of the screen for setting preferences. There is also a button 'Favorites' where you can put the responsibilities that you access frequently. You can even add your browser favorites here. Say if you need to check your Yahoo or Gmail account very frequently, you can go directly to these accounts from the favorite section; you need not open a new browser every time and type the mail address.

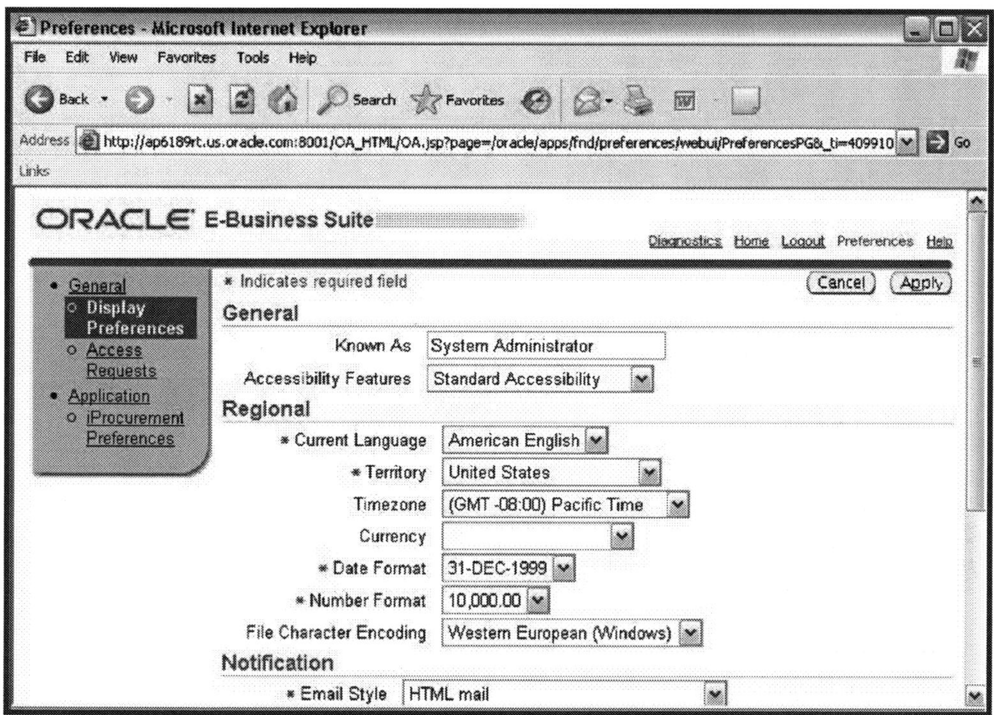

Fig. 5.15 The Preference Screen

Using Profiles for Customization

You can also customize the Oracle Application for areas which are not there in the preference section, like color scheme, look and feel, etc. by changing a couple of profile options. In Oracle Applications there are four types of profiles:

- Site—affects all applications installed at a site
- Application—affects a specific application
- Responsibility—affects the applications assigned to a specific responsibility
- User—normally set by the users, it affects the applications run by a specific user

A user-level setting overrides a responsibility-level setting, which in turn overrides an Application-level setting. The Application-level setting can override a site-level setting.

The System administrator sets options at all four levels. The user can change only the user-level profiles.

The steps are given here to set a profile option.

1. The Profile Values window displays the Profile Name, Default Value, and User Value.

   To view a specific profile, query for that particular profile, use the button F11 from your keyboard. It puts the Forms into query mode and Cntrl+F11 executes the query. Use the button F3 for canceling the query.

2. Enter a value in the User Value field, or choose a value from the list of values (if available). To accept the default setting, clear the User Value field.
3. Choose Save from the File menu or select the Save toolbar icon.

Please note that some profile option changes do not take effect until you change responsibilities or restart the session.

Profiles used for customization of Oracle Applications at user level

- **`Flex fields: Open Descr Window`**

  This profile controls whether or not a descriptive flex field window automatically opens when you navigate to it. The values are either "Yes" or "No".

- **`FND`: Indicator Colors**

  This profile is set to Yes by default. The default color scheme is
  - The fields are displayed in yellow
  - When the query mode is entered, the field is displayed in light blue
  - The field which cannot be changed, viz. which is read only is set in dark grey

  The valid values are "Yes" or "No"

- **Java Color Scheme**

  When the Java 'Look and Feel' profile option is set to "oracle", you can select a color scheme option to enhance the usability of the Forms-based interface.

- **Java Look and Feel**

  This profile is used for Forms-based applications. This profile has two values:
  - "Oracle look and feel" provides a predefined set of color schemes used by Oracle Applications by default
  - "Generic Look and feel" adheres to the color scheme of your operating system

  This option must be set to "oracle" to specify the Java Color Scheme

- **Printer**

  This option is used to define your printer.

- **Sign-On: Notification**

  This profile has two values, "Yes" and "No". If "Yes" is selected, then it displays a message at the time of log in giving details of:

  The number of concurrent requests failed (if any) since your last session
  - How many times an incorrect password was used with your user name since you last logged on.
  - If the default printer identified in your user profile is unregistered or not specified.

- **Viewer: Application for Text**

  In case the system administrator has registered other applications for viewing text output, select the application from the list of values. The option Viewer: Text must be set to "Browser" to use this option.

- **Viewer: Text**

  This profile sets the display viewer for text report output.

  The valid values are "Browser" and "Report Viewer".

Launching Direct Forms

The launch of direct Forms is not supported in Oracle Applications by default. If you still want to launch the Forms directly then you must switch off the security. The direct Forms can be accessed using the given URL:

```
http://<Apache_hostname>.<domain>:<Web_Port>/dev60cgi/f60cgi
```

If you try to access the direct Forms without turning off the authentication, you will get this message:

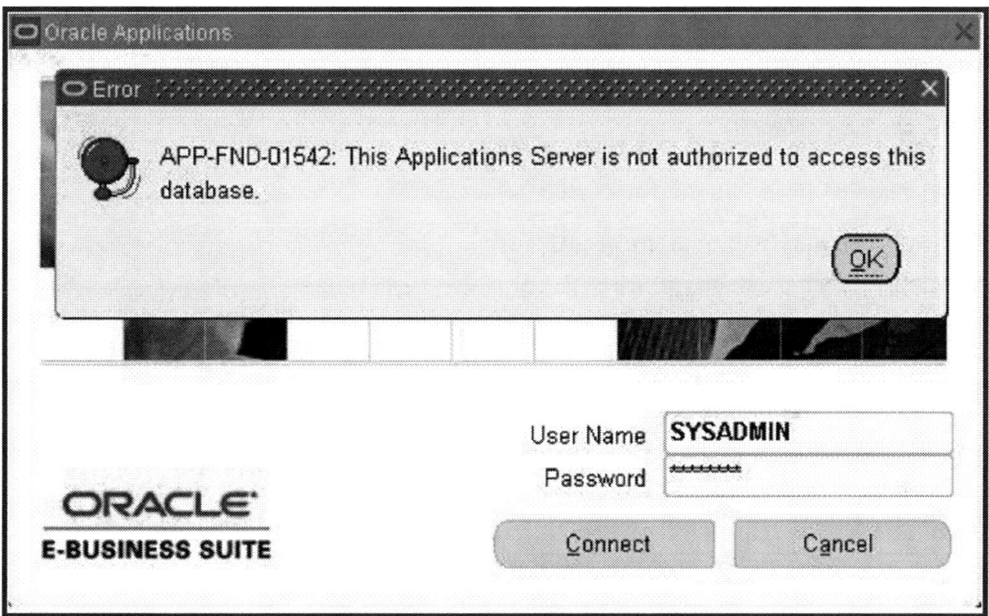

Fig. 5.16 Error Information

The following command is used to turn off the authentication:

```
java oracle.apps.fnd.security.AdminAppServer apps/apps AUTHENTICATION OFF
DBC=<name of dbc file>
```

Configuring TCF Socket Server

The TCF Socket Server is implemented as a servlet that runs within the Apache Jserv engine framework. It helps in communicating certain java components of Oracle Applications with the middle tiers and the database. The Java Component includes BOM Flow Routing Network Designer, AK Object Navigator and the Function Security Menu Viewer.

The minimum requirement of running the TCF socket server is Apache and Apache Jserv. Since Rapid Install takes care of installing these along with Oracle Application, no user action is required here. You just need to make sure that the Apache configuration is proper and it can run servlets. The only manual step involved is adding the TCF Socket Server to the list of servlets that are automatically started.

The importance of this server is such that it should always be up and running.

Checking the Apache Jserv engine configuration

You can find out if the Apache Jserv engine is configured properly to run servlets or not in the following ways:

- You can run `AOL/J` setup test to check that the Apache JServ engine is configured properly to run servlets
- The Application Servlet Agent (`APPS_SERVLET_AGENT`) profile should be set to point to a proper servlet zone
- The `TCF:HOST` and `TCF:PORT` profile options should be updated so that the TCF Socket Server uses the same zone

Please note that the profiles are only updated at the site level.

Starting the TCF Socket Server automatically

In order to start the TCF server automatically you need to add it to the list of servlets started automatically with the Apache Jserv. So you need to edit the zone.properties file in `$IAS_ORACLE_HOME/Apache/Jserv/etc` directory and add the following line:

```
servlets.startup=oracle.apps.fnd.tcf.SocketServer
```

After doing it, you have to bounce the Apache in order to reflect the change.

Updating the PL/SQL, Log and Out Directory

The directory in which the concurrent programs create their output files is defined in the `utl_file_dir` parameter in the `init.ora` file of the database and the `APPLTMP` and `APPLPTMP` parameter in the `APPLSYS.env` or `<envname>.env` in the `APPL_TOP`. In order to concurrent manager to create the output files these three values should be `inn sync` and should point to the same directory.

The value of the `APPLTMP` and `APPLPTMP` can be checked from the `APPL_TOP` by firing the following command

```
appmgr01) appmgr - -bash $ echo $APPLTMP
/slot01/appmgr/emstestcomn/temp

(appmgr01) appmgr - -bash $ echo $APPLPTMP
/slot01/appmgr/emstestcomn/temp
```

The value for `utl_file_dir` can be checked from `sqlplus` by connecting as a `sysdba`

```
SQL> show parameter utl

NAME              TYPE          VALUE
-----------------------------------------------

utl_file_dir     string     /slot01/appmgr/emstestcomn/temp
```

The location of these directories should be given in such a way that they are mounted and accessible from the database server as well as the `APPL_TOP`. Its default location is set to `/usr/tmp` directory, which you should change. To change the values in the database, you can edit the `init.ora` file from `$ORACLE_HOME/dbs` location from your database server. To change the two variables in the `APPL_TOP`, you can change the `APPLSYS.env` or `<envname>.env` file from the `$APPL_TOP` location. Another method is to use the '`edit parameter`' feature of Oracle Application Manager to update the variables and then run the autoconfig script located in `$COMMON_TOP/admin/scripts` (`adautocfg.sh`) to recreate the environment file.

6

Managing Oracle Applications

In this chapter, we will discuss how to manage Oracle Applications. This is divided into two sections, managing the database and managing the middle tiers. Since all the Database Administrators know how to manage the former, we won't discuss that in detail. The chapter will mainly deal with managing the Application system.

MANAGING THE DATABASE

An Oracle DBA is generally very familiar with the database. For the novice, we will discuss how to start and stop the database and the database listener.

Starting the Oracle Database

To start the database, log in to the database server as the owner of the Oracle software, and source the environment file named `<sidname>.env`. This is normally stored in `$ORACLE_HOME`. After sourcing the environment file, do an `echo $ORACLE_HOME` to crosscheck that it's pointing the right database. Then log in as '`sysdba`' and issue the command 'startup' (see Fig. 6.1).

```
(oracle01) 9.2.0 - -bash $ sqlplus '/ as sysdba '

SQL*Plus: Release 9.2.0.5.0 - Production on Fri Nov 18 07:14:57 2005

Copyright (c) 1982, 2002, Oracle Corporation. All rights reserved.

Connected to an idle instance.

SQL> startup
ORACLE instance started.

Total System Global Area     598283852 bytes
Fixed Size                      452172 bytes
Variable Size                419430400 bytes
```

Contd

Fig. 6.1 Contd

```
Database Buffers              167772160 bytes
Redo Buffers                   10629120 bytes
Database mounted.
Database opened.
SQL>
```

Fig. 6.1 Starting the Oracle Database

Various stages in database startup

The three steps to start an Oracle database and make it available for system wide use are:

- Start an instance
- Mount the database
- Open the database

Start an instance

First, the initialization parameter file is read to determine the values of the initialization parameters. Then Oracle allocates an SGA (this is the shared area of memory used for database information), and creates background processes. At this point, no database is associated with the memory structures and processes.

Mount the database

A database is mounted in order to associate the instance with it. The instance finds the database control files and opens them. These are specified in the `CONTROL_FILES` initialization parameter of the parameter file used for starting the instance. Oracle then reads the control files for the names of the data files and redo log files of the database.

At this point, the database is still closed. It is accessible only to the database administrator, who can keep the database closed while completing specific maintenance operations.

Open the database

Opening a mounted database makes it available for normal database operations. This is usually done by a database administrator, after which any valid user can connect to the database and access its information.

When you open the database, Oracle opens the online data files and redo log files. If a tablespace was offline when the database had previously been shut down, the tablespace and its corresponding data files will still be offline when you reopen the database.

If any of the data files or redo log files are not present when you attempt to open the database, then Oracle returns an error. You must perform recovery on a backup of any damaged or missing files before you can open the database.

Various startup options

There are a number of startup options available to start an Oracle Database, each of which are discussed further.

- `STARTUP`

  Normal database startup means starting an instance, and mounting and opening a database. This mode allows any valid user to connect to the database and perform typical data access operations.

- `STARTUP NOMOUNT`

  You can start an instance without mounting a database. Typically, you do so only during database creation.

- `STARTUP MOUNT`

  You can start an instance and mount a database without opening it, allowing you to perform specific maintenance operations.

- `STARTUP RESTRICT`

  You can start an instance and mount and open a database in restricted mode. Then, the database is available only to administrative personnel and not general database users. Use this mode of database startup when you need to accomplish one of the following tasks:

  - Export or import of database data
  - A data load (with SQL*Loader)
  - Temporarily prevent typical users from using data
  - During certain migration and upgrade operations

  Typically, all users with the `CREATE SESSION` system privilege can connect to an open database. Opening a database in restricted mode allows database access only to those users who have both the `CREATE SESSION` and `RESTRICTED SESSION` system privileges. However, only database administrators should have the `RESTRICTED SESSION` system privilege.

  Start an instance (and, if you want, mount and open the database) in restricted mode by using the `STARTUP` command with the `RESTRICT` option. Later, use the `ALTER SYSTEM` statement to disable the `RESTRICTED SESSION` feature:

  ```
  ALTER SYSTEM DISABLE RESTRICTED SESSION;
  ```

- `STARTUP FORCE`

  In unusual circumstances, you might experience problems while attempting to start a database instance. Then you have to force the instance to start. You should not force a database to start unless you are faced with the following problems:

  - You cannot shut down the current instance with the `SHUTDOWN NORMAL`, `SHUTDOWN IMMEDIATE`, or `SHUTDOWN TRANSACTIONAL` commands
  - You experience problems when starting an instance

  If either of these situations arises, you can usually solve the problem by starting a new instance using the `STARTUP` command with the `FORCE` option.

  If an instance is running, `STARTUP FORCE` shuts it down with mode `ABORT` before restarting it.

- `STARTUP OPEN RECOVER`

  If you know that media recovery is required, you can start an instance, mount a database, and have the recovery process start automatically using this option. But if you attempt a recovery when none is required, Oracle issues an error message.

Shutting Down Oracle Database

For stopping the database one needs to be logged in as a sysdba and issue a shut down command. We will discuss the various shut down options in the next section

Stages in database shut down

The three steps to shutting down a database and the associated instance are:

- Close the database
- Un-mount the database
- Shut down the instance

A database administrator can perform these steps using Enterprise Manager or as a sysdba. Oracle automatically performs all three steps whenever an instance is shut down.

Close a database

When you close a database, Oracle writes all database and recovery data in the SGA to the data files and redo log files respectively. Next, Oracle closes all online data and redo log files. At this point, the database is closed and inaccessible for normal operations. The control files remain open even after the database is closed, if it is still mounted.

Close the database by terminating the instance

In an emergency, you can terminate the instance of an open database to close and completely shut down instantaneously. This process is fast as the operation of writing all data in the buffers of the SGA to the data files and redo log files is skipped. The subsequent reopening of the database requires recovery, which Oracle performs automatically.

Un-mount a database

Oracle un-mounts the database after closing it. This is done so that it is disassociated from the instance. At this point, the instance remains in the memory of your computer. After a database is un-mounted, Oracle closes the control files of the database.

Shut down an instance

The final step in database shut down is the shutting down of the instance. When this is done, the SGA is removed from memory and the background processes are terminated.

Abnormal instance shut down

In unusual circumstances, shut down of an instance might not occur cleanly; all memory structures might not be removed from memory or a background process might not be terminated. When remnants of a previous instance exist, a subsequent instance startup most likely will fail. In such situations, the database administrator can force the new instance to start up either by first removing the remnants of the previous instance or by issuing a `SHUTDOWN ABORT`.

Various shut down options

There are four options available for a database shut down, as given here.

- Shut down normal
- Shut down immediate
- Shut down transactional
- Shut down abort

Shutting down with the Normal option

This commend is used to shut down a database in normal situations.

```
SHUTDOWN NORMAL
```

It then proceeds, provided the following conditions are taken into account.

- No new connections are allowed after the statement is issued.
- Before the database is shut down, Oracle waits for all users connected at the time to disconnect from the database.
- The next startup of the database will not require any instance recovery procedures.

Shutting down with the Immediate option

Use immediate database shut down only in the following situations:

To initiate an automated and unattended backup

- When you know a power shut down is going to occur soon
- When the database or one of its applications is functioning irregularly and you cannot contact users to ask them to log off or they are unable to log off

The command for this is:

```
SHUTDOWN IMMEDIATE
```

Immediate database shut down proceeds with the following conditions.

- No new connections or new transactions are allowed after the statement is issued.
- Any uncommitted transactions are rolled back. (If long uncommitted transactions exist, this method of shut down might not finish quickly, despite its name.)
- The next startup of the database will not require any instance recovery procedures.

Shutting down with the Transactional option

When you want to perform a planned shut down of an instance while allowing active transactions to be completed first, use this option:

```
SHUTDOWN TRANSACTIONAL
```

Transactional database shut down proceeds with the following conditions:

No new connections or new transactions are allowed after the statement is issued

- After all transactions have completed, any client still connected to the instance is disconnected
- At this point, the instance shuts down just as it would when a `SHUTDOWN IMMEDIATE` statement is submitted
- The next startup of the database will not require any instance recovery procedures

A transactional shut down prevents clients from losing work and at the same time, does not require all users to log off.

Shutting down with the Abort option

You can shut a database down instantaneously by aborting the database's instance. If possible, this type of shut down should only be done when:

- The database or one of its applications is functioning irregularly and none of the other types of shut down work
- You need to shut down the database instantaneously (for example, if you know a power shut-down is going to occur in a minute)
- There are problems while starting a database instance

When any such situation occurs, issue this command:

```
SHUTDOWN ABORT
```

An aborted database shut down proceeds with the following conditions:

- No new connections or new transactions are allowed after the statement is issued
- Current client SQL statements being processed by Oracle are immediately terminated
- Uncommitted transactions are not rolled back
- Oracle does not wait for users currently connected to the database to disconnect, but implicitly disconnects all of them
- The next startup of the database will require instance recovery procedures

Starting/Stopping Database Listener

Oracle Listener is a server-based process that provides basic connectivity for clients, application servers and other databases.

Table 6.1 Relevant Files for Oracle TNS Listener

$ORACLE_HOME/bin/lsnrctl	Listener control program
$ORACLE_HOME/network/admin/listener.ora	Configuration file for the listener
$ORACLE_HOME/bin/tnslsnr	Server listener process

The lsnrctl program is the mechanism for starting and stopping the listener process (tnslsnr). The command 'listener start' is used for starting and for stopping the listener the command 'listener stop' is used.

MANAGING APPLICATIONS

Oracle Applications consists of a number of middle tiers, viz. — `Apache`, `Jserv`, Forms, Concurrent Manager, Reports server and Discoverer. In this section, we will explore how to manage all the middle tiers and discuss the components of each.

The scripts for managing the middle tiers are located in `COMMON_TOP/admin/scripts/<sid>` directory for 11*i* and `$INST_TOP/admin/scripts` for R12. To run these scripts, log in to the application tier as the owner of the application file system and source the environment (using, as mentioned earlier, the environment `<sid>.env` located in the `$APPL_TOP`). All the scripts create a log file that shows the status of the server. The log files are written in the directory `$COMMON_TOP/admin/log/<sid>` for 11*i* and `$INST_TOP/logs/appl/admin/log` for R12. Each component of the middle tier has a separate log file.

Managing the Middle Tier Listener

The first step in starting the middle tier is starting its listener. The name of the listener is generally `APPS_<sid>`. It can be started/stopped using script `adalnctl.sh`

```
adalnctl.sh { start | stop | status }
```

```
(appmgr01) emstest - -bash $ adalnctl.sh start

adalnctl.sh version

Checking for FNDFS executable.
Starting listener process APPS_emstest.

Adalnctl.sh: exiting with status 0

(appmgr01) emstest - -bash $
```

Fig. 6.2 Starting the Middle Tier Listener

This can also be manually controlled using the `lsnrctl` command.

```
LSNRCTL> start apps_emstest
Starting/slot01/appmgr/emstestora/8.0.6/bin/tnslsnr: please wait...

TNSLSNR for Linux: Version 8.0.6.3.0 - Production
Log messages written
to/slot01/appmgr/emstestora/8.0.6/network/admin/apps_emstest.log
Listening on:
(ADDRESS=(PROTOCOL=tcp)(DEV=6)(HOST=144.20.198.56)(PORT=1527))

Connecting to (ADDRESS=(PROTOCOL=TCP)(Host=ap6189rt)(Port=1527))
STATUS of the LISTENER
______________
Alias                    apps_emstest
Version                  TNSLSNR for Linux: Version 8.0.6.3.0 -
Production
Start Date               19-NOV-2005 00:14:21
Uptime                   0 days 0 hr. 0 min. 0 sec
Trace Level              off
Security                 OFF
SNMP                     OFF
Listener Log File
/slot01/appmgr/emstestora/8.0.6/network/admin/apps_emstest.log
Services Summary...
  FNDFS     has 1 service handler(s)
  FNDSM     has 1 service handler(s)
The command completed successfully
```

Fig. 6.3 Manual Starting of Middle Tier Listener

Managing the Web Server (Apache)

The Apache server can be started with the script `adapcctl.sh`. The parameters that accepts is start stop and status.

```
adapcctl.sh { start | stop | status }
```

The Apache startup script is customized for the Oracle Applications in such a way that and it takes of starting the `Jserv`, `modplsql` and the TCF socket server automatically once the Apache is started for 11*i* Application systems but for R12 application system the `adapcctl.sh` script starts only the Apache. The other component OC4J is taken care with a seperate script.

```
(appmgr01) emstest - -bash $ adapcctl.sh start

adapcctl.sh version 115.43

Starting Apache Web Server Listener (dedicated HTTP) ...
Starting Apache Web Server Listener (dedicated PLSQL) ...

adapcctl.sh: exiting with status 0

 (appmgr01) emstest - -bash $ adapcctl.sh stop

adapcctl.sh version 115.43

Stopping Apache Web Server Listener (dedicated HTTP) ...
Stopping Apache Web Server Listener (dedicated PLSQL) ...
/slot01/appmgr/emstestora/iAS/Apache/Apache/bin/apachectl stop: httpd
stopped

adapcctl.sh: exiting with status 0

(appmgr01) emstest - -bash $
```

Fig. 6.4 Apache Startup for 11*i*

```
(appmgr01) scripts - -bash $ adapcctl.sh start

You are running adapcctl.sh version 120.6

Starting OPMN managed Oracle HTTP Server (OHS) instance ...

adapcctl.sh: exiting with status 0

adapcctl.sh: check the logfile /slot01/appmgr/inst/apps/emstest/logs/
appl/admin/log/adapcctl.txt for more information ...

(appmgr01) scripts - -bash $
```

Fig. 6.5 Apache Startup for R12

The log file created by the script is adapcctl.txt and it is located with the log files.

Oracle Applications also uses all the advanced features provided for managing the Apache. Apart from starting and stopping, the Apache can be configured to run SSL (Secured Socket Layered) and restricted mode.

The Apache server can be started in the restricted mode using the scripts also and can be controlled with the script `adaprstctl.sh`

```
adaprstctl.sh { start | stop | status }
```

```
(appmgr01) emstest - -bash $ adaprstctl.sh start
adaprstctl.sh version 115.1
Starting Apache Restricted Web Server Listener ...
adaprstctl.sh: exiting with status 0
(appmgr01) emstest - -bash $
```

Fig. 6.6 Control of Apache in Restricted Mode

Managing the Forms

The Forms server can be controlled with the script 'adfrmctl.sh', for 11*i* and for 'adformsctl.sh' for R12.

```
adfrmctl.sh  { stop |start | status }
adformsctl.sh (stop |start | status )
```

The log file created by the scripts is 'f60svrm.txt' for 11*i* and 'adformsctl.txt' for R12 available at the common location of the log files.

For 11*i* application systems, the Forms server can also be started manually with the f60ctl executable which is located at $ORACLE_HOME/bin. This is the 8.0.6 Oracle Home, and should not be confused with the Oracle Home of the database server. The command for starting the Forms server manually is:

```
f60ctl start port=<port name> mode=socket exe=f60webmx logfile=/location of
logfile.
```

For R12 Application systems the forms is managed using OPMN so manual start of the same is not advisable.

Socket, HTTP, and HTTPS connection modes of Forms

The initial releases of the Oracle Forms Server were based on client server architecture. They used a simple method for connecting the client to the server, using a direct socket connection. This was suitable for companies providing thin client access to Forms applications within their corporate LANS/WANS. In the direct socket connection mode, the client has to be able to see the server machine and get permission to establish a direct network connection.

This mode is not the best choice for application deployment via unsecured network paths such as the Internet, since it exposes the company to potential invasions. This is because the true identity of the client can be hard to determine. A company that is connected to the Internet thus usually has a strict policy defining the types of network connections that can be made to safeguard valuable information and infrastructure assets.

With the widespread adoption of HTTP as the standard protocol for data transmission on the Internet, most companies permit HTTP traffic in their corporate networks. Therefore, Oracle Forms Server 6i was extended to support data transmission using HTTP and HTTPS. With this, structured messages sent to and from the client and servers are encapsulated in standard HTTP messages. Companies that permit Internet access to their corporate servers through the firewall using HTTP can also deploy Forms applications.

```
(appmgr01) scripts - -bash $ adformsctl.sh start

You are running adformsctl.sh  version 120.12

Starting OPMN managed FORMS OC4J instance  ...

adformsctl.sh: exiting with status 0

adformsctl.sh: check the logfile /slot01/appmgr/inst/apps/emstest/logs/
appl/admin/log/adformsctl.txt for more information ...

(appmgr01) scripts - -bash $
```

Fig. 6.7 Starting Forms

In release 12 the forms are started in servlet mode by default. In case if you want to start the same in socket mode then you can use the script 'adformsrvctl.sh'.

This script also takes the three parameters start, stop and status.

In 11*i* you can always start the forms in servlet or socket mode using the f60ctl executable as discussed earlier.

The status of the Forms server can also be checked at the operating system level by enquiring with the Forms port number.

```
netstat -a | grep <forms port number>
```

The output for this query is given in Fig. 6.8.

```
(appmgr01) emstest - -bash $ netstat -a | grep 9000
tcp  0 0 *:9000                      *:*                         LISTEN
tcp  0 0 ap6189rt.us.oracl:19000 *:*                             LISTEN
tcp  0 0 ap6189rt.us.oracl:19000 ap6189rt.us.oracl:40129 TIME_WAIT
(appmgr01) emstest - -bash $
```

Fig. 6.8 Quering the Status of Forms Server

Managing the Forms Metric Client (Only for 11*i*)

The Forms Metric Client is used for Forms load balancing. The Forms Metric Client is managed by the script adfmcctl.sh, which has the same three parameters, viz. start, stop and status.

```
adfmcctl.sh { start | stop | status }.
```

The Forms Metric Client uses 'd2lc60 executable' for controlling the same. The log file name of the Forms Metric Client is 'd2lc60.txt'. It is available at the locations of the log files.

Managing the Reports Server (Only for 11*i*)

The reports server can be controlled with a script 'adrepctl.sh'. It uses the executable FNDSVCRG located at $FND_TOP/bin. The default name of the report server log file is rep60_<sid>.txt.

Reports Server can be controlled by:

```
adrepctl.sh { start | stop | status }
```

```
(appmgr01) emstest - -bash $ adrepctl.sh start

You are running adrepctl.sh version 115.26

starting Reports Server for emstest on port 7000.

adrepctl.sh: exiting with status 0

(appmgr01) emstest - -bash $
```

Fig. 6.9 Control of Reports Server

Managing the Discoverer Server (Optional Component)

The discoverer server is controlled by the script 'addisctl.sh'. Unlike other scripts, this script also uses the parameters start stop and status for controlling the same. The log file name of the discoverer is 'addisctl.txt' and it can be found in the log locations.

```
addisctl.sh { start | stop | status }
```

```
appmgr01) emstest - -bash $ addisctl.sh start

addisctl.sh version 115.14

/slot01/appmgr/emstestora/8.0.6/vbroker/bin/osagent
Started osagent.
Osagent logs messages to the file /slot01/appmgr/emstestora/8.0.6/
discwb4/util/osagent.log.
Waiting for OAD to start...
Started OAD.
OAD logs messages to the file
/slot01/appmgr/emstestora/8.0.6/discwb4/util/oad.log.
Discoverer Locator Started.
Locator logs messages to the file
/slot01/appmgr/emstestora/8.0.6/discwb4/util/locator.log.

addisctl.sh: exiting with status 0
```

Fig. 6.10 Managing the Discoverer Server

Managing the Concurrent Manager

The Concurrent Manager can be started with the script adcmctl.sh. It takes the parameters abort and status apart from the start/stop parameter. Only in this script, the apps user ID and apps password need to be given.

```
adcmctl.sh {start | stop | abort |status} <APPS username/APPS password>
```

```
(appmgr01) emstest - -bash $ adcmctl.sh start apps/apps

You are running adcmctl.sh version 115.19

Starting concurrent manager for emstest ...
Starting emstest_1119@emstest Internal Concurrent Manager
Default printer is noprint

adcmctl.sh: exiting with status 0

(appmgr01) emstest - -bash $
```

Fig. 6.11 Managing the Concurrent Manager

Alternatively, it can also be started using the '`startmgr`' executable for 11*i* and `startmgr.sh` script for R12, which is located in the `$FND_TOP/bin` directory.

This command starts the internal Concurrent Manager, which in turn starts all the Concurrent Managers defined. There are some parameters which can be parsed along with the command.

- `Sysmgr` The apps user ID and password (default— apps/apps)
- `Mgrname` The name of the manager (default— Standard Manager)
- `Diag` This is used for diagnosis. If the CM is started with the parameter 'diag=y', then full diagnostic output is produced. (default— N)
- `Logfile` The log file of the manager (default— `std.mgr`)
- `mailto` If the Concurrent Manager goes down it will notify this by mail
- `Printer` The default printer for sending the output files
- `Restart` If the CM goes down abnormally it will automatically restart (default— N)
- `Sleep` The number of seconds the ICM should wait before checking a new request from the table `FND_CONCURRENT_REQUESTS` (default— 60 seconds)
- `PMON` The number of cycles ICM will wait before checking failed Managers (default— 20)
- `Quesiz` Number of pmon cycles the ICM waits while checking for normal changes in CM operation. Normal changes include the start or end of a work shift and changes to the CM definitions entered in the Define Concurrent Manager form (default— 1).

```
(appmgr01) emstest - -bash $ cd $FND_TOP/bin
(appmgr01) bin - -bash $ startmgr sysmgr=apps/apps logfile=/tmp/log
Starting icm@emstest Internal Concurrent Manager
Default printer is
(appmgr01) bin - -bash $ tail -f /tmp/log

Starting icm@emstest Internal Concurrent Manager — shell process ID 7345
     logfile=/tmp/log
      PRINTER=
       mailto=appmgr01
     restart=N
          diag=N
         sleep=60 (default)
          pmon=20 (default)
        quesiz=1  (default)
Found dead process: spid=(21928), cpid=(750413), ORA pid=(19),
manager=(201/222)
Found dead process: spid=(21931), cpid=(750414), ORA pid=(41),
manager=(535/1023)
Found dead process: spid=(22019), cpid=(750417), ORA pid=(46),
manager=(0/1071)
Found dead process: spid=(20749), cpid=(750400), ORA pid=(16),
manager=(0/1)
Application Object Library: Concurrent Processing version 11.5
Copyright (c) 1979, 1999, Oracle Corporation. All rights reserved.
Internal Concurrent Manager started: 17-AUG-2005 08:47:13

Process monitor session started: 17-AUG-2005 08:47:13
Found dead process: spid=(21993), cpid=(750415), Service Instance=(1051)
Found dead process: spid=(22016), cpid=(750416), Service Instance=(1054)
Found dead process: spid=(22030), cpid=(750418), Service Instance=(1095)
Found dead process: spid=(22042), cpid=(750419), Service Instance=(1096)

Starting STANDARD Concurrent Manager            : 17-AUG-2005 08:47:15
Starting STANDARD Concurrent Manager            : 17-AUG-2005 08:47:15
Starting STANDARD Concurrent Manager            : 17-AUG-2005 08:47:15
Starting XDP_MANAGER Concurrent Manager         :17-AUG-2005 08:47:15
Starting OAMCOLMGR Concurrent Manager           : 17-AUG-2005 08:47:15
```

Contd

Fig. 6.12 Contd

```
Starting FNDCRM Concurrent Manager                    : 17-AUG-2005 08:47:15
Starting INVTMRPM Concurrent Manager                  : 17-AUG-2005 08:47:15
Starting CRPINQMGR Concurrent Manager                 : 17-AUG-2005 08:47:15
Starting PODAMGR Concurrent Manager                   : 17-AUG-2005 08:47:15
Starting RCVOLTM14 Concurrent Manager                 : 17-AUG-2005 08:47:15
Starting RCVOLTM Concurrent Manager                   : 17-AUG-2005 08:47:15
Starting XDP_MANAGER Concurrent Manager               : 17-AUG-2005 08:47:15
Starting XDP_Q_EVENT_SVC Concurrent Manager           : 17-AUG-2005 08:47:15
Process monitor session ended: 17-AUG-2005 08:47:18
Process monitor session started: 17-AUG-2005 08:49:18
Process monitor session ended: 17-AUG-2005 08:49:19
```

Fig. 6.12 Starting the Concurrent Manager Manually

Managing the OC4J (Only for R12)

In 11*i* the script adapcctl.sh use to take care of starting the Apache as well as `Jserv` but in R12 the `Jserv` has been replaced by OC4J and the script `adapcctl.sh` no longer manages the OC4J. It is now being managed by separate scripts.

For managing the OACORE OC4J the script is '`adoacorectl.sh`'

This script also takes the three parameters start, stop and status.

```
(appmgr01) scripts - -bash $  adoacorectl.sh start

You are running adoacorectl.sh version 120.11

Starting OPMN managed OACORE OC4J instance  ...

adoacorectl.sh: exiting with status 0

adoacorectl.sh: check the logfile
/slot01/appmgr/inst/apps/emstest/logs/appl/admin/log/adoacorectl.txt for
more information.
```

Fig 6.13 Starting the OACORE OC4J

For managing the OAFM (Oracle Applications Fusion Middleware) OC4J the script is '`adoafmctl.sh`'.

This script also takes the three parameters start, stop and status.

```
(appmgr01) scripts - -bash $ adoafmctl.sh start

You are running adoafmctl.sh version 120.6

Starting OPMN managed OAFM OC4J instance  ...

adoafmctl.sh: exiting with status 0

adoafmctl.sh: check the logfile
/slot01/appmgr/inst/apps/emstest/logs/appl/admin/log/adoafmctl.txt for
more information ...

(appmgr01) scripts - -bash $
```

Fig 6.14 Starting the OAFM OC4J

Managing the OPMN (Only for R12)

For managinng the OPMN the script is 'adopmnctl.sh'. This script also takes the three paremeters start, stop and status.

The logfile created by the script is 'adopmnctl.txt' and is stored at the central location of all the logs.

```
(appmgr01) scripts - -bash $  adopmnctl.sh start

You are running adopmnctl.sh version 120.4

Starting Oracle Process Manager (OPMN) ...

adopmnctl.sh: exiting with status 0

adopmnctl.sh: check the logfile
/slot01/appmgr/inst/apps/emstest/logs/appl/admin/log/adopmnctl.txt for
more information ...

(appmgr01) scripts - -bash $
```

Fig 6.15 Starting the OPMN

Starting/Stopping all the Middle Tiers

All these scripts for starting and stopping the middle tiers need not be manually run. Oracle provides two different scripts that take care of starting and stopping all the middle tiers in one go. For starting, the script is 'adstrtal.sh'. It takes the apps user ID and apps password as parameter.

```
adstrtal.sh <appsusername/appspassword>
```

Similarly, for stopping all the middle tiers simultaneously the script is 'adstpall.sh'. This also takes the apps user ID and apps password as parameter.

```
adstpall.sh <appsusername/appspassword>
```

Both these scripts create a log file containing detailed information about the components started, already running, disabled and not running. The log file name is in the following format:

```
<Month><Date><Hour><Minute>.log
```

7

Concurrent Processing and Concurrent Manager

A user typically performs two types of activities in Oracle Applications—one online transaction and the other batch processing. The batch processing job is also known as Concurrent Processing which allows the Oracle Application users to schedule jobs in background while the user can work with online data entry operations.

When an Oracle Application user submits a request to run a program it's called concurrent requests. Concurrent Manager are the programs, which are responsible for running the concurrent requests. When a user submits a report to be run as a concurrent request, the job enters in a request queue. The Concurrent Managers continuously read request from this master queue and run the requests based on the request's schedule, priority, and compatibility rules. The Concurrent Managers runs in background and they take care of initiating and completing the concurrent requests. Concurrent Managers act as administrators of job processing in Oracle Applications and employ workers at the operating system to process the application user requests by running concurrent programs. Each manager can run any program or can be specialized to run only certain programs.

Oracle Application consists of several types of Concurrent Managers. That doesn't mean that you can't define any Concurrent Manager. You can define any number of Concurrent Managers as per your requirement. The key managers predefined by Oracle includes Internal Concurrent Manager (ICM), Conflict Resolution Manager, and Standard Manager. We will discuss each of them in details.

INTERNAL CONCURRENT MANAGER

The Internal Concurrent Manager controls all the other Concurrent Managers. Its main task is to ensure that all the other Concurrent Managers are up and running. The Internal Concurrent Manager starts, sets the number of active processes, monitors, and terminates all other concurrent processes through requests made to the Service Manager, including restarting any failed processes. The ICM also starts and stops, and restarts the Service Manager for each node. The Internal Concurrent Manager is in turn monitored by Internal Monitor which is responsible for starting the failed Internal Concurrent Manager in a local node. There should be an Internal Monitor defined on each node.

CONFLICT RESOLUTION MANAGER

The Conflict Resolution Manager (CRM) takes care of resolving the program incompatibilities and checks if a request in queue can be run in parallel with the running request.

STANDARD MANAGER

The Standard Manager is the master Concurrent Manager. This manager is always running and it can take care of processing any concurrent request, it has no specialization rules. This manager runs 24 hours a day for 365 days. The definition of this manager should never be altered. In case if you alter the definition of the standard manager and you have not defined additional managers to run your requests, some of the program may not run in a proper way.

CONCURRENT PROGRAM

A Concurrent Program is a program which is registered with AOL. When registering a program with AOL certain informations like program name, execution method and argument needs to be given. A concurrent program can be written in

- Oracle Tools: PL/SQL, SQL*Loader, SQL*Plus, and Oracle Reports
- Pro*C
- Host Language (i.e., shell or DCL)

When defining a concurrent program the following thing needs to be taken care.

- Selecting an executable file to run the program.
- Choosing the execution method for the program (when defining your executable in Define Concurrent Program executable).
- Defining parameters for the program, if any.
- Defining printing information.
- Specifying any incompatible programs that must not run while the program runs
- Choosing whether to allow users to run this report from the Run Reports form or from within a form. If the latter option is chosen, the form from which you want to kick-off your program needs to be modified. If the first option is chosen, the program needs to be added to a report security group.

CONCURRENT PROGRAM LIBRARIES

A program library contains programs that can be called by the manager when Concurrent Managers are in operation. The workers (the OS background processes) of Concurrent Managers are the running instances of these program library executables.

Each Concurrent Manager can only run immediate concurrent programs from its own program library. In addition to this, it can run any spawned or Oracle Tool concurrent programs as spawned processes.

The system administrator may create a concurrent program library and assign it to a manager, or link in bespoke immediate program(s) to one of the existing program libraries. The advantage of linking in programs to a program library is, the assigned manager does not have to spawn another process to execute your job, hence, it will be faster to process.

To create a new concurrent program library, the application developer/system administrator needs to perform various steps including:

- Creating the immediate programs
- Defining the concurrent program executable
- Defining the concurrent programs
- Defining the concurrent program library
- Assigning the program library to a manager

STARTING CONCURRENT MANAGER

There are two main ways of starting Concurrent Manager

1. Using the `script adcmctl.sh`
   The Concurrent Manager can be started using the script `adcmctl.sh` which is located at `$APPLCSL/scripts/<sid>` directory for 11*i* and `$INST_TOP/admin/scripts` for R12. The following command needs to be given for starting the Concurrent Manager.

   ```
   adcmctl.sh start apps/apps passwd
   ```

```
(appmgr01) emstest - -bash $ adcmctl.sh start apps/apps
You are running adcmctl.sh version 115.19
Starting Concurrent Manager for emstest ...
Starting emstest_0817@emstest Internal Concurrent Manager
Default printer is noprint
adcmctl.sh: exiting with status 0
```

Fig. 7.1 Starting Concurrent Manager

2. Using `startmgr` utility for 11*i* and `startmgr.sh` for R12
   The Concurrent Manager can also be started by the utility `startmgr/startmgr.sh` which is available at `$FND_TOP bin. startmgr/startmgr.sh` starts the Internal Concurrent Manager which in turn starts all the Concurrent Managers which are defined. There are a couple of parameters which can be parsed along with the command startmgr which are given below in Table 7.1.

Table 7.1

Parameters	Description	Default
sysmgr	Sqlplus sername/password that owns the foundation tables	Applsys/<passwd>
Mgrname	The name of the Manager	Internal Manager
Logfile	The logfile of the Manager	$FND_TOP/$APPLLOG/ $mgrname.mgr or $APPLCSF/$APPLLOG/ $mgrname.mgr
Sleep	The number of seconds the ICM should wait before checking new request from the table FND_CONCURRENT_REQUESTS	60 Seconds
Restart	If the CM goes down abnormally it will automatically restart the manager. Y= the number of minutes the ICM waits before restarting the manager	N=not to restart after abnormal termination
Mailto	MAILTO is a list of users who should receive mail whenever the manager terminates	Current user
Printer	The default printer for sending the output files	
Diag	This is used for diagnosis. If the CM is started with the parameter diag=y then full diagnostic output is produced in the logfile	N
Pmon	The number of sleep cycles ICM will wait before checking failed Managers	20
Quesiz	Number of pmon cycles the ICM waits between times it checks for normal changes in Concurrent Manager operation. Normal changes include the start or end of a work shift and changes to the Concurrent Manager definitions entered in the Define Concurrent Manager form. (Default 1)	1

```
(appmgr01) emstest - -bash $ cd $FND_TOP/bin
(appmgr01) bin - -bash $ startmgr sysmgr=apps/apps logfile=/tmp/log
Starting icm@emstest Internal Concurrent Manager
Default printer is
(appmgr01) bin - -bash $ tail -f /tmp/log
========================================================================
Starting icm@emstest Internal Concurrent Manager — shell process ID 7345
    logfile=/tmp/log
    PRINTER=
    mailto=appmgr01
    restart=N
    diag=N
    sleep=60 (default)
    pmon=20 (default)
    quesiz=1 (default)
Found dead process: spid=(21928), cpid=(750413), ORA pid=(19),
manager=(201/222)
Found dead process: spid=(21931), cpid=(750414), ORA pid=(41),
manager=(535/1023)
Found dead process: spid=(22019), cpid=(750417), ORA pid=(46),
manager=(0/1071)
Found dead process: spid=(20749), cpid=(750400), ORA pid=(16),
manager=(0/1)
+----------------------------------------------------------------------+
Application Object Library: Concurrent Processing version 11.5
Copyright (c) 1979, 1999, Oracle Corporation. All rights reserved.
Internal Concurrent Manager started : 17-AUG-2005 08:47:13
+----------------------------------------------------------------------+
Process monitor session started : 17-AUG-2005 08:47:13
Found dead process: spid=(21993), cpid=(750415), Service Instance=(1051)
Found dead process: spid=(22016), cpid=(750416), Service Instance=(1054)
Found dead process: spid=(22030), cpid=(750418), Service Instance=(1095)
Found dead process: spid=(22042), cpid=(750419), Service Instance=(1096
```

Contd

Fig. 7.2 Contd

```
Starting STANDARD Concurrent Manager          : 17-AUG-2005 08:47:15
Starting STANDARD Concurrent Manager          : 17-AUG-2005 08:47:15
Starting STANDARD Concurrent Manager          : 17-AUG-2005 08:47:15
Starting XDP_MANAGER Concurrent Manager       : 17-AUG-2005 08:47:15
Starting OAMCOLMGR Concurrent Manager         : 17-AUG-2005 08:47:15
Starting FNDCRM Concurrent Manager            : 17-AUG-2005 08:47:15
Starting INVTMRPM Concurrent Manager          : 17-AUG-2005 08:47:15
Starting CRPINQMGR Concurrent Manager         : 17-AUG-2005 08:47:15
Process monitor session ended                 : 17-AUG-2005 08:47:18
Process monitor session started               : 17-AUG-2005 08:49:18
Process monitor session ended                 : 17-AUG-2005 08:49:19
```

Fig. 7.2 Manually Starting Concurrent Manager

LOCATION OF CONCURRENT MANAGER LOGFILES

The Concurrent Manager log files can be located in one of the following places:

1. For 11*i* if the environment variable `$APPLCSF` is set, the default location is `$APPLCSF/$APPLLOG`
2. For 11*i* if the environment variable `$APPLCSF` is not set, the logs go to `$FND_TOP/$APPLLOG`

   The default name of the Concurrent Manager log files is `std.mgr`. You can change these by setting the parameter `logfile=<name>`
3. On NT the log files are called `CM_<SID>.LOG`
4. In R12 the location of CM logs is `$INST_TOP/logs/appl/conc/log`

QUERYING THE CONCURRENT MANAGER

There are many ways to find out if the Concurrent Manager is running or not and a `Apps DBA` should be aware of all the methods for checking if the Concurrent Manager is up and running. There are mainly three ways.

1. Checking from the Operating System: The Concurrent Manager can be queried from the operating system level by querying for the process `FNDLIBR`. If the process of `FNDLIBR` is up and running it means the Concurrent Manager is also up and running.

```
(appmgr01) emstest - -bash $ ps -ef | grep FNDLIBR |grep appmgr01
appmgr01 13152 13147  0 08:46 /tmp/log 00:00:00 FNDLIBR

appmgr01 13346 13291  0 08:47 ?       00:00:00 FNDLIBR
appmgr01 13347 13291  0 08:47 ?       00:00:01 FNDLIBR
appmgr01 13348 13291  0 08:47 ?       00:00:00 FNDLIBR
appmgr01 13364 13291  0 08:47 ?       00:00:00 FNDLIBR
```

Fig. 7.3 Checking Concurrent Manager from Operating System

2. Checking from the forms: The Concurrent Manager can also be checked from the Forms by the following navigation > System Administration > Concurrent > Manager > Administer. If the actual is equal to the target it means the Concurrent Manager is up and running. The value of Actual and Target should be greater or equal to 1. From the given screenshot we can also see weather the specific Concurrent Managers are up and running or not. We can see from the below figure that the Internal Manager, Conflict Resolution Manager, Service Manager, Inventory Manager are running. From the screen itself we can terminate, deactivate and restart any of these managers.

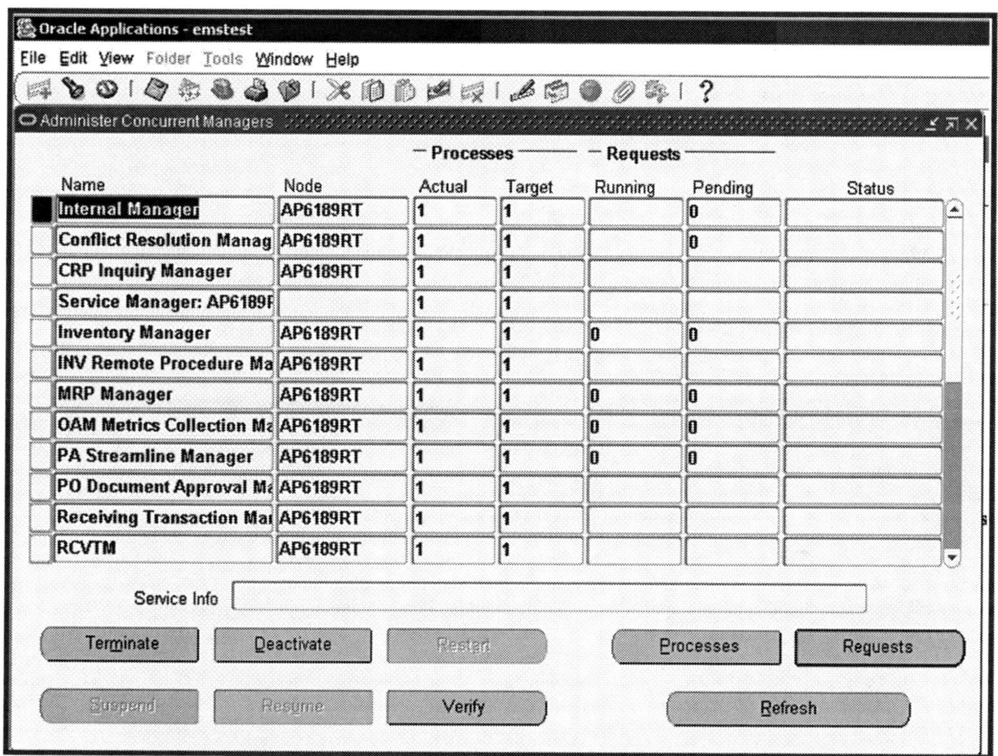

Fig. 7.4 Administer Concurrent Manager Screen

3. Checking by running the `sqlfile`: The status of the Concurrent Manager can also be checked by running `afimchk.sql` available at the `FND_TOP/sql`.

```
(appmgr01) sql - -bash $ cd $FND_TOP/sql
(appmgr01) sql - -bash $ pwd
/SLOTS/slot01/appmgr/emstestappl/fnd/11.5.0/sql
(appmgr01)sql -bash $sqlplus -s apps/apps @afimchk.sql
Status                                   Since                                Method
----------------------------------------------------------------------------------------
Internal Conc Manager is running on - AP6189RT  23-AUG-05 09:42:10 AM
LOCK
Log File - /slot01/appmgr/emstestcomn/admin/log/emstest/emstest_0823.mgr
```

Fig. 7.5 Checking CM Using sql

4. Checking from Oracle Application Manager: We can also check for the Concurrent Manager by login into the Oracle Application Manager and then by navigating to the Application Dashboard. The overview page give information about all the middle tiers components which are up and running. As shown in Fig. 7.6 there is a ✓ mark in the concurrent processing tab. It means the Concurrent Manager is up and running.

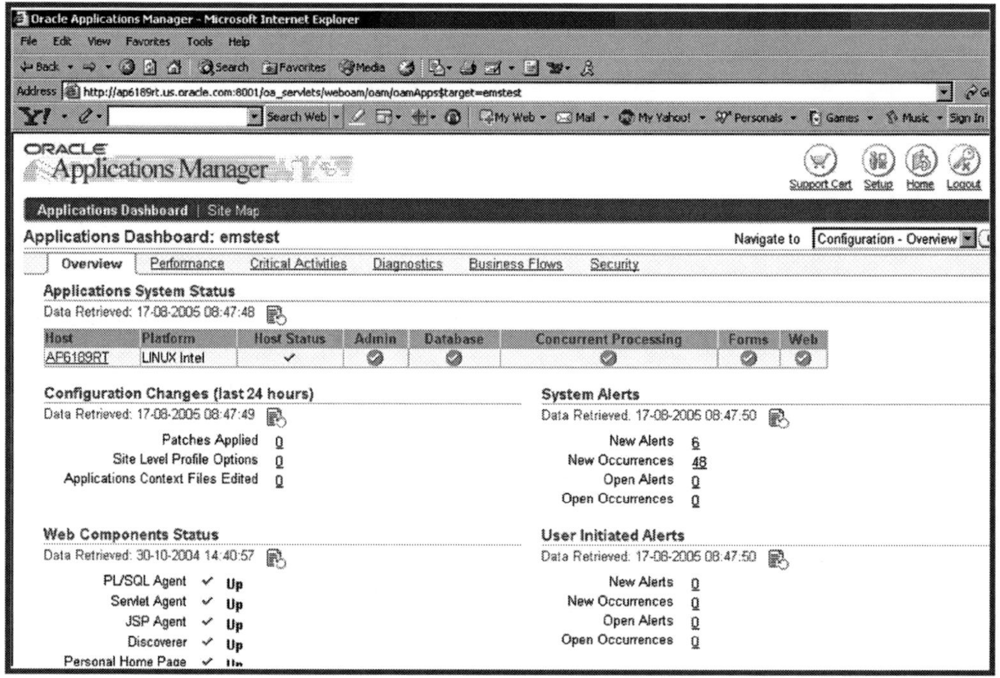

Fig. 7.6 Checking CM from OAM

If we click the tick mark it will show in details which of the managers are up and running as shown in Fig. 7.7.

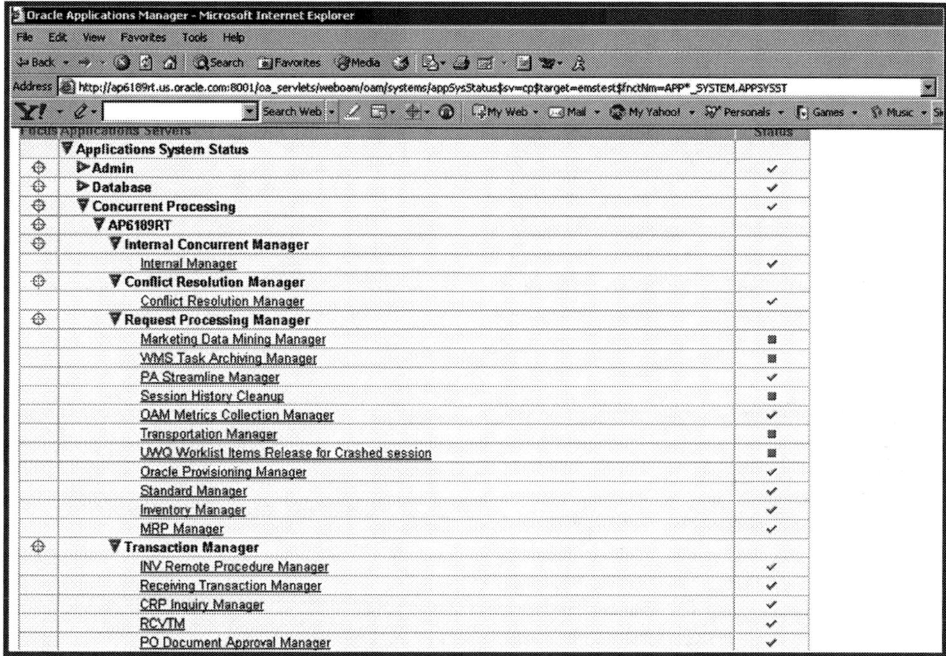

Fig. 7.7 Status of all the CM's from OAM

STOPPING CONCURRENT MANAGER

The stopping of Concurrent Manager is very simple

1. Using the script `adcmctl.sh`.

   The Concurrent Manager can be stopped by using the script `adcmctl.sh`. The script is run in the following way

```
adcmct.sh stop apps/<apps passwd>
```

```
(appmgr01) emstest - -bash $ adcmctl.sh stop apps/apps

You are running adcmctl.sh version 115.19

Shutting down Concurrent Managers for emstest ...
Submitted request 2750788 for CONCURRENT FND SHUTDOWN

adcmctl.sh: exiting with status 0

(appmgr01) emstest - -bash $
```

Fig. 7.8 Stopping Concurrent Manager

2. By querying for the process `FNDLIBR` and killing the same by issuing a kill –9.
3. Individual Concurrent Managers can be deactivated from the Forms using the navigation > Concurrent > Manager > Administer.
4. Using the `CONCSUB` utility about which we will discuss in details later in this chapter. The syntax for the same is

```
$CONCSUB username/password SYSADMIN 'System Administrator'
SYSADMIN WAIT=Y CONCURRENT FND ABORT
```

SUBMITTING CONCURRENT REQUEST

The concurrent requests can be submitted via forms using the navigation View > Request > Submit a New request. It then opens a window and then prompts for type of request which you want to run a single request or a request set.

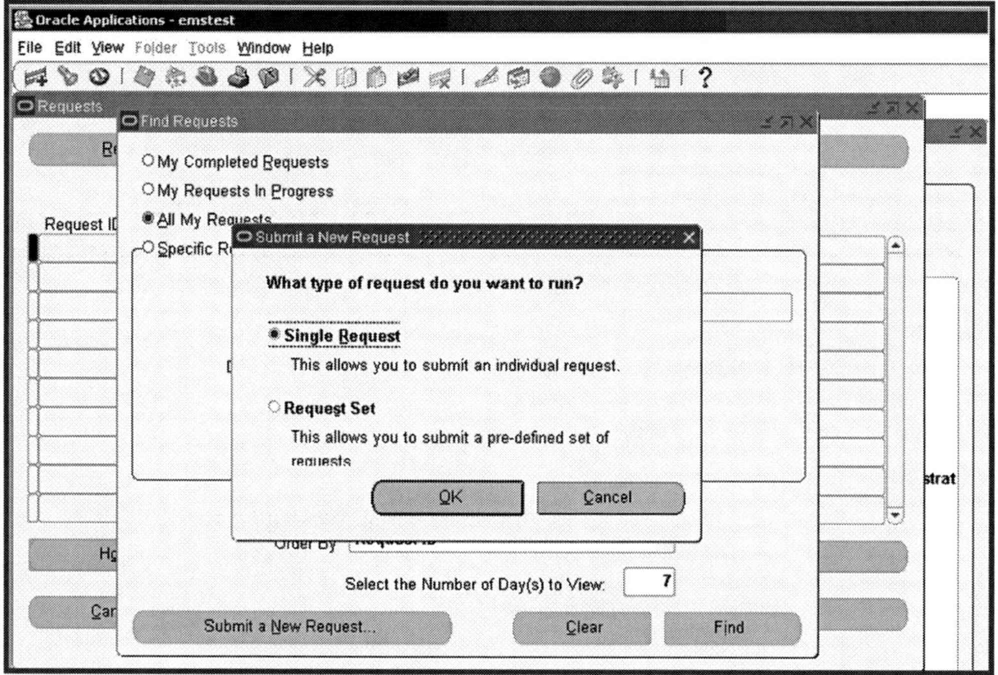

Fig. 7.9 Submitting Concurrent Request

The option single request allows to submit only one single request at a time whereas the option Request Set allows to run multiple concurrent programs and reports at one go. The request set can be further classified into two types—private and public. Private request sets are created by the users who have not logged with system administrator responsibility whereas public request sets are created by the system administrators. System administrators can also update any request set, regardless of who the owner is.

Select the Single Request button and click ok. It opens the submit request form as shown in Fig. 7.10. Select the program which needs to be run from the list.

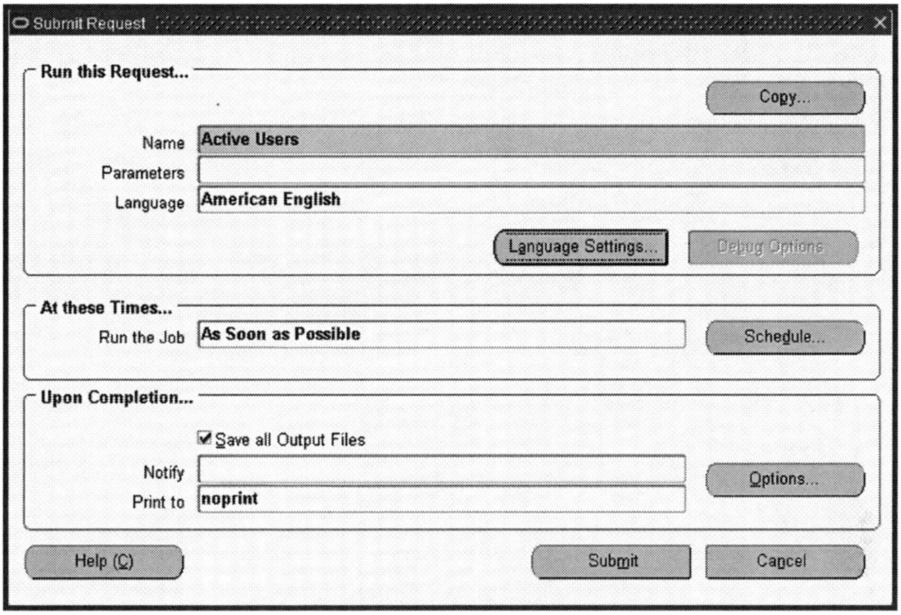

Fig. 7.10 Submit Request Screen

The request can either be submitted immediately or can be scheduled for a later period of time. Click the button schedule for scheduling the same for a later period of time. By default the concurrent request are submitted immediately.

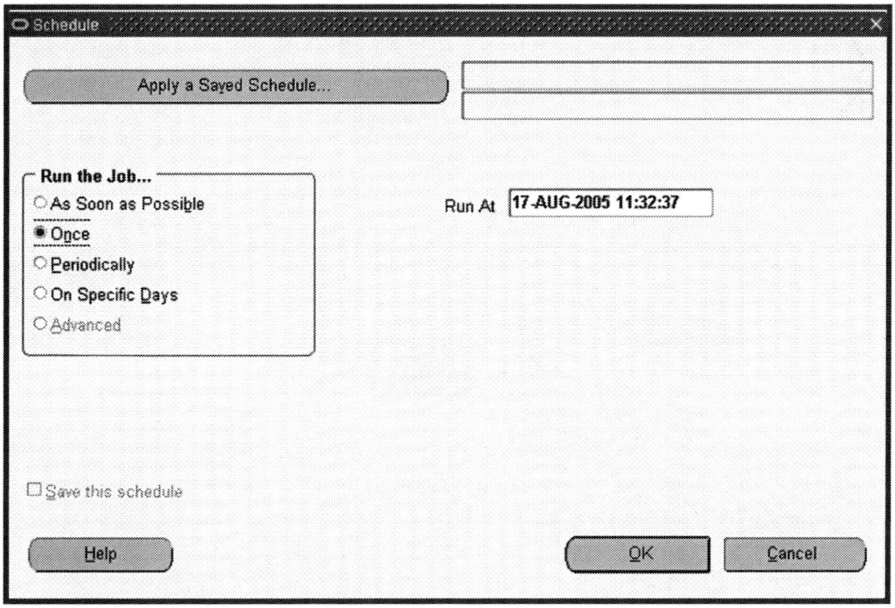

Fig. 7.11 Scheduling Concurrent Request

The concurrent program can be run immediately, only once, periodically or on some specific days. You can also save this schedule for future reference and can use the same schedule for a different Concurrent Program by using the option apply a Saved Schedule.

The Completion option refers to what Oracle Application will do once the request is completed. It can notify people via email, can save the output in a file, can take a print out of the same or simply won't do anything.

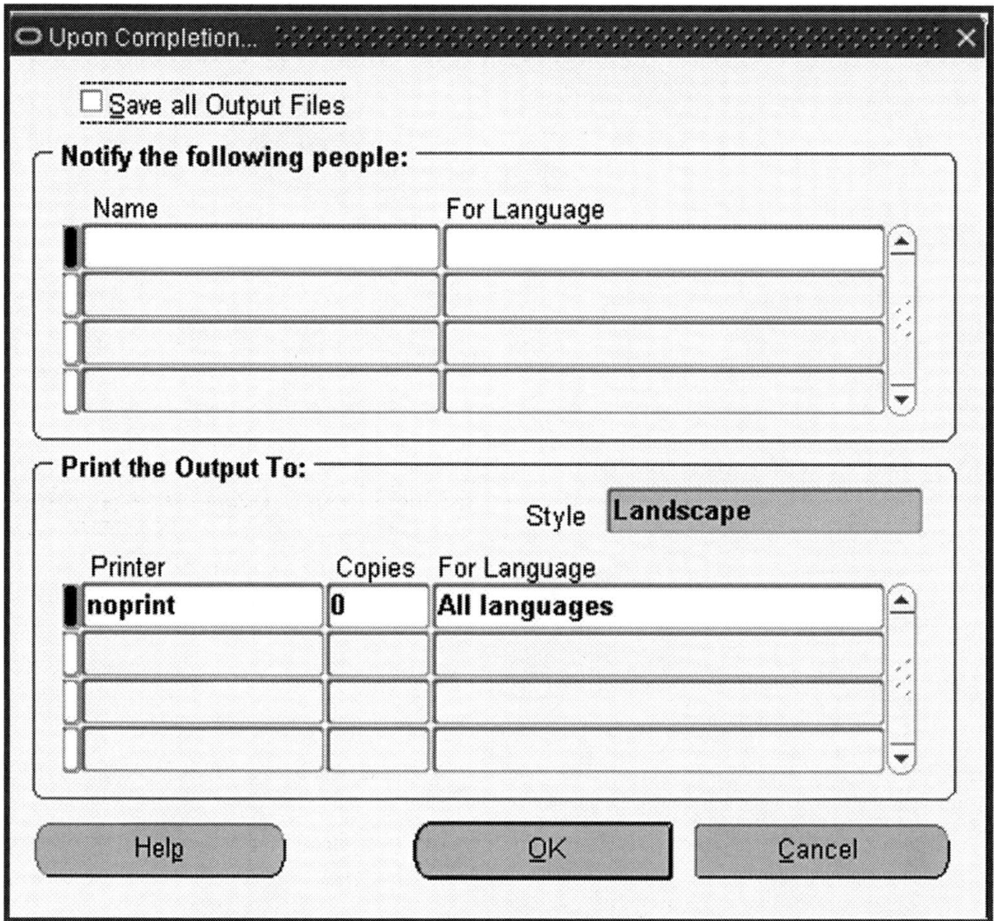

Fig. 7.12 Completion Options

Once the request is submitted it gives a request ID and prompts if we want to submit a new request.

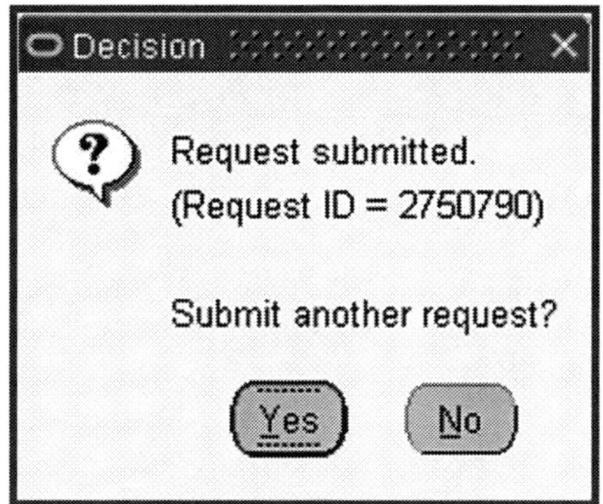

Fig. 7.13 Request ID

THE CONCSUB UTILITY

The concurrent request can also be submitted from the command line syntax using the Concurrent Submission utility CONCSUB. It allows the users to submit the concurrent request at the OS level without login to the forms. This utility submits a concurrent request from the command line and returns to the command line once the request is completed.

The syntax for the CONCSUB is given below

- Syntax: CONCSUB <ORACLE ID> <Responsibility Application Short Name> <Responsibility Name> <User Name> [WAIT=<Wait Flag] CONCURRENT <Concurrent Program Application Short Name> <Concurrent Program Name> [START=<Requested Start Date>] [REPEAT_DAYS=<Repeat Interval>] [REPEAT_END=<Request Resubmission End Date>] <Concurrent Program Arguments ...>
- Example: CONCSUB SCOTT/TIGER SYSADMIN 'System Administrator' SYSADMIN WAIT=Y CONCURRENT FND FNDMNRMT START='"01-JAN-2000 23:00:00"' REPEAT_DAYS=1 REPEAT_END='"01-JAN-2001 23:59:00"' Y 0 0
- ORACLE ID: Username and password of the ORACLE ID for Applications, separated by a slash ("/").
- Responsibility Application Short Name: Enter the short name of the application for your responsibility. This name, along with your responsibility name, will be used to select a responsibility for your concurrent request to run in.
- Responsibility Name: This name, along with your responsibility application short name, will be used to select a responsibility for your concurrent request to run in.
- User Name: Enter the name of your Application Object Library user. This name will be used to update the Who information for any data your concurrent program changes.
- Wait: This means if you want CONCSUB to wait till the request get completes before returning to the prompt. The default is N which means it waits until the job completes. The Y returns to the prompt immediately and "n" is the number of seconds to wait before it exits.

FLOW OF A CONCURRENT REQUEST

Once a Concurrent request is submitted by the user, the table FND_CONCURRENT_REQUESTS is automatically updated with the details of the request. The table is also updated with the information about the schedule of the concurrent request weather its immediately scheduled or scheduled at a fixed time. Once the request is scheduled to run the Concurrent Manager checks the FND_CONCURRENT_TABLES to find out if the request is incompatible with any other request. If the request is incompatible then the Conflict Resolution Manager takes care of the request and find out what are the incompatibilities and it resolves the incompatibilities. If there are no incompatibilities then it's checked weather any special manager is there to take care of this request. If there is any special manager to take care of this request then it goes to the queue of that manager else the standard manager takes care of the same. Once the request is processed the FND_CONCURRENT_REQUEST table is updated with the status.

The concurrent request can have many phases when it's being processed by the manager.

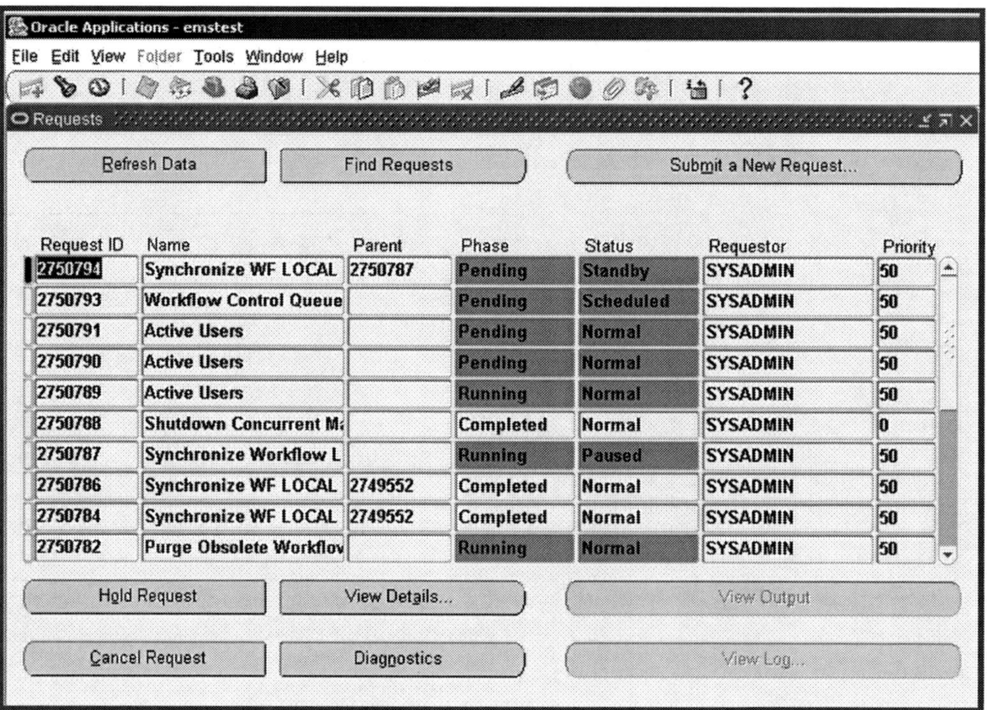

Fig. 7.14 Various Phases of Concurrent Request

From the above figure we can see three phases of a Concurrent request viz Pending, Running, and Completed. Apart from these three phases there is one more phase which is inactive which comes into picture when the Concurrent Manager is down.

The figure given below shows the phase when the concurrent request is inactive. We can see from these figures for every phase there is a corresponding status. We will discuss the combination of the phase and the status in details.

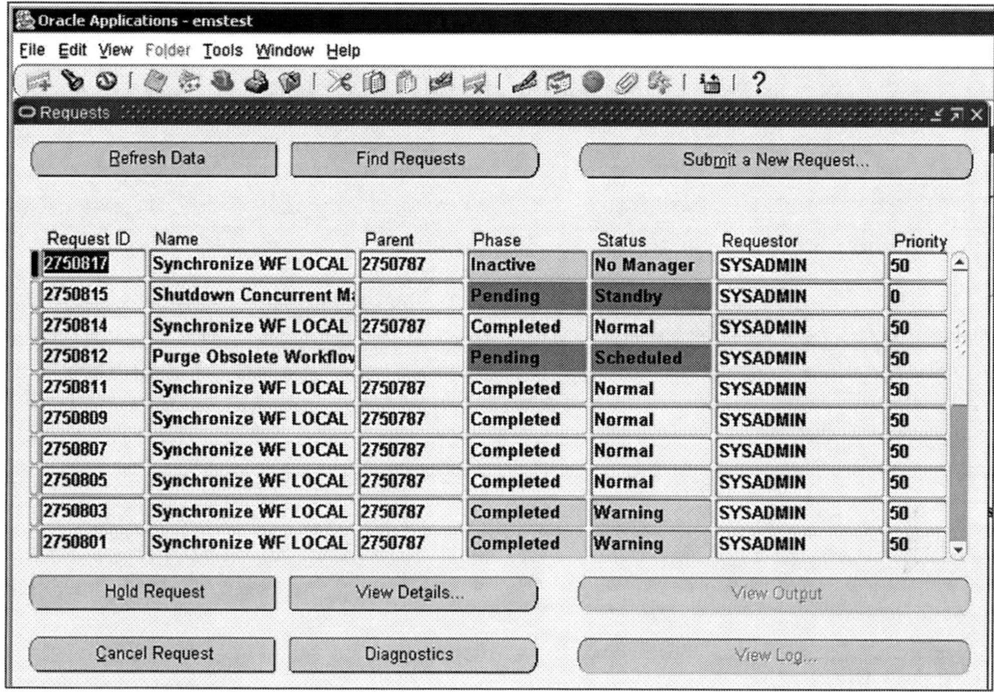

Fig. 7.15 Showing the Inactive Phase of CM

COMBINATION OF PHASE AND STATUS

The Completed Phase

This phase has five status which are discussed below

- Normal: The request completed normally.
- Error: The request failed. The details about the error can be checked from the logfile.
- Warning: The request completed with a warning. The warnings are generated when the upon completion task don't complete successfully.
- Cancelled: The request was cancelled before it was started.
- Terminated: When a running request was terminated.

The Running Phase

This phase has four status which are discussed below

- Normal: This means that the request is running normally and no interfere is required.
- Paused: This means that this request is waiting for some other request to be finished. This usually happens when the completion of this request depends on the completion of the other.

- Resuming: This means that the paused request is resuming. This takes place once the dependent request completes and the request which was paused can now be taken care.
- Terminating: This happens when the user or sysadmin chooses to terminate the request from the forms by clicking the terminate button.

The Pending Phase

This phase has four status which are discussed below

- Normal: This phase is very common which means the requests are waiting for the Concurrent Manager.
- Standby: If the concurrent request is incompatible with some other request then they are put in the standby status till the Conflict Resolution Manager resolves the incompatibility and the manager is allotted.
- Waiting: This usually happens when this request depends on completion of some other requests so that once the other request is finished the output for the same can be used to complete this request.
- Scheduled: This means that the concurrent request are scheduled to run at a point of time in near future.

The Inactive Phase

This phase has three status which are discussed below

- No Manager: This means either the Concurrent Manager is down or no specialized manager is defined to run this request.
- Disabled: This means that though the concurrent program has been requested but it has not been enabled yet.
- On Hold: This means that a pending request has been kept on hold for the time being.

DEFINING CONCURRENT MANAGERS

For defining Concurrent Managers we need to login to the ebusiness suite as sysadmin and need to choose the System Administration responsibility. Then select the tab Define under the heading Concurrent Manager in the right hand side.

The exact screen shot of the same is shown in Fig. 7.16.

Adding new Concurrent Managers is one of the crucial decisions which the Apps DBA needs to take. Before adding new Concurrent Managers a lot of factors need to be examined. One of the major area which needs to be analyzed properly is the resource. If you have less number of managers then your over all concurrent processing gets delayed with a lot many requests having the status pending. On the other hand if you have too many managers then there will be a heavy load on your operating system and online transactions will suffer which would result in performance issues. Thus before adding any new managers a proper analysis needs to be done to obtain the optimum performance.

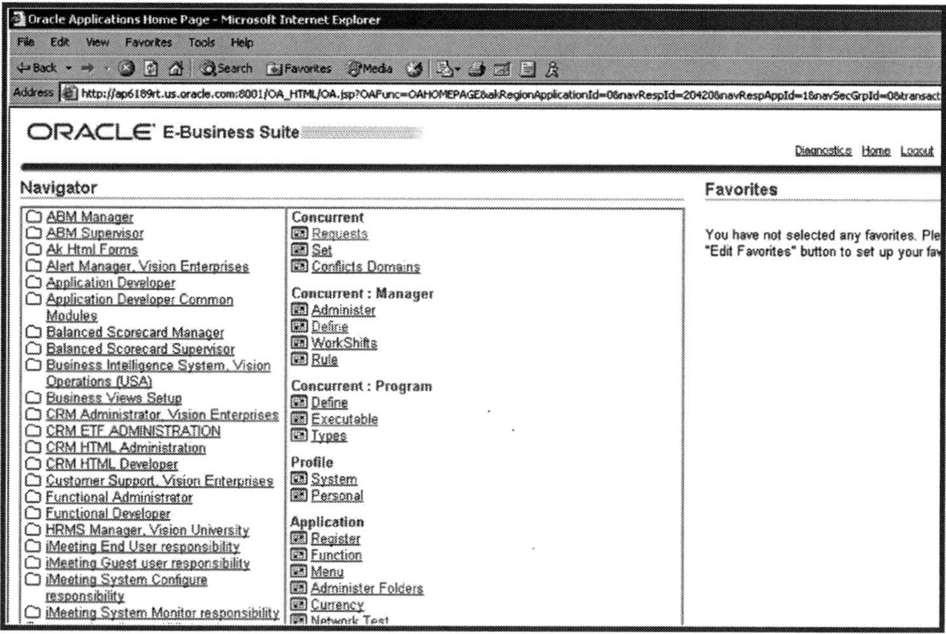

Fig. 7.16 The Sysadmin Responsibility Screen

Once clicked on the Define Concurrent Manager link the forms launch and the window for defining the Concurrent Manager opens.

Oracle Applications - emstest
File Edit View Folder Tools Window Help
Concurrent Managers

Manager	APPS DBA		☐ Enabled
Short Name	AD		
Application	Applications DBA		
Description	APPS DBA MANAGER		
Type	Concurrent Manager		
Data Group		Cache Size	4
Consumer Group	LOW_GROUP		

Parallel Concurrent Processing Details

	Node	System Queue	Platform
Primary	AP6189RT		LINUX Intel
Secondary			

Program Library

Name	FNDLIBR	Application	Application Object Library

Specialization Rules | Work Shifts

Fig. 7.17 Define Concurrent Manager Screen

- Manager: The first field is Manager in which the name of the Concurrent Manager needs to be given which you would be adding.
- Short Name: The second field is Short Name in which a short name of the Concurrent Manager needs to be given.
- Application: The Application column helps to identify which application this Concurrent Manager would be running but this doesn't mean that this Concurrent Manager won't be able to run programs associated with other applications.
- Description: In this field put short description of this Concurrent Manager.
- Type: In this field you need to define what type of Concurrent Manager you are going to define. You cannot update this field once defined. There are several types which are available at the LOV which are Concurrent Manager, Transactional Manager, Internal Monitor etc. Select the manager which you need to define.
- Cache Size: This refers to the number of requests the manager remembers each time it reads which requests it needs to run. If a manager has a cache value of five then it will read five requests at a time and wait till these five requests have been completed before it starts any new request. This parameter is used to tune the Concurrent Manager to work in an effective manner.

  Note: Oracle suggests to enter a value of 1 when defining a manager that runs long and 3 or 4 for the managers which run small quick jobs.
- Data Group: This is used only by the Transaction Manager. This is used by the transaction manager to connect the database.
- Consumer group: Resource consumer groups and resource plans provide a method for specifying how to partition processing resources among different users. A resource consumer group defines a set of users who have similar resource usage requirements. An overall resource plan specifies how resources are distributed among the different resource consumer groups. Oracle Applications allows the system administrator to assign individual Oracle Applications users to resource consumer groups. In addition, concurrent programs and Concurrent Managers can be assigned to resource consumer groups.

Parallel concurrent processing details

- Node: This field is applicable only if you have enabled parallel concurrent processing. Here you define the node from which your manager will operate. The node must be registered with the Oracle Applications and an entry of the node should be there in the table `FND_NODES`.
- System Queue: If you are operating in a parallel concurrent processing environment and you want your manager to use a platform-specific queue management system instead of generic concurrent processing queue management, specify the queue or class name of that system.

Program Library

- Name: You need to assign a predefined Library for your manager. The Concurrent Manager runs only those programs which are listed in their program libraries. If the specialization rule includes any other type of concurrent programs then the Concurrent Manager can also run those programs. The following are a few libraries.

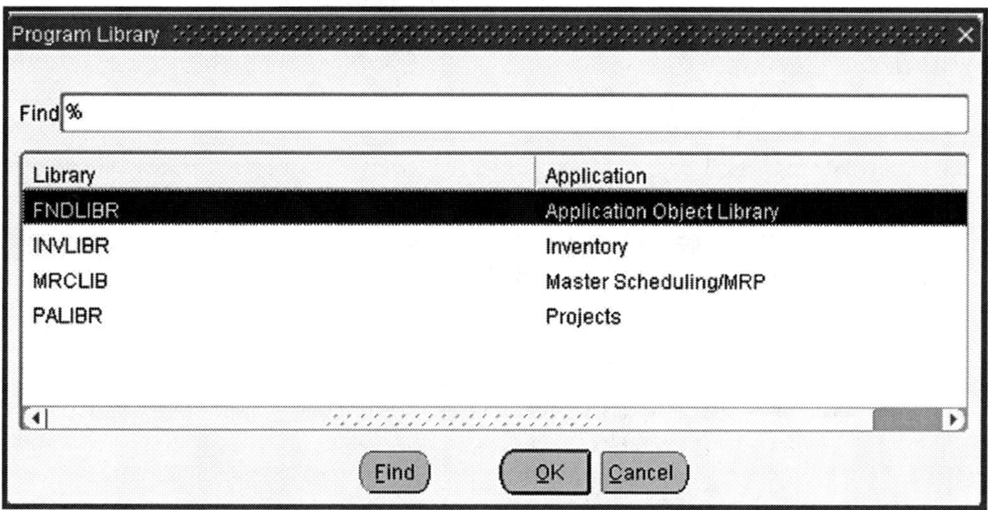

Fig. 7.18 Program Library Screen

Specialization Rules

From here you can specialize your manager to run only certain types of requests. If you don't define specialization rules then the manager can process any kind of concurrent request.

- Include: Use this drop down button to include or exclude those requests which your manager will/won't run.
- Type: Here you specify the type of specialization rule you want to assign to your manager. There are five types which are available in the drop down list viz Combined Rule, Oracle ID, Program, Request Type and User.
- Application: The Application refers to the various Applications which will be either included or excluded for processing by this Concurrent Manager. You can add as many applications you want this manager to take care.
- Name: This is the actual name of the concurrent program which will be either included or excluded by this Concurrent Manager.

The Specialization rule screen is shown in Fig. 7.19.

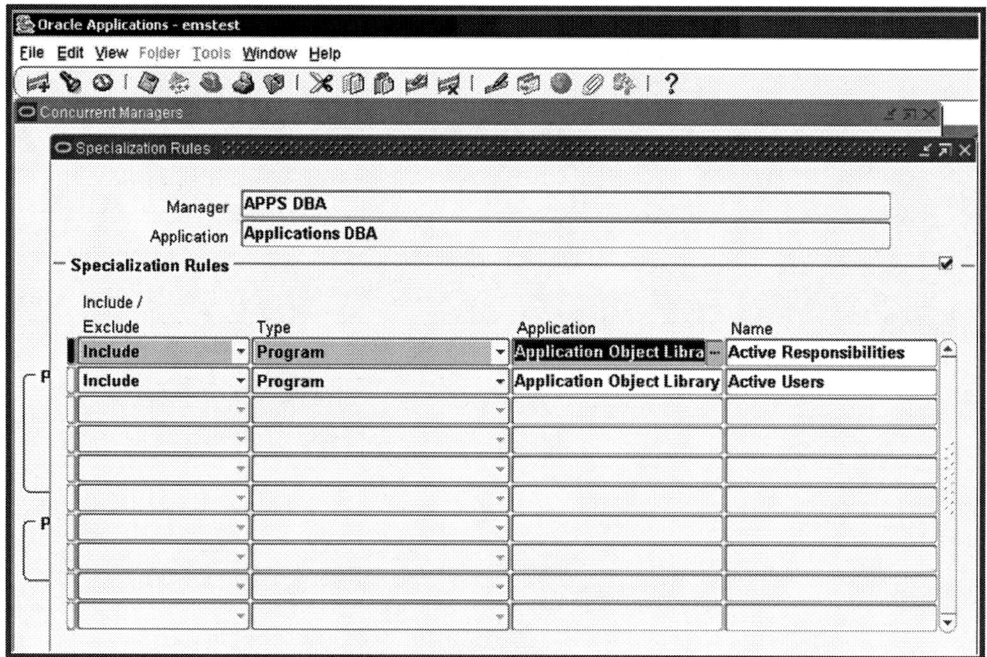

Fig. 7.19 Specialization Rules Screen

Work Shifts

The Work Shift defines the time for which the Concurrent Manager is active. You can define some fixed date or time for or can make the manager run 24*7 making it active all the times.

The Work Shifts are defined by using the Work Shift form (see Fig. 7.20) which we will discuss later in this chapter.

The Process tab defined the number of the operating system process which will run to process the concurrent requests. Each process can run a concurrent request.

The Parameter tab is used for Generic Service Management.

The Sleep Seconds is the sleep time for your manager during the work shifts. This is the number of seconds the Concurrent Manager waits between checking the list of pending concurrent requests.

DEFINING WORK SHIFTS

For defining the workshift for the first time follow the following Navigation > Concurrent > Manager > Work Shifts which is shown in Fig. 7.21.

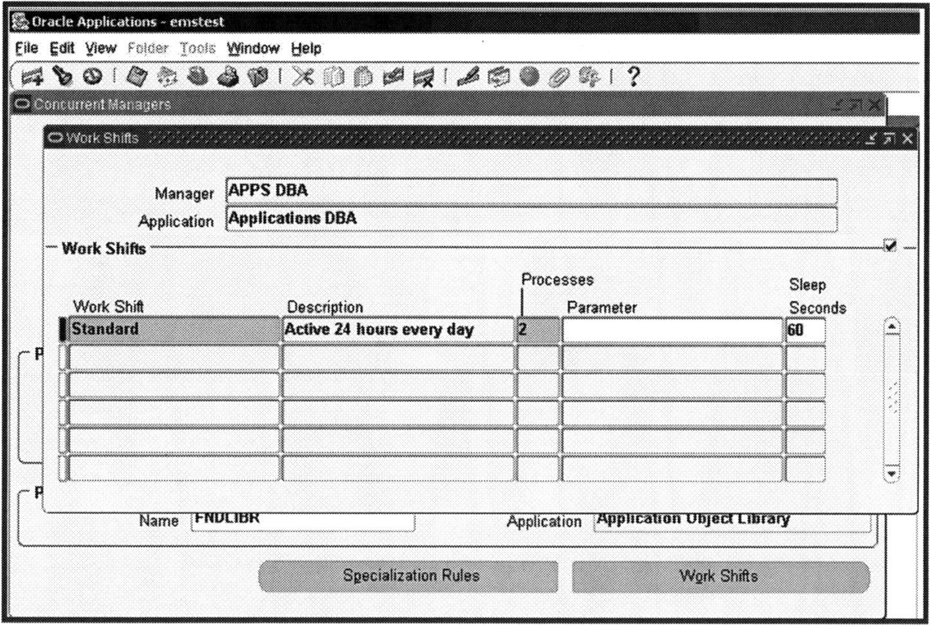

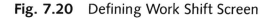

Fig. 7.20 Defining Work Shift Screen

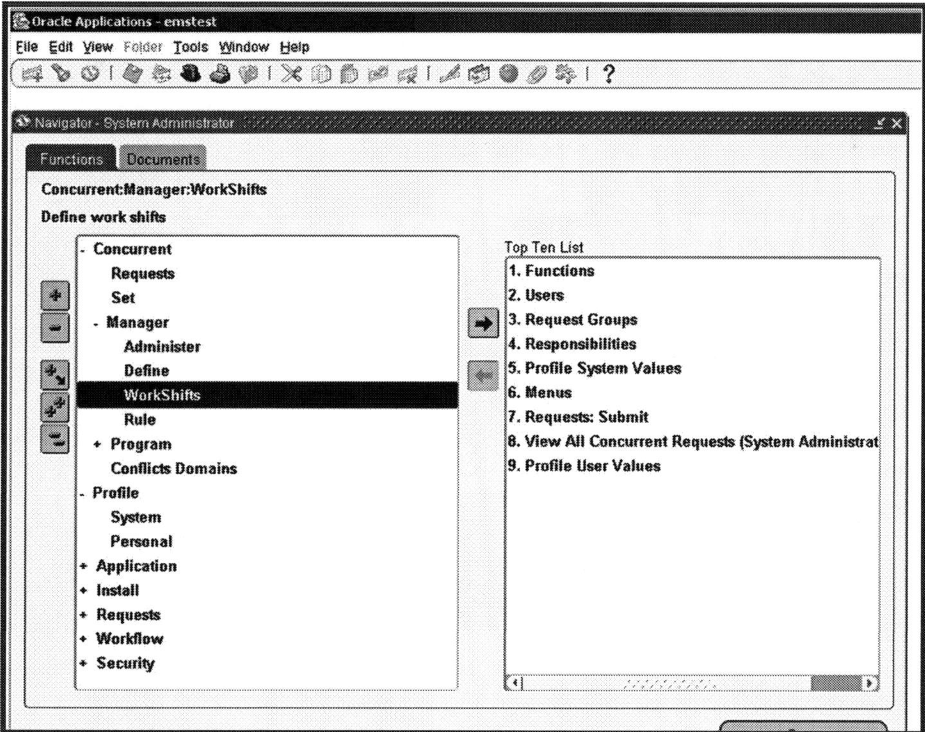

Fig. 7.21 Navigation of Work Shift

Once the Work Shifts button is pressed it opens a new window from where we can define the various work shifts which we can use while defining new Concurrent Managers.

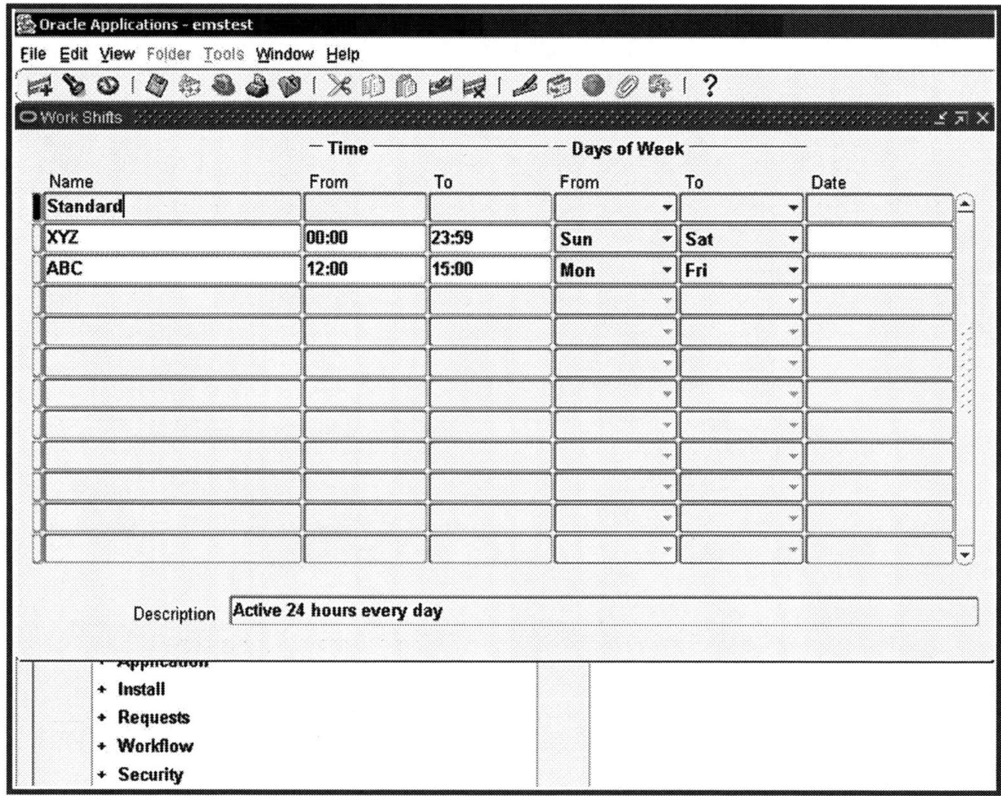

Fig. 7.22 Workshift Screen

We can define as many work shifts we want and can define a work shift to run at any particular day or time.

- Name: This refers to the name of the work shift which you will be defining.
- From/To: This is the time at which your concurrent shift begins and ends.
- Days From/To: This refers to weekdays from which your concurrent shift will begin and end. From the figure given above we can see the shift of ABC starts from Monday and ends in Friday.
- Date: Enter a date if you want to define a date specific work shift.

ADMINISTRATING CONCURRENT MANAGERS

You can administer any Concurrent Manager from the screen below. You can view the status of the Concurrent Manager, You can restart the Concurrent Manager can deactivate a manager and do a number of other controls from this screen (see Fig. 7.23).

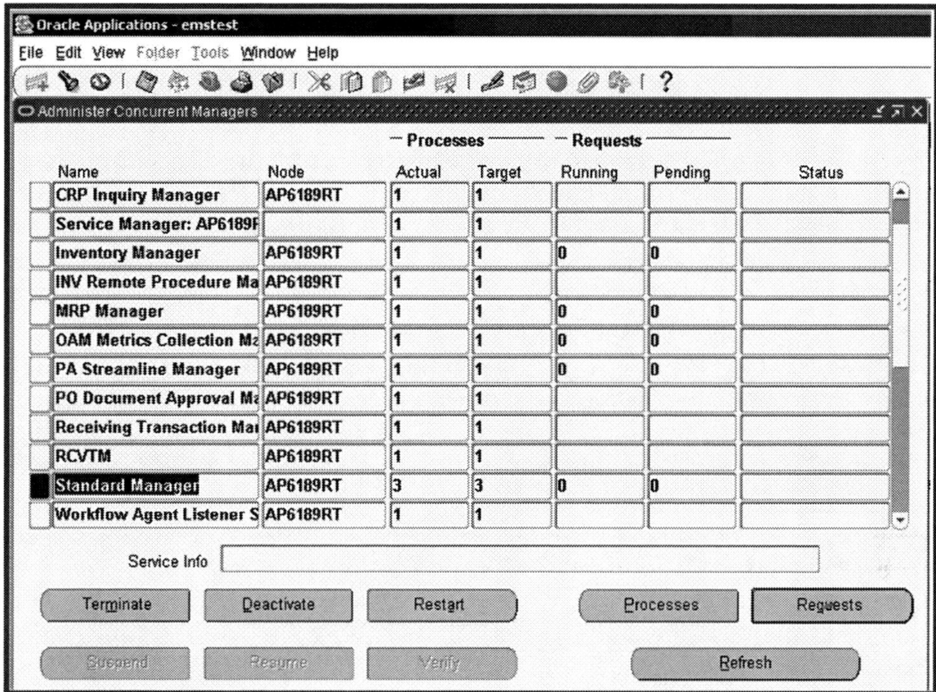

Fig. 7.23 Administrating Concurrent Managers

- Name: This is the first column which contains the name of the Concurrent Manager. We can see from the figure the highlighted one is standard manager.
- Node: Node refers to the node from which the Concurrent Manager is started. In parallel concurrent processing where you configure multiple node the node information is obtained from this column.
- Process Actual: The process actual refers to the actual number of the processes running for that Concurrent Manager. Each process can run one concurrent request. So normally for Standard manager the process is always greater than all the other managers.
- Process Target: The process target refers to the maximum number of the processes that can be active for this manager. Sometimes the actual process may be less than of Target process due to manager deactivation.
- Request Running: This shows the number of the requests currently being processed by the Concurrent Managers.
- Request Pending: This shows the number of requests which are pending are waiting for the Concurrent Managers to complete the running requests. If the actual process for the Concurrent Manager is less and too many concurrent requests are submitted together then this number goes up.
- Status: This field shows the status of the manager after you have chosen a particular action which are shown in the buttons below. For example if you select a particular manager and click on the restart button below then the status field will have the value restarting.

CONTROLLING SPECIFIC MANAGERS

There are certain actions that are shown in the bottom of the Administer Concurrent Manager, which are used for controlling the Concurrent Manager.

- Terminate: When you terminate Internal Manager then all the managers are automatically gets deactivated and all the running requests are terminated. If you want to terminate a particular manager then select the manager and click the button terminate. The status of the manager changes to deactivate after a few seconds and all the requests processed by that manager are immediately terminated. Once a manager is terminated it doesn't restart automatically, you have to manually restart the same using the Restart button.
- Deactivate: For deactivating a particular manager select the manager and press the button deactivate. In case of deactivation all the requests processed by the manager are allowed to complete before the manager shut down. If you deactivate the Internal Manager then all the managers automatically gets deactivate but all the running requests are allowed to complete before the manager is shut down. This is the only difference between termination and deactivation. In termination all the running requests are terminated immediately whereas in case of deactivation all the running requests are allowed to complete at first.
- Restart: The restart option is available when you select a particular manager. With the restart button you can restart a particular manager. Whenever you change the definition of the Concurrent Manages you need to restart the same in order to make the change effective. You may also need to restart if you have changed the work shift for a particular manager or you modify the number of the target processes. In case of parallel concurrent processing if you change the Node of a particular manager then also you have to restart the manager in order to reflect the change.
- Verify: The verify button becomes enable only when you select the Internal Manager which means that this option is only available for the Internal Manager. One of the functions of the internal manager is to monitor the processes of each Concurrent Manager. The process of monitoring the other Concurrent Manager by internal manager is known as the `PMON` cycle. When you click the verify button you can force the process monitoring or the `PMON` activity to occur.
- Suspend: The suspend option is available only for services managed by Generic Service Management (GSM). We will discuss GSM later in this chapter. The suspend option suspends the operations of the service.
- Resume: Like Suspend this option is also available for services managed by GSM. The resume option resumes the operation of the service.
- Refresh: This button refreshes the current window and once this button is clicked you can get the updated status of the manager. Suppose you have selected a manager and have clicked the control button terminate then by pressing the refresh button you can come to know when the manager gets actually terminated.
- Request: This button will open the Request Submission Form which we had already discussed earlier with which Concurrent Requests can be submitted.
- Process: The process button shows the details of the processes of the given Concurrent Manager. It displays all the processes which are active, terminating, migrating as well as those processes that have been terminated or deactivated.

PARALLEL CONCURRENT PROCESSING

Parallel Concurrent Processing is the way to distribute Concurrent Managers across a multiple nodes in a cluster, massively parallel, or networked environment. Parallel Concurrent Processing helps in distributing the load across multiple nodes thereby fully utilizing the hardware resource.

The following are the advantages of the parallel concurrent processing.

- Load Distribution: Since the concurrent processing is distributed among multiple servers as a result the load is distributed across various nodes which results in high performance.
- Fault Tolerance: When a node fails the concurrent processes continues to run on the other nodes as a result the work is not hampered.
- Single Point of Control: The ability to administer Concurrent Managers running on multiple nodes from any node in a cluster, massively parallel, or networked environment.

PARALLEL CONCURRENT PROCESSING ENVIRONMENTS

Parallel concurrent processing runs in multi-node environments, such as cluster, massively parallel, and networked environments. In these environments, each node consists of one or more processors (CPUs) and their associated memory. Each node has its own memory that is not shared with other nodes and each node operates independently of other nodes, except when sharing a resource such as a disk.

With parallel concurrent processing, one or more Concurrent Managers run on one or more nodes in a multi-node environment. You decide where Concurrent Managers run when configuring your system.

Environments in which parallel concurrent processing can run:

Cluster Environments

In a cluster environment, multiple computers, each representing a single node, share a common pool of disks. With parallel concurrent processing in a cluster environment, a single ORACLE database resides in the common disk pool, while multiple instances of Real Application Cluster (RAC) run simultaneously on multiple nodes in the cluster. Multiple Concurrent Managers are also distributed across the nodes in the cluster.

Massively Parallel Environments

In a massively parallel environment, multiple nodes are housed in a single computer. All nodes share access to a common pool of disks. The IBM SP/2, for example, is a massively parallel computer. With parallel concurrent processing in a massively parallel environment, separate RAC instances run simultaneously on multiple nodes, with multiple Concurrent Managers also distributed across nodes.

Networked Environments

In networked environments, multiple computers of the same type are connected via a local area network (LAN) to a single database server, or alternatively, to a cluster of database servers.

HOW PARALLEL CONCURRENT PROCESSING WORKS

In case of parallel concurrent processing all the managers are assigned a primary and a secondary node. The managers are started in their primary node by default. In case of node failure or Oracle Instance failure all the Concurrent Managers on that node are switched to their secondary nodes. Once the primary node is available again the Concurrent Managers on the secondary nodes are migrated back to the primary node. It may happen that during the migration process a manager may be spread across both primary and secondary node.

In case of parallel concurrent processing it may happen that in a node where parallel concurrent processing is configured the Oracle Instance may or may not be running. The node which is not running Oracle the Concurrent Managers connects via Net8 to a node which is running Oracle.

The Internal Concurrent Manager can run on any node, and can activate and deactivate Concurrent Managers on all nodes. Since the Internal Concurrent Manager must be active at all times, it needs high fault tolerance. To provide this fault tolerance, parallel concurrent processing uses Internal Monitor Processes. The job of the internal monitor process is to constantly monitor the internal manager and start when once it fails. Only one Internal Monitor Process can be active on a single node. You decide which nodes have an Internal Monitor Process when you configure your system.

The internal monitor keeps an eye on the internal manager and restarts the same when the internal manager fails. There can be only one internal monitor process on a single node. You can also assign each Internal Monitor Process a primary and a secondary node to ensure fail over protection. Internal Monitor Processes, like Concurrent Managers, can have assigned work shifts, and are activated and deactivated by the Internal Concurrent Manager.

The concurrent log and output files from requests that run on any node are accessible on-line from any other node. Users need not log onto a node to view the log and output files from requests run on that node.

MANAGING THE PARALLEL CONCURRENT PROCESSING ENVIRONMENTS

We will discuss how to manage the environments which have parallel concurrent processing configured in it.

Defining Concurrent Manager

For parallel concurrent processing environments the Concurrent Managers can be defined exactly in the same way like normal environments. Here also you define the Concurrent Manager using the define Concurrent Manager form. When you define a manager, you specify the manager type, which may be either Concurrent Manager, Internal Manager, or Transaction Manager.

There are three other types of managers that Oracle Applications predefines viz the Internal Concurrent Manager, the Conflict Resolution Manager, and the Scheduler. For the CRM and Scheduler you can assign the primary and secondary nodes. For the Internal Concurrent Manager you assign the primary node only.

To each Concurrent Manager and each Internal Monitor Process, you may assign a primary and a secondary node. You may also assign primary and secondary system queue names, if a platform-specific queue management system is available on your platform.

Administering Concurrent Managers

Target Nodes

Using the Administer Concurrent Managers form, you can view the target node for each Concurrent Manager in a parallel concurrent processing environment. The target node is the node on which the processes associated with a Concurrent Manager should run. When a manager's primary node and ORACLE instance are available, the target node is set to the primary node. Otherwise, the target node is set to the manager's secondary node (if that node and its ORACLE instance are available.) During process migration, processes migrate from their current node to the target node.

Control Across Nodes

Using the Administer Concurrent Managers form, you can start up, shut down, restart, and monitor Concurrent Managers and Internal Monitor Processes running on multiple nodes from any node in your parallel concurrent processing environment. You do not need to log onto a node to control concurrent processing on it. You can also terminate the Internal Concurrent Manager or any other Concurrent Manager from any node in your parallel concurrent processing environment.

Starting Up Managers

You start up parallel concurrent processing by invoking the `STARTMGR` command from the operating system prompt. Regardless of the node from which you activate the Internal Concurrent Manager, it starts up on its assigned node (assuming that you operate from a node whose platform supports remote process startup.)

After the Internal Concurrent Manager starts up, it starts all the Internal Monitor Processes and all the Concurrent Managers. It attempts to start Internal Monitor Processes and Concurrent Managers on their primary nodes, and resorts to a secondary node only if a primary node is unavailable.

Shutting Down Managers

You shut down parallel concurrent processing by issuing a "Deactivate" command against the Internal Concurrent Manager from the Administer Concurrent Managers form. All Concurrent Managers and Internal Monitor Processes are shut down before the Internal Concurrent Manager shuts down.

Terminating a Concurrent Process

You can terminate a running concurrent process on the local node or on remote nodes by issuing a "Terminate" command from the Administer Concurrent Managers form.

Migrating Managers

Most process migration occurs automatically in response to the failure or subsequent availability of a primary node. However, you may migrate processes manually by changing the node assignments for a Concurrent Manager or Internal Monitor Process using the Concurrent Managers form. To effect your changes, you issue a "Verify" command against the Internal Concurrent Manager from the Administer Concurrent Managers form.

GENERIC SERVICE MANAGEMENT

An Oracle Applications system depends on a variety of services such as Forms Listeners, HTTP Servers, Concurrent Managers, and Workflow Mailers. Such services are composed of one or more processes that must be kept running for the proper functioning of the applications. Previously many of these processes had to be individually started and monitored by system administrators. Management of these processes was complicated by the fact that these services could be distributed across multiple host machines. The new Service Management feature for Release 11*i* helps to greatly simplify the management of these processes by providing a fault tolerant service framework and a central management console built into Oracle Applications Manager 11*i*.

Service Management is an extension of concurrent processing, which provides a powerful framework for managing processes on multiple host machines. With Service Management, virtually any application tier service can be integrated into this framework. Services such as the Oracle Forms Listener, Oracle Reports Server, Apache Web Listener, and Oracle Workflow Mailer can be run under Service Management. With Service Management, the Internal Concurrent Manager (ICM) manages the various service processes across multiple hosts. On each host, a Service Manager acts on behalf of the ICM, allowing the ICM to monitor and control service processes on that host. System administrators can then configure, monitor, and control services though a management console which communicates with the ICM.

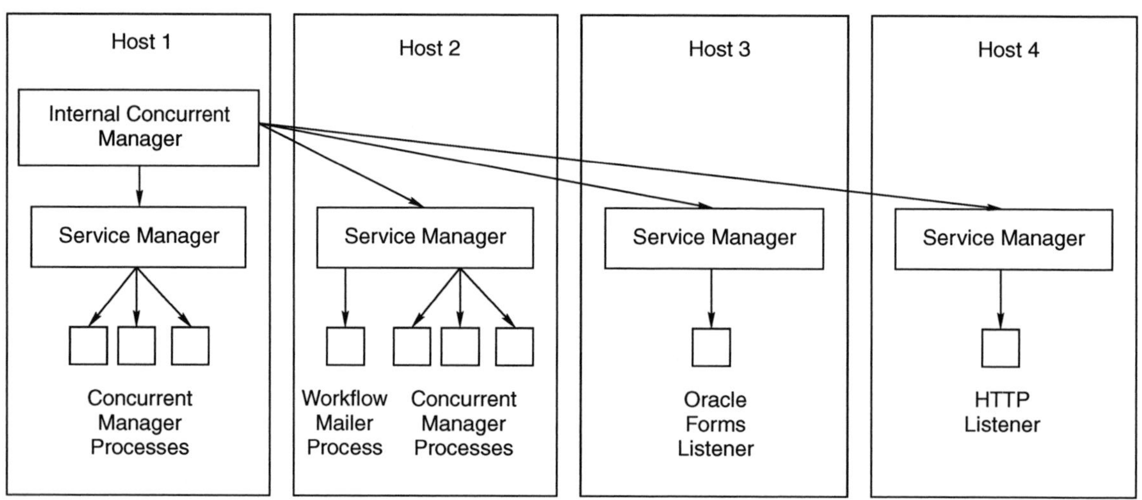

Fig. 7.24 Generic Service Management

Service Management provides a fault tolerant system. If a service process exits unexpectedly, the ICM will automatically attempt to restart the process. If a host fails, the ICM may start the affected service processes on a secondary host. The ICM itself is monitored and kept alive by Internal Monitor processes located on various hosts.

Service Management provides significant improvements in the manageability of Oracle Applications. System administrators can now use the central console in Oracle Applications Manager 11*i* to manage a variety of services that formerly had to be managed independently on separate hosts. The entire set of system services may be started or stopped with a single action. Service Management also provides a great benefit by automatically compensating for certain system failures.

Service processes are very much like Concurrent Manager and transaction manager processes. They must be kept running on a middle tier for the proper functioning of their respective products. The concurrent processing management feature has been built for Concurrent Managers and transaction managers, to provide fault tolerance, process distribution, and simplified configuration and control.

Benefits of Service Management

- The service processes will no longer need to be manually and individually started and monitored by Oracle Applications system administrators.
- Services can take advantage of the process distribution and fault tolerance capabilities that have been developed for concurrent processing.
- As with Concurrent Manager processes, system administrators can use work shifts to determine the number of processes that will be active for a service on a given node for a given time period.

To extend process management support to the various Applications services, the Internal Concurrent Manager must be able to start, monitor, and control processes on all Applications tiers. Every node of every tier will have an Oracle RPC-based Service Controller installed. The ICM will use the Service Controller to manage processes.

IMPORTANT DIAGNOSTIC SCRIPTS

The following SQL scripts located under `$FND_TOP/sql` are useful when diagnosing Concurrent Manager problems:

1. `afimchk.sql`: Tells the status of the `ICM` and `PMON` method.
2. `afcmstat.sql`: Lists active manager processes.
3. `afrqrun.sql`: Lists all the running, waiting and terminating requests.
4. `afrqwait.sql`: Lists requests that are constrained and waiting for the `ICM` to release them.
5. `afrqscm.sql`: Prints log file name of managers that can run a given request. It can be used to check for possible errors when a request stays in pending status. It requires a request ID value.
6. `afcmcreq.sql`: Prints the log file name of the manager that processed the request.
7. `afrqstat.sql`: Summary of completed concurrent requests grouped by completion status and execution type. It requires number of days prior to today on which to report parameter.
8. `afimlock.sql`: Lists locks that the `ICM` is waiting to get.
9. `afcmrrq.sql`: Lists managers that currently are running a request.

Apart from this the Metalink note **213021.1** also lists a couple of other important scripts which are very useful for diagnosing the issues with Concurrent Manager.

8

PATCHING ORACLE APPLICATIONS

Patching is one of the most frequent tasks undertaken by Apps DBA. Oracle provides a utility Auto Patch (commonly known as adpatch), which patches as well as upgrades Oracle Application installations. Patching is generally done in order to upgrade to higher versions, to fix an issue and/or add new features. This chapter deals with how Auto Patch works, how to run it in interactive as well as non-interactive modes, and what are the different options available for running Auto Patch.

PATCH CLASSIFICATION

There are several types of patches:

- Individual patches
- Mini packs
- Maintenance packs
- Family rollups
- Family consolidated upgrade patches

Patches, Mini-packs and Maintenance Packs

In simple language,

Patch + patch = Mini-pack
Mini-pack + mini-pack = Maintenance pack

Patches are created by Oracle whenever there are enhancements in its Applications or there are any problems with the existing ones. A patch may contain a fix for a single issue or for a collection of issues.

During a release cycle, a product combines individual patches into a mini-pack. When these mini-packs are combined, they form a maintenance pack. In earlier releases, mini-packs were referred to as patch sets and maintenance packs as release updates.

Mini-packs and maintenance packs are always cumulative. The latest mini-pack contains all the prior mini-packs; so if a latest mini-pack for a product is used, there is no need to apply a prior mini-pack.

FAMILY PACKS AND FAMILY CONSOLIDATED UPGRADE PATCHES (FCUP)

In simple language:

Product mini-pack + product mini-pack = Family pack
Product upgrade patches + product upgrade patches = FCUP

During a release cycle, all the minipacks of a product family are combined. The consolidated patch results in a family rollup patch or a family pack.

To improve the performance of the upgrade process, Oracle has introduced the family consolidated upgrade patch (FCUP). The FCUP combines all product patches that update all known issues during the 'Auto Upgrade' portion of the upgrade. These patches are packed by the product family and applied before the upgrade using the pre-install mode of Auto Patch.

PATCH FILE STRUCTURE

Patches generally consist of a top-level directory with several files and one or more sub-directories. The top-level directory is named '`<patchnum>`', denoting the number of the patch. The most important files in the top-level directory are: `README.txt`, `README.html` and the driver files (`c<patchnum>.drv`, `d<patchnum>.drv`, `g<patchnum>.drv`, and `u<patchnum>.drv`). For most patches, applying the patch drivers is the only action required.

The `README.txt` or `README.html` files for each patch describe what the patch does, list files in the patch and indicate the servers on which the patch should be run. It also explains any steps required to apply the patch, including prerequisite patches or manual steps.

Patch Drivers

A patch may contain one more driver files. In some cases, a patch contains one single unified driver called u driver or split driver. This includes three driver files—a copy driver (c driver), a database driver (d driver) and a generation driver (g driver).

For patches having split drivers, the entire patch should be applied; for example, if the c driver is applied, the d and g drivers also should be applied.

Copy driver

The naming convention that Oracle Application follows for patches is '`c<patch number>.drv`' for each driver. The copy driver contains commands to change Oracle Application files. It copies all the new files in the patch to `$APPL_TOP`.

For a multi-nodal installation, the c driver should be applied to all the nodes of `$APPL_TOP`.

The c driver does the following work:

- Copies the files that are there in the patch to the `$APPL_TOP`
- Extracts the appropriate files from each product's c library
- Re-links the Oracle Application Products
- Regenerates the JAR files and compiles the Java Server Pages (JSP) files

- Compares the files in the patch with those in the `$APPL_TOP`; if the files in the patch are a higher version, then adpatch copies the files from patch to `$APPL_TOP`

Database driver

Like the copy driver, the database driver is also named '`d<patch number>.drv`'. The database driver contains all the commands to change the database object. In multi-nodal installations, the d driver is run only from the `$APPL_TOP`, which implements the admin server.

The database driver applies all the scripts copied by the copy driver to the database. Here is a brief description of all the scripts that are run by the d driver:

- Makes a list of all the invalid objects in the database
- Runs SQL scripts, which make changes to the database objects
- Compiles all the invalid objects that are there in the database.

Generate driver

A similar naming convention is followed for the generate driver also, which is named '`g<patch number>.drv`'. The generation driver regenerate all Forms, reports and PL/SQL libraries that have been effected by the patch.

Unified driver

The unified driver is named '`u<patch number >.drv`'. It is combination of all three drivers, viz. c, d and g. The actions of each drive are performed by the unified driver, following the order of c, d and g.

HOW AUTO PATCH WORKS

The Auto Patch extracts the appropriate files from the product library. It compares the extracted object modules with their corresponding files in the patch directory. If a file in the patch directory is a more recent version than the product's current file, Auto Patch backs up the product's current file in a sub-directory of the patch directory.

Specifically, it backs up

```
<PROD>_TOP/<subdir(s)>/<old_file_name>
```

to

```
<patch_dir>/backup/<env_name>/<appl_top_name>/<prod>/<subdir(s)>/ \
<old_file_name>.
```

Where,

```
<patch_dir> is the patch directory,
<env_name> is the Applications Environment name,
<appl_top_name> is the APPL_TOP name, and
<prod> is the name of the product being patched
```

The various actions of Auto Patch are briefly mentioned here.

- It replaces each product's outdated files with newer files from the patch directory.
- It applies changed Java class files and regenerates JAR files as needed.
- It loads the new object modules into the libraries.
- It re-links the Oracle Application products with the Oracle server.
- It runs SQL scripts and exec commands in parallel, which change Oracle Applications database objects.
- It copies specified HTML or media files to their respective destinations.
- It generates Oracle Forms files.
- It generates Oracle Reports files.
- It generates Oracle Graphics files.
- It appends a record of how it changed your system to `applptch.txt` in the `$APPL_TOP/admin/<SID>` directory.
- It records summary information of actions actually performed to `applpsum.txt` located under `APPL_TOP/admin`.
- It updates the various ad tables, viz. `ad_applied_patches` and `ad_bugs` with the status of the patch.

FEATURES OF AUTO PATCH

Platform aware: If you try to apply a Linux patch on a Solaris-based system, it warns you regarding this action.
Translation aware: If a language translation patch needs to be applied in addition to the base version, Auto Patch notifies you of the same.

DOWNLOADING A PATCH

You can download patches from Oracle Metalink *http://www.metalink.oracle.com*. These are the steps to download a patch.

- Log in to Metalink
- Select the patches option
- Query for the patches
- Download the patches

The first step in downloading a patch is to log in to the Metalink (see Fig. 8.1).

Metalink Log in Page

The Metalink log in page is shown in Fig. 8.2. Log in to this page using your Metalink user ID and password.

Once logged in, you are taken to the main page. This contains News and notes, Search button from where one can find the solutions for Oracle Applications-related problems. It also contains a tab 'Service

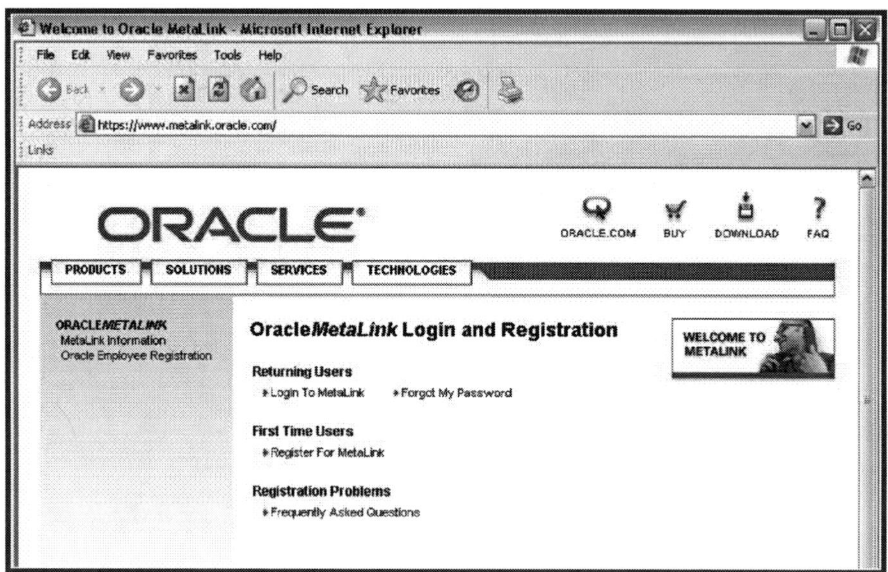

Fig. 8.1 Metalink Home Page

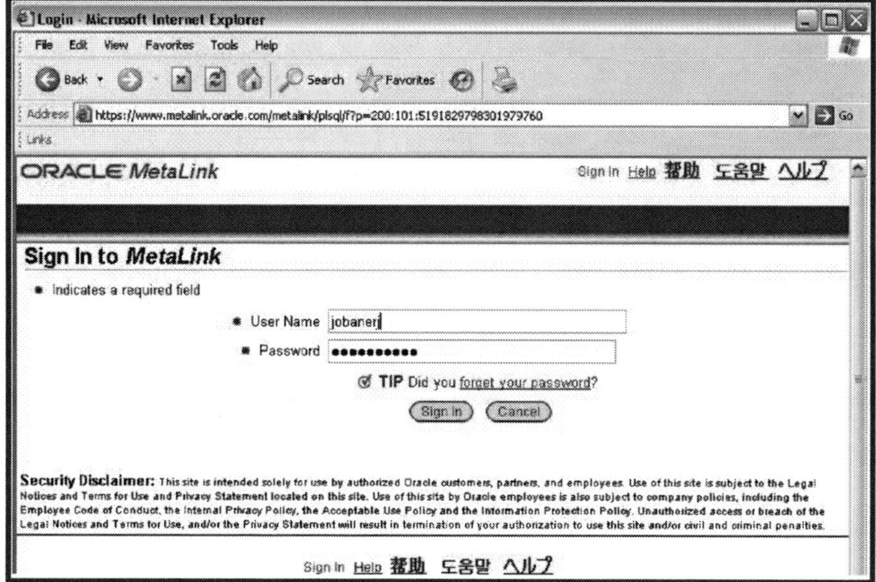

Fig. 8.2 Metalink Log in Page

Request' from where you can log service requests against Oracle for all your issues. There is also a tab 'Forums' from where you can discuss issues with other members of Metalink or with a technical expert of Oracle.

To download patches, click on the button 'Patches'. The screen is shown in Fig. 8.3.

Patch Download Screen

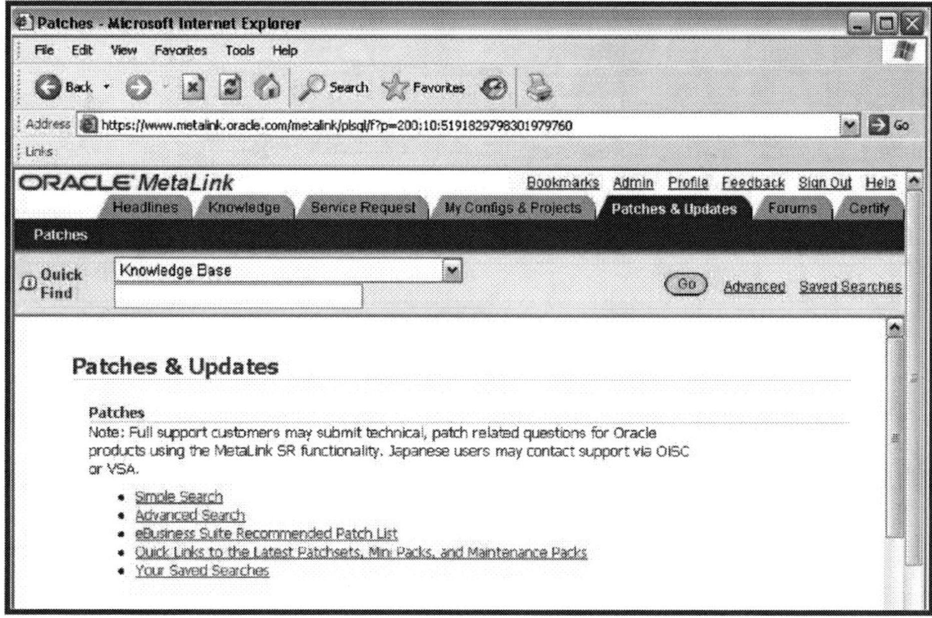

Fig. 8.3 Patch Download Screen

The patch download screen shows the following options.

- Simple Search—with this button you can download the patch simply by giving the patch number and the platform for which you want to download the patch.
- Advanced Search—helps to search for patches across various Oracle products between various versions, platforms, etc.
- E-Business Suite Recommended Patch List—from this link, you can find the patches recommended for your version of Oracle Applications.
- Quick Links to latest Patch set, Mini-packs and Maintenance packs—from this link you can get information about the latest patches of Oracle Applications in a product-wise list.
- Your Saved Searches—from this tab, you can view all your earlier searches in the Metalink.

Querying for Patches

For querying patches, click on the 'Simple Search' tab. Enter the patch number in the screen as shown in Fig. 8.4 and select the platform. Click 'Go' to query for the patch.

Downloading a Patch

Once the 'Go' button is pressed as shown in Fig. 8.4, it will show the details of the patch. It will show the size of the patch and the readme of the patch. There will be a download button on the lower right hand side of the screen. Click the button to download the patch (see Fig. 8.5).

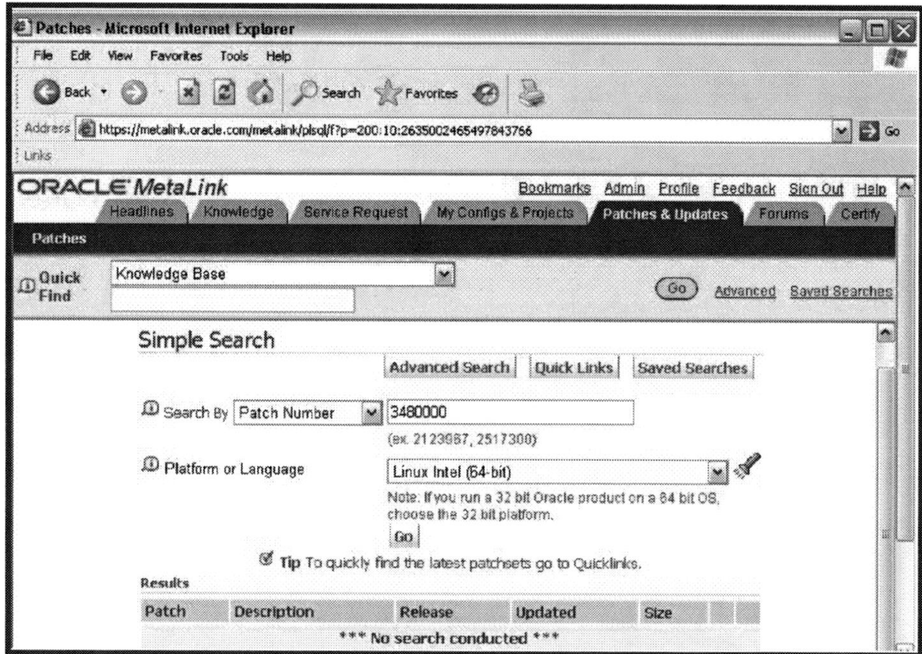

Fig. 8.4 Querying Patches

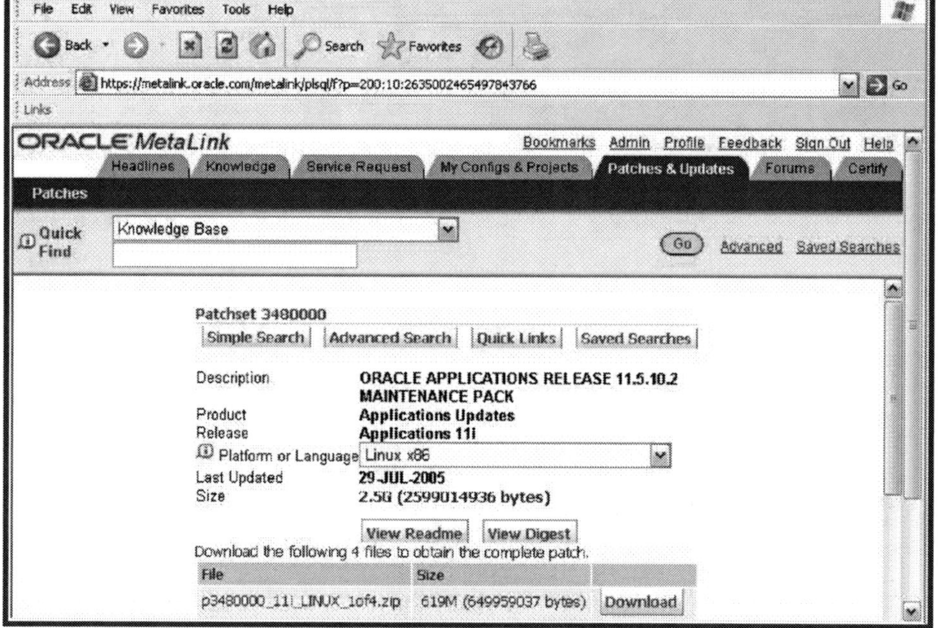

Fig. 8.5 Downloading a Patch

The patches can also be downloaded alternatively directly from linux server by doing a ftp to *updates.oracle.com* and then entering your metalink user id and password

APPLYING A PATCH

1. To apply a patch, log in to the application system (`Appl_Top`) as the owner of the application files system (`appmgr`).
2. Source the environment file to point to the correct `APPL_TOP`. This file is normally present in the `$APPL_TOP` directory with the name `<db_name.env>` or `APPSORA.env`.
3. Verify the `$APPL_TOP, $ORACLE_HOME`, `$ORACLE_SID` and the `$TWO_TASK`.
4. Place the patch in a patch top directory. If the directory doesn't exist, then create it and download the patch there. Unzip the patch in the patch top.
5. Verify that `$AD_TOP/bin` and `$ORACLE_HOME/bin` are there in the `$PATH`.
6. Verify that there is enough disk space.
7. Read the readme file carefully to find the prerequisite patches as well as the post-install or manual steps if any. This file is located in the directory created by unzipping the patch.
8. Shut down the middle tiers. This step is not mandatory but depends on the type of patch being applied. If the patch modifies or re-links the files of the Forms server or the concurrent processing server, then the concerned servers (i.e. Forms server or Concurrent Managers) need to be shut down.
9. Use adpatch from the command line to start the patching. The adpatch asks a number of questions. When prompted, specify the driver name. The Auto Patch applies that particular driver. If it's needed for all, then start adpatch for all drivers.
10. Review the log files. By default, the log files are located in `$APPL_TOP/admin/<SID>/log` directory. The default name of the log file is '`adpatch.log`', but it is advisable to name the log files in patch-number.log. Check for any errors or warnings in the logs. If the patching process has used multiple workers, then the workers create their own log files (`adwork01.log`). Here is a list of the log files in which the patch writes all the details:
    - `adpatch.log`: The patch log file
    - `adworkerxx.log`: Patch workers log
    - `adpatch.lgi`: Contains additional patching information
    - `adrelink.log`: Re-linking details are updated in this file
11. Post-install steps, if included in the readme of the patch, should be followed.
12. Restart the services.

If you are using 11.5.10 release, then you need to enable the maintenance mode from adadmin before starting the adpatch session. In this mode, user log in is not possible, and users are informed about the maintenance when they log in to the application system. A patch can be applied without going to maintenance mode using `options=hotpatch`. But applying a patch using `hotpatch` causes performance degradation and is therefore not advisable.

```
      AD Administration Main Menu
   ----------------------------------

   1.    Generate Applications Files menu

   2.    Maintain Applications Files menu

   3.    Compile/Reload Applications Database Entities menu

   4.    Maintain Applications Database Entities menu

   5.    Change Maintenance Mode

   6.    Exit AD Administration

Enter your choice [6] :5

           Change Maintenance Mode
   --------------------------------------

Maintenance Mode is currently: Disabled.

Maintenance mode should normally be enabled when patching
Oracle Applications and disabled when users are logged on
to the system.  See the Oracle Applications Maintenance
Utilities manual for more information about maintenance mode.

Please select an option:

   1.    Enable Maintenance Mode

   2.    Disable Maintenance Mode

   3.    Return to Main Menu

Enter your choice [3] :1

sqlplus -s &un_apps/*****

@/slot01/appmgr/emstestappl/ad/11.5.0/patch/115/sql/adsetmmd.sql ENABLE

Successfully enabled Maintenance Mode.

Review the messages above, then press [Return] to continue.
```

Fig. 8.6 Enabling Maintenance Mode from Adadmin

After successful application of the patch, restart all the middle tiers and allow access to the users.

If an additional language apart from US English is installed, the NLS patch needs to be applied in all the nodes immediately after the patching.

Applying a Patch in a Multi-node System

A multi-node installation is one where the Oracle Applications installation is spread across different machines or `APPL_TOPs`. If your system is configured on multiple nodes then you must run Auto Patch on each node to update the necessary files. The Auto Patch needs to be run only once from the `admin` server to upgrade the database objects, but the copy driver and the generation driver must be run from all the nodes that require the changed files.

Table 8.1 shows which driver needs to be run from which server.

Table 8.1 Applying a Patch in a Multi-node Installation

	Admin Server	Forms Server	Web Server	Conc Proc Server
C<patch>.drv	✓	✓	✓	✓
D<patch>.drv	✓	×	×	×
G<patch>.drv	✓	✓	✓	✓

If the patch only has a unified driver then you need to run that from all the nodes. Auto Patch will take care of applying the required driver on the particular node.

Applying a Patch in a Two-node or Multi-node System

In a two-node or multi-node installation, the middle tier is installed across two different nodes. The admin server and concurrent server are installed in one node and the web server and Forms server are installed on a separate node. In such an installation, Auto Patch should be applied in the manner given in Fig. 8.7.

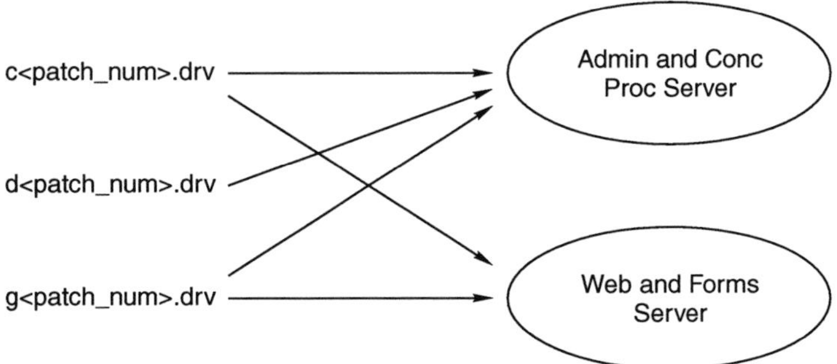

Fig. 8.7 Applying a Patch in a Two-node/Multi-node Installation

INTERACTIVE AND NON-INTERACTIVE PATCHING

Auto Patch can be run in interactive mode, where user intervention is needed, or in non-interactive mode where no such intervention is required. We will discuss each of these modes further.

Interactive Patching (Standard Mode)

The Auto Patch (adpatch) executable is located at $AD_TOP/bin. Run the Auto Patch from the PATCH_TOP directory.

For example,

```
$ cd $APPL_TOP/patches/3480000
$ adpatch
```

Where,

```
$APPL_TOP/patches/3480000 is the PATCH_TOP directory
```

The Auto Patch prompts a number of questions which need to be answered. The default selection for the question is provided in [ ]. Here is a sample of what Auto Patch prompts.

```
(appmgr01) appmgr - -bash $ adpatch

                    Copyright (c) 2002 Oracle Corporation
                       Redwood Shores, California, USA

                        Oracle Applications AutoPatch

                               Version 11.5.0

NOTE: You may not use this utility for custom development unless you have
written permission from Oracle Corporation.

Your default directory is '/slot01/appmgr/emstestappl'.
Is this the correct APPL_TOP [Yes] ?

AutoPatch records your AutoPatch session in a text file you specify.
Enter your AutoPatch log file name or press [Return]
to accept the default file name shown in brackets.

Filename [adpatch.log] :

You can be notified by email if a failure occurs.
Do you wish to activate this feature [No] ?
```

Fig. 8.8 Example of Auto Patch Prompting in Interactive Mode

As seen in the Fig. 8.8, the patch at first verifies whether or not it's pointing to the correct $APPL_TOP. Then it prompts for the log file, which is by default adpatch.log. It is recommended to name the log file in a manner similar to the patch number, viz. if applying the c driver then name the log file 'c3480000.log'. Adpatch provides the option of email notification in case of patch failure. To activate this feature we need to give an email address. This option is set to 'No' by default.

```
Please enter the batchsize [1000] :

Please enter the name of the Oracle Applications System that this
APPL_TOP belongs to.

The Applications System name must be unique across all Oracle
Applications Systems at your site, must be from 1 to 30 characters long,
may only contain alphanumeric and underscore characters,and must start
with a letter.

Sample Applications System names are: "prod", "test", "demo" and
"Development_2".

Applications System Name [emstest] : emstest *
```

Fig. 8.9 Naming the Log File

The batch size refers to the number of rows to commit at a time when certain scripts run. If we don't enter a specific value, Auto Patch takes the default, which is normally set to a relatively smaller value to accommodate systems with a small rollback segment. To take advantage of higher rollback segment, you must specify a larger batch commit size than the default value. The next question it asks is the Oracle Application system name, which is usually the same as that of the `SID`. Normally, Auto Patch answers this question by looking at the configuration file. All answers marked with an asterisk (*) are answered by Auto Patch itself by looking at the configuration file created at the time of installation.

```
NOTE: If you do not currently have certain types of files installed in
this APPL_TOP, you may not be able to perform certain tasks.

Example 1: If you don't have files used for installing or upgrading the
database installed in this area, you cannot install or upgrade the
database from this APPL_TOP.

Example 2: If you don't have forms files installed in this area, you
cannot generate them or run them from this APPL_TOP.

Example 3: If you don't have concurrent program files installed in this
area, you cannot relink concurrent programs or generate reports from this
APPL_TOP.

Do you currently have files used for installing or upgrading the database
installed in this APPL_TOP [YES] ? YES *

Do you currently have Java and HTML files for HTML-based functionality
installed in this APPL_TOP [YES] ? YES *

Do you currently have Oracle Applications forms files installed in this
APPL_TOP [YES] ? YES *
```

Fig. 8.10 Questions Answered by Auto Patch Automatically

These questions are relevant if we have a multi-nodal installation. For a single node installation all the program files are installed in the same APPL_TOP, and so the answer is yes for all of the questions in Fig. 8.10. The Auto Patch answers them automatically, as we can see there is an asterisk (*) next to each of the answers.

```
Please enter the name Oracle Applications will use to identify this
APPL_TOP.

The APPL_TOP name you select must be unique within an Oracle Applications
System, must be from 1 to 30 characters long, may only contain
alphanumeric and underscore characters, and must start with a letter.

Sample APPL_TOP Names are: "prod_all", "demo3_forms2", and "forms1".

APPL_TOP Name [emstest] : emstest *


You are about to apply a patch to the installation of Oracle Applications
in your ORACLE database 'emstest' using ORACLE executables in '/slot01/
appmgr/emstestora/8.0.6'.

Is this the correct database [Yes] ?

AutoPatch needs the password for your 'SYSTEM' ORACLE schema in order to
determine your installation configuration.

Enter the password for your 'SYSTEM' ORACLE schema: manager

The ORACLE username specified below for Application Object Library
uniquely identifies your existing product group: APPLSYS

Enter the ORACLE password of Application Object Library [APPS] :

AutoPatch is verifying your username/password.
Connecting to APPLSYS......Connected successfully.

Connecting to SYSTEM......Connected successfully.

Connecting to APPLSYS......Connected successfully.
```

Fig. 8.11 Further Auto Patch Prompts

We can see from Fig. 8.11 that the name of the APPL_TOP is also taken from the configuration file and is answered automatically. It then prompts for the system and apps schema passwords. When the passwords are given, it connects to the database to continue the processing.

```
Enter the directory where your Oracle Applications patch has been
unloaded

The default directory is [/slot01/appmgr/emstestappl/patches/3480000] :

Please enter the name of your AutoPatch driver file :u3480000.drv

Enter the number of parallel workers [6] :14
```

Fig. 8.12 Auto Patch Prompt for Patch Driver

The Auto Patch verifies the PATCH_TOP, i.e. the directory where the patch is uploaded. It then asks for the name of the driver file to be applied. If d driver or g driver is selected then we need to give the number of the workers that will run the various files of the patch.

If the patch is one that can be applied in parallel, then Auto Patch asks the user to specify the number of parallel workers to be used for parallel processing. It automatically determines the default value as being two plus the number of CPU's on the node where your database server is running. For example, if your server has a single CPU then the default number of workers is three.

Auto Patch then initiates the required number of workers, which it manages through the use of the FND_INSTALL_PROCESS table, which has all information about the files assigned to specific workers.

```
Updating the Patch History file...

AutoPatch is complete.

AutoPatch may have written informational messages to the file
/slot01/appmgr/emstestappl/admin/emstest/log/adpatch.lgi


You should check the file
/slot01/appmgr/emstestappl/admin/emstest/log/adpatch.log
for errors.
```

Fig. 8.13 Log File Information

Once all the information is given Auto Patch starts applying the patch. The screen displays the process and the phases of execution. Once the patching is completed, it gives the message to check all the logs.

Non-interactive Patching

The non-interactive mode of running Auto Patch means applying a patch without user intervention. This mode helps in automating the patching process and in avoiding patching prompts. Once the PATCH_TOP location is specified, Auto Patch will run all the drivers from there. For this, we need to initially create an Auto Patch defaults file for the Application system.

To create this file for the first time, at the prompt we need to give:

```
(appmgr01) bash $ adpatch\ defaultsfile=$APPL_TOP/admin/$TWO_TASK/def.txt
```

This will prompt all the questions normally asked during interactive patching. Answer all of them; when asked for the directory where your patch has been unloaded, enter an abort at the command prompt. This will create a def.txt file at the location specified in the command prompt. Verify that this defaults file has been created properly. Once the defaults file is created for the application system, we can start running Auto Patch in a non-interactive way.

The command to run Auto Patch in non-interactive mode is:

```
(appmgr01) - -bash $ adpatch defaultsfile=$APPL_TOP/admin/$TWO_TASK/def.txt \
logfile=d3480000.log \
patchtop=$APPL_TOP/patches/3480000 \
driver=c3480000.drv,d3480000.drv,g3480000.drv \
workers=14 \
interactive=no \
```

The Auto Patch will run the patch drivers in the order of the names given.

Alternatively, you can copy `$APPL_TOP/admin/adalldefaults.txt` to `APPL_TOP/admin/<SID>/<new_file>.txt`, and edit it as needed.

AUTO PATCH MODES

In addition to the interactive and non-interactive modes, Auto Patch can also be run in two specialized modes—test mode and pre-install mode.

Test Mode

The test mode is used to determine the action of the patch without actually applying it. When the patch is run in this mode it does not perform any action as such, but documents the operations it would have performed while running. In other words, it lists each file it would have copied, generated, executed or re-linked.

Applying a patch in test mode is like applying a patch interactively, with the following exceptions. It does not:

- Copy any files from the patch directory to the installation area
- Archive any object modules into the product libraries
- Re-link any executables
- Generate any Forms, reports, PL/SQL libraries, or menu files
- Run any SQL or exec commands (commands that change the database)
- Update the patch history file
- Update patch information in the database

To run the adpatch in test mode, we need to give the following command.

```
(appmgr01)  -bash $ adpatch apply=no
```

Pre-install Mode

The pre-install mode is normally used to update AD utilities before an upgrade to Oracle Applications. This is run from the command prompt by giving the following command:

```
Adpatch preinstall=y
```

In this mode also the `adpatch` prompts for all default questions except those related to database driver. This mode should be used only if the readme of the patch advises application of the patch in pre-install mode.

A patch in pre-install mode performs the following actions:

- Checks the versions of the files
- Re-linking of AD and FND executables
- Copying files
- Saving the patch history information in the file applptch.txt

At any time, you can stop the `adpatch` session by typing abort at the `adpatch` prompt. But you can't stop the patching once it has started.

```
(appmgr01) appmgr - -bash $ adpatch

                    Copyright © 2002 Oracle Corporation
                      Redwood Shores, California, USA

                      Oracle Applications AutoPatch

                              Version 11.5.0

NOTE: You may not use this utility for custom development
      unless you have written permission from Oracle Corporation.

Your default directory is '/slot01/appmgr/emstestappl'
Is this the correct APPL_TOP [Yes] ?

AutoPatch records your AutoPatch session in a text file you specify.
Enter your AutoPatch log file name or press [Return] to accept the
default file name shown in brackets.

Filename [adpatch.log] : abort
(appmgr01) appmgr - -bash $
```

Fig. 8.14 Aborting Adpatch

MERGING PATCHES

Sometimes many patches have to be applied one after another. It is advisable at such times to merge all the patches into a single consolidated patch and then apply it. This allows us to save a lot of time, and reduces the task duplication overhead of patches. Merging makes patching easier and the time-consuming process of package revision cache is done only once for the entire merged patch bundle, again saving more time. Oracle Application provides a utility called **admrgpch** for merging patches.

The steps to running admrgpch are:

1. In `Patch_top`, create two directories called source and target
2. Download all the patches which need to be merged in the source directory
3. Unzip all the patches
4. Run AD Merge Patch with the parameter '`admrgpch -s source -d destination -merge_name <name for the patch/driver>`'

Where

'`Source`' is the full path name of the source directory where all the patches are downloaded and unzipped

'`Target directory`' refers to the full path name of the directory where the merged patch will be created

'`Merge name`' refers to the merged driver name, viz. `cmerged.drv`

It is always recommended to check the log file of merged patch for any errors after merging. The default log file name is '`admrgpch.log`'. It is located in the directory from which the AD merge patch was run.

Applying Merged Patches

The merged patch can be applied like any normal patch with adpatch utility. A readme file also gets created once a patch is merged. It contains information about how to apply the merged patch. The NLS patches also can be merged into a single patch. AD merge patch doesn't merge patches of different releases, platforms or parallel modes. It supports patches having unified drivers as well as those having copy, database and generate drivers.

ADPATCH COMMAND LINE OPTIONS

There are several command line options available with adpatch that are frequently used by apps dba.

The '`options=`' argument is used to pass generic options to Auto Patch. It takes the form of a comma-separated list. The user can enter one option or a comma-separated list of options, e.g. `options=nocopyportion,nogenerateportion`. Do not include a space after the comma.

Table 8.2 Command Line Options Available with Adpatch

Option	Description
`autoconfig`	Purpose: Tells Auto Patch to run AutoConfig automatically. Default: `autoconfig`. Use `options=noautoconfig` if you are applying a number of patches in sequence and want to run `AutoConfig` only once, after applying the last patch of the sequence. Comments: The more common method is to merge the patches first with AD merge patch.
`checkfile`	Purpose: Tells Auto Patch to either skip running `EXEC`, `SQL`, and `EXECTIER` commands if they are recorded as already run, or to record them as having run after running them. Default: `checkfile`. Use `options=nocheckfile` to turn off the `checkfile` feature. Comments: `checkfile` provides significant performance benefits.
`compiledb`	Purpose: Tells Auto Patch to automatically compile invalid objects in the database after running actions normally found in the database driver. Default: `compiledb` for standard patches. nocompiledb for standard patch translations, documentation patches, and documentation patch translations. Use `options=nocompiledb` to save time when multiple non-merged patches are applied in a maintenance window. Comments: Merging multiple patches and applying a single merged patch is usually a better strategy.
`compilejsp`	Purpose: Tells Auto Patch whether to automatically compile out-of-date JSP files. JSP files are only compiled if the patch contains copy actions for at least one JSP file. Default: `compilejsp` for standard patches. nocompilejsp for standard patch translations, documentation patches, and documentation patch translations. Use `options=nocompilejsp` to save time when multiple non-merged patches are applied in a maintenance window. Comments: Merging multiple patches and applying a single merged patch is usually a better strategy.
`copyportion`	Purpose: Tells Auto Patch whether to run commands normally found in a copy driver. Default: `copyportion`. Use `options=nocopyportion` to tell Auto Patch not to perform copy driver actions. Comments: Useful mostly with unified drivers.

Contd

Table 8.2 Contd

Option	Description
databaseportion	Purpose: Tells Auto Patch whether to run commands normally found in a database driver. Default: `databaseportion`. Use options=nodatabaseportion to tell Auto Patch not to perform database driver actions. Comments: Useful mostly with unified drivers.
generateportion	Purpose: Tells Auto Patch whether to run commands normally found in a generate driver. Default: `generateportion`. Use `options=nogenerateportion` to tell Auto Patch not to perform generate driver actions. Comments: Useful mostly with unified drivers.
hotpatch	Purpose: Tells Auto Patch to apply a patch regardless of whether the Oracle Applications system is in maintenance mode. Auto Patch aborts the patching session if maintenance mode is disabled and the `options=hotpatch` command is not used. Default: `nohotpatch`.
integrity	Purpose: Tells Auto Patch to verify that the version of each file referenced in a copy action matches the version present in the patch. Default: `nointegrity` Comments: Using `options=nointegrity` is safe and avoids some Auto Patch overhead.
parallel	Purpose: Tells Auto Patch whether to run actions that update the database in parallel (like SQL) and actions that generate files in parallel (like genform). Default: `parallel` Comments: We do not recommend changing the default, as Oracle Applications patches are tested on systems using parallel processing.
prereq	Purpose: Tells Auto Patch whether to check that prerequisite patches have been applied prior to running patch driver files that contain actions normally found in the copy driver. Default: `prereq` Comments: We do not recommend changing the default.
validate	Purpose: Tells Auto Patch whether to connect to all registered Oracle Applications schemas at the start of the patch. Default: `novalidate`. Use options=validate to validate password information for all Oracle Applications schemas. Comments: Useful for finding problems with incorrectly registered Oracle Applications schemas or schemas with invalid passwords.

There are few additional `adpatch` options available, described in Table 8.3.

Table 8.3 Additional Adpatch Options

Option	Description
`apply=no`	`Adpatch` only displays which files it will replace and the actions it will take, but doesn't make any changes.
`preinstall=y`	This mode is mainly used during upgrades or when patching `adpatch` itself so that it won't make some of the checks it normally would during start up.
`options=nolink`	Won't link updated executables after applying a patch in `Apps filesystem`.
`options=nogenrpll`	Won't generate .pll-s after applying a patch.
`options=nogenform`	Won't generate Forms after applying a patch.
`options=nogenrep`	Won't generate reports after applying a patch.

PATCH FAILURES

Oracle recommends backing up the entire application system before starting any upgrade. There could be several reasons for patch failure and the apps dba has to troubleshoot to fix the issue.

When a patch fails, the first step is to look at all the patch log files to find out what exactly is the issue. If the patch says that some worker has failed then we need to check the worker log. As discussed earlier, the worker log is available at `$APPL_TOP/admin/$TWO_TASK/log`.

Patch can fail before, during or after the worker processing. The course of action differs depending on which phase the patch fails in.

If a patch is applied in parallel mode, Auto Patch operates with the number of workers specified. When the Auto Patch fails before or after the worker processes, a message appears asking whether you would like to continue the process.

```
An error occurred while .....
Continue as if it were successful [No] :
```

It is better that you review the log files to determine the exact error and then decide whether to continue or exit. If you think the error can be fixed afterwards then continue with the patching. For example, if the patch fails while generating a form then continue; once the patching is over, generate the form manually.

If the worker fails then log in to another terminal, source the environment and check the worker log in the `$APPL_TOP/admin/$TWO_TASK/log` directory for the exact issue. Once the issue is fixed, the patching can be started from the point it had failed earlier using the ad utility `adctrl`. This utility will be discussed in detail in Chapter 9.

RESTARTING AUTO PATCH

You can exit from the Auto Patch session anytime by typing 'abort' at the prompt. The Auto Patch can be restarted as many times as required until the patch is successfully applied. It is restarted using the command:

```
$ adpatch
```

```
(appmgr01) - -bash $ adpatch

                    Copyright (c) 2002 Oracle Corporation
                       Redwood Shores, California, USA

                        Oracle Applications AutoPatch

                               Version 11.5.0

NOTE: You may not use this utility for custom development
        unless you have written permission from Oracle Corporation.

Your default directory is '/slot01/appmg/emstestappl'.
Is this the correct APPL_TOP [Yes] ?

Filename [adpatch.log] :

Backing up restart files, if any......Done.

Your previous AutoPatch session did not run to completion. Do you wish to
continue with your previous AutoPatch session [Yes] ?
```

Fig. 8.15 Resumption of Auto Patch

Once 'Yes' is typed, the patching will start from the point it had failed. If the patching needs to be done afresh, at this stage we then need to type 'No', and the patching will again start from scratch.

ENHANCEMENTS IN PATCHING UTILITIES IN R12

Manual Steps Infrastructure

The Release 12 has introduced some significant enhancements in the patching related stuffs. A major enhancement is the elimination of the manual steps after patching. Earlier a couple of the patches use to have some manual steps in the readme of the patch, which the `APPS DBA` had to perform manually. R12 eliminates all those manual steps and ships a script with all the patch which has manual steps which takes care of performing the manual steps.

The script is known as `admsi.pl` is shipped with the patch which takes care of performing the manual steps. All the information about the manual steps is stored in the patch in an xml file in the `patch/115/manualsteps/ad_run_grants.xml` file. Once the `admsi.pl` script is run it creates a custom readme for that particular patch in an html format.

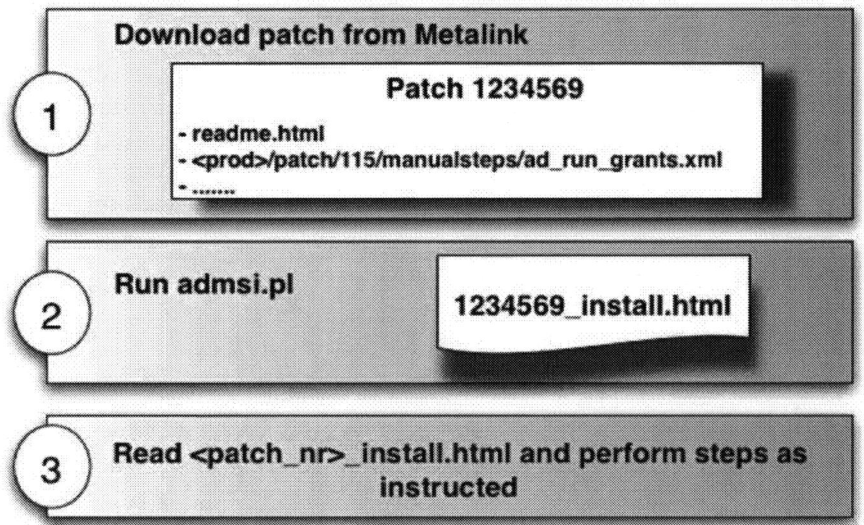

Fig. 8.16 Overview of Manual Steps

The `admsi.pl` script creates a `patch_number.html` that has the details of the steps that needs to be performed.

A sample readme file generated by the `admsi.pl` is shown in Fig. 8.17.

If a patch is merged using the admerge then AD Merge patch make sure that all the manual steps from all the source patches are present in the target patch.

Once the patching is done all the information about the manual steps is updated in the database as well.

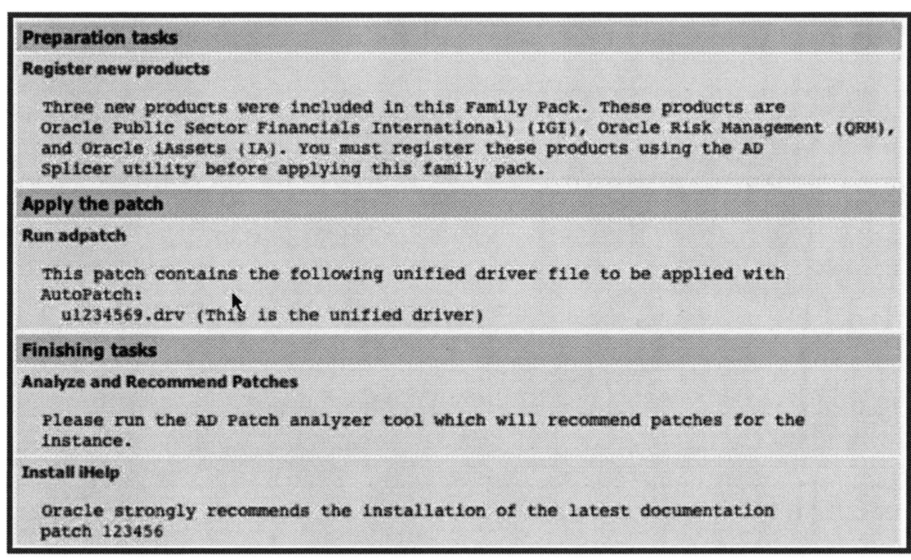

Preparation tasks

Register new products

Three new products were included in this Family Pack. These products are Oracle Public Sector Financials International) (IGI), Oracle Risk Management (QRM), and Oracle iAssets (IA). You must register these products using the AD Splicer utility before applying this family pack.

Apply the patch

Run adpatch

This patch contains the following unified driver file to be applied with AutoPatch:
u1234569.drv (This is the unified driver)

Finishing tasks

Analyze and Recommend Patches

Please run the AD Patch analyzer tool which will recommend patches for the instance.

Install iHelp

Oracle strongly recommends the installation of the latest documentation patch 123456

Fig. 8.17 Sample Readme File Generated by `admsi.pl`

Monitoring Patches in Progress

Release 12 provides enhancements in functionality to monitor all the patches which are currently being applied from the Oracle Application Manager. Normally when the patching takes place the Application system is in maintenance mode and the application tier including the Apache is shut down. This prevents the access to the application system . In order to monitor the patches the Apache needs to be started in the restricted mode using the script `adaprstctl.sh` which is available in the scripts location which we have already discussed earlier.

Before this the `ad_monitor` account needs to be set up . The `ad_monitor` is the account which needs to used for login to the Oracle Application Manager in restricted mode. The `ad_monitor` account needs to be unlocked before one can login to OAM . Do the following for unlocking the `ad_monitor` account.

- Login to the database as `SYSTEM` or `SYSDBA`
- At the `sqlplus` promot issue the following command

```
SQL > alter user ad_monitor account unlock;
```

- The default password for the account `ad_monitor` is lizard. You may want to change the password.

The following are the steps for monitoring the patches through the Oracle Application Manager.

- Shutdown the middletiers
- Enable maintenance mode using `adadmin`
- Start the Apache in the maintenance mode using the following command
  - UNIX

```
$ adaprstctl.sh start
```

  - Windows

```
C:\> adaprstctl.cmd start
```

- Run the Auto Patch session using adpatch
- Launch the Oracle Applications URL

```
host>:<port>/servlets/weboamLocal/oam/oamLogin
```

- Login to the Oracle Applications Manager using the `ad_monitor` account.
- Navigate the following path
- Sitemap >Maintenance>Patching and Utilities>Timing Reports. From the following navigation you will be able to monitor the progress of the patch . The timing reports screen is shown in Fig. 8.18.

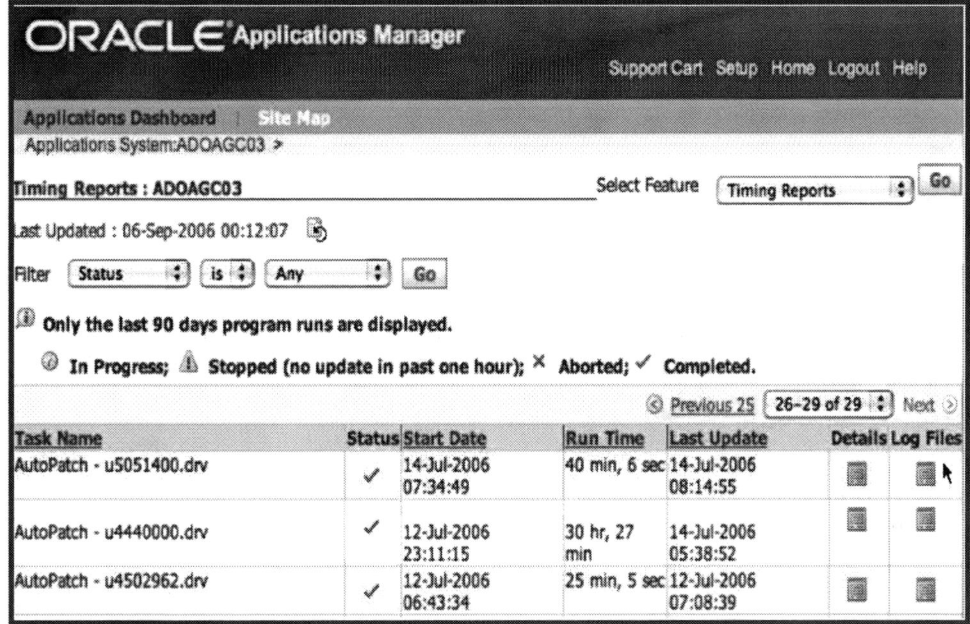

Fig. 8.18 The Timing Reports Screen Showing the Patch Details

You can also monitor the progress of the patching process by reviewing the following files

- AutoPatch messages
  As AutoPatch runs, it displays messages on the screen about the status and progress of the patching process. The message file is in the format patch `number.lgi`

- Patch log files
  AutoPatch creates log files in the current directory. Each log file contains information about completed patching actions. The patch log is normally in the format patch `number.log`

- Relink log files
  All the information about the relink is stored in the `adrelink.log` file which can also be moniroted from the OAM

- Workers Log
  All the information about the various workers can also be checked from the OAM . The workers log are in the format `adwork001.log`, `adwork002.log` and so on.

Figure 8.19 shows the screen shot from where all the logfiles can be monitored.

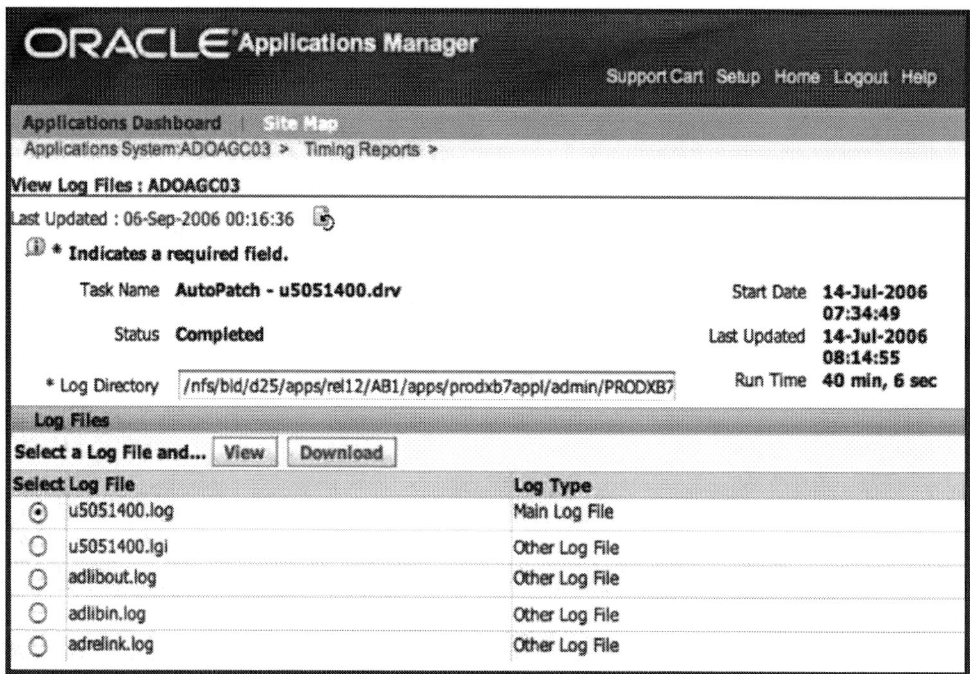

Fig. 8.19 The Various Patch Logfiles

9

AD UTILITIES

Oracle AD utilities are a set of tools that are shipped with Oracle Applications to ensure their proper functioning. They are used to upgrade, patch, install and maintain Oracle Applications. There are around 15 AD utilities, and an Application DBA is supposed to know all of them. We will examine each of the AD utilities.

AUTO PATCH

This is a utility for applying patches to Oracle Applications. It has already been discussed in detail in Chapter 8.

ADADMIN

AD administration is used to perform a number of administrative tasks to maintain the Oracle Application and ensure it runs smoothly.

It performs two types of works—one is performed at the database level and the other is performed at the file system level. The user is required to provide all the inputs at the adadmin prompt, which normally involves choosing from the various options in the adadmin menu. This doesn't mean that adadmin can't be used non-interactively. Some tasks can be run non-interactively also. This is really useful for scheduling routine tasks that require little or no intervention.

The steps to starting the adadmin are:

1. Login to the `APPL_TOP` as the owner of the application file system
2. Run the environment file (`APPLSYS.env`) for sourcing the environment
3. Ensure that there is sufficient disk space
4. Check whether the application system is sourced properly

Adadmin can be invoked simply by typing 'adadmin' from the prompt. Once started, the `adadmin` asks a number of questions, just like `adpatch`. It then asks for the log file name (which is `adadmin.log` by default), the system and `apps` password. Once given these inputs, we are taken to the main menu of `adadmin`. If the previous session of the `adadmin` was not successful, then at the beginning you are asked whether you want to continue from the previous session or start a fresh one.

```
(appmgr01) appmgr - -bash $ adadmin

                 Copyright (c) 2002 Oracle Corporation
                    Redwood Shores, California, USA

                 Oracle Applications AD Administration

                           Version 11.5.0

NOTE: You may not use this utility for custom development
      unless you have written permission from Oracle Corporation.

Your default directory is '/slot01/appmgr/emstestappl'.
Is this the correct APPL_TOP [Yes] ?

AD Administration records your AD Administration session in a text file
you specify.  Enter your AD Administration log file name or press
[Return] to accept the default file name shown in brackets.

Filename [adadmin.log] : adadmin.log

You can be notified by email if a failure occurs.
Do you wish to activate this feature [No] ?

Please enter the batchsize [1000] :


Please enter the name of the Oracle Applications System that this
APPL_TOP belongs to.

The Applications System name must be unique across all Oracle
Applications Systems at your site, must be from 1 to 30 characters long,
may only contain alphanumeric and underscore characters, and must start
with a letter.

Sample Applications System names are: "prod", "test", "demo" and
"Development_2".

Applications System Name [emstest] : emstest *

Do you currently have Oracle Applications forms files installed
in this APPL_TOP [YES] ? YES *


Do you currently have concurrent program files installed
in this APPL_TOP [YES] ? YES *
```

Contd

Fig. 9.1 Contd

```
You are about to use or modify Oracle Applications product tables
in your ORACLE database 'emstest' using ORACLE executables in '/slot01/
appmgr/emstestora/8.0.6'.

Is this the correct database [Yes] ?

AD Administration needs the password for your 'SYSTEM' ORACLE schema in
order to determine your installation configuration.

Enter the password for your 'SYSTEM' ORACLE schema: manager


The ORACLE username specified below for Application Object Library
uniquely identifies your existing product group: APPLSYS

Enter the ORACLE password of Application Object Library []:

AD Administration is verifying your username/password.
```

Fig. 9.1 Unix Session 1: Invoking Adadmin

Once all the answers are given at this prompt, the `adadmin` main menu appears. This is shown in Fig. 9.2.

```
          AD Administration Main Menu
   ____________________________________________

   1.    Generate Applications Files menu

   2.    Maintain Applications Files menu

   3.    Compile/Reload Applications Database Entities menu

   4.    Maintain Applications Database Entities menu

   5.    Change Maintenance Mode

   6.    Exit AD Administration
```

Fig. 9.2 Unix Session 2: Adadmin Main Menu

We can see from Fig. 9.2 that there are six main options displayed in the main menu. The first two deal with maintaining application files system. This means they handle all the issues related to the `APPL_TOP`, viz. re-linking the applications, generating the Forms, regenerating the JAR files, etc. The next two deal with maintaining database objects, viz. compiling and validating the schema, compiling the flexfields, etc. The fifth option changes the maintenance mode, and the sixth one is to exit. We will examine all the options one by one.

Generate Applications Files Menu

If this option is selected, the following options are shown.

```
Enter your choice [6]: 1

        Generate Applications Files
   ______________________________________

   1.    Generate message files

   2.    Generate form files

   3.    Generate report files

   4.    Generate graphics files

   5.    Generate product JAR files

   6.    Return to Main Menu
```

Fig. 9.3 Unix Session 3: Generate Applications Files

Generate message file

This option takes care of generating all the Oracle message files. Oracle Application uses this file to display messages. This task generates message binary files (`extension .msb`) from Oracle Application Library tables.

```
Enter your choice [6]: 1

AD utilities can support a maximum of 999 workers. Your current database
configuration supports a maximum of 241 workers. Oracle recommends that
you use between 8 and 16 workers.

Enter the number of workers [8]: 14

Your current character set is "UTF8".

Do you want to generate Oracle Message files using this character set
[Yes]?

Enter list of products ('all' for all products) [all]:

The current set of installed languages is: US AR KO

Please select languages for generating Oracle Message files.
You may select all of the above languages, or just a subset.
```

Contd

Fig. 9.4 Contd

```
Enter list of languages ('all' for all of the above) [all]: US

You selected the following languages: US

Is this the correct set of languages [Yes]?
```

Fig. 9.4 Unix Session 4: Adadmin Prompts

From this figure, we can see that once the option for generating message files is selected, it asks a number of questions. It first asks for the number of workers for parallel processing, then it displays the current character set and ask if you want to generate the message files using this character set or not. It then asks for the list of products for which the message files need to be generated. This is really helpful if we want to generate message files for a particular product, say for `fnd` or `ad`. Then it displays all the installed languages and asks which of these need message files to be generated. Once all the inputs are given, the `FND_INSTALL_PROCESS` table is created and workers are assigned for generation of message files.

```
Creating FND_PROCESS_INSTALL table

Done reading jobs from FND_INSTALL_PROCESSES table ...

Telling workers to read 'todo' restart file.
Done.

Starting phase 1000 (admin): Administration


There are now 124 jobs remaining (current phase=admin):
    0 running, 124 ready to run and 0 waiting.


 Assigned: file US.msb on worker  1 for product fnd username APPLSYS.

 Assigned: file US.msb on worker  2 for product alr username APPLSYS.
 Assigned: file US.msb on worker  3 for product ax  username AX.
 Assigned: file US.msb on worker  4 for product ak  username AK.
 Assigned: file US.msb on worker  5 for product xla username XLA.
 Assigned: file US.msb on worker  6 for product gl  username GL.
 Assigned: file US.msb on worker  7 for product rg  username RG.
 Assigned: file US.msb on worker  8 for product ap  username AP.
 Assigned: file US.msb on worker  9 for product fa  username FA.
```

Fig. 9.5 Unix Session 5: Creating FND INSTALL Process Table

Once all the message files are generated, it returns to the menu of adadmin.

```
        Generate Applications Files
    ______________________________________

    1.     Generate message files
    2.     Generate form files
    3.     Generate report files
    4.     Generate graphics files
    5.     Generate product JAR files
    6.     Return to Main Menu
```

Fig. 9.6 Unix Session 6: Generate Applications Files

Generate Forms files

This options takes care of generating the Forms files (`extension .fmx`) from binary Forms definition files (`extension .fmb`). These files are normally located at `$AU_TOP`, and the executables files are stored under each product's directory. Oracle Applications uses the binary form files to display data entry forms. Like the previous option, this also asks a couple of questions before generating the Forms. This task should be performed whenever you have issues with a Form or set of Forms.

```
Enter your choice [6]: 2

AD utilities can support a maximum of 999 workers. Your current database
configuration supports a maximum of 240 workers. Oracle recommends that
you use between 8 and 16 workers.

Enter the number of workers [8]: 14

Your current character set is "UTF8".

Do you want to generate Oracle Forms objects
using this character set [Yes]?

Do you want to regenerate Oracle Forms PL/SQL library files [Yes]?

Do you want to regenerate Oracle Forms menu files [Yes]?

Do you want to regenerate Oracle Forms executable files [Yes]?

Enter list of products ('all' for all products) [all]:
```

Contd

Fig. 9.7 Contd

```
Generate specific forms objects for each selected product [No]?

The current set of installed languages is: US AR KO

Please select languages for generating Oracle Forms files.
You may select all of the above languages, or just a subset.

Enter list of languages ('all' for all of the above) [all]:

You selected the following languages: US AR KO

Is this the correct set of languages [Yes]?
```

Fig. 9.7 Unix Session 7: Generating Forms Files

As can be seen from this figure, it first asks for the number of the workers to be used for parallel processing. It then displays the current character set of the database and asks if you want to generate the Forms using the same character set. It subsequently asks if you want to regenerate the Oracle Forms PL/SQL library files, menu files and Forms executable files. Finally, it asks for which products and languages you want to generate the Forms. Once all the inputs are given, it creates the `FND_INSTALL_TABLE` and assigns the workers. Once the Forms are generated, it returns to the previous menu.

Generate report files

This option generates the binary Oracle reports file (`extension .rdf`). The set of questions asked here is identical to that asked for Forms generation. The details of the adadmin prompts at the time of generation of report file are given in Fig. 9.8.

```
AD utilities can support a maximum of 999 workers. Your current database
configuration supports a maximum of 237 workers.Oracle recommends that
you use between 8 and 16 workers.

Enter the number of workers [8]: 14

Your current character set is "UTF8".

Do you want to generate Oracle Reports objects
using this character set [Yes]?

Do you want to regenerate Oracle Reports PL/SQL library files [Yes]?

Do you want to regenerate Oracle Reports executable files [Yes]?

Enter list of products ('all' for all products) [all]:

Generate specific reports objects for each selected product [No]?
```

Contd

Fig. 9.8 Contd

```
The current set of installed languages is: US AR KO

Please select languages for generating Oracle Reports files.
You may select all of the above languages, or just a subset.

Enter list of languages ('all' for all of the above) [all]:

You selected the following languages: US AR KO

Is this the correct set of languages [Yes]?
```

Fig. 9.8 Unix Session 8: Generating Reports

Once the products are selected, it displays the list of the products which need report generation.

```
Selecting reports for Public Sector Financials International...

Selecting reports for Internet Procurement Enterprise Connector...

Selecting reports for Install Base...

Selecting reports for Enterprise Install Base...

Selecting reports for E Records...

Selecting reports for Sales...

Selecting reports for Transportation Planning...
```

Fig. 9.9 Unix Session 9: Displaying List of Products

Once the products are displayed, it assigns the workers and starts the generation of reports.

```
Creating FND_INSTALL_PROCESSES table...

Telling workers to read 'todo' restart file.Done.

Starting phase 1000 (admin): Generate Report Libraries

Starting worker processes.

Worker process 1 started.

Worker process 2 started.

Worker process 3 started.
```

Contd

Fig. 9.7 Contd

```
There are now 8547 jobs remaining (current phase=admin):
    0 running, 15 ready to run and 8532 waiting.
 Assigned: file FABAL.pll  on worker  1 for product au  username APPLSYS.
 Assigned: file FARSV.pll  on worker  2 for product au  username APPLSYS.
 Assigned: file fadolif.pll  on worker  3 for product au  username
APPLSYS.
 Assigned: file HRREPORT.pll on worker  4 for product au  username
APPLSYS.
```

Fig. 9.10 Unix Session 10: Assigning Workers

Once the reports are generated, it returns to the previous menu.

Generate graphics files

This generates the Oracle Graphics files (`extension .ogd`) from the graphics definition files. Like the previous option, this also prompts for some questions while generating the graphics files. There are some questions which are specific to graphic generation.

```
Enter your choice [6]: 4

Your current character set is "UTF8".

Do you want to generate Oracle Graphics objects using this character set
[Yes]?

Do you want to regenerate Oracle Graphics PL/SQL library files [Yes]?

Do you want to regenerate Oracle Graphics executable files [Yes]?

Enter list of products ('all' for all products) [all]:

Generate specific graphics objects for each selected product [No]?

The current set of installed languages is: US AR KO

Please select languages for generating Oracle Graphics files.
You may select all of the above languages, or just a subset.

Enter list of languages ('all' for all of the above) [all]:
```

Fig. 9.11 Unix Session 11: Prompts of Generating Graphics File

Once all the answers are given, it starts generating the graphics. This is done as shown in Fig. 9.12.

```
Generating graphics "CNCMTRD.ogd" with command:
/slot01/appmgr/emstestappl/ad/11.5.0/bin/adogdgen.sh    userid=APPS/*****
source=/slot01/appmgr/emstestappl/cn/11.5.0/graphs/CNCMTRD.ogd dest=/
slot01/appmgr/emstestappl/admin/emstest/out/tmp.ogd
stype=OGD dtype=OGD resdir=/slot01/appmgr/emstestappl/ad/11.5.0/graphs
logdir=/slot01/appmgr/emstestappl/admin/emstest/out
tmpdir=/slot01/appmgr/emstestappl/admin/emstest/out logfile=adogdtmp.txt
g60batm exit status is 0
Copying output file back to source file:
  Output: /slot01/appmgr/emstestappl/admin/emstest/out/tmp.ogd
  Source: /slot01/appmgr/emstestappl/cn/11.5.0/graphs/CNCMTRD.ogd
```

Fig. 9.12 Unix Session 12: Generation of Graphic Files

Generate product JAR (Java Archive) files

This is the last option in this menu. It takes care of generating JAR files whenever you upgrade the Developer6i technology stack. It signs the JAR files and regenerates the product JAR files in JAVA_TOP and copies them to APPL_TOP. It also generates other Java related files under APPL_TOP and JAVA_TOP. It also recreates Java libraries under APPL_TOP and JAVA_TOP. Generation of JAR files prompts for only one question, given in Fig. 9.13.

```
Enter your choice [6]: 5
Do you wish to force regeneration of all jar files? [No]?
```

Fig. 9.13 Unix Session 13: JAR Force Regeneration Prompt

If you choose 'No', it generates only JAR (Java archive) files that are missing or out-of-date. If you choose 'Yes', all JAR files are generated. Once this choice is made, adadmin starts generation of JAR files.

```
Generating any out of date or missing jar files.
  Signing product JAR files in  JAVA_TOP -
  /slot01/appmgr/emstestcomn/java
   using entity Development and certificate 1.
Successfully created javaVersionFile.
  Generating product JAR files in JAVA_TOP -
  /slot01/appmgr/emstestcomn/java with command:
adjava -mx512m -nojit oracle..ad.jri.adjmx
@/slot01/appmgr/emstestappl/admin/emstest/out/genjars.cmd
```

Fig. 9.14 Unix Session 14: Actual Generation of JAR

Maintain Applications Files

The next option in the `adadmin` main menu is Maintain Applications Files. This option takes care of the maintenance tasks required to keep your application files up-to-date. As seen in Fig. 9.15, this menu has a couple of sub-menus, which will be discussed further.

```
            Maintain Applications Files

1.    Relink Applications programs

2.    Create Applications environment file

3.    Copy files to destination

4.    Convert character set

5.    Maintain snapshot information

6.    Check for missing files

7.    Return to main menu

Enter your choice [7]:
```

Fig. 9.15 Unix Session 15: Maintain Application Files Menu

Relink Application programs

This option relinks Oracle Applications programs with the Oracle server libraries, so that they function with the Oracle database. It prompts for a couple of questions as shown in Fig. 9.16.

```
Do you wish to proceed with the relink [Yes]?

Enter the name of your Oracle Applications environment file below.
File name [emstest.env]:

Reading product executable information...

Reading product executable information...

Enter list of products to link ('all' for all products) [all]:

Generate specific executables for each selected product [No]?

AD Administration can relink your Oracle Applications programs with debug
information.  Oracle recommends that you do not relink your programs
with debug information unless asked to do so by Oracle Support Services.

Relink with debug information [No]?
```

Fig. 9.16 Unix Session 16: Relink Prompts

This option should be used only when asked for specifically by Oracle support.

Create Applications environment file

This option creates an environment file that defines your system configuration. It prompts for Oracle Applications environment name.

```
Enter your choice [7]: 2

Enter the name of your Oracle Applications environment file below. File
name [emstest.env]:
```

Fig. 9.17 Unix Session 17: Prompting Environment File

Copy files to destinations

This option copies files from each product area to central locations, where they can be easily referenced by non-Applications programs. It prompts for only one question.

```
Enter your choice [7]: 3

Do you wish to copy UNCONDITIONALLY when a target file exists [No]?
```

Fig. 9.18 Unix Session 18: Prompting Copying Details

Using force copy option to overwrite existing files is not recommended unless it is instructed by Oracle support services. The file types copied to the respective destinations are given here.

- JAVA files are copied to `$JAVA_TOP`
- HTML files are copied to `$OAH_TOP`
- Media files are copied to `$OAM_TOP`

The directories for these variables are specified in the file '`adovars.env`', which is present in `$APPL_TOP/admin` directory.

Convert character set

This option at first prepares the files in `APPL_TOP` for conversion to another character set and then converts the same. Once this option is chosen, it prompts for a small sub-menu containing three options.

```
Enter your choice [7]: 4

 1. Scan the APPLTOP for exceptions
 2. Scan a CUSTOM directory for exceptions
 3. Convert character set
 4. Return to previous menu
```

Fig. 9.19 Unix Session 19: Convert Character Set Details

The first option scans the APPL_TOP for exceptions. It prompts for a couple of questions which is shown in Fig. 9.20.

```
Enter your choice [1]: 1

UTF8 is the character set in NLS_LANG

Please enter the source character set [UTF8]:

Please enter the target character set: US7ASCII

You are about to check your APPL_TOP for lossy conversion of files when
converting from UTF8 to US7ASCII.

Run the check [Y]?

AD Administration will create a manifest file under
"/slot01/appmgr/emstestappl/admin/emstest/out"
with the list of convertible files.
If a file with that name already exists, it will be overwritten.

You should use this manifest file later for character set conversion.

Please enter a name for the manifest file [admanifest.lst]:
```

Fig. 9.20 Unix Session 20: Details of Scan

It scans the APPL_TOP and creates three files in $APPL_TOP/admin/$TWO_TASK/out directory. These are the files it creates:

- admanifest_excp.lst—lists files that will not be converted because of lossy conversion
- admanifest.lst—lists files that can be converted
- admanifest_lossy.lst—lists files with lossy conversions, including line by line detail

Review the files listed in admanifest_excp.lst. Fix the files that report lossy conversion before you convert the character set. Repeat this task until there are no entries in admanifest_excp.lst.

The second option scans a custom directory for exceptions. It also collects the same information as the previous one, but it scans only for the custom applications directories, rather than the whole APPL_TOP. This option prompts for the full path of the custom directory where the scan has to be done.

```
Enter your choice [1]: 2

UTF8 is the character set in NLS_LANG

Please enter the source character set [UTF8]:
```

Contd

Fig. 9.21 Contd

```
Please enter the target character set US7ASCII

Please enter the FULLPATH of the custom directory:
```

Fig. 9.21 Unix Session 21: Prompting Full Path of Custom Directory

The third option actually converts the character set. Run this task only if `admanifest_excp.lst` has no entries. It prompts you as to whether or not you have created the manifest file and for the name of the manifest file (`admanifest.lst`) created when you ran the scan option(s).

```
Enter your choice [1]: 3

You need a manifest file to run this option.
The manifest file has the list of convertible files.
You can create a manifest file by using the Scan options.
The scan options will create the manifest file under your
"/slot01/appmgr/emstestappl/admin/emstest/out"
directory.

Have you created the manifest file [Y]?

Please enter the name of the manifest file [admanifest.lst]:

Converting from character set 'UTF8' to character set 'US7ASCII'.
```

Fig. 9.22 Unix Session 22: Prompting Manifest File

Maintain snapshot information

Basically there are two types of snapshots—`APPL_TOP` and global snapshots. An `APPL_TOP` snapshot lists patches and versions of files in the `APPL_TOP`. A global snapshot lists patches and latest versions of files in the entire Applications system (i.e. across all `APPL_TOP`'s). Both `APPL_TOP` and global snapshots may be either current view or named view snapshots. A current view snapshot is created once and updated when appropriate to maintain a consistent view. A named view snapshot is a copy of the current view snapshot at a particular time (not necessarily the latest) and it is not updated.

A complete current view snapshot is required to operate automatic prerequisite patch checking. During the installation, Rapid Install created a current snapshot as a baseline. Each time you run Auto Patch, it automatically creates a new (updated) snapshot, so that the information is current.

```
      Maintain Snapshot Information
    ______________________________________

   1.     List snapshots

   2.     Update current view snapshot

   3.     Create named snapshot

   4.     Export snapshot to file

   5.     Import snapshot from file

   6.     Delete named snapshot(s)

   7.     Return to Maintain Applications Files menu
```

Fig. 9.23 Unix Session 23: Maintain Snapshot Information

From this menu, you can:

- List snapshots stored in the system
- Update current view snapshots (APPL_TOP and global)
- Create named snapshots (select a current view snapshot to copy and name)
- Export snapshot to file (select one to export to a text file)
- Import snapshot from (a text) file
- Delete named snapshot (select a snapshot for deletion)

Check for missing files

This option verifies that all the files needed to run Oracle Applications for the present configuration are there in the APPL_TOP, and checks if any are missing.

```
Enter your choice [7]: 6

AD Administration records the output from
"verifying that all required files exist" in a file in the
/slot01/appmgr/emstestappl/admin/emstest/out directory.
If the file already exists, it will be overwritten.

Please enter the filename you wish to use or press [RETURN] to accept
the default filename [admvrf.lst] :

Verifying all files needed by all installed applications...
  Reading driver files...
```

Fig. 9.24 Unix Session 24: Checking Missing Files

The information about the missing file is written in a file called `admvrf.lst` which is created at `$APPL_TOP/admin$TWO_TASK/`out directory.

Compile/Reload Applications Database Entities

This is the third option in the adadmin main menu. This option has a couple of sub-menus.

```
        Compile/Reload Applications Database Entities
    ____________________________________________________

    1.     Compile  APPS schema

    2.     Compile menu information

    3.     Compile flex fields

    4.     Reload JAR files to database

    5.     Return to Main Menu

Enter your choice [5]:
```

Fig. 9.25 Unix Session 25: Compile/Reload Applications Database Entities Menu

Compile APPS schema

This option takes care of compiling the invalid objects (program units of PL/SQL and Java) in the `APPS` schema. Invalid objects in other schemas such as Sys and System are not necessarily compiled. This task can be performed with multiple workers for parallel processing, and is normally performed after patch application. It prompts for two questions, as shown in Fig. 9.26.

```
Enter your choice [5]: 1

AD utilities can support a maximum of 999 workers. Your
current database configuration supports a maximum of 234 workers.
Oracle recommends that you use between 8 and 16 workers.

Enter the number of workers [8]: 14

Run Invoker Rights processing in incremental mode [No]?

Creating FND_INSTALL_PROCESSES table...
```

Fig. 9.26 Unix Session 26: Compile Apps Schema Prompts

Typing 'Yes' at this prompt causes invoker rights processing to run only on the packages that have changed since it was last run.

Compile menu information

This option compiles the menu data structure. It needs to be done if compile security concurrent requests submitted from the menus form fail or if you have uploaded menu entries to the FND_MENU_ENTRIES table. This prompts if you want to force compilation of all menus. Choosing 'no' results in the compilation of only those menus that are changed, whereas choosing 'yes' compiles all.

```
Enter your choice [5]: 2

Do you wish to force compilation of all menus? [No]?

Generating any out of date menus.

sqlplus -s APPS/***** @/slot01/appmgr/emstestappl/fnd/11.5.0/sql/
fndscmpi.sql
```

Fig. 9.27 Unix Session 27: Compiling Menu Prompt

Compile flex fields

This task compiles flex field data structures in Applications Object Library (AOL) tables. This needs to be done if the patch application changes the setup of the flex fields.

```
Enter your choice [5]: 3

Deleting existing compiled flexfield information.

Compiling all application flexfields.

/slot01/appmgr/emstestappl/fnd/11.5.0/bin/fdfcmp APPS/***** 0 Y
```

Fig. 9.28 Unix Session 28: Compile Flex Fields

Reload JAR files to database

This task reloads all the Oracle Application JAR files to the database. Choose this option if the patch readme says so or if all Oracle Applications Java classes are removed from your database. It loads the JAR files to database in the following way.

```
  Temporarily resetting CLASSPATH to:
  "/slot01/appmgr/emstestappl/ad/11.5.0/java/adjri.zip:/local/java/
jdk1.4.2_04/lib/rt.jar:/local/java/jdk1.4.2_04/lib/i18n.jar:/local/java/
```

Contd

Fig. 9.29 Contd

```
jdk1.4.2_04/lib/tools.jar:/slot01/appmgr/emstestcomn/java/appsborg.zip:/
slot01/appmgr/emstestcomn/java/apps.zip:/slot01/appmgr/emstestora/8.0.6/
forms60/java:/slot01/appmgr/emstestcomn/java"

  Calling /local/java/jdk1.4.2_04/bin/java ...

Loading contents of archive file into database with arguments

-ms128m -mx256m -nojit oracle.aurora.server.tools.loadjava.LoadJavaMain -
f -thin -user "APPS/*****@AP6189RT.us.oracle.com:1521:emstest" /slot01/
appmgr/emstestappl/admin/emstest/out/a000ldjva.jar

  Calling /local/java/jdk1.4.2_04/bin/java ...
```

Fig. 9.29 Unix Session 29: Reloading JAR Files

Maintain Applications Database Entities

The fourth option in the adadmin main menu is Maintain Applications Database Entities menu. This maintains the integrity of the database entities. It has five sub-menus shown in Fig. 9.30.

```
          Maintain Applications Database Entities
      ____________________________________________________

1.  Validate  APPSschema

2.  Re-create grants and synonyms for  APPSschema

3.  Maintain multi-lingual tables

4.  Check DUAL table

5.  Maintain Multiple Reporting Currencies schema

6.  Return to Main Menu

Enter your choice [6]:
```

Fig. 9.30 Unix Session 30: Maintain Applications Database Entity

Validate APPS schema

Validating `APPS` schema means verifying the integrity of the `APPS` schema. It checks whether the `APPS` schema has proper roles and privileges or not. It determines both the problems specific to `APPS` schema as well as the problems not specific to the schema that need to be fixed. This task produces a report named `<APPS schema name>.lst`, which is located at `$APPL_TOP/admin/$TWO_TASK/`out.

Validation of the `APPS` schema is in turn taken care of by an SQL script '`advrfapp.sql`' which is located in `$AD_TOP/admin/sql`. The same script can also be run from the SQL prompt.

```
Enter your choice [6]: 1

Validating APPS schema "APPS"...

sqlplus -s SYSTEM/*****

@/slot01/appmgr/emstestappl/ad/11.5.0/admin/sql/advrfapp.sql APPS APPLSYS

Done validating APPS schema "APPS".

Validation output is recorded in
/slot01/appmgr/emstestappl/admin/emstest/out/APPS.lst

Successful completion of the SQL scripts above does not
guarantee that any or all of your APPS schemas are correct.

You must review the output from this validation step and fix
all indicated problems.  You should then re-run this step to
ensure that all problems have been corrected.

Review the messages above, then press [Return] to continue.
```

Fig. 9.31 Unix Session 31: Validating APPS Schema

Re-create grants and synonyms for APPS schema

This task takes care of recreating grants and synonyms for APPLSYSPUB, for APPS schema and for recreating grants on some packages from System to APPS. This task is usually done when validation of APPS schema reports an issue with missing grants and synonyms.

```
Enter your choice [6]: 2

AD utilities can support a maximum of 999 workers. Your
current database configuration supports a maximum of 241 workers.
Oracle recommends that you use between 8 and 16 workers.

Enter the number of workers [8]: 14

 Recreating grants and synonyms needed by all installed applications...

sqlplus -s APPS/*****

@/slot01/appmgr/emstestappl/fnd/11.5.0/admin/sql/afpub.sql &un_apps
&pw_apps &un_pub &pw_pub
```

Fig. 9.32 Unix Session 32: Recreating Grants and Synonyms

Each product's data objects are created in its own schema (such as the GL schema) but the user accesses all data objects through the APPS schema. Therefore the APPS schema must have the appropriate grants and synonyms for those objects.

This task run two SQL files:

1. $FND_TOP/admin/sql/afpub.sql to set up grants and synonyms for the Applications Public Schema (APPLSYSPUB by default)
2. $AD_TOP/admin/sql/adgs.pls for every Oracle Applications base product schema

Grants and synonyms could be missing due to several reasons, like if there is incomplete database migration, if some custom developments have been done, if patches have failed or if new components have been installed in the database.

Maintain multi-lingual tables

This task needs to be done after you add a new language. It calls PL/SQL routines that maintain multi-lingual tables for Oracle Applications by adding any missing, un-translated rows. This task runs the <PROD>NLINS.sql script for every product and prompts for the number of workers.

```
Enter your choice [6]: 3

AD utilities can support a maximum of 999 workers. Your
current database configuration supports a maximum of 241 workers.
Oracle recommends that you use between 8 and 16 workers.

Enter the number of workers [8]:

Creating FND_INSTALL_PROCESSES table...
```

Fig. 9.33 Unix Session 33: Maintain Multi-lingual Tables Prompting Workers

Check dual table

The dual table is created automatically by Oracle along with the data dictionary. It is there in the schema of Sys. This table has one column named Dummy of type Varchar2 and contains one row with a value of 'X'. This task ensures that the dual table exists and has exactly one row.

```
Enter your choice [6]: 4
SYS.DUAL has the correct number of rows.
Granting privileges on SYS.DUAL ...
```

Fig. 9.34 Unix Session 34: Checking Dual Table

```
SQL> desc dual
 Name                                  Null?    Type
 ----------------------------------------------------
 DUMMY                                           VARCHAR2(1)

SQL> select * from dual;

D
-
X

SQL>
```

Fig. 9.35 Oracle Session 1: Describing Dual Table

Maintain multiple reporting currencies schema

This task varies depending on whether or not you have currently enabled Multiple Reporting Currencies (MRC). If you have MRC, the option looks like the screen in Fig. 9.36. If MRC functionality is not implemented in your database, the option will read 'Convert to Multiple Reporting Currencies schema'.

The Multiple Reporting Currencies feature allows you to:

- Report and maintain accounting records at the transaction level in more than one functional currency
- Define one or more reporting sets of books in addition to your primary set of books
- Store data for the reporting set of books in the standard product schemas
- Access each reporting set of books data through the adjunct `APPS_MRC` schema

Convert to multi-org

This option appears as a menu choice only if multi-org is not installed in your database. Using this, you can convert to multi-org architecture.

- Can reflect different sets of books, business groups, legal entities, operating units, and inventory organizations.
- Stores data for all operating units in a base product table with `_ALL` suffix for example, (`SO_HEADERS_ALL`).
- It is a virtual partitioning solution that secures information by operating unit by using views within the schema.
- Uses the values in the `ORG_ID` column to guarantee that only the information appropriate for the chosen organization is returned to the user.

Converting to multi-org prompts for the number of parallel workers, confirms that you want to run this task, then creates scripts to disable and re-enable triggers in the `APPS` schema. It then disables all triggers in the `APPS` schema, converts seed data and transaction data to multiple organizations in parallel and finally re-enables all previously disabled triggers in the `APPS` schema.

CHANGING MAINTENANCE MODE

This is the last option in the main menu of the adadmin. It has been introduced with the 11.5.10 release, in which the Oracle Applications system is made accessible only for patching activities. This provides optimal performance for Auto Patch sessions, and minimizes downtime needed. Maintenance mode is only needed for Auto Patch sessions. Other AD utilities do not require maintenance mode to be enabled.

Change maintenance mode has two sub-menus, enable and disable maintenance mode. The former enables the maintenance and the user's access is restricted, while the latter disables the maintenance mode and full access is given to the users.

```
              Change Maintenance Mode
    ------------------------------------------

Maintenance Mode is currently: Disabled.

Maintenance mode should normally be enabled when patching
Oracle Applications and disabled when users are logged on
to the system.  See the Oracle Applications Maintenance
Utilities manual for more information about maintenance mode.

Please select an option:
   1.    Enable Maintenance Mode
   2.    Disable Maintenance Mode
   3.    Return to Main Menu

Enter your choice [3]: 1
sqlplus -s &un_apps/*****
@/slot01/appmgr/emstestappl/ad/11.5.0/patch/115/sql/adsetmmd.sql ENABLE

Successfully enabled Maintenance Mode.
Review the messages above, then press [Return] to continue.
Enter your choice [3]: 2
sqlplus -s &un_apps/*****
@/slot01/appmgr/emstestappl/ad/11.5.0/patch/115/sql/adsetmmd.sql DISABLE
```

Fig. 9.36 Unix Session 36: Changing Maintenance Mode

Running AD Administration in Non-interactive Mode

Running adadmin in non-interactive mode allows one to schedule the running of routine tasks. To run adadmin in non-interactive mode, you must first create a defaults file. You can then run the adadmin in non-interactive mode using this file.

Creating an AD administration defaults file

To create a defaults file, specify defaultsfile= <filename> at the AD Administration command line. The file must be located under APPL_TOP/admin/<SID>. For example, type:

```
$ adadmin defaultsfile=APPL_TOP/admin/emstest /default.txt
```

In order to choose which task the defaults file will run, you add menu_option= <menu choice> to the utility start command. This overrides any menu-specific key stroke information stored in the defaults file initially, and allows you to use the defaults file for any of the AD Administration menu items.

The menu options to run adadmin in non-interactive mode is given in Table 9.1.

Table 9.1 Different Menu Options of Adadmin

Menu options	Details
GEN_MESSAGES	Generate message files
GEN_FORMS	Generate Form files
GEN_GRAPHICS	Generate graphics files
GEN_REPORTS	Generate reports files
GEN_JARS	Generate product JAR files
RELINK	Relink Applications programs
CREATE_ENV	Create Applications environment file
COPY_FILES	Copy files to destinations
CONVERT_CHARSET	Convert character set
SCAN_APPLTOP	Scan the APPL_TOP for exceptions
SCAM_CUSTOM_DIR	Scan a CUSTOM directory for exceptions
LIST_SNAPSHOT	List snapshots
UPDATE_CURRENT_VIEW	Update current view snapshot
CREATE_SNAPSHOT	Create named snapshot
EXPORT_SNAPSHOT	Export snapshot to file

Contd

Table 9.1 Contd

Menu options	Details
IMPORT_SNAPSHOT	Import snapshot from file
DELETE_SNAPSHOT	Delete named snapshot
CHECK_FILES	Check for missing files
CMP_INVALID	Compile APPS schema
CMP_MENU	Compile menu information
CMP_FLEXFIELDS	Compile flex field data in AOL tables
RELOAD_JARS	Reload JAR files to database
VALIDATE_APPS	Validate APPS schema
CREATE_GRANTS	Recreate grants and synonyms for APPS schema
MAINTAIN_MLS	Maintain multi-lingual tables
CHECK_DUAL	Check dual table
MAINTAIN_MRC	Maintain Multiple Reporting Currencies schema
CONVERT_MCURR	Convert to Multiple Reporting Currencies
CONVERT_MULTI_ORG	Convert to multi-org
ENABLE_MAINT_MODE	Enable maintenance mode
DISABLE_MAINT_MODE	Disable maintenance mode

ADCTRL

`Adctrl` is the utility that displays the status of the workers, and is used to restart or play with the workers. This option is normally used if some worker fails or hangs using `adpatch` or `adadmin`. The steps to use `adctrl` are:

1. Open a new terminal
2. Log in as the owner of the application file system and source the environment
3. Start the AD controller with adctrl command
4. This will prompt you to:
   - Confirm the `APPL_TOP` name
   - Specify a log file (by default, this is `adctrl.log`)
   - Give user name of `AOL APPLSYS`
   - Provide password of `AOL APPS`
5. This will take you to the main menu of the AD control

```
                 AD Controller Menu
    ---------------------------------------------

    1.     Show worker status

    2.     Tell worker to restart a failed job

    3.     Tell worker to quit

    4.     Tell manager that a worker failed its job

    5.     Tell manager that a worker acknowledges quit

    6.     Restart a worker on the current machine

    7.     Exit
Enter your choice [1]:
```

Fig. 9.37 Unix Session 37: Adctrl Main Menu

Show worker status

This is the first option in the menu of `adctrl`. This option shows which file has been assigned to each worker, whether the workers are running, have failed or completed.

```
Enter your choice [1]: 1

        Control
  Worker   Code     Context          Filename        Status
  ------   ------   -------------    ------------    ------------
       1   Run      Generic R115     FABAL.pll       Completed
       2   Run      Generic R115     FARSV.pll       Completed
       3   Run      Generic R115     fadolif.pll     Completed
       4   Run      Generic R115     REPORT.pll      Completed
       5   Run      Generic R115     INVISMMX.pll    Running
       6   Run      Generic R115     inv.pll         Running
       7   Run      Generic R115     cst.pll         Completed
       8   Run      Generic R115     BISRPRT.pll     Completed
       9   Run      Generic R115     GGMREP.pll      Completed
      10   Run      Generic R115     JTFBCHBN.pll    Completed

Review the messages above, then press [Return] to continue.
```

Fig. 9.38 Unix Session 38: Showing Worker Status

The different status possibilities of workers are given in Table 9.2

Table 9.2 Different Status of Workers

Status	Details
Assigned	The manager assigned a job to the worker
Completed	The worker completed the job
Failed	The worker has encountered a problem and has failed
Fixed, Restarted	You fixed the problem and the failed job has restarted
Restarted	The worker has restarted a job
Running	The worker is running a job
Wait	The worker is idle

If a worker fails, check the log file `adwordXXX.log` under the `$APPL_TOP/admin/$TWO_TASK/log` directory to find out the exact error.

Tell worker to restart a failed job

This option restarts the failed worker. For example, suppose an SQL file fails due to a space issue in the database while applying a patch. You log in to some other terminal and add some space in the data files. Then you can use this option to restart the failed SQL file. Select the second option from the adctrl main menu. This will prompt for the worker number that needs to be restarted. Give the number of the failed worker and then select the option 'Show worker status' to find out whether it has actually been started or not.

Many times, while applying a patch the worker fails and cannot be restarted. If this happens, the only option is to stop the patching, fix the issue and then restart. In this scenario, the third, fourth and fifth options should be used in the following order:

- Option 3: Tell worker to quit
- Option 4: Tell manager that a worker failed its job
- Option 5: Tell manager that a worker acknowledges quit
- Option 7: Quit

Restart a worker on the current machine

This option also restarts the worker on the machine from which the patching is occurring.

Running AD Controller Non-interactively

Like `adpatch` and `adadmin`, `adctrl` can also be run in non-interactive manner by creating a defaults file. The defaults file used for `adadmin` can also be used for running `adctrl` in non-interactive manner.

But the menu option of running the adctrl using defaults file needs to be added. If you want to create a new defaults file, it can be created in the same way as for adadmin.

The menu options for the defaults file for adctrl are listed in Table 9.3.

Table 9.3 Menu Options for Adctrl

Menu options	Details
ACKNOWLEDGE_QUIT	Tell manager that a worker acknowledges quit
INFORM_FAILURE	Tell manager that a worker failed its job
RESTART_JOB	Tell worker to restart a failed job
SHOW_STATUS	Show worker status
SHUTDOWN_WORKER	Tell worker to quit
START_WORKER	Restart a worker on the current machine

Given below is the example of running adcrtl in the non-interactive mode.

```
adctrl interactive=n \
defaultsfile=$APPL_TOP/admin/emstest/ctrldefs.txt \
menu_option=SHOW_STATUS \
logfile=adctrl.log
```

ADSPLICE

Oracle often releases new products after the base release of the Application. These products are known as off cycle products. AD splicer is the utility that incorporates off cycle products into Oracle Applications so that they are recognized by AD utilities as a valid Oracle Application product. Then you can use adpatch to install the product's component file system and database object. AD splicer cannot be used to add custom non-Oracle products to your APPL_TOP.

AD Splicer Control Files

AD splicer requires two types of control files.

Product definition file: There are two product definition files per sliced product—(prod_name) prod.txt, which contains language-independent information for the product and (prod_name) terr.txt, which contains language-dependent information for the product.

Since both the files define the product and the associated language, they must not be edited. The AD splicer control files must copied to the APPL_TOP/admin directory.

Product configuration file: The product configuration newprods.txt file contains all the parameters required to splice a new product. The following is the entry for the newprods.txt:

```
product=alr
base_product_top=*APPL_TOP*
oracle_schema=alr
sizing_factor=100
main_tspace=*Product_Name*D
index_tspace=*Product_Name*X
temp_tspace=*Temporary_Tablespace*
default_tspace=*Product_Name*D
```

These entries are explained here.

- `Product`: This is the new product to be spliced by adsplice. This entry should not be edited.
- `Base_product_top`: This is the base directory, which contains the new product. It is normally the `APPL_TOP`.
- `Oracle_schema`: This identifies the Oracle schema where the database objects for this product are created. This should be the same as product name.
- `Sizing factor`: This is used when creating the tables and index for the product. The default value of 100 means 100%. This is recommended, as it denotes that the objects are created with the defaults size as determined by Oracle.
- `Main_tspace`: The default table space for the product.
- `Index_tspace`: The default index table space for the product.
- `Temp_tspace`: This is the table space for the Oracle schema's temporary segments, for example, `TEMP`.
- `Default_tspace`: Specifies the default table space where this product's objects are created.

Once the configuration files are modified, the `adsplice` can be run from the command line as '`adsplice`'. This will prompt for the file names as shown in Fig. 9.39. Once spicing is completed, the new product will be installed.

```
(appmgr01) admin - -bash $ adsplice

                    Copyright (c) 2002 Oracle Corporation
                       Redwood Shores, California, USA
                                 AD Splicer

                               Version 11.5.0

NOTE: You may not use this utility for custom development
        unless you have written permission from Oracle Corporation.

Your default directory is '/slot01/appmgr/emstestappl'.
Is this the correct APPL_TOP [Yes]?
```

Contd

Fig. 9.39 Contd

```
AD Splicer records your AD Splicer session in a text file
you specify.  Enter your AD Splicer log file name or press [Return] to
accept the default file name shown in brackets.

Filename [adsplice.log]:

You are about to install or upgrade Oracle Applications product tables in
your ORACLE database 'emstest'
using ORACLE executables in '/slot01/appmgr/emstestora/8.0.6'.

Is this the correct database [Yes]?

AD Splicer needs the password for your 'SYSTEM' ORACLE schema
in order to determine your installation configuration.

Enter the password for your 'SYSTEM' ORACLE schema: manager

The ORACLE username specified below for Application Object Library
uniquely identifies your existing product group: APPLSYS

Enter the ORACLE password of Application Object Library [APPS]:

AD Splicer is verifying your username/password.

Please enter the directory where your AD Splicer control file is located.

The default directory is [/SLOTS/slot01/appmgr/emstestappl/admin]:

Please enter the name of your AD Splicer control file [newprods.txt]:

Processing file /SLOTS/slot01/appmgr/emstestappl/admin/newprods.txt...
  Loading information for product 'lr'...

Connecting to SYSTEM......Connected successfully.
  Loading information for product 'ec'...

Successfully read file /SLOTS/slot01/appmgr/emstestappl/admin/
newprods.txt.

Adding new languages into FND_LANGUAGES...

Connecting to APPS......Connected successfully.

Saving module actions...done.

Saving product actions...done
```

Fig. 9.39 Unix Session 39: Adsplice

AD RELINK (ADRELINK.SH)

Ad relink is the executable used to relink AD executables with Oracle product libraries contained in the Oracle Applications technology stack, `Oracle_Home`. All product executables can be linked using the 'Relink Application executables' menu on the 'Adadmin Maintain Application files' sub-menu. The only exception is an AD executable that has to be manually relinked using `Ad` relink. Normally, any programs that need to be updated after a patch are automatically relinked by Auto Patch.

Running the AD Relink

- Log in to the environment as the owner of the application file system
- Source the environment and ensure that it is pointing to the correct `APPL_TOP`
- Relink the executables with the following command:

```
$ adrelink.sh force={y | n } ad " executable name "
```

For example, to relink `adpatch`, the command line argument will be as shown in Fig. 9.40.

```
(appmgr01) appmgr - -bash $ adrelink.sh force=y " ad adpatch"

Start of adrelink session

Date/time is  Wed Jun 22 10:07:27 PDT 2005

Log file is  /slot01/appmgr/emstestappl/admin/log/adrelink.log

Command line arguments are    "force=y" "ad adpatch"


Operating System Information (output of 'uname -a'):

Linux ap6189rt 2.4.21-20.Elhugemem #1 SMP Wed Aug 18 20:32:11 EDT 2004
i686 i686 i386 GNU/Linux


Backup Mode is "file"

Removing extra variables from the environment...
  adrelink will save the following variables (if set - Generic: "PATH
ORACLE_HOME TMPDIR TZ APPL_TOP APPLFENV PLATFORM LD_LIBRARY_PATH COBDIR
LIBPATH NLS_LANG JAVA_TOP

PERL5LIB"    - Shell-Specific: "PS1 PS2 PS3 PS4 IFS MAILCHECK _ LOGNAME
A__z"
  Beginning pass 1.
   Processing 354 environment variables...

Creating prefix makefiles ...
Done creating prefix makefiles
```

Contd

Fig. 9.40 Contd

```
Starting  link of product ''ad' on Wed Jun 22 10:07:48 PDT 2005
Current product is  ad
Current product _TOP is  $AD_TOP
Current prodarea is  /slot01/appmgr/emstestappl/ad/11.5.0

Backing up or removing executables...

adrelink is exiting with status 0

End of adrelink session
Date/time is  Wed Jun 22 10:07:54 PDT 2005
**********************************************************

Line-wrapping log file for readability ...
Done line-wrapping log file.

Original copy is
/slot01/appmgr/emstestappl/admin/log/adrelink.lsv
New copy is /slot01/appmgr/emstestappl/admin/log/adrelink.log
```

Fig. 9.40 Unix Session 40: Adrelink

The option '`force=y`' will relink the executables regardless of the status of the libraries or the object files. '`Force=n`' will relink only if the libraries or object files are more recent that the current executable program.

The adrelink log file is created in `$APPL_TOP/admin/log` and the name of the log file is `adrelink.log`. Once the relinking is complete, this file should be checked for any errors.

FILE CHARACTER SET CONVERSION (ADNCNV)

This utility is used to convert the character set of Oracle Application files. Though usually the character of the files is automatically converted either by Rapid Install or Auto Patch, in some cases you might need this utility. With it, you can change the character set of the following files:

- ODF files
- Loader files
- Driver files
- SQL files
- Header files
- HTML files
- PL/SQL scripts

The conversion of the character set is very simple, with just four parameters necessary.

```
(appmgr01) bin - -bash $ adncnv
Usage: adncnv <source file> <source char set> <dest file> <dest char set>
(appmgr01) bin - -bash $
```

Fig. 9.41 Unix Session 41: Adncnv

- `Source file`—refers to the full path name of the source file whose character set needs to be changed
- `Source Char set`—refers to the present character set of the source file
- `Dest File`—refers to the full path name of the of the converted file
- `Dest Char set`—refers to the new character set of the converted file

ODF COMPARISON (ADODFCOMP)

ODF refers to Object Description file. Each Oracle Application product is made up of one or more building blocks. For example, journal entry is a building block of Oracle General Ledger. There is an object description file (ODF) describing the tables, views, indexes, sequences and privilege sets for that particular building block.

The ODF comparison utility compares an Object Description File with the database objects in an Oracle account. It detects any differences in database structure and runs SQL statements to remove the differences so that the objects in the account will match the descriptions in the ODF file. This utility is used to compare the data model of a customer's data to a standard set of data model files from the current Oracle Application release. It can optionally modify the database to match the standard data model.

```
(appmgr01) bin - -bash $ adodfcmp

                    Copyright (c) 2002 Oracle Corporation
                      Redwood Shores, California, USA

              ODF (Object Description File) Comparison Utility

                              Version 11.5.0

NOTE: You may not use this utility for custom development
      unless you have written permission from Oracle Corporation.

Usage: adodfcmp keyword=value [,keyword=value,...]

Valid Keywords:
userid         – ORACLE username/password to be compared with ODF file
mode           – Type of objects to compare
odffile        – File name of ODF file to use
touser         – Userid to grant to [or list of APPS schemas]
```

Contd

Fig. 9.42 Contd

```
priv_schema      – ORACLE username/password with DBA privileges
logfile          – File name of log file
 (Default adodfcmp.log)
changedb         – Automatically change the database?
 (Default No)
listmissing      – Report missing objects?
 (Default Yes)
listmatch        – Report matching objects?
 (Default Yes)
listextra        – Report extra objects?
 (Default No)
sizingfactor     – Sizing factor to apply
 (Default 100)
tspace           – Tablespace to store tables
indextspace      – Tablespace to store indexes
log_index        – Create indexes in LOGGING mode
 (Default Yes)
parindxthres     – Parallel index creation threshold [num blks]
alternext        – Alter next extent [No, Yes, Force]
 (Default No)
batchsize        – How many rows to update at a time
 (Default 1000)
oldviews         – Replace, rename, or drop existing views
 (Default replace)
defer            – List of indexes to process later [if any]
rel106mode       – Run in 10.6.0 compatible mode
 (Default No)
parfile          – Filename of a parameter file [if any]
 (Default NONE)

You can specify command-line parameters either by position or by
keywords.
(appmgr01) bin - -bash $
```

Fig. 9.42 Unix Session 42: Adodfcmp Prompt

- `Userid`—refers to the Oracle user name/password for the base schema. Base schema is that schema where the product table and index are located.
- `Mode`—refers to the type of objects in ODF to compare against the database.
- `Odffile`—the name of the ODF file to compare against the database.
- `Touser`—the Oracle user name and password of the Oracle Applications product to grant to.
- `priv_schema`—Oracle schema that has DBA privileges, along with its password. It is normally the APPS schema.
- `Logfile`—the file in which the comparison results are written. The log file resides in the directory from which you start the `adodfcmp` utility. The default name of the log file is `adodfcmp.log`.
- `Changedb`—the default value of this option is set to no. If set to yes, the database objects will be changed to match the definitions in ODF.
- `Listmissing`—this is set to yes by default. If this is set to no, the utility will ignore missing objects.
- `Listmatch`—this is also set to yes by default. Specify `listmatch=no` to prevent the utility from reporting objects that match their descriptions.
- `Listextra`—this is set to no by default. So by default it will not report extra objects. If you want to report extra objects then set this parameter to yes.
- `Sizingfactor`—sets the sizing factor at which the utility creates missing objects. This is by default 100.
- `Tspace`—sets the table space for tables created by the utility.
- `Indextspace`—sets the table space for indexes created by the utility.
- `log_index`—this creates indexes in `LOGGING` mode.
- `Parindxthres`—refers to Parallel Index Creation Threshold in a number of blocks.

Example of adodfcmp.:

```
    adodfcmp odffile=gllk.ODF userid=GL/GL touser=/ priv_schema=system/manager
tspace=GL_TABLE indextspace=GL_INDEX grants=Yes parfile=cmppf.dat listextra=No
```

10

CLONING

Cloning is the process of creating an identical copy of the Oracle Application System. It is one of the most frequent tasks of an APPS DBA. Oracle provides a couple of methods for cloning an Application system, the most popular being the adclone and rapid clone. You can also clone an Application system using the Oracle Application Manager (this will be discussed in further detail in Chapter 11). You can even clone a single node Application to a multi-node Application system and vice versa; it is also possible to make a clone of a cloned Application system.

Cloning of Application system is required for the following reasons:

- Creating a test copy of your production system before upgrading
- For testing patches
- Periodically refreshing a test system from your production system in order to keep the test system up-to-date
- Creating a development copy of your environment
- Moving an existing system to a different machine

ADCLONE

Adclone is an Oracle-provided utility to clone Application systems for release 11.5.1–11.5.5 for systems which are not autoconfig enabled. Cloning with adclone involves four simple steps:

- Running Rapid Install
- Copying the source database
- Copying the source Application file system
- Updating the configuration information

The first step is to download and apply patch #2115451 in pre-install mode in all the nodes of the APPL_TOP of the source environment. This patch contains the latest adclone utility. Oracle recommends changing of the passwords of APPS, APPLSYS and APPLSYSPUB to their defaults before starting the clone.

The passwords of the above schema can be changed by using the FNDCPASS utility. Its syntax is:

```
FNDCPASS logon 0 Y system/password mode username new_password
```

For example,

```
FNDCPASS apps/apps 0 Y system/manager SYSTEM APPLSYS WELCOME
FNDCPASS apps/apps 0 Y system/manager ORACLE GL      GL1
FNDCPASS apps/apps 0 Y system/manager USER   VISION  WELCOME
```

Running Rapid Install

Rapid Install needs to be run for cloning an Application system using adclone. Use the Rapid Install you originally used to create the source Application system, regardless of the current version being used. This means that if you originally installed 11.5.1 and later on upgraded to 11.5.2, then run the Rapid Install of 11.5.1 in the target environment. Select the option 'Install Oracle Applications' and choose 'Install a fresh database'. When prompted, enter the target database name and create a new configuration file to be used during the cloning.

Before starting the cloning, make sure that the following options of the source Application system matches with that of the target one.

1. The database type, e.g. if the source database is a vision, then the target system must be a vision.
2. Server node and configuration— say if you have three node installations in the source, then the target should have three nodes with the same configurations.
3. The platform should be the same for the source as well as the target. It is not possible to clone an instance having source APPL_TOP on Unix and target APPL_TOP on Windows.
4. The base language should be the same as the source; if you want to install an additional language in the target you can always do that at a later stage.
5. The default territory should be same for both source and the target.
6. The APPL_TOP character set should be same for both source and target.

Make sure your source environment is running properly without any issues before cloning. If you face any environment issue with the source environment, it is advisable to resolve the issues first, otherwise you will get the same issues with the target environments also.

Changing file ownership

If the base version of your source environment is 11.5.1, then you need to change the ownership of the COMMON_TOP to the Application file system owner (applmgr). To do this you first need to shut down all the middle tiers. This is done by using the scripts available at $COMMON_TOP/admin/scripts. Once the middle tiers are stopped, change the file permission as Oracle user.

```
$  cd     $COMMON_TOP
$  chown -R (applmgr username) ./util/apache
$  cd admin/scripts <applmgr username> adaprctl.sh adcmctrl.sh
   admctrl.sh adfmsctrl.sh adfroctl.sh adrepctrl.sh adalnctrl.sh
```

Applying patch 2115451

Download and apply the patch in pre-install mode to all the `$APPL_TOPs` of the target Application system. This patch contains the `adclone` utility.

Before starting the `adclone` utility, ensure that you have `perl` in your path. In the 11.5.1 release, it is available at `$COMMON_TOP/Apache/perl/bin/perl`. If this is not there in the path, then add it.

```
$ echo $PATH
$PATH=<Apache directory>/perl/bin:$PATH
$export PATH
```

You can also check whether the environment is picking the correct path for perl using the command:

```
$which perl
```

This will show the path from where the environment is picking the `perl`. Once the `perl` is there in the path, you are ready to run the `adclone` utility.

Running Adclone

Run the `adclone` in pre-clone mode from a temporary directory using the following command:

```
perl <ad_top>/bin/adclone.pl -mode=preclone \
-env_name=<SID> \
-node_name=<hostname> \
-config_file=<config file> \
-ad_top=<ad_top>
```

The arguments used to run the `adclone` are explained further.

- Mode— refers to the mode of the operation. Choose 'Pre-clone' when beginning the clone process and 'Post-clone' when at the end of the clone process.
- `Env_name`— refers to the name of the environment or the SID.
- `Node_name`—the host name of target system excluding the domain.
- `Config_file`— the full path name of the config file created by the Rapid Install (its default name is `config.txt`).
- `Ad_top`— the full path name of the `AD_TOP` directory.

Running `adclone` in the pre-install mode does the following.

- It shuts down any running services on the current node (this needs to be done before starting the `adclone` utility as a standard practice).
- It saves all the configuration files from the `APPL_TOP` and the `COMMON_TOP` to the `COMMON_TOP/admin/`clone directory.
- It deletes `$APPL_TOP, JAVA_TOP` and the `OA_HTML` directory.

Upgrading the database (conditional)

If you have upgraded the source database to a higher version than that shipped with the Rapid Install then you must upgrade the database of the target Application system to bring it at par. If this is not done, the target database may not start properly because of different versions in the data file headers and the Oracle home. This may result in ORA errors.

Removing the data files

Shut down the target database created by running the Rapid Install. Once this is done, you can delete all the data files, log files and control files, as they will be cloned with the source database.

Shut Down the Source Database

Take a trace backup of the control file, as it will be helpful in creating the target database's control file. This can be done using the command, `alter database backup control file to trace`. Once the trace backup has been taken, shut down the database normally.

Copy the data files

Copy all the data files and the log file to the target location of the data files. Verify the '`init.ora`' file of the target database and check that all entries are correct. Check the location of the control files and the rollback segments.

Create the control file

Make a list of all the data and log files that are copied to the target Application system and create the control file. The 'create control file' script created earlier in the source database before shut down can be used to create the new control file script. Just copy the trace control file script from the source database and change all the entries to reflect the correct path and database name. Create the control file at the 'no mount' phase.

```
SOL> startup nomount
SQL>@create_control.sql
Control file created.
```

Starting the database

Once the control file is created you can start the database:

```
SQL> Alter database open resetlogs
Database opened
```

You can then add some space in the temp file and check if all the rollback segments are online.

Creating DBID for RMAN (optional)

If you have RMAN (Oracle Recovery Manager) then you need to reset the database identifier. RMAN necessitates that each database should have a unique ID; so we need to change the ID of this instance as it is the same as that of the source instance.

The database ID is stored in the file header of the control file, data files and log files. It therefore has to be reset in all these locations. Shut down the database normally to accomplish this.

```
SQL> shutdown immediate;
```

Start the instance till the mount stage. Do not open the database.

```
SQL> startup mount
```

Create a new DBID by executing the following command as a SYS user.

```
SQL> exec sys.dbms_backup_restore.zerodbid(fno => 0);
```

Since the database name is changed at the time of control file creation, the Global database also needs to be renamed. This can be done using the command:

```
SQL> alter database rename global_name to <desired_name>
```

Start the database by issuing the command:

```
SQL> alter database open;
```

Once the database is opened, start the database listener and check if you can connect to the database through a remote desktop. If both these actions occur, it means you are done with the database part.

Copying the APPL_TOP

Copy the entire APPL_TOP, JAVA_TOP and OA_HTML from the source Application system. Before copying, make sure you have shut down all the middle tiers and no services are running. Log in to the machine as the owner of the Application file system, viz. APPLMGR and start copying the files. If the source and target are on different boxes, then NFS mounting (Network File System) of the file system will enable the copying across the two different servers. In case NFS mounting is not possible, you can tar or zip the source directories and then FTP the same to the target server, where they can be restored.

Once the copying of the files is complete, try to connect to the database server from the middle tiers server. If you are able to connect, you are ready to finish the adclone process.

Running Adclone in Post-clone Mode

Log in as the owner of the Application file system (APPLMGR) and run the adclone in the post-clone mode. Don't run any configuration file to source the environment before running the adclone. This is necessary, as the environment configuration is not complete till the adclone is run in this mode. The adclone utility is available at $AD_TOP/bin directory.

Use the following syntax for running the adclone in post-clone mode:

```
perl adclone.pl -mode=postclone -env_name=<SID>
-node_name=<hostname> -config_file=<config file>
-ad_top=<ad_top>
```

It will prompt for the SYSTEM and the APPS passwords, and you must enter the same.

The `adclone` in the post-clone option does the following tasks.

- It updates the various profile options in the `fnd_profile_options` table of the database.
- It changes all the configuration files in the `APPL_TOP` with the proper values of the port and path name for the target environment.
- It changes the configuration files in the `COMMON_TOP` with the proper values of the port and path name for the target environment.
- It creates the DBC file in the `$FND_TOP`/secure location.
- It updates the libraries path.
- It starts up all the middle tier components.

In case of a multi-node installation, all these steps need to be done on all the nodes of the environment.

It is not necessary to copy the `APPL_TOP` once the database copy is done. Since they are separate you can always copy them simultaneously in order to save time.

Post Cloning Tasks

Technology stack patching (conditional)

During cloning we copy only the `APPL_TOP`, `JAVA_TOP` and the `OA_HTML` directories, and not the technology stack created by the Rapid Install. If you have applied any technology stack patch in the source environments, they need to be applied in the target environment as well so that both the environments are in sync. Even if you have changed a parameter in some configuration file of the technology stack, the same file needs to be changed in the target environment. Some examples of technology stack updates are upgrading the Oracle Developer patch set, upgrading the iAS versions, etc.

Sign the Java archive files

Oracle Application 11*i* requires all the JAR (Java Archive) files used in the client tier to be certified using a customer specific digital certificate. You can use the digital certificate that is there in the source Application system by copying the `identitydb.obj` file from there. This file is located in the home directory of the Application user (`$HOME`).

If you want to create a new digital certificate, this can be done by issuing the command '`adjkey -initialize`' as shown in Fig. 10.1.

```
(appmgr01) appmgr - -bash $ adjkey -initialize

                    Copyright (c) 2002 Oracle Corporation
                       Redwood Shores, California, USA

                           AD Java Key Generation

                               Version 11.5.0
```

Contd

Fig. 10.1 Contd

```
NOTE: You may not use this utility for custom development
      unless you have written permission from Oracle Corporation.

Reading product information from file...

Reading language and territory information from file...

Reading language information from applUS.txt ...

Successfully created javaVersionFile.

adjkey will now create a signing entity for you.

Please specify a common name to be assigned to certificate [CUSTOMER]:

Please specify an organization unit to be assigned to certificate
[ORGANIZATION UNIT]: Oracle

Your digital signature has been created successfully and imported into
the keystore database. This signature will now be used to sign
Applications JAR files whenever they are patched.

  IMPORTANT: If you have multiple web servers, you must copy
  files to each of the remaining web servers on your site.
  See the documentation reference for more information.


adjkey is complete.
```

Figure 10.1 Creation of New Digital Certificate

Relinking executables

Once the cloning is done, you must relink all the executables using `adamin` and then choosing the option 'Relink Applications programs'.

Modifying the appsweb.cfg (conditional)

If the `appsweb.cfg` file was modified by any patch in the source Application system, it must be updated in the target system as well. The `appsweb.cfg` exists in two different locations on the Application system— `$OA_HTML/bin` and `$FND_TOP/`resource. Take a backup of the file at both locations and then copy the file from the source to the target Application system. Edit the file and modify the port number, host name and the name of the environment to reflect the values of your target system.

Updating session_cookie_domain (conditional)

If you use Internet Explorer as a default browser, you need to alter the default `session_cookie_domain` from null to some other value and update the self-service parameters directly using SQL*Plus:

```
sqlplus <APPS username>/<APPS password>
SQL> update ICX_PARAMETERS
2> set SESSION_COOKIE_DOMAIN = '<domain>';
```

Sanity check

Now you are done with the cloning. To do a sanity check, first shut down the Application and then start the Application system. If you are able to start all the components of the middle tiers then you are half done. You then need to check various log ins.

- Database PL/SQL Cartridge Connection: With Apache single listener (11.5.2 and later or migrated 11.5.1), go to *http://<apache host>:<apache port>/pls/<dad name>/FND_WEB.PING*.

  With WebDB 2.5 (default configuration for 11.5.1), go to *http://<webdb host>:<webdb port>/<dad name>/FND_WEB.PING*.

  If it is correct, you will see a table with information about your database.
- Apache Jserv: Go to *http://<apache host>:<apache port>/servlets/IsItWorking*. You should see a message that Apache Jserv is working.
- Applications log on and Apache server: Go to the Rapid Install portal page, *http://<apache host>:<apache port>*. Click on Apps Logon Links> personal home page link>. Log in as `SYSADMIN` and click on System Administrator Responsibility. This will launch the Forms. This means the Forms are up and running.

Once the sanity check is complete, your target Application system is ready for use.

AUTOCONFIG

Since `autoconfig` is a prerequisite for Rapid Clone, we will discuss this first. `autoconfig` is a tool which supports automated configuration of an Application system. It collects the information to support the automation into two repositories, called the application context and the database context. When the `autoconfig` runs on the database tier, it takes the information from the database context file to generate all configuration files to be used for the database tier. Similarly, when it runs in the application tier, it takes the information from the application context file to generate all the configuration files.

The `autoconfig` consists of several components that are explained in Table 10.1.

Table 10.1 Components of Autoconfig

Autoconfig components	Details
Application Context	This is an xml repository which is located in the `APPL_TOP/admin` directory for 11*i* and `$INST_TOP/appl/admin` for R12 that contains all information related to the `APPL_TOP`. The name of the file is `<SID>.xml`.
Database Context	This is also an xml repository which is located in the `RDBMS ORACLE_HOME` of the database tier. It contains information specific to the database. The location

Contd

Table 10.1 Contd

Autoconfig components	Details
	and name of the database context file is `<RDBMS ORACLE_HOME>/appsutil/<CONTEXT_NAME>.xml`.
Autoconfig Template	Template files that include name tags, which are replaced with instance-specific information from the relevant context (this process is called instantiation).
Autoconfig Driver	Each product in the `APPL_TOP` has a driver file used by the autoconfig. The driver file lists the autoconfig file templates and their destination locations.
Autoconfig Scripts	These are a set of scripts that provide a simplified interface to the autoconfig APIs.

You must be on `AD.F` or later to migrate to `autoconfig`.

Once `autoconfig` is enabled, you can use it to start and stop the Application system. You must have the following software components in your database and/or the middle tiers to run `autoconfig`.

Table 10.2 Software Components Necessary to Run Autoconfig

Software	Version	Location/Node	Details
Perl	5.004	Application and the database tier	You can use the perl shipped with iAS1022 and 9*i* database. Alternatively, you can download it from www.perl.com. Perl must be there in your path.
Perl	5.6	Only for Tru64 users. Application and database tier	You can download the perl 5.6 from www.perl.com. Perl must be there in the path for running autoconfig.
JRE	1.3.1	Database tier	This is only for Windows users. Install JRE 1.3.1 into the `<RDBMS ORACLE_HOME>/jre/1.3.1` directory.
JDK	1.3.1	Application tier	The metalink note 130091.1 contains detailed information about upgrading and installing the JDK1.3.1.
Zip	2.3	Application and database tier	This can be downloaded from *www.info-zip.org*. Zip must be there in your path for cloning.
Unzip	5.x	Application tier	The same can be downloaded from *www.info-zip.org*. Unzip must be there in your path for cloning.

Migrating to Autoconfig

Since R12 Application system are already autoconfig enabled so this section is irrelevant for R12 based application system.

Requirement for 11*i*

If the application system was created using an 11.5.1 Rapid Install, you must do the following:

- Migrate to Apache 1.3.12s (the details are available at metalink document 161779.1)
- Migrate to xmlparser2 version 11.5.1 using the patch 1379677

Requirements for Windows users

If you use Windows then you need to apply three additional patches:

- 2237858 — Provides support for long file names (8.3)
- 3320237 — Provides specific Windows executables
- 4445697 — Provide the Windows Service Control Wrapper (OaMkSvc)

Applying Autoconfig Patch

For enabling `autoconfig`, you need to apply the patches 4175764 and 4244610 to all application tier nodes in the Application instance. Both patches contain the unified driver. Apply them using the `adpatch` utility.

Migrating to AutoConfig on the Database Tier

Once the `autoconfig` patch has been applied, the following tasks need to be done in the database tier.

Copying files

- In the `APPL_TOP`, log in to the Application tier (`APPL_TOP`) as the owner of the application file system (`APPLMGR`).

  Create the `appsutil.zip` file in `$APPL_TOP/admin/out` by issuing the following command:

  ```
  perl <AD_TOP>/bin/admkappsutil.pl
  ```

- In the database, copy or FTP the `appsutil.zip` file to the `<RDBMS ORACLE_HOME>`.

  ```
  cd <RDBMS ORACLE_HOME>
  unzip -o appsutil.zip
  ```

Generating database context file

Execute the following commands to create your database context file:

- On Unix:

  ```
  cd <RDBMS ORACLE_HOME>
  . <CONTEXT_NAME>.env
  cd <RDBMS ORACLE_HOME>/appsutil/bin
  adbldxml.sh tier=db appsuser=<APPSuser> appspasswd=<APPSpwd>
  ```

- On Windows:

```
cd /d <RDBMS ORACLE_HOME>\appsutil\bin
adbldxml.cmd tier=db appsuser=<APPSuser> appspasswd=<APPSpwd>
```

Generate and apply autoconfig configuration files

This step will convert the database to `autoconfig`. Once this step is completed, the old configuration will no longer be available.

- On Unix:

```
cd <RDBMS ORACLE_HOME>/appsutil/bin
adconfig.sh contextfile=<CONTEXT> appspass=<APPSpwd>
```

- On Windows:

```
cd /d <RDBMS ORACLE_HOME>\appsutil\bin
adconfig.cmd contextfile=<CONTEXT> appspass=<APPSpwd>
```

Migrating to Autoconfig on the Application Tier

Once these steps are completed in the database tier, you are ready to migrate the `autoconfig` on the database tier.

Generating the Oracle Applications context file

This is the xml file available at the `$APPL_TOP/admin/sid_hostname.xml`. If this file doesn't exist, it can be generated in this manner:

- On Unix:

```
cd  <AD_TOP>/bin
adbldxml.sh tier=apps appsuser=<APPSuser> appspasswd=<APPSpwd>
```

- On Windows:

```
cd /d <AD_TOP>\bin
adbldxml.cmd tier=apps appsuser=<APPSuser>appspasswd=<APPSpwd>
```

If you are on 11.5.1 release then you need to change the ownership of the application tier `ORACLE_HOME` from Oracle user to `APPLMGR` user by running the `adownmt.sh` available at `$AD_TOP/bin`.

If you are on 11.5.7 release, then you must patch the Oracle HTTP Server (OHS) component using the OHS patch 2674529. You must update the `oprocmgr_port` value in the Applications context file with a free port number. You can use the port chosen in `<IAS_HOME>/Apache/Apache/conf/httpd.conf file`, under the `<IfModule mod_oprocmgr.c>` section.

Generate and Apply Autoconfig Configuration Files

Before doing this, shut down all the middle tiers and run the following commands.

- On Unix

```
<AD_TOP>/bin/adconfig.sh contextfile=<CONTEXT> appspass=<APPSpwd>
```

- On Windows

```
<AD_TOP>\bin\adconfig.cmd contextfile=<CONTEXT> appspass=<APPSpwd>
```

RAPID CLONE

Rapid Clone is another technique of cloning an application system. To use this, you must have the minimum required software as given in Table 10.3.

Table 10.3 Software Necessary to Use Rapid Clone

Software	Version	Location/Node	Details
Oracle Universal Installer	2.2.0.19	All the nodes	You need to have this version of Oracle Universal Installer. You can download and apply the patch 4017155 on every iAS and RDBMS ORACLE_HOME to be cloned.
Perl	5.005	The source and target database nodes	You can use the perl shipped with iAS1022 and 9*i* database. Alternatively you can download it from www.perl.com. Perl must be there in your path.
JRE	1.1.8	Source database node	If the RDBMS ORACLE_HOME was not installed using Rapid Install, install JRE 1.1.8 into the <RDBMS ORACLE_HOME>/jre/1.1.8 directory.
JRE	1.3.1	Source database node	This is only for Windows users. Install JRE 1.3.1 into the <RDBMS ORACLE_HOME>/jre/1.3.1 directory.
JDK	1.3.1	Target system in the middle tiers	The metalink note 130091.1 contains the detailed information about upgrading and installing the JDK1.3.1.
Zip	2.3	All nodes in the source	This can be downloaded from *www.info-zip.org*. Zip must be there in your path for cloning.

If you are in Windows, you need to apply the patch 2237858 to enable support of long file names.

Apply the Rapid Clone Patch

In order to enable the cloning of your file system using Rapid Clone, you must apply the patch 4175764 to all the middle tiers of the source application system.

Running autoconfig

The `autoconfig` must be implemented in the database tier as well as the application tier before starting the Rapid Clone. We have already discussed the `autoconfig` in the previous section. Follow the instructions there to implement the `autoconfig` in the database and application tiers.

Preparing the Template

The first step in the cloning process is to prepare the template in the source application system. Once the source is copied to the target, Rapid Clone updates these templates to contain the new target system configuration settings. Rapid Clone will not change the source system configuration. Run the following commands to create the template.

- At database tier: log in as Oracle user and run the following:

```
cd <RDBMS ORACLE_HOME>/appsutil/scripts/<CONTEXT_NAME>
perl adpreclone.pl dbTier
```

- At the application tier: log in as `APPLMGR` and run the following:

  For 11*i*

```
cd <COMMON_TOP>/admin/scripts/<CONTEXT_NAME>
-perl adpreclone.pl appsTier
```

  For R12

```
cd $INST_TOP/admin/scripts
perl adpreclone.pl appsTier
```

Copying the Files from the Source to the Target Application System

Copying the APPL_TOP

The next step is to copy the file system of the `APPL_TOP` from the source to the target application system. Make sure that in the target node, the owner of the `APPL_TOP` is `APPLMGR`. The following files need to be copied:

For 11*i*

- `APPL_TOP`
- `OA_HTML`
- `OA_JAVA`
- `OA_JRE_TOP`
- `COMMON_TOP>/util`
- `COMMON_TOP>/clone`
- `COMMON_TOP>/_pages` (when this directory exists)

- 806 ORACLE_HOME
- iAS ORACLE_HOME

For R12

- APPL_TOP
- COMMON_TOP
- AS Tools ORACLE_HOME
- AS Web IAS_ORACLE_HOME

Copying the database

The following steps need to be followed to copy the database.

Shut down the source database

Take a trace backup of the control file, which will be helpful in creating the control file of the target database. This is done using the command, `alter database backup controlfile to trace.` After that, shut down the database normally.

Copy the data files

Copy all the data files and the log file to the target location. Verify the init.ora file of the target database and check all the entries are correct. Check the location of the control files and the rollback segments

Create the control file

Take a list of all the data files and the log files copied to the target application system and create the control file. The 'create control file' script made earlier in the source database before shut down can be used to create a new control file script. Just copy the trace control file script from the source database and change all the entries to reflect the correct path and database name. Create the control file at the 'no mount' phase.

```
SOL> startup nomount
SQL>@create_control.sql
Control file created.
```

Starting the database

Once the control file is created, you can start the database.

```
SQL> Alter database open resetlogs
Database opened
```

Then add some space in the temp file and check if all the rollback segments are online.

Configuring the Target Application System

Configuring the target database

Log in to the database tier as Oracle user and execute the following command:

```
cd <RDBMS ORACLE_HOME>/appsutil/clone/bin
perl adcfgclone.pl dbTier
```

Configuring the target APPL_TOP

Log in to the `APPL_TOP` as the owner of application file system and execute the following command.

```
cd  $COMMON_TOP/clone/bin
perl adcfgclone.pl appsTier
```

Post-cloning Tasks

Updating profile options

Rapid Clone only takes care of the site-level profile options. All other options need to be manually updated.

Updating printer settings

If you are going to use different printers for your target application system, you have to do the printer configuration for the target application system.

Updating session_cookie_domain (conditional)

If you use Internet Explorer as the default browser then you need to alter the default `session_cookie_domain` from null to some other value and update the self-service parameters directly using SQL*Plus:

```
sqlplus <APPS username>/<APPS password>
SQL> update ICX_PARAMETERS
2> set SESSION_COOKIE_DOMAIN = '<domain>';
```

Updating Workflow Configuration

Table Name	Column Name	Column Value Details
WF_NOTIFICATION_ATTRIBUTES	TEXT_VALUE	Starts with *http://<old web host>*: Update to new web host
WF_ITEM_ATTRIBUTE_VALUES	TEXT_VALUE	Starts with "*http://<old web host>*: Update to new web host
WF_SYSTEMS	GUID	Create a new system defined as the new global database name using the Workflow Administrator Web Applications responsibility.
WF_SYSTEMS	NAME	Value needs to be replaced with the database global name.
WF_AGENTS	ADDRESS	Update database link with the new database global name.
FND_FORM_FUNCTIONS	WEB_HOST_NAME	Update with the new web host name.
FND_FORM_FUNCTIONS	WEB_AGENT_NAME	Update to point at the new PL/SQL listener name.
FND_CONCURRENT_REQUESTS	LOGFILE_NAME	Update with the correct path to the log file directory.
FND_CONCURRENT_REQUESTS	OUTFILE_NAME	Update with the new directory path on the target system

Sanity Check

First shut down the Application and then start the application system. If you are able to start all the components of the middle tiers, your sanity check is half done. Once all the middle tiers are up and running, you need to check all the different logins like Apache, Forms and middletier components like concurrent manager.

If the application system is working perfectly fine then you can announce the same to the users.

11

ORACLE APPLICATION MANAGER

Oracle Application Manager (OAM) is used to monitor and manage your application system. OAM is an HTML-based user interface through which you can manage the entire Oracle E-Business Suite. Once a user logs in to OAM, he is directed to the application dashboard from where he can get a quick overview of the application system.

APPLICATION DASHBOARD

The first screen of the application dashboard shows all components of the middle tiers that are up and running.

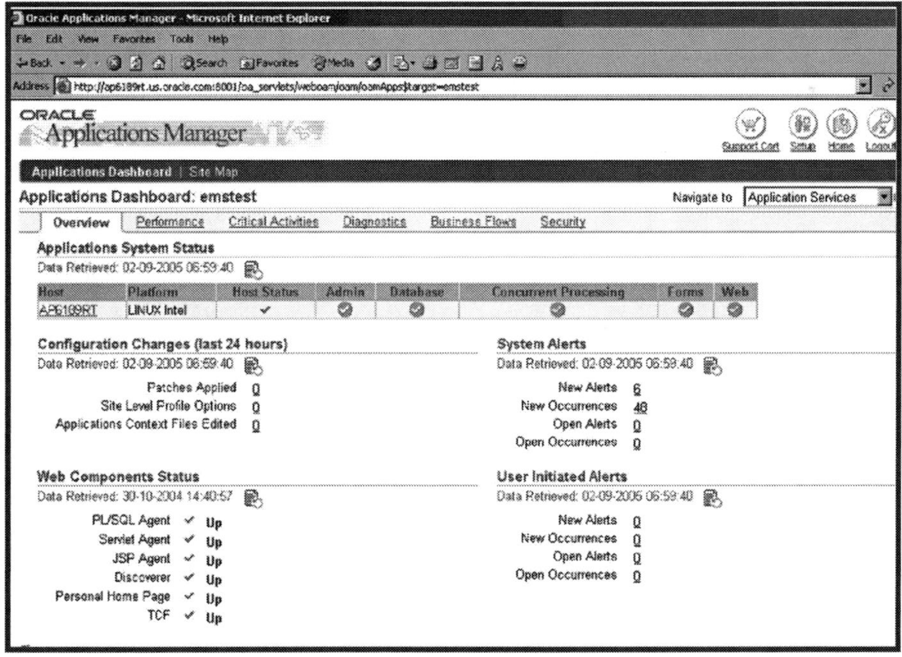

Fig. 11.1 Application Dashboard

From this figure, it can be seen that there some tabs, viz. overview, performance, critical activities, diagnostics, business flows and security. We will discuss each of them.

Overview

This tab gives a lot of information about the application system.

Application system status

This has information about all the components installed in the host machine.

Box 11.1

Host—shows the name of the host. In Fig. 11.1, it is showing AP6189.
Platform—the operating platform of the host (here Linux).
Host Status—this shows if the host is up and running or not.
Admin—shows if the admin tier is installed in this host.
Database—shows the status of the database and the host in which it is installed.
Concurrent Proc—gives the status of the Concurrent Managers and the node from where they have been started.
Forms—this shows the status of the Forms and the server from which they have been started.
Web—this shows the status of the Apache and the server from which it has been started.

In Fig. 11.1, the same host name is given for all the components, as this is a single node installation. If it had been a multi-node installation then it would have shown the host names followed by the server running on that host. If you click on the '✓' on a particular server, it shows the details of that particular server, e.g. if you click on Concurrent Processing, you will know the status of the standard manager and Internal Manager and the host from which the managers are running.

Configuration changes

This shows the changes that have occurred in the application system in the last 24 hours. This is really helpful in diagnosing what went wrong if, all of a sudden, the application system behaves abnormally. This contains the following details.

- Patches Applied—this shows the number of the patches that were applied to the application system in the last 24 hours. If you click on the number of patches, it will show the details.
- Site Level Profile—this shows the number of changes made on the site level profile options in the last one day. Click on the number to see the details of the same.
- Application Context Files Edited—this will show the number of the application context files that were changed in the last 24 hours. Click on the number to see the details.

System alerts

If something goes wrong in the application system, it immediately sends an alert. The alerts are classified into four categories.

- New alerts are those which have not yet been checked by the administrator.
- New occurrences are the additional occurrences of the alerts that are new in status. Say if the same alter comes 5 times then new alert field will be updated with count 1 whereas the new occurrences will be updated with the count 5.
- Open alerts are those which are not yet fixed.
- Open occurrences are additional occurrences in the alerts that are open in status.

Web component setting

This shows the status of web components. It should be either up of warning. OAM shows the status of the following web components:

- PL/SQL agent
- Servlet agent
- JSP agent
- Discoverer
- Personal home page
- TCF

User initiative alert

These are alerts that are not a part of the system alerts. They are created and customized by the users in order to notify them on the occurrence of particular events. These alerts are also of four types:

- New alerts
- New occurrences
- Open alerts
- Open occurrences

Performance

This lists the activities presently going on in the system in detail.

Figure 11.2 shows the session details of the following.

- 'Forms Session' shows the number of Forms sessions currently active.
- 'Database Session' shows the number of active database sessions. Clicking on the number shows the details of the active session. This is shown in Fig. 11.3.

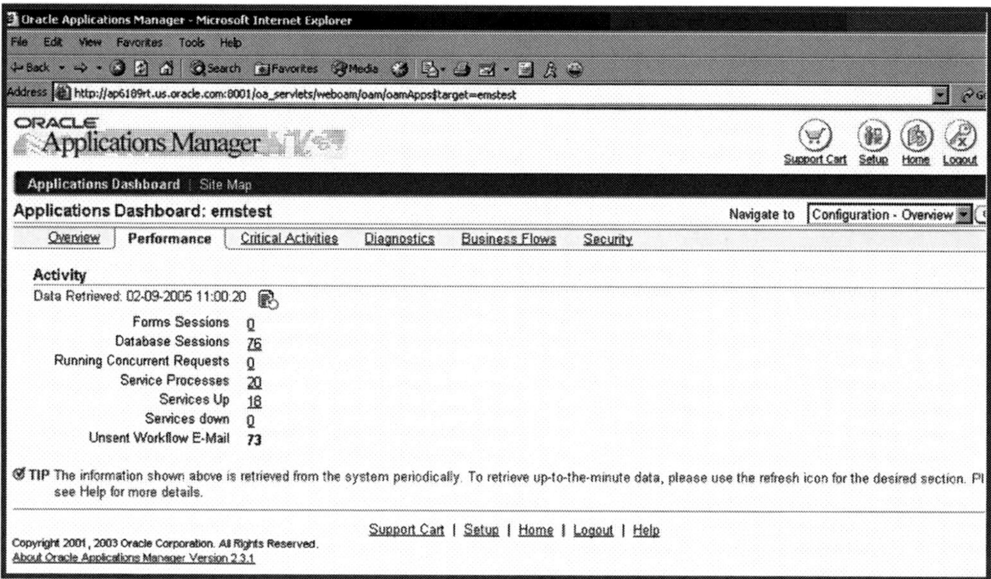

Fig. 11.2 Performance Screen

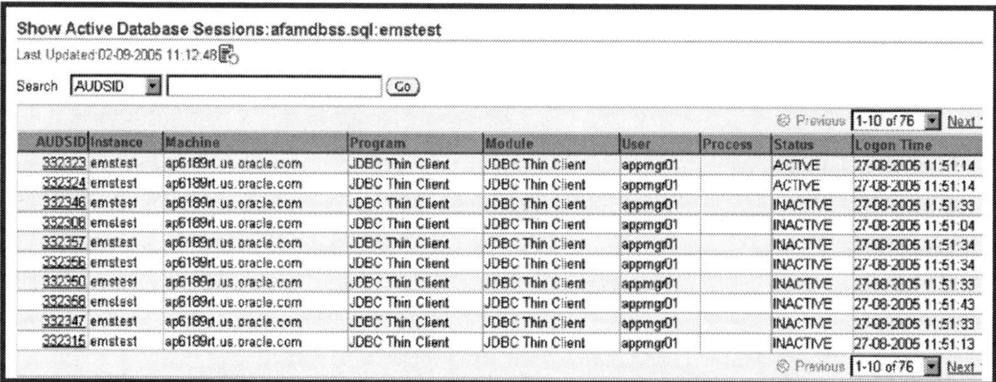

Show Active Database Sessions:afamdbss.sql:emstest

Last Updated 02-09-2005 11:12:48

Search AUDSID Go

Previous 1-10 of 76 Next

AUDSID	Instance	Machine	Program	Module	User	Process	Status	Logon Time
332323	emstest	ap6189rt.us.oracle.com	JDBC Thin Client	JDBC Thin Client	appmgr01		ACTIVE	27-08-2005 11:51:14
332324	emstest	ap6189rt.us.oracle.com	JDBC Thin Client	JDBC Thin Client	appmgr01		ACTIVE	27-08-2005 11:51:14
332346	emstest	ap6189rt.us.oracle.com	JDBC Thin Client	JDBC Thin Client	appmgr01		INACTIVE	27-08-2005 11:51:33
332308	emstest	ap6189rt.us.oracle.com	JDBC Thin Client	JDBC Thin Client	appmgr01		INACTIVE	27-08-2005 11:51:04
332357	emstest	ap6189rt.us.oracle.com	JDBC Thin Client	JDBC Thin Client	appmgr01		INACTIVE	27-08-2005 11:51:34
332356	emstest	ap6189rt.us.oracle.com	JDBC Thin Client	JDBC Thin Client	appmgr01		INACTIVE	27-08-2005 11:51:34
332360	emstest	ap6189rt.us.oracle.com	JDBC Thin Client	JDBC Thin Client	appmgr01		INACTIVE	27-08-2005 11:51:33
332358	emstest	ap6189rt.us.oracle.com	JDBC Thin Client	JDBC Thin Client	appmgr01		INACTIVE	27-08-2005 11:51:43
332347	emstest	ap6189rt.us.oracle.com	JDBC Thin Client	JDBC Thin Client	appmgr01		INACTIVE	27-08-2005 11:51:33
332315	emstest	ap6189rt.us.oracle.com	JDBC Thin Client	JDBC Thin Client	appmgr01		INACTIVE	27-08-2005 11:51:13

Previous 1-10 of 76 Next

Fig. 11.3 Screen of Active Database Sessions

- 'Running Concurrent Request' shows the number of concurrent requests presently running. Click the number to check the details (see Fig. 11.4).
- 'Service Processes' shows all the Concurrent Managers' processes, including all the processes managed by the Internal Manager. It also shows information about the services managed by the GSM if it is configured (see Fig. 11.5).

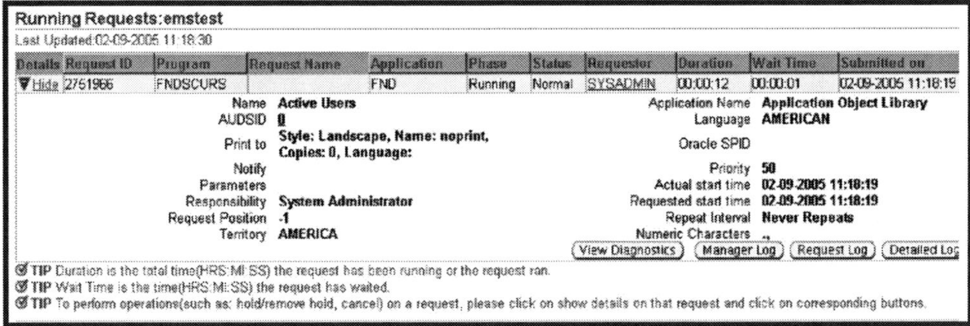

Fig. 11.4 Running Requests Screen

Select Service and ... (View Details) Previous 1-10 of 28 Next

Select	Name	Status	Actual Processes	Target Processes	Message
◉	Internal Concurrent Manager		1	1	
○	Conflict Resolution Manager		1	1	
○	Scheduler/Prerelease Manager		0	0	
○	Request Processing Manager		8	8	
○	Transaction Manager		5	5	
○	Internal Monitor		0	0	
○	Service Manager		1	1	
○	SFM Controller Services		0	0	
○	Forms Listener		0	0	
○	SFM SM Interface Test Services		0	0	

Select Service and ... (View Details) Previous 1-10 of 28 Next

Fig. 11.5 Service Processes Screen (All the Concurrent Managers)

- 'Services Up' gives the number of services that are up and whose target services match the actual services.
- 'Services Down' shows the number of the services which are down and whose target services don't match the actual services.
- 'Invalid Database Objects' displays the number of invalids in the APPS schema.
- 'Unsent Workflow Emails' will show in detail the number of the workflow mails that are yet to be sent.

Critical Activities

This is a list of those concurrent programs that perform maintain activities. Concurrent programs are grouped on the basis of the programs they run. In Fig. 11.6, the focus icon shows the different groups.

There are two main sub-tabs in the critical activities tab, viz. 'Update Frequency' and 'Modify Monitored Program'.

With the first button, you can modify the frequency of the concurrent program according to your requirement. The screen for this action is given in Fig. 11.7. Click the button 'ok' after entering the new frequency.

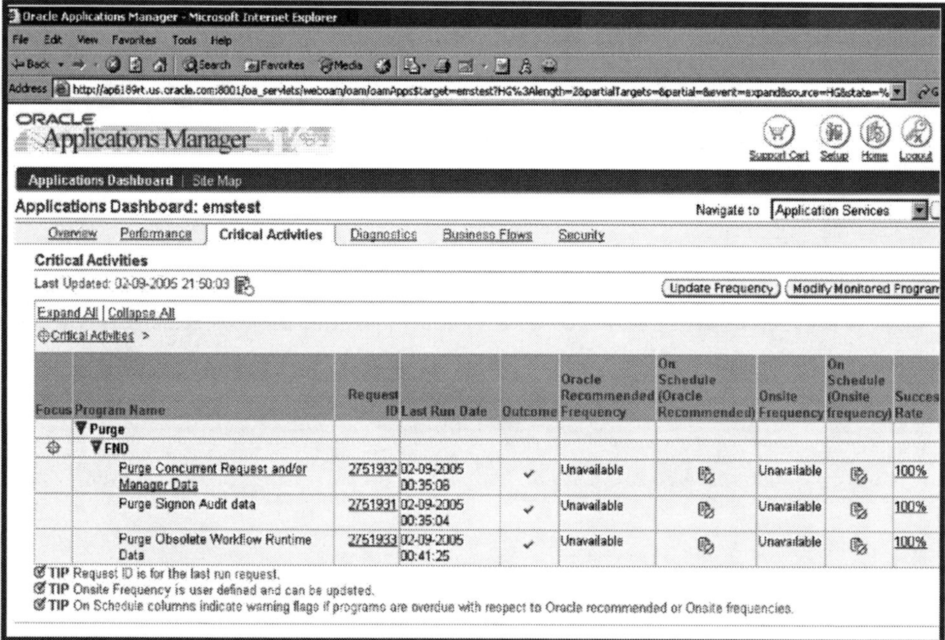

Fig. 11.6 Critical Activities Screen

Update Frequency for Monitored Critical Activities: emstest

(Cancel)

Program Name	Application	Program Type	Oracle Recommended Frequency	Onsite Frequency (days)
Purge Concurrent Request and/or Manager Data	FND	Purge	Unavailable	
Purge Obsolete Workflow Runtime Data	FND	Purge	Unavailable	
Purge Signon Audit data	FND	Purge	Unavailable	

TIP Onsite Frequency is a target frequency and may not be the frequency at which the program actually runs.

Fig. 11.7 Update Frequency Screen

With the 'Modify Monitored Program List' tab, you can add or remove any program you want in the category of the critical activities. To add any program to the category of critical activities select the program and click the button 'Move'. To add all the programs just press the 'Move All' button. To remove a particular program, click the 'Remove' button; in order to remove all the programs, click the 'Remove All' button. This is shown in Fig. 11.8.

For each critical activity, the following list is displayed.

- Focus categorizes the concurrent programs into different groups.
- Program Name shows the name of the concurrent program which constitutes the critical activity.
- Request ID—for every submitted concurrent program, there is a unique request ID that helps to identify that program.
- Last Run Date refers to the time the program was last run.

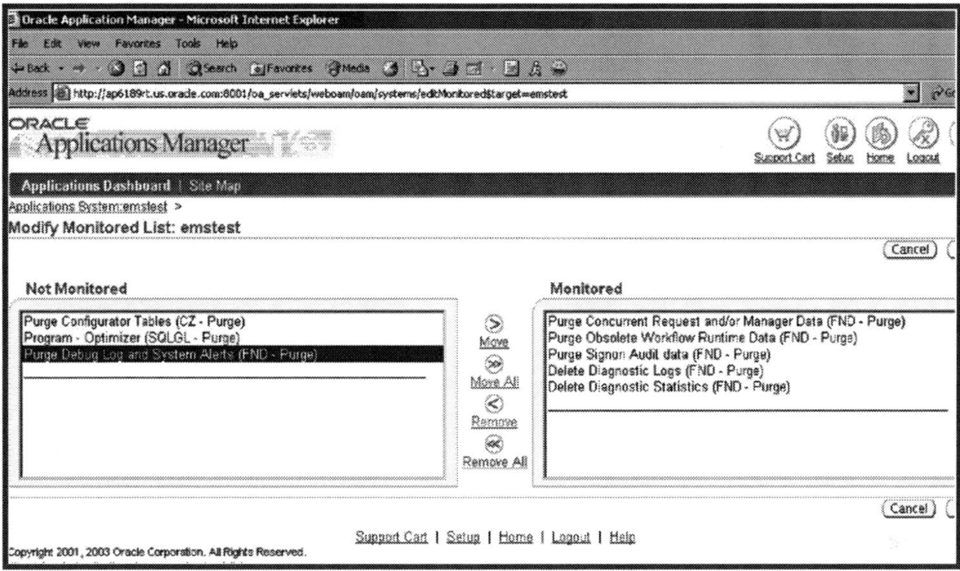

Fig. 11.8 Modify Monitored List Screen

- Outcome indicates the completion status of the program.
- Oracle Recommended Frequency is the pre-defined frequency recommended by Oracle.
- On Schedule (Oracle Recommended) indicates whether the Oracle recommended schedule has been met or not.
- Onsite Frequency refers to the actual running frequency of the concurrent program.
- On Schedule (On Site) refers to whether the on-site frequency has been met.
- Success Rate shows the percentage of successful completed requests.

Diagnostics

The diagnostics tab provides a summary of the tests carried out on the environment at regular intervals of time, and the results of each test. You can view all at one go, view the failures in the past week or of one day. You can even launch a diagnostic session to find out what exactly is going wrong with the environment. Figure 11.9 shows the diagnostic screen.

In the table, the test names are given along with the details. All these columns are described here.

The 'Focus' function is used to focus on a particular test. Say, if you want to view only the details of AOL sessions, click on the focus button of AOL Session and only that test will be shown.

- 'Test Name' signifies the name of the test run by diagnostics.
- 'Times Run' shows the number of times the test was run.
- 'Times Failed' is the number of times the test failed.
- 'Status' shows the status of the tests collectively. If a test was carried out 45 times, the collective status of these tests would be displayed.

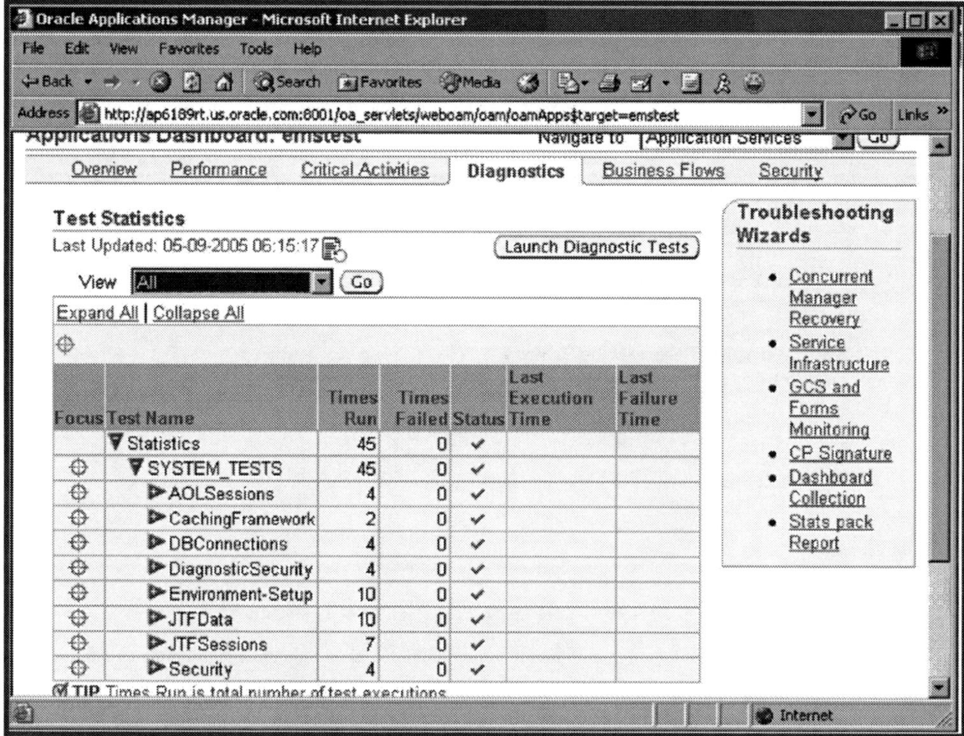

Fig. 11.9 Diagnostic Screen

- 'Last Execution Time' shows the time when the same test was last executed.
- 'Last Failure Time' is the last time the same test failed.

You can see from Fig. 11.9, there is a button called 'Launch Diagnostic Tests', which can be used to launch new tests to troubleshoot environment issues (see Fig. 11.10).

This page shows the module name followed by the number of the tests available for that particular module. Click the module you want to test and then click the button 'Run all Groups'. The tests taken will be on the left and the output will be on the right side of the screen. A sample output of the tests of HTML Platform is shown in Fig. 11.11.

Business Flow

With this page, you can see the details of a particular business flow. You can define as many business flows as you want; you can also see the sub-flows and the components of the business flows. For each business flow, you can view and enable/disable monitoring.

OAM provides the following concurrent program to help you maintain your business flow setup. Schedule requests for the concurrent program from the link provided.

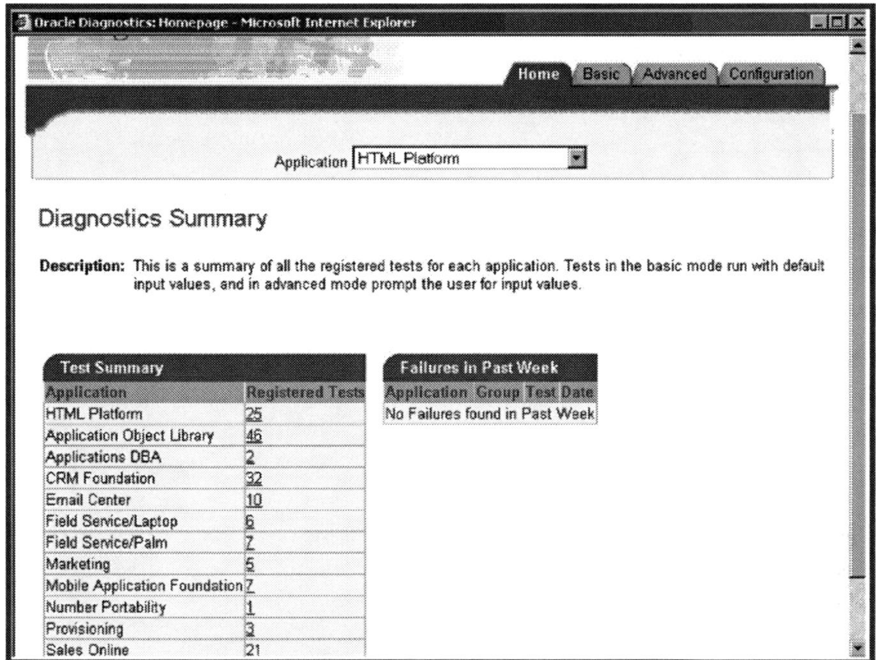

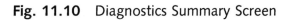

Fig. 11.10 Diagnostics Summary Screen

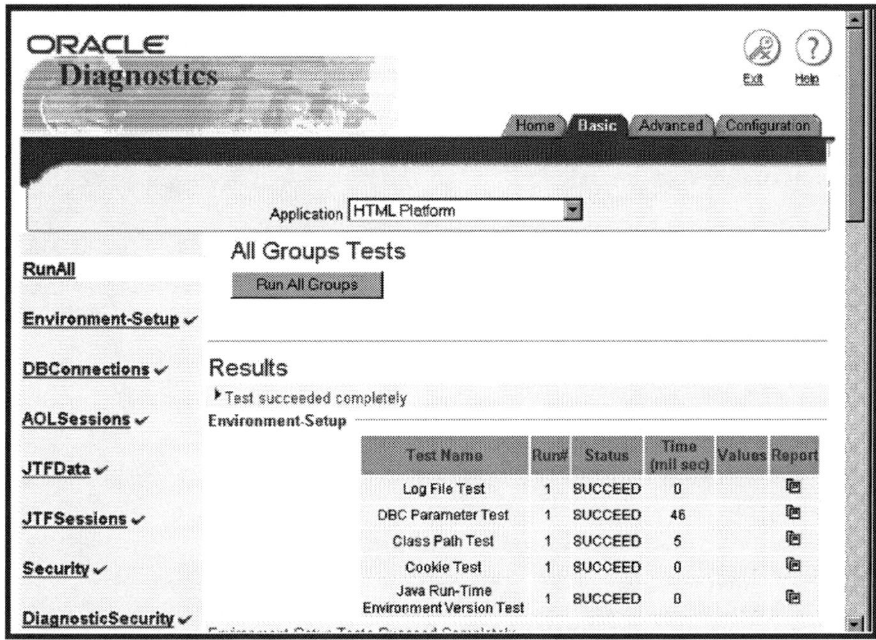

Fig. 11.11 Diagnostic Tests of HTML Platform

Metrics Refresh—schedule requests for the OAM: KBF Metrics Rollup Program to update the setup status of your business flows.(It means KBF Metrics Rollup Program is the name of the concurrent program which updates you with all the business flows of the company. The same can be scheduled through the OAM)

Security

The security page provides a summary of security-related system alerts and diagnostic test results. You can use this page to monitor important security metrics, such as failed log on attempts, blocked and inactive user accounts, etc. There are three main headings in the security page (see Fig. 11.12).

- Security Alerts are raised either at the failure of security-related diagnostic tests or at runtime by the application code. There are three categories of alerts, viz. critical, error and warnings. Critical lists the critical errors, which should be resolved immediately. Error lists the non-critical errors and warning is for informational purposes.
- Security Test Failures will show the details of the tests failed at the time of execution. This table contains details of the name of the test, time of failure and the error.
- Resource tab will link to the security-related documents on metalink. The metalink credentials need to be supplied first by giving the metalink user ID and the password.

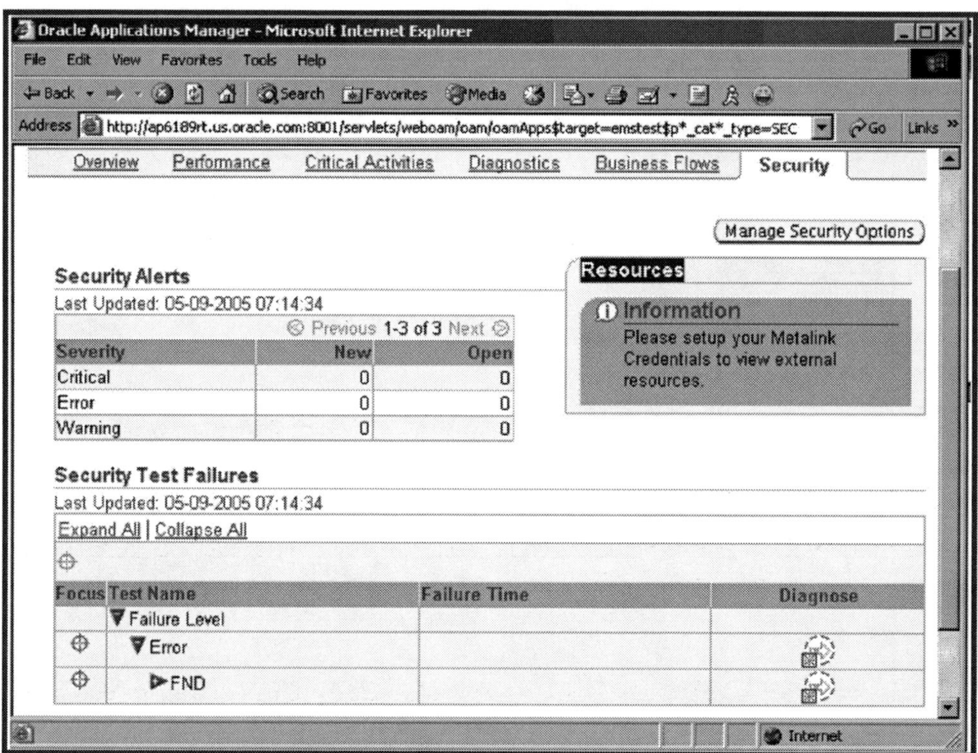

Fig. 11.12 Security Screen

SITE MAP

The site map lists all the features and applications available in Oracle Applications Manager. It has the following tabs:

- Administration
- Monitoring
- Maintenance
- Diagnostics and repair

We will discuss all these features and applications one by one.

Administration

The features in the administration tab are grouped in the following categories shown in Fig. 11.13.

Fig. 11.13 Administration Screen

System configuration

The feature provides detailed information on the configuration of your system. You can update many of your configuration settings from the links here as well.

Hosts

The host page shows the details of the hosts where the Oracle Application is installed. It will show from which host each service is running (see Fig. 11.14).

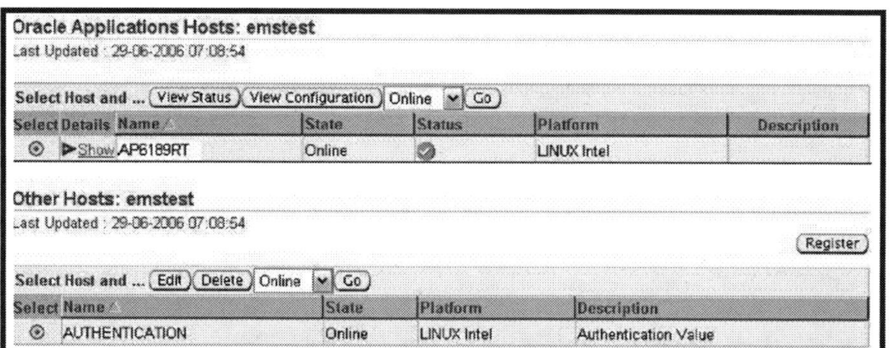

Fig. 11.14 Host Screen

To view information about a host's application services and processes from the Hosts page, select a host and click the 'View Status' button.

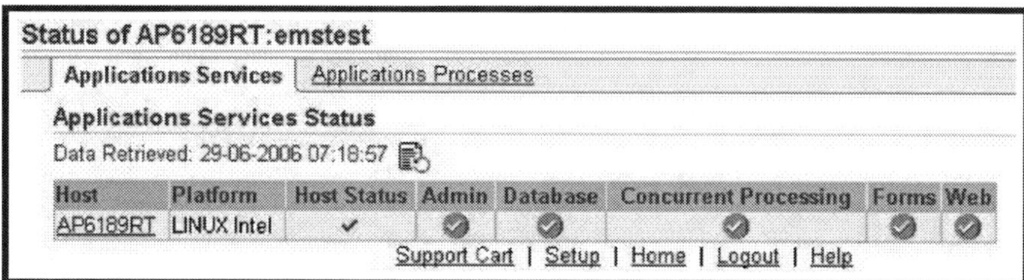

Fig. 11.15 Status of Host

The 'Application Services' tab shows all the components of Oracle Applications and which component is running from each host. Since this is a single node installation, the figure is showing all the components as running from a single host. In a multi-node installation, there will be multiple hosts.

Applications Services | Applications Processes

Concurrent Managers Active Processes
Last Updated : 29-06-2006 07:53:34

Expand All | Collapse All

Focus	Service Processes	Status	AUDSID	Oracle SPID	Start Date
	▼ Services				
	▼ Internal Concurrent Manager				
	▼ Internal Manager				
	26375	Active	1675762	11	04-06-2006 05:03:30
	▶ Standard Manager				
	▶ Transaction Manager				
	▶ Conflict Resolution Manager				
	▶ SFM Event Manager Queue Services				
	▶ SFM Application Monitoring Services				
	▶ Generic Service Component Container				

Fig. 11.16 Concurrent Manager Processes Screen

The 'Applications Processes' tab provides a table of active Concurrent Manager processes, as well as links to Forms runtime processes and Jserv processes.

In the 'Concurrent Manager Active Processes' table, you can expand the table to see the OS Process ID, AUDSID, Oracle SPID, and start date for any active service processes. For each active process, you can drill down on the OS Process ID or AUDSID to open more detailed process or session data.

Viewing and editing host configuration settings

To view or edit host configuration settings from the Hosts page, select a host and click the 'View Status' button.

The Host Configuration page displays a summary of the Applications services and ports that have been configured. To view or modify the associated autoconfig context file, click the 'Edit Configuration' button.

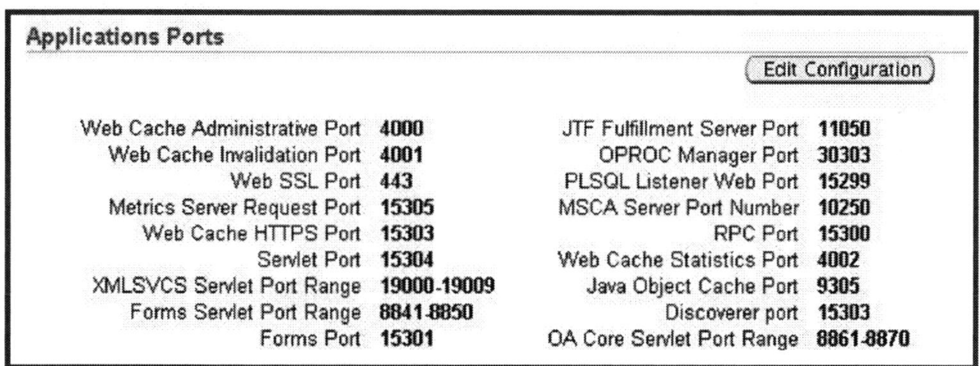

Applications Ports

Edit Configuration

Web Cache Administrative Port	4000	JTF Fulfillment Server Port	11050
Web Cache Invalidation Port	4001	OPROC Manager Port	30303
Web SSL Port	443	PLSQL Listener Web Port	15299
Metrics Server Request Port	15305	MSCA Server Port Number	10250
Web Cache HTTPS Port	15303	RPC Port	15300
Servlet Port	15304	Web Cache Statistics Port	4002
XMLSVCS Servlet Port Range	19000-19009	Java Object Cache Port	9305
Forms Servlet Port Range	8841-8850	Discoverer port	15303
Forms Port	15301	OA Core Servlet Port Range	8861-8870

Fig. 11.17 Applications Ports

Setting the state of a host

On the Hosts page, the 'State' column indicates whether a host is online or offline. Select a host, choose a value from the drop-down list, and click 'Go' to change the state of a host. Disabling a host means that none of its services will be monitored in Oracle Applications Manager.

Autoconfig

Rapid Install stores all the configuration parameters for both the `APPL_TOP` and the database in central repositories called context files. There is one context file each for the `APPL_TOP` and the database. When you subsequently run the `autoconfig` script during maintenance tasks, it uses the parameters in the context files to generate updated configuration files and database profiles.

Oracle Applications Manager `autoconfig` is the tool used to view the current context files, edit the parameters contained there, view previous context files and compare the current context files against previous ones. You can use OAM `autoconfig` to edit the configuration parameters, then run the `autoconfig` script on the file system to instantiate the changes.

When you edit application tier configuration parameters with OAM `autoconfig`, the changes are initially made to a database table. When you finish editing and save the changes, the context file is synchronized with the parameters in the database table.

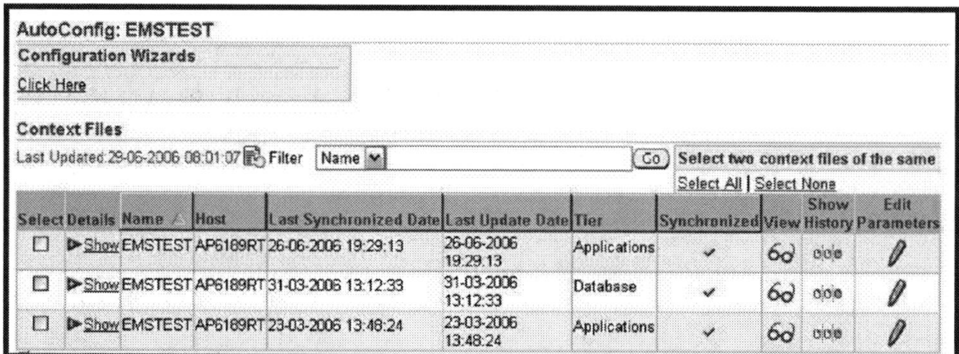

Fig. 11.18 Autoconfig Screen

There is a row for each context file in the table. It has the following columns.

- Select—click the check boxes of two context files on the same tier and then click 'Compare' to compare them.
- Details—click 'Show' to see more details about when the context file was created, who created it, and if it was successfully written.
- Name—the name of the context file.
- Host—the node on which the context file is located.
- Last Update Date—this is the date and time of last changes to the database.
- Tier—the context file may be either an application tier or a database tier context file.
- Synchronized—indicates whether the values in the database and in the file system have been synchronized.
- Last Synchronized Date—indicates the date the database and file system were synchronized.
- View—click this icon to view the context file as a text file. You can set up any text editor to view it.
- Show History—this shows all previous versions of the context file. You can compare the current version with previous ones on this page.
- Edit Parameters—you can search for and edit parameters on this page, and create a new version of the context file.

It can be seen from Fig. 11.19, that there is a tab, 'Configuration Wizard'. This wizard helps to configure some advanced features of Oracle Applications. From the figure, you can easily understand which features of Oracle Applications can be configured.

License manager

The license manager is used to license additional products, country-specific functionalities and languages. You can also generate reports on the licenses for your installation (see Fig. 11.20).

Configuration Wizards

Configuration Name	Description	Action
HTTP Load balancing	Use this option to configure HTTP Load Balancing for an E-Business Suite Release 11i system if you have a third party HTTP load balancer. Use this option to also disable HTTP Load Balancing.	Enable Disable
SSL	Use this option to configure SSL for an E-Business Suite Release 11i system.	Enable Disable
SSL Accelerator	Use this option to configure an E-Business Suite Release 11i system with a SSL accelerator.	Enable Disable
Forms Listener Servlet	Use this option to enable or disable the Forms Listener Servlet for an E-Business Suite Release 11i system.	Enable Disable
Apache JServ load balancing	Use this option to enable or disable Apache Jserv Load Balancing across multiple Web nodes for an E-Business Suite Release 11i system.	Enable Disable

Fig. 11.19 Configuration Wizard Screen

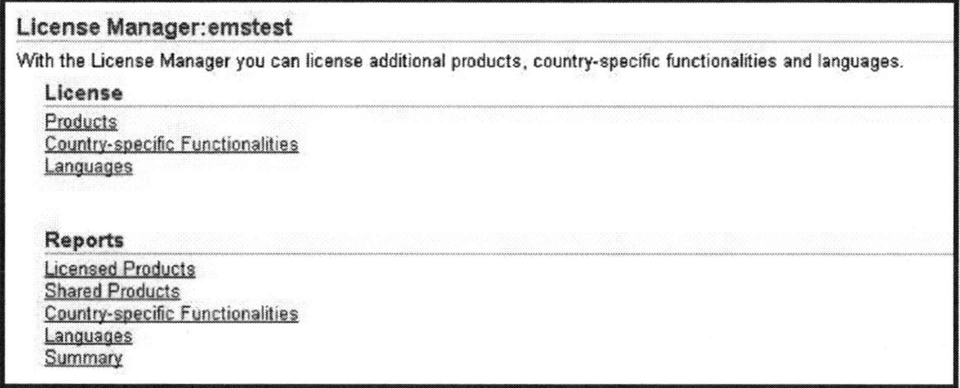

Fig. 11.20 License Manager Screen

There are two tabs under the license manager.

- License—from here you can actually license new products, add new languages to your existing installation and add country-specific functionalities.
- Report—you can generate the reports of the licensed products installed in your application system from here.

The APPS DBA may be required to add new products and languages in the existing application system. The same process is followed for licensing additional products.

To add additional languages, click on the tab 'Languages' as seen in Fig. 11.20. The list of languages is displayed in the next screen. Those languages which have a '✓' in the check box indicate that they are already installed in the application system. The ones without this sign are not installed in the application system.

Select the languages which you want to install. Figure 11.21 shows the list of languages. In the given figure, American English, Arabic and Korean are already installed; we will select Canadian French and Dutch for our installation.

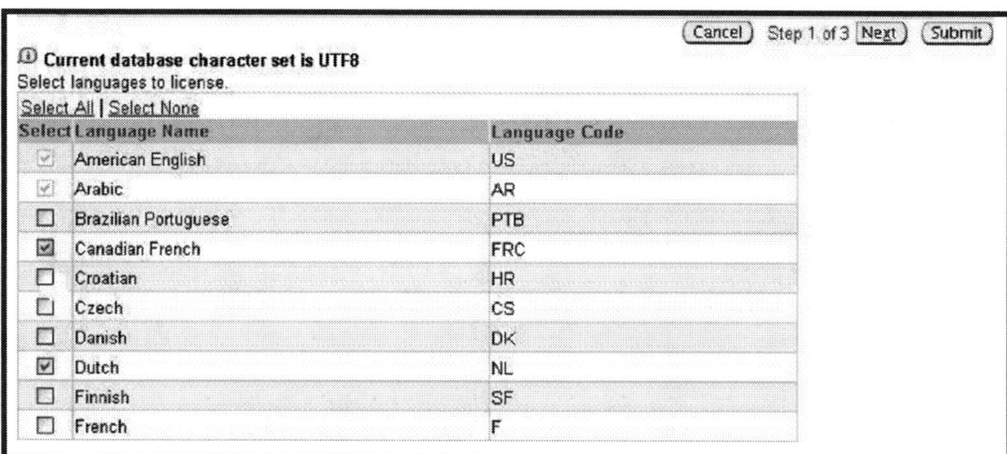

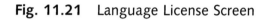

Fig. 11.21 Language License Screen

Once additional languages are added, it will prompt you to choose the base language. You can change the base language as shown in Fig. 11.22.

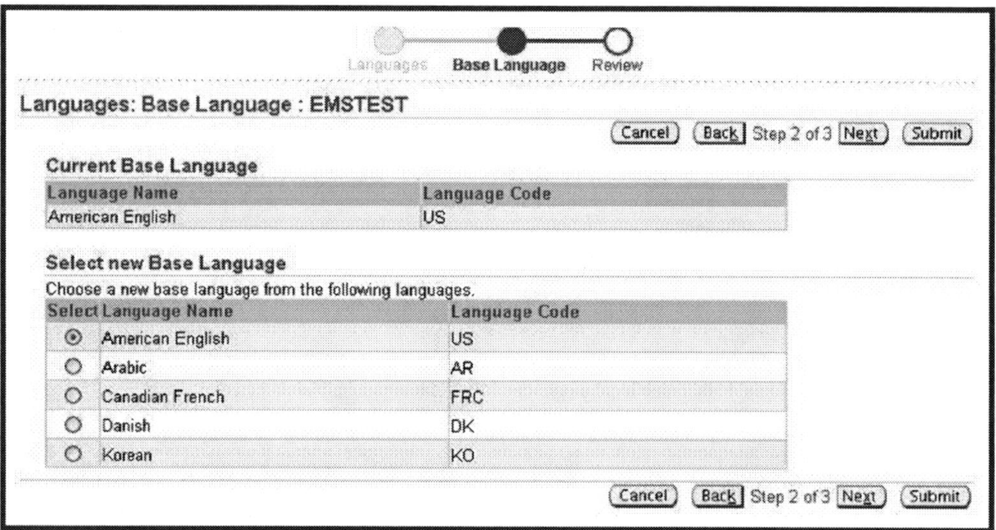

Fig. 11.22 Changing Base Language

Select the language that you want as base language and press 'Next'. The last screen shows the details of the languages that will be added to the application system and the new base language (see Fig. 11.23).

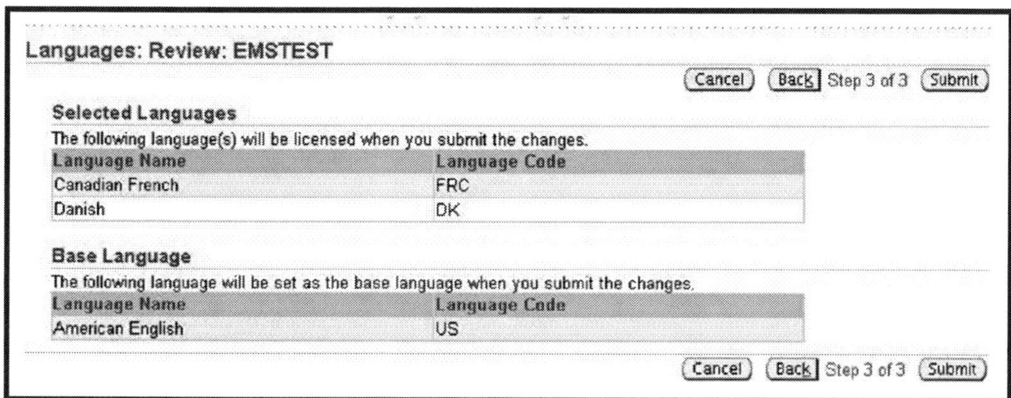

Fig. 11.23 Details of Languages Added

Review the languages which you want to add. If there is any mismatch, you can rectify it by pressing the 'Back' button. Click 'Submit' to add the languages.

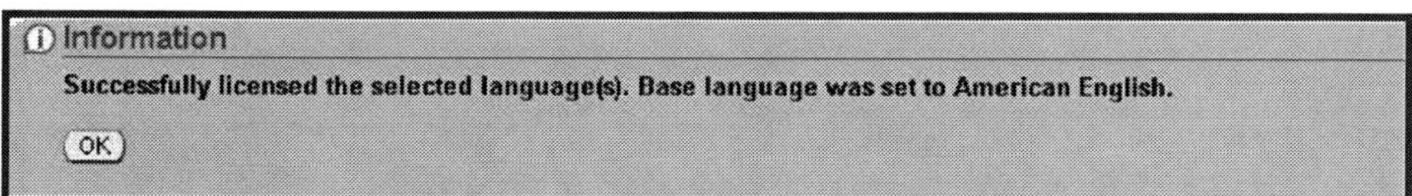

Fig. 11.24 Completion of Licensing

The alert that the languages have been successfully added in the application system will be displayed.

Adding an additional language through OAM does not install the language, but simply marks it as active. You have to install the NLS software in the application system to install new languages.

Concurrent request

This is the second tab under Administration. From here, the following activities can be done/monitored.

Submit new

New concurrent requests can be submitted from here. These can be submitted in the same way as discussed in Chapter 7. The only difference here is that it doesn't launch Forms-based application for submitting a new request. It can be submitted in a web-based UI from Oracle Applications Manager.

Pending

This shows all the requests that are in pending state.

Running

This shows the requests that are currently running.

Completed (last hour)

This shows the completed requests in the last one hour.

Since we have already discussed the Concurrent Manager, we won't be repeating it here. The next tab under administration is Application Services and Service Fulfillment Manager, which also talks about Concurrent Manager.

Application services

This gives information on various types of application services, like Generic Services, Request Processing Manager and Transaction Manager (which we have already discussed in Chapter 7).

Service fulfillment manager

Service Fulfillment Manager (SFM) provides a complete set of tools to automate fulfillment activities and integrate business flows for any type of service across multi-vendor application systems. SFM is beyond the scope of this book.

Workflow

Oracle workflow managers allow the system administrator to manage Oracle workflow for multiple Oracle Applications instances from a single console. The administrator can control workflow system services such as the agent listeners, notification mailers, background engines and other service components using the workflow manager. Administrators can also monitor work item processing by viewing the distribution of all work items by status and drilling down to additional information. They can also monitor event message processing for local business event system agents by viewing the distribution of event messages by status as well as queue propagation schedules. Discussion of workflow in detail is beyond the scope of this book.

Oracle Application Manager Log

The Oracle Application Manager log displays the log file generated by Oracle Applications Manager. There are three levels of log, viz. USER, SUPPORT and DEV.

- USER includes messages related to Oracle Applications Manager initialization routines, trace information about the error message, and any diagnostic messages related to customizations or extensions that have been added.
- SUPPORT has the user-level messages and additional information useful to support diagnosis of problems (for example, configuration setting details, prerequisite patch-related issues, and module-related information).
- DEV (Development) includes trace information related to code paths (for example, "Inside method A") and any code-related information that could be useful to the developer to diagnose a problem. This level also includes performance-related log messages.

The default is USER. You need to change the 'zone.properties file' to change the log level. The parameter is: `oracle.apps.oam.logger.level`.

For example:

- `servlet.weboam.initArgs=oracle.apps.oam.logger.level=USER`
- Bounce Apache/Jserv for your changes to take effect.

Monitoring

With Oracle Applications Manager, you can monitor the components of the Oracle Application. This divided into separate sections as can be seen from Fig. 11.25.

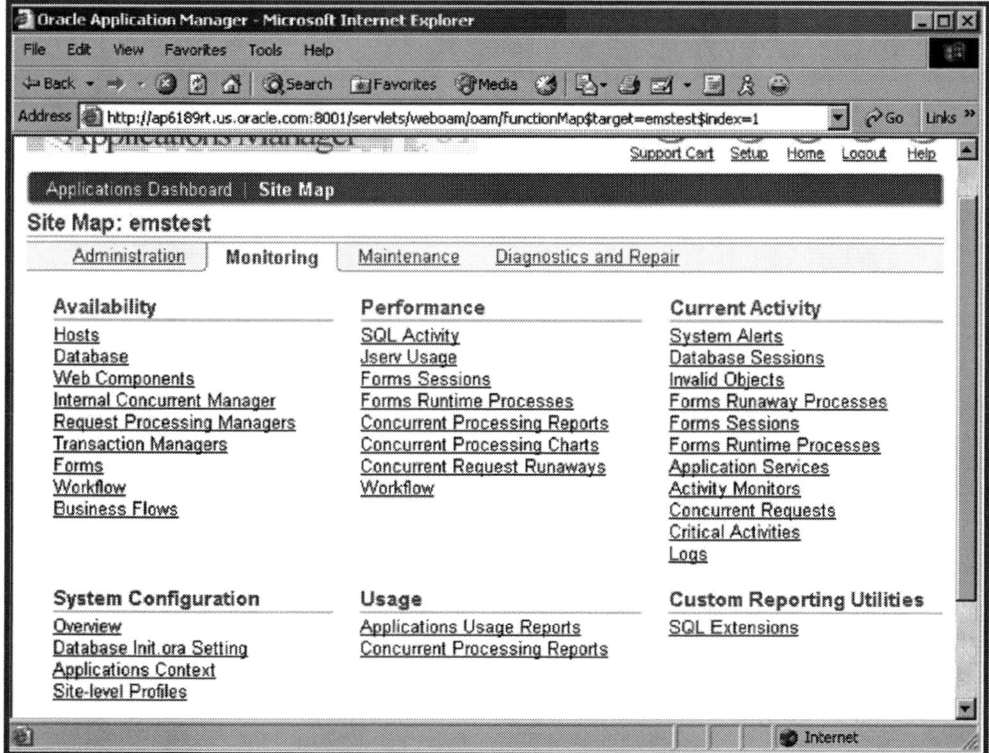

Fig. 11.25 Monitoring Screen

Availability

We can check the availability of the database as well as each of the middle tiers from this section. Since we have already discussed the same in the earlier section on dashboard, we won't repeat it.

System configuration

The system configuration shows the important configuration details for the environment at the database as well as the application level.

Overview

It shows the details of the database host name, operating system platform, the version of the database, the database node, the node of the concurrent processing server, the host name and port number of the Forms server, host name and port number of the web server.

Database Init.ora settings

The init.ora file is the initialization file which is used by the Oracle database. The location of this file is `$ORACLE_HOME/dbs`. One can easily check the initialization parameters of the database from here without logging into the database directly. The OAM not only displays the actual value but also shows the Oracle recommended value for that parameter.

Previous 1-25 of 56 Next 25

Parameter Name	Current Value	Recommended Value	Mandatory
db_cache_size	167772160	163577856	no
java_pool_size	67108864	52428800	no
pga_aggregate_target	1073741824	1074789376	no
processes	500	200	no
sessions	555	400	no

Resources

- Database Init Parameters Recommendations for E - Business Suite

Fig. 11.26 Database Init Parameters

Application context

Oracle Application context file is the 'sid.xml' file, which contains all the information of the application system. This file is automatically created during the Rapid Install or by running autoconfig; it acts as metadata of the application system. This file is located at `$APPL_TOP/admin` directory in the `$APPL_TOP` and `$ORACLE_HOME/appsutil` directory of the database server. Oracle Application Manager shows the details of the context file, both of the `APPL_TOP` and the database. You can check as well as edit the parameters of the context file OAM.

Site level profiles

This option displays all the site level profile options used by Oracle Applications (see Fig. 11.27). It also shows in a tabular manner when the profile was last modified and who modified it. There is also a filter available to search for a particular profile or a profile with a specific string. The best advantage of this feature is that you can check all the site level profiles at one place, and need not log in to the Forms for this.

Performance

Oracle Application Manager helps in resolving performance issues faced by an application system. It is no longer necessary to write complex queries to check what is wrong in the database. The areas in which Oracle Application Manager helps in finding the performance-related issues are discussed further.

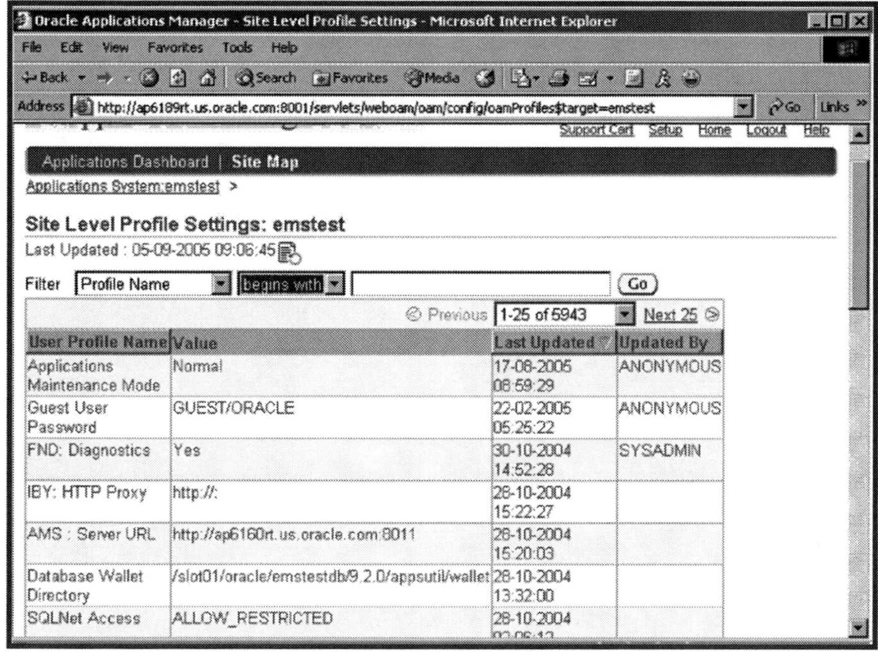

Fig. 11.27 Site Level Profile Settings

SQL activity

Figure 11.28 shows the following details

- `SQL_HASH`
- Physical reads
- Logical reads
- Total sorts
- Execs
- Total loads
- Load

Jserv usage

OAM provides a summary of the running Jserv instances, giving an overview of memory usage, connections, and AM pools for the distributed Jservs in your Application system. Jserv usage data may be useful when fine-tuning system performance or investigating performance problems. Every HTML page generated by Oracle Applications Framework is associated with an Application Module that runs in Jserv and manages the transaction state data and database connection for the page. To enhance application performance, these Application Modules are maintained in a shared pool on the web server. OAM allows you to view the Application Modules currently in this pool. For each Application Module, you can find the E-Business Suite user currently using the module, the database session details associated

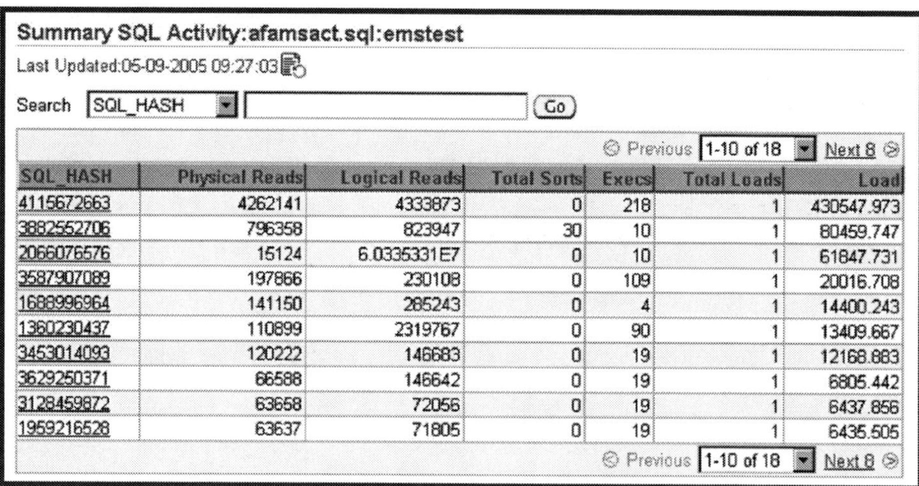

Summary SQL Activity:afamsact.sql:emstest

Last Updated:05-09-2005 09:27:03

Search SQL_HASH [ ] Go

Previous 1-10 of 18 Next 8

SQL_HASH	Physical Reads	Logical Reads	Total Sorts	Execs	Total Loads	Load
4115672663	4262141	4333873	0	218	1	430547.973
3882552706	796358	823947	30	10	1	80459.747
2066076576	15124	6.0335331E7	0	10	1	61847.731
3587907089	197866	230108	0	109	1	20016.708
1688996964	141150	285243	0	4	1	14400.243
1360230437	110899	2319767	0	90	1	13409.667
3453014093	120222	146683	0	19	1	12168.883
3629250371	66588	146642	0	19	1	6805.442
3128459872	63658	72056	0	19	1	6437.856
1959216528	63637	71805	0	19	1	6435.505

Previous 1-10 of 18 Next 8

Fig. 11.28 Summary SQL Activity

with the module, and other technical and performance-related data. Additionally, OAM can now be configured to take periodic snapshots of Jserv memory usage. This allows you to identify trends in memory usage and compare the values from different points in time. With the help of Jserv summary page, you can check the following details.

The table on the Jserv Usage Summary page shows the following Application Module (AM) pool data, viz. total and available.

Select an Item and View ... AM Pools | Connections | Memory | Environment

Expand All | Collapse All

Select	Focus	Server:Port	Memory			Connections		AM Pools	
			Total (KB)	Used (KB)	Available (%)	Total	Available	Total	Available
		▼Active OACore Jserv							
	⊕	▼AP6189RT:8001							
◉		JServ:11678	146908	78432	47	11	8	0	0

Fig. 11.29 Jserv Usage Screen

The table also shows the available and total connection pool data. The 'Connection Pool Statistics' page shows the following details:

- Creation time
- Restart time
- Configuration parameters
- Current statistics
- Lifetime statistics

Memory page shows the memory usage in terms of Total Memory, Used Memory and % Free Memory (see Fig. 11.30).

Fig. 11.30 Memory Screen

Environment page shows the environment details for a particular Jserv. The environment details are divided into three categories:

- System properties (contains general details)
- Class Path Settings
- Process Environment (contains information about `PATH LD_LIBRARY_PATH, LIBPATH, DISPLAY`, etc.)

Forms sessions

This page displays information about the Forms session only when the profile option 'Sign-On: Audit Level' is set to 'Form'. Every open form constitutes an open forms session.

This will show the details of each open form session like the user name, who has launched the Forms, the responsibility chosen while launching the Forms, the form name, etc.

Forms Sessions: emstest

Last Updated:06-09-2005 05:43:42

Select Form and View ... (Session Details)

Select	Form Name	AUDSID	RTI_PID	Username	Responsibility	Application	LRs	PRs	CPU	PGA	UGA	Duration
◉	Update System Profile Values	340440	23233	SYSADMIN	System Administrator	Application Object Library	330	13	5	1465	459	0:16:22
○	Administer Concurrent Managers	340452	24320	SYSADMIN	System Administrator	Application Object Library	813	56	9	1593	587	0:2:57

Fig. 11.31 Forms Session Screen

The following details are shown on the Forms session screen, as shown in Fig. 11.31.

- Form Name is the name of the form that constitutes a Forms session.
- AUUDSID is the Auditing Session ID. For each opened Forms session, a unique ID is assigned which gives detailed database session information.
- RTI_PID is the runtime process ID. This shows the operating process ID of that particular form. From the figure, we can see that the RTI_PID for the Concurrent Manager Administer Forms is 24320. We can query this process from the backend Forms server.

```
(appmgr01) appmgr - -bash $ ps -ef | grep 24320
appmgr01 24320 12035  0 05:27 ?
        00:00:01 f60webmx webfile=5,7,ap6189rt_9000_emstest
```

- User name: This shows the user name who has logged in the Forms.
- Responsibility: This shows the responsibility that was chosen for logging.
- Application: This shows the module to which this Forms belongs.
- LRs: This shows the Logical data block reads. This includes data block reads from both memory and disk. The limits are set and measured in the number of block reads performed by a call or during a session.
- PRs: This shows the total number of data block reads from the session or from the disc.
- CPU: This shows the CPU usage in seconds.
- PGA: This is the Program Global Area memory used by the Forms session.
- UGA: This is the User Global Area memory that is used by the Forms session.
- Duration: This shows the duration in HH:MM:SS of the time since the Forms were open.

You can select a Forms process and click on the 'Session Details' button to find more details about a particular Forms session. The session details screen is shown in Fig. 11.32.

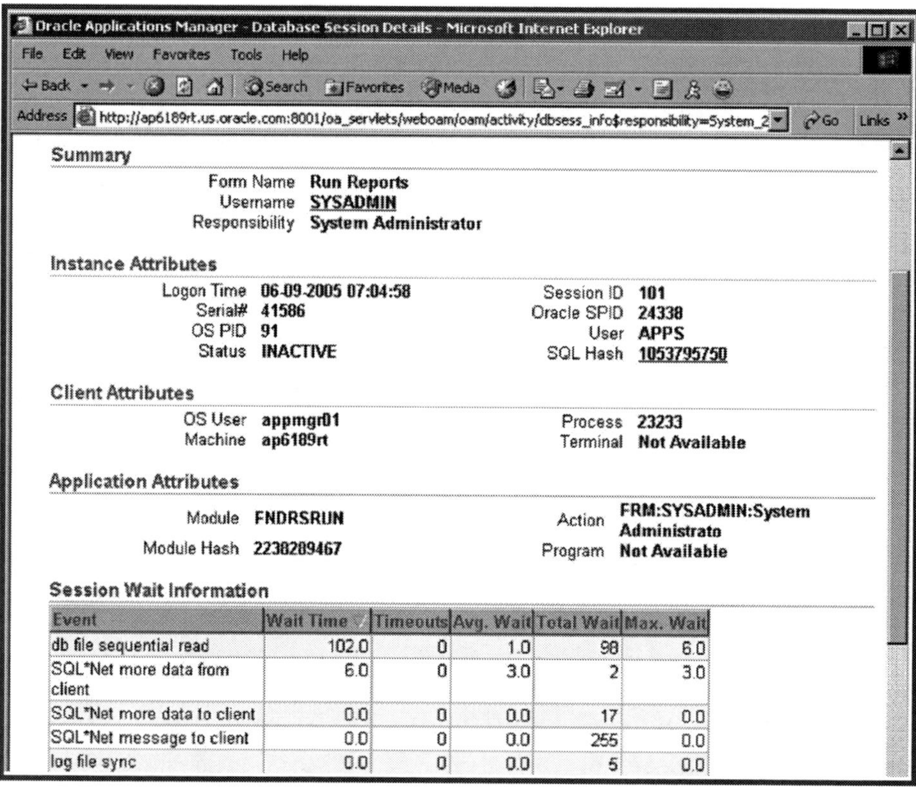

Fig. 11.32 Details of Particular Forms Session

Forms runtime process

This page gives information about the Forms runtime processes. To get this information, you must start a service instance of the OAM Generic Collection Service. This can be done from the Administer Concurrent Manager form by selecting it and clicking the 'Activate' button. This is shown in Fig. 11.33.

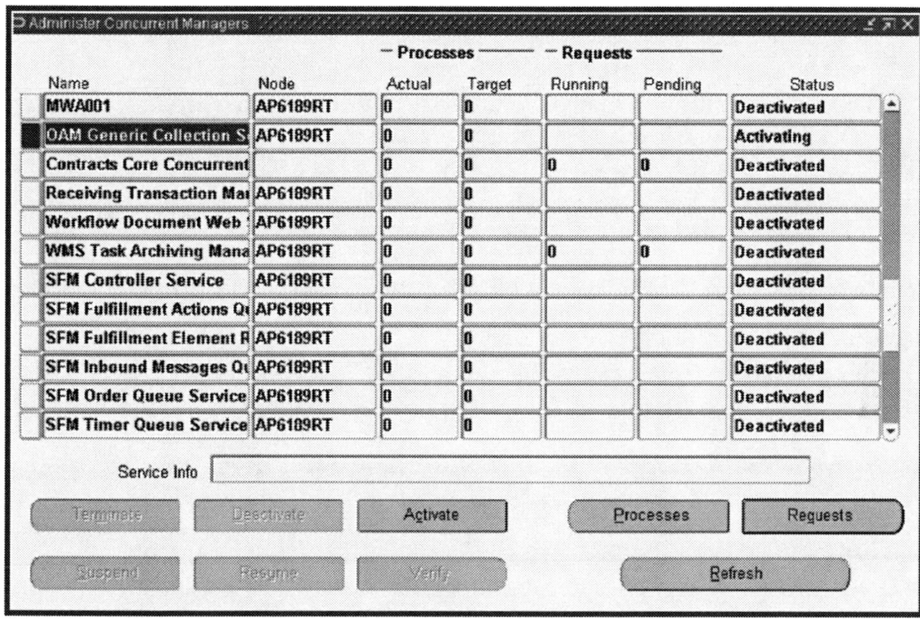

Fig. 11.33 Administer Concurrent Manager Screen

Once the OAM Generic Collection Service is up and running, it will show actual and target processes equal to one. Once it is started you will be able to view the runtime process of the Forms.

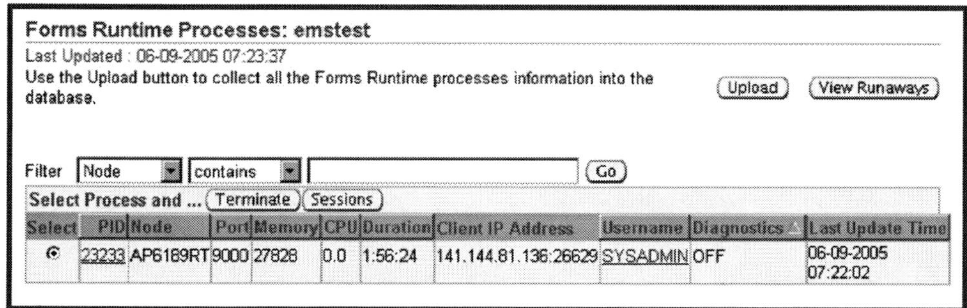

Fig. 11.34 Forms Runtime Process

The following details are shown.

- PID—shows the Forms runtime process ID, which is running in the backend Forms server.
- Node—the host name of the Forms server.

- Port—shows the Apache port of the servlet listener.
- Memory—the memory used by the Forms runtime process in Kilobytes.
- CPU—shows the CPU used by this session in seconds.
- Duration—the duration for which the Forms are running in HH:MM:SS.
- Client IP Address—the IP address of the terminal from which the Forms are launched.
- User name—the one used to log in.
- Diagnostics—used to view the Forms Runtime Diagnostics log (FRD). If this is on then FRD logs can be viewed. To enable diagnostics, set the Forms listener environment variable '`FORMS60_OAM_FRD`' to ON and restart the listener.
- Last Update time—the time the form was last updated.

Concurrent processing reports

This page shows the concurrent processing reports. The reports can be divided into three categories:

- Concurrent Request Statistics by Program
- Concurrent Request Statistics by User name
- Programs Usage Statistics

Concurrent request statistics by program The statistics for the concurrent requests by program are taken from the `fnd_concurrent_requests` table. The following details are given:

- Application: The application for which the concurrent requests are run
- Program: The name of the concurrent program
- Total: This shows the total of all individual runtimes for the program
- Average: The average runtime for this request
- Minimum: This shows the minimum time taken to run this program
- Maximum: This shows the maximum time taken to run this program

Select a Program and View... (Requests)

Select	Application	Program	Total	Average	Minimum	Maximum	Times Run
◉	Application Object Library	Purge Obsolete Workflow Runtime Data	0:12:4	0:4:1	0:2:55	0:6:11	3
○	Application Object Library	Synchronize WF LOCAL tables	0:1:38	0:0:5	0:0:1	0:0:14	18
○	Application Object Library	OAM Applications Dashboard Collection	0:0:22	0:0:4	0:0:4	0:0:5	5
○	Application Object Library	Active Users	0:0:14	0:0:7	0:0:5	0:0:9	2
○	Application Object Library	Purge Concurrent Request and/or Manager Data	0:0:6	0:0:2	0:0:2	0:0:2	3
○	Application Object Library	Purge Signon Audit data	0:0:5	0:0:3	0:0:2	0:0:3	2
○	Application Object Library	Workflow Control Queue Cleanup	0:0:2	0:0:1	0:0:1	0:0:1	5

Fig. 11.35 Concurrent Request Statistics by Program

Concurrent request statistics by user name This shows the user name, total number of requests completed by the user and the total runtime of the requests (see Fig. 11.36).

Select a Username and View... (Requests)

Select	Username	Requests Completed	Total Runtime
◉	SYSADMIN	67	0:15:46
○	OPERATIONS	6	0:0:39

Fig. 11.36 Programs Usage Statistics

This shows the statistics of concurrent programs on the basis of each program. It shows the program name, average, maximum and minimum time taken to run the program (in seconds), number of times the program is run, success rate and the total time that the program was run.

Concurrent processing charts This page shows the concurrent processing details in three charts.

- Concurrent requests
- Concurrent Managers
- Utilization

The concurrent request group shows a few charts, viz. concurrent requests by status, running requests per user, pending requests per user, running requests per application, pending requests per application, running requests per responsibility, etc.

The Concurrent Manager group shows the following charts, viz. pending requests per manager and sessions blocking CRM/ICM activity.

The utilization group shows how many running requests and available processes exist per manager.

Click the 'Chart Settings' button to create a chart. You can select the chart type—a vertical bar, horizontal bar, pie or table. You can also select the interval for refreshing the chart. Once the chart setting is configured, it will be displayed.

Focus	Name	Description	Setting
	▼ Concurrent Processing Chart Group		
⊕	▼ Concurrent Requests		
	Concurrent Requests by Status	The counts of concurrent requests grouped by status	▦
	Running Requests per User	The counts of running requests grouped by user	▦
	Pending Requests per User	The counts of pending requests grouped by user	▦
	Running Requests per Application	The counts of running requests grouped by application	▦
	Pending Requests per Application	The counts of pending requests grouped by application	▦
	Running Requests per Responsibility	The counts of running requests grouped by responsibility	▦
	Pending Requests per Responsibility	The counts of pending requests grouped by responsibility	▦
	Completed Requests by Status	The completed requests for the last hour grouped by status	▦
	Top Running Requests by Buffer Gets	The top running requests by buffer gets	
	Top Running Requests by Disk Reads	The top running requests by disk reads	
	Top Running Requests by CPU	The top running requests by CPU	
	Top Running Requests by PGA	The top running requests by PGA memory	
	Top Running Requests by UGA	The top running requests by UGA memory	
	Longest Running Requests	The longest running requests	
	Requests Waiting on Locks	The requests waiting on locks	
	All Running Requests	All running requests	
	All Pending Requests	All pending requests	
⊕	▼ Concurrent Managers		
	Pending Requests per Manager	The count of pending requests for each manager	▦
	Sessions Blocking CRM/ICM Activity	Sessions blocking CRM/ICM activity	
⊕	▼ Utilization		
	Running Requests and processes per Manager	The count of running requests and processes for each manager	▦

Fig. 11.37 Creating a Chart

Once the chart is configured the chart will be as shown in Fig. 11.38.

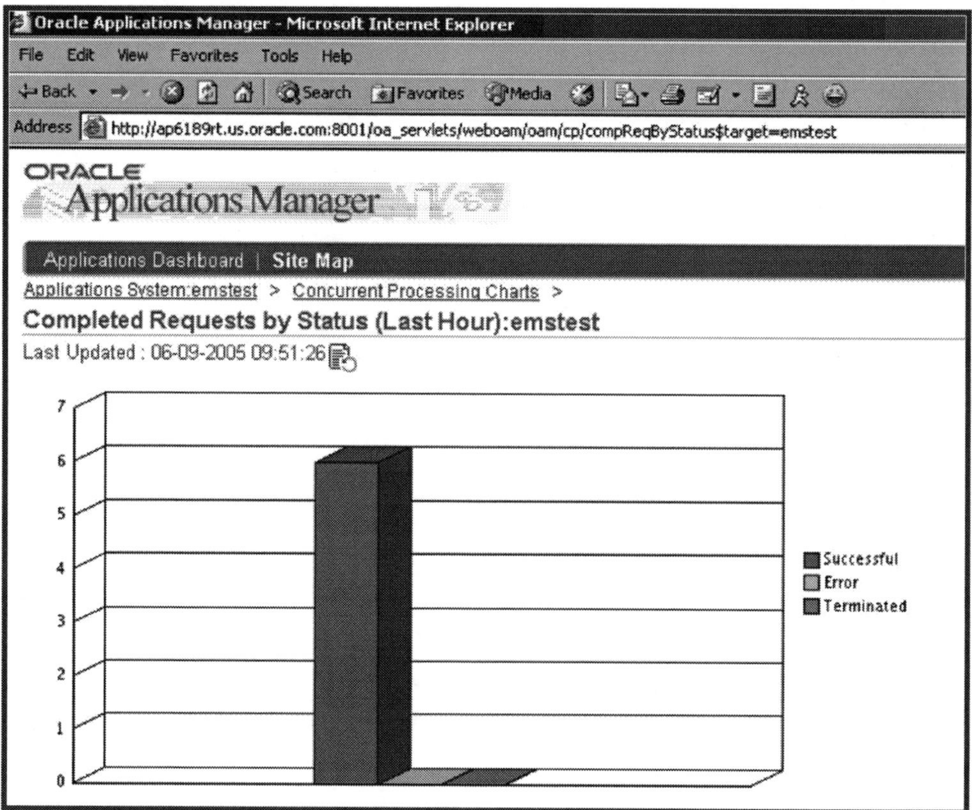

Fig. 11.38 Configured Chart

Concurrent request runaways

It happens many times that when a concurrent request is cancelled, the database session that was supposed to come to an end doesn't cause many issues in the system. If any such database sessions are currently active, they will be reported on this page. The table supplies context information for each session: request ID, AUDSID, program, user name, start time, phase, status, Oracle SPID, and PID. You can delete a session by selecting it in the table and clicking 'Terminate'. You can drill down on the links in the request ID, AUDSID, program, and user name columns to view the details of each.

MAINTENANCE

The maintenance is divided into three categories—patches and utilities, cloning and purging, as shown in Fig. 11.39.

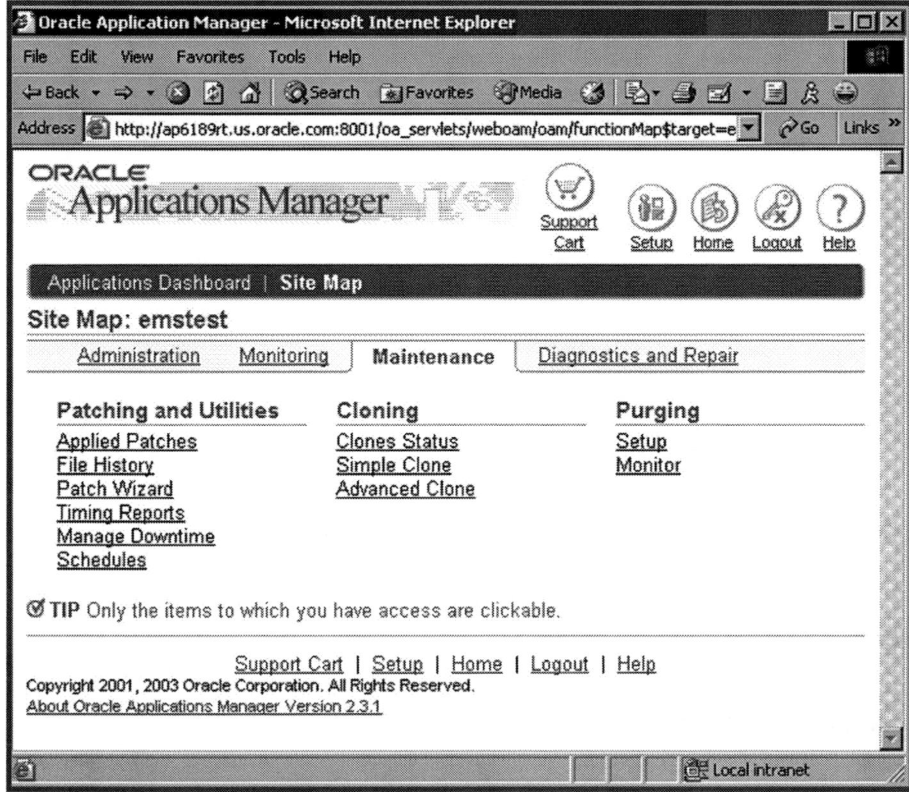

Fig. 11.39 Maintenance Screen

Patching and Utilities

This topic has been divided into five sub-topics, which are discussed further.

Applied patches

You can search for patches that were applied to a particular environment from this page (see Fig. 11.40). Whenever a patch is applied, the patch history information is uploaded in the database. This page queries the tables containing the patch history and shows the output. With the applied patch feature, you can find the following information:

- The patch number
- Patches applied on a specific date
- Patches applied within a range of dates
- Whether it was a merged or stand alone patch
- The node of the `APPL_TOP` from which the patch was applied
- NLS details of translation patches applied
- The completion date

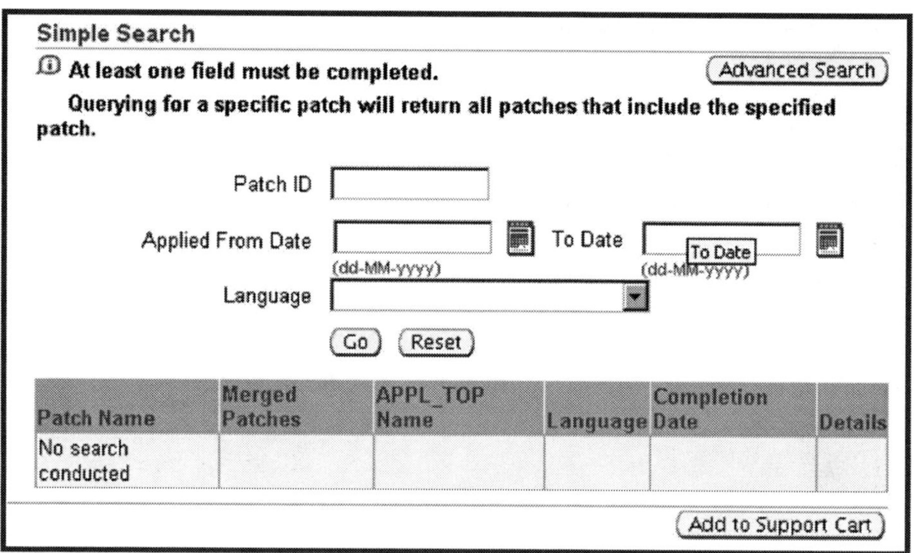

Fig. 11.40 Patch Search Screen

File history

This page gives the history of the file, like how many times the file was changed, which patch changed the file version, the dates on which the file was changed.

There are three main fields in the simple search page.

- File name: Enter the name of the file, not its full path. The file name is case sensitive. You can use wild cards.
- Change from date: Enter the date from which you want to know the file version changes.
- To date: Enter the date till when you want to know the file version changes.
- Language: Select the language from the drop-down list. You can select only one language at a time. If you want to select more than one language, go to the advanced options.

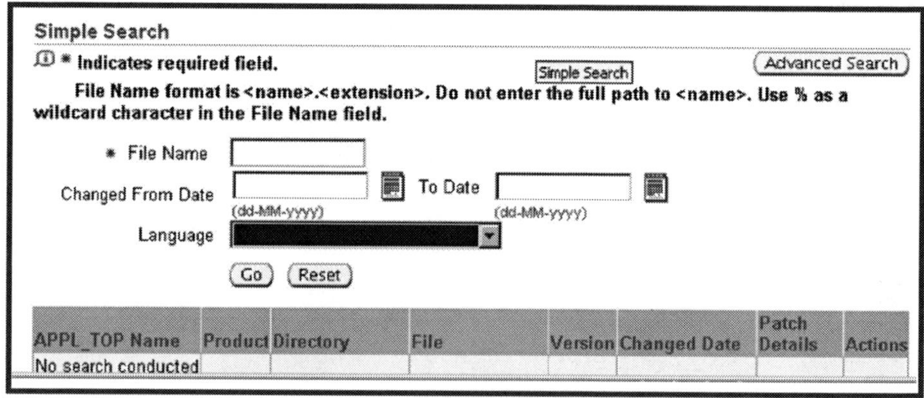

Fig. 11.41 File History Screen

The search result gives the following output:

- `APPL_TOP` name is the name of the `APPL_TOP` containing the file
- Product is the product code to which the file belongs
- The directory where the file is located
- The file name that was searched
- The version number of the file
- Changed Date is the date on which the file was changed with this version
- Patch Details shows the details of the patch which has changed this file
- Action: Summary report gives the action that updated the file

Patch wizard

Patch wizard is the utility shipped with the 11.5.10 version of Oracle Application. It replaces the Patch Advisor shipped with earlier versions. With this wizard you can determine patches that have not been applied in the application system. It makes a comparison between the patches already applied against a list of all recommended Oracle Applications patches. It also tell the impact of applying these patches.

The first step before running the patch wizard is to setup your metalink credentials in the Update Metalink Credentials page.

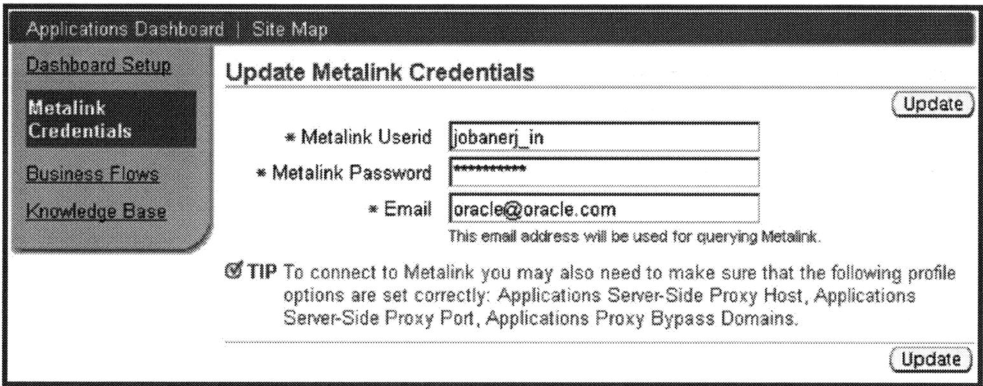

Fig. 11.42 Update Metalink Credentials

Patch wizard tasks

The patch wizard table lists the tasks available here (see Fig. 11.43). It contains the following information about each task:

- Task Name
- Description of the task
- Tasks (the actual link for the task)
- Job Status shows the exact status of the task

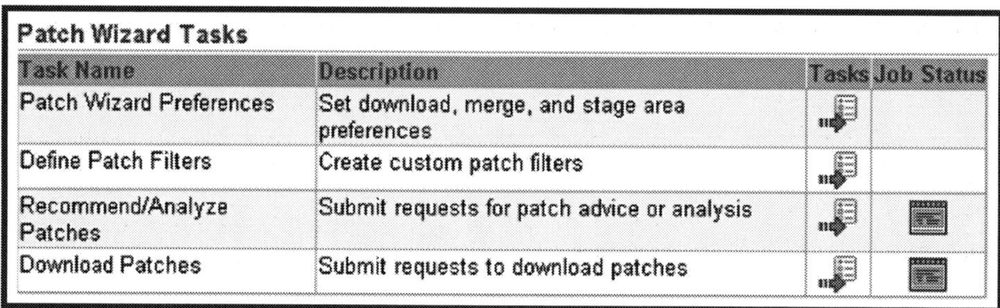

Patch Wizard Tasks

Task Name	Description	Tasks	Job Status
Patch Wizard Preferences	Set download, merge, and stage area preferences		
Define Patch Filters	Create custom patch filters		
Recommend/Analyze Patches	Submit requests for patch advice or analysis		
Download Patches	Submit requests to download patches		

Fig. 11.43 Patch Wizard Tasks

Patch wizard preference

This page stores the patching preference for the patch wizard.

Last Updated : 07-09-2005 02:22:40
Oracle MetaLink User ID **jobanerj_in**

Staging Directory
* Staging Directory /slot03/appmgr/emstestappl/patches
(Example: /user01/applmgr/stage)

Merge Option Defaults
To download patches, you must setup your MetaLink Credentials page in OAM Site Map.
Automatically merge downloaded patches
* Merging Strategy
One merged patch: US and non-US
Two merged patches: US; non-US
Multiple merged patches: US; language1;language2;..

Language and Platform Defaults
Select default Languages and Platform for downloading patches.

Languages
Available Languages: Brazilian Portuguese, Canadian French, Croatian, Czech, Danish, Dutch, Finnish, French, German, Greek
Move / Move All / Remove / Remove All
Selected Languages: Arabic, Korean

Platform
LINUX Intel
HP Tru64 UNIX
Sun Solaris OS (SPARC)
MS Windows NT/2000 Server
IBM RS/6000 AIX
HP-UX 11.0/32 bit

Fig. 11.44 Patch Wizard Preference Screen

Staging Directory is the one where the patches are downloaded. The same directory stores files used by the patch wizard. Oracle recommends using the same staging directory each time you run the patch wizard.

Merge Option Defaults is the option chosen to merge the patches automatically after the download. You can merge all of them into one single patch, create two merged patches—one for US and one for non-US patches (NLS)—or you can create multiple merged patches, one for each language.

Language and Platform Details shows the information regarding whichever languages the patch wizard will download. You can set the platform details from this window only.

In Display Option Defaults, you can select the Show Hidden Patches in order to see all patches. If you download a patch and don't want that patch to be included in the report, this is a hidden patch.

Define patch filters

The patch wizard has the ability to analyze and compare the list of recommended patches with the patches that are already applied in the system. The patch Information Bundle contains information for all recommended patches for all products. The patch wizard compares this file against the patch history database to compare and list the recommended patches. If the patch wizard makes a comparison between these two then the number of recommended patches would be unnecessarily large and the results might not be useful. To avoid this, patch wizard provides filters so that only those patch types and products in the meta data that apply to your system are included in the comparison.

Click the 'Tasks' icon for Define Patch Filters. This allows you to see all filters created for the current system. Patch wizard has three pre-seeded filters and the option of creating custom filters.

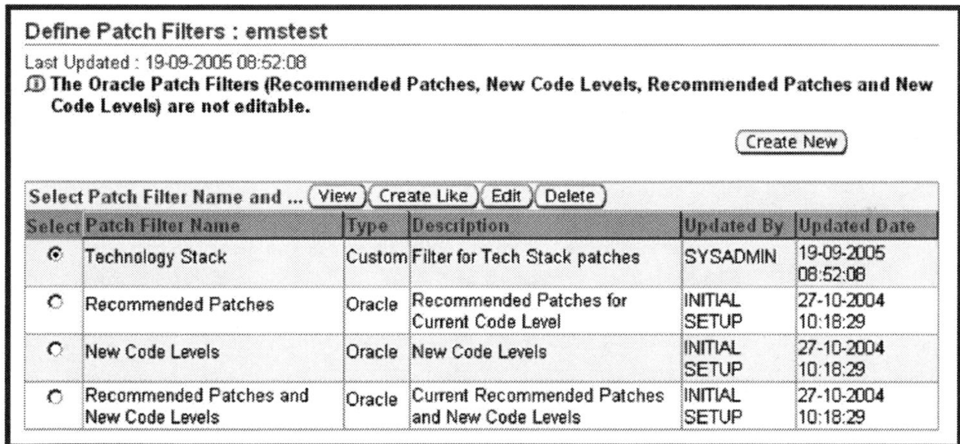

Define Patch Filters : emstest

Last Updated : 19-09-2005 08:52:08

The Oracle Patch Filters (Recommended Patches, New Code Levels, Recommended Patches and New Code Levels) are not editable.

(Create New)

Select Patch Filter Name and ... (View) (Create Like) (Edit) (Delete)

Select	Patch Filter Name	Type	Description	Updated By	Updated Date
◉	Technology Stack	Custom	Filter for Tech Stack patches	SYSADMIN	19-09-2005 08:52:08
○	Recommended Patches	Oracle	Recommended Patches for Current Code Level	INITIAL SETUP	27-10-2004 10:18:29
○	New Code Levels	Oracle	New Code Levels	INITIAL SETUP	27-10-2004 10:18:29
○	Recommended Patches and New Code Levels	Oracle	Current Recommended Patches and New Code Levels	INITIAL SETUP	27-10-2004 10:18:29

Fig. 11.45 Define Patch Filters Screen

Figure 11.45 shows six columns.

- Select—this option selects which filter to view, create like edit, delete. Just check the Figure 11.45. Select a filter and then click on either view, create like or edit or delete.
- Patch filter name.
- Type—tells which type of filter it is a custom created or Oracle predefined.
- Description of the filter.
- Updated by—the user who made recent updates to this filter.
- Updated Date—The date when the filter was last updated.

Three filters come with the application system by default. They can neither be edited nor deleted. These filters can be seen in the patch filter name column with the Type as 'Oracle'. These are described as follows.

1. Recommended Patches: This determines the recommended patches for the present code level.
2. New Code Levels: This filter determines the recommended patch for code levels higher than that of the application system.
3. Recommended Patches and New Code Levels: This filter determines recommended patches for the current as well as for new code levels.

For creating a custom filter you need to click 'Create New' on the top right corner of the screen. It prompts for a name and description of the filter you would like to create. You need to select the product from the list and check either or both the check boxes (Recommended Patches and New Code Level) to define your patch filters. We will create a filter for Human Resource patches as shown in Fig. 11.46.

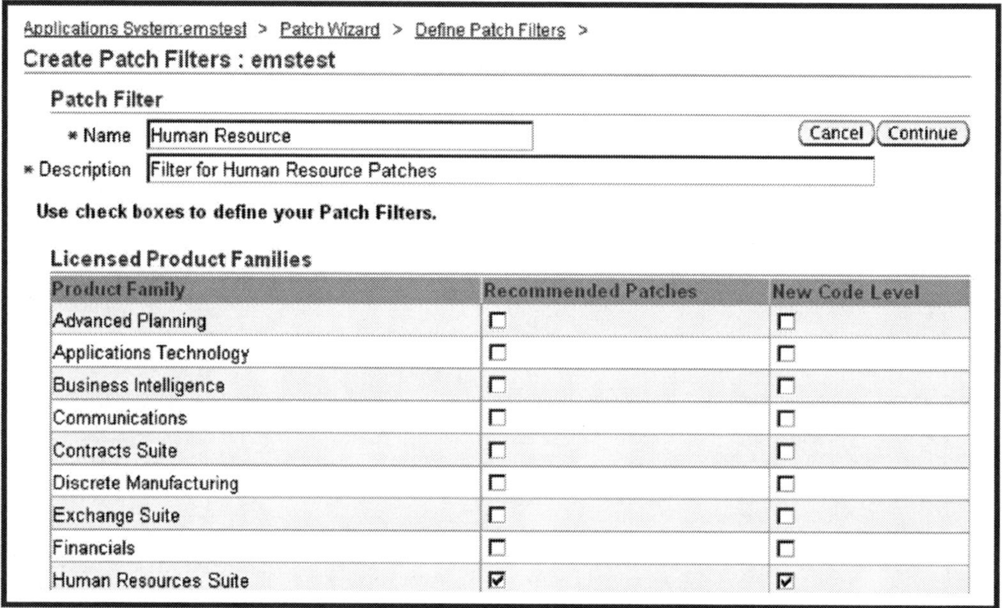

Fig. 11.46 Create Patch Filters

Once the filter is created, it can be seen in the patch filter screen.

Recommend/analyze patches

Once the stage area setup is over and the patch filters are created, you can submit the request to create recommendations or analyze specific patches or upload a patch information bundle to the database. The request can be submitted from the Recommend/Analyze patch main screen. This screen shows three actions.

- Create Recommendations: You can select one of the patch filters and then submit the request for a list of recommended patches of the product in your patch filter.

- Analyze Specific Patches: You can also put the patch numbers separated by a comma in the text box and then make an analysis of the impact of specific patches on your system.
- Upload Patch Information Bundle (no analysis): This task updates the system with the latest patch information bundle without an analysis.

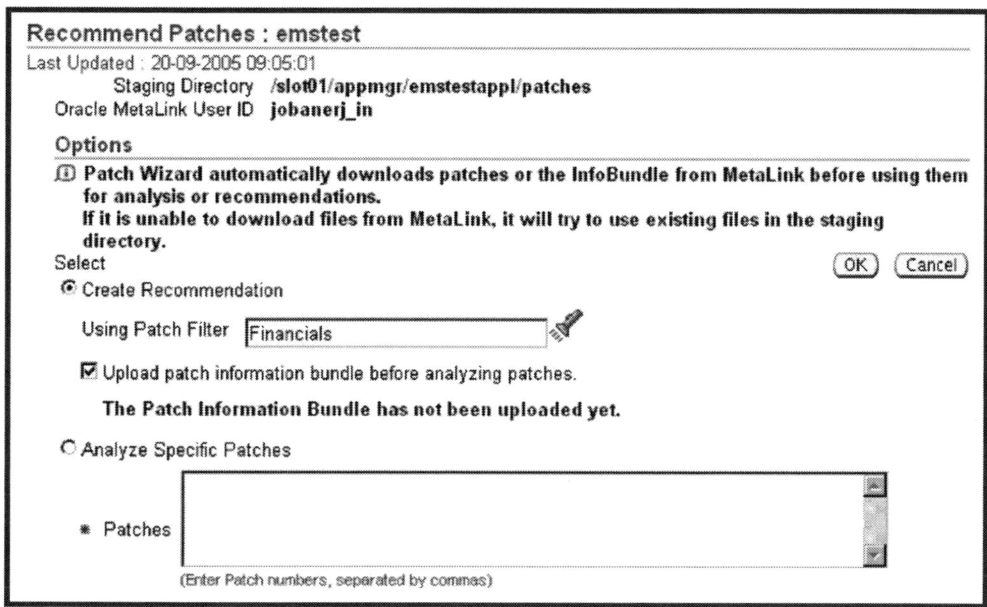

Fig. 11.47 Recommend Patches

Select a patch filter and press 'Ok' to create a recommendation. It prompts for a confirmation as shown in Fig. 11.48.

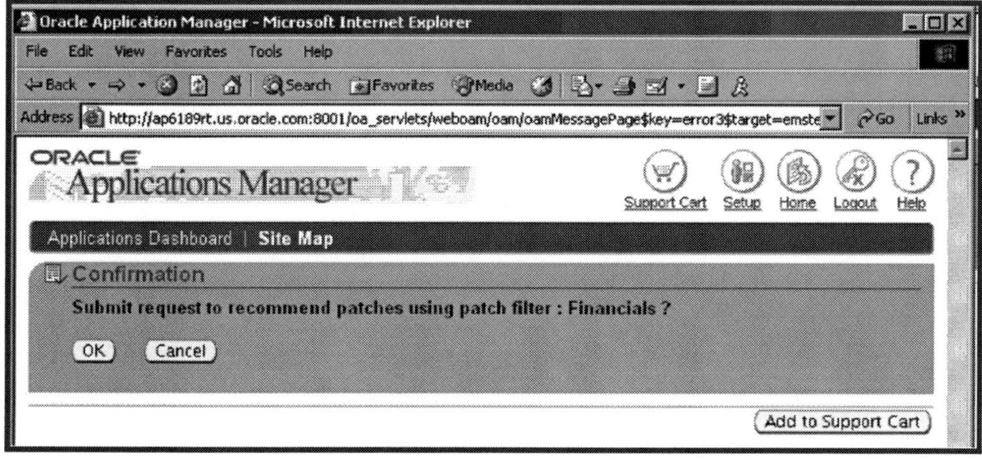

Fig. 11.48 Confirmation Screen for Recommending Patches

Once confirmed, it gives a request ID and the navigation path for viewing the status of the request.

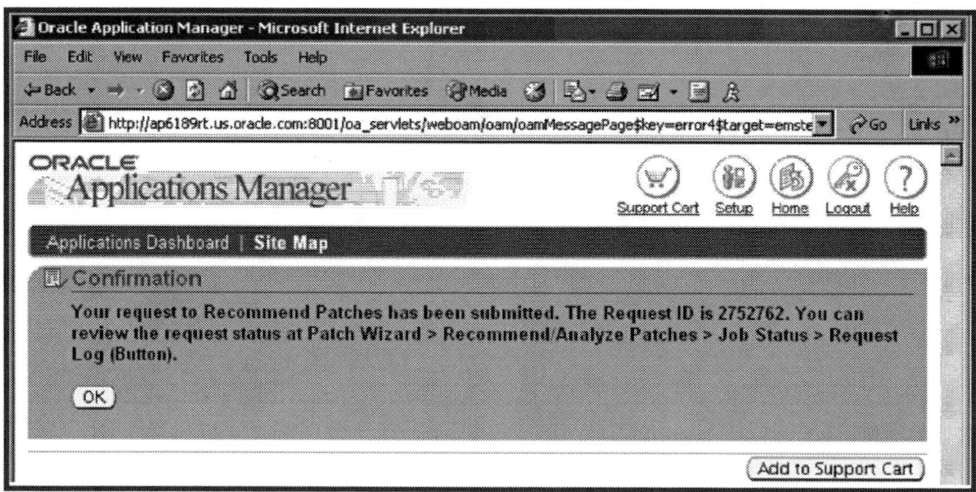

Fig. 11.49 Request ID for Recommend Patches

If the request is successful, the job is displayed in the 'Results' section of the patch wizard main page. If not, the job will not appear here. Check the request log from the 'Job Status Request' page to identify the issue.

Download patches

This is the last option in the patch wizard tasks menu (see Fig. 11.50). It is useful as OAM will take care of the headache of downloading patches. It can even merge the patches if required. You can also schedule the downloading for a later time. The download patch has four sections.

- Patch selection—enter the patch number that you would like to download separated by a comma. There are two options available for download, 'Download only' and 'Download and analyze'. The former simply downloads and the latter downloads as well as analyzes.
- Automatically merge downloaded patches—this option automatically merges the patches only if the download is successful. In merge options, there are three fields.
  - Automatically merge download patches. Check this box if you want to merge the patches automatically once the download is complete.
  - Merged patch name. The default is Merged_(date)(time).
  - Merging strategy is where you specify how you want the patches to be merged. There are three options available.
    - One merged patch: It's a single merged patch containing all the US and NLS patches.
    - Two merged patch: Here you specify the creation of two merged patches, one for US and other for NLS.
    - Multiple merged patch: Here you specify the creation of multiple patches, one for US and one for each language installed.

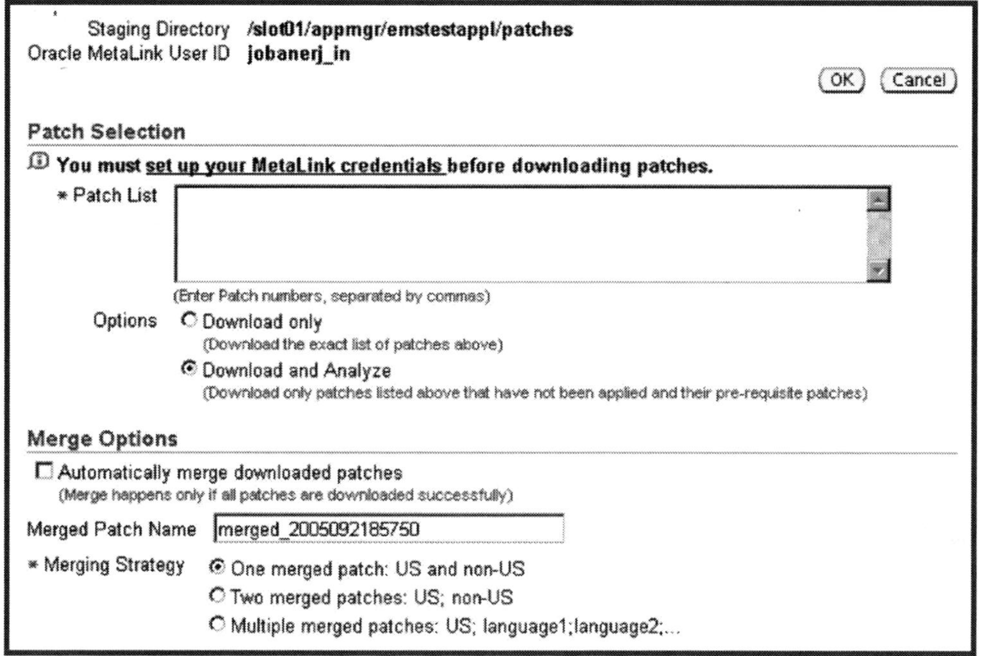

Fig. 11.50 Download and Analyze Screen

- Language and Platform: Here you specify the languages for which you want to download the patch. You can download patches of more than one language at a time. Here you also specify the platform for which you would like to download the patch. You can't download a patch for more than one platform.
- Schedule: If you want to schedule the download on a specified date and time you can do so.

Recommended patches results

Clicking the 'Details' icon associated with a patch request in the patch wizard main page accesses the 'Recommended Patches Results' page. This page lists the results of the selected recommend patches requests submitted.

The set of recommended patches are divided in two sections:

- Recommended patches for current code level
- Patches that introduce a new code level

Timing reports

This gives a detailed report about the Autopatch and adadmin sessions. This includes details of the time each job was started, how long the job continued, the number of failures in the job, the number of jobs skipped, details of the job run successfully (see Fig. 11.51). This report is very useful for the management as it contains the detailed information of the downtime. This report is also useful for doing a root cause analysis if there is a delay in deliverables.

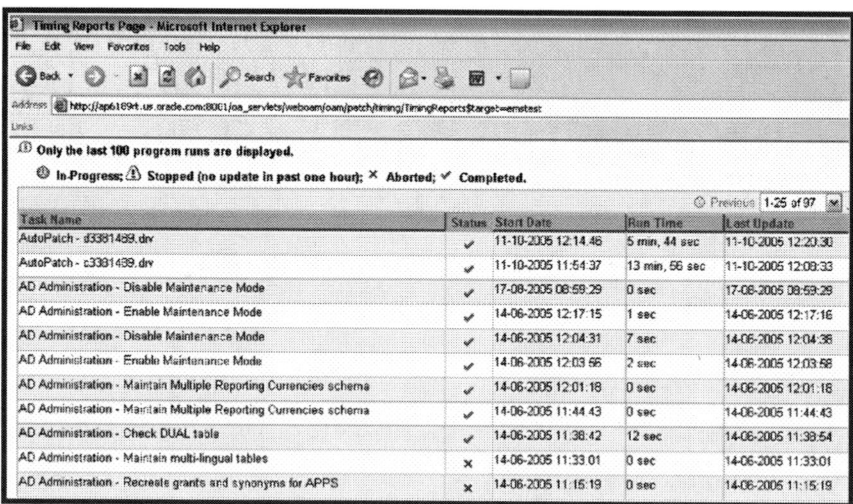

Timing Reports Page - Microsoft Internet Explorer

Only the last 100 program runs are displayed.

In-Progress; Stopped (no update in past one hour); ✕ Aborted; ✓ Completed.

Previous 1-25 of 97

Task Name	Status	Start Date	Run Time	Last Update
AutoPatch - d3381489.drv	✓	11-10-2005 12:14:46	5 min, 44 sec	11-10-2005 12:20:30
AutoPatch - c3381489.drv	✓	11-10-2005 11:54:37	13 min, 56 sec	11-10-2005 12:08:33
AD Administration - Disable Maintenance Mode	✓	17-08-2005 08:59:29	0 sec	17-08-2005 08:59:29
AD Administration - Enable Maintenance Mode	✓	14-06-2005 12:17:15	1 sec	14-06-2005 12:17:16
AD Administration - Disable Maintenance Mode	✓	14-06-2005 12:04:31	7 sec	14-06-2005 12:04:38
AD Administration - Enable Maintenance Mode	✓	14-06-2005 12:03:56	2 sec	14-06-2005 12:03:58
AD Administration - Maintain Multiple Reporting Currencies schema	✓	14-06-2005 12:01:18	0 sec	14-06-2005 12:01:18
AD Administration - Maintain Multiple Reporting Currencies schema	✓	14-06-2005 11:44:43	0 sec	14-06-2005 11:44:43
AD Administration - Check DUAL table	✓	14-06-2005 11:38:42	12 sec	14-06-2005 11:38:54
AD Administration - Maintain multi-lingual tables	✕	14-06-2005 11:33:01	0 sec	14-06-2005 11:33:01
AD Administration - Recreate grants and synonyms for APPS	✕	14-06-2005 11:15:19	0 sec	14-06-2005 11:15:19

Fig. 11.51 Timing Reports Page

The timing report contains the following information.

- Task Name: This contains information about the exact task, viz. Auto Patch or adadmin. It also give details about the driver of the Auto Patch and the module of the adadmin.
- Status: Whether it completed successfully or not.
- Start Date: The date and the time the task was started.
- Runtime: The total duration for which the task was run.
- Last Update: When the timing information was last updated.
- Details: This contains a link to the details of the task for the maintenance session. Figure 11.52 shows the snapshot of the details screen.

Focus	Task Name	Elapsed Time	Start Date	End Date
	▼ AutoPatch			
⊕	▼ AutoPatch startup after aimini	1 min, 5 sec	11-10-2005 12:14:46	11-10-2005 12:15:51
⊕	▼ Run a single patch driver file	4 min, 36 sec	11-10-2005 12:15:54	11-10-2005 12:20:30
	Steps before copy portion	5 sec	11-10-2005 12:15:54	11-10-2005 12:15:59
⊕	▼ Database portion steps	4 min, 27 sec	11-10-2005 12:15:59	11-10-2005 12:20:26
	Get initial list of invalid objects in DB	14 sec	11-10-2005 12:15:59	11-10-2005 12:16:13
⊕	▼ Run SQL scripts and EXEC commands	2 min, 12 sec	11-10-2005 12:16:13	11-10-2005 12:18:25
⊕	▼ Running database update commands	2 min, 11 sec	11-10-2005 12:16:14	11-10-2005 12:18:25
⊕	▼ Running SQL and EXEC commands in parallel	2 min, 10 sec	11-10-2005 12:16:14	11-10-2005 12:18:24
⊕	▼ Running parallel SQL and EXEC commands	2 min, 10 sec	11-10-2005 12:16:14	11-10-2005 12:18:24
	con	10 sec	11-10-2005 12:18:03	11-10-2005 12:18:13

Fig. 11.52 Snapshot of Details Screen

Manage downtime schedules

You can manage downtimes schedules for doing maintenance activity in your application system. You can fill in all the details about the downtime, viz. the cause, when it starts and ends, the point of contact of the application system at the downtime, the message that will be displayed if the users try to log in during the downtime.

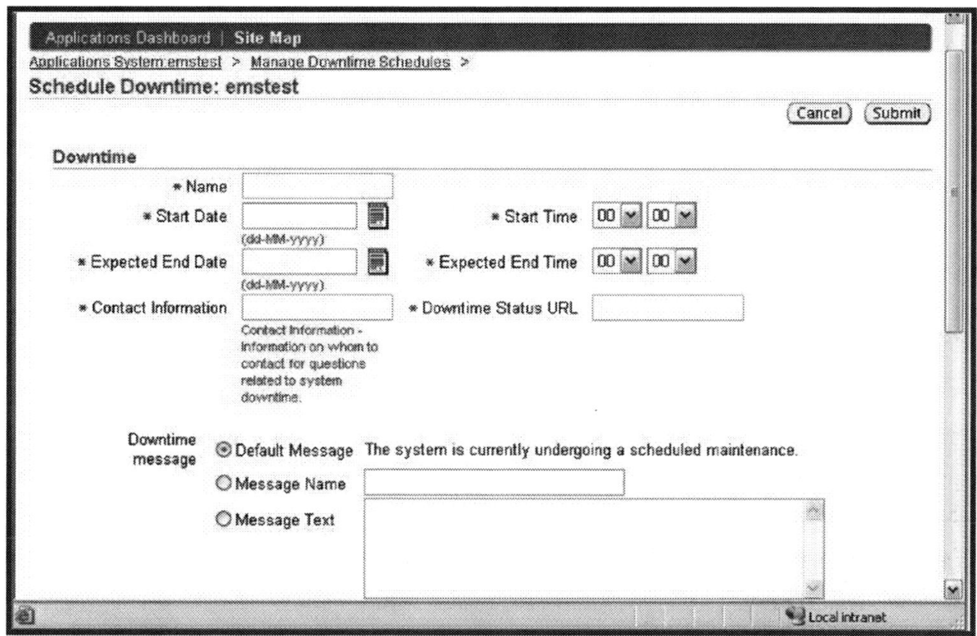

Fig. 11.53 Manage Downtime Schedules

Cloning

Cloning is the process of creating an identical copy of the Oracle application system. You can do this with OAM also. This is the easiest mode of cloning, where you only have to enter the source and target application system details. OAM takes care of cloning and configuring the target application system. It is a web-based process.

The process of cloning via OAM is divided into two categories, simple and advanced.

Simple clone

Simple clone creates an exact copy of your source information system. The following information needs to be given for a simple clone.

- Clone Name: Name of the clone process used to identify the clone job.
- Description: A brief description about the clone, why the new application system would be used, etc.

- Target: Name of the target application system.
- Priority: There are three types of priority available, high, medium and low.
- Requester: The user ID of the person initiating the clone.
- Database Tier Details: The hostname and the SID need to be given.
- Application Tier Details: The target hostname of the Application tier.

Once all the details are entered, the next screen appears where it shows the details of the database host, database port, hostname of the Application tier, the various port numbers of the middle tiers and all the configuration details. In simple cloning you can only view the parameters; you cannot change any of them. On clicking the button, it starts the actual cloning and the exact status of the cloning is displayed. Figure 11.54 shows the details of the simple clone process.

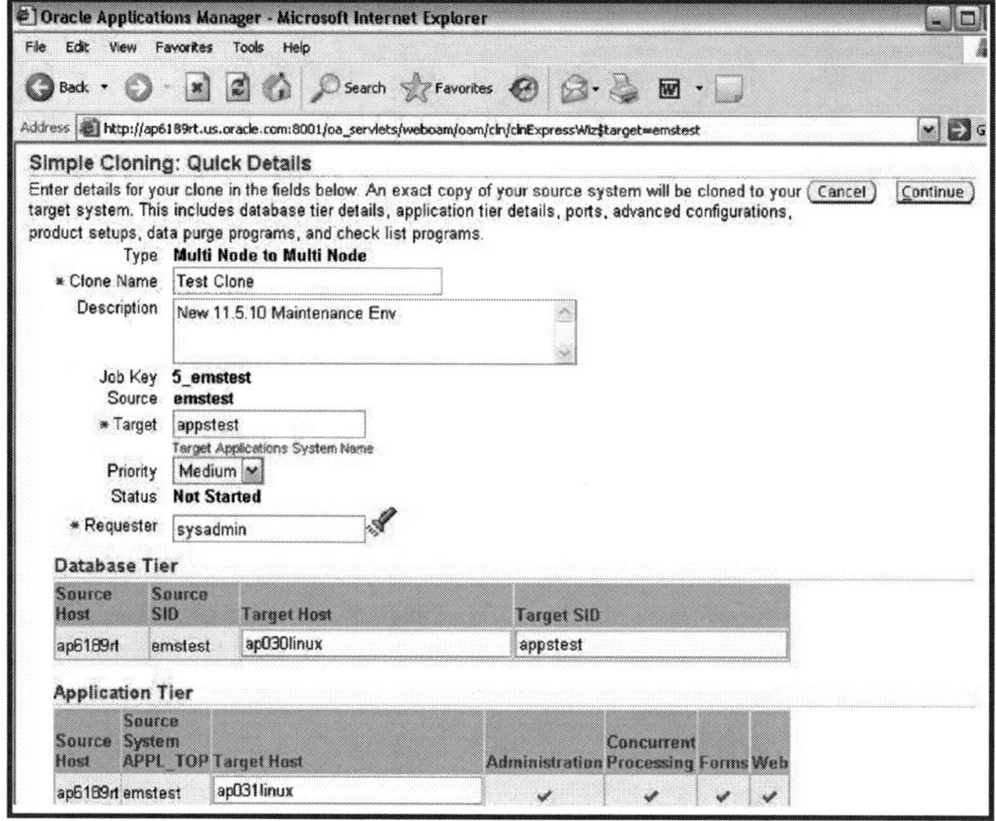

Fig. 11.54 Simple Cloning Screen

Figure 11.54 shows the values required for a simple clone.

The next screen of the simple clone is seen in Fig. 11.55. It shows the various servers and the details of the source and target instance. The next figure shows the details of all the ports of the target instance. In simple clone you cannot change any values of the ports and other parameters.

General Clone Information

Clone **Complete Applications System: Application Tier (APPL_TOP, Tech Stack) and Database Tier (RDBMS Home, Database)**

Type

Cloning Type **Multi Node to Multi Node**

Database Tier

Source System Nodes

Source Host	Domain	Port	SID	Details
ap6189rt	us.oracle.com	1521	emstest	

Available Target System Nodes

Source Host	Target Host	Domain	Port	SID	Details
ap6189rt	ap030linux	us.oracle.com	1521	appstest	

Application Tier

Source System Nodes

Source Host	Source System APPL_TOP	Platform	Administration	Concurrent Processing	Forms	Web	Details
ap6189rt	emstest	Linux	✔	✔	✔	✔	
ap6189rt	emstest	Linux	✔	✔	✔	✔	

Available Target System Nodes

Source Host	Source System APPL_TOP	Target Host	Platform	Administration	Concurrent Processing	Forms	Web	Details
ap6189rt	emstest	ap031linux	Linux	✔	✔	✔	✔	

Fig. 11.55 General Clone Information

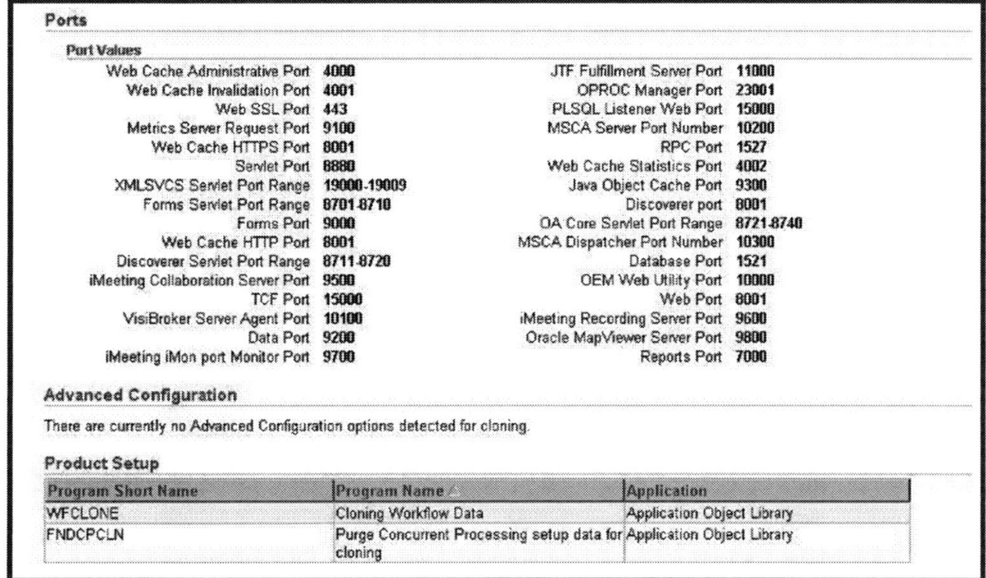

Ports

Port Values

Port	Value	Port	Value
Web Cache Administrative Port	4000	JTF Fulfillment Server Port	11000
Web Cache Invalidation Port	4001	OPROC Manager Port	23001
Web SSL Port	443	PLSQL Listener Web Port	15000
Metrics Server Request Port	9100	MSCA Server Port Number	10200
Web Cache HTTPS Port	8001	RPC Port	1527
Servlet Port	8880	Web Cache Statistics Port	4002
XMLSVCS Servlet Port Range	19000-19009	Java Object Cache Port	9300
Forms Servlet Port Range	8701-8710	Discoverer port	8001
Forms Port	9000	OA Core Servlet Port Range	8721-8740
Web Cache HTTP Port	8001	MSCA Dispatcher Port Number	10300
Discoverer Servlet Port Range	8711-8720	Database Port	1521
iMeeting Collaboration Server Port	9500	OEM Web Utility Port	10000
TCF Port	15000	Web Port	8001
VisiBroker Server Agent Port	10100	iMeeting Recording Server Port	9600
Data Port	9200	Oracle MapViewer Server Port	9800
iMeeting iMon port Monitor Port	9700	Reports Port	7000

Advanced Configuration

There are currently no Advanced Configuration options detected for cloning.

Product Setup

Program Short Name	Program Name	Application
WFCLONE	Cloning Workflow Data	Application Object Library
FNDCPCLN	Purge Concurrent Processing setup data for cloning	Application Object Library

Fig. 11.56 Ports Screen

Once the finish button is clicked it starts the clone and the status page appears. From this, we can obtain the status of the clone.

Advanced clone

In advanced cloning you can change all the configuration parameters. Another feature of advanced clone also is that it allows the replication of only a certain component of Oracle Applications in the target system. The following details need to be given for an advanced clone.

- Clone name that will be used for identifying the clone.
- Description of the clone.
- The name of the target application system.
- Priority of the task, high, low or medium.
- Requester/initiator of the cloning.

Apart from entering the details, there are seven steps in an advanced cloning.

Establish cloning parameters

In this step, you enter the details of the cloning parameters. You need to click the button 'Go to Task' as shown in Fig. 11.57.

Name	Required	Last Updated	Go To Task	Status	Details
Task 1: Establish Cloning Parameters	Yes			Not Started	
Task 2: Prepare the Source System	Yes			Not Started	
Task 3: Copy Application Tier Files from Source to Target	Yes			Not Started	
Task 4: Copy Database Tier Files from Source to Target	Yes			Not Started	

Fig. 11.57 Enter Cloning Parameters

This takes you to the next screen shown in Fig. 11.58.

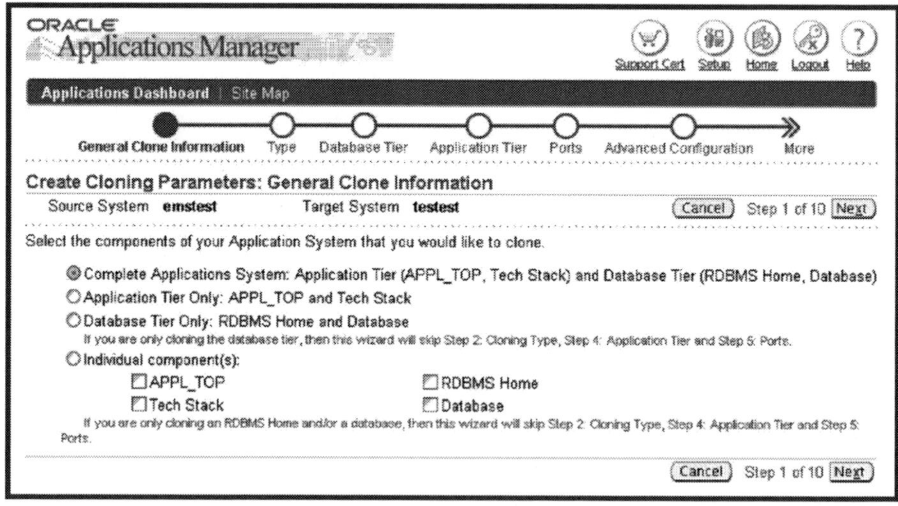

Fig. 11.58 Selection of Cloning Components

In this screen, you specify the components of the application system you would like to clone. You can clone a complete application (including the database and the `APPL_TOP`) or choose to clone only individual components like the `APPL_TOP`, the Tech Stack or the database tier.

In the next screen you define the type of cloning, viz. single node to single node, single to multi-node or multi- to multi-node.

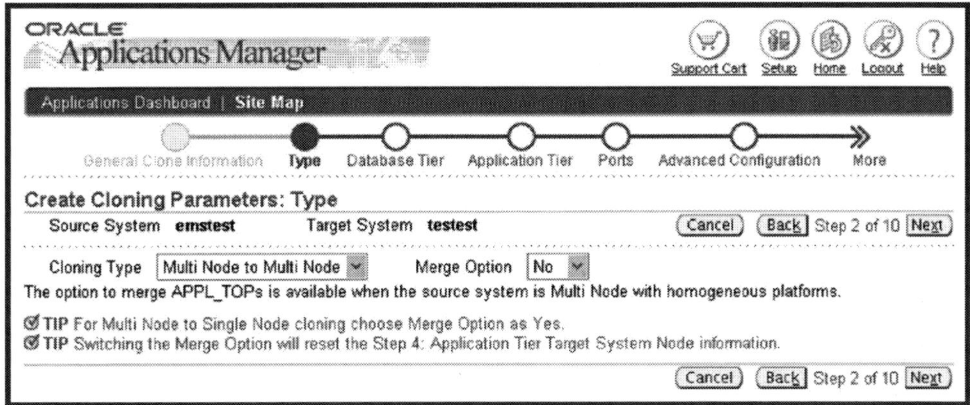

Fig. 11.59 Type of Cloning

You then need to give the details of the target database in the next screen.

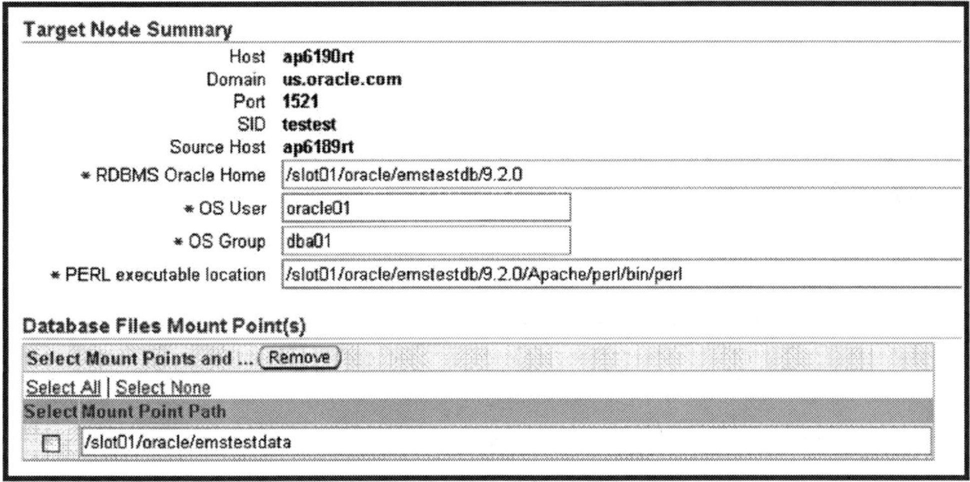

Fig. 11.60 Target Node Details

- Hostname: Hostname of the target database.
- Domain: The domain of the target database
- Port: The port of the target database.
- SID: The SID of the target database.

- Source host: The hostname of the source database.
- Oracle Home: The Oracle Home of RDBMS database.
- OS User: The owner of the Oracle files system.
- OS Group: The group of the Unix Oracle user.
- Perl executable Loc: The location of the perl executable.
- Data files Location: The location of the data files of the target instance.

In the next screen, you define the cloning the parameters of the `APPL_TOP`. In this screen you define target host for Forms, Concurrent Manager, Apache and admin tier. If it is a multi-node `APPL_TOP` you also define the nodes that will host each server.

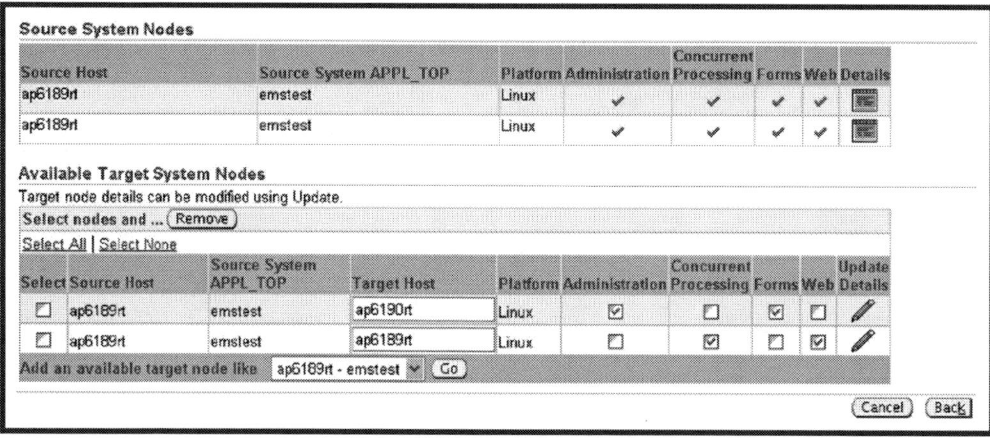

Fig. 11.61 Source System Nodes

You can specify the mount points of various top level directories of the `APPL_TOP` by clicking the 'Update details' button (Fig. 11.62). You can specify the following details of the `APPL_TOP`:

- Hostname: The hostname of the `APPL_TOP`
- Domain: The domain name
- `APPS OS` User: The operating system owner of the `APPL_TOP`
- `APPS OS` Group: The operating system group of the OS user
- Common Top Dir: The mount point of the common top
- 8.0.6 Oracle Home: The mount point of 8.0.6 Oracle Home
- iAS Oracle Home: The mount point of Apache Oracle Home
- JDK1.3.1 Location: The full pathname of the JDK1.3.1 executable
- Perl Exe Location: The full pathname of the perl executable
- `APPL_TOP` mount point: The full pathname of the `APPL_TOP` mount point.

Application Tier: Update Target Node Details

Source System **emstest** Target System **testest** (Cancel) (OK)

Target Node Summary

Host	**ap6189rt**
Platform	**Linux**
Source Host - APPL_TOP Name	**ap6189rt - emstest**
Supported Application Services	**Administration, Concurrent Processing, Forms, Web**
* Domain	us.oracle.com
* Apps OS User	appmgr01
* Apps OS Group	applgp01

Locations

* COMMON_TOP directory	/slot01/appmgr/emstestcomn
* 8.0.6 Oracle Home	/slot01/appmgr/emstestora/8.0.6
* iAS Oracle Home	/slot01/appmgr/emstestora/iAS
* JDK 1.3.1 Location	/local/java/jdk1.4.2_04
* PERL executable location	/slot01/appmgr/emstestora/iAS/Apache/perl/bin/perl

APPL_TOP Mount Point(s)

* APPL_TOP mount point	/slot01/appmgr/emstestappl
Auxiliary mount point 2	/slot01/appmgr/emstestappl
Auxiliary mount point 3	/slot01/appmgr/emstestappl

Fig. 11.62 Update Target Node Details

In the next screen shown in Fig. 11.63, you can assign the various ports to the components of the middle tiers. In the simple clone option, you can't change the ports, but in advance clone you can allocate the various ports. You can either manually change all the ports or change them using the port pool option. This option increases the value of the port number by the number chosen in port pool; say, if you choose a port pool of five then all the default ports will be increased by five.

You can do product-specific task from the next screen, like cloning the workflow data from the source to the target application system.

Since you are cloning the application system from a source you don't want unnecessary data from the source application system. In the next screen, you can purge the unnecessary data from your source application system.

Once the cloning is done, you can run diagnostic tests to check the process. You can schedule the test at the time of cloning itself. In the next screen, you define the products for which you want to run the diagnostic tests.

The last screen is the review where all the information you have entered can be viewed at one place. If you think you have entered any wrong information you can go back and change it. Pressing 'Ok' completes the entry of the cloning parameters.

Port Pool

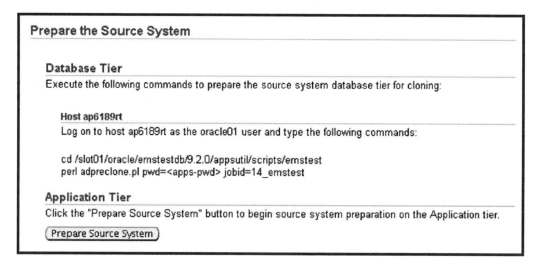

Select the port pool number to populate the ports that you want to use on the target system.

Port Pool [0] (Go)

Port Values

Port	Value	Port	Value
* Web Cache Administrative Port	4000	* JTF Fulfillment Server Port	9300
* Web Cache Invalidation Port	4001	* OPROC Manager Port	8100
* Web SSL Port	443	* PLSQL Listener Web Port	8200
* Metrics Server Request Port	9200	* MSCA Server Port Number	10200
* Web Cache HTTPS Port	8000	* RPC Port	1626
* Servlet Port	8800	* Web Cache Statistics Port	4002
* XMLSVCS Servlet Port Range	19000-19009	* Java Object Cache Port	12345
* Forms Servlet Port Range	18000-18019	* Discoverer port	8000
* Forms Port	9000	* OA Core Servlet Port Range	16000-16009
* Web Cache HTTP Port	8000	* MSCA Dispatcher Port Number	10300
* Discoverer Servlet Port Range	17000-17009	Database Port	**1521**
* iMeeting Collaboration Server Port	9500	* OEM Web Utility Port	10000
* TCF Port	15000	* Web Port	8000
* VisiBroker Server Agent Port	10100	* iMeeting Recording Server Port	9600
* Data Port	9100	* Oracle MapViewer Server Port	9800
* iMeeting iMon port Monitor Port	9700	* Reports Port	7000

Fig. 11.63 Assigning Ports

Prepare the source system

In this phase, you prepare the source application system to kickoff the clone process. The preparation of the source is divided into two parts, automatic and manual. Both of these are explained in Fig. 11.64.

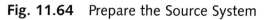

Prepare the Source System

Database Tier

Execute the following commands to prepare the source system database tier for cloning:

Host ap6189rt

Log on to host ap6189rt as the oracle01 user and type the following commands:

```
cd /slot01/oracle/emstestdb/9.2.0/appsutil/scripts/emstest
perl adpreclone.pl pwd=<apps-pwd> jobid=14_emstest
```

Application Tier

Click the "Prepare Source System" button to begin source system preparation on the Application tier.

(Prepare Source System)

Fig. 11.64 Prepare the Source System

The preparation of the database clone part is manual, as one has to log in to the database server and execute the command for preparing the clone process. The preparation of the clone of the `APPL_TOP` is automatic and can be started by clicking 'Prepare Source System'. At the time of the preparation of the source application system it makes various templates. The following is an excerpt from the log file.

```
Completed 20 templates...
Making
inventory/Components21/oracle.sysman.sqlserver/9.2.0.1.0/context.xml
@ 07:16
Templatizing '/SLOTS/slot01/oracle/emstestdb/9.2.0/inventory/
Components21/oracle.sysman.perfman/9.2.0.1.0/context.xml' to '/SLOTS/
slot01/oracle/emstestdb/9.2.0/appsutil/template/inventory/Components21/
oracle.sysman.perfman/9.2.0.1.0/context.xml'
Templatizing '/SLOTS/slot01/oracle/emstestdb/9.2.0/inventory/
Components21/oracle.sysman.capacity/9.2.0.1.0/context.xml' to '/SLOTS/
slot01/oracle/emstestdb/9.2.0/appsutil/template/inventory/Components21/
oracle.sysman.capacity/9.2.0.1.0/context.xml'
Templatizing '/SLOTS/slot01/oracle/emstestdb/9.2.0/inventory/
Components21/oracle.sysman.events/9.2.0.1.0/context.xml' to '/SLOTS/
slot01/oracle/emstestdb/9.2.0/appsutil/template/inventory/Components21/
oracle.sysman.events/9.2.0.1.0/context.xml'
Templatizing '/SLOTS/slot01/oracle/emstestdb/9.2.0/inventory/
Components21/oracle.rsf.platform_rsf/9.2.0.1.0/context.xml' to '/SLOTS/
slot01/oracle/emstestdb/9.2.0/appsutil/template/inventory/Components21/
oracle.rsf.platform_rsf/9.2.0.1.0/context.xml'
```

Fig. 11.65 Excerpt from Log File

Copy application tier files from source to system

Here you copy the files of the Application tier, viz. the `APPL_TOP` from the source to the target environment. You need to log in the source system Application tier nodes and shut down all the middle tier services. Once this is done, copy the following directories from the source to the target (Fig. 11.66).

The following directories need to be copied from the source to the target:

- `$APPL_TOP`
- `$COMMON_TOP/html`
- `$COMMON_TOP/java`
- `$COMMON_TOP/util`
- `$COMMON_TOP/clone`
- `$COMMON_TOP/_pages`

This takes us to the next step.

Applications System:emstest > Advanced Cloning >

Copy Application Tier Files from Source to Target

Back Done

Manual Instructions:

Log on to the source system application tier nodes.
Shut down the application tier server processes.
Copy the following application tier directories from the source to the target application tier host(s). The application tier directories on the target hosts should be owned by user appmgr01.

Expand All | Collapse All

Focus	Source Path	Type	Target Host	Target Path
	▼Application Tier			
	▼ap6189rt			
	/slot01/appmgr/emstestappl	APPL_TOP Mount Point(s)	ap6190rt	/slot01/appmgr/emstestappl
	/slot01/appmgr/emstestcomn/html	OA_HTML	ap6190rt	/slot01/appmgr/emstestcomn/html
	/slot01/appmgr/emstestcomn/java	OA_JAVA	ap6190rt	/slot01/appmgr/emstestcomn/java
	/slot01/appmgr/emstestcomn/util	COMMON_TOP/util	ap6190rt	/slot01/appmgr/emstestcomn/util
	/slot01/appmgr/emstestcomn/clone	COMMON_TOP/clone	ap6190rt	/slot01/appmgr/emstestcomn/clone
	/slot01/appmgr/emstestcomn/_pages	COMMON_TOP/_pages	ap6190rt	/slot01/appmgr/emstestcomn/_pages

Fig. 11.66 Copying Application Tier Files

Copy database tier files from source to target

In this step you copy the data files, log files and control files from the source to the target. Log into the DB tier and shutdown the database with a proper shutdown. Then copy all the files and press 'Done'.

Configure the target system

To configure the target system you need to log in to the target system as Oracle user and run the following commands from the DB as well as the Application tier.

Execute the following command:

```
cd <RDBMS ORACLE_HOME>/appsutil/clone/bin
perl adcfgclone.pl dbTier <full path of context file>
```

Log in to the `APPL_TOP` as the owner of the application file system, viz. `applmgr` and execute the following command.

```
cd $COMMON_TOP/clone/bin
perl adcfgclone.pl apps Tier <full path of the context file>
   as shown in the pic below
```

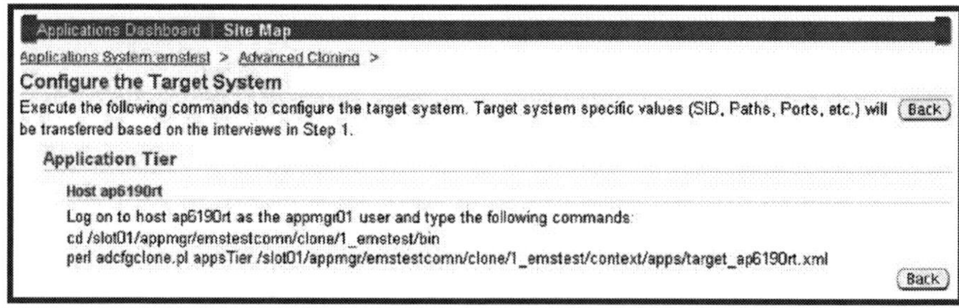

Fig. 11.67 Configuring the Target System

Initiate data purge

These are the data purge parameters you set in the first step. Click the 'Submit Request' icon next to each program to run the program. You can click 'Outcome' to review this.

Review checklist

These are the diagnostic programs that you chose in the first step, which can now be run. Click the 'View Results' tab to see the results of the tests.

Once these steps are completed, start the target application and do a complete sanity check.

12

Upgrading Oracle Applications

If you want to explore the full potential of Oracle Applications, the best way is to upgrade your application system to the latest version of Oracle Applications, which is now Release 12. Upgrading to 11.5.10 is a pre-requisite for upgrading to R12 in a few situations. So, in this section we will be discussing upgrading to 11.5.10 and in the next section, we will be discussing upgrading to R12.

SECTION 1

UPGRADING TO 11.5.10

The 11.5.10 database tier consists of an Oracle9*i* version 9.2.0.6 (9.2.0 Oracle home) for both new installations and upgrades.

The 11.5.10 Applications technology stack includes:

- Oracle Internet Application Server iAS 1.0.2.2.2—includes Oracle HTTP Server
- RDBMS 8.0.6 (Oracle Home)
- Oracle Developer6i (6.0.8.2.4)
- Oracle Forms
- Oracle Reports
- Oracle Graphics
- Discoverer (4.1.48)
- JInitiator (1.3.1.18)

We will discuss the upgrade of Oracle Application in two sections—one, upgrading from Release 10.7 or 11.0 of Oracle Applications and the other, upgrading from a previous release 11*i* version of Oracle Applications.

UPGRADING FROM RELEASE 10.7 OR 11.0 OF ORACLE APPLICATIONS

If you are upgrading from release 10.7 or 11.0.X then Rapid Install is used in both pre-upgrade and post-upgrade processing steps. You also need to fulfill the minimum software requirement for 11.5.10 CU2, which has already been discussed in Chapter 4.

The Pre-upgrade Process

The upgrade process consists of several steps which we will discuss one by one.

Announcing downtime

The first step towards an upgrade is announcing a downtime. All the users must be aware of it well in advance and the downtime should be planned in such a way that it has the least effect in terms of revenue. Ideally, the upgrade should be planned for weekends or holidays.

Backing up the application system

A full backup of the database and the `APPL_TOP` must be taken before starting the upgrade process. Then, in case of any upgrade failures you can revert to the existing system. A cold backup of the database should be taken with the normal shutdown.

Running TUMS utility

TUMS is a utility to help customers reduce the number of steps in the upgrade. It looks at a customer's specific situation, and identifies which steps are relevant for that customer. The Upgrade Manual Script (TUMS) is used to create a report that lists the upgrade steps that don't apply to your Oracle Application installation. You can ignore these steps.

Apply patch 3422686

You need to download and apply the TUMS 3422686 patch from Metalink using the adpatch utility to generate the TUMS report. The TUMS patch needs to be applied for both 10.7 and 11.0.x versions of Oracle Applications.

Run adtums.sql

Once the patch is applied successfully the adtums.sql script is used to generate the TUMS report. For the `<DIRECTORY>` value, enter the full path of the directory where you want the TUMS report. This directory must be listed in the `UTL_FILE_DIR` parameter of your init.ora before TUMS can write the report and must have the appropriate permissions to write the report (`tums.html`).

If you are upgrading from release 10.7

For Unix users:

```
$ cd $AD_TOP/patches/107/sql
$ sqlplus <APPS username>/<APPS password> @adtums.sql <DIRECTORY>
```

For Windows users:

```
C:\> cd %AD_TOP%\patches\107\sql
C:\> sqlplus <APPS username>/<APPS password> @adtums.sql <DIRECTORY>
```

If you are upgrading from release 11.0

For Unix users:

```
$ cd $AD_TOP/patch/110/sql
$ sqlplus <APPS username>/<APPS password> @adtums.sql <DIRECTORY>
```

For Windows users:

```
C:\> cd %AD_TOP%\patch\110\sql
C:\> sqlplus <APPS username>/<APPS password> @adtums.sql <DIRECTORY>
```

Review the TUMS report

The `adtums.sql` script creates a report called `tums.html`, which lists the Category 1–6 steps in the 11.5.10 upgrade that *do not* apply to your installation. You may safely ignore any steps listed in this report.

The sample report of the TUMS is given in Box 12.1.

Box 12.1

Oracle Applications Release 11*i*

Based on analysis of your installation it has been determined that you do not need to perform the following upgrade steps.

You may cross these steps out of the upgrading Oracle Applications Release 11.5.10 manual before you begin your upgrade.

If you are upgrading to a version of 11*i* other than 11.5.10, you must refer to the Metalink note 230538.1 for more details about the TUMS.

Maintain multilingual table (optional)

In case your application system has additional language than American English then you must ensure the validity and the accuracy of the multilingual table by running the adadmin and selecting the option Maintain Multilingual Table. The adadmin is discussed in more details in the adutilities chapter. There should not be any Oracle errors while performing this step.

Renaming custom database objects with application prefix (optional)

In case if you have custom database objects then you are required to rename the custom database objects with Applications prefix. The custom database must have been created as per the naming standard given in the Oracle Application Developers Guide, which is available for download from OTN.

Checking attachment file upload directory (optional)

You should check this directory if you have used Oracle Applications attachment to attach a file-type document to any application entity. In the previous releases of Oracle Applications, you could attach file-type documents in this manner. The files were stored in a directory on the application tier and the location was stored in the attachment file directory profile option. In release 11*i*, file-type attachments are stored in the database. You need to determine and note the location of the existing attachment file so that you can load them in the database at a later stage.

The steps for finding the location are:

- Log in as system administration
- Choose the 'Profile > System'
- In the Find System Profile Values window, type 'Attachment File Directory' in the Profile field and click 'Find'
- If it displays any profile option write down its path name
- Log in to the `APPL_TOP` and verify that the files exist in the directory specified
- If no results are displayed on the search, you can simply ignore this step

Saving the custom.pll

If you have done any customizations in Oracle Applications you must preserve the custom library (`custom.pll`), which will be used at a later stage.

The Oracle Applications upgradation is jointly done by the Applications DBA and the Oracle Applications Functional Consultants. Apart from the steps mentioned here, many product-related tasks also need to be performed by the Functional Consultant, which is beyond the scope of this book. The `APPS DBA` must coordinate with the Functional Consultant to ensure that all the steps are accomplished before running the Rapid Install.

The Upgrade Process

The upgrade starts with running Rapid Install. It needs to run twice, once for the actual upgrade and then to configure all Application systems once the upgrade is complete. This is the sequence in which the upgrade works from a 10.7 or 11.0.x release to 11.5.10CU2:

- Enter configuration parameters and run Rapid Install
- Run Auto Upgrade to upgrade products and database objects
- Run Auto Patch to apply the patches
- Run Rapid Install to configure and start all the servers and services

Running Rapid Install

The first time, Rapid Install is run to upgrade the Application file system and tech stack.

Specifying the configuration

The first step for upgradation is to specify the configuration values that the Rapid Install needs to create for a new file system and technology stack. This is done by typing *rapidwiz* at the command prompt. The welcome screen is shown in Fig. 12.2.

```
(appmgr01) rapidwiz - -bash $ ./rapidwiz

Rapid Install Wizard is validating your file system......
Preparing to start up Rapid Install...
Rapid Install Wizard will now launch the Java Interface.....

If you are performing a DVD/CD install, you must change directories in
your session to a directory outside of the DVD/CD-ROM mount point before
you will be able to eject the DVD/CD and proceed.

(appmgr01) rapidwiz - -bash $
```

Fig. 12.1 Unix Session 12.1

The welcome screen

The Rapid Install launches the Java Interface and the welcome screen is displayed.

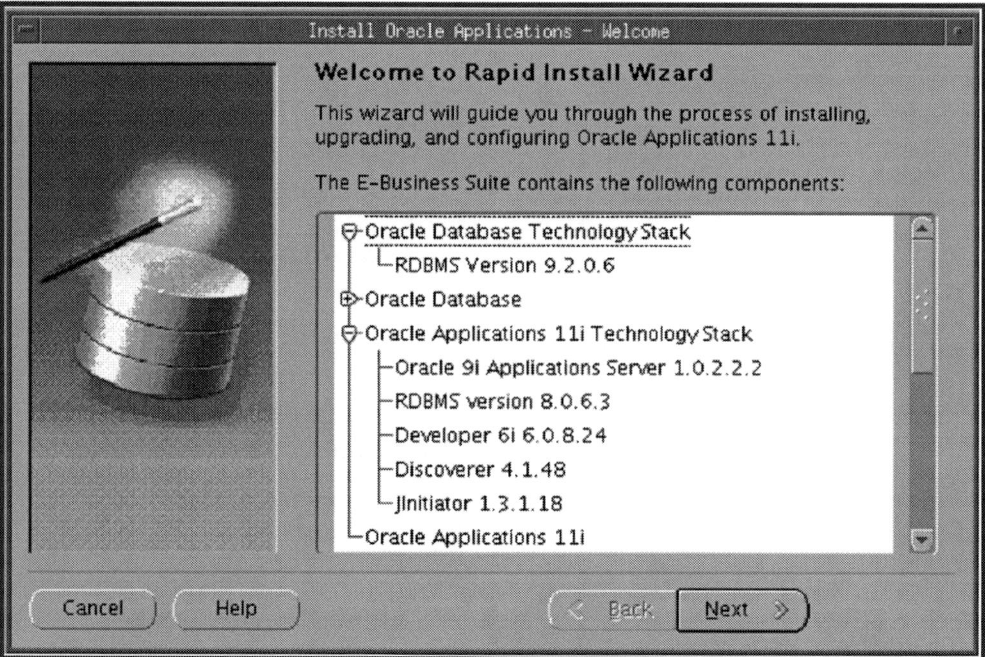

Fig. 12.2 Welcome Screen

The figure shows all the components that will be installed in the application system. The iAS technology stack is installed for the 1.0.2.2.2 version. It also installs Oracle 9.2.0.6 RDBMS Oracle home without a database. You are not required to give any input in this screen, so continue by pressing 'Next'.

Selecting wizard operation

The next screens displays two options—'Install Oracle Applications E-Business 11*i*' and 'Upgrade to Oracle Applications E-Business 11*i*'. The install option sets up a new, fully configured system. It is used when you are installing the Oracle Application system for the first time. There is one more check box, 'Use Express Configuration' along with the install option. This sets up a fully configured, single user/single node application system with either a Vision Demo or a fresh database. Since express configuration is used while installing the Oracle Application for the first time, it has already been discussed in an earlier chapter and so we won't discuss it here.

Since we are upgrading the existing installation, we will select the second option. Press 'Next' to continue.

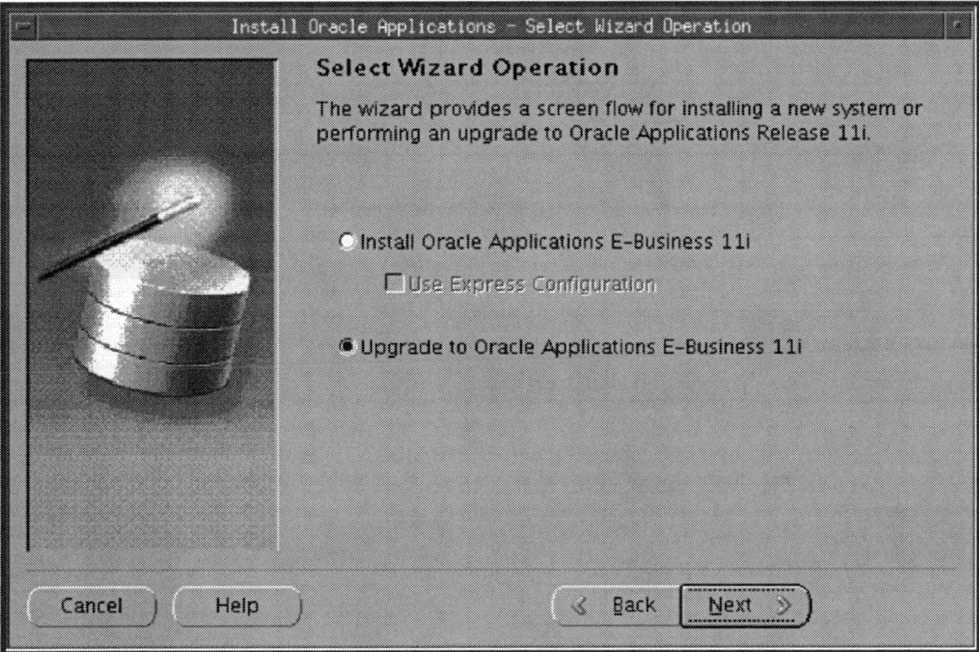

Fig. 12.3 Select Wizard Operation

Select upgrade action

There are two options here (Fig. 12.4):

1. Create upgrade file system
2. Configure upgraded 11*i* Instance

The first option is chosen while running the Rapid Install during the upgrade stage. Here Rapid Install collects the configuration parameters for your application system and stores them in a configuration file (`config.txt`). When you run the Rapid Install, it creates a context file (`envname.xml`) containing the details of your application system.

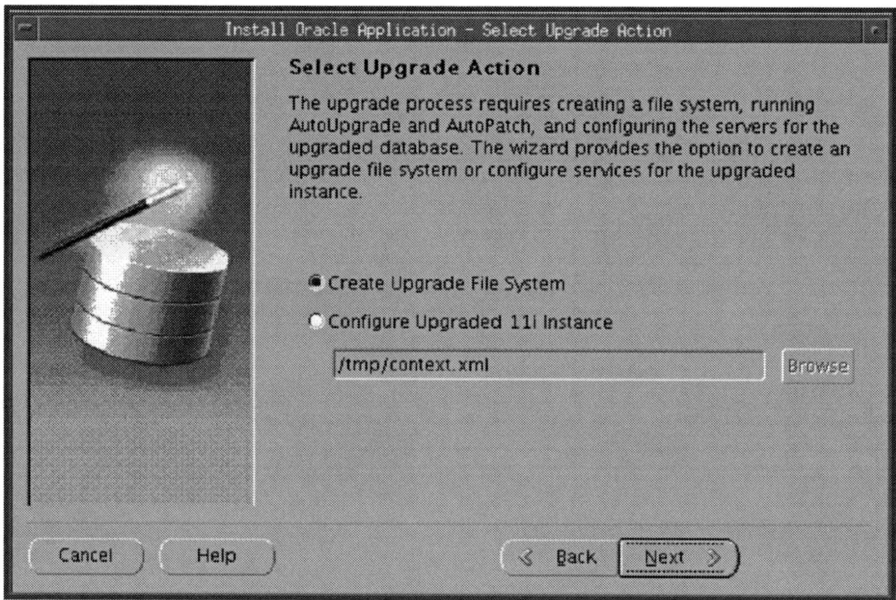

Fig. 12.4 Select Upgrade Action

The second option is chosen when running Rapid Install during the post-upgrade stage. Here you specify the location and name of the context file created while running the Rapid Install earlier.

Here, we will choose the first option.

Load configuration

This screen shown in Fig. 12.5 prompts whether or not you will be using an existing configuration file. If you select 'No' Rapid Install creates a new configuration file '`config.txt`' and stores all the information in it. Rapid Install uses this file to configure the application file system and install the technology stack components.

If you select 'Yes' the Rapid Install prompts for the full location of the file and uses the parameters given there. This option is used typically when a previous run is unsuccessful and Rapid Install is being run for the second time. It can also be chosen when copying the configuration file to other nodes in a multi-node upgrade.

Since we are doing the upgrade for the first time, choose 'No' and click 'Next' to continue.

Selecting install type

The next screen shown in Fig. 12.6 prompts you to select the type of installation. Here, you indicate whether your existing system is a single node or multiple node installation.

In a single node upgrade, the database and `APPL_TOP` as well as all the middle tier components are installed on one server.

In a multi-node upgrade, the database, middle tier components and the `APPL_TOP` are distributed across multiple servers. All the nodes can be configured to share a common `APPL_TOP`.

We will first do a single node upgrade and then a multi-node one.

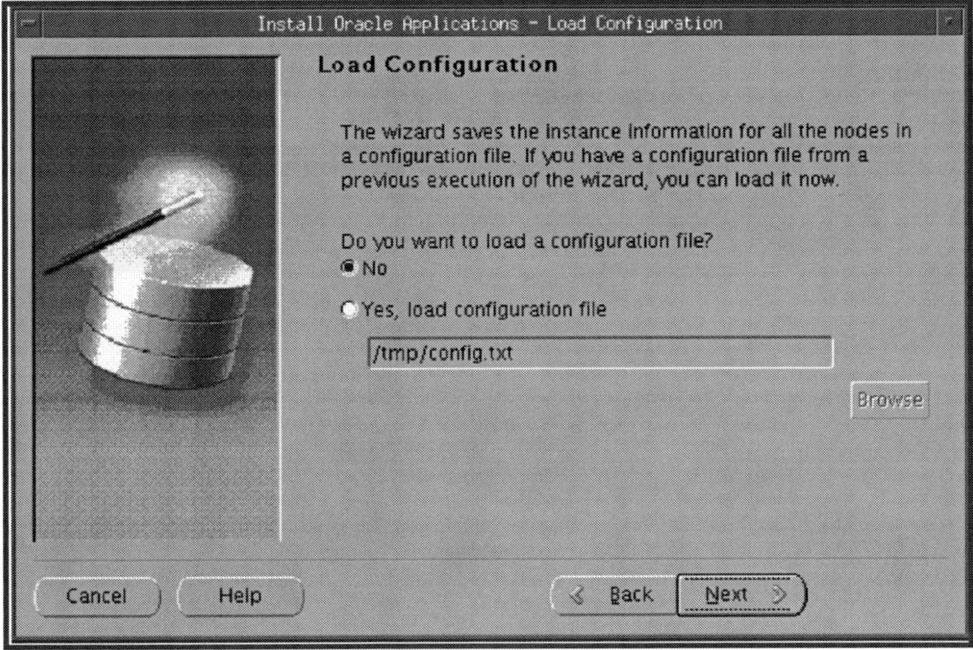

Fig. 12.5 Load Configuration

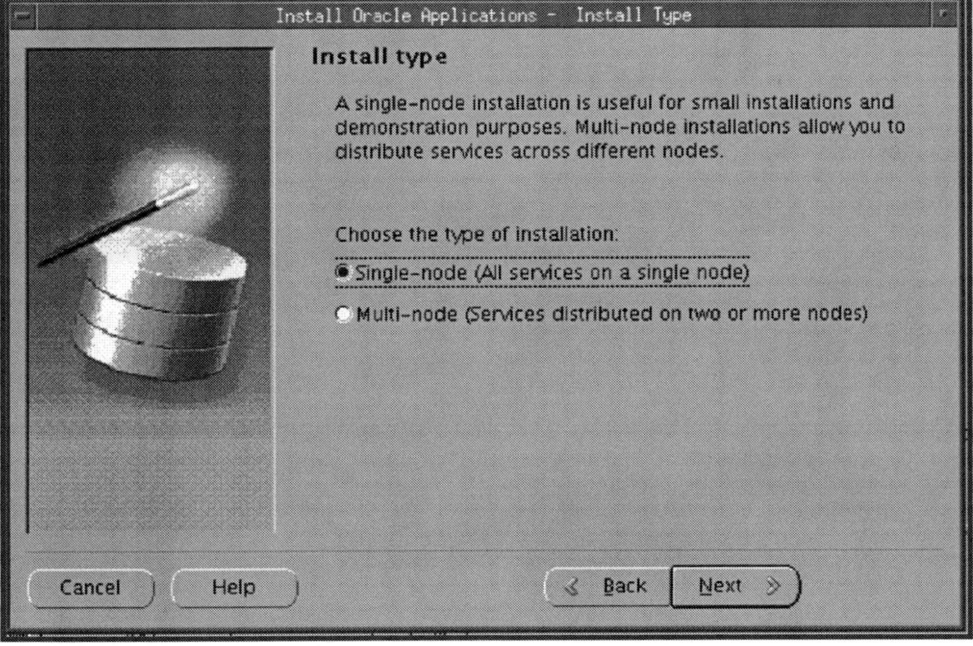

Fig. 12.6 Selecting Install Type

Define database type

In this screen you describe your existing database (see Fig. 12.7). Upgrading Oracle Application to the latest version (i.e. 11.5.10 CU2) upgrades the database to the 9.2.0.6 version. In this screen, you indicate the name of your existing database in the database name field. Since the database upgrade is a part of Oracle Applications upgrade, the database type field is grayed out. The database name that you enter should be exactly similar to the existing one.

Enter the value of the domain name. The domain name when combined with the hostname must produce a fully qualified domain name.

Enter the port number of your database port in the respective field. This port number is used to connect to your database.

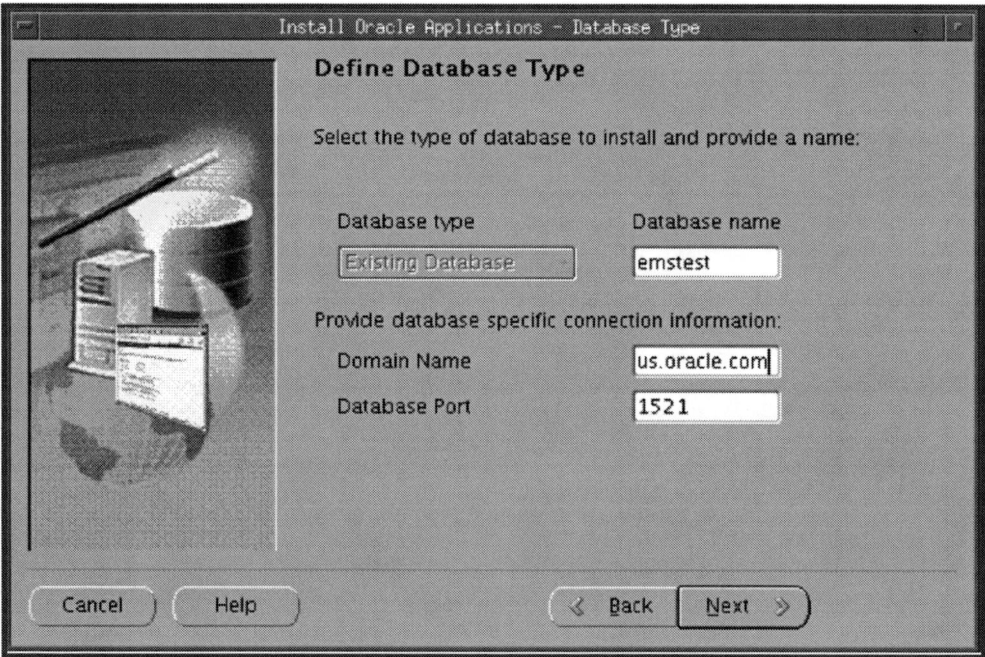

Fig. 12.7 Define Database Type

Reviewing user information

The next screen shown in Fig. 12.8 displays the user name and the default password for it. If your actual passwords are different from the defaults then you must enter them for your existing application system.

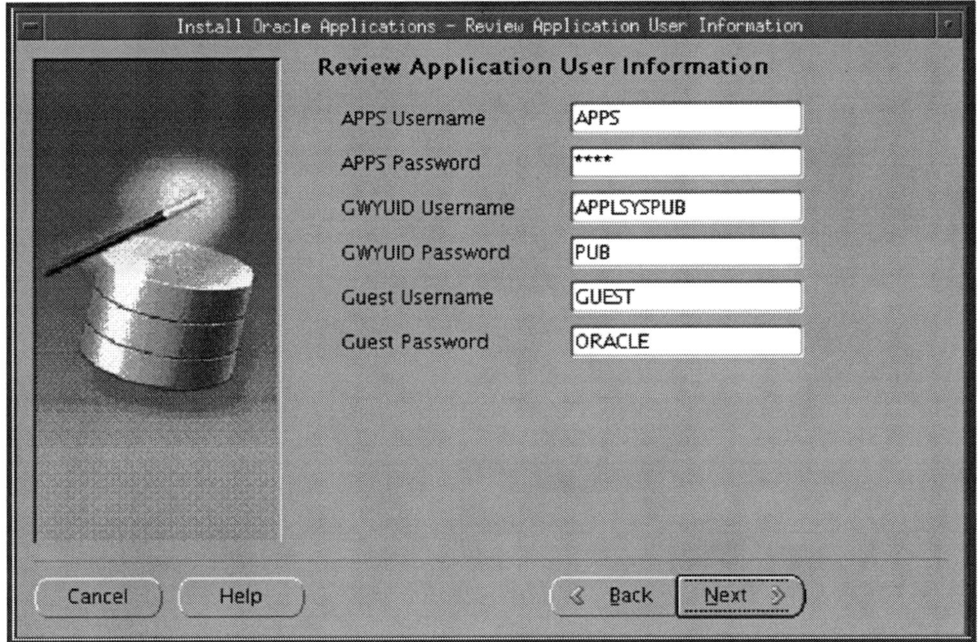

Fig. 12.8 Reviewing User Information

The default user names and passwords are given in Table 12.1.

Table 12.1 Default User Names and Passwords

User name	Password
APPS	APPS
APPLSYSPUB(GWYUID)	PUB
GUEST	ORACLE

Database install information

In this screen you enter the database information in more detail (see Fig. 12.9). The Oracle OS user is the operating system user name who will own the Oracle file system. The Oracle OS group is the Unix group name of the Oracle user. The Base Install directory is the top level directory used to derive the mount points associated with the database. Please note that this is *not* the ORACLE_HOME.

You can feed the base install directory and proceed further. If you want to refine the directory path for the derived mount points then click the button 'Advanced Edit'. This opens a new screen where you can give the details (see Fig. 12.10).

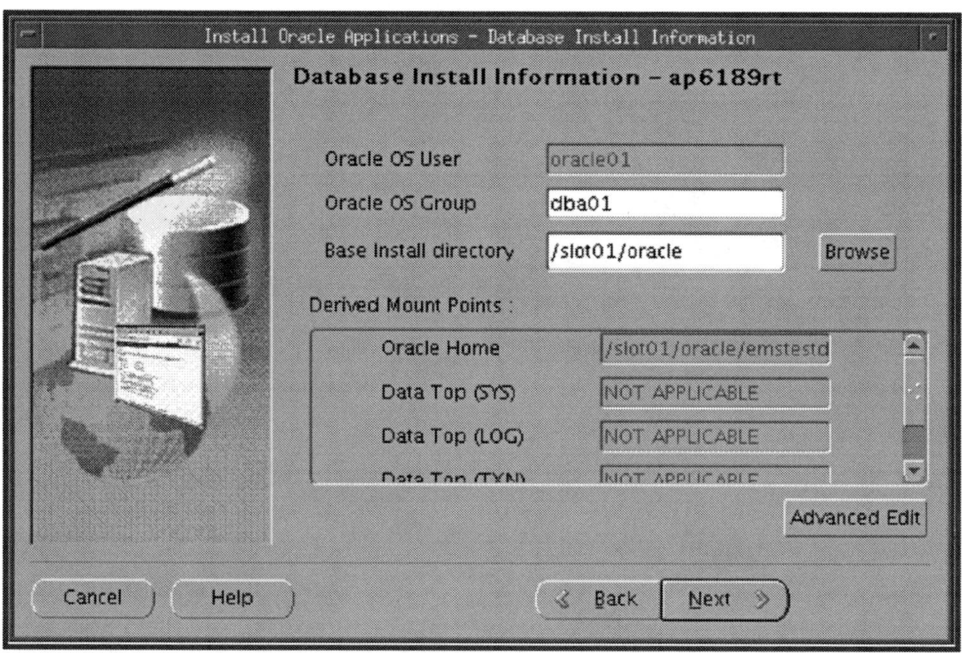

Fig. 12.9 Database Install Information

Database Mount Points

Database Install Information

Oracle Home /slot01/oracle/emstestdb/9.2.0 Browse

Data Top (SYS) Browse

Data Top (LOG) Browse

Data Top (TXN) Browse

Data Top (ARCHIVE) Browse

OK Cancel

Fig. 12.10 Database Mount Points

In this screen you can edit the individual mount points if their values differ from the default ones. Click 'OK' to return to the database information screen and press 'Next' to continue.

From Figs 12.9 and 12.10, it can be seen that you can edit only the Oracle Home field and not the Data Top (which is the location of the data files). It can also be seen from the figure in the Data Top locations it's a blank field. This is because Rapid Install doesn't create any database during an upgrade process, just a new Oracle Home.

If all the parameters given are correct in the database information screen then the Rapid Install connects to the existing database and determines the active and additional languages installed in the application system. If this is possible the additional language screen doesn't appear.

If Rapid Install is not able to connect to the existing database, it opens the 'Select Additional Language' screen as shown in Fig. 12.11.

Selecting additional languages

The default language of the application system is American English. If you have more than one language installed in your existing application system, select them using the '>' button. You cannot add or delete new languages from this screen. You must have the NLS software available for all the additional languages as well as the Rapid Install for the translated software.

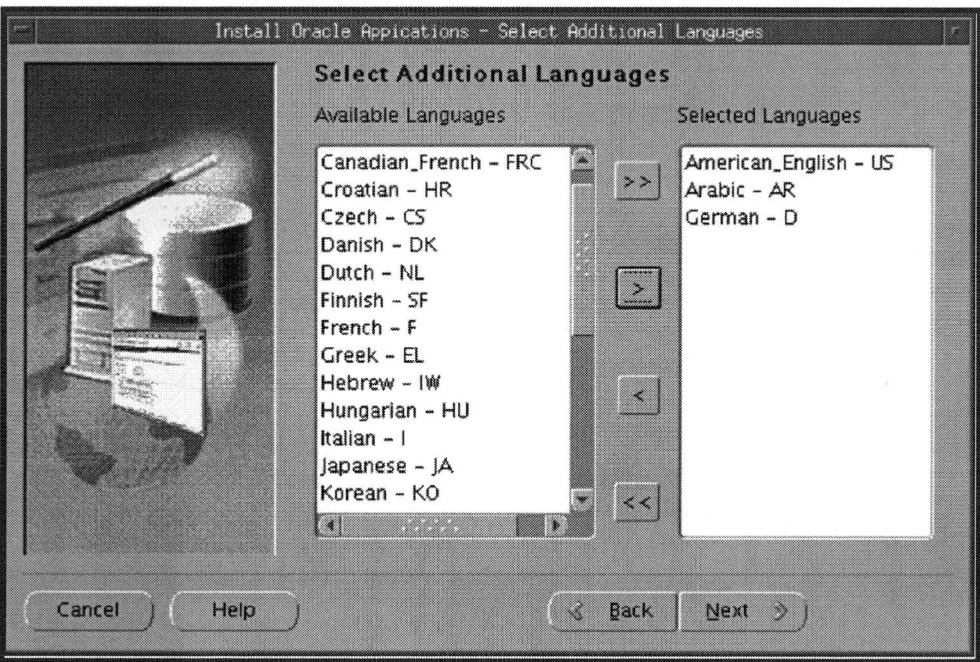

Fig. 12.11 Selecting Additional Languages

If you want to add more languages it can be done once the upgrade is over. You can use the License Manager from OAM to register additional languages and then install it by downloading the appropriate language software from Oracle Technology Network, *http://www.oracle.com/technology/index.html.*

Selecting internationalization settings

If you have the software for additional languages installed in your application system then you can review the internationalization settings in the next screen shown in Fig. 12.12.

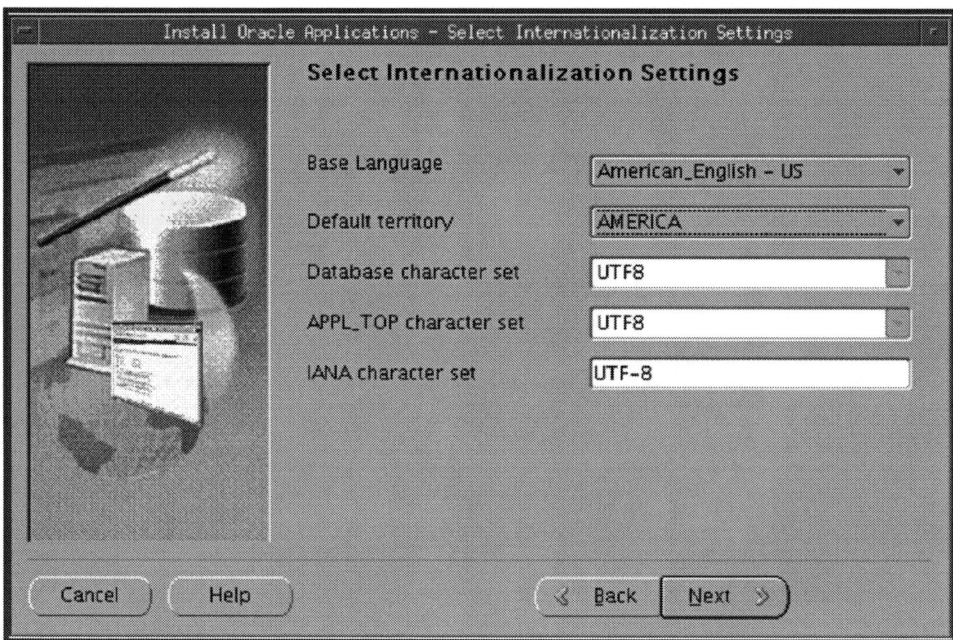

Fig. 12.12 Selecting Internationalization Settings

If the Rapid Install is able to connect with the existing database, it queries for internationalization details from your database and displays the Base Languages, Default Territory, Database character set, APPL_TOP character set and IANA character set. If the rapid install is able to connect to the database then all the fields are grayed out. If it is unable to do so, if the Rapid Install is not able to connect to the existing database it displays the default values.

- Base Language: The base language is the default language of your application system. If you have more than one language the base language field is not grayed out, and you can change it. If you have only American English as the active language then this field is grayed out and cannot be changed.
- Default Territory: This is set to AMERICA by default and should remain so during the upgrade.
- Database Character: This refers to the common character set of the database, which is compatible with all the additional languages installed in your application system.
- APPL_TOP Character: This refers to the common character set of the APPL_TOP, which is compatible with all the additional languages installed in your application system.
- IANA Character: This refers to the Internet Assigned Number Authority character set. For more information about this, visit *http://www.iana.org/assignments/character-sets.*

APPL_TOP node information

Here you specify the top level directory and the mount points for the APPL_TOP (see Fig. 12.13).

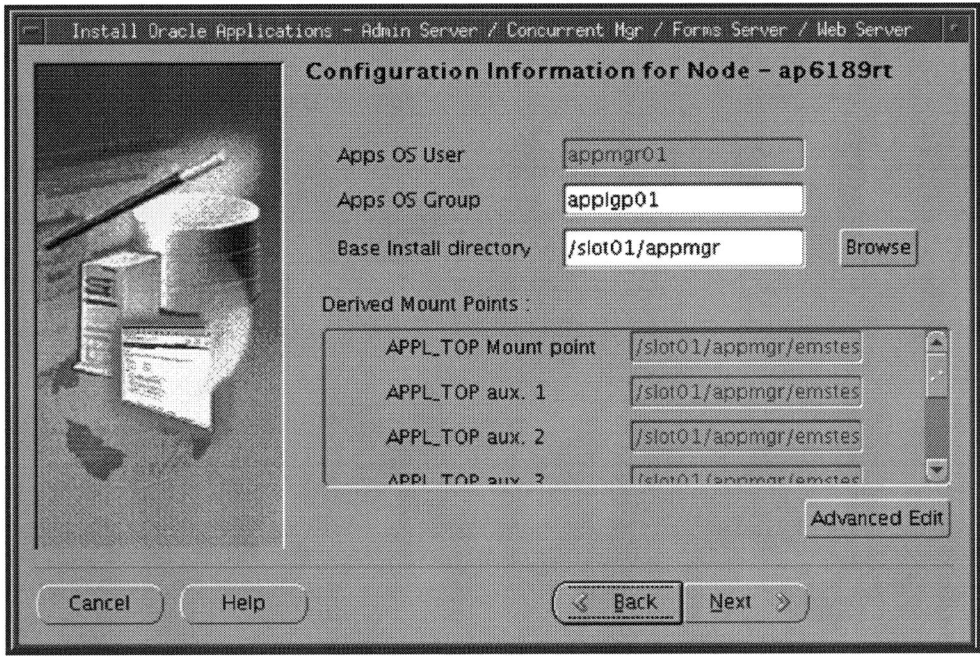

Fig. 12.13 APPL_TOP Node Information

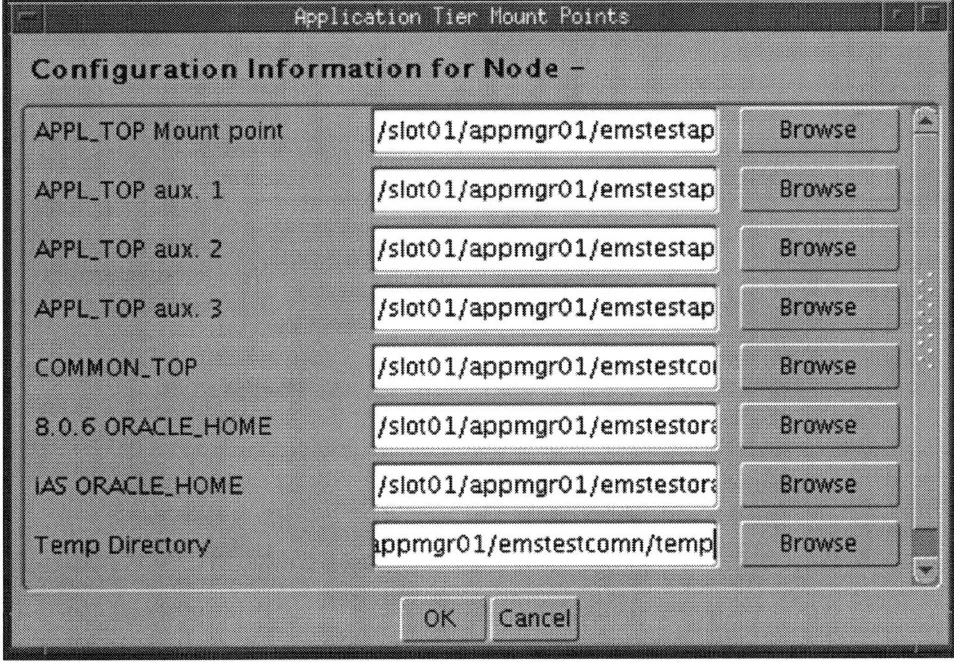

Fig. 12.14 Application Tier Mount Points

From the screen shown in Fig. 12.14 you can change the mount points of the following:.

- `APPL_TOP`
- `COMMON_TOP`
- `8.0.6 ORACLE_HOME`
- `iAS ORACLE_HOME`
- Temp Directory

Global system settings

The next screen prompts for the global domain name that your system will use to connect the services and listeners.

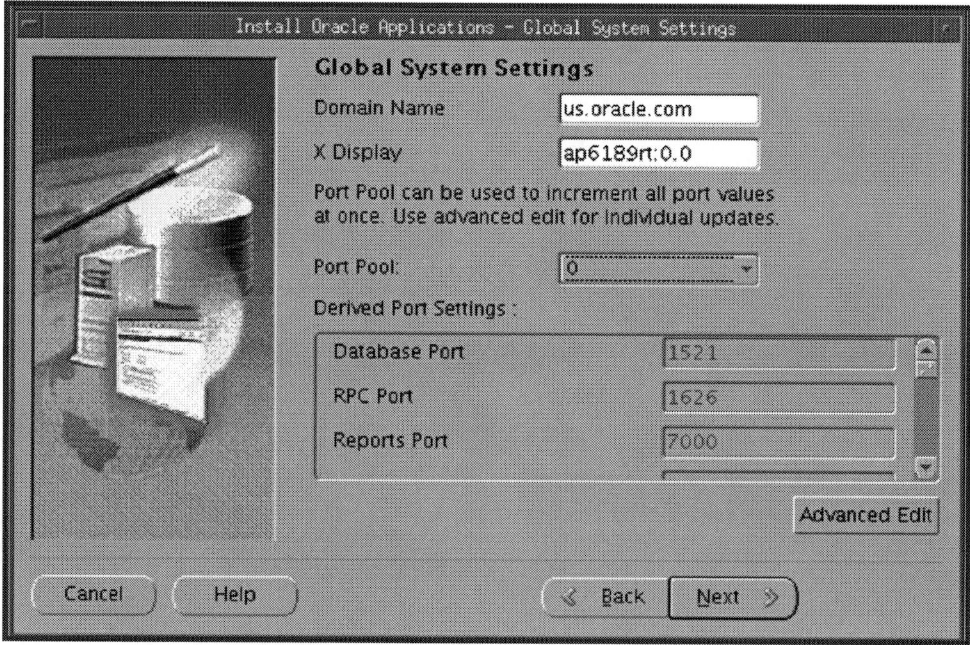

Fig. 12.15 Global System Settings

The domain name should be such that when combined with the hostname it produces a fully qualified domain name, viz. in *ap6189rt.us.oracle.com*, the domain name is `us.oracle.com`.

X Display is the default of the operating system, which should be Hostname:0,0.

The screen shown in Fig. 12.16 also shows the port numbers that Rapid Install will be assigning for various components. Port pool option increases the default values by adding a counter to the default port.

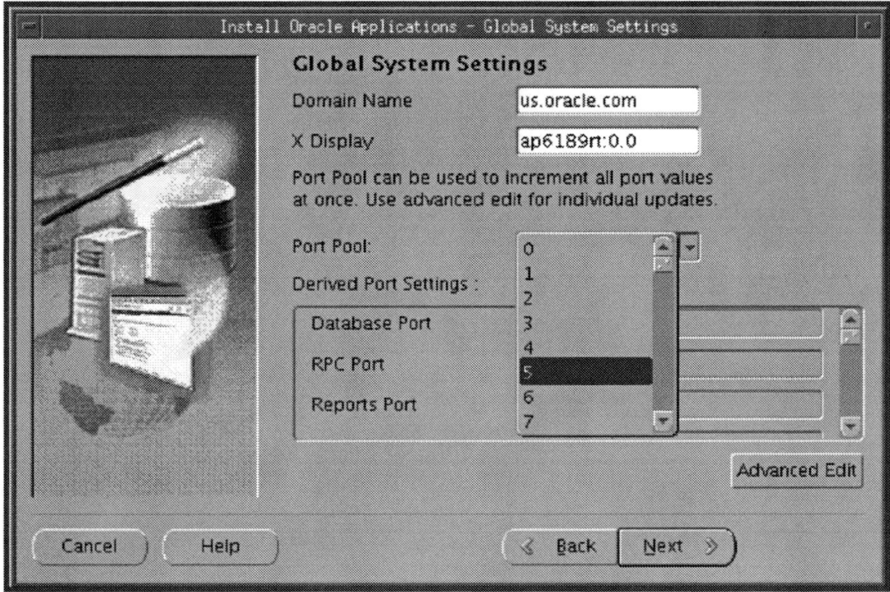

Fig. 12.16 Port Pool Details

If you want to assign totally different values, click on the 'Advanced Edit' button. This shows all the ports that the Rapid Install assigns.

Port Values

Port Values

Database Port	1521
RPC Port	1631
Reports Port	7005
Web Listener Port	8005
OProcMgr Port	8105
Web PLSQL Port	8205
Servlet Port	8805
Forms Listener Port	9005
Metrics Server Data Port	9105
Metrics Server Req. Port	9205

OK Cancel

Fig. 12.17 Various Ports

Saving the configuration file

By now, you have given all the information required to run the Rapid Install. All the information is stored in a configuration file '`config.txt`' used to configure a specific Oracle Application Instance. Rapid Install uses these values during the installation to create the file system, install the database, and configure and start the server processes. The default location of the file is temp directory. It is always advisable to save the `config.txt` file to some other location as it can be used for re-installation or if the installation errors out at a later stage.

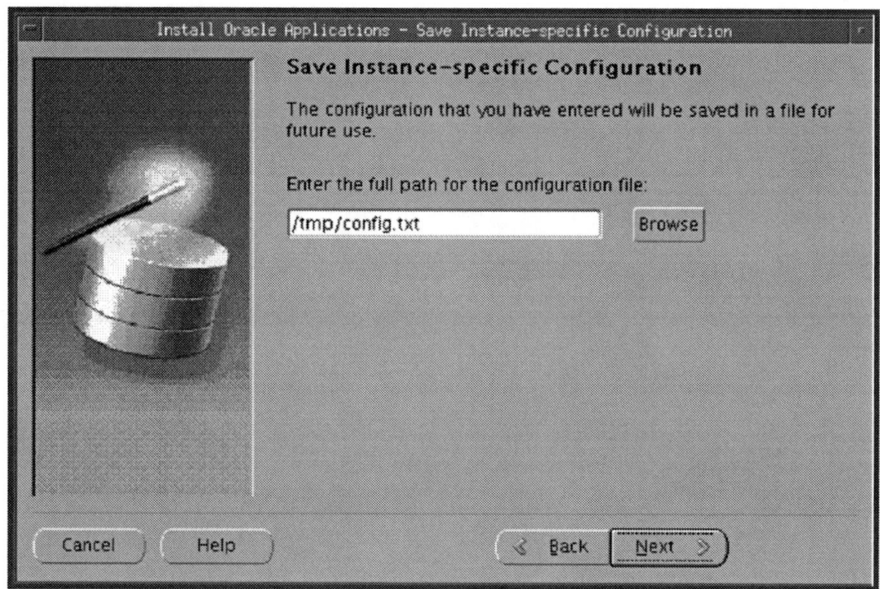

Fig. 12.18 Saving the Configuration File

Pre-install checking

Before starting the installation the Rapid Install performs a number of checks to ensure the process is smooth (see Fig. 12.19).

It checks the system on the following parameters.

- Port Uniqueness: There is no duplicate defined port for the processes
- File Space Check: It ensures that the file system have sufficient space
- OS Patch Check: It ensures that the right Operating System patches are there
- File System Check: It checks whether the files are mounted properly and have correct permission
- Host/Domain Check: It verifies the hostname and the domain name
- System Utilities Check: It checks whether the linking utilities, viz. make, ld and cc are available or not

The results of each test are labeled with check marks (✓) or exclamation marks (!) or a cross (×) mark. The significance of these symbols have been explained earlier. Click 'Yes' to continue and 'No' to review the issues.

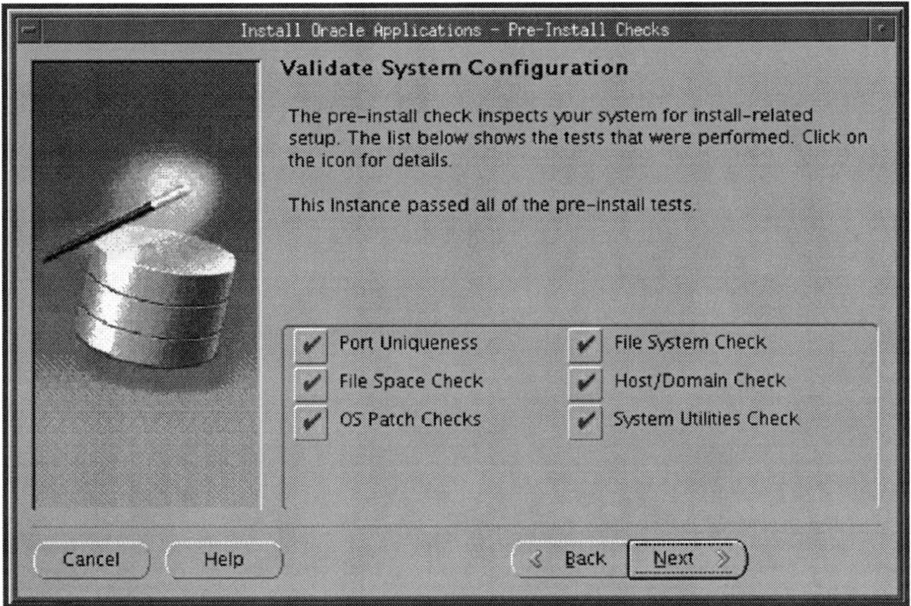

Fig. 12.19 Pre-install Checks

Component installation review

Rapid Install now lists all the components that it will install based on the parameters entered earlier.

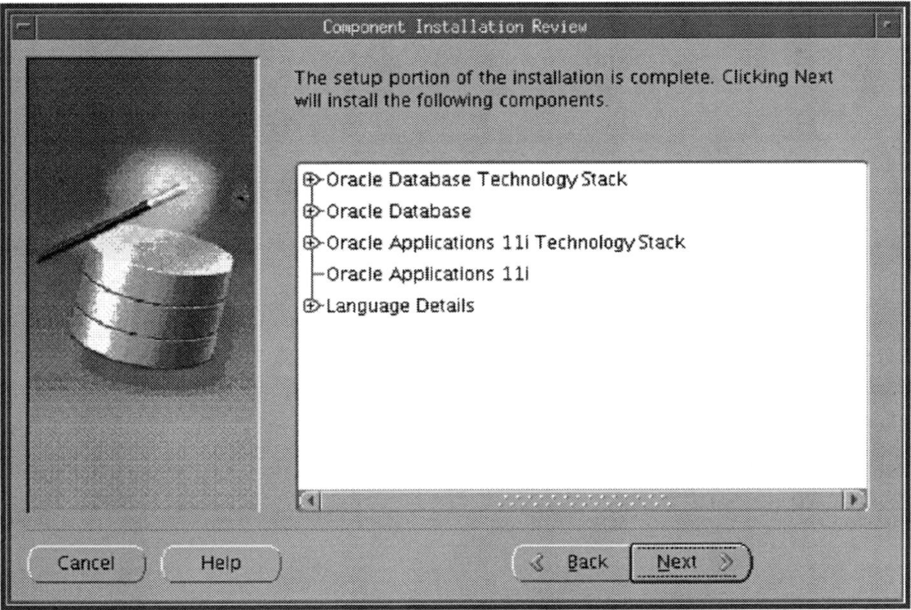

Fig. 12.20 Component Installation Review

On clicking 'Next' it displays an alert asking if you want to start the Rapid Install now.

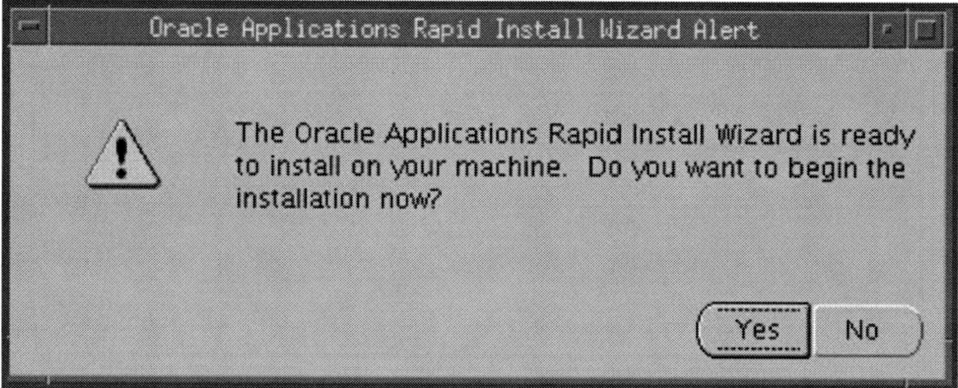

Fig. 12.21 Confirming to Start Installation

Click 'Yes' to start the installation. Rapid Install creates a new file system for the `APPL_TOP` and the technology stack `ORACLE_HOME`. It also creates `ORACLE_HOME` for the database.

Once the installation is started, the status bar is displayed.

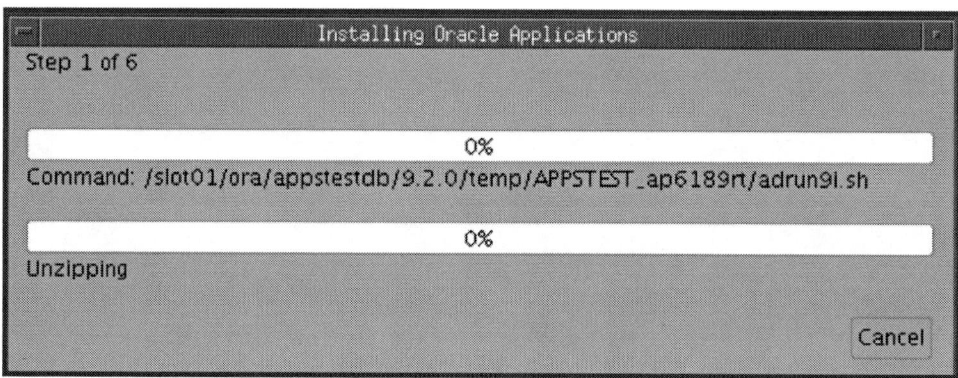

Fig. 12.22 Showing Progress

Once the process is complete, Rapid Install displays the post-installation status screen.

Multi-node upgrade

If we want the multi-node upgrade option, we need to select it when prompted for the type of the upgrade by the Rapid Install.

Choosing installation type

In this screen you indicate whether to install Oracle Application on a single node or distribute it across multiple nodes (see Fig. 12.23).

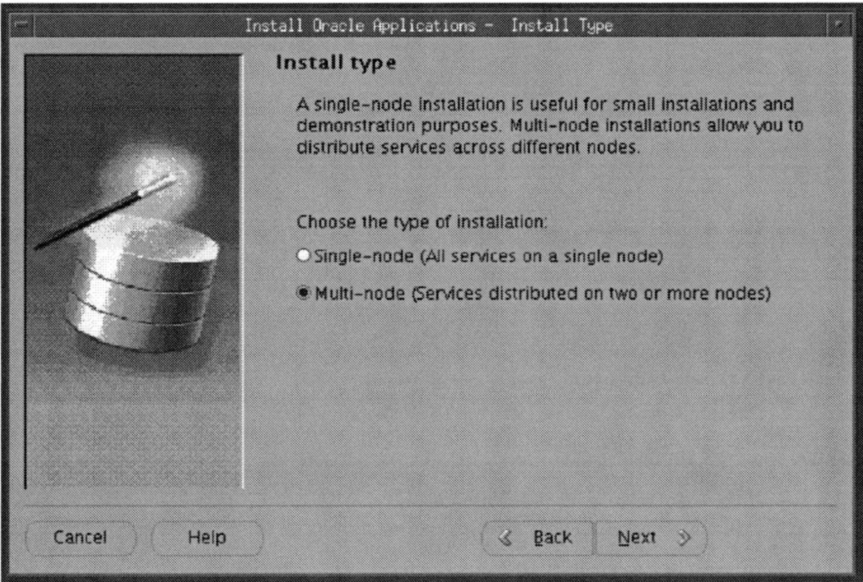

Fig. 12.23 Choosing Install Type

Here, we will select the multi-node option. As mentioned earlier, in a multi-node installation we can distribute the database, Forms, concurrent processing server and Apache across multiple nodes.

Load balancing is the feature where you can distribute the load of Forms and concurrent processing across multiple nodes. Here, the requests are automatically directed to server having the least load. The next figure shows the load balancing screen.

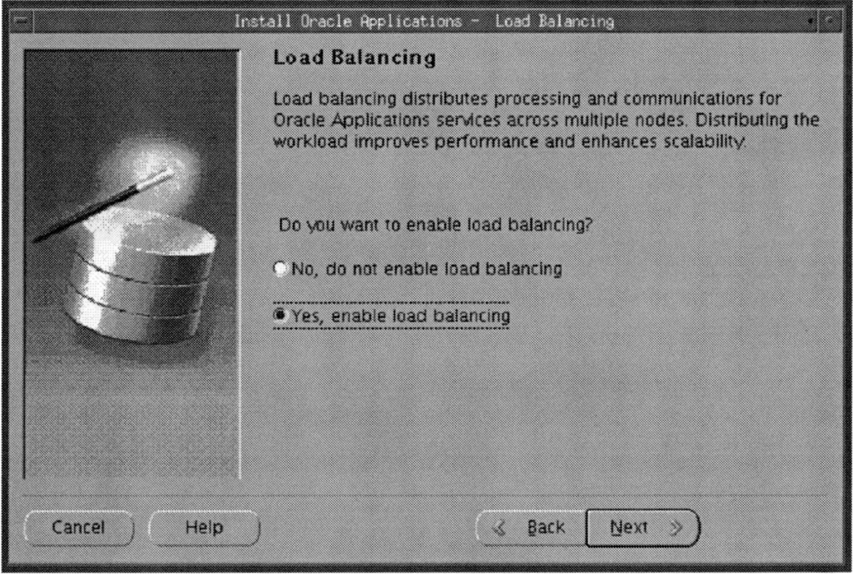

Fig. 12.24 Load Balancing

We will discuss both options, viz. enabling and not enabling load balancing.

Case 1: Load balancing is enabled

Press 'Yes' to enable load balancing. Then Rapid Install will ask how many nodes will be assigned for Forms and concurrent processing server. Choose more than one node for each service type to enable load balancing of that service.

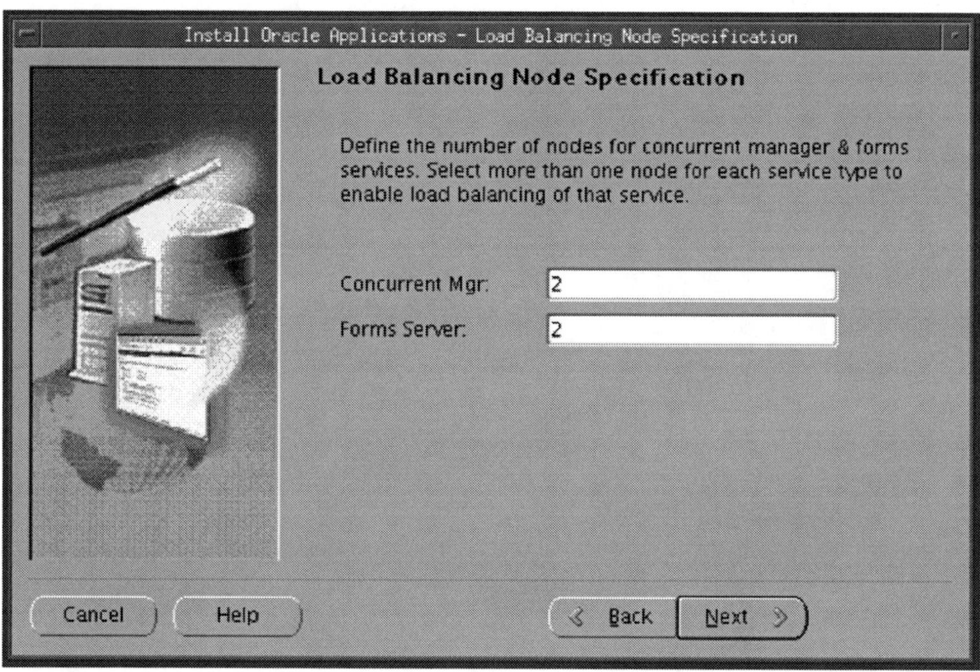

Fig. 12.25 Node Information

Once the number of nodes has been defined, Rapid Install will prompt for server details in the next screen shown in Fig. 12.26.

Case 2: Load balancing is not enabled

If you choose not to enable load balancing, Rapid Install straightaway goes to the server information screen without checking the details of primary and secondary servers, as they are not applicable in this case (see Fig. 12.27).

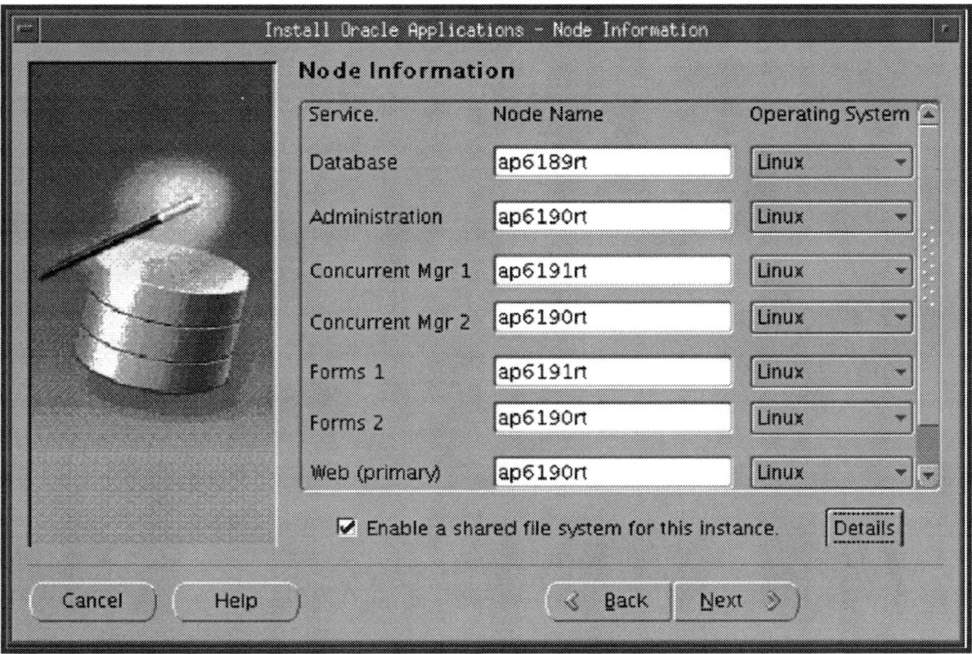

Fig. 12.26 Node Details

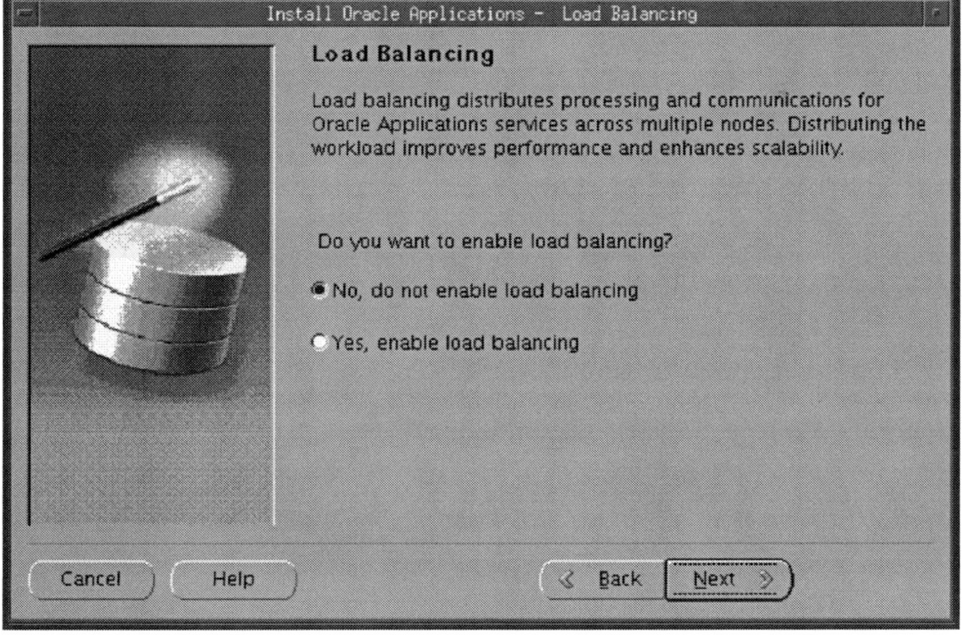

Fig. 12.27 Load Balancing

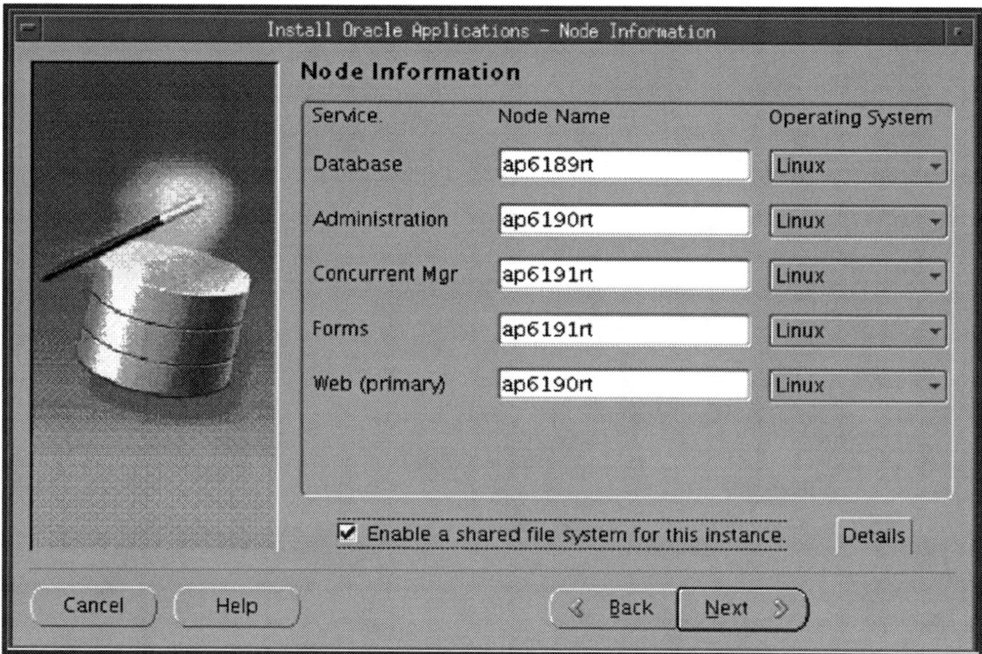

Fig. 12.28 Node Details

In this screen (Fig. 12.28) you assign the various servers to individual nodes using the 'Node Name' field. The first option is for database and in the node name field you give the name of the server that will be your database server. We have selected 'ap6189rt' as our database server. The next option is administration, which is the admin tier of the APPL_TOP. This has been taken as 'ap6190rt'. The next option is for Concurrent Manager, which will host the concurrent processing server. 'ap6191rt' is our Concurrent Manager node. The next option is where the forms server will run; this we have chosen as 'ap6191rt'. The last option is web and in this example, the Apache will be hosted from 'ap6190rt' server.

It can clearly be seen here that we are doing a three node installation, with DB on one server, Forms-CM on one and Admin-Web on one.

There is also a check box 'Enable a shared APPL_TOP for this instance'. This means the APPL_TOP will be installed only in one node (which is also called the admin tier) but will be accessible from the other nodes also. With the 11.5.10 release, the APPL_TOP is shared by default. Shared APPL_TOP is possible only if all the nodes have the same operating system.

There is a 'Details' button after the check box. If this box is clicked, it opens a screen from where you can define which node you will be installing the APPL_TOP in and which ones you will be sharing the APPL_TOP.

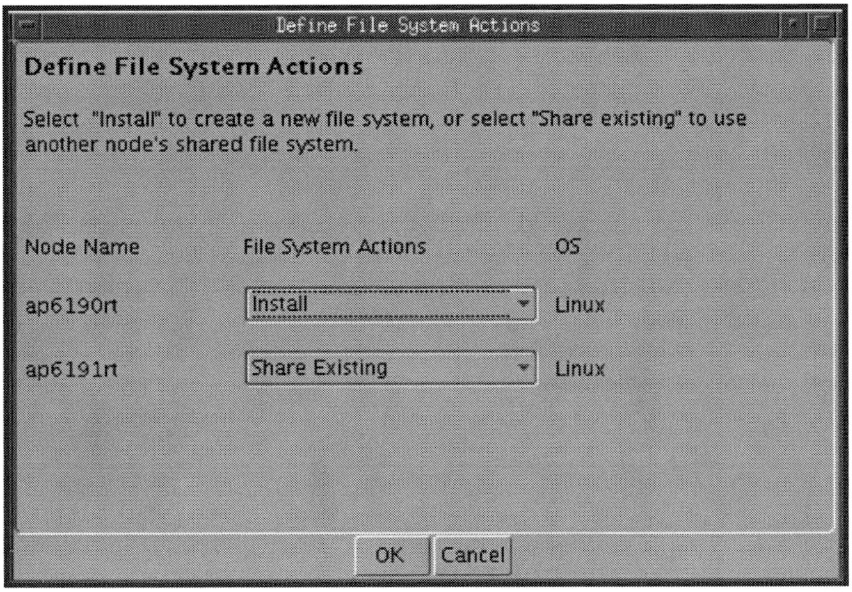

Fig. 12.29 Install/Share APPL_TOP

The above screen (Fig. 12.29) shows three options—Node Name, File System Actions and OS. The node name is the physical server from where your Forms, Apache and CM are hosted. The 'file system actions' shows two options, 'Install' and 'Share existing'. The former actually installs the `APPL_TOP` on that particular node. All the `APPL_TOP` files will be installed in this node. It will serve as the `admin` tier and all activities like patching and running Adutilities will take place from this node. 'Share existing' means that it won't have its own `APPL_TOP` but will use the `APPL_TOP` shared by the node marked 'Install'.

In this example, we have chosen to install the `APPL_TOP` in the node `ap6190rt`. The server `ap6191rt` will be sharing its `APPL_TOP`.

Setting environment variable and adding custom setting

Log in to the new `APPL_TOP` and source the environment file. Crosscheck that it is pointing to the new `APPL_TOP` and all its reflecting the product top's correctly. If you had any customized environment variables in the `adovars.env` of your previous `APPL_TOP` then change them in all `adovars.env` files in the new `APPL_TOP` in all the servers.

Apply the upgrade patches

Apply all the consolidated upgrade patches listed in the most current release notes of Oracle Applications. The patches should be applied in the pre-install mode of the new `APPL_TOP`. Don't apply any AD minipack even if it is listed in the current release notes.

Checking custom schema conflicts

If you originally installed the Oracle Application with release 9.3 or earlier versions, you must check that the custom schemas that you have created are not in conflict with the new schema that will be created with the Auto Upgrade. To check this, run the following script from the new `APPL_TOP`:

```
cd $APPL_TOP/admin/preupg
sqlplus apps/apps password
sql>@adpuver.sql
```

If there is a conflict, then contact the Oracle Support immediately.

Enable the SYSADMIN user

Since the Auto Upgrade accesses the AOL user name using the application user SYSADMIN, the application user must exist and should be enabled. The SYSADMIN user should have the responsibility of System Administrator and the password of this user should be SYSADMIN only before running the Auto Upgrade.

Migrate or upgrade the database to 9i

Perform the migration or upgrade using the Oracle9*i* ORACLE_HOME created by Rapid Install. Consult the Oracle manual to do the database upgrade.

Convert existing tablespaces to local extent management

Oracle recommends converting the tablespaces to locally managed ones to increase the performance. Run the following script for this:

```
$ cd $APPL_TOP\admin\preupg
$ sqlplus <SYSTEM username>/<SYSTEM password> @adtbscnv.pls
<SYSTEM password>
```

Creating new product tablespaces

There are two options available to create new product tablespaces. The first option is to keep the existing model and create the product tablespace; the second option is to migrate to the Oracle Application tablespace model (OATM). Ensure that the system tablespace is at least 9 GB in size before you run the scripts.

If you are planning to keep the existing tablespace model, you need to run the 'adgnofa.sql' script as follows. On the command line, indicate the <MODE> as NEW to create new product tablespaces, or ALL to create tablespaces for new products and resize existing product tablespaces.

To run this script go to

```
$ cd $AD_TOP/patch/115/sql
$ sqlplus <APPS username>/<APPS password> @adgnofa.sql <MODE>
```

If you are planning to use the new OATM model, you need to run the adgncons.sql as follows.

```
$ cd $AD_TOP/patch/115/sql
$ sqlplus <APPS username>/<APPS password> @adgncons.sql \
<APPS username> <APPS password> APPLSYS
```

Once the upgrade is complete you must finish the process by moving the pre-release 11*i* objects to the new tablespace.

Running both the scripts generates the `adcrtbsp.sql`. The `adcrtbsp.sql` needs to be run from the database server as system user to add new product tablespace and to resize the existing tablespace. This script automatically converts the newly created tablespaces to local extent management.

Running Auto Upgrade to upgrade products and database objects

Once the Rapid Install is run successfully, the next step is to run Auto Upgrade. It is used to upgrade Oracle Applications from the earlier to the base version of the latest release. It can be started from the command prompt by typing *adaimgr*.

Steps for running the Auto Upgrade are:

1. Log in to the `APPL_TOP` as the owner of the application file system
2. Run the environment file (`APPLSYS.env`) for sourcing the environment
3. Check whether the application system is sourced properly

Once the environment is sourced properly, you can invoke the Auto Upgrade utility as mentioned. If you want to use the OFA-compliant (old) tablespace model then type—

```
$ adaimgr consolidated_tablespace=N
```

To use the (new) OATM tablespace model, type—

```
$ adaimgr
```

This will start the Auto Upgrade utility. The `adaimgr` prompts are given in the following figure.

```
(appmgr01) appmgr - -bash $ adaimgr

                  Copyright (c) 2002 Oracle Corporation
                     Redwood Shores, California, USA

                   Oracle Applications Auto Upgrade

                            Version 11.5.0

NOTE: You may not use this utility for custom development unless you have
written permission from Oracle Corporation.

Your default directory is '/slot01/appmgr/emstestappl'.
Is this the correct APPL_TOP [Yes]?

AutoUpgrade records your AutoUpgrade session in a text file
you specify. Enter your AutoUpgrade log file name or press [Return]
to accept the default file name shown in brackets.

Filename [adaimgr.log]:
```

Fig. 12.30 Unix Session 12.2

The Auto Upgrade verifies whether or not it is pointing to the correct `APPL_TOP`. Next, it prompts for the name of the log file, which is by default `adaimgr.log`. Like other log files, the location of the autoupgrade log file is `$APPL_TOP/admin$TWO_TASK/log` in the `APPL_TOP`.

```
It is critical that your Oracle Applications, RDBMS and related tools are
compatible and certified combinations. If you are uncertain whether a
combination is certified please contact Oracle Support Services.

Are you certain you are running a certified release combination [No]? Yes

You can be notified by email if a failure occurs.
Do you wish to activate this feature [No]?

Please enter the batchsize [1000]:

Please enter the name of the Oracle Applications System that this
APPL_TOP belongs to.

The Applications System name must be unique across all Oracle
Applications Systems at your site, must be from 1 to 30 characters long,
may only contain alphanumeric and underscore characters, and must start
with a letter.

Sample Applications System names are: "prod", "test", "demo" and
"Development_2".

Applications System Name [emstest]:
```

Fig. 12.31 Unix Session 12.3

Adaimgr checks whether the application system we are going to upgrade consists of compatible and certified combinations. It should not happen, for example, that you are using an 8.0.5 database for an 11.5.10 version of Oracle Applications. It then asks if you would like an email notification if there is any failure during the run of `adadmin`. Then it prompts for the batch size and the name of the application system.

```
NOTE: If you do not have or choose not to have certain types of files
installed in this APPL_TOP, you may not be able to perform certain tasks.

Example 1: If you don't have files used for installing or upgrading the
database installed in this area, you cannot install or upgrade the
database from this APPL_TOP.

Example 2: If you don't have forms files installed in this area, you
cannot generate them or run them from this APPL_TOP.
```

Contd

Fig. 12.32 Contd

```
Example 3: If you don't have concurrent program files installed in this
area, you cannot relink concurrent programs or generate reports from this
APPL_TOP.

Do you currently have or want to install files used for installing or
upgrading the database in this APPL_TOP [YES]?

Do you currently have or want to install Java and HTML files for HTML-
based functionality in this APPL_TOP [YES]?

Do you currently have or want to install Oracle Applications forms files
in this APPL_TOP [YES]?

Do you currently have or want to install concurrent program files in this
APPL_TOP [YES]?
```

Fig. 12.32 Unix Session 12.4

The installation of Oracle Applications is normally spread across different nodes with the `admin` tier on one node, CM on another and Apache hosted from a third. `Adaimgr` checks the components installed from each node and processes them accordingly. If you have multiple-node architecture then you need to run the `adaimgr` from each node.

```
APPL_TOP Name [emstest]:

You are about to install or upgrade Oracle Applications product tables in
your ORACLE database 'emstest' using ORACLE executables in '/slot01/
appmgr/emstestora/8.0.6'.

Is this the correct database [Yes]?

AutoUpgrade needs the password for your 'SYSTEM' ORACLE schema in order
to determine your installation configuration.

Enter the password for your 'SYSTEM' ORACLE schema: manager

There exists one FND_PRODUCT_INSTALLATIONS table. AutoUpgrade will
upgrade the existing product group.

The ORACLE username specified below for Application Object Library

uniquely identifies your existing product group: APPLSYS
```

Contd

Fig. 12.33 Contd

```
Enter the ORACLE password of Application Object Library [APPS]:
                              AutoUpgrade Main Menu
___________________________________________________________________________

   1.  Choose database parameters
   2.  Choose overall tasks and their parameters
   3.  Run the selected tasks
   4.  Exit AutoUpgrade
   * Please use License Manager to license additional
     products or modules after the upgrade are complete
Enter your choice:
```

Fig. 12.33 Unix Session 12.5

`Adaimgr` prompts for the application system name, crosschecks the Oracle Home, verifies the system and `APPS` password and then takes us to the main menu of `adaimgr`.

The main menu shows the options for configuring as well as for running the upgrade. The first and second options are used to configure the upgrade. The third option starts the upgrade process.

To select an option, type the option number and press enter. The options are normally selected in numeric order.

Choosing database parameters

The first option in the `adaimgr` main menu is used for choosing the database parameters. From this screen you can do the following:

- Change the default Oracle user ID and password for each product
- Set the sizing factor for new objects of a product or for new products
- Set the tablespaces for new products
- Change the tablespaces for existing products

The screen is shown in Fig. 12.34.

At the top of this screen, you can see O, S, M, I and D written. These are the options out of which one chooses to configure the database parameters. These options are discussed further.

```
                  AutoUpgrade - Choose database parameters

                                 - O -    - S -  --- M ---   --- I ---    --- D ---
  Product                  Action ORACLE  Sizing Main        Index        Default
# Name                          | User ID Factor Tablespace  Tablespace   Tablespace
- ------------------------   --  -------  ------ ----------  ----------   ----------
1 Application Object Lib        APPLSYS    100   USER_DATA   USER_IDX     USER_DATA
2 Application Utilities         APPLSYS    100   USER_DATA   USER_IDX     USER_DATA
3 Applications DBA              APPLSYS    100   USER_DATA   USER_IDX     USER_DATA
4 Oracle Alert                  APPLSYS    100   USER_DATA   USER_IDX     USER_DATA
5 Global Accounting Engi        AX         100   USER_DATA   USER_IDX     USER_DATA
6 Oracle Common Modules         AK         100   USER_DATA   USER_IDX     USER_DATA
7 Oracle Common Accounti        XLA        100   USER_DATA   USER_IDX     USER_DATA
8 Oracle General Ledger         GL         100   USER_DATA   USER_IDX     USER_DATA
 There are 191 Oracle Applications. Enter U/D to scroll up/down.

 <Product #><Letter>  - To change a database parameter for a product;
                        INCLUDE the LETTER ABOVE the COLUMN you want
                        to change
 U / D / T / B        - Press up/down/top/bottom to see other products
    [Return]          - To return to the AutoUpgrade Main Menu
 Enter your choice (for example, 1M):
```

Fig. 12.34 Unix Session 12.6

Option O—Oracle user ID This column displays the Oracle user ID for each product. You cannot change this for currently installed products. Oracle also recommends not changing the default user ID.

To change the user ID, type the product number followed by O. The product numbers are displayed in the first column. You can scroll across the list of products by typing 'U' to go up and 'D' to go down, or 'T' to go to the top and 'B' for the bottom of the product list. The new user name can be any word of up to 30 characters. To change only the password, press enter when Auto Upgrade prompts for the user name, and enter the new password at the next prompt.

Option S—sizing factor The option shows the sizing factor applied by Auto Upgrade to the new product tables and index. The default sizing factor is 100. To change it, type the product number followed by S and then the new sizing factor at the prompt.

Option M—main tablespace This option shows the main tablespace allocated to the product in the database. You can change it by typing the product number followed by M at the prompt.

Option I—index tablespace This option shows tablespace where the index are created for that particular product. You can change the index tablespace by typing the product number and then 'I' at the prompt.

Option D—default tablespace This option shows the default tablespace for the product. It is used for operations that do not specify a tablespace, and defaults to the main tablespace for that product. You can change the default tablespace by typing the product number followed by D at the prompt.

You can also change a particular option of all the products at one go by typing 'A' followed by the option at the prompt. For example, if you want to change the sizing factor for all the products then you need to type AS at the prompt.

Choose overall tasks and their parameters

This is the second option in the Auto Upgrade main menu and it displays the tasks undertaken by Auto Upgrade during the upgrade process.

```
Enter your choice: 2

        AutoUpgrade – Choose overall tasks and their parameters

  # Task                                        Do it?    Parameters
  — ——————————————————————————————————————————  ——————    ——————————————
  1 Create Applications environment file        YES       emstest.env
  2 Verify files necessary for install/upgrade  YES
  3 Install or upgrade database objects         YES

    There are 3 tasks.  Enter U/D to scroll up/down.

    <Task #>    - To change YES to NO or NO to YES
                  (You cannot change a task marked with a *)
    <Task #>P   - To change the parameters of a task
    U/D         - To page up/down to see other tasks
    [Return]    - To return to the AutoUpgrade Main Menu

Enter your choice (for example 2 or 2P):
```

Fig. 12.35 Unix Session 12.7

Create Application file Auto Upgrade creates an environment file during its running. The default name of the environment file is `<SID>.env`. If you want to change the name of the environment file, enter the new file name at the prompt and press enter. The file name can be up to 30 characters.

Verify files necessary for install/upgrade This option verifies that all the files, which are required for the Auto Upgrade are present. In case some files are missing, it alerts the user about this. This option is generally run as a pre-upgrade step to identify if there are any missing files.

Install or upgrade database objects This option verifies files, upgrades database objects for existing product groups and installs new database objects.

Running the selected task

Once the first and the second options of the Auto Upgrade have been run, the next step is to run the selected task. The third option of Auto Upgrade asks a series of questions related to configuration of the environment. This is given below.

```
Enter your choice: 3

How do you wish to enable Parallel Concurrent Processing:

1. Not enabled
2. Enable generic parallel concurrent processing
3. Enable parallel concurrent processing with operating system queue

The default choice is 1 - Not enabled.

Enter your choice [1]:

The concurrent managers can create output files which use a name that is
no longer than 8 characters and an extension which is no longer than 3
characters.

Do you wish to use the 8.3 file name convention [No]:
```

Fig. 12.36 Unix Session 12.8

Auto Upgrade first checks if you want to enable parallel concurrent processing or not, which we have already discussed in Chapter 7. It then checks if you want to use the 8.3 file name convention. 8.3 file name convention means the output files of the Concurrent Manager will have eight digits with an extension of three digits, for example, `standard.mgr`.

```
The concurrent managers can put all the log and report files in a common
area where the client machines can view them.

Enter the name of this common area below, or press [Return] if you want
log and report files for each application to go in that application's log
and output subdirectories. Enter the name of the common area:

Enter the log subdirectory name for this product group [log]:

Enter the output subdirectory name for this product group [out]:

Enter the directory for Applications temporary files [/slot01/appmgr/
emstestcomn/temp]:
```

Contd

Fig. 12.37 Contd

```
Enter the directory for Oracle Reports temporary files [/tmp]:

Some PL/SQL programs produce temporary log/output files. The directories
used for this must be listed in the init.ora parameter "utl_file_dir".
The value of utl_file_dir for this database is:
"/usr/tmp, / slot01/oracle/emstestdb/8.1.7/appsutil/outbound/emstest"

Enter the directory for temporary log/output files from PL/SQL programs.
Directory:
```

Fig. 12.37 Unix Session 12.9

Auto Upgrade then prompts for the location of the log files, where log and output files will be stored. The location of the log files is given below.

If the environment variable `$APPLCSF` is set, the default location is `$APPLCSF/$APPLLOG`.

1. If the environment variable `$APPLCSF` is not set, the logs go to `$FND_TOP/$APPLLOG`. The default name of the Concurrent Manager log files is `std.mgr`. You can change this by setting the parameter `logfile=<name>`.
2. On NT the log files are called `CM_<SID>.LOG`.

It then prompts for the directories for temporary files of Applications and for Oracle reports. The temporary directories are those where the temporary files are stored. The PL/SQL programs also produce temporary log/output files. Auto Upgrade then prompts for the PL/SQL program log/output directory. The directories used for this must be listed in the `init.ora` parameter "`utl_file_dir`". Auto Upgrade displays the parameter of the `init.ora` and the PL/SQL program log/output directory must match with the "`utl_file_dir`" parameter of the `init.ora`.

```
What is the name of the machine, including domain name, hosting the web
server that will be used for accessing Applications forms?

Applications forms web server host machine[ ]? ap6090rt.us.oracle.com

What port is the Applications forms web server running on [80] ? 8000

Reading topfile.txt ...

AutoUpgrade records the output from
"verifying files needed for install/upgrade" in a file in the
/slot01/appmgr/emstestappl/admin/emstest/out directory.
If the file already exists, it will be overwritten.

Please enter the filename you wish to use or press [RETURN] to accept
the default filename [adiuvf.lst]:
```

Fig. 12.38 Unix Session 12.10

AutoUpgrade then asks for the web server's name, domain and port.

As Auto Upgrade verifies files, it asks for the name of the log file in which the output from these tasks should be stored.

The log file (`adiuvf.lst`) is stored in `$APPL_TOP/admin/<SID>/out` (UNIX), or `%APPL_TOP\admin\<SID>\out` (Windows). You can accept the default name or enter a new one at this prompt.

Once all the information is given, Auto Upgrade starts running and verifies the files for each of the products.

```
Running sub driver "adupfpi.drv"..

sqlplus -s APPS/*****

@/slot01/appmgr/emstestappl/ad/11.5.0/patch/115/sql/adsetdf.sql
&systempwd &un_fnd

Verifying all files needed by all installed or planned applications...
   Reading driver files...

Checking files needed in Receivables...
All needed files present.

Checking files needed in Order Entry...
All needed files present.

SYS.DUAL has the correct number of rows.
Granting privileges on SYS.DUAL...
```

Fig. 12.39 Unix Session 12.11

If Auto Upgrade finds any file missing, it displays a failure message and stops. It lists the missing files in the `adaimgr.log` file. Review the missing files, correct the problems, and restart Auto Upgrade.

If the main menu appears, it means Auto Upgrade has finished all the tasks. To exit Auto Upgrade, type the fourth option.

The next step is to apply the latest updates and then run the Rapid Install to configure all the servers.

Applying the updates

Before running the Auto Upgrade, we had applied all the consolidated upgrade patches listed in the most current release notes of Oracle Applications. But at that time we didn't apply the AD mini-pack. There are a few other things that we need to take care of now. The following updates need to be applied now.

- AD mini-pack: Apply the latest AD mini-pack (US version) to upgrade the database. Even if you have additional languages installed, don't apply the NLS patch now.
- Unified driver: For bringing the database to the latest release of Oracle Applications 11*i*, apply the unified driver (US version) on the node with the admin server. The patch driver is located in `$AU_TOP/patch/115/driver`. The patch must be applied with the options 'nocopyportion' and 'nogenerateportion'.

```
$adpatch options=nocopyportion,nogenerateportion
```

- NLS version: Install the NLS version of the AD mini-pack followed by the NLS software to bring your translations up to the full maintenance pack level for this release.

Running Rapid Install for configuring server

The final step in an upgrade process is to run the Rapid Install to configure the server. Invoke Rapid Install by typing '*rapidwiz*' at the command prompt. The welcome screen is shown in Fig. 12.41.

```
(appmgr01) rapidwiz - -bash $ ./rapidwiz

Rapid Install Wizard is validating your file system......
Preparing to start up Rapid Install...
Rapid Install Wizard will now launch the Java Interface.....

If you are performing a DVD/CD install, you must change directories in
your session to a directory outside of the DVD/CD-ROM mount point before
you will be able to eject the DVD/CD and proceed.

(appmgr01) rapidwiz - -bash $
```

Fig. 12.40 Unix Session 12.12

Welcome screen

The Rapid Install launches the Java Interface and the welcome screen is displayed at the first place.

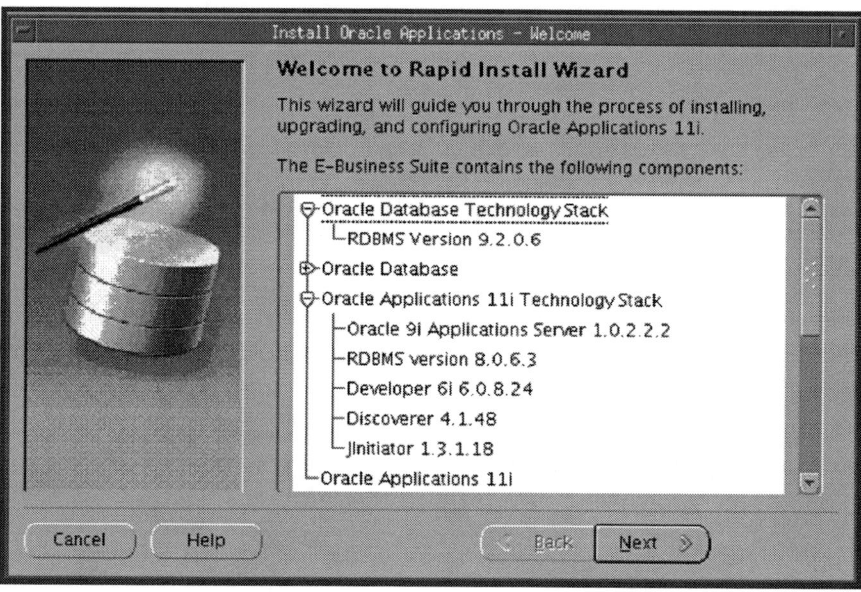

Fig. 12.41 Welcome Screen

The figure shows all components that will be installed in the application system. Rapid Install configures the iAS technology stack to the 1.0.2.2.2 version. It also installs Oracle 9.2.0.5 RDBMS Oracle Home without a database. You are not required to give any input in this screen, so press 'Next' and continue.

Selecting wizard operation

The next screens displays two options, 'Install Oracle Applications E-Business 11*i*' and 'Upgrade to Oracle Applications E-Business 11*i*'. The first option sets up a new, fully configured system.

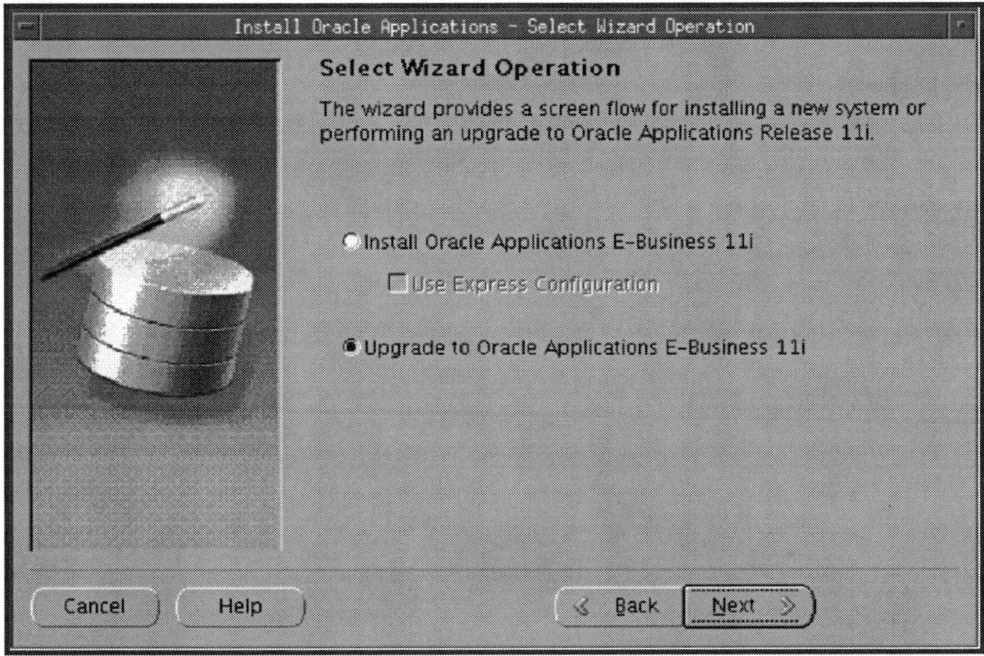

Fig. 12.42 Select Wizard Operation

Since we are configuring an upgraded instance, we will select the second option. Press 'Next' to continue.

Select upgrade action

The 'Select Upgrade Action' screen shows two options: (see Fig. 12.43).

1. Create Upgrade file system
2. Configure Upgraded 11*i* Instance

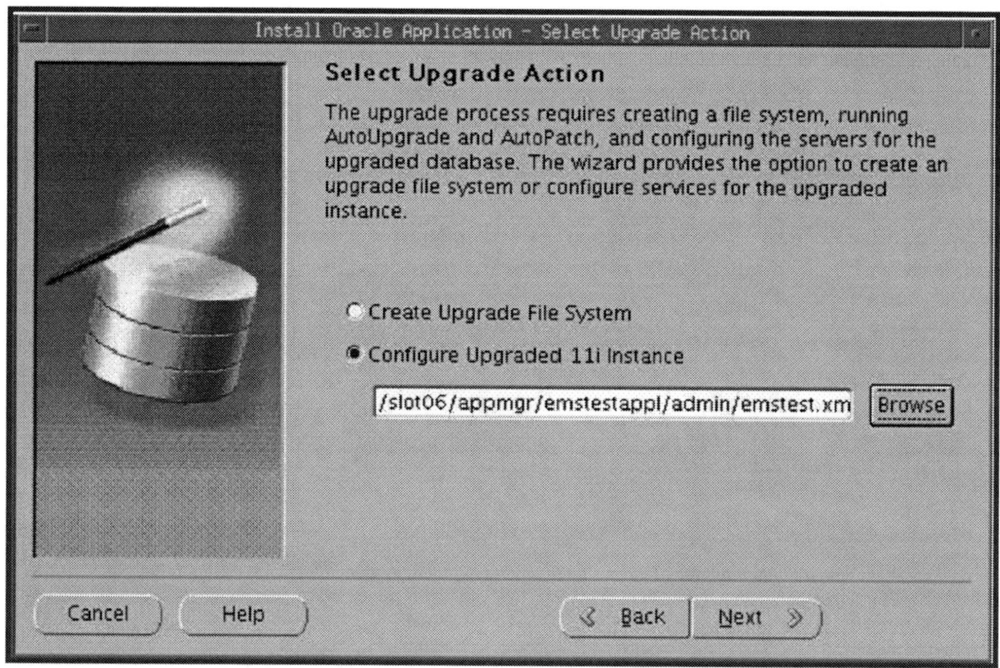

Fig. 12.43 Select Upgrade Action

The first option is chosen while running Rapid Install during the upgrade stage. Here, Rapid Install collects the configuration parameters for your application system and stores them in a configuration file (`config.txt`). When you run the Rapid Install, it creates a context file (`envname.xml`), which contains all the details of your application system.

The second option is chosen when running the Rapid Install during the post-upgrade stage. Here you specify the location and name of the context file created while running the Rapid Install during the upgrade stage. The location of the context file is `$APPL_TOP/admin/$TWO_TASK/<SID.xml>`.

Since we are configuring the upgraded instance we will select the second option, viz. 'Configure Upgraded 11*i* instance'.

Beginning the configuration

Due to security issues, the passwords are not stored in the context file. Rapid Install prompts for the APPS password (see Fig. 12.44).

Install Oracle Applications - Review Application User Information

Review Application User Information

APPS Username	APPS
APPS Password	****
GWYUID Username	APPLSYSPUB
GWYUID Password	PUB
Guest Username	GUEST
Guest Password	ORACLE

Cancel Help Back Next

Fig. 12.44 Review Information

Once the details are given, Rapid Install prompts that it is going to run Autoconfig for the server.

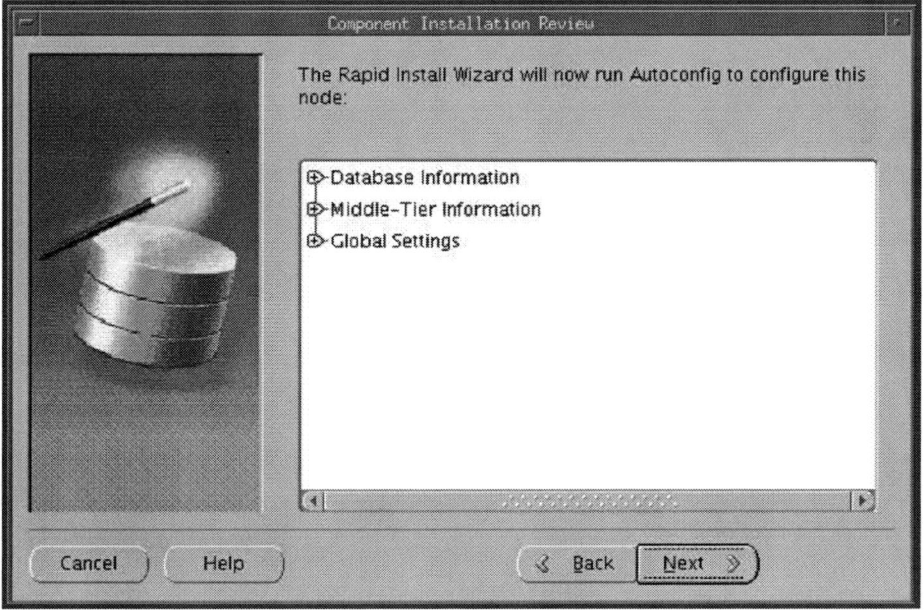

Fig. 12.45 Component Install Review

It then prompts whether or not you want to start the installation.

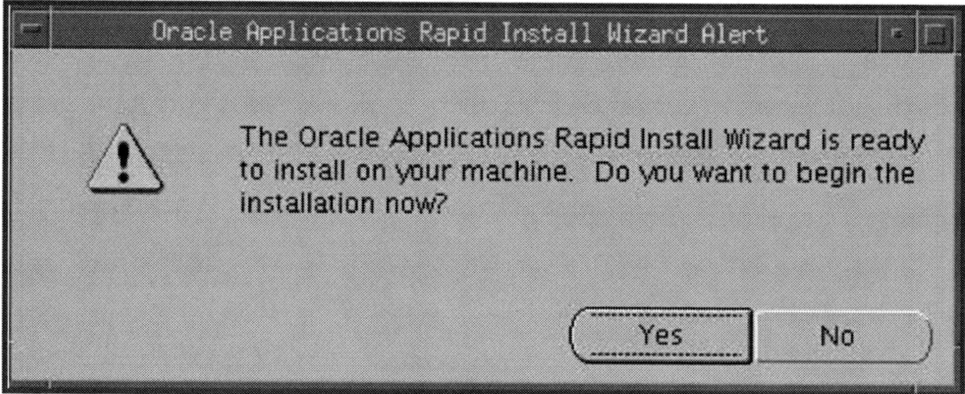

Fig. 12.46 Alert

Once 'Yes' is clicked, it starts configuring the various servers and displays the status. The status screen is shown in the following figure.

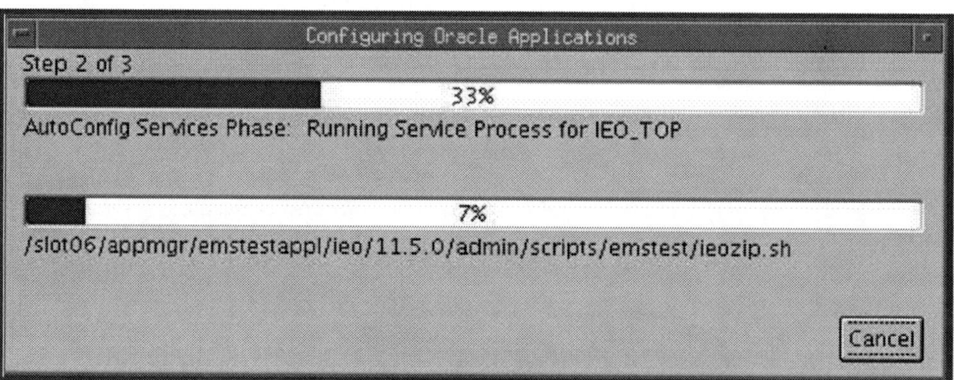

Fig. 12.47 Installation Status

Once the configuration is done, it validates the system configuration by checking all the components. Once the validation is completed, it gives the output in the post-install check screen (see Fig. 12.48). These are the components of the post-install check.

- Database Availability Check
- Environment File Check
- DBC File Check
- HTTP Check
- JSP Check
- PHP Check

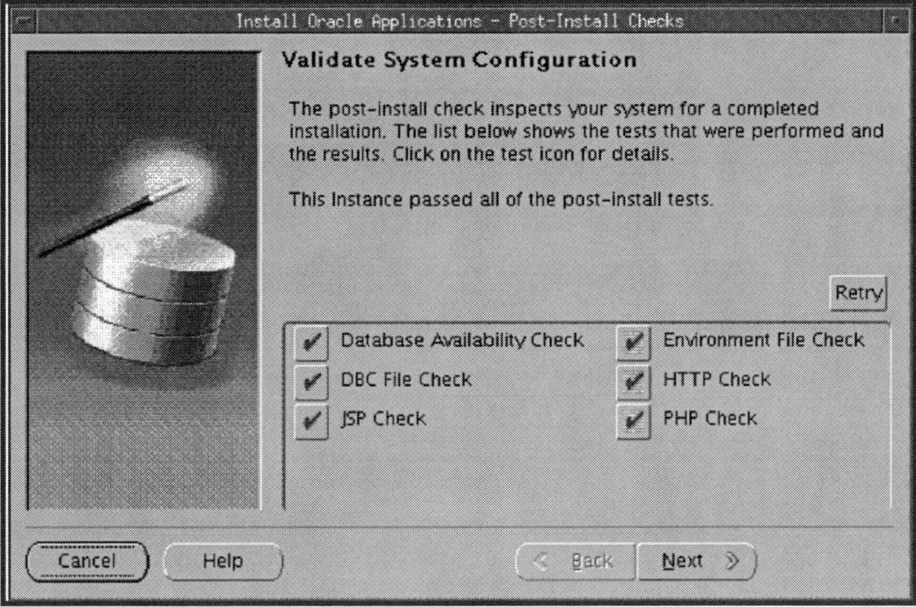

Fig. 12.48 Validate Configuration

Click 'Next' and the finish screen appears. Press 'Finish' to complete the installation process.

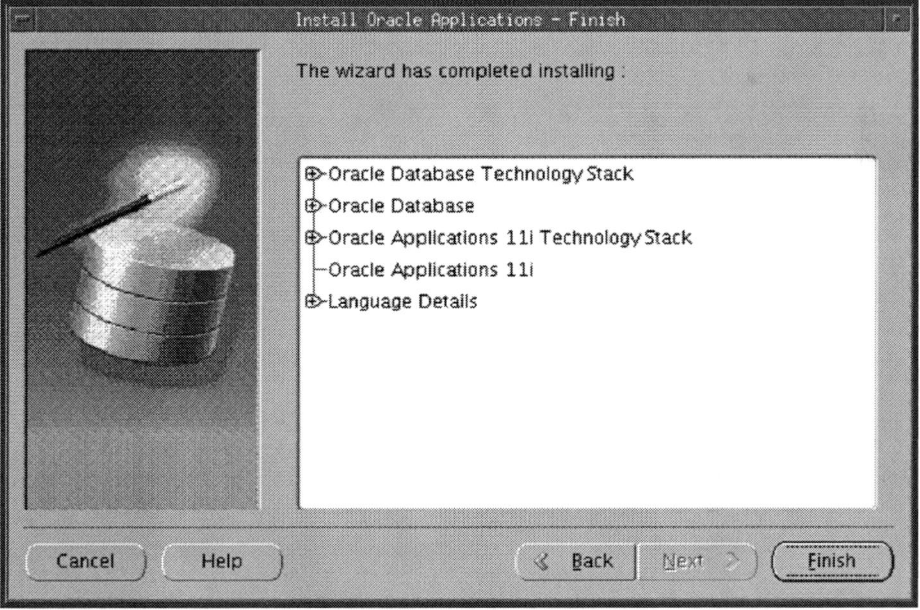

Fig. 12.49 Finish Screen

UPGRADING ORACLE APPLICATIONS TO 11.5.10 CU 2 FOR 11*i* APPLICATION SYSTEMS

If you have a release 11*i* Application then you need to follow the steps given here to upgrade your application system to 11.5.10 CU 2.

Pre-upgrade Process

The upgrade process consists of several steps, which we will discuss in detail.

Announcing downtime

The first step is announcing a downtime. All users must be aware of the downtime well in advance and it should be planned in such a way that it has the least effect in terms of revenue. Ideally, the upgrade should be planned for weekends or holidays.

Backing up the application system

A full backup of the database and the `APPL_TOP` must be taken before starting the upgrade process so that if there are any upgrade failures you can revert to the existing system. A cold backup of the database should be taken with the normal shutdown.

Running TUMS utility

TUMS is a utility to help customers reduce the number of steps necessary in the upgrade. It looks at a customer's specific situation, and identifies the irrelevant steps for that customer. The output of TUMS can be used to reduce upgrade time. The Upgrade Manual Script (TUMS) is used to create a report that lists the upgrade steps that don't apply to your Oracle Application installation. You can ignore the steps generated with the report of TUMS.

Apply patch 4238286 TUMS utility for the 11.5.10 maintenance pack.

To generate the TUMS report you need to download and apply the TUMS 4238286 patch from Metalink using the adpatch utility.

The TUMS for 11.5.10 maintenance pack report will be created in the directory `UTL_FILE_DIR`. So make sure that this directory has proper write permission.

Once the patch is applied successfully, the TUMS report can be generated using the following command:

```
$ cd $AD_TOP/patch/115/sql
$ sqlplus <APPS username>/<APPS password> @adtums.sql <DIRECTORY>
```

The report file '`tumsmp.html`' will be created in the `UTL_FILE_DIR`, which is mentioned in the `init.ora` parameter of the database. Make sure that the `UTL_FILE_DIR` is not a symbolic link as some problems may then occur at this point.

Figure 12.50 shows a sample output of TUMS.

Oracle Applications Release 11.5.10 TUMS-MP Report

Report generated on 11/25/2005, 06:10 am

Summary Information
Based on your current configuration, you must perform the following steps from the *Maintenance Pack Installation Instructions*:

Section 1:Pre-Update Tasks
Perform steps 2,3,4,6,7,11a,13,1cl45,16,9,18,20,21,22,23

Section 2:Applying the Release 11.5.10 Maintenance Pack
Perform steps 1,2,3,4

Section 3:Post-Update Tasks
Perform steps 1,2,3,4,5,6

Section 4:Product-Specific Tasks
Perform the steps for:
Activity Based Management
Oracle Enterprise Install Base
Install Base
iProcurement
Advanced Planning
Workflow
eCommerce
Oracle Human Resources
Oracle Payroll

Fig. 12.50 TUMS

At first, the summary of the information is given and then the detailed information is given at the bottom (see Fig. 12.51).

Applying the AD mini-pack

To apply the latest Applications DBA mini-pack 4337683 you should have implemented `autoconfig` in your environment. If you have not done so, it can be done as a part of AD mini-pack application. You need to refer to the Metalink note 233044.1 to apply this patch.

Updating autoconfig tech stack components

For this, you need to apply the patch 4489303. Make sure you follow all the steps mentioned in the 'readme' of the patch.

Running tech stack validation utility

Apply the patch 4318672 in all the nodes of the `APPL_TOP` to install the utility. This verifies the minimum technology stack components version and the other configuration requirements associated with the 11.5.10 CU 2 Maintenance Pack. Once this patch is applied, you need to run the technology

Detailed Information
Steps that you must perform are colored *GREEN*
Steps that you do need not to perform are colored BLACK

Section 1:Pre-Update Tasks
You must apply the AD Minipack
You must implement or update AutoConfig
You must run the 11.5.10 technology stack validation utility
You need to perform this RI step only if you have a Windows Install
You may choose to convert to the new tablespace model based on Database object type
You must configure the database for new products and new tablespace requirements
You need not perform the Audit Trail shadow tables step
You need not perform the Oracle Payables step
You must perform this step as you are using Oracle Service
You need not perform the Oracle Install Base step
You need not migrate the Oracle Service Contract rules
You must perform this Oracle Shipping Execution step
You must perform this Oracle Depot Repair step
You need not review the Oracle Interaction Center Certifications
You must synchronize data for Oracle Mobile Field Service
You must perform the ILOG Install step
You need not perform this Process Manufacturing Step
You may choose to prepare Marketing and Sales modules for update
You need not perform the Leads migration step
You may choose to do this TCA contacts unmerge process now to reduce downtime
You must upgrade Applications Desktop Integrator
You must unzip the American English Maintenance Pack zip file
You must unzip and merge NLS Maintenance packs

Section 2:Applying the Release 11.5.10 Maintenance Pack
All steps are mandatory

Section 3:Post-Update Tasks
All steps are mandatory

Fig. 12.51 Detailed Information from TUMS Utility

stack validation utility at the APPL_TOP as well as at the database. The utility can be run with the following command:

At APPL_TOP

```
$ADPERLPRG $FND_TOP/patch/115/bin/TXKScript.pl
    -script=$FND_TOP/patch/115/bin/txkVal11510MP.pl
    -txktop=$APPLTMP
    -appspass=<apps_password>
    -outfile=$APPLTMP/txkVal11510MP.html
```

At database

```
$ADPERLPRG $ORACLE_HOME/appsutil/bin/TXKScript.pl
    -script=$ORACLE_HOME/appsutil/bin/txkVal11510MP.pl
    -txktop=$ORACLE_HOME/appsutil
    -appspass=<apps_password>
    -outfile=$ORACLE_HOME/appsutil/temp/txkVal11510MP_DB.html
```

The utility must return '[ALLPASS]' status on each application tier server node as well as database server nodes in order to continue with the installation of the release 11.5.10 Maintenance Pack. If '[FAIL]' is returned for any test on any node, you must take the specified action to fix the problem, re-run the utility on each node that reported a failure, and ensure that the [ALLPASS] status is returned.

Converting to OATM model (optional)

The 11.5.10 release of Oracle Application introduces a new Oracle Application Tablespace Model (OATM) consisting of only 12 tablespaces. In this model, each database object is mapped to a tablespace based on its Input/Output characteristics. These characteristics include object size, life span, access methods and locking granularity. This model facilitates easier maintenance, reduced space usage, and runtime performance gains for Oracle Applications. The OATM uses locally managed tablespaces. In previous releases of 11*i*, each product was allocated two separate tablespaces, one for index and the other for data. But with OATM, the total number of tablespaces has been reduced to 12, including temporary and system tablespaces, and undo segments. If your application system is on a previous release, you can switch to the OATM model using this utility. This is optional.

Configuring database for new products

The database must be configured for the new products added since the release of 11*i*. You need to apply the patch 3180164, which take cares of adding new product details in your environment.

Product-specific steps

Apart from these, there are many product-specific pre-install steps that need to be carried out before the application of the maintenance pack. Since these tasks are specifically related to products that are installed, we are not discussing them here. You must check the Oracle manual for these while doing an upgrade.

Upgrade Process

Stop the middle tiers

Shut down all the components of the middle tiers before starting the patching. You can use the script adstpall.sh located in the `$APPLCSF/scripts/<sid>` directory for this.

Upgrading the database

Before applying the 11.5.10 CU2 the database must be upgraded to 9*i* release 2 or a higher version of Oracle RDBMS. If you are planning to upgrade to 9.2.0 version then you must follow the steps given in the Metalink note 216550.1, and if to the 10g release 1, then follow the steps given in the metalink note 282038.1.

Apply the 11.5.10 CU 2 maintenance pack

Apply the 11.5.10 CU 2 patch 3480000. If you have a multiple node `APPL_TOP`, the patch should be applied to the admin tier first and then in all the other nodes one by one. If there are any languages other than American English installed, you must apply the NLS patch immediately after the base patch. If you are upgrading from release 11.5.4 or earlier then you must run the adadmin and choose the option 'Maintain multi-lingual tables'. The NLS patch also needs to be applied from all the nodes in case of a multiple node installation.

The Auto Patch also takes care of the post-installation steps during patching itself like compiling `APPS` schema, flex fields, and JSPs, maintaining MRC, generating JAR files and Forms, etc. which earlier had to be done manually after patching.

Post-upgrade Steps

Start the middle tiers

Once the 11.5.10 CU 2 patch has been successfully applied, you can start all the middle tiers for testing purpose only. Therefore the access to users should not be given till you complete all the steps.

Registering new products

The new products don't get registered in the database automatically, but need to be done manually. You have to use the license manager for this, which can be invoked using the Oracle Applications Manager.

Dropping MRC schema

The Multiple Reporting Currencies schema is no longer used. You can safely drop the schema. This can be done online also and no downtime is required. The following script needs to run.

```
$ cd $APPL_TOP/admin
$ sqlplus SYSTEM/<SYSTEM password> @addrpmrc.sql <APPLSYS_USERNAME> SAFE
```

Product-specific tasks

There are many product-specific tasks also that need to be performed as a part of Oracle Application Upgradation. Consult the Oracle Manual for a list of all such tasks.

Sanity testing

Once all the product-specific tasks are done, conduct a sanity test to check the working of the environment. If you are facing any issue after the upgradation then contact Oracle Support with full details of the error.

Announce the environment to the users

Once the sanity testing is done and all log ins are working then announce the environment to the users. Take a complete backup of the environment as soon as possible.

Upgrading Technology Stack Components

Rapid Install can be used to upgrade the database as well as the technology stack components. Rapid Install can also be used to install a new `ORACLE_HOME` for an upgrade to a 9*i* database.

Upgrading the database

To start the database upgrade using the Rapid Install, the screen is invoked by typing '`rapidwiz -techstack`' at the command prompt. The tech stack screen that appears is shown in the following figure.

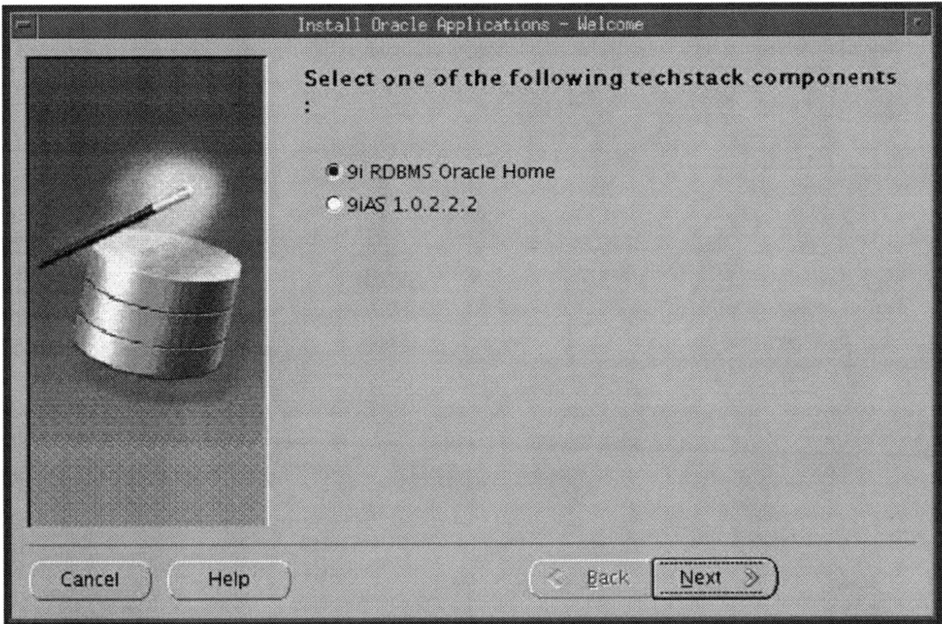

Fig. 12.52 Tech Stack Welcome Screen

This screen lists the tech stack components that the wizard can install. To install a new `ORACLE_HOME` for an Oracle 9*i* database or to upgrade the database to 9*i*, select 9*i* RDBMS Oracle Home.

Click 'Next' to continue.

The next screen shown in Fig. 12.53 prompts for the details of the database you want to upgrade or where you would like to create the new `ORACLE_HOME`.

The following information needs to be given in this screen:

- SID: The name of the database instance
- Database Port: The port number of the database
- Base Install Directory: The top-level directory that Rapid Install uses to install the RDBMS. All sub-directories (mount points) associated with the RDBMS are derived from this directory.
- Oracle OS User: The operating system user who is the owner of oracle files.
- Oracle OS Group: The OS Group of the Oracle OS user.

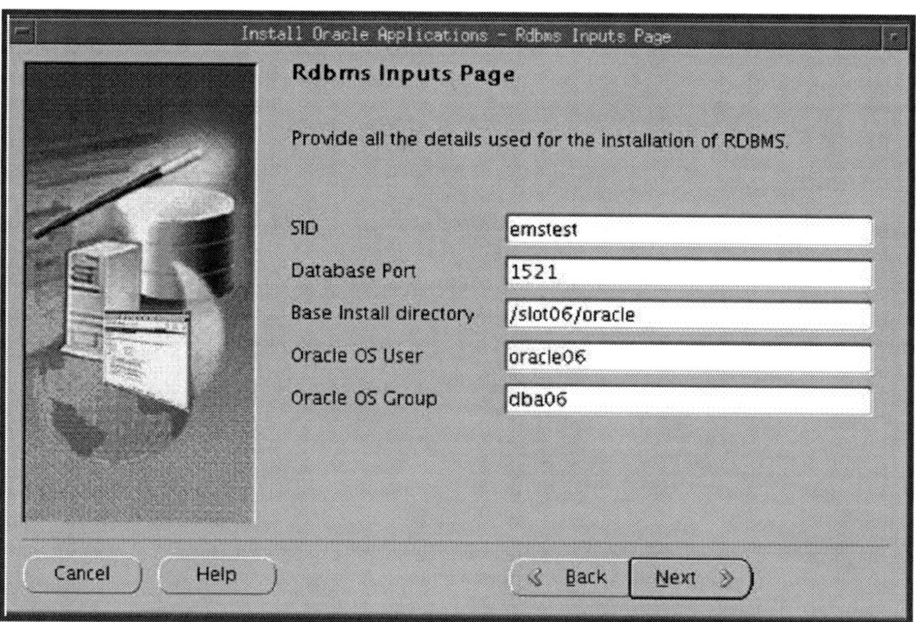

Fig. 12.53 RDBMS Inputs Page

Press 'Next' to continue.

The next screen displays the components that Rapid Install is going to install.

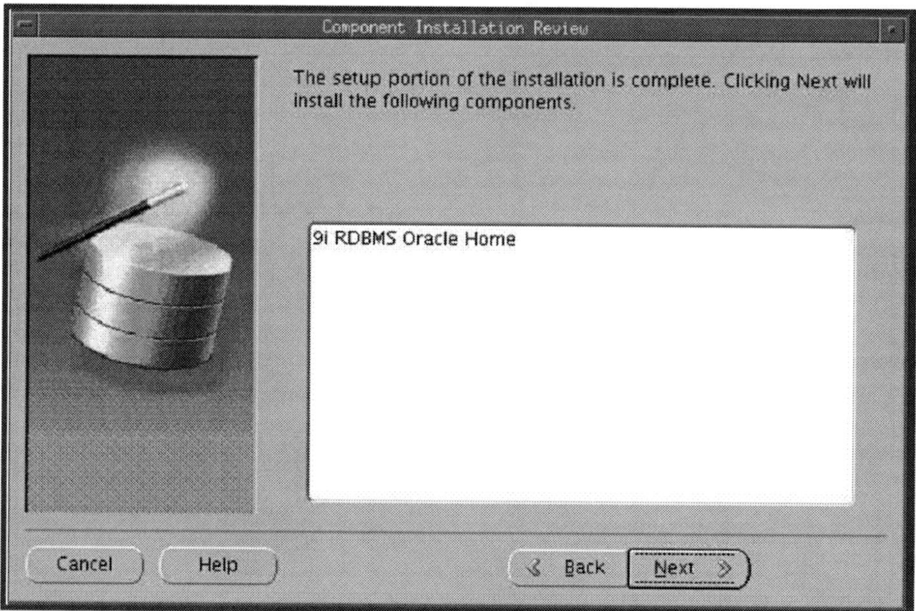

Fig. 12.54 Review

The wizard then prompts you to begin the installation with an alert.

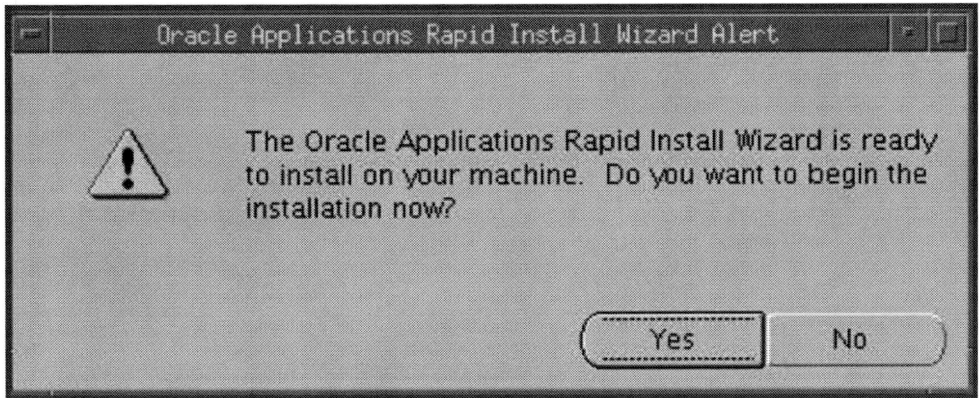

Fig. 12.55 Alert

Click 'Yes' to start the installation.
Rapid Install displays the progress of the installation as shown here.

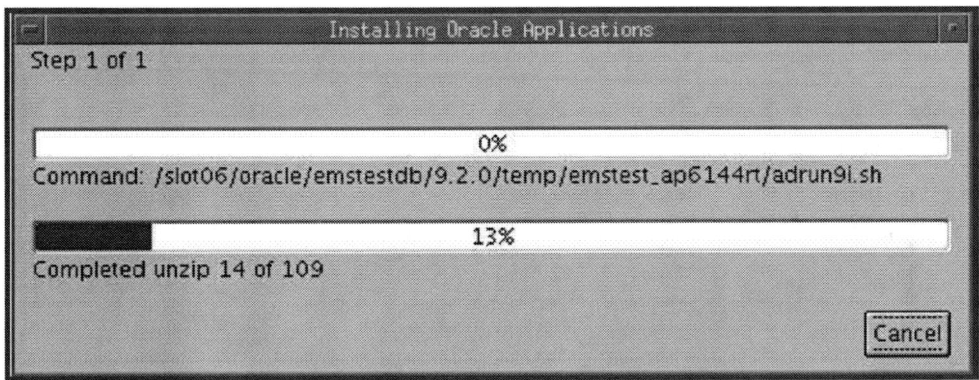

Fig. 12.56 Progress

Once the components are installed, Rapid Install displays the post-install checks screen.

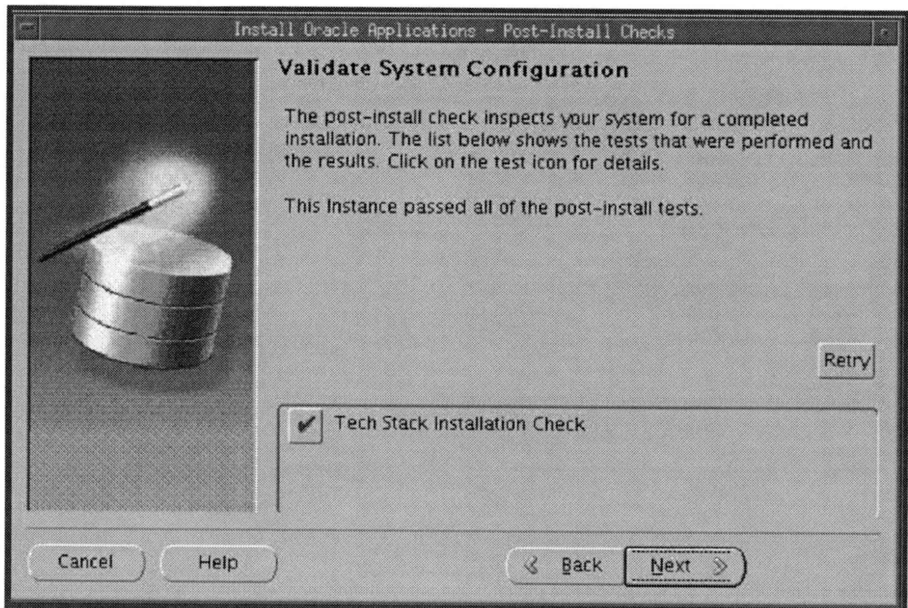

Fig. 12.57 Validate Configuration

This screen verifies that the configuration is correct (see Fig. 12.57). Click 'Next' to continue. The finish screen displays the components installed. Click 'Finish' to end the Rapid Install session.

Rapid Install then displays the finish screen.

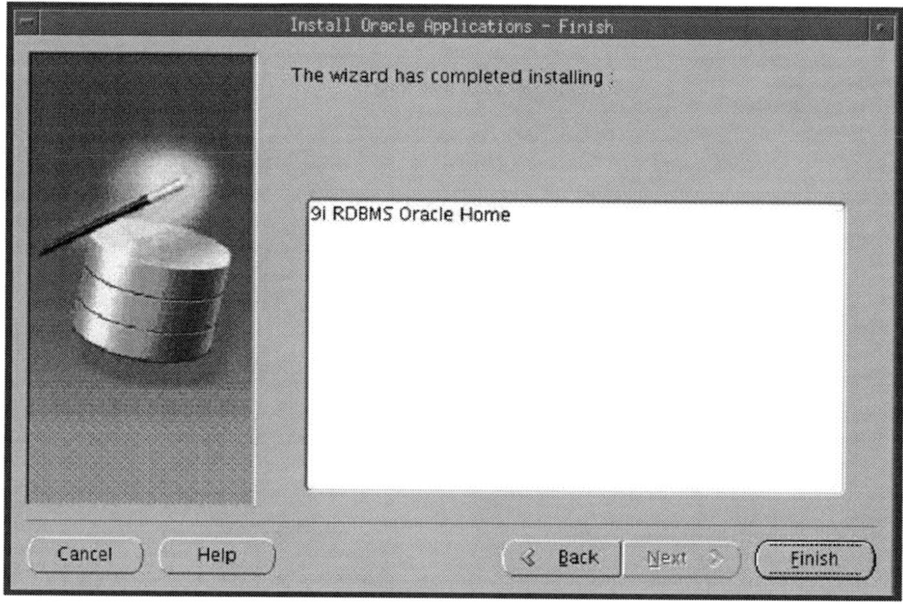

Fig. 12.58 Finish Screen

Click 'Finish' to complete the installation.

Once the database upgrade is done, you must perform the necessary post-install steps. These include applying patches, compiling the objects, and verifying certain parameters (like `init.ora`).

Upgrading the tech stack

The Rapid Install is also used to upgrade the existing application tier node to Oracle 9*i* Application Server (9*i*AS) 1.0.2.2.2. This includes the following components.

Oracle HTTP Server powered by Apache (Web server)

- Oracle Discoverer
- Oracle Portal
- Oracle Log in Server, supporting Enterprise Single Sign-on

Pre-install steps

Follow the instructions as per the document on Oracle Metalink (Doc ID: 146468.1) for installing Oracle 9*i* Application Server 1.0.2.2.2 with Oracle Applications.

Starting Rapid Install

The Rapid Install screen is invoked by typing '`rapidwiz - techstack`' at the command prompt. The selected tech stack screen appears.

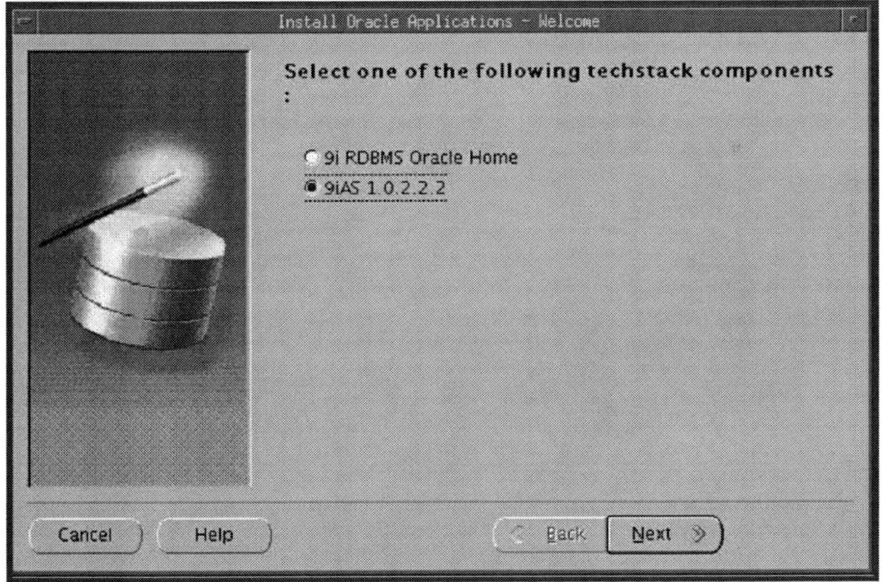

Fig. 12.59 Upgrade Tech Stack

To install or upgrade the tech stack, select the 9*i*AS 1.0.2.2.2. Autoconfig has previously stored configuration parameters in a context file. To modify this configuration, you need to change the parameters so that they point to the new `ORACLE_HOME`.

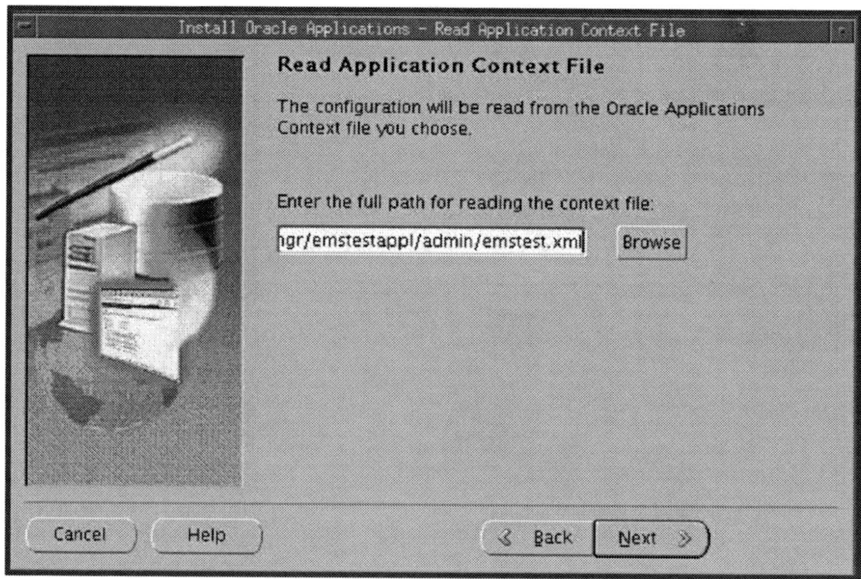

Fig. 12.60 Read Context File

Enter the path and file name directly in the text box, or click 'Browse' and navigate to the file. Highlight the file and click 'OK' to return to this screen.

Click 'Next' to continue.

The next screen prompts for the new `ORACLE_HOME` locations. Here, you need to provide the locations of the `ORACLE_HOME` associated with the updated application tier technology stack.

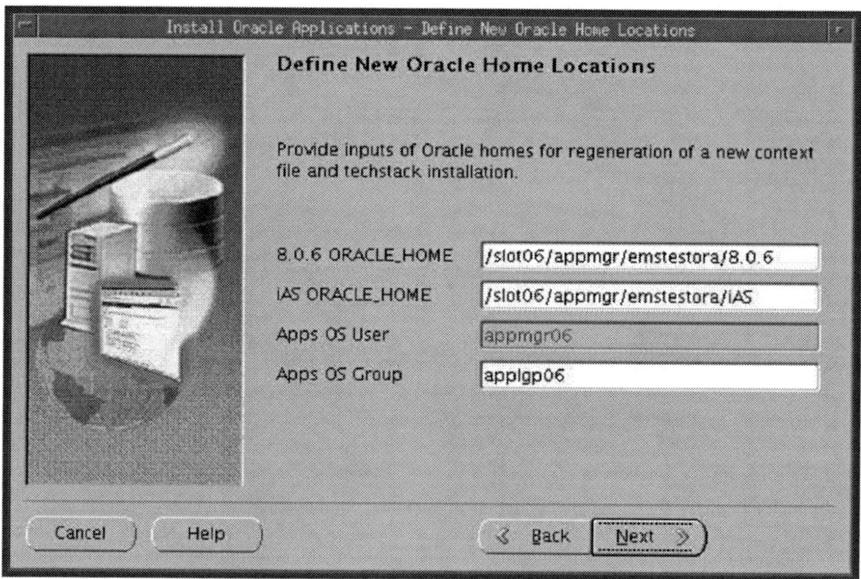

Fig. 12.61 Define Oracle Home

In this screen you enter the name of the new ORACLE_HOME that will be associated with the upgraded iAS tech stack and stored in the regenerated context file. Techstack upgrade will create two new ORACLE_HOME one for 8.0.6 and other for iAS. Here we give the location of the path name where the two new ORACLE_HOME will be created. Once the new ORACLE_HOME is generated it will update the context file (the xml file) with the details of these two new ORACLE_HOME.

The following inputs need to be given.

- 8.0.6 ORACLE_HOME: The location for the new 8.0.6 ORACLE_HOME
- iAS ORACLE_HOME: The location of the new iAS ORACLE_HOME
- APPS OS User: The owner of the APPL_TOP file system
- APPS OS Group: The OS group of the APPL_TOP owner

Click 'Next' to continue.

The 'Component Installation Review' screen lists the components that the wizard will install.

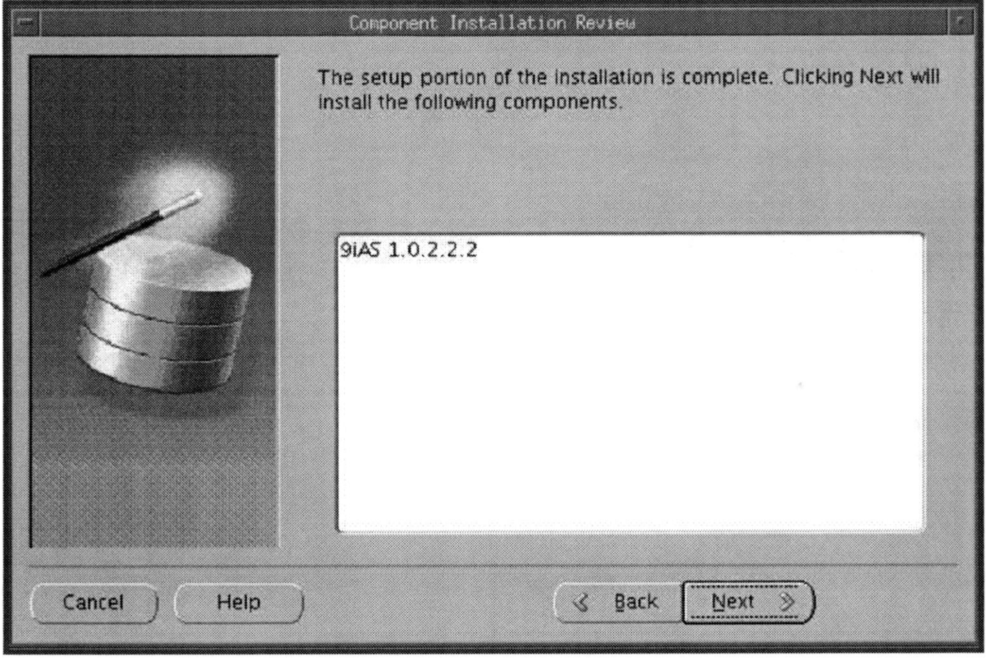

Fig. 12.62 Review

The wizard then prompts you to begin the installation.

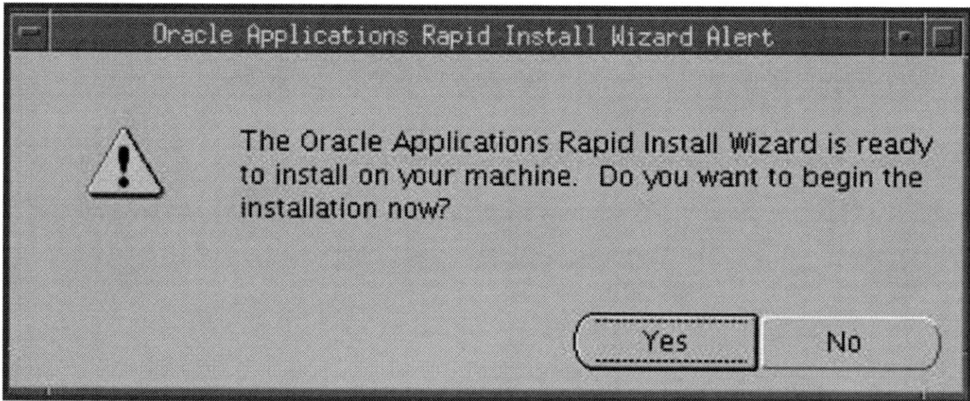

Fig. 12.63 Alert

Click 'Yes' to start the installation.

Rapid Install displays the progress of the installation in the following manner.

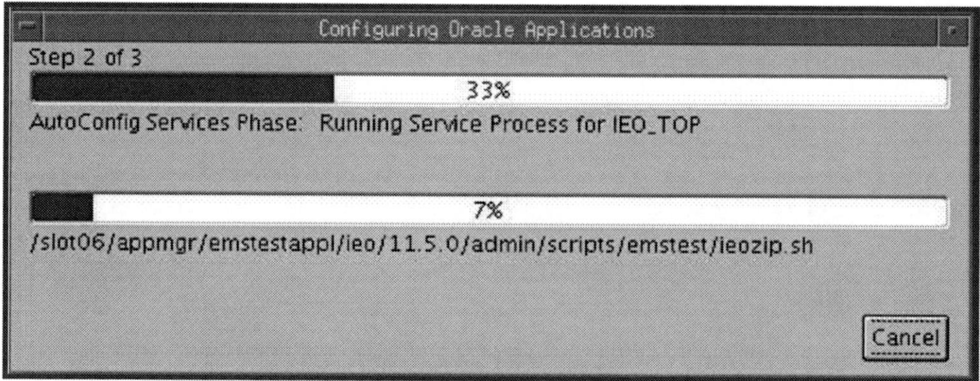

Fig. 12.64 Progress

Once the components are installed, Rapid Install displays the post-install checks screen.

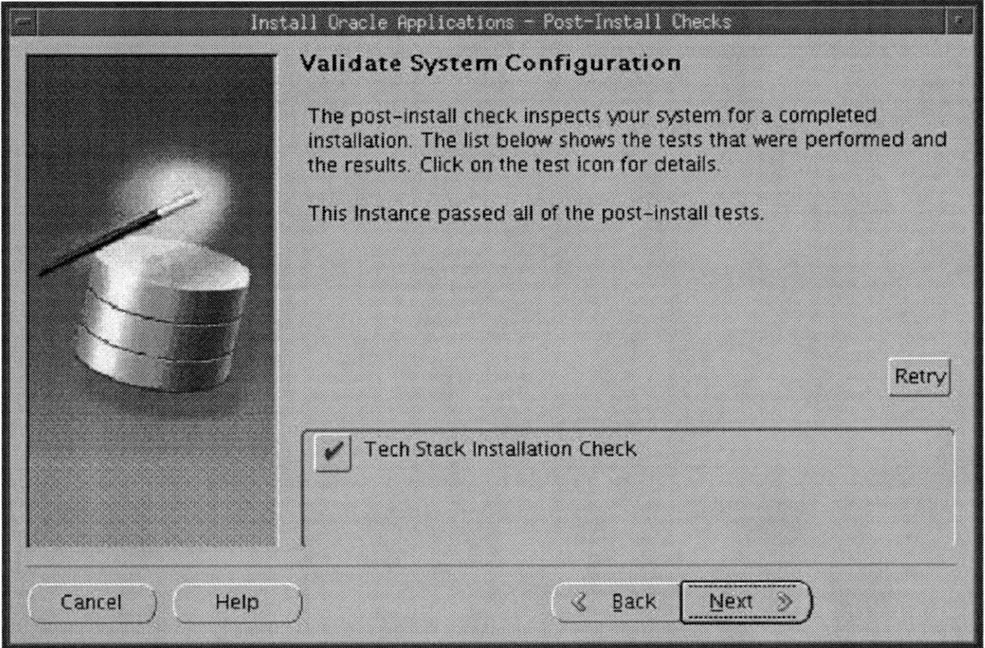

Fig. 12.65 Validate System Configuration

This screen verifies that the configuration is correct. Click 'Next' to continue. The finish screen displays the components installed. Click 'Finish' to end the Rapid Install session.

Once the installation is complete, follow the Metalink note 146468.1 to complete the post-install steps. This includes applying patches, manually updating other context file parameters and so on.

SECTION 2

UPGRADING TO RELEASE 12

The Oracle Applications Release 12 was launched in Jan 2007, which comes with the latest technology stack components.

The R12 database consists of the Oracle 10gR2 database and the application tier contains the following components:

- Oracle 10g Application Server (AS) 10.1.2
- Oracle 10g Application Server (AS) 10.1.3
- Oracle Developer 10g (includes Oracle Forms)
- Java (J2SE) native plug-in 1.5.0_08
- Java Developer Kit (JDK) 5.0

Direct upgrade to Release 12 is possible only if you have Release 11.5.7 or higher. If you have Release 11.5.6 or lower, you need to upgrade to 11.5.10 CU2 first and only then you can upgrade to Release 12. We have already discussed upgrading to 11.5.10 CU2 in the previous sections, so in this section we will discuss upgrading to Release 12 for application system in 11.5.7 or higher level.

Software and Memory Requirement

The software and memory requirement for a Release12 upgrade is same as we discussed in the chapter *Installing Oracle Applications R12.*

The Pre-upgrade Process

The upgrade process consists of several steps which we will discuss one by one.

Announcing downtime

The first step towards an upgrade is announcing a downtime. All the users must be aware of it well in advance and the downtime should be planned in such a way that it has the least effect in terms of revenue. Ideally, the upgrade should be planned for weekends or holidays.

Backing up the application system

A full backup of the database and the `APPL_TOP` must be taken before starting the upgrade process, so that in case of any upgrade failure you can revert to the existing system. A cold backup of the database should be taken with the normal shutdown.

Adding space

Before starting the upgrade you must ensure that you have enough sufficient tablespace. If you do not have enough space, you need to add more space in the tablespace. You can also go through the metalink note 399362.1 for sizing on the various tablespaces.

Database initialization parameters

Some of the upgrade scripts take a long time to complete. Their performance can be significantly improved by changing a few initialization parameters in the database for the duration of the upgrade.

We can change the following parameters:

Table 12.2

Parameter	Purpose	Recommended Value
`db_file_multiblock_read_count`	Specifies the maximum number of blocks read in one I/O operation during a sequential scan.	Remove this parameter permanently from the init.ora file. Do not restore this parameter even after the upgrade

Contd

Table 12.2 Contd

Parameter	Purpose	Recommended Value
`_db_file_optimizer_read_count`	It represents the maximum number of blocks read in one I/O operation during a sequential scan for the purposes of calculating the cost of operations like full table and fast full index scans. The actual number of blocks read in one I/O operation during a sequential scan is independently controlled by this parameter	Default is 8. Keep the default
`job_queue_processes`	Specifies the maximum number of processes that can be created for the execution of jobs	It should be equal to the number of CPUs.
`parallel_max_servers`	Controls the maximum number of parallel query server processes running in the database.	The value should be equal to 2 times the number of the CPU's.
`pga_aggregate_target`	`PGA_AGGREGATE_TARGET` controls workareas allocated by both dedicated and shared connections.	The value should be equal to 1G
recyclebin	Used to control whether the Flashback Drop capability is turned on or off. If the parameter is set to OFF, dropped tables do not go into the recycle bin	OFF

Create temporary tablespace

Create a temporary tablespace (`TEMP`) as a locally managed tablespace using the temporary file option with a uniform allocation size. In case if you already have a temporary tablespace but extent management is not local or allocation type is not uniform then simply drop the temporary tablespace and recreate the same.

```
SQL> drop tablespace TEMP;
SQL> create TEMPORARY tablespace TEMP tempfile 'temp.dbf' size 2048M EXTENT
MANAGEMENT LOCAL UNIFORM SIZE 1M;
```

To verify that the temporary tablespace has been created, run the following:

```
SQL> select CONTENTS, EXTENT_MANAGEMENT, ALLOCATION_TYPE from dba_tablespaces
where tablespace_name='TEMP';
```

The output should be:

CONTENTS	EXTENT_MANAGEMENT	ALLOCATION_TYPE
TEMPORARY	LOCAL	UNIFORM

Apply 11*i*.AD.I

You need to apply the 11*i*.AD.I minipack if it is not in your application system. If you have already applied the AD.I then you can ignore this step. The latest version of the AD.I is 11*i*.AD.I (AD.I.5) the patch number for which is 5161676. Metalink note 233044.1 contains detailed information regarding how to apply the AD patch.

Running TUMS utility

TUMS is a utility to help customers reduce the number of steps in the upgrade. It looks at a customer's specific situation, and identifies which steps are relevant for that customer. The Upgrade Manual Script (TUMS) is used to create a report that lists the upgrade steps that do not apply to the Oracle Application installation. You can ignore these steps.

```
Apply patch 5120936
```

You need to download and apply the TUMS 5120936 patch from metalink using the `adpatch` utility to generate the TUMS report.

```
Run adtums.sql
```

Once the patch is applied successfully the adtums.sql script is used to generate the TUMS report. For the `<DIRECTORY>` value, enter the full path of the directory where you want the TUMS report. This directory must be listed in the `UTL_FILE_DIR` parameter of your init.ora before TUMS can write the report and must have the appropriate permissions to write the report (`tumsr12.htm`).

```
$ cd $AD_TOP/patch/115/sql
$ sqlplus <APPS username>/<APPS password> @adtums.sql <DIRECTORY>
```

Saving the custom.pll

If you have done any customizations in Oracle Applications you must preserve the custom library (`custom.pll`), which will be used at a later stage.

The Oracle Applications upgradation is jointly done by the Applications DBA and the Oracle Applications Functional Consultants. Apart from the steps mentioned here, many product-related tasks also need to be performed by the Functional Consultant, which is beyond the scope of this book. The APPS DBA must coordinate with the Functional Consultant to ensure that all the steps are accomplished before running the Rapid Install.

Convert to multiple organizations architecture

Multiple organizations architecture supports performance improvements across all Oracle Applications. It also supports Multiple Organizations Access Control, which enables an Application's responsibility to access multiple operating units if desired. Release 12 requires multiple organizations to be enabled. If you already have converted to multiple organizations architecture, you can ignore this step else you need to convert to this architecture. You can use the metalink note Doc ID: 210193.1 for converting to the multiple org.

Drop event alert triggers in custom schemas

If you have event alert database triggers in custom schemas then you need to drop the same. You can drop them using the script `alrdtrig.sql` located at `ALR_TOP/patch/115/sql`. If you don't have any event alert triggers in the custom schemas then you can ignore this step.

Run AD preparation scripts

Release 1G12 mandates to migrate to the new tablespace model, which is known as Oracle applications tablespace model (OATM). OATM consists of only twelve tablespaces. In this model, each database object is mapped to a tablespace based on its Input/Output characteristics, which include object size, life span, access methods and locking granularity. This model facilitates easier maintenance, reduced space usage, and run-time performance gains for Oracle applications. The new tablespace model also supports Real Application Cluster (RAC) implementation on Linux, especially considering current Linux limitation of 255 raw devices. The OATM uses locally managed tablespaces. In previous release of 11*i*, each product was allocated two separate tablespaces, one for index and the other for data. But with OATM the total number of tablespace has been reduced to twelve including temporary tablespace, system tablespace, and undo segments.

To prepare your system for the Oracle Applications Tablespace Model in Release 12, you must run some preparation scripts. Download and unzip patch 5726010. Follow the instructions in the *readme* file for running the following scripts:

- *adgncons.sql*: The tablespace model for Release 12 (OATM) is based on database object type rather than product affiliation. The adgncons.sql script prepares `adcrtbsp.sql`, configures the database to hold the new products to be added during the upgrade, and switches your system to use the new tablespace model.
- *adcrtbsp.sql*: Generated by adgncons.sql, this script creates the new tablespaces, allocates unlimited tablespace to all `APPS` users, updates `fnd_product_installation` table with correct data and index tablespace information, assigns default tablespace to all `APPS` users, and sets the `new_ts_mode flag in fnd_product_groups` to Y
- *adgrants.sql*: (`adgrants_nt.sql` for Windows) Grants SYS privileges needed by Applications, and creates required views in SYS.

Note: Running the preparation scripts creates tablespaces and prepares the database objects only for new products it does not migrate to OATM. Once the upgrade is complete you have to manually migrate to OATM.

Run gather schema statistics

Before starting the upgrade you need to run the gather schema statistics concurrent program to utilize the cost based optimization feature. For running the gather statistics concurrent program login to Oracle Applications as sysadmin and submit the gather statistics program with the schema name ALL in order to gather the statistics of all the schemas.

The Upgrade Process

Running Rapid Install for creating the file system

Rapid Install needs to be run to lay down the R12 file system and the new technology stack. For upgradation to R12 the Rapid Install needs to be run twice for the first time to create the file system and for the second time to configure the various servers. We will go through all the screen shots of upgrade for better understanding.

As discussed earlier the rapidinstall can be invoked by typing the command rapidwiz at the unix prompt.

```
bash $ ./rapidwiz

Rapid Install Wizard is validating your file system......
      4 dvd labels found
Rapid Install Wizard will now launch the Java Interface.....
```

The welcome screen appears as shown in the Fig. 12.66

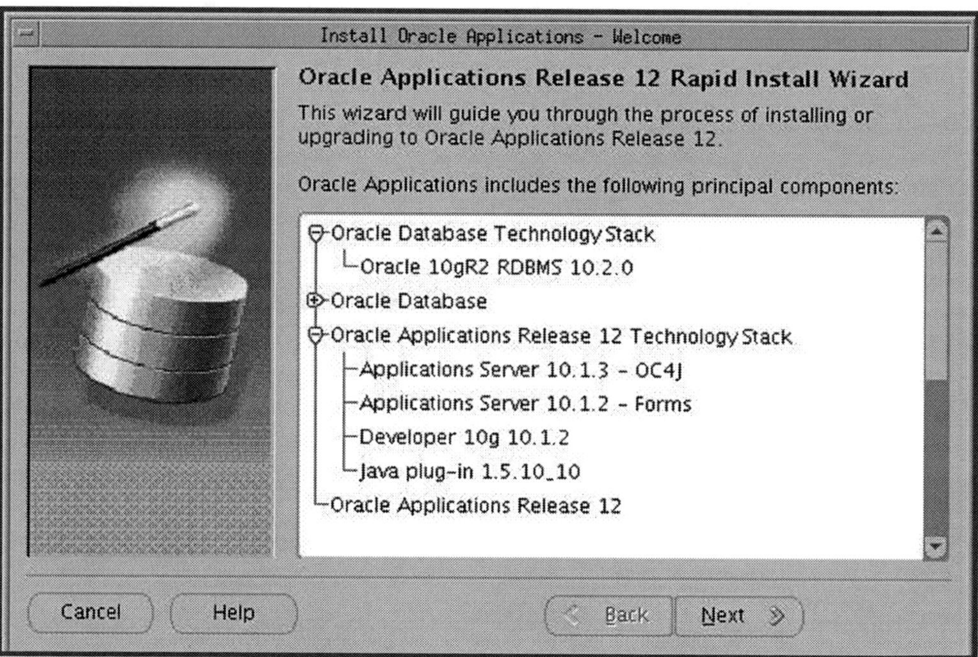

Fig. 12.66 The Welcome Screen

Press 'Next' to proceed with the upgrade

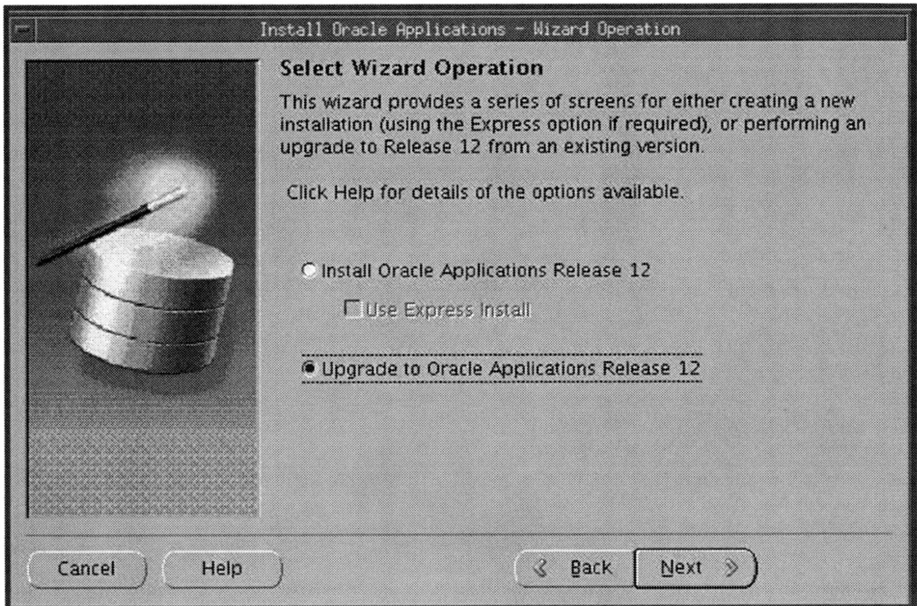

Fig. 12.67 Selecting Wizard Operation

This screen prompts for two options Install Oracle Applications Release 12 and Upgrade to Oracle Applications Release 12. Since now we are doing an upgrade so select the option Upgrade to Oracle Applications Release 12 and press Next

Fig. 12.68 Oracle Configuration Manager

The next screen is of Oracle Configuration Manager (OCM). It is a new component that is included in the R12 Rapid Install which is designed to facilitate support for your Oracle products. It provides continuous tracking of key Oracle and system statistics of the machine it is running on. Data collected by the Configuration Manager is sent via secured HTTPS back to Oracle Support, who can thereby maintain an updated view of your Oracle instance. OCM also automatically discovers the installed components and their configuration information.

Though Oracle recommends deploying the OCM, it is an optional component. So you can either accept or decline to proceed with the OCM.

If you choose Accept, you are presented with another OCM screen as shown in Fig. 12.69.

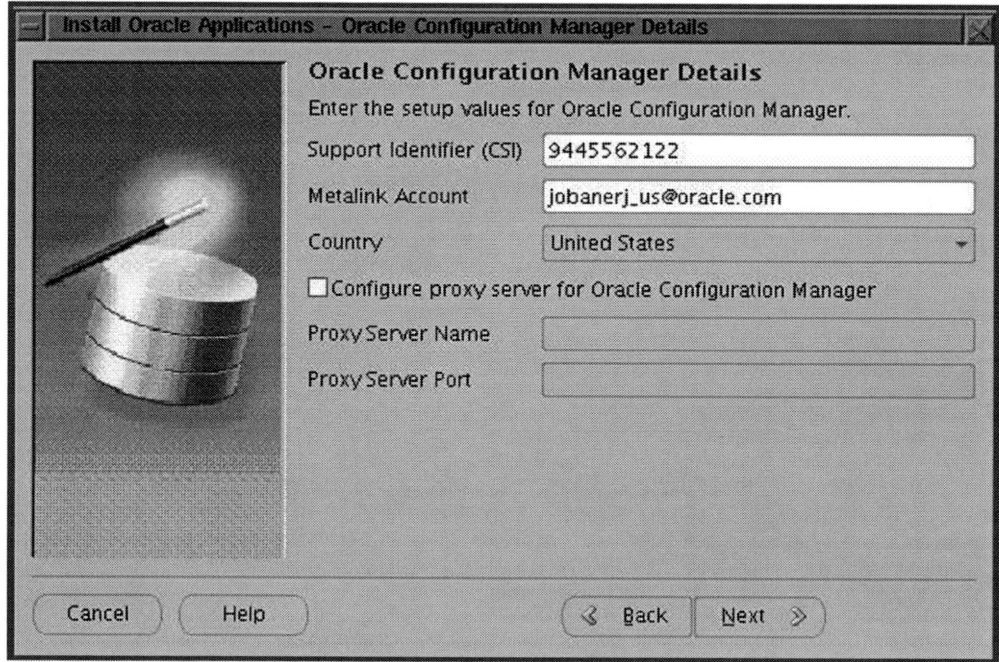

Fig. 12.69 Oracle Configuration Manager Details

The following details need to be given in this screen:

Support Identifier (CSI Number): it is the unique Customer Support Identifier number which is provided from Oracle.

Metalink Account: it is the email address by which your company is registered to metalink.

Country: Select the country from the drop down list.

If you intend to use proxy server for OCM, you need to check the check box saying Configure proxy server for Oracle Configuration Manager and need to give the proxy server name and the port number.

Enter all the details and proceed.

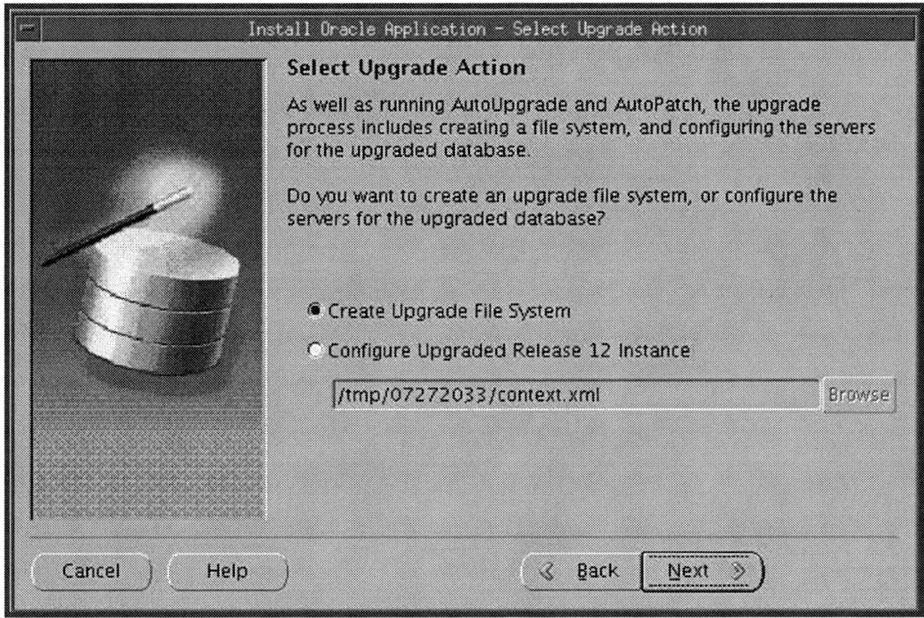

Fig. 12.70 Select Upgrade Action

As already discussed, while upgrading to R12, Rapid Install needs to be run twice for the first time to create the file system and for the second time to configure the R12 instance. Since we are creating the file system first, click on the option Create upgrade file system and press Next.

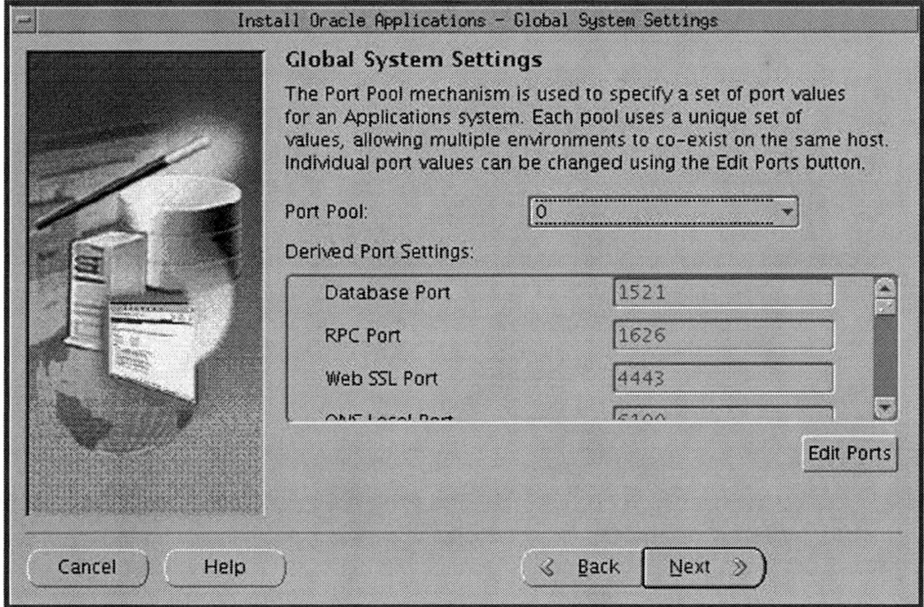

Fig. 12.71 Global System Settings

In the Global System Settings you choose the port values for the various services for your upgraded environment. You can use the port pool of your choice from the port pool drop down list. To assign some specific ports to some of the component, click on the Edit Ports button.

Choose a port pool and press Next.

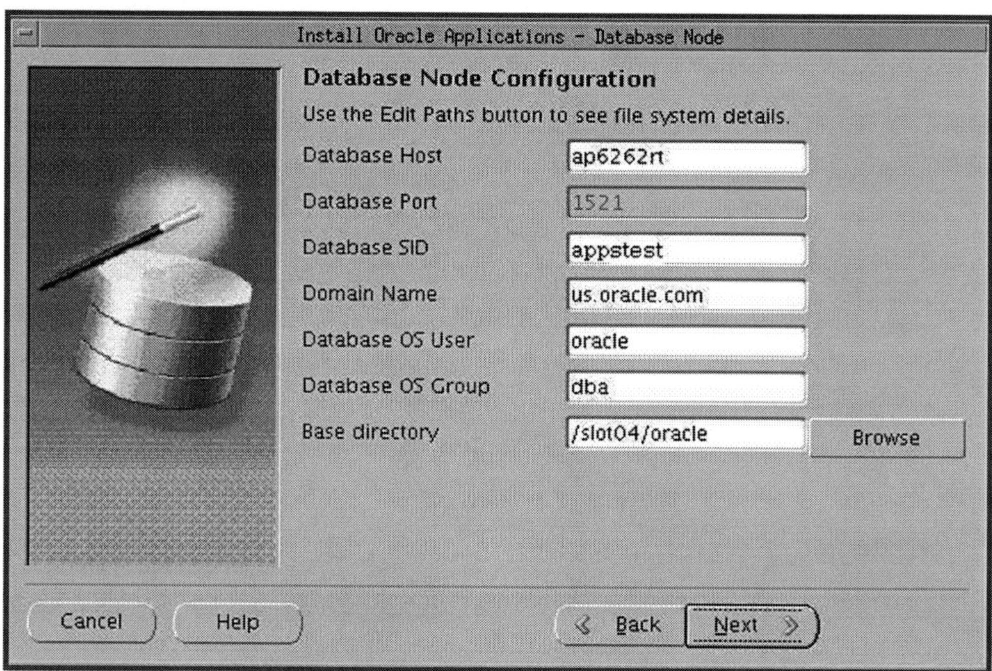

Fig. 12.72 Database Node Configuration

The next screen is the database node details. It shows the details of your existing database of the 11*i* application system. You are required to provide the following values to connect with the existing database: the hostname of the database, the port of the database, SID, the domain of the host, the owner of the Oracle software and the group of the owner of the oracle software and the base directory of Oracle.

On the next screen, provide the username and password of the existing system. The screen shows the default username and the password. You are required to provide the actual values which is being used by the database. Press Next to continue.

On the next screen, provide the details of the internationalization settings. If your existing application system has more than one language installed, you can choose the additional languages on this screen. As it can be seen from Fig. 12.74 the default territory is set to America. It should be set to America only during the upgrade. You can always change the same to other values after the upgrade, if necessary.

Database character set and `APPL_TOP` character set defaults to a common character set that is compatible with the active languages indicated on the Select Additional Languages screen. If these character sets are not there in your existing system, select the correct ones from the drop-down list.

Install Oracle Applications - Review Application User Information

Review Application User Information

APPS Username APPS
APPS Password ****
GWYUID Username APPLSYSPUB
GWYUID Password PUB
Guest Username GUEST
Guest Password ORACLE

Cancel Help Back Next

Fig. 12.73 Review Application User Information

Fig. 12.74 Select Internationalization Setting

IANA character set: The Internet Assigned Numbers Authority character set is the Internet assigned standard used by the web server. You can get more information about IANA character set from the following URL http://www.iana.org/assignments/character-sets

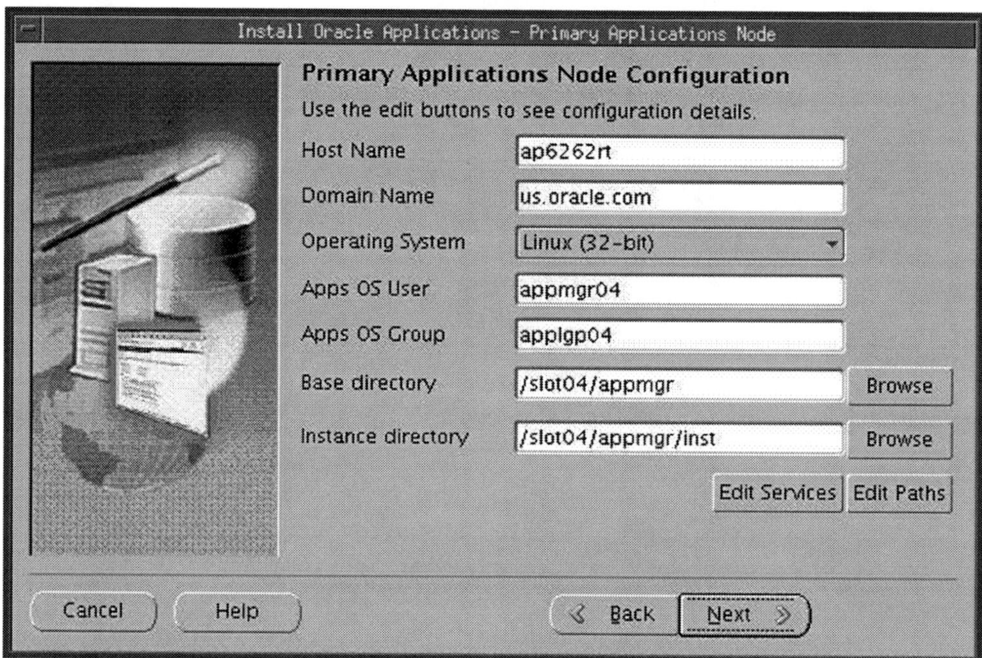

Fig. 12.75 Application Node Details

On this screen, provide the details where you would like to create the application file system. You are required to give the following details:

- Hostname: Hostname of the applications node
- Domain Name: The domain of the hostname
- Operating System: The operating system of your applications node
- Apps OS User: The operating system user who will own the application file system
- Apps OS Group: The unix group of the OS user.
- Base directory: The base directory of the application file system.

  Rapid Install automatically creates the mount points of `APPL_TOP, COMMON_TOP`, and technology stack `ORACLE_HOME` from the information derived from the base directory. You can always change the path of the default location. For changing the path click on the button Edit Paths. Figure 12.76 shows the default mount points. Edit Services button enables you to choose which services are enabled on this Applications node.
- Instance directory: The Instance directory stores instance-specific files, including runtime generated files, log files, and configuration files. This is also known as `INST_TOP`. It can be a local directory and may not be in a shared location. As discussed earlier, the concept of the `INST_TOP` came in Release 12 only.

Primary Application Node Paths

Primary Applications Node Configuration

APPL_TOP Mount point	/slot04/appmgr/apps/apps_st/appl	Browse
APPL_TOP aux. 1	/slot04/appmgr/apps/apps_st/appl	Browse
APPL_TOP aux. 2	/slot04/appmgr/apps/apps_st/appl	Browse
APPL_TOP aux. 3	/slot04/appmgr/apps/apps_st/appl	Browse
COMMON_TOP	/slot04/appmgr/apps/apps_st/comn	Browse
Tools Oracle Home	/slot04/appmgr/apps/tech_st/10.1.2	Browse
Web Oracle Home	/slot04/appmgr/apps/tech_st/10.1.3	Browse
Temp Directory	/slot04/appmgr/inst/apps/PROD_ap6262rt/	Browse

OK Cancel

Fig. 12.76 Advance Edit of Mount Points

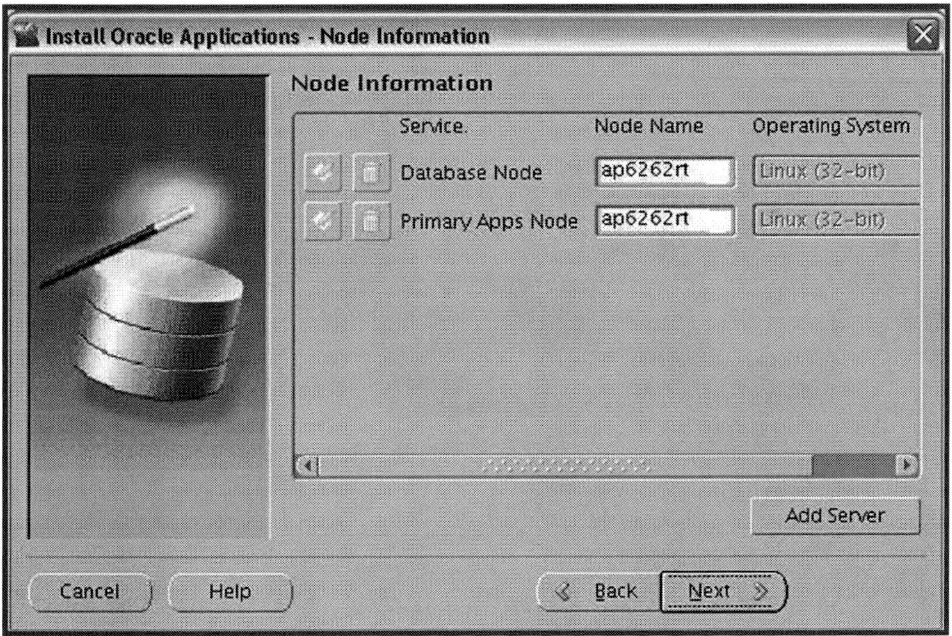

Fig. 12.77 Review Node Information

The next screen displays information about the database and the application nodes. To add more nodes for the applications, click on the Add Server button. In case of a multi node installation, you can add the additional servers from here only. Press Next to continue

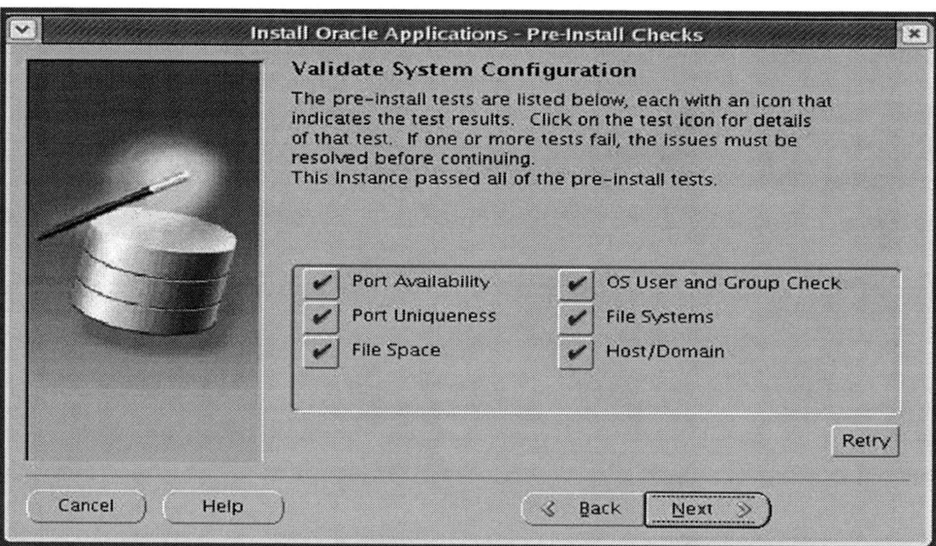

Fig. 12.78 Pre-install Checks

Now the Rapid Install does all the validations to check if it is feasible to start with the installation. If the Rapid Install displays errors in the screen then you are required to fix it before proceeding. Press Next to continue.

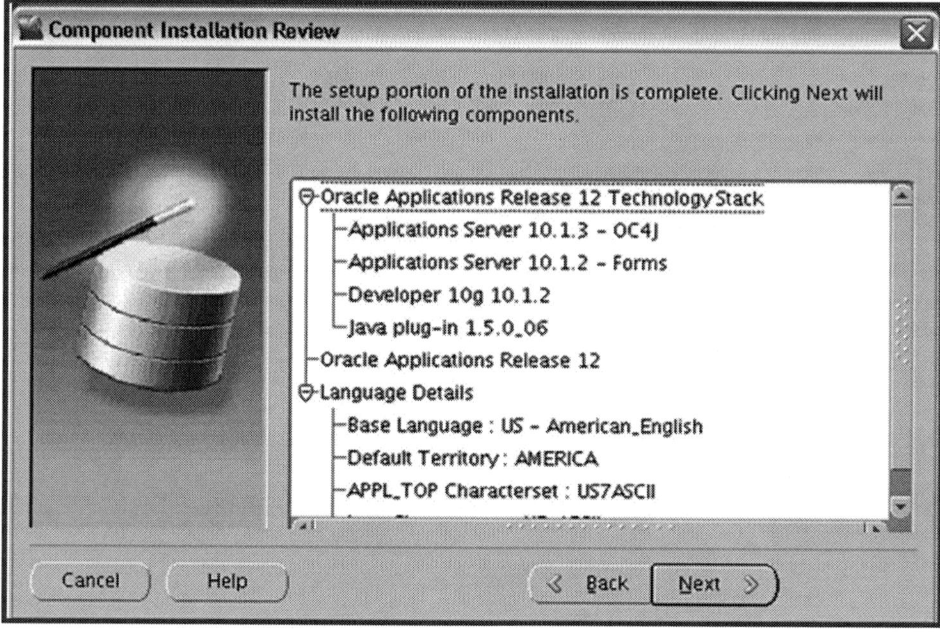

Fig. 12.79 Components Review

Rapid Install displays the various components to be installed. Click Next to continue. Rapid Install displays another alert screen asking you to verify that you are ready to begin the installation. Click Yes to continue.

Rapid Install creates the new file systems for the Applications tier and the 10g R2 `ORACLE_HOME` for the database.

Shutting down the middletier

Since we would be doing the database upgrade in the next step so shut down the middletier in both 11*i* and R12 instance. Also If you use the Oracle Applications Object Library Audit Trail feature, you must disable it before the upgrade.

Upgrading the Database

After the new file system is created and configured, the next step is to upgrade the existing database to 10gR2. If you have already upgraded your database to 10gR2, you can skip this step. You can refer to the metalink note Doc ID: 403339.1 (Oracle 10gR2 Database Preparation Guidelines for Oracle E-Business Suite Release 12 Upgrade) to get started with the upgrade.

Updating the init.ora

Since we would be upgrading the database with the R12 patches in the next section so it is required to change the init.ora parameters of the database for any performance bottlenecks. You can refer to metalink note 396009.1 for the details of the initialization parameters.

Disable custom triggers, constraints, and indexes (optional)

Disable custom triggers or constraints on Oracle Applications tables. Re-enable these triggers after the upgrade. If you have custom indexes on Applications tables, determine whether they can affect performance during the upgrade, and drop them if necessary. If you are not sure, it is better to drop the indexes and add them after the upgrade, if the new release has not created a similar index. If you do not have any of these, this step can be ignored.

Drop MRC schema (optional)

Since there is no `MRC_APPS` schema in Release 12 and all programs and reports use the `APPS` schema, you can drop it as it frees space and reduces processing overhead during the upgrade.

Apply Release 12 AD minipack

Apply the R12 AD minipack on all the application tier server nodes on your release 12 `APPL_TOP`. Before applying the patch make sure that the maintenance mode is enabled. Alternately you can also apply the patch using `options=hotpatch`.

Run the American English upgrade patch driver

We have upgraded the database to 10gR2 previously but the database does not have any R12 objects in it. To bring the database to the full Oracle Applications Release 12 level, use AutoPatch to run the

(American English) unified driver (u4440000.drv). It is located in $AU_TOP/patch/115/driver. Run the driver on the administration server node on your Release 12 APPL_TOP.

Since the patch contains only the unified drive and it is required to run only the database driver, it can be applied using the command

```
$ adpatch options=nocopyportion,nogenerateportion
```

If you have more language other than US English, it is required to apply the NLS patch also. Download the NLS Release 12 patch (4440000) for each active language in your system, and run each driver (u4440000.drv) on your Release 12 APPL_TOP. Note that the NLS patch driver has the same name as the American English patch driver.

Apply latest product patches

Determine the latest product specific patches. Then, download the American English patches. Using AD Merge patch, create a merged patch and apply it to your Release 12 APPL_TOP. If you have more than one language, you must apply the NLS equivalents of each American English product-specific patch.

Once all the patches are applied you are required to disable the maintenance mode.

Reset init.ora parameters

Reset the init.ora parameters which were changed before the upgrade.

Running autoconfig on database tier.

When Rapid Install was run for the preparation for upgrade, it created and stored an instance specific context by replacing system variables you entered on the wizard screens with the specific values you saved in the configuration file (config.txt). At this point in the upgrade, Rapid Install is pointed to the Applications context file. Rapid Install (using Autoconfig) updates your system configuration using the values it finds in the context file.

Update the RDBMS ORACLE_HOME file system with AutoConfig files.

On the application tier (as the applmgr user):

Log on to the APPL_TOP environment (source the environment file).

Run the following Perl script to create appsutil.zip in $INST_TOP/admin/out.

```
perl $AD_TOP/bin/admkappsutil.pl
```

On the database tier (as the ORACLE user):

Copy or FTP the appsutil.zip file to the <RDBMS ORACLE_HOME>.

```
cd $ORACLE_HOME
unzip -o appsutil.zip
```

Run AutoConfig on the database tier nodes.

```
<RDBMS ORACLE_HOME>/appsutil/scripts/<CONTEXT_NAME>/adautocfg.sh
```

The Post-upgrade Process

Running Rapid Install for configuring the various servers

Once the database is upgraded with R12 the next step would be to configure the R12 instance as a whole. For configuring all the services Rapid Install needs to be run again. During the installation Rapid Install creates an xml file in `$APPL_TOP/admin` directory where it stores all the information about the various services. This xml file is also known as context file. For configuring the various servers you are required to point to the xml file when prompted.

Start Rapid Install with the `./rapidinstall command`. In the Select Upgrade Action screen as shown in Fig. 12.80, select Configure Upgraded Release 12 Instance.

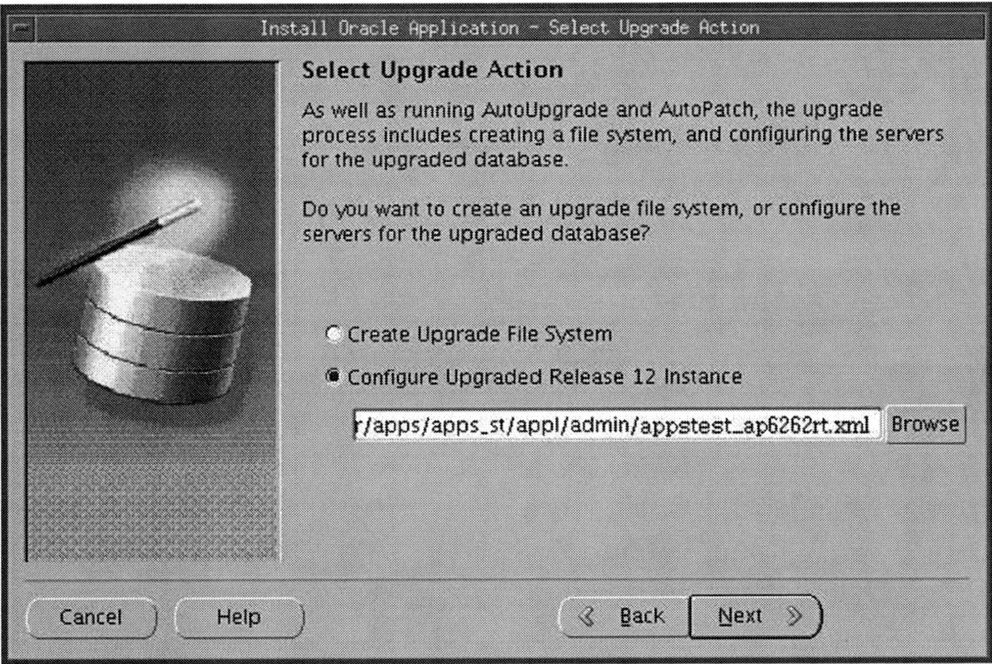

Fig. 12.80 Choosing Configure Upgraded Release 12

In the box give the details of the applications context file. You can either enter the path directly in the box, or click Browse and highlight the path in the directory. Press Next to continue.

For security reasons, the `APPS` password is not saved in the context file, so you will be prompted to re-enter it on the Review Application User Information screen.

Rapid Install notifies you of the components and processes it will configure and start. Click Next to continue. At the prompt about beginning the installation now, click Yes. Rapid Install creates server process control scripts and starts all server processes.

Reapplying customizations

If you have done any customizations in Oracle applications you need to integrate all of them at this stage. Though it may be done by functional consultants and Oracle application developers but an `Apps DBA` is often required to integrate these customizations with the apps schema.

During the upgrade, custom triggers or constraints may have been modified. If you have disabled these triggers and constraints, identify any data updates that must be made before you re-enable them.

If you have dropped any custom indexes, review the new data model to determine if the index is necessary before you redefine it.

Changing passwords

Though Rapid Install keeps all the existing passwords of the schemas but for those new products which Rapid Install installs, it creates a new schema and the default password is the product's short name. Review and change the passwords for all the new schemas that are created with this upgrade.

Sanity testing

Before releasing the environment to the users, perform a complete sanity testing of the environment and ensure that all the middletiers are running and you are able to navigate properly in without any issues.

13

PRINTER SETUP

Whenever any report is generated, Oracle Reports formats the output. When the formatting is over, the Concurrent Manager sends it to the operating system, which in turn either issues an operating system print command or calls a custom print program that issues the print command.

Oracle Applications provides two kinds of printing solutions. One is Pasta Utility, which is very easy to setup and maintain and provides the complete printing solution. Oracle Applications also allows the user to define own printers to cater to custom requirements.

To explain the overall printing process in more detail, the Oracle Application user submits a request to run a report. This is most commonly done from the 'Submit Request Form' (`shortname =FNDRSRUN`). The request is written into the concurrent queue/request table(s) (e.g. `FND_CONCURRENT_REQUESTS`). The CM that eventually picks up the request will read it and its definition from the queue. It will then start off Oracle reports. Oracle Reports will look at a setting for the number of copies you want. If copies is not equal to 0, then Oracle reports will look at the print style definition to know which SRW file to use. If copies is not equal 0, then Oracle Reports will look at the print driver definition to know the SRW file to use. In either case, Oracle Reports will look at the print style to determine the rows and columns contained in the report. These override both the print style and print driver SRW files (which contain rows and columns as well). After the file has been generated using the appropriate SRW file and row/columns settings, the Concurrent Manager will pre-pend the initialization string and append the reset string to the output. As a general rule, the first component of the initialization string should be the reset string. Do not assume that the printer has been properly reset; it is the responsibility of the System Administrator to configure the initialization and reset strings properly.

Oracle reports utility looks at the print driver to determine which output method is being used. It has two primary methods for output, Command and Program. Most (around 95%) of all reports are via the command method. Here, Oracle Reports generates the output file and then uses operating system commands to send the file to the printer. In the other method, program, the output from Oracle Reports is sent to a program/script that then makes additional changes to the file. Then the program is responsible for printing the report. This kind of processing is typically referred to as 'filter'. PASTA, the executable `FNDPSTAX` present in `$FND_TOP/bin` is an example of such a program. The first course of action for a system administrator trying to get a print is to ensure that one can print from the machine. Also, check to see that you can print from the servers. Setting up printers within Oracle Applications assumes that printing has already been set up at the operating system level. If this hasn't already been done, it must be at this point, as Oracle Applications does not control printers and will not be able to set them up.

The printer needs the following information for printing a report.

- The information about the text it is going to print. The formatting of the text is taken care of by Oracle reports (this includes page break, carriage return, line feed, text bold on/off, text underline on/off). The values for these are retrieved from an SQL*Report Writer (SRW) Driver file.
- The information about the document formatting, viz. the dimensions for a report output file in terms of width and height. The print style defines the dimensions for a report output file.
- The information about printer formatting, viz. the orientation, like landscape or portrait.

To summarize, these are the printer definition components:

- Printer Type describes the printer
- Printer Style formats the document
- Printer driver formats the output
- The SQL* Report Writer Driver formats the text

DEFINING PRINTERS

There are two ways of defining a printer—one, using the predefined components, and two, using the custom components. In the first method, you just need to register the printer as a predefined type. To define a printer using custom components, the following steps need to be followed:

- Define the new type
- Define the new style
- Define the new driver
- Register the printer as new type

Defining New Type

The first step in defining a printer is deciding its type. This describes the kind of printer you have or the model of the manufacturer, for example, a Canon Laser Jet Printer.

For adding a new type, you have to assign a style and driver. The printer type form can be queried to find the existing combinations of style and drivers to decide whether an existing printer type supports the new printer.

You can navigate via `Sysadmin > Install > Printer > Types` and then run 'Query by example' to see all the existing definitions (see Fig. 13.1).

These are the detailed steps in creating a printer type:

- Log in to Applications as the system administrator
- Navigate the path `Install > Printer > Register`
- In the 'Type' field, put the type of the printer preferably as Manufacturer + Model

- In the 'Description' field, put any distinguishing information that you want about this type of printer
- Save the record

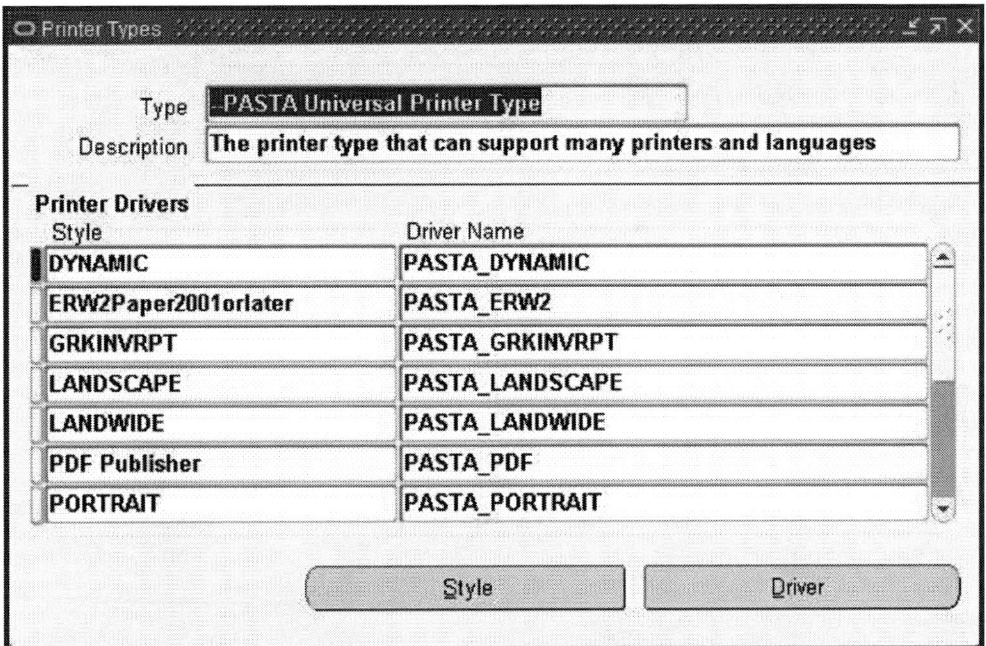

Fig. 13.1 Printer Types

Defining New Style

Print style is used to define the rows, columns and orientation of the report. It is also used to define which SRW driver is used when the number of copies is equal to zero (see Fig. 13.2).

- Log on to Applications as the system administrator responsibility.
- Navigate `Install > Printer > Style`.
- In the 'Style Name' field, type a unique name. Once you have created a style, it can not be deleted.
- In the 'Seq' field, type a unique number. This number is only used to display a sequence when you query print styles from this form.
- In the 'User Style' field, put the same value as that of the Style Name field. This field is not used anywhere but in this form.
- In the 'SRW Driver' field, put the name of the SRW file that you expect Oracle Reports to use when the number of copies = 0. At this point, Applications will not validate that the SRW file actually exists.
- In the 'Description' field, put any distinguishing information about the style.

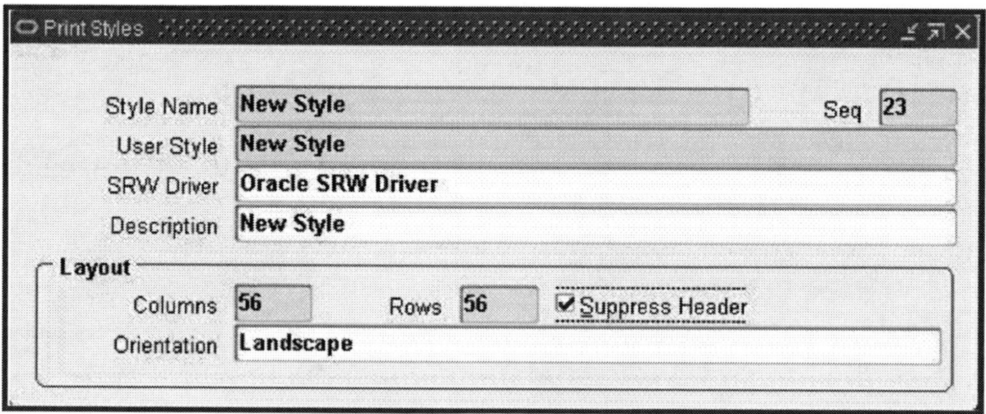

Fig. 13.2 Defining New Style

- In the 'Columns' field, put the number of character wide for your style.
- In the 'Rows' field, put the number of lines long for your style.
- Select the 'Suppress Header' checkbox when you do not want Oracle reports to print an identifier header page prior to printing the report.
- In the 'Orientation' field, put either 'Portrait' or 'Landscape', as appropriate for your style. This field is used for bit-mapped reports.
- Save the record.

Defining New Driver

The printer driver communicates with the printer and provides information needed to print the reports in the required style. You can also create custom printer drivers to support print styles for new or existing printer drivers (see Fig. 13.3). You need to define a new printer driver in the following situations:

- When a printer type needs different control characters
- When the control characters have different meanings because of differences in operating system and platform
- When the language translation changes the meaning of the control characters
- When the printer needs special control characters to select different characters sets

The following are the steps to create a new driver.

- Log on to Applications as the system administrator.
- Navigate `Install > Printer > Driver`.
- In the 'Driver Name' field, put a name for your print driver. This must be unique for a given platform.
- In the 'User Driver' field, put the same name as your driver name. The field must be unique.
- In the 'Description' field, put any additional information specific to this print driver.

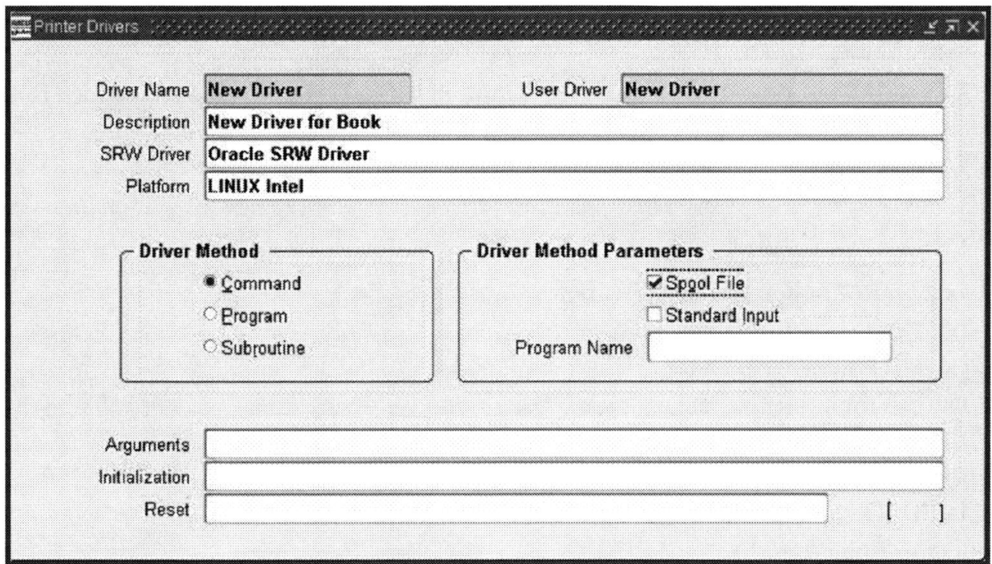

Fig. 13.3 Defining New Printer Drivers

- In the 'SRW Driver' field, put the name of the SRW file that you expect Oracle reports to use when the number of copies > 0.
- At this point, Applications will not validate the actual existence of the SRW file.
- In the 'Platform' field, put the name of the platform being used only if you have multiple drivers of the same name on differing platforms. Otherwise, leave the field null. Also leave it null for Windows NT.
- In the 'Driver Method' option group, you can choose Command, Program or Sub-routine. Most of your reports will use the command method. This method uses the operating system command, as described in the field 'Arguments'. The program method uses the program described in the 'Program Name' field to output the file. The sub-routine method is essentially identical to the command method. Here, the Concurrent Manager calls a predefined Oracle Applications sub-routine that passes a print command and arguments to the printer via the operating system. The sub-routine name appears in the name field of the printer driver form. The difference between this and the command method is that it does not spawn an operating system shell to execute printing. An example of this is using `SYS$PRINT` on a VMS platform. This method is OS-specific, and may not be supported for your operating system.
- The 'Spool File' checkbox is used when the driver method is set to program. The program will create its own spool file.
- The 'Standard Input' checkbox should be left unchecked when the driver method is program, unless the program accepts standard input.
- In the 'Program Name' field, put the name of the program or of the sub-routine, depending on the driver method being used.
- In the 'Arguments' field, put the full operating system print command and its arguments when the driver method is command (see the command method argument parameters discussed later

in this chapter). When the driver method is program, enter the arguments that you would like to pass to the program.

- In the 'Initialization' field, put the initialization string that you want pre-pended to the output.
- In the 'Reset' field, put the reset string that you want appended to the output.
- Save the changes.

Registering New Printer

- Log on to Applications as the system administrator.
- Navigate `Install > Printer > Register`.
- In the 'Printer' field, put the OS name of the printer. Even though you would have already defined the printer to the operating system, Oracle Application does not validate the information in this field.
- In the 'Type' field, choose the printer type from the available LOV.
- In the 'Description' field, put any distinguishing information about this printer.
- Commit the record.

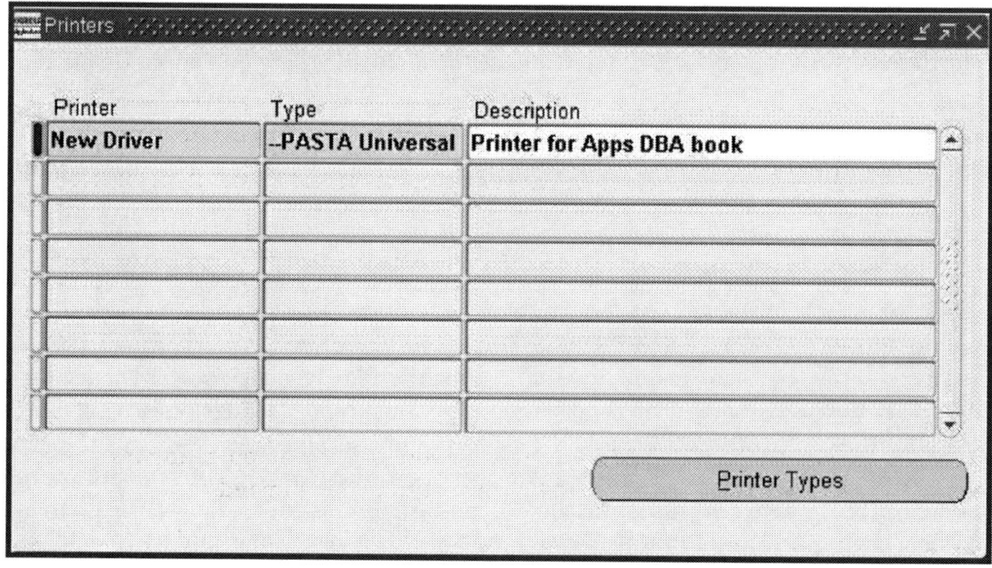

Fig. 13.4 Registering New Printer

Assigning a Printer Driver

You must have a registered printer, a style, and a driver to complete this step.

- Log on to Applications as the system administrator.
- Navigate `Install > Printer > Types`.

- Query your printer type.
- Move to the printer drivers region and go to the row-oriented fields labeled 'Style' and 'Driver Name'.
- Insert a new row.
- In the 'Style' field, type or select (via the LOV) the style you want assigned to this printer.
- In the 'Driver Name' field, type or select the print driver that you want assigned to this printer.
- Save the changes.

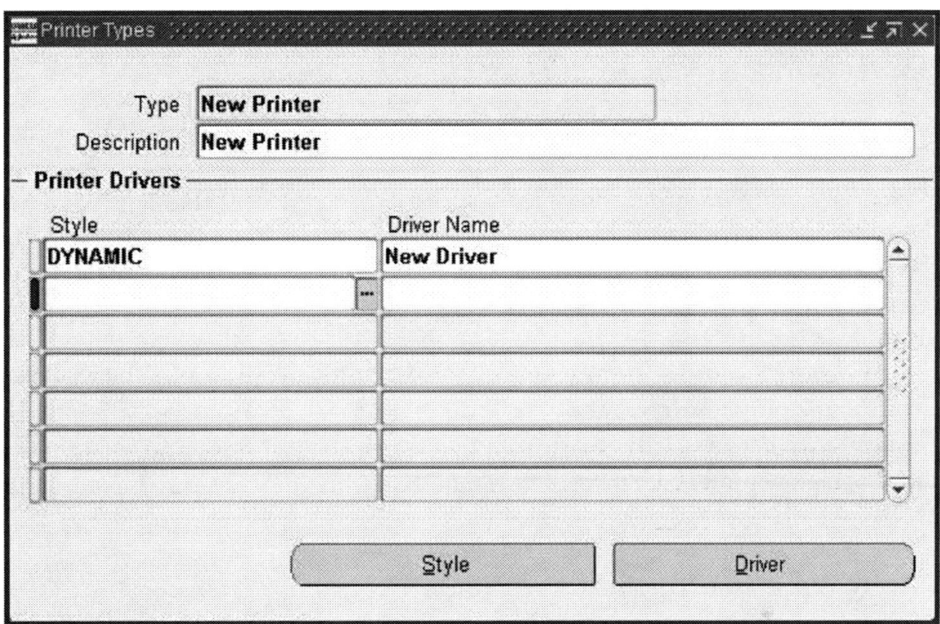

Fig. 13.5 Assigning a Printer Driver

Command method argument parameters

There are four different parameters you can pass in addition to the operating system command for printing. These are listed in the 'Arguments' field after the O/S command.

1. `-d$PROFILES$.PRINTER`: '-d' calls out the destination printer, and `$PROFILES$.PRINTER` retrieves the operating system name of the printer associated with the request.
2. `-n$PROFILES$.CONC_COPIES`: '-n' calls out the number of copies to print. `$PROFILES$.CONC_COPIES` retrieves the value of the profile option Concurrent: Report Copies, unless this value is updated at runtime.
3. `-t"$PROFILES$.TITLE"`: '-t' calls out the report title to print on a banner or header page and `-t$PROFILES$.TITLE` retrieves the title of the output file, typically titled as Application user name. Request ID. For example, if user Joyjeet Banerjee ran a report with concurrent request ID 154221, the title would be JOBANERJ. 154221. This is operating system-dependent.

4. `$PROFILES$.FILENAME`: `$PROFILES$.FILENAME` calls out the filename of the report to be printed. The value retrieved is the output file name, including the path to the file.

Here are the corresponding arguments for Unix and Windows.

Unix:

```
lp -c -d$PROFILES$.PRINTER -n$PROFILES$.CONC_COPIES -t"$PROFILES$.TITLE"
$PROFILES$.FILENAME
```

Windows:

```
PRINT /D:$PROFILES$.PRINTER $PROFILES$.FILENAME
```

ORACLE REPORTS AND REPORT GENERATION

The activities of Oracle reports include page break, carriage return, line feed, text bold on/off, and text underline on/off instructions within the output file. The values are retrieved from an SQL*Report Writer (SRW) driver file.

When the report is generated for online viewing, Oracle Reports uses the SRW driver named by the print style in the relevant form.

When the report has to be printed, it uses the SRW driver named by the Oracle Applications printer driver in the printer drivers form.

The dimensions of a report are determined by the values given for columns and rows in the print style, defined using the print styles form. These values override the width and height values in an SRW driver file.

SRW Drivers and Oracle Applications Printer Drivers

When the report does not have to be printed (number of copies = 0 and the target printer field is blank), Oracle reports feature uses the SRW driver named by the print style defined in the respective form.

When the report is to be printed (number of copies > 0), it uses the SRW driver named by the Oracle Applications printer driver in the printer drivers form.

The dimensions of a report are determined by the columns and rows values in the print style, defined using the print styles form. These values override the width and height values in an SRW driver file.

Concurrent Manager Issues or Calls a Print Command

When a report is completed, the CM pre-pends an initialization string to the output file. The initialization string is defined using the printer drivers form. The CM appends a reset string to the output file, which is also defined by the same form.

An Oracle Applications printer driver is typically executed by either issuing a print command or calling a print program.

When the printer driver method is command, the Concurrent Manager can issue an operating system print command and arguments, entered in the arguments field of the printer drivers form.

When the printer driver method is program, the CM can call a custom print program, named (along with its path) in the name field of the printer drivers form. Arguments to the program may be entered in the form's arguments field.

Concurrent Manager can provide values for arguments

The CM may provide values for the four arguments of an operating system print command or custom print program:

- The name of the file to be printed

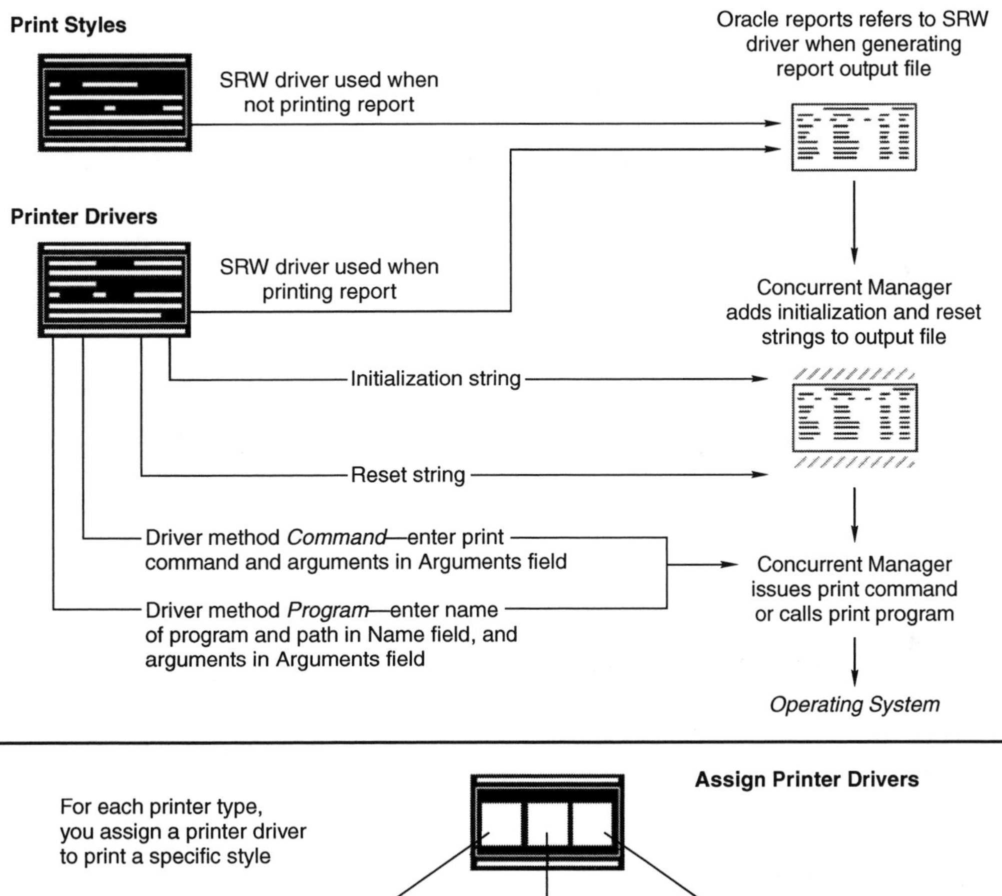

Fig. 13.6 Summary of Oracle Applications Printing

- The operating system name of the target printer
- The title of the file, which appears on a header page if it is printed
- The number of copies to be printed

Configuring Pasta Printer

Pasta is an Oracle Applications utility that simplifies the standard printing set up procedure. The only set up required here for basic printing is the registration of the printer. The following are the steps for configuring the pasta printer:

1. Apply Pasta 2.5.1 (Patch 2460859)
2. The printer type, printer driver, and SRW driver files are provided by patch 465094
3. Use the Printers window to register your printer:
   - Enter your printer's name as defined in the operating system and applications
   - Select 'Pasta Universal Printer' from the list of values for the printer type
4. Bounce the Concurrent Manager

You are now ready to print text and postscript reports from your postscript printer using the default Pasta configuration in the following styles: Landscape, Land-wide, Portrait and Dynamic.

14

MANAGING APPLICATION SECURITY

One of the important tasks of the system administrator is to manage the security of Oracle Applications. He must ensure that the users are logged in with proper responsibility. The responsibilities separate users with different access levels. Even a small mistake while providing proper responsibility may lead to severe damages, like if a user has system administration responsibility, he can mess up the entire application system. In Oracle Application, the first level of security is implemented by creating users and providing them responsibilities.

CREATING USERS

An Oracle Application user is created using the `navigation > Security > User > Define.`

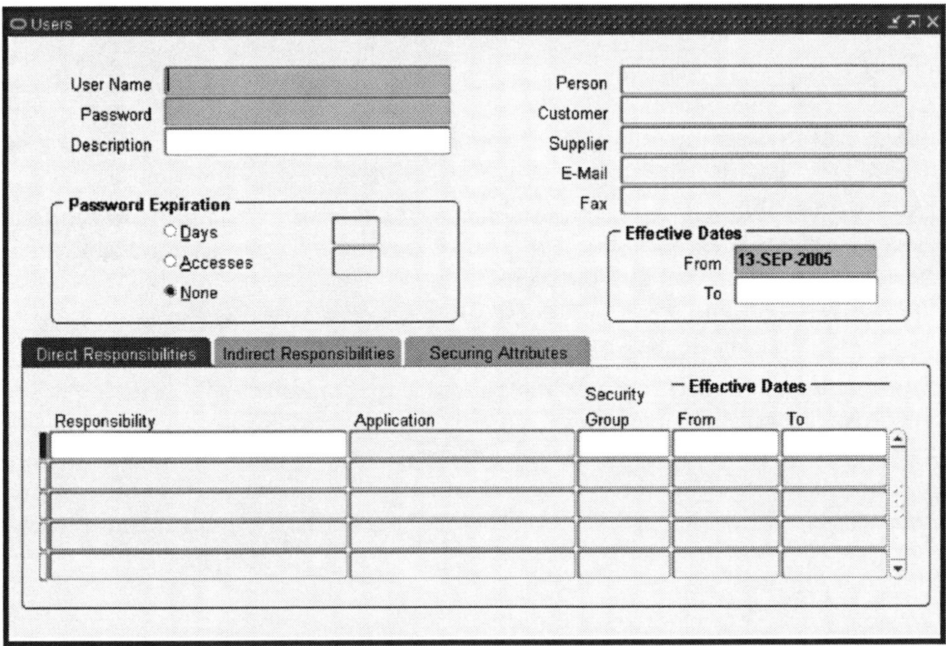

Fig. 14.1 Defining the Application Users

The terms used on this screen are explained further.

- User name: Enter a user name for the user you are trying to create. The name must be unique in Oracle Applications. The user name you enter will be displayed in capital letters.
- Password: Enter the password for the application user. It needs to be entered twice and must be of five characters. The password entered during the creation of the user is a temporary one, as the application user will be asked to change the password when he logs in for the first time. For security reasons, the password window doesn't display the password.
- Description: In this field you may enter the description of the user. This is an optional field.
- Password expiration: Here, you specify how the password of the user will expire. This rule applies to the password entered by the user. If you want the password to expire after a certain date, click on the date button and enter the number of days after which the password will expire. You can also choose a selected number of accesses for this. Check the 'accesses' button and enter the number of accesses. You can also choose not to have the password expire automatically and leave it to the user. When the password of the user expires, a pop-up window prompts him/her to change the password. Oracle recommends application users to change their password frequently, as it reduces the likelihood of unauthorized access.
- Person: If you choose to put a person to associate with the application user name then the person must be an employee already defined in the system.
- Customer: You can also choose to put a customer to associate with the application user name. Then, the customer must be a customer contact already defined in the system.
- Supplier: You can choose a supplier to associate with the application user name as long as he is a supplier contact already defined in the system.
- Email: Enter the email address of the application user (optional).
- Fax: Enter the fax number of the user (optional).
- Effective dates: The effective dates define the period till when the application user is valid. You cannot delete an application user, but you can enter an effective end-date that falls before the system date in order to deactivate an application user. If you wish to reactivate a user, change the date to later than the current date, or clear the end date field.
- Direct responsibilities: Direct responsibilities are those assigned directly to the users at the time of user creation. A responsibility is uniquely identified by an application name and a responsibility name. An application user can be given more than one responsibility.
- Indirect responsibilities: A user inherits these through membership of a group to which the responsibility has been assigned.
- Securing attributes: Securing attributes are used by Oracle HTML-based applications to allow rows (records) of data to be visible to specified users or responsibilities based on the specific data (attribute values) contained in that row. You may assign one or more values for any of the securing attributes assigned to the user. If a securing attribute is assigned to both a responsibility and to a user but the user does not have a value for that securing attribute, no information is returned for it.

DEFINING RESPONSIBILITIES

A responsibility determines all the modules an application user can access, the application functions he can use, and the reports and concurrent programs he can run. Different application users assigned the same responsibility will have the same application privileges.

All the Oracle Application products are installed with pre-defined responsibilities. You can check the reference guide of Oracle Application products while assigning them.

You need to assign data group, request security group and menu to assign responsibilities. This is shown in the following figure. We will discuss these first before explaining responsibility.

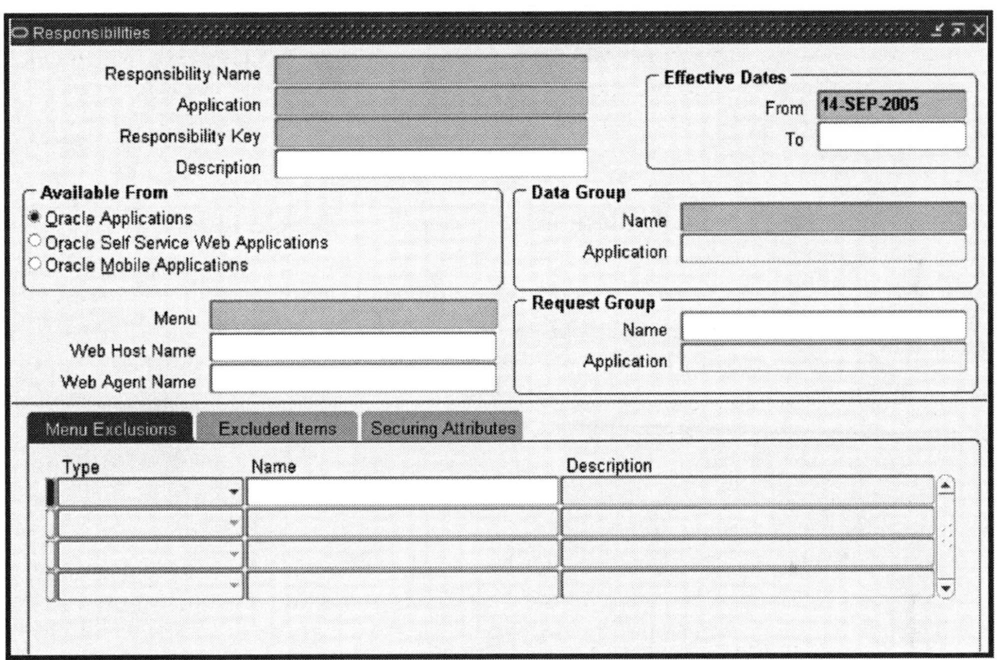

Fig. 14.2 Defining Responsibilities

Data Group

A data group defines the mapping between Oracle Application products with Oracle ID. It is a collection of pairings of an Application with an Oracle ID. The Oracle database user ID determines the database tables and other objects the user can access through Oracle Applications Forms, reports, or concurrent programs. Data group support concurrent processing and cross application reporting.

A data group is a list of Oracle Applications and the Oracle user name assigned to each one. Each application in a data group must have an Oracle user name assigned to it. An application may be listed only once in a data group.

The data group serves two main purposes:

- It identifies the Oracle user name to which the Forms connect when the user selects the responsibility
- Concurrent Manager uses data group to match the application that owns a concurrent program or report with an Oracle ID

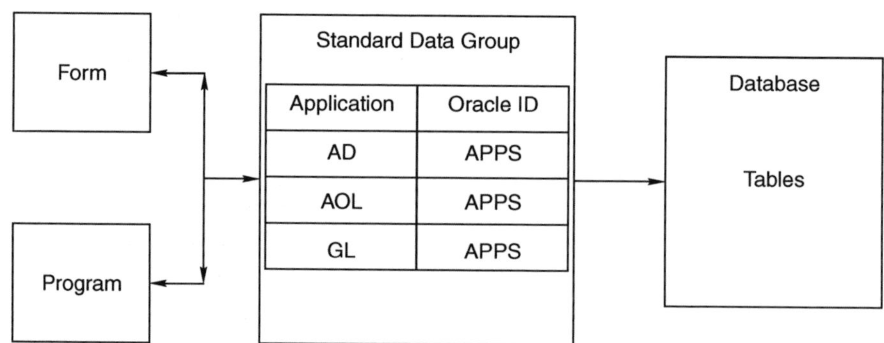

Fig. 14.3 Relating Data Group to Form and Programs

With an Oracle ID and password you can access the application tables in a database if it's a part of the data group. From Fig. 14.3, we can see that the APPS ID has access to the tables of AD, AOL and GL. By defining a data group, you can control the relationship between Forms, applications and concurrent programs.

All the Applications need access to Application Object Libraries (AOL) tables, as AOL owns the database tables referred to during concurrent processing and the standard report submission by any Oracle Application. Whenever you define a data group, the AOL is automatically included. The AOL's Oracle ID can neither be updated nor deleted.

During installation, the data groups are automatically defined for Oracle Applications. If you wish to utilize any other data groups you only need to define them. To do this, follow the navigation > Security > Oracle > Data group (refer Fig. 14.4).

The following details need to be given to create a data group.

- Data Group: In this field, you enter the name of the data group you wish to create.
- Description: Here you enter the description of the data group.
- Application: You select the application that you want to include in your data group from the list.
- Oracle ID: Select the Oracle ID you want to assign to an application. This is used to access tables in the database. Each Oracle ID allows access to a pre-defined set of tables in the database.
- Copy Applications From: Use this button to copy an existing data group, then add or delete application-Oracle user name pairs to create a new data group.

Request Security Group

The system administrator groups reports, request sets and concurrent programs to create a request group. When defining a request group, the following can be included:

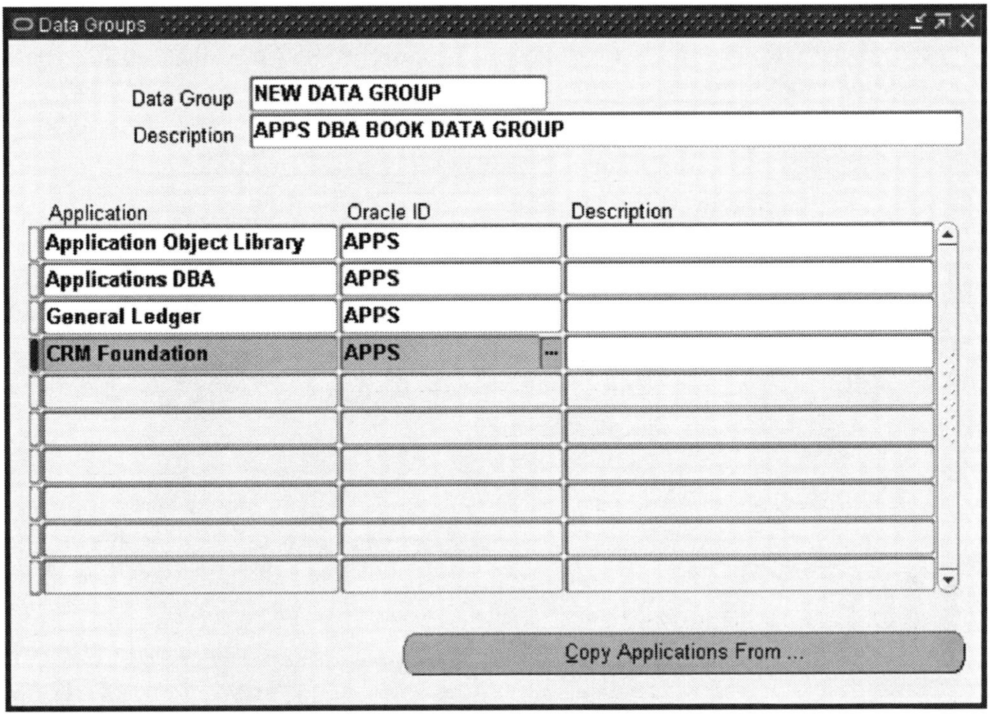

Fig. 14.4 Creating New Data Groups

- All the reports and concurrent programs owned by an application
- Individual reports and concurrent programs
- Request sets (which are collections of reports and concurrent programs that may be selected from an application user's request security groups)
- Request set stage functions (which are used to calculate the status of stages within a request set)

When a request group is assigned to a responsibility, the request group is referred to as a request security group. Any user signed on under a responsibility can run the reports and concurrent programs (including requests and request sets) contained in their responsibility's request security group.

For defining the request groups, follow the navigation

System Administrator > Security > Responsibility > Request

To create a request group, first you need to enter the group (request group name) and the application. You can also include requests from any application in your request group, regardless of the application attached to your request group.

- Group: This is the name of the group by which you will identify this request group.
- Application: This means the applications whose concurrent program and reports are included. You can include any request from any application in your request group.

- Code: This is optional. This code is used for a custom SRS form so that only programs or reports in this request group could be processed by the custom SRS form. The code—together with the application module— must be unique.
- Description: This is optional. Here, you can enter a description of the request group.
- Type: The type can be Application, Program, Set or Stage Function.
- Name: The Application, Program name.

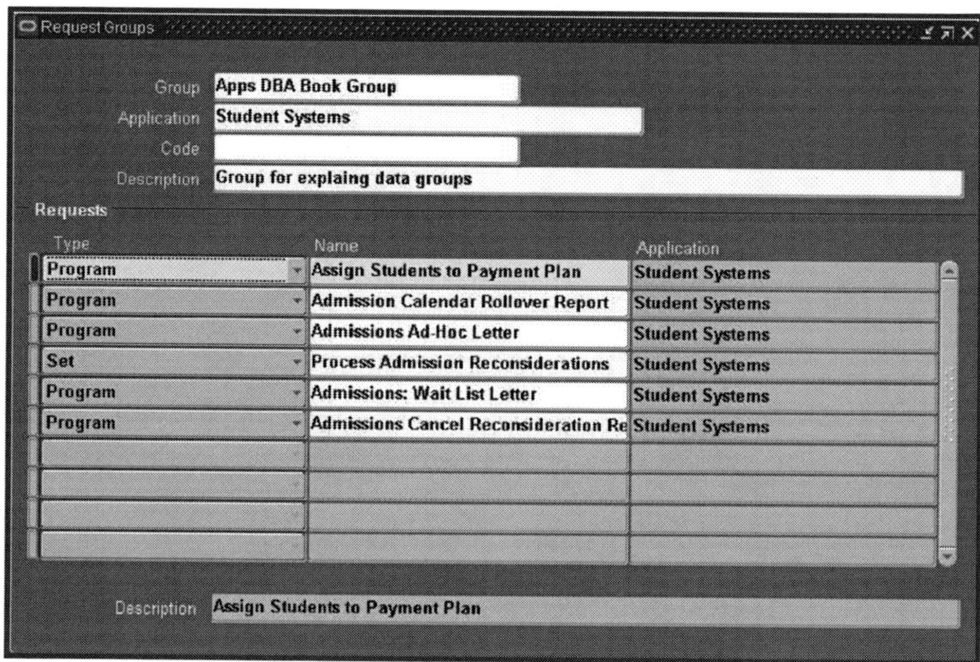

Fig. 14.5 Creating Request Groups

Menu

A menu is a hierarchical arrangement of functions and menus of functions. Each responsibility has a menu assigned to it. A menu entry is a menu component that identifies a function or a menu of functions. In some cases, both a function and a menu of that function correspond to the same menu entry. For example, both a form and its menu of sub-functions can occupy the same menu entry.

Components of responsibility

As discussed earlier, the responsibility has three components, two of which are required (data group and menu) and one that is optional(request security group).

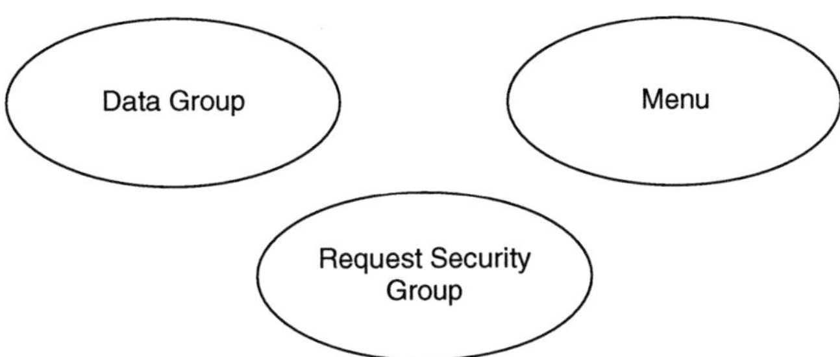

Fig. 14.6 Components of Responsibility

Responsibility creation process

These are the steps in creating a responsibility:

- Enter Application and the responsibility name
- Enter start date and the end dates
- Select data group (to supply the form, report and program connect privilege)
- Select menu (to supply access to forms within an application)
- Select request group (to control access to the functionalities of the application)
- Enter menu or function exclusions (to control access to the functionality of the application)

Box 14.1

Responsibility Creation Process

Data Groups
Security
ORACLE
Data Group

Users
Security
User
Define

Responsibilities
Security
Responsibility
Define

Request Groups
Security
Responsibility
Requests

Menus
Application
Menu

INDEX

Made in the USA